International Directory of
COMPANY
HISTORIES

International Directory of
COMPANY
HISTORIES

VOLUME 70

Editor

Tina Grant

ST. JAMES PRESS

An imprint of Thomson Gale, a part of The Thomson Corporation

Detroit • New York • San Francisco • San Diego • New Haven, Conn. • Waterville, Maine • London • Munich

THOMSON

GALE

International Directory of Company Histories, Volume 70
Tina Grant, Editor

Project Editor
Miranda H. Ferrara

Editorial
Virgil Burton, Donna Craft, Louise Gagné,
Peggy Geeseman, Julie Gough, Linda Hall,
Sonya Hill, Keith Jones, Lynn Pearce,
Maureen Puhl, Holly Selden,
Justine Ventimiglia

Imaging and Multimedia
Randy Bassett, Lezlie Light

Manufacturing
Rhonda Dover

Product Manager
Gerald L. Sawchuk

LIBRARY OF CONGRESS CATALOG NUMBER 89-190943
ISBN: 1-55862-545-3

BRITISH LIBRARY CATALOGUING IN PUBLICATION DATA
International directory of company histories. Vol. 70
I. Tina Grant
33.87409

Printed in the United States of America
10 9 8 7 6 5 4 3 2 1

CONTENTS

Company Histories

PREFACE

The St. James Press series *The International Directory of Company Histories (IDCH)* is intended for reference use by students, business people, librarians, historians, economists, investors, job candidates, and others who seek to learn more about the historical development of the world's most important companies. To date, *IDCH* has covered over 7,050 companies in 70 volumes.

Inclusion Criteria

Most companies chosen for inclusion in *IDCH* have achieved a minimum of US$25 million in annual sales and are leading influences in their industries or geographical locations. Companies may be publicly held, private, or nonprofit. State-owned companies that are important in their industries and that may operate much like public or private companies also are included. Wholly owned subsidiaries and divisions are profiled if they meet the requirements for inclusion. Entries on companies that have had major changes since they were last profiled may be selected for updating.

The *IDCH* series highlights 10% private and nonprofit companies, and features updated entries on approximately 50 companies per volume.

Entry Format

Each entry begins with the company's legal name, the address of its headquarters, its telephone, toll-free, and fax numbers, and its web site. A statement of public, private, state, or parent ownership follows. A company with a legal name in both English and the language of its headquarters country is listed by the English name, with the native-language name in parentheses.

The company's founding or earliest incorporation date, the number of employees, and the most recent available sales figures follow. Sales figures are given in local currencies with equivalents in U.S. dollars. For some private companies, sales figures are estimates and indicated by the abbreviation *est.* The entry lists the exchanges on which a company's stock is traded and its ticker symbol, as well as the company's NAIC codes.

Entries generally contain a *Company Perspectives* box which provides a short summary of the company's mission, goals, and ideals, a *Key Dates* box highlighting milestones in the company's history, lists of *Principal Subsidiaries, Principal Divisions, Principal Operating Units, Principal Competitors,* and articles for *Further Reading.*

American spelling is used throughout *IDCH*, and the word "billion" is used in its U.S. sense of one thousand million.

Sources

Entries have been compiled from publicly accessible sources both in print and on the Internet such as general and academic periodicals, books, annual reports, and material supplied by the companies themselves.

Cumulative Indexes

IDCH contains three indexes: the **Index to Companies**, which provides an alphabetical index to companies discussed in the text as well as to companies profiled, the **Index to Industries**, which allows researchers to locate companies by their principal industry, and the **Geographic Index**, which lists companies alphabetically by the country of their headquarters. The indexes are cumulative and specific instructions for using them are found immediately preceding each index.

Suggestions Welcome

Comments and suggestions from users of *IDCH* on any aspect of the product as well as suggestions for companies to be included or updated are cordially invited. Please write:

The Editor
International Directory of Company Histories
St. James Press
27500 Drake Rd.
Farmington Hills, Michigan 48331-3535

AB	Aktiebolag (Finland, Sweden)
AB Oy	Aktiebolag Osakeyhtiot (Finland)
A.E.	Anonimos Eteria (Greece)
AG	Aktiengesellschaft (Austria, Germany, Switzerland, Liechtenstein)
A.O.	Anonim Ortaklari/Ortakligi (Turkey)
ApS	Amparteselskab (Denmark)
A.Š.	Anonim Širketi (Turkey)
A/S	Aksjeselskap (Norway); Aktieselskab (Denmark, Sweden)
Ay	Avoinyhtio (Finland)
B.A.	Buttengewone Aansprakeiijkheid (The Netherlands)
Bhd.	Berhad (Malaysia, Brunei)
B.V.	Besloten Vennootschap (Belgium, The Netherlands)
C.A.	Compania Anonima (Ecuador, Venezuela)
C. de R.L.	Compania de Responsabilidad Limitada (Spain)
Co.	Company
Corp.	Corporation
CRL	Companhia a Responsabilidao Limitida (Portugal, Spain)
C.V.	Commanditaire Vennootschap (The Netherlands, Belgium)
G.I.E.	Groupement d'Interet Economique (France)
GmbH	Gesellschaft mit beschraenkter Haftung (Austria, Germany, Switzerland)
Inc.	Incorporated (United States, Canada)
I/S	Interessentselskab (Denmark); Interesentselskap (Norway)
KG/KGaA	Kommanditgesellschaft/Kommanditgesellschaft auf Aktien (Austria, Germany, Switzerland)
KK	Kabushiki Kaisha (Japan)
K/S	Kommanditselskab (Denmark); Kommandittselskap (Norway)
Lda.	Limitada (Spain)
L.L.C.	Limited Liability Company (United States)
Ltd.	Limited (Various)
Ltda.	Limitada (Brazil, Portugal)
Ltee.	Limitee (Canada, France)
mbH	mit beschraenkter Haftung (Austria, Germany)
N.V.	Naamloze Vennootschap (Belgium, The Netherlands)
OAO	Otkrytoe Aktsionernoe Obshchestve (Russia)
OOO	Obschestvo s Ogranichennoi Otvetstvennostiu (Russia)
Oy	Osakeyhtiö (Finland)
PLC	Public Limited Co. (United Kingdom, Ireland)
Pty.	Proprietary (Australia, South Africa, United Kingdom)
S.A.	Société Anonyme (Belgium, France, Greece, Luxembourg, Switzerland, Arab speaking countries); Sociedad Anónima (Latin America [except Brazil], Spain, Mexico); Sociedades Anônimas (Brazil, Portugal)
SAA	Societe Anonyme Arabienne
S.A.R.L.	Sociedade Anonima de Responsabilidade Limitada (Brazil, Portugal); Société à Responsabilité Limitée (France, Belgium, Luxembourg)
S.A.S.	Societá in Accomandita Semplice (Italy); Societe Anonyme Syrienne (Arab speaking countries)
Sdn. Bhd.	Sendirian Berhad (Malaysia)
S.p.A.	Società per Azioni (Italy)
Sp. z.o.o.	Spólka z ograniczona odpowiedzialnoscia (Poland)
S.R.L.	Società a Responsabilità Limitata (Italy); Sociedad de Responsabilidad Limitada (Spain, Mexico, Latin America [except Brazil])
S.R.O.	Spolecnost s Rucenim Omezenym (Czechoslovakia
Ste.	Societe (France, Belgium, Luxembourg, Switzerland)
VAG	Verein der Arbeitgeber (Austria, Germany)
YK	Yugen Kaisha (Japan)
ZAO	Zakrytoe Aktsionernoe Obshchestve (Russia)

$	United States dollar	ISK	Icelandic krona
£	United Kingdom pound	ITL	Italian lira
¥	Japanese yen	JMD	Jamaican dollar
AED	Emirati dirham	KPW	North Korean won
ARS	Argentine peso	KRW	South Korean won
ATS	Austrian shilling	KWD	Kuwaiti dinar
AUD	Australian dollar	LUF	Luxembourg franc
BEF	Belgian franc	MUR	Mauritian rupee
BHD	Bahraini dinar	MXN	Mexican peso
BRL	Brazilian real	MYR	Malaysian ringgit
CAD	Canadian dollar	NGN	Nigerian naira
CHF	Swiss franc	NLG	Netherlands guilder
CLP	Chilean peso	NOK	Norwegian krone
CNY	Chinese yuan	NZD	New Zealand dollar
COP	Colombian peso	OMR	Omani rial
CZK	Czech koruna	PHP	Philippine peso
DEM	German deutsche mark	PKR	Pakistani rupee
DKK	Danish krone	PLN	Polish zloty
DZD	Algerian dinar	PTE	Portuguese escudo
EEK	Estonian Kroon	RMB	Chinese renminbi
EGP	Egyptian pound	RUB	Russian ruble
ESP	Spanish peseta	SAR	Saudi riyal
EUR	euro	SEK	Swedish krona
FIM	Finnish markka	SGD	Singapore dollar
FRF	French franc	THB	Thai baht
GRD	Greek drachma	TND	Tunisian dinar
HKD	Hong Kong dollar	TRL	Turkish lira
HUF	Hungarian forint	TWD	new Taiwan dollar
IDR	Indonesian rupiah	VEB	Venezuelan bolivar
IEP	Irish pound	VND	Vietnamese dong
ILS	new Israeli shekel	ZAR	South African rand
INR	Indian rupee	ZMK	Zambian kwacha

International Directory of
COMPANY HISTORIES

Acme United Corporation

1931 Black Rock Turnpike
Fairfield, Connecticut 06825
U.S.A.
Telephone: (203) 332-7330
Fax: (203) 332-1588
Web site: http://www.acmeunited.com

Public Company
Incorporated: 1982 as Acme Shear Company
Employees: 90
Sales: $43.4 million (2004)
Stock Exchanges: American
Ticker Symbol: ACU
NAIC: 332211 Cutlery and Flatware (except Precious)
    Manufacturing

Acme United Corporation is a publicly traded manufacturing company based in Fairfield, Connecticut, that is devoted to production in three product groups: cutting instruments, measuring devices, and safety products. The company has been involved in the manufacture of scissors since the 1800s and continues to make a wide range of scissors for the home, school, and office markets. Other cutting instruments include shears, guillotine and rotary paper trimmers, hobby knives and blades, utility knives, and medical cutting instruments. Acme United measuring devices, such as rulers, tape measures, and math tools, are marketed under the venerable Westcott brand name. Safety products include First Aid kits, biohazard response products, and over-the-counter medication refills. Acme United maintains a major manufacturing plant in North Carolina as well as facilities in Canada, Germany, and Hong Kong. The company's major customers are Staples, Inc., Office Max, and United Stationers, Inc., which, combined, comprise nearly half of Acme United's annual revenues.

Company Roots Date to Civil War Era

The seeds of Acme United were planted in 1867 when German immigrant Leo Renz bought an old grist mill powered by the Beacon Hill Brook in Naugatuck. Here he opened Renz Shear Shop, which specialized in the making of cast iron shears and scissors. Over the next 20 years he grew the business and sold it to his brother, Robert. After his death, his heirs sold the company to a younger relation named Mitchell Renz. He moved the operations to Fairfield in 1880, and two years after that incorporated it as The Acme Shear Company. He was also responsible for bringing the brothers David C. Wheeler and Dwight Wheeler into the business. They bought out Renz, who decided in 1883 to quit New England and try his luck in Florida. Under Wheeler family management, Acme Shear expanded its product lines to include nut crackers and axe blades and later began manufacturing steel shears.

A second generation of the Wheeler family took over management of the company in the form of David Wheeler's son, Dwight C. Wheeler. A third generation, Henry C. Wheeler, joined the business in 1939 after graduating from Yale University. Just two years later, his father died and because the family wanted a Wheeler to head the business, he was made president when just 25 years of age. Although years later he would admit to being too young for the role, he was able to build on the momentum achieved by the previous generations of the Wheeler family, as well as the world-changing events of World War II, so that by 1946 Acme Shear was the world's largest maker of shears and scissors.

Medical Field Entered in 1960s

Henry Wheeler added a new title, chief executive officer, in 1953. Then, in the 1960s, he expanded the company in a number of directions. A scissors' subsidiary, Surmano Ltd., was established in the United Kingdom to sell directly to the European market. Because of increasing demand for disposable medical scissors, Acme Shear became involved in the medical field. In 1965, it introduced a line of disposable medical scissors and surgical instruments, selling them to other companies that packaged them for the hospital market. This business did so well that in 1969 Acme Shear opened a major manufacturing plant in Fremont, North Carolina, one that met government requirements for the production and packaging of medical equipment. The 1960s were also noteworthy because a fourth generation of

+---+
| **Company Perspectives:** |
| |
| *We aspire to be the leading supplier of |
| cutting, measuring and safety products to |
| offices, school and homes worldwide.* |
+---+

the Wheeler family became involved as Dwight C. Wheeler II, Henry Wheeler's son, joined the company in 1966. A graduate of the University of Bridgeport with a degree in manufacturing engineering, he worked as an industrial engineer at the Producto Machine Company in Bridgeport before coming to Acme United. The company marked its 100th anniversary in 1967, the same year that Acme United ceased to be a pure family business. Acme Shear conducted an initial public offering of stock, which then began trading on an over-the-counter (OTC) basis.

During the 1970s, Acme Shear continued its efforts at diversification. In 1970, it became involved in a school product kindred to scissors, rulers, by acquiring Westcott Rule Company, which had been founded in 1872 in Seneca Falls, New York. To better reflect the company's new business mix the 100-year-old Acme Shear name was dropped in June 1971 in favor of Acme United Corporation. The 1970s also saw continued growth in the medical field. In 1972, Acme United acquired One Time Package Products Inc., maker of single-use consumer package products, a deal that allowed Acme United to market its own line of products rather than rely on third parties. The medical products division now offered One Time disposable procedure trays, Reposable stainless steel instruments, and povidone-iodine microbicide, a germicide sold under the ACU-Dyne brand. In the late 1970s, Acme United brought out wound dressings, including a sterile, non-absorbent, self-adhering polyurethane dressing called ACU-Derm and an absorbent version sold under the Lyo Foam name. Also of note during the decade, in 1979 the company's stock graduated from the OTC and began trading on the American Stock Exchange.

Struggles and Successes: 1980s to Mid-1990s

Much of Acme United's growth was due to its thriving medical business, but that would begin to change in the 1980s. The company was overly dependent on a single customer, American Hospital Supply, which by 1983 accounted for $22 million in sales. Then, American Hospital elected to manufacture many of the products themselves. To make the loss of this business even worse, hospitals began to pool their orders so that they were able to demand steeper discounts, thus cutting into Acme United's margins. Moreover, the company faced strong new competition from a United Kingdom medical supplier, Smith & Nephew. Acme United spent much of the 1980s adjusting to these realities, but by the end of the decade was ready to resume expansion.

The company looked overseas to fuel growth. In January 1990, Acme United closed on the $2.8 million acquisition of Emil Schlemper G.m.b.H., a leading West German maker of scissors, shears, manicure products, and surgical instruments. With Schlemper complementing the United Kingdom division, Surmanco, Acme United was now one of the largest manufac-

turers of cutting instruments in the European Common Market. Several months later, it increased its market share while expanding Surmanco by paying some $900,000 to acquire Homeric Ltd., a Sheffield, England-based maker of scissors, rulers, household shears, and surgical equipment. The next major acquisition was completed in October 1991, when Acme United bought Peter Altenbach and Sons GmbH for approximately $1.9 million. Founded in 1900, Altenbach was Germany's third largest manufacturer of quality knives and scissors, with annual sales of about $7 million. As had been the case with the Schlemper and Homeric acquisitions, Altenbach was expected to become immediately profitable, as Henry Wheeler told the press that Altenbach was "an efficient, well-managed business." Unfortunately for Acme United, that assessment was not accurate. According to the *New Haven Register,* in a 1995 profile of Acme United, "The Altenbach purchase turned into a disaster as labor problems and poor cost controls drained earnings. Acme moved to restructure the division and cut employment by 30 percent, which proved more costly considering the high severance costs built into German labor laws."

On other fronts during the early 1990s, Acme United offered the Kleen Earth line of "green" scissors and rulers made from recycled plastic and packaged in recycled cardboard. At a cost of $5.4 million in cash and stock, it expanded its medical division in early 1992 by acquiring SePro Healthcare, Inc., the U.S. subsidiary of a United Kingdom firm, Seton Healthcare Group PLC. As a result, Acme United picked up inventory, a New Jersey facility, and exclusive distribution rights to Seton's pressure therapy bandages and specialized wound dressings, as well as an opportunity to distribute Seton's future medical products. Later in 1992, Acme United reached an exclusive marketing and distribution agreement with a New York City company, OPCO Medical Products Ltd., for the OPCO line of patented intravenous therapy products, serving both the hospital and after-care market. These products included a patented IV Bubble, an inflatable item used to keep a catheter from being accidentally dislodged, and an IV board, a companion product that immobilized a limb with a molded arm board and finger support to provide a more stabile intravenous site. Also in 1992, Acme United acquired the exclusive U.S. marketing and distribution rights for the Royal-Derm lines of skin care and wound-care products, designed to increase moisturization and provide pain relief for patients suffering from burns as well as the ulcers and wounds suffered by the bedridden.

The problems with Altenbach led to a $468,000 restructuring charge in 1992. In addition, Acme United also encountered problems with the launch of the Royal-Derm and OPCO product lines. Attempts to market the latter failed completely, leading to a $264,000 charge for leftover inventory and licensing rights, while Royal-Derm met with stiff new competition, resulting in price cutting and a $415,000 charge for dated inventory. In an attempt to address Acme United's mounting difficulties, reorganization was begun in January 1994. The company was now divided into three business units: North American consumer products, European consumer products, and U.S. Medical products. Management teams were assigned to each unit and given the authority to make sweeping changes, including headcount reduction and other cost-cutting measures. In addition, 78-year-old Henry Wheeler stepped down as CEO,

Key Dates:

1867: Benz Shear Shop is founded.
1882: The business is incorporated as The Acme Shear Company.
1883: Brothers Dwight and David C. Wheeler buy the company.
1941: Henry Wheeler is named president.
1965: The company offers disposable surgical instruments.
1967: The company goes public.
1971: The company changes its name to Acme United Corporation.
1979: Acme lists on the American Stock Exchange.
1990: Emil Schlemper GmbH is acquired.
1995: Walter C. Johnson is named CEO.
2004: Clauss Cutlery is acquired.

replaced by his 51-year-old son, Dwight C. Wheeler II. The elder Wheeler retained the chairmanship, however.

New Leadership and Challenges: Mid-1990s–2000s

After Acme United appeared to hit bottom in 1993, the company showed some improvement in 1994, when it barely returned to profitability, before experiencing a disappointing setback the following year. The company's stock, which had been trading in the neighborhood of $25 during the 1980s, slumped to around $3, leading to increasing pressure from shareholders to make major changes in management. In November 1995, Dwight Wheeler was replaced as CEO by Walter C. Johnson, who had been hired earlier in the year to head the medical products division. Johnson had previously served as vice-chairman of Marshall Products Inc., an Illinois medical supply distributor whose revenues he had helped to double in four years before it was sold to a Japanese company. Johnson was also named to the Acme United board of directors, where at the age of 44 he was considerably younger than his colleagues, whose average age was 66.

After losing more than $8.7 million on sales of $52.2 million in 1995, Acme United initiated a cost reduction program in 1996. The Westcott plant in Seneca Falls, closed in 1995, was sold in 1996. The company's Bridgeport, Connecticut, plant was also shut down in 1996, with all production moved to Acme United's more modern, lower cost, facilities in North Carolina. Altenbach was also sold off in May 1996. As planned, Acme United also began reducing its inventory company-wide in order to free up money for investment in the company. Moreover, Johnson shook up his management team. All four of his direct reports, along with five other senior managers, were terminated in 1996. The company lost another $3.2 million in 1996, much of which was the result of restructuring charges, but it also saw revenues dip to $47.5 million, with the medical products unit experiencing a 12 percent drop in business and European sales that, excluding Altenbach, was off by 4 percent.

Acme United expanded its North American office products business in 1997 by acquiring the Rotex Division of Esselte

Canada. Also in 1997, Acme United sold the marketing rights for Seton Healthcare products for $2 million, a harbinger of what was to come, as Johnson decided to focus the company's attention on consumer products. Less than two years later, in March 1999, Acme United sold its medical unit for $8.2 million to Medical Action Industries, a Long Island-based supplier of medical and disposable surgical products. Also in March 1999, Henry Wheeler died, some 60 years after first joining the company.

Although the loss of the medical division significantly lowered the company's total revenues, Acme United slowly returned to profitability, posting net income of $1.1 million in 2000 after losing $156,000 from continuing operations in 1999 and $1.7 million in 1998. The company shied away from low margin products, concentrating instead on value-added products, such as the Tagit! line of student scissors, rulers, staplers, and staple removers introduced in 2000. In addition, the company made inroads into the office market by achieving greater penetration with such retailers as Staples and Office Max. Sales improved to $36.2 million in 2001, a 5 percent improvement over the previous year, and net income grew to $1.3 million.

Poor economic conditions caused another setback in 2002, leading to the restructuring of the European unit, with the operations of the United Kingdom plant transferred to Germany. Acme United also increased its focus on core products and regained some momentum in 2003, during which sales increased 13 percent over the previous year to $35 million and net income increased 85 percent to $1.2 million. A new titanium scissor line performed well enough to warrant the application of the technology to new products, such as paper trimmers. In addition, in 2003 Acme United opened a Hong Kong subsidiary.

With business once again on an upswing, Acme United was in a position to grow externally. In June 2004, it acquired Clauss Cutlery from Alco Industries. Almost as old as Acme United, Clauss, founded in Fremont, Ohio, in 1877, was once the world's largest scissor manufacturers. Its scissors and cutting tools now primarily served the floral market as well as such industrial customers as auto, textile, food processing, and electronics, providing Acme United with a solid platform on which to expand into other areas of the cutting trade. The company's turnaround under Johnson's leadership appeared complete when the results for 2004 were released in March 2005. Acme United experienced a 24 percent increase in sales to $43.4 million, while net income grew to $3.2 million. With sales showing improvement in all markets, Acme United was well positioned to now enjoy sustained growth.

Principal Subsidiaries

Acme United Ltd.; Emil Schlemper GmbH; Acme Untied (Asia Pacific), Ltd.

Principal Competitors

Aearo Corporation; Esselte Corporation; Fiskars Corporation.

Further Reading

"Acme United Acquires Germany Cutlery Maker," *Fairfield Count Business Journal*, November 4, 1991, p. 20.

"Acme United to Acquire Major Portion of SepRo's Medical Products," *Fairfield Count Business Journal,* January 20, 1992, p. 4.

"Acme United to Distribute New Line of Wound and Skin-Care Products," *Fairfield Count Business Journal*, September 21, 1992, p. 3.

Davies, Paul, "Scissor-Maker Cutes New Hope," *New Haven Register*, May 28, 1995, p. 1.

Strempel, Dan, "Acme United Corp. Acquires Clauss Cutlery Assets," *Fairfield Count Business Journal*, June 28, 2004, p. 8.

—Ed Dinger

Air Pacific Ltd.

Maintenance & Administration Centre
Nasoso Road
Nadi Airport
Fiji
Telephone: +679 673 7382/673 7354
Toll Free: (800) 227-4446
Fax: +679 672 0704
Web site: http://www.airpacific.com

Private Company
Incorporated: 1947 as Katafaga Estates Ltd.
Employees: 700
Sales: FJD 421.7 million ($250 million) (2004)
NAIC: 481111 Scheduled Passenger Air Transportation;
   481112 Scheduled Freight Air Transportation; 488190
   Other Support Activities for Air Transportation;
   561599 All Other Travel Arrangement and
   Reservation Services

Air Pacific Ltd. of Fiji is a leading airline in the South Pacific. Its main international markets are Australia and New Zealand. The airline maintains a fleet of up to a half-dozen jets. Its base, Nadi International Airport, is an important stopover on transpacific routes. Air Pacific participates in a number of codesharing arrangements.

Origins

Air Pacific Ltd. was not the first airline to connect the islands of Fiji. Fiji Airways, an airline backed by Guinea Airways, was established in Adelaide, South Australia, in 1932. It began short-lived services in the spring of 1933, according to *A History of the World's Airlines* by R.E.G. Davies.

In 1947 New Zealand National Airways Corporation (NZNAC) began a flying boat service connecting New Zealand with Fiji, Tonga, Samoa, and the Cook Islands. This was called the "Coral Route." The Australian airline Qantas also began flying to Fiji in the late 1940s.

Harold Gatty, the famous aviator dubbed "the Prince of Navigators" by Charles Lindbergh, established a second airline called Fiji Airways in September 1951. It was originally named after Gatty's coconut farm, registered in 1947 as Katafaga Estates Ltd.

Gatty had flown to fame with Wiley Post in their 1931 circumnavigation of the globe. He had then helped Pan American Airways set up its South Pacific routes. He then settled in Fiji with his Dutch-born wife.

Fiji Airways was acquired by Qantas in August 1958. Air New Zealand and British Overseas Airways Corporation had acquired stakes in the mid-1960s, as did the governments of Tonga, Western Samoa, Nauru, Kiribati, and the Solomon Islands. The intent was to make Fiji Airways a regional airline.

Fiji Airways used small de Havilland Dragon Rapide and Drover aircraft at first. The fleet soon included Douglas DC-3s. Several de Havilland Herons were added after the acquisition by Qantas, and the network spread throughout neighboring islands.

In 1971, the fleet was standardized to include BAC1-11 jets and Hawker Siddeley 748 turboprops. The airline's first international flight, to Brisbane, Australia, came on June 1, 1973. (Its flight engineer was future Air Pacific CEO Andrew Drysdale.)

In the 1970s, tourism surpassed agriculture as Fiji's leading industry, making Air Pacific's role in the country's economy even more important. The government of Fiji acquired a controlling interest in Air Pacific in 1974. Services to Auckland, New Zealand were launched in 1975, followed by Brisbane (via Noumea) in 1975.

Challenges in the 1980s

A 1981 *New York Times* profile of the region's aviation industry described some of the challenges of operating in the South Pacific. The long over-ocean stretches required more catering, and salt spray made corrosion an issue.

Around 1984, the government of Fiji, planning to buy out some of its partners in Air Pacific, stopped requiring the airline to maintain loss-making jet connections with neighboring isles.

Company Perspectives:

Fiji is a wonderful place for a holiday, whether for relaxing, taking a romantic break, absorbing different cultural experiences or getting away with the whole family. Air Pacific can take you there with an instant feeling of being part of Fiji from the moment you step on board, greeted with a friendly "Bula!" We offer a range of fares with varying conditions, depending on what your travel style is. There is something to suit everyone— children can become Captain Bula Club members with activity kits to keep them busy and we deliver full service, entertainment and meals so you are well attended to. Come join us in our "Island in the Sky" and let us show you OUR Fiji.

The airline received no subsidies. It also had to finance its own aircraft. While there was little competition at home, international routes were contested by larger rivals. The company's main market was Australia, which saw Fiji as an exotic yet affordable vacation spot.

Air Pacific used a DC-10 jet to begin flying to Honolulu in 1983. This adventure, dubbed "Project America," produced disastrous results, however, and was canceled after 14 months.

Air Pacific was losing $4–$7 million a year and had accumulated losses of more than $20 million when Qantas began a ten-year management contract with the airline in 1985. Its fortunes were soon reversed, when in 1986, it posted a profit of nearly $100,000. According to the *Journal of Commerce*, the association with Qantas helped Air Pacific win business from travel agents. Qantas paid a reported $3.5 million for a 20 percent stake in Air Pacific in 1987.

Two coups in 1987 disturbed the local travel industry. As Air Pacific CEO Andrew Drysdale told *Airline Business,* however, the importance of Fiji having its own national airline was underscored when other international carriers temporarily withdrew from the market.

Forging Alliances in the 1990s

Operating profit hit a record $11 million in fiscal 1989–90. Revenues were up 52 percent to about $100 million. The airline was carrying about 300,000 passengers a year. The fleet then included two leased jets, a Boeing 747 and Boeing 767, and two ATR-42 turboprops, bought in 1988. There were about 650 employees.

Air Pacific relocated its headquarters from the capital city of Suva to the coastal town of Nadi, site of the main international airport. The company also constructed an elaborate aircraft maintenance center there.

The airline tried the American market again in 1994, adding a service to Los Angeles. By this time, Continental Airlines had abandoned its South Pacific routes. There was also increasing awareness of Fiji in the United States.

Air Pacific also soon added flights to Melbourne as Qantas reorganized its transpacific services. In a unique cooperation with another Polynesian carrier, Air Pacific jointly leased a Boeing 737 with Royal Tongan Airlines. The two airlines' colors were painted on opposite sides of the plane.

Qantas raised its equity in Air Pacific from 17.45 percent to 46 percent in 1998. It paid FJD 27 million for the additional shares. The government of Fiji owned 51 percent.

Qantas was a member of the oneworld global airline alliance, and deals with fellow oneworld members followed its increased participation in Air Pacific. Air Pacific signed a codeshare agreement with Canadian Airlines, allowing it to transport traffic from Toronto on to Auckland, New Zealand. A codeshare with American Airlines soon followed.

By this time, the airline had 730 employees. The fleet included up-to-date Boeing 737 and 767 jets. ATR-42 turboprops were used on flights to neighboring islands.

By the late 1990s, the airline had experienced something of a turnaround in the main direction of its cargo trade. Whereas inbound freight of consumer goods had dominated previously, the airline then had trouble filling the belly capacity of its passenger airliners with westbound cargo. Air Pacific had little cargo marketing support in the United States, reported the *Journal of Commerce*. Its flights from Fiji to Los Angeles were, however, full of fresh fish, fruits, and clothing.

The airline was thriving on the strength of passenger traffic. Revenues were FJD 371 million in the fiscal year ended March 31, 1999, with profits rising 60 percent to FJD 13 million. These impressive results were achieved in the face of a currency devaluation. Air Pacific carried 412,000 passengers during the year.

Air Pacific was beginning a large expansion program, raising the fleet to six aircraft (three mid-sized Boeing 737s—two of them the latest -800 series variant, a widebody 767, and two 747s) and adding flights to Australia and North America.

New Planes, New Challenges in 2000 and Beyond

While some airlines worried about whether to cancel flights during the changing of the millennium because of possible Y2K computer issues, Air Pacific used Fiji's location on the International Date Line to offer passengers a flight with two New Year's celebrations. In spite of this auspicious beginning, the year was to be a very challenging one. There was another coup in May 2000, which devastated the economy and led tourists to avoid the country. Faced with a falloff in traffic, Air Pacific returned one of its two leased Boeing 747 jumbo jets. Such measures were not enough to avoid the worst loss in its history, which totaled FJD 38.5 million ($15 million) in fiscal 2000–01.

Air Pacific was soon in the black again, however, and made FJD 10 million ($3 million) in the fiscal year ending March 31, 2002. By 2003, tourist arrivals, which fell to 270,000 after the 2000 coup, reached record levels (about 400,000). Fiji seemed to benefit from its relative isolation from world events following the 9/11 terrorist attacks on the United States.

Air Pacific was replacing its remaining 747 with two newer ones leased from Singapore Airlines. Two Airbus A330s were being bought to add to the fleet in 2005. These deals, worth

Key Dates:

1951: Fiji Airways is founded by famed aviator Harold Gatty.
1958: Qantas acquires Fiji Airways.
1971: The airline is renamed Air Pacific Ltd.
1973: The airline schedules its first flight to Australia.
1974: The Fiji government acquires a controlling interest.
1985: Qantas begins managing Air Pacific through a turn-around.
1987: Coups upset Fiji tourism.
1994: Air Pacific begins service to Los Angeles.
2000: Another coup rattles the local tourist industry.
2004: A new FJD 1.3 billion airliner order is the largest commercial investment in Fiji history.

FJD 1.3 billion, were the largest business investment in Fiji's history, according to New Zealand's *National Business Review.* This amounted to nearly two-thirds the country's annual GDP.

The additional capacity allowed for more frequencies on long-haul routes. Managing director John Campbell told Wellington, New Zealand's *Dominion Post* that the airline expected strong price competition from Air New Zealand, which also was adding capacity, and new entrant Virgin Blue. Air Pacific also faced being undercut by charter operators and tour packagers.

Air Pacific remained profitable and reached another record in fiscal 2003–04, posting net income of FJD 24.5 million for the year. Weaker U.S. currency against the Aussie and Kiwi dollars contributed.

Principal Operating Units

Air Pacific Charters; Air Pacific Holidays; Airport Ground Services.

Principal Competitors

Air New Zealand; Virgin Blue.

Further Reading

"Airline Fights Hard to Get Back in the Black," *Australian Financial Review,* October 11, 1982, p. 28.

"Air Pacific to Relocate," *New Zealand Herald,* April 5, 1990, p. 10.

"Air Pacific Wants Three-Way Alliance," *Dominion Post* (Wellington), January 18, 2003, p. 7.

Barnett, Chris, "Fiji's Air Pacific Struggles to Fill Cargo Space," *Journal of Commerce,* May 18, 1999, p. 8A.

Davies, R.E.G., *A History of the World's Airlines,* London: Oxford University Press, 1964.

"Fiji Signs Qantas Sale Deal," *The Dominion* (Wellington), Bus. Sec., May 18, 1998, p. 16.

Hollie, Pamela G., "New Pacific Industry: Airlines," *New York Times,* Sec. 2, October 24, 1981, p. 29.

Keith-Reid, Robert, "Birds of a Feather: Joint Venture Buoys Pacific Carriers," *Far Eastern Economic Review,* April 6, 1995, p. 73.

——, "Fiji's Time, Country's Economy Undergoes a Quiet Revolution," *National Business Review* (New Zealand), January 23, 2004, p. 19.

Kennedy, Graeme, "Airline Expansion Takes Off," *National Business Review* (New Zealand), February 8, 2003, p. 23.

——, "Air Pacific Makes Short Work of Coup in Effecting Big Turnaround," *National Business Review* (New Zealand), June 14, 2002, p. 56.

——, "Air Pacific Moves to Consolidate Place As Top Carrier in Pacific Is.," *National Business Review* (New Zealand), November 27, 1998.

Shrimpton, James, "Silver Jubilee of Flight into Airline Big Time," *Adelaide Advertiser,* May 30, 1998, p. 31.

Stone, David, "NZ-Fiji Aviation Accord Opens Skies for Qantas," *Independent Business Weekly,* May 27, 1998.

Stove, Vincent W., "Qantas Buys 20 Percent of Fijian Airline," *Journal of Commerce,* November 19, 1987, p. 5B.

Tait, Nikki, "Qantas, Air Pacific Reach New Accord," *Financial Times* (London), June 8, 1995, p. 34.

Thomas, Tony, "Air Pacific Holds a Steady Course," *Business Review Weekly,* November 6, 1992, p. 30.

Van den Bergh, Roeland, "Air Pacific Profit Takes Off with 59% Rise," *The Dominion* (Wellington), Bus. Sec., May 29, 1999, p. 13.

——, "Fiji's Air Pacific Boosts Fleet to Life Passenger Numbers," *The Dominion* (Wellington), Bus. Sec., June 2, 1999, p. 22.

——, "Tiny Airline Fears 'Pincer Movement,'" *Dominion Post* (Wellington), July 12, 2003, p. 9.

Vandyk, Anthony, "A High Roll on L.A.," *Air Transport World,* September 1, 1994, p. 119.

——, "Stoking Up the Home Fires: 'Project America' Drove Air Pacific into Bankruptcy; The Fijian Carrier Is Profitable Now and Wants No Part of Any More Routes to the U.S.," *Air Transport World,* November 1, 1990, p. 96.

"Worldly Thinking—Air Pacific Fights for Share of Increased Passenger Traffic," *Airline Business,* October 1, 1990, p. 54.

—Frederick C. Ingram

Andronico's Market

1109 Washington Avenue
Albany, California 94706
U.S.A.
Telephone: (510) 559-2800
Fax: (510) 524-3601
Web site: http://www.andronicos.com

Private Company
Incorporated: 1955
Employees: 1,000
Sales: $250 million (2003)
NAIC: 445110 Supermarkets & Other Grocery Stores,
722211 Limited Service Restaurants

Andronico's Market is a chain of supermarkets in Northern California. The ten Andronico's outlets serve a mostly upscale clientele in an area that radiates out from San Francisco's Bay 15 miles north to San Anselmo, 35 miles east to Walnut Creek and Danville, and 45 south to Los Altos. Stores average about 40,000 square feet with sales areas of about 29,000 square feet. They are geared toward the gourmet shopper, and each features a wide range of specialty grocery items, out-of-the-ordinary produce and herbs, full-service meat and fish service, fresh flowers, a deli with freshly cooked foods, kitchen gadgets, and tableware.

1929–89: From Neighborhood Market to Chain

Frank Andronicos emigrated to San Francisco from his native Greece in 1906 at the age of 15. After working with his older brothers as a produce buyer, and trying his hand as a railroad laborer and in the hotel and sugar industries, he struck out on his own. His first solo venture, undertaken with his wife, Eva, was a produce stand in Alameda, California. In 1929, he opened F. Andronicos, a full-service market on Solano Avenue in Berkeley, California. (He later dropped the ''s.'')

''He was always quality-oriented and believed passionately in delivering the best quality to his customers,'' reflected Bill Andronico, Andronico's grandson, in a 2004 *Supermarket News* article. The store became a focal point of the community, a place where everyone knew everyone else and where quality customer service was assured. Andronico held a contest to name the store, and customers chose to call it the Park and Shop Market.

The business grew slowly for the first three decades. In 1957, the year in which John Andronico, Frank's son, joined the business, the family opened a second Park and Shop Market in Berkeley. John Andronico had worked in the family store stocking shelves as a child and liked to joke that he had been in the grocery business from before birth. According to Bill Andronico, John's son, in the 2004 *Supermarket News* article, John brought ''the whole notion of good food'' to the company. ''He loved to buy and sell quality produce, and he also liked eating good food.'' A third Park and Shop opened in San Francisco in 1959. Two more stores opened in the 1960s but later were closed.

John Andronico became president of the three-store company in 1978, the year in which Frank Andronico died. John's son, Bill, began working for the company in 1975, during his second year of senior high school and continued working while he earned a bachelors degree in economics at the University of California at Berkeley. After graduating with a masters in food industry management from the University of Southern California in the 1980s, Bill Andronico joined the business full time.

In the early 1980s, Park and Shop introduced innovations that became industry standards: refrigerated ''waterfall'' produce cases with staggered shelves and a built-in misting supply and Metro shelving—metal grocery shelves—that allowed for shelves of variable depth. The company also began installing in-store kitchens in 1984. In 1986, while remodeling its second store, the company changed its name to Andronico's Park and Shop Market ''because we thought it was important to differentiate ourselves from other supermarkets that had generic names or less-than-imposing banners,'' according to Bill Andronico in *Supermarket News* in 2004. Bill became president of the company in 1988. A year later, prompted by a booming economy, the company began a growth spurt, opening two new stores in Berkeley, one in 1989 and another in 1990.

1989–99: A Decade of Growth in Food Service

In the early 1990s, Andronico's entered the home meal replacement market, introducing prepared meals at several of its locations. The chain's emphasis on service ran against the su-

Company Perspectives:

We are a family of passionate people committed to providing a unique and exciting shopping experience. Out mission is to offer unsurpassed customer service and superior quality food.

permarket industry trend at the time and presented some real challenges. "If you think you can put in a décor package, hire a chef, and it starts and ends there, it isn't going to happen," said Bill Andronico in 1995 *Supermarket Business* article. The typical home meal replacement, consisting of an entrée and side dishes, cost as much as its restaurant counterpart to prepare, but customers were not willing to pay the same prices for supermarket meals. Andronico's installed commercial kitchens staffed with restaurant people at each of its markets and began to advertise aggressively, billing its stores as providing restaurant-quality foods "for every occasion." Its efforts paid off as many of its customers from dual-income households shopped daily in its foodservice sections.

In 1994, Andronico's remodeled its San Francisco store, in part because it was dissatisfied with the store's leased deli, according to Bill Andronico, John Andronico's successor. To that end, the store's International Food Court, a 100-foot run of prepared foods, introduced high-service features, such as a fresh pasta station, a grilling station, and deli-bakery. The deli displayed 20 to 40 salads and 15 to 20 entrees daily, most of which it sold out. The San Francisco store also had a banquet room with seating for 18 in which it catered for company and community groups.

In 1995, with five stores, the independent grocery chain purchased the 70-year-old Guasco's Market, one of the Bay Area's oldest supermarkets, and the 22-year-old Rancho Market in Los Altos, California. Both of these independent markets had fallen victim to big grocery store chains, joining the more than one dozen Bay Area independent supermarkets to close in the early 1990s. Guasco's management cited the cost of health benefits for its unionized labor forces and the need to upgrade to remain competitive as its reasons for closing. Andronico's closed Guasco's in 1996 for extensive remodeling. The cost of upgrading smaller independents to include new food counters and in-store kitchens ran more than $2 million at the time.

Increasingly, Andronico's convenience-oriented philosophy came to be typified by its bakeries and deli express counters. "You can literally come into this store, go straight to the counter, order your coffee drink, grab a self-serve muffin or pastry, do your bagel or buy something our of the service bakery right in front there and get the heck out of Dodge in no time at all . . . You don't have to deal with the checkstands whatsoever. It's a store-within-a-store," said Bill Andronico of the remodeled Rancho Market in a 1996 *Supermarket Business* article. "I think our foodservice philosophy has evolved, and this store is an unveiling of the most developed food service offering that we've gotten together . . . We are gearing more to the convenience side, and so we're doing a lot of self-serve, but we're not cutting away from the service aspect."

The reopened Rancho became Andronico's sixth store in Los Altos in 1996 followed by the remodeled Guasco's as the seventh in San Anselmo in 1997. That year, the company changes its name to Andronico's Market, Inc. Each of its stores looked a little different and catered to the needs and flavor of local clientele, in keeping with the original Park and Shop's emphasis on being a neighborhood grocery.

What unified all Andronico's markets was in part their produce sections. "We've always done things a little differently in produce . . . We've dealt with and developed programs with a lot of small growers . . . "Bill Andronico described his company's Food Labeling and Nutritional Information program in a *Supermarket Business* article in July 1996. The program had blue shelf talkers to identify local produce, purple shelf talkers to identify IPM produce (produce grown with integrated pest management), and orange shelf talkers to identify organic produce. Customers were encouraged to sample items. "It ties in with our philosophy to take care of the customer in any way we can and make sure that they walk out of the store 100 percent satisfied that they received attention when they wanted it and that we went beyond their expectations," Andronico went on to explain in the article. The special emphasis on produce paid off in 1998 when Andronico's was named Best Grocery Store in the *San Francisco Chronicle's* Reader's Choice poll.

It fact, it was Andronico's produce section that provided it with a competitive edge against the supermarket giants in the late 1990s. As a small chain, the company was in a better position to capitalize on the factors that make for a signature produce section, such as quality control (buying produce at just the right time from local growers), variety (buying smaller amounts of a large number of items), and selecting items in response to customer demand. Andronico's produce buyers scoured San Francisco's warehouse districts every day to find a variety of top-quality produce.

John Andronico worked in the company until shortly before his death at age 76 in 1999. "He backed away from the business slowly," Bill Andronico recalled in a 2004 *Supermarket News* article. "He knew his succession plan for me needed to evolve, and so he divested responsibility over several years." Bill Andronico became chairman and chief executive officer of Andronico's in 1999. Connie Andronico, John's daughter, was company vice-president involved with in-store demo programs and special events.

Bill Andronico oversaw the opening of the company's ninth store in Danville in the East Bay in 1999. Also that year, the company installed a web-accessible system to monitor and replenish stock. The elaborate Danville market cost about $3.5 million to build and occupied more than 40,000-square-feet. It featured an extensive supply of wine with a wine-tasting bar, an in-house bakery called Forno di Andronico, a kitchen for hosting cooking classes and private parties; a farmer's market-style produce area, and a housewares department. A full third of the store was devoted to prepared foods sold at the delicatessen, salad bars, and grill area. A state-of-the-art audio system created eight different sound "zones," ranging from rainforest noises in the produce area to Frank Sinatra in the wine bar. The store's industrial kitchen hosted a cooking school, called Ingredients, that featured chefs Bradley Ogden, Alice Medrich, and Nancy Oakes in 2000. Its Living Healthy Center employed a full-time, certified nutritionist.

Andronico's new flagship store won *Supermarket Business's* Award of Excellence in 1999, although Andronico, pre-

Key Dates:

1929: Frank Andronicos opens the Park and Shop Market in Berkeley, California.

1957: The second Park and Shop opens in Berkeley; John Andronico joins the family business.

1959: The third Park and Shop opens in San Francisco.

1975: Bill Andronico joins the company.

1978: John Andronico heads the company after the death of Frank Andronico.

1984: The company begins to install in-store kitchens for preparing meals.

1986: Park and Shop changes its name to Andronico's Park and Shop Market; the company opens its headquarters in Albany, California.

1988: Bill Andronico becomes president of the company

1989: The company opens a new store in Berkeley.

1994: The company remodels its San Francisco market.

1995: Andronico's buys Guasco's Super in San Anselmo and the Rancho Market in Los Altos.

1997: Andronico's opens a store in Palo Alto; the company changes its name to Andronico's Market, Inc.

1999: John Andronico dies; Bill Andronico becomes chairman and chief executive officer; the Danville market opens.

2002: Andronico's opens a store in Walnut Creek.

occupied with *kaizen*, the Japanese term for continuous improvement, aimed for ever better. In 1998, he and key people in the company had taken a cross-country trip to visit 87 grocery stores in 15 cities and 11 states. He also belonged to a ''share group'' whose members, including John Zagara of Zagara's in New Jersey and John Campbell of HEB's Central Market, aimed to stay abreast of and to anticipate industry trends.

2000 and Beyond: A Focus on Continued Improvement

Andronico implemented a variety of leadership training initiatives to create connections within the company and with shoppers and their communities. These included a program called ''400 percent,'' which measured results in the form of sales and profits, leadership, and communication and honesty among employees. ''The key to it all is that we go high tech so that we can be high touch,'' explained Bill Andronico in a 1999 *Supermarket Business* article. ''We collect appropriate data and bring it into report form so that we can go out there and touch the people. . . .'' There was an employee mentoring program and an Employee Appreciation Day. A team-building course for meat managers included duck hunting and hot coal walking. Wine stewards were taken on regular jaunts to Napa Valley wineries.

The company's aggressive expansion mode continued in 2000 with the addition of a new, smaller format, New York-style store in a former warehouse building in Emeryville, the company's ninth. Part supermarket, part convenience store, part café, and part New York deli, the Emeryville Central Market bucked the industry trend toward larger stores, which in 1998 averaged 40,000 square feet, by occupying fewer than 10,000

square feet. There was also an adjacent 15,000-square-foot warehouse and room for the company's headquarters. Central Market had food preparation stations at the center of the store—including a sushi bar, noodle bowl station, grill station, assorted hot foods, service salads, pannini and pizza stations, bakery, and espresso bar—and outdoor seating. Located in a neighborhood that was a mix of residential lofts and apartments and small dot.com businesses and corporations, Central Market was more food service center than retail store. However, the biggest part of the Emeryville project was its backroom production and distribution center with high-tech, high-speed preparation equipment. Emeryville's state-of-the art bakery and kitchen offered Andronico's the possibility of reducing its dependence upon deli vendors throughout its stores.

In 2002, Andronico's opened its 11th store, a large-format, 40,000-square-foot store, with 28,000 square feet of retail space in downtown Walnut Creek. As with Emeryville, the emphasis in this store was on perishables and prepared foods from its large working kitchen. The store as a whole was distinguished by floor to ceiling windows on two of its sides, and windows opened onto the food preparation area.

Neither of these two new stores fared well, however. The Emeryville store fell victim to the burst dot.com bubble. Evening sales had never met expectations for this store, and with the departure of the neighborhood's lunch-time crowd, Andronico's could not afford to keep the store open. The Emeryville store closed in 2004, while the Walnut Creek store, continued to operate below expectations.

Andronico's also had to contend with the fact that its sales figures did not grow much between 2000 and 2003, remaining at approximately $250 million annually. Meanwhile, soaring health care and workers' compensation insurance costs led the company to fire 100 of its workers. However, despite such setbacks, the company continued to gain recognition and to invest in its growth. In 2003, Andronico's was chosen as the National Association for the Specialty Food Trade's retailer of the year. That same year, the San Francisco store underwent a remodeling that allotted 800 square feet of its selling area to housewares, which included the company's own brand. The Palo Alto store also expanded its housewares section to 10,000 square feet in 2003. In 2004, the San Francisco store won *Gourmet News* magazine's Retail Leadership Award for superior cross-merchandising of its housewares.

Andronico's would need to take time to take stock of recent market trends and in-store developments, as Bill Andronico announced in a 2004 *East Bay Business Times* article. According to Andronico, the business had ''a great brand that could easily be successful in other parts of the Bay Area, including the . . . wine country, and even in nearby markets like Sacramento, which doesn't really have anything like out store today . . .'' The decision to come was whether to grow organically or to seek outside investment to fuel the construction of new stores or to acquire independent grocers or smaller chains.

Principal Competitors

Albertson's Inc.; Raley's Inc., Safeway Inc., Trader Joe's Company, Inc., Whole Foods Market Inc.

Further Reading

Goll, David, "Entrepreneur Bill Andronico: From Neighborhood Roots to Top Niche," *East Bay Business Times*, September 3, 2004, p. 23.

Hammel, Frank, "A True Foodservice Commitment: Tomorrow's Meal-Shoppers Won't Met You Halfway," *Supermarket Business*, June 1995, p. 89.

Ingram, Bob, "A Self-Service Assault on the Senses," *Supermarket Business*, May 1996, p. 169.

——, "Strength Through Sophistication and Spirit," *Supermarket Business*, December 15, 1999, p. 21.

Lewis, Len, "At Your Service," *Progressive Grocer*, March 2000, p. 54.

——, "Oasis in Emeryville," *Progressive Grocer*, July 2000, p. 62.

Temple, James, "Albany, California-based Grocery Chain Carves Out Fresh Niche," *Knight Ridder Tribune Business News*, July 25, 2004, p. 1.

Zwiebach, Elliot, "Extreme Food Retailing: After 75 Years, Andronico's Passion for Food Retailing, Showcasing Top-Quality Foods, and Creating an Exciting Shopping Experience Continues Strong," *Supermarket News*, April 19, 2004, p. 12.

——, "Three Generations of Andronicos," *Supermarket News*, April 19, 2004, p. 20.

—Carrie Rothburd

Atlanta Bread Company International, Inc.

1955 Lake Park Drive, Suite 400
Smyrna, Georgia 30080
U.S.A.
Telephone: (770) 432-0933
Toll Free: (800) 398-3728
Fax: (770) 444-1991
Web site: http://www.atlantabread.com

Private Company
Incorporated: 1993
Employees: 1,500
Sales: $200 million (2004)
NAIC: 445299 All Other Specialty Food Stores; 311811
    Retail Bakeries

Atlanta Bread Company International, Inc., operates and franchises a chain of bakery-cafés, relying almost entirely on franchisees to expand the chain. The company operates more than 160 restaurants in 27 states, offering a menu of baked goods, such as muffins, croissants, bagels, and cookies, as well as sandwiches and salads. Select units offer an expanded menu of pizza, pasta, calzones, and omelettes, part of the company's attempt to cultivate more breakfast and dinner business (lunchtime business accounts for 75 percent of the company's sales). Atlanta Bread's restaurants are served by a central commissary in Smyrna, Georgia. The company hopes to have as many as 800 stores nationwide by at least 2015.

Origins

Atlanta Bread was founded by two St. Louis natives, brothers Bob and Rick Auffenburg, but the chain owed its existence entirely to another pair of brothers, Jerry and Basil Couvaras. The Couvaras brothers were born and raised in South Africa, the sons of Stavros Couvaras, a second-generation South African with Greek ancestry. Stavros Couvaras worked as a dealer of provisions and supplies to ships, earning his fortune in the port of Durban following the closure of the Suez Canal. With the money he made as a ship chandler, Stavros sent his sons to college. Both attended the University of Witwatersrand in

Johannesburg, where Jerry earned a degree in political science and economics and Basil earned a degree in industrial psychology. Jerry, nine years older than his brother, worked as an investment banker in Johannesburg and teamed up with Basil to manage two investment companies. Next, the brothers embarked on careers in the franchised foodservice business. Jerry operated as a franchisor of a 12-unit casual steakhouse chain called Digger's Grill. Basil worked as the director of a multi-store franchise of Chicken Licken, a chain of 260 quick-service restaurants based in Johannesburg. The pair left South Africa in the early 1990s, arriving in Atlanta in 1993.

The Couvaras brothers became joint venture partners with the Auffenburg brothers, who had opened two sandwich cafés in Sandy Springs, a suburb of Atlanta. Jerry was in his mid-30s and Basil was in his mid-20s at the time the agreement was made. When the Couvaras brothers inked the deal with the Auffenburgs, a third unit opened that drove home the potential of the Atlanta Bread concept in the minds of the two South Africans. The third unit, located in suburban Norcross, Georgia, was an immediate success, generating more sales than the other two units combined. Jerry Couvaras, in a January 25, 1999 interview with *Nation's Restaurant News,* remembered the success of the Norcross restaurant. ''Basil and I were both working the unit,'' he said. ''We saw what they had and knew we could improve it by setting up the right systems. Of course, it helped that they were looking to sell the entire thing at that stage.'' The Couvaras brothers bought the Atlanta Bread concept from the Auffenburg brothers in 1994, and immediately set about turning the concept into a sprawling chain.

During their first years in business, the two brothers revamped much of what they had purchased. Sweeping changes were made, as new designs, menus, marketing methods, and operational controls were tested, enabling the Couvaras brothers to fine-tune the concept. The brothers relied on their business experience in South Africa, using the managerial, marketing, and operational models of Chicken Licken and Digger's Grill to help guide them. To achieve expansion, the Couvaras brothers intended to franchise their concept, something they began to do in 1995. That year, Atlanta Bread signed its first franchisee, Dino Bylos, the first of scores of franchisees who would create a chain of Atlanta Bread bakery-café restaurants. A decade later, virtually all of the units bearing the Atlanta Bread banner were operated by franchisees.

As the Couvaras brothers worked to develop their perfect franchise model, expansion of the chain occurred at a fairly rapid pace considering the nascence of the concept. By 1997, there were 33 bakery-cafés in operation, most of them located in the greater Atlanta area. By the end of 1998, Atlanta Bread Co. was a 47-unit chain, with restaurants stretching from Florida to New York and from Georgia to Texas. By this point, many of the lasting characteristics of the concept had developed, yielding what the Couvaras brothers believed was a successful blueprint for accelerated expansion. The brothers had developed a hybrid breakfast, lunch, and dinner concept, featuring wood floors, open fireplaces, and classical music piped through sound systems. The menu included the company's signature sourdough "Loaf of Soup," zucchini muffins, jalapeno bagels, and almond croissants. The brothers intended to roll out the concept nationally, making Atlanta Bread Co. a fixture in markets across the country. "Our unwritten mission is to be the McDonald's for baby boomers, selling fast, affordably priced meals and artisan baked goods in homey neighborhood ambience," Jerry Couvaras explained in his January 25, 1999 interview with *Nation's Restaurant News*.

New Facilities Provide Support for Expansion in the Late 1990s

The Couvaras brothers approached expansion more aggressively at the end of the 1990s, assembling the franchisees to fuel the chain's growth and establishing the infrastructure to serve the new units. The 47 units in operation at the end of 1998 were operated by 35 franchisees, a total that was expected to grow quickly because the company had signed agreements with 35 more franchisees to open 51 new restaurants. The majority of these new units were slated to open by the end of 1999. To provide support for the growing chain, the brothers invested $5 million in a new headquarters and commissary facility, the construction of which was finished in January 1999. The 68,000-square-foot complex replaced a 14,000-square-foot facility, giving the company the capability to supply at least four times the number of stores it had in operation at the time. "As far as storage and mixing machinery, our commissary is a League of Nations," Jerry Couvaras remarked in his interview with *Nation's Restaurant News*. "The $195,000 flour silos, including scales, are German; the pastry line equipment, costing $150,000 and capable of producing 5,000 cinnamon rolls or similar pieces an hour, is Swiss; the mixers are French."

As Atlanta Bread began pressing forward with its expansion plans, work continued on improving the bakery-café concept. The Couvaras brothers wanted Atlanta Bread to be a breakfast, lunch, and dinner destination, but the majority of the company's business was lunchtime business, accounting for 75 percent of its sales. The brothers wanted a more balanced business base, so they turned to their director of operations and corporate executive chef, Peter Teimori, to help cultivate more breakfast and dinner business. Teimori, who joined Atlanta Bread in 1997, began his culinary career in Tehran, Iran, studying with his grandfather, a French-trained baker and chef. Teimori received his formal education in the United States, earning his Master's degree in management from Indiana State University. He became a certified chef, pastry chef, bakery chef, and chocolatier, serving as a senior chef instructor at the California Culinary Academy and as corporate pastry chef for the Ritz-Carlton Hotel chain. Teimori began experimenting with menu changes in 2000, attempting to build upon Atlanta Bread's soup and sandwich base. He developed a test menu that added five new sections to the chain's menu, creating hot entrees that included a variety of pizzas, pasta entrees, calzones, hot breakfast specialties, and omelettes. The work begun in 2000 would not be unveiled publicly for several years, but when the changes were introduced, their influence created a new type of restaurant.

As Teimori worked on the recipes, logistics, and training to introduce a more comprehensive menu, the Atlanta Bread chain expanded. The company generated nearly $70 million in revenues in 2000, a total that marched upward as new units opened. By the spring of 2001, there were 93 restaurants in operation scattered across 18 states. The Couvaras brothers hoped to open 60 more units by the end of 2001 and 100 additional restaurants in 2002—goals that would not be reached. The beginning of 2002, however, saw Teimori's months of experimentation unveiled to the public. Atlanta Bread entered its ninth year of business with a new prototype unit.

Debut of Prototype Restaurants in 2002

In early 2002, the expanded menu was introduced in three new units in Atlanta and Dallas. The addition of pizzas, pasta entrees, calzones, hot breakfast specialties, and omelettes necessitated a change in store design. To prepare the new items, a grill and wood-burning oven were added to the design format, as well as 500 additional square feet for a total of 5,200 square feet. The prototype cost 15 percent more to build, but Jerry Couvaras expected the new format to generate an additional 20 percent in revenue. "My term for this is 'casual chill-out' breakfast and dinner," he said in a September 30, 2002 interview with *Nation's Restaurant News*. "This is a chef-designed concept that's been in the planning for three years. It creates a tremendous point of difference. We can offer dinner for 20 to 30 percent less than Olive Garden. That's what quick casual is all about." When the new units were opened, there were 132 units in operation in 25 states. Short-term expansion plans called for opening an additional 110 units by the end of 2003, expansion that was to include the debut of 18 prototype units by mid-2003.

The Couvaras brothers again failed to reach their ambitious expansion objective, but the shortfall did not detract from the chain's success. The business press hailed the achievements of the Couvaras brothers, but in 2004 the brothers attracted

Key Dates:

1993: Jerry and Basil Couvaras invest in a small sandwich shop business in Sandy Springs, Georgia.
1995: The Couvaras brothers begin franchising the Atlanta Bread concept.
1999: The construction of a new commissary is completed, giving the company the ability to supply at least 200 restaurants.
2000: Experiments begin on an expanded menu.
2002: Prototype restaurants, featuring an expanded menu, first appear.
2004: Atlanta Bread announces the goal of 500 stores in 50 states by 2008.

attention for all the wrong reasons. Atlanta Bread's franchisees, who enjoyed a particularly close relationship with the central office in Smyrna, Georgia, were shocked by the news. On March 21, Jerry Couvaras, while visiting in Johannesburg, was arrested and detained, charged with multiple counts of securities fraud and theft. The charges stemmed from the collapse of the Couvaras brothers' South African investment companies in the early 1990s, a collapse that allegedly cheated approximately 2,000 investors of ZAR 38 million, or $5.8 million. Following the arrest of Jerry Couvaras, who was released on bail but not allowed to leave South Africa, senior investigators in Johannesburg issued an arrest warrant for Basil Couvaras for related charges. After issuing the warrant on May 18, South African officials began working with the Federal Bureau of Investigation (FBI) to arrest Basil Couvaras in the United States. Initially, Basil Couvaras refused to return to South Africa, but in late June he agreed voluntarily to join his brother in Johannesburg. An interim president took over at Atlanta Bread while the company's two senior executives were detained. By the fall of 2004, the threat that the company might lose its senior management disappeared. All the charges were dropped except for one count that Jerry Couvaras settled in court through a plea agreement. The brothers returned to their offices in Smyrna, ready to enter the most ambitious expansion phase in Atlanta Bread's history.

When the brothers returned to Atlanta Bread's helm, they presided over a $200 million business. There were 160 restaurants in existence, operating in 27 states. Expansion plans announced at the end of 2004, if fulfilled, promised the emergence of a truly national chain, one whose reach extended into scores of markets. In 2005, the company planned to open up to 30 stores in the northeastern United States and in Florida. By 2008, the Couvaras brothers hoped to have 500 locations in 50 states. Ultimately, they envisioned a chain with roughly 1,000 restau-

rants, a long-range goal they hoped to meet between 2010 and 2015. In a January 31, 2005 interview with *Nation's Restaurant News,* Jerry Couvaras offered his thoughts on the company's future, expressing the confidence that underpinned the company's ambitious growth plans. ''We just have a lot of confidence in the brand,'' he said. ''We have a lot of dedicated franchisees who have been with us for a decade and continue to grow and give us a lot of inspiration. Although we've been one of the fastest growing companies in Georgia, the most important thing to us is to open up strong stores that can withstand competition and withstand time. It's more sustainable than being fashionable and going with the trade winds. We're building this company to last, rather than being a fad.''

Principal Subsidiaries

Atlanta Bread Company.

Principal Competitors

Panera Bread Company; New World Restaurant Group, Inc.; ABP Corporation.

Further Reading

Ashburn, Elyse, ''Executive of Bakery-Café Chain Atlanta Bread Co. to Surrender in Africa,'' *Atlanta Journal-Constitution,* June 29, 2004, p. B1.
——, ''South Africa Seeks Arrest of Atlanta Bread Co. Executive,'' *Atlanta Journal-Constitution,* June 23, 2004, p. B1.
Cavanaugh, Bonnie Brewer, ''Atlanta Bread Co.: System Improvements Allow Ga.-Based Chain to Continue to Rise,'' *Nation's Restaurant News,* January 31, 1995, p. 24.
Crary, David, ''Atlanta Bread Co. Official to Face Charges in South Africa,'' *American Intelligence Wire,* June 29, 2004, p. 34.
Hayes, Jack, ''Atlanta Bread Co. Eyes Rise in Sales: Prototype Takes Aim at Breakfast, Dinner,'' *Nation's Restaurant News,* September 30, 2002, p. 10.
——, ''Atlanta Bread Roiled by CEO Couvaras' Arrest in S. Africa,'' *Nation's Restaurant News,* May 17, 2004, p. 4.
——, ''Jerry & Basil Couvaras,'' *Nation's Restaurant News,* January 25, 1999, p. 58.
LaHue, Polly, ''Atlanta Bread Company on the Rise,'' *Restaurant Hospitality,* October 2000, p. 132.
Lovel, Jim, ''Bakery Readies New '05 Strategy,'' *ADWEEK,* November 1, 2004, p. 13.
Poole, Sheila M., ''Smyrna, Ga.-Based Restaurant Company Plans to Open 60 New Locations,'' *Atlanta Journal-Constitution,* March 22, 2001, p. B3.
Rogers, Monica, ''Not by Bread Alone: Chef Peter Teimori Extends Atlanta Bread Company's Menu Beyond Soups and Sandwiches,'' *Chain Leader,* July 2002, p. 44.

—Jeffrey L. Covell

Berwick Offray, LLC

9th and Bomboy Lane
Berwick, Pennsylvania 18603
U.S.A.
Telephone: (570) 752-5934
Toll Free: (570) 752-6531
Fax: (570) 752-6531
Web site: http://www.berwickindustries.com

Wholly Owned Subsidiary of CSS Industries, Inc.
Founded: 1945
Employees: 1,600
Sales: $230 million (2003)
NAIC: 336360 Motor Vehicle Seating and Interior Trim
Manufacturing

A subsidiary of CSS Industries, Inc., Berwick Offray, LLC, is the world's largest manufacturer and distributor of decorative ribbons and bows produced by both woven and non-woven methods. The business of the Berwick, Pennsylvania-based company is divided among seven divisions. The Christmas Retail division offers a wide variety of bows and ribbons for wrapping Christmas presents. The Trim Time Retail division is devoted to home décor, tree, and wreath decorating. Berwick's Everyday Retail division produces gift packaging and party decorations for non-Christmas holidays such as Valentine's Day and Easter, as well as birthdays and other gift-giving occasions. The Floral Wholesale division produces decorative ribbon used by florists in creating bouquets. The company also offers a variety of ribbons and bows through its Craft Retail division suitable for craft projects. Berwick's Packaging Wholesale division sells bulk orders of bows, ribbons, and accessories and primarily serves customers such as department stores that offer gift-wrapping services. Finally, Berwick has a Custom division, producing customized ribbons and bows on request. The Berwick Offray name is the result of a 2002 acquisition that brought together the rival firms of Berwick Industries and C.M. Offray and Son, Inc.

American Ribbon Industry Dates to the Early 1800s

Popular in Europe for many years, decorative ribbons were not commonplace in colonial America because of their association with the hated nobility, for whom the wearing of ribbons among both men and women indicated social rank. In England, Parliament actually passed a law that limited the wearing of ribbons to members of the aristocracy. As the United States grew older, the stigma attached to ribbons diminished and a small cottage industry emerged. Around 1815, ribbon making entered a new era with the introduction of the jacquard loom, which allowed the incorporation of floral designs and pictures in ribbons and increasingly spurred the use and popularity of ribbons in America.

C.M Offray and Son was the older of the two companies that would one day combine to create Berwick Offray. The company was founded in 1876 in the New York City area by a 17-year-old French fabric designer dispatched to the United States to serve as a representative of a French textile and fancy ribbon company. He stayed and launched his business by importing ribbons from France to New Jersey. Offray created his own ribbon designs, some of which continue to inspire the designers of today's firm. The company established a mill in Paterson, New Jersey, in 1900. A second generation also joined the company when the founder's son, Claude V. Offray, eventually took over the helm. In 1922, the company moved its plant to Hagerstown, Maryland, and it was here that Offray was completely renovated for war production during World War II, when the plant produced parachute tapes and webbings. With it new technical capabilities, Offray was able after the war to make important advances in the production of ribbons using manmade fabrics. It became the first U.S. manufacturer to produce wire-edge ribbon, as well as the first company to meet government standards for flame retardancy without the use of chemicals.

Claude V. Offray, Jr. succeeded his father as president of the family company in 1962. Under his leadership, Offray became more vertically integrated in its marketing approach, expanding into a wide range of industries that used ribbon. The company made a misstep in the late 1980s, however, when it acquired the tape and braid division of Talon, America. The business never fit in, and after just a year the assets were sold to Coats & Clark, Inc. A few months later, in 1989, Offray made a more appropriate acquisition, paying $38 million for Lion Ribbon Co., a ribbon manufacturer based in Chester, New Jersey. The extra production capacity would soon be put to good use, as the demand for ribbon, in particular yellow ribbon, soared in 1990 and 1991, a ten-fold increase over the previous year, due to the Persian Gulf War and people wearing and displaying yellow ribbons in support of the troops. To keep up with demand, Offray plants were operated 24 hours a day, six days a week.

Offray Closes Plants in the Late 1990s

Offray again tried to branch out from ribbons in 1992 when it formed a new division, Fototextiles, to do full-color photographic transfers to fabrics. Other diversification efforts, which took advantage of the company's manufacturing expertise, included the introduction of webbing used by firefighters and a woven tube for vein replacement. Nevertheless, Offray's core business remained decorative ribbon. It declined to participate in the bow business, which was highly competitive and price sensitive because of large offshore bow manufacturers. By the end of the 1990s, Offray manufactured its ribbon in the United States in plants located in Hagerstown, Maryland; Danville, Virginia; Anniston, Alabama; Leesville, South Carolina; and Watsontown, Pennsylvania. One plant was also located in Ireland, two in Argentina, and contract work performed in Mexico. At the close of the decade, Offray shut down the plants in Ireland and Virginia as part of an effort to re-engineer its workflow process and achieve greater efficiencies and improved turnaround time.

Offray was hit with another surge in demand following the terrorist attacks on the United States on September 11, 2001. Within a day, all of the available stock of red, white, and blue ribbon were sold, and the company was swamped with back orders, forcing management to convene constant strategy meetings to determine how to meet the needs of regular customers and their non-patriotic uses of ribbons with the new patriotic needs. The manufacturing plants, which normally operated two shifts, five days a week, now ran around the clock, seven days a week. Management was further distracted because the company was in the process of being sold. In February 2002, an agreement was reached to sell Offray to rival Berwick Industries, a CSS Industries subsidiary, for $45 million.

Berwick Industries was founded in 1945 in the central Pennsylvania town of Berwick. Unlike Offray, which produced woven ribbon, Berwick used a non-woven method to make its ribbons and bows. The company's first manufactured ribbon was called Satinette, followed later by a plastic ribbon, Splendorette. In short, the ribbons started out as small polypropylene balls, melted and dyed, then cooled, pressed into a 16-inch-wide sheet, and rolled onto large spools. Slitting machines unwound the spools and cut the ribbon into a variety of widths. Some of the ribbon was rolled onto smaller spools for sale, and some was processed into printed ribbons or loaded onto bow-making machines and converted into bows in a variety of shapes and sizes. Berwick was sold to CSS in 1993 for $35 million, a year after the ribbon and bow manufacturer had been forced to restructure its operations, eliminating two unprofitable divisions and initiating other cost-saving measures. At this point, Berwick was generating close to $60 million a year in annual revenues.

CSS was no stranger to reorganization, having recently transformed itself following bankruptcy. The company started out in 1923 as City Stores Company, a department store holding company for three department stores located in Memphis, New Orleans, and Birmingham, Alabama. Other stores soon became part of this ownership group, which allowed individual stores to operate separately while enjoying the benefits of group buying power. The company first went bankrupt during the Great Depression but emerged reorganized in 1934. After the economy rebounded with the advent of World War II, City Stores resumed expansion mode in the postwar years, acquiring department stores in Memphis, Miami, New York City, Hartford, Connecticut, and Washington, D.C., while opening new stores in other urban locations.

The 1970s saw many of City Stores' markets become the victims of urban decay, resulting in a steady erosion in department store sales and the forced closure of many CSS operations. By 1979, the company was again forced into bankruptcy and filed for Chapter 11 protection. During the reorganization process, City Stores was gutted. Some retail operations were discontinued, some stores consolidated, and an assortment of real estate and other assets unloaded for cash. A private investment company, Philadelphia Industries Inc., acquired a controlling interest and its president, Jack Farber, installed himself as City Stores chief executive officer in 1980. He continued to reshape the company, hacking off unprofitable operations, and returned CSS to profitability through the resulting cost savings and the continued divestiture of assets. In 1985, Faber changed the name from City Stores to CSS Industries and began to pursue an acquisition strategy that completely transformed the nature of the company. The first major acquisition came in 1985 with the purchase of Rapidforms, a maker of business forms, followed by Ellisco Co., a metal container manufacturer. In 1988, CSS moved into the gift wrap sector by acquiring Paper Magic Group for $38 million. Among the many products Paper Magic produced were ribbons and bows. In 1991, Paper Magic expanded by acquiring Spearhead Industries, which produced Halloween masks, costumes, and holiday novelties.

After CSS acquired Berwick in 1993, the ribbon and bow manufacturer was originally integrated into Paper Magic, which was then supplemented by further acquisitions. Halloween product assets from Topstone Industries and Illusive Concepts expanded part of the business, while the Christmas business was beefed up with the 1995 acquisition of Cleo, Inc., a major manufacturer of Christmas wrapping paper and trim, as well as gift wrap for other occasions. At this point, CSS divided its assets into two divisions: Direct Mail Business Products Group and

---

Key Dates:

1876: C.M. Offray and Son is founded.
1922: Offray opens a plant in Hagerstown, Maryland.
1945: Berwick Industries is founded.
1989: Offray acquires Lion Ribbon Co.
1993: CSS Industries acquires Berwick.
1999: Berwick acquires bow assets from 3M and Affinity Diversified Industries.
2002: Berwick acquires Offray.

Consumer Products Group, the latter of which housed Berwick. During the second half of the 1990s, it was Consumer Products that became the main emphasis at CSS. Within that group, Berwick was allowed to operated as a standalone company.

Berwick Becomes Separate CSS Product Group in the Mid-1990s

In 1996, Berwick Industries completed an acquisition on its own, purchasing Ribbon Magic Inc., a Minneapolis-based maker of upscale ribbons and bows that specialized in foil hot-stamped items. A year later, CSS restructured its operations. Part of its plan called for the sharing of some administrative functions between Berwick and Paper Magic. The benefits failed to materialize, however, and CSS soon returned to its decentralized approach. By the end of the 1990s, CSS recast its two divisions as four product-oriented groups: The Paper Magic Group, Fall Spring—and Everyday Product Division; The Paper Magic Group—Winter Product Division; Cleo, Inc.; and Berwick Industries.

Before acquiring Offray, Berwick completed a pair of acquisitions in 1999. First, it bought the pull-bow assets of Minnesota Mining and Manufacturing Company (3M), including butterfly and pom-pom pull bows sold under the Bow Magic label to the wholesale floral and retail packaging markets. Berwick then acquired Minnesota-based Affinity Diversified Industries Inc.'s Balloon-in-a-Bow product line, which was then expanded to offer new seasonal design and other designs and the use of licensed characters. However, both deals paled in comparison to the 2002 acquisition of Offray.

At the time of the purchase, Offray had annual sales approaching $100 million, and Berwick slightly more. The two companies appeared to be a good fit. Berwick concentrated on extruded polypropylene ribbon and Offray focused on woven ribbon. While they both sold to major retail chains, there was not much of an overlap. Berwick counted among its major customers big box discounters Wal-Mart, Kmart, and Target. Offray, on the other hand, did less business with Wal-Mart and did not sell at all to Target. Soon after the Offray acquisition, a restructuring plan was put into effect, and over the course of the next two years an Offray distribution facility in Quebec, Canada, and an associated warehouse in Antietam, Maryland, were closed, moves that resulted in the termination of about 125 employees.

Berwick Offray emerged as the world's largest maker of ribbons and bows, posting annual sales well above $225 million. Those numbers improved when the United States became involved in another war, this time in Iraq. Once more the display of yellow ribbon to show support for U.S. troops, and red, white, and blue ribbons to demonstrate patriotism, forced Berwick Offray factories to ramp up production to meet the demand. In general, the use of commemorative ribbons and decorative bows showed no indication of going out of favor, ensuring the company of steady business for many years to come.

Principal Divisions

Christmas Retail; Trim Time Retail; Everyday Retail; Floral Wholesale; Craft Retail; Packaging Wholesale; Custom.

Principal Competitors

Artistic Ribbon & Novelty Company Inc.; Fu Hua Industrial Co., Ltd.; M&J Trimming.

Further Reading

"Berwick—50 Years in Ribbons," *Gifts & Decorative Accessories*, July 1995, p. 10.
Dishneau, David, "Ribbon Maker Goes Extra Mile to Meet Holiday Demand," *Associated Press*, December 2, 1999.
Heerwagen, Peter, "Maryland Ribbon Sold to Public Company," *Quad-State Business Journal*, March 2002, p. 22.
Lewerenz, Dan, "This Town Has Ties to Your Holiday Gifts," *Associated Press*, November 29, 2000.
Morley, Hugh R., "Not Enough Red, White, and Blue," *Record* (Bergen County, N.J.), September 26, 2001, p. B3.

—Ed Dinger

Birthdays Ltd.

Dumers Lane
Bury
BL9 9UR
United Kingdom
Telephone: + 44 161 763 7353
Fax: + 44 161 763 7354
Web site: http://www.birthdays.co.uk

Wholly Owned Subsidiary of Clinton Cards plc
Incorporated: 1969 as Ron Wood Greeting Cards
    Holdings
Employees: 3,260
Sales: £144.7 million ($228 million) (2003)
NAIC: 453220 Gift, Novelty and Souvenir Stores;
    424110 Printing and Writing Paper Merchant
    Wholesalers; 424120 Stationery and Office Supplies
    Merchant Wholesalers

Birthdays Ltd. is one of the leading retailers and wholesalers of greeting cards and related gifts in the greeting card-made United Kingdom. Indeed, the United Kingdom is said to boast the world's highest per capita greeting card market, sending an average of 52 greeting cards per year. Based in Bury, near Manchester, Birthdays operates more than 500 stores throughout the United Kingdom and Ireland, selling an extensive range of branded and own label greeting card designs. The company also sells party supplies through a second retail format, Party Land. In addition to its U.K. and Irish networks, Birthdays operates five stores in Cyprus. The company, which originated as a wholesale supplier of greeting cards and gift wrapping in the 1960s, maintains this activity and is one of the United Kingdom's leading suppliers to supermarkets, department stores, and other retailers. Rising greeting card sales at supermarkets, however, have placed Birthdays under pressure to maintain its market share. To shore up its position, the company agreed to be acquired by rival Clinton Cards at the end of 2004. Birthdays is expected to remain a separate business, positioned at the value end of the sector to complement Clinton's own mid-level to high-end customer target. Clinton also has pledged to expand the Birthdays chain to more than 600 stores into the second half of the 2000s. Birthdays last reported sales of £144.7 million ($228 million) in 2003.

Wholesale Greetings in the 1960s

Britain's passion for greeting cards stretched back to the 1840s when Sir Henry Cole commissioned artist John Calcott Horsley to engrave and color 1,000 cards as a means of replacing the letters Cole habitually wrote to send holidays greetings. Cole then sold the leftover cards for a shilling each. The idea caught on quickly, helped by the passage of the Postage Act of 1846 three years later. That legislation reduced postage on letters to just one penny.

The United Kingdom remained one of the world's largest markets for greeting cards into the second half of the 20th century. Yet the greeting card industry itself remained relatively modest in comparison with its booming growth toward the end of the century. A significant factor in the rise of the greeting card industry in the United Kingdom was the appearance of the first dedicated greeting card shops at the end of the 1960s. The new retail market in turn stimulated the demand for new greeting card designs and, especially, the development of a whole new range of "occasions" for card giving.

The rising demand in greeting cards, and the new retail outlets, opened opportunities in the wholesale sector as well. In 1966, husband-and-wife team Ron and Gail Wood launched a wholesale business providing greeting cards and gift wrap to retailers in the region around Manchester. The Bury-based business not only handled greetings cards from the major publishers, it also began designing its own cards. The company incorporated as Ron Wood Greeting Cards Holdings in 1969.

Witnessing the success of the greeting card retail sector, the Woods decided to enter that market as well. In 1975, the company opened its first three Ron Wood Greeting Cards stores in the Manchester area. The company's format proved a strong success and by the mid-1980s, the company had opened more than 30 stores. The company also opened its first purpose-built warehouse and office facility in Bury, with some 180,000

Company Perspectives:

The Birthdays Group is the leading retailer of greeting cards and related products in the UK. Birthdays is building on its background of solid retail experience and is able to offer you many new and exciting ventures. Our new concept stores are designed to provide you with a unique shopping experience, combined with the best possible prices! No ifs, no buts! We aim to provide only quality products. Birthdays' goal is to be as famous for its service to its customers, as it is for its high quality shops and 'value for money' merchandise.

Key Dates:

1966: Ron Wood and wife Gail establish a wholesale greeting card and gift wrap business.
1969: The company is incorporated as Ron Wood Greeting Cards Holdings.
1975: The first three retail stores are launched.
1986: The Birthdays retail format is launched.
1996: The company changes its name to Birthdays Greeting Cards after Wood sells out to a management buy-in.
1999: 3i becomes a major investment, with a 39 percent stake.
2000: The Ecardsforyou.co.uk web site is launched.
2001: The Party Land retail format is launched.
2003: Tom Hunter and Chris Gorman acquire control of Birthdays.
2004: Birthdays is acquired by Clinton Cards.

square feet of space. That site also served as an introduction into the property development market for Ron Wood himself.

A significant milestone in the company's development came in 1986 with the launch of a new format for its retail operations. Called Birthdays, the new stores featured not only greetings cards and gift wrap, but also gifts and, of importance, party supplies. Over the next decade, Ron Wood Greeting Cards added to its range of retail merchandise, and Birthdays stores came to feature goods such as plush toys, ornaments and decorations, and novelty items.

New Owners in the New Century

The expanding range of greeting cards—celebrating a raft of newly invented holidays such as Secretaries' Day and Grandparents' Day, as well as cards celebrating unlikely occasions such as divorces—provided the foundation for the growth of the retail greeting card industry. At the same time, a new generation of greeting card publishers, many of them small companies, enabled stores to fill more shelf space and to attract a more diversified customer base.

Ron Wood profited doubly from the rising interest in greeting cards. On the one hand, the company's wholesale wing developed a new market providing greeting cards to confectionery shops, as well as to newsstands and tobacco stores. The company's retail side, meanwhile, began a national expansion. Helping to fuel the group's growth was its decision to sell its Bury headquarters and warehouse facility, in a sale-leaseback arrangement that gave the company the capital to invest in new locations.

By the middle of the 1990s, the company operated nearly 400 stores, including 50 franchised stores, throughout the United Kingdom and in Ireland. With sales of more than £99 million (approximately $160 million), the company was able to claim a leading share of the British specialist retail greeting card market.

The success of the Bury headquarters and warehouse development, and its subsequent sale, encouraged Ron Wood to launch a new career as a property developer in the mid-1990s. In 1996, Wood decided to sell most of his holding in Ron Wood Greeting Cards to a management buy-in led by John Lovering, formerly with the Tarmac Group, backed by Prudential and Schroders. The deal cost the buy-in team some £90 million.

Following the acquisition, the company's name was changed to Birthdays Greeting Cards Ltd. Lovering now led the company on a new expansion drive, promising to boost the group's retail network past the 500 mark in the early 2000s. In 1999, Birthdays took on additional capital backing when 3i paid £25 million for a 39 percent stake in the company.

The company also began looking for new business opportunities at the dawn of the 21st century. In 2000, for example, Birthdays launched a new web site, Ecardsforyou.co.uk, created by design consultants Tableau, in order to capture the rising interest in virtual greeting cards. The site included a library of more than 1,000 different cards, including greetings featuring animations and videos. Birthdays also sought to capitalize on its successful range of party supplies. In 2001, the company launched Party Land, a retail format focused on the party planning market. The first Party Land opened as a section of a Birthdays store in Solihull in 2002. By the beginning of 2003, the company began making plans to roll out the Party Land concept to other stores in the Birthdays chain.

Yet Birthdays had been struggling in the early years of the century. While the company's revenues remained strong, topping £144 million in 2003, its profits were slipping. At the same time, the company's market share was being eroded by new competition from the supermarket sector, as well as by the rise of new challengers, especially Clinton Cards. That company, which laid claim to have founded the United Kingdom's first specialist greeting card shop in 1969, had grown rapidly though the 1990s. A series of large-scale acquisitions, including the purchase of Hallmark's U.K. retail network, had boosted Clinton's own network to more than 600 stores. In 2002, Clinton even approached Birthdays with a buyout offer reportedly worth some £100 million. The two sides, however, were unable to reach an agreement.

In September 2003, 3i and Birthdays' other investors instead sold the company to Scottish entrepreneur Tom Hunter, in partnership with Chris Gorman, owner of the Gadget Shop chain of retail novelty stores. The pair paid an estimated £60 million to acquire the company, and began making plans to cross-market Birthdays' and Gadget Shops' product ranges in each other's stores. Hunter and Gorman also attempted to reposition Birthdays by launching a new value format of discount greeting card stores.

Hunter and Gorman soon discovered that Birthdays required a larger capital injection than they were willing to provide. In November 2004, the pair announced that they had agreed to sell Birthdays to Clinton Cards for a total of just £50 million. Although Clinton declared its intention of retaining Birthdays as an independent operation, the group nonetheless was able to claim a combined retail network of more than 1,200 stores and a leading market share of more than 21 percent. The two formats also were in large part complementary, with Birthdays pegged to fill the niche of lower-end and value cards, while the Clinton Cards format targeted the mid-level and upper-end markets. With its own 40th birthday approaching, Birthdays appeared set to remain a fixture in the U.K. greeting card market.

Principal Subsidiaries

Party Land.

Principal Competitors

Card and Party Stores Ltd.; Clinton Cards plc; Retail Variations plc; QD Stores Ltd.; David Patton Holdings Ltd.; Rippleglen Ltd.; Retail Stores plc.

Further Reading

"Birthdays (Stationery and Gifts)," *UK Retail Briefing,* October 2003, p. 73.

"Birthdays Takeover on the Cards," *Printing World,* September 11, 2003, p. 10.

"Clinton Cards Launches Birthdays Acquisition Bid," *UK Retail Briefing,* December 2004, p. 22.

Creasey, Simon, "Wood Work: After Catching the Property Bug While Running National Card Retailer Birthdays, Ron Wood Has Turned Himself into One of the North's Top Developers," *Property Week,* January 30, 2004, p. 89.

Moore, Sheryl, "Birthdays Takes Greeting Cards Back to 1966 Prices," *Manchester Evening News,* December 1, 2003.

Nelson, Fraser, "Happy Pounds 90m Return for Birthdays Group," *The Times,* October 22, 1996, p. 29.

"Prudential and Schroders Wrap Birthdays Buyout," *European Venture Journal,* December 1, 1996.

Wallop, Harry, "Scotland's 'Richest Man' Loses Millions by Selling Birthdays," *Daily Telegraph,* November 19, 2004.

—M.L. Cohen

Bobs Candies, Inc.

1315 West Oakridge Drive
Albany, Georgia 31707
U.S.A.
Telephone: (229) 430-8300
Toll Free: (800) 569-4033
Fax: (229) 430-8331
Web site: http://www.bobscandies.com

Private Company
Incorporated: 1922 as Famous Candy Company
Employees: 410
Sales: $41.3 million (2004)
NAIC: 311340 Nonchocolate Confectionery
   Manufacturing; 311320 Chocolate and Confectionery
   Manufacturing from Cacao Beans

Bobs Candies, Inc., makes and distributes candies, ranking as the largest candy cane maker in the world. The company sells its products to discount stores, supermarkets, convenience stores, and drug stores, as well as online through three web sites—bobscandies.com, americancandy.com, and sweetstripes.com. Bobs Candies offers candy canes in a variety of flavors and makes an assortment of other candies, including stick candy, hard candy, sugar free candy, and bag candy. The company is family-owned, led by the third generation of the McCormack family.

Origins

Albany, Georgia became the candy cane capital of the world with seed money from Birmingham, Alabama. The investors who provided the capital for Albany's first commercial candy-making business—a group the Albany newspaper referred to as "Birmingham capitalists"—were persuaded to back the venture by a young candy factory worker named Bob McCormack. In 1919, McCormack left his job at the Nashville, Tennessee-based Martin Biscuit Company to explore the possibility of starting a candy-making operation in Albany. He solicited the financial help of his former boss, E.L. Martin, two Martin Biscuit workers, R.E. (Bob) Mills and Charles Meyer, and his uncle, Lawrence McCormack, a candy salesman. McCormack, in a letter excerpted on Bobs Candies' web site, wrote to his fiancée in February 1919, confident

that his entrepreneurial career would be a success. "If conscientiousness and hard work, gall, nerve, stickability, and persistence are any of the roads that lead to success," McCormack wrote, "I do believe I will get by with the very large undertaking of starting a candy making business."

McCormack made good on his claim, beginning production two months after he wrote to his fiancée (the pair were wed the following year). In May 1919, McCormack's Famous Candy Company began production of its first batch of candy, relying on a three-person workforce, some secondhand equipment brought in from Birmingham, and basic supplies procured by McCormack to get started. McCormack succeeded from the beginning, a difficult achievement for any fledgling business, but particularly hard for a candy company starting out amid sugar shortages stemming from World War I. Famous Candy Company initially made and sold coconut, peanut, stick, and hard candy, as well as taffy, but soon chocolate and pecan candies were added to the company's product line. Pecan candies, which later were marketed as "Bobs Pe-Kons" and "Bobs Pe-Kon-ettes," drove the company's sales during its formative decades, serving as a mainstay product until World War II.

Business was brisk during McCormack's first years in business. His workload soon required proactive help from his investors, resulting in the arrival of Bob Mills from Birmingham to assist in running the company. Mills took over the administrative duties in Albany, freeing McCormack to concentrate on sales and production. The division of labor between the two Bobs invigorated sales, enabling the pair to buy out the other investors, an event marked by a change in the company's name to the Mills-McCormack Candy Company. In 1924, the co-owners dropped their surnames from the company's corporate title, opting for the name they had in common, yielding Bobs' Candy Company (the apostrophe was dropped several years later).

The Albany candy operation faced its greatest challenge during its second decade of business. The Great Depression delivered economic blows to industries nationwide, causing companies of all types to reel from its effects and, in many cases, collapse. The candy industry was no exception, its ranks winnowed drastically by the bleak economic conditions, leaving only the hardiest members to survive the decade-long catastrophe. By 1933, as the Great Depression reached its trough, candy sales throughout the country were down 45 percent and nearly 900 candy makers had declared bankruptcy. The Albany candy operation stood as an exception to the pervasive trend of financial collapse surrounding it, not only surviving through the decade but demonstrating the ability to expand during the harshest of economic times. McCormack increased the production of low-cost pecan candies, a luxury Southerners continued to budget for as a relief from the strife of poverty. The company changed its name again as a result, calling itself Bobs Candy & Pecan Company. McCormack also introduced a line of snack foods during the 1930s, selling salted peanuts and peanut butter crackers, items that would help his company stay afloat when the next calamity arrived a decade later. Last, in a move that belied the economic conditions of the time, Bobs Candy & Pecan Company moved into larger facilities, having outgrown the accommodations of its original quarters during the black years of the Great Depression.

Persevering During World War II

McCormack barely had the chance to celebrate his fortune at surviving through the 1930s when misfortune struck the company. As the 1940s neared, consumers had begun to act as the consumers of a decade earlier, enjoying discretionary income that allowed them to spend more freely. McCormack's sales began to rise robustly, driven in large part by the popularity of Bobs Candy & Pecan Company's line of traditional candies and its snack line of salted peanuts, peanut candies, peanut brittle, and peanut butter candies. On February 11, 1940, all of that was lost, both the company's products and its ability to make products. Early in the morning, a tornado swept through Albany's business district, killing and injuring more than 500 residents, and completely destroying Bobs Candy & Pecan Company, a company without tornado insurance. It took 256 truckloads to remove the rubble at the Bobs Candy & Pecan Company site.

McCormack was forced to start from scratch after the tornado. By using his cash reserves, he was able to rebuild his business within six months. The company stopped making chocolate candy after the tornado, but introduced a candy bar that paid homage to the natural disaster. Bobs Tornado Bar, a peanut, coconut, and popcorn bar that was advertised as "worth a dime but costs five cents," sold well, helping the company to gain its footing.

Stability was elusive during the war years, as McCormack and his company had to adapt to changing dynamics within the candy industry. Again, the company faced a sugar crisis, as rationing measures were implemented, but the most defining change was engendered by the price of pecans. Within months, the price of pecans tripled, forcing the company to stop using pecans, which had been a mainstay ingredient in its products. McCormack fell back on his snack food line for financial support, focusing on the sale of peanut butter crackers and vacuum-packed peanuts. The switch in product emphasis was enough to warrant a change in the company's name, marking the end of Bobs Candy & Pecan Company in 1943 and the beginning of Bobs Candy and Peanut Company.

Innovations highlighted the company's postwar years, enabling it to record robust sales growth in the 1950s and 1960s. Hard candies were particularly popular during the late 1940s, but high humidity in southern Georgia meant the candies had to be shipped quickly and remain on store shelves for only a short time or else they would become gummy and bleed color. In 1946, McCormack solved the problem by installing large air conditioners to de-humidify the company's wrapping room. In 1949, further improvements in product quality were achieved when a new machine was introduced that sealed candy stick in moisture-proof wrappers. A third innovation arrived as the 1950s began, its creation the work of Father Harding Keller, McCormack's brother-in-law. During the 1940s, Keller invented a machine to dispense ribbons of peanut butter on the company's peanut butter crackers, an invention that greatly improved the consistency and quality of the product. In 1950, Keller scored another success with the invention of a machine that twisted soft candy into the spiral striping that defined the look of candy canes. The Keller Machine, combined with the improvements in wrapping, allowed for mass production. Soon, the company's candies and snacks were stocked in 600 A&P stores throughout the southern United States.

McCormack's company ended the 1950s having evolved past its stature as a regional wholesaler to become a nationally-oriented enterprise. Break-proof packaging, developed in 1956, the year the company changed its name to Bobs Candies, Inc., enabled the company to distribute its candy canes on a national basis. In 1958, the refinement of a machine first developed by Keller accelerated national distribution, giving the company the ability to create the crook in candy canes automatically. By the end of the decade, when the company claimed to be the largest candy cane producer in the world, annual sales eclipsed $3 million, a total derived from the production of 1.8 million sticks of candy and 500,000 candy canes on a daily basis.

Growth and Leadership Changes in the Late 20th Century

The 1960s brought an end to McCormack's longstanding leadership, paving the way for a new generation of McCormacks to guide the company. McCormack relinquished the title of president in 1963, passing control to his son, Bob McCormack, Jr. One of the first projects undertaken by McCormack, Jr., was to move the company to larger quarters. Bobs Candies occupied six buildings in downtown Albany, using nearly 100,000 square feet of space, but the rapid growth of the company demanded more space. Construction began in 1967 and production at the new 130,000-square-foot facility began the following year. The new facility, which boasted 260 tons of air conditioning units, doubled the company's production capacity.

Bobs Candies expanded its production facility twice in the 1970s, once at the beginning of the decade and again at the end of the decade. As it had during the 1960s, production capacity doubled during the 1970s, a decade that witnessed another packaging innovation, shrink-wrapping. Shrink-wrapping provided a more aesthetically pleasing look to the company's candies, which attracted more customers. The company's customers eyed the new shrink-wrapped selections from Bobs Candies at a different type of retail outlet during the 1970s. Although supermarkets remained the biggest purchasers of the company's candies, Bobs Candies increasingly was selling its products to convenience stores, which became the primary outlet for the company's individually wrapped candies. The 1970s also witnessed the emergence of large discount chains such as Wal-Mart Stores, which supplanted supermarkets as the biggest purchasers of the company's candies in the 1980s.

Leadership passed to the third generation of the McCormack family in the 1980s as Bobs Candies neared its 70th anniversary. Greg McCormack was named president in 1988, but, like others in the McCormack family, he spent years working for the family business. Before being named president, Greg McCormack was selected to oversee a major new addition to the company's operation. A second production facility was opened in 1984, a facility that gave the company its first overseas presence. The facility was located in Kingston, Jamaica, where Greg McCormack spent nearly three years managing the operation of the 13,000-square-foot plant that produced unwrapped, pure-sugar stick candy. Not long after returning home, Greg McCormack was named president, assuming the post the same year Bobs Candies acquired Fine Candy. A competitor, Fine Candy generated more than $4 million in annual sales when it was acquired by Bobs Candies, adding a substantial boost to the company's sales. "Our sales grew fairly dramatically when we acquired them," Greg McCormack confirmed in a May 1998 interview with *Candy Industry*.

After the spike in sales from the Fine Candy acquisition, Bobs Candies' revenue growth leveled out, but at a robust rate, increasing between 10 percent and 15 percent annually throughout much of the 1990s. Revenue growth was fueled, in part, by another expansion program in 1994, one that increased the size of the company's production facility by 175,000 square feet. Greg McCormack, in his first full decade in charge, concentrated on long-range planning, something he believed his predecessors in large part had ignored. Part of his strategic outlook involved increasing the business generated by the company's non-candy cane products. Bobs Candies distributed its candy canes nationwide, but the company could not claim the same for its line of other hard candies. Further, the sale of candy canes was a seasonal business, leaving Bobs Candies less well-rounded than Greg McCormack would have liked. To give the company a broader, more reliable business base, Greg McCormack focused on pure sugar candies, a segment of the company's business that first began to grow in the 1970s. After numerous rebranding efforts, the company unveiled its line of pure sugar candies under the Sweet Stripes banner in 1997. "Sweet Stripes is what we're focusing on now," McCormack explained in his May 1998 interview with *Candy Industry*. "That is an evolving strategy that we are continuing to work on. We're expanding our production capabilities of it by more than 100 percent to keep up with demand and expected demand."

As Bobs Candies entered the 21st century, the growth of the 1990s had created a candy maker with more than $40 million in sales. Although the company was nearing its 90th anniversary, it employed modern marketing and production techniques, ensuring that Bobs Candies would remain the world's preeminent candy cane manufacturer in the years ahead. At the company's production facility in Albany, cooling and de-humidifying systems developed by the National Aeronautics and Space Administration (NASA) ensured product quality and consistency. On the marketing front, the company used three web sites to sell its candies, maintaining an online presence through bobscandies.com, sweetstripes.com, and americancandy.com. With its proven ability to adapt to changing times and market conditions, the company promised to play a prominent role in the candy business well into the future.

Principal Subsidiaries

Click Foods, LLC; Sweet Stripes, Inc.

Principal Competitors

See's Candies, Inc.; Russell Stover Candies Inc.; Kraft Foods Inc.

Further Reading

Amire, Roula, "Rain or Shine, Bobs Candies Delivers," *Candy Industry,* May 1998, p. 20.
"Bobs Candies," April 5, 1999, p. 17.
"Bobs Candies Moves Candy Cane Production to Mexico," *Candy Industry,* December 2001, p. 11.
"Bobs Candies Saves with 'Space Age' Heat Pipes," *Air Conditioning, Heating & Refrigeration News,* January 22, 1990, p. 64.

—Jeffrey L. Covell

Bristow Helicopters Ltd.

Redhill Aerodrome
Redhill
Surrey
RH1 5JZ
United Kingdom
Telephone: (+44) 1737-822353
Fax: (+44) 1737-822694
Web site: http://www.bristowhelicopters.com

Private Company
Incorporated: 1953 as Air Whaling Limited
Employees: 873
Sales: £145.92 million ($229.7 million) (2003)
NAIC: 213112 Support Activities for Oil and Gas
    Operations; 481211 Nonscheduled Chartered
    Passenger Air Transportation; 481212 Nonscheduled
    Chartered Freight Air Transportation; 481219 Other
    Nonscheduled Air Transportation; 621910 Ambulance
    Services

Bristow Helicopters Ltd. (BHL) is one of the world's top helicopter services companies. BHL provides transportation to offshore oil rigs, search and rescue operations, and other services, including training for military pilots. The company's worldwide fleet numbers about 120 helicopters. Bristow has a headquarters in Surrey, a European unit based in Aberdeen, and about a dozen bases overseas. The company is affiliated with Offshore Logistics, Inc. (OLOG) of the United States. Together, the two firms offer a truly global reach.

Origins

Bristow Helicopters Limited dates back to 1953, when Air Whaling Ltd. was founded by Alan Bristow, a former Royal Navy helicopter pilot. After World War II, he became the first helicopter test pilot employed by Westland Aircraft Ltd. He then went to work for the newly formed Compagnie Helicop-Air in Paris for another two years. He left when French unions objected to a foreigner holding this position. Next, Bristow

joined the French Foreign Legion and won a Croix de Guerre for helping the French Army set up a helicopter squadron.

Bristow then formed his own company. He leased a hangar from the Royal Navy at Henstridge Airfield in Somerset, England, and set up Air Whaling Ltd. on June 6, 1953. The firm specialized in spotting whales for the whaling industry. Alan Bristow credited Ted Wheeldon, who had helped him get his Westland test pilot job, with arranging Air Whaling's sideline as a distributor of Westland helicopters to the whaling industry.

According to company literature, the firm has a long history of innovation. For example, it was Bristow's request for an offshore refueling method that prompted Flight Refuelling Ltd. (part of Cobham plc) to develop one of the aerial refueling systems used by modern military aviators.

The company spent considerable effort developing a technology for harpooning whales by helicopter. However, the firm's prospects for this were scuttled by International Whaling Commission regulations in the mid-1950s.

The company soon built up a trade ferrying men and material to and from oil rigs in the North Sea, its first small contract coming from the Shell Oil Company in 1955. A new company called Bristow Helicopters Ltd. (BHL) was created. Working for British Petroleum brought Bristow into the Persian Gulf in 1957. This contract allowed the company to buy its own helicopters for the first time, two Westland Widgeons. Bristow also ventured into Iran and Bolivia that year (the original Bolivian adventure lasted till 1962). The limited number of companies that could afford helicopter services prompted the firm to look for work on a global basis, said Bristow in the company history *Leading from the Front.*

Acquired by Airwork in 1959

BHL relocated from Henstridge to Redhill Aerodrome in the late 1950s. By 1959, BHL employed 100 people and had more than 14 helicopters in the field. That year, the business—which then included Bristow Helicopters (Eastern), Bristow Helicopters (Bermuda), and Helicopter Rentals—was sold to Airwork Ltd. Airwork had been maintaining aircraft for the Royal Air

Company Perspectives:

As part of the Offshore Logistics Group, Bristow Helicopters strives to conduct all of our business in an atmosphere that emphasizes trust, integrity, respect and results. We work together with a firm commitment to safety, reliability and value for our customers.

Force since before World War II. It had acquired several operators before buying BHL, which it combined with helicopter operator Fison-Airwork. Fison had extensive experience in Nigeria, where it performed crop dusting and other jobs.

In 1960, Airwork merged with Hunting-Clan to create British United Airways (BUA), which the next year merged with Silver City Airlines and then British Aviation Services. Air Holdings was created as a holding company.

Alan Bristow and three of his colleagues acquired a 49 percent holding in two of the subsidiaries, BHL and Airwork. Helicopter Contractors, later Bristow Helicopter Group Ltd., was formed to oversee these interests.

Bristow began training helicopter pilots for the Royal Navy at Redhill in 1961. This was followed by contracts from India, Australia and New Zealand. The company had started its training operations in Kuwait several years earlier. By the end of the 1960s, BHL had also established a training joint venture in Iran.

George Fry became head of BHL in December 1967 as Alan Bristow began a two-year stint as joint managing director of British United Airways. During Fry's tenure, the fleet grew to 80 helicopters. BHL's stature was such that it was able to buy 15 state-of-the-art Jet Rangers from Agusta Bell. The company was also putting new turbine engines in its older Whirlwinds. Operations expanded to Trinidad, Nigeria, Egypt, Morocco, Indonesia, Malaysia, and Australia.

BHL was also becoming active in the North Sea. It began its first tentative operations from Aberdeen in 1969 and established a base there two years later. BHL began flying large Sikorsky S61Ns that could carry two-dozen passengers. Another workhorse was the 15-passenger Bell 212.

1970s Rescues

BHL set up a school to train its own pilots at Redhill in 1970. This business was contracted out to a U.S. firm in 1998. Another important service was begun in 1971—search and rescue (SAR) over the Straights of Dover. Public outcry caused this duty to be reassigned to the Royal Air Force within three years. The civil-run approach eventually prevailed, however.

BHL's North Sea operations led to rescue work. In 1974, the company evacuated 150 people from two rigs that had come unmoored. BHL also participated in the massive rescue of more than 500 crew members from the derrick barge *Hermod* on December 15, 1979.

Since the mid-1970s, a number of countries had been nationalizing the helicopter services once provided by BHL. These included Abu Dhabi (1975), Malaysia (1983), and Dubai (1984). In the case of Malaysia, BHL retained a management contract to run the operation for several years.

Operations in Iran, where BHL had been active since 1957, came to a more dramatic end. By 1979, BHL's Iran-based operation employed 300 people and 23 helicopters. After the Shah of Iran was deposed following the revolution headed by the Ayatollah Khomenei, BHL was able to start removing these assets and the expatriate personnel. However, seven aircraft worth $15 million and 22 people had to be surreptitiously evacuated on March 9, 1979 in "Operation Sandstorm," a dramatic rescue that made tabloid headlines in the United Kingdom.

Busy in the 1980s

BHL acquired a small operator, British Executive Air Services (BEAS), in 1978. By 1980, Bristow's operations had spread to the Gulf Coast of the United States and the fleet numbered about 170 helicopters. It was flying about 150,000 passengers a year in the early 1980s.

The Gulf of Mexico operations were started in 1979 with Bristow's acquisition of Texas-based Offshore Helicopters Inc. Renamed Bristow Offshore Helicopters Inc. (BOHI), the operation closed down within two years, however.

BHL kept its fleet up to date with the newest helicopter types. In 1980, this meant the Sikorsky S76, followed in 1982 by the Aerospatiale 332L Super Puma. Bristow ordered $100 million worth of Pumas specially modified for oilrig crew transport. These were dubbed "Tigers" by BHL.

The company's innovative engineering was not limited to the Tigers. BHL had developed a number of unique technologies to meet its operating needs, that is, auto-hover systems. It was also a pioneer of Health and Usage Monitoring Systems (HUMS), which monitored for unusual vibration on various components in order to prevent accidents.

BHL was kept busy in the early 1980s supporting military operations in the Falklands (BHL maintained a presence there through the late 1990s). Another, smaller southern hemisphere mission was the support of the British Antarctic Survey in 1984. Unfortunately, one of the two Jet Rangers dispatched was wrecked on the ice on the way back to its ship.

Consolidation in the 1980s and 1990s

The company began a relationship with China's CITIC Offshore Helicopter Co. Ltd. in the mid-1980s, soon before oil was discovered in the South China Sea. Times were leaner elsewhere. A plunge in oil prices in 1986 in particular led to a thinning of the ranks of helicopter services companies. Bristow managed to survive, acquiring British Caledonian Helicopters in 1987. By 1990, Bristow was flying more than 200 helicopters and 40 fixed-wing aircraft. It employed 2,000 people. The oil industry accounted for more than two-thirds of revenues.

Financial services company British & Commonwealth Holdings acquired BHL in June 1988 through its Bricom unit. British & Commonwealth was bought out by Sweden's Gamlestaden group in July 1990. A 1991 management buyout

Key Dates:

1955: Bristow Helicopters Limited (BHL) is formed by Alan Bristow.
1959: BHL becomes part of the Airwork Ltd./Air Holdings family.
1961: Bristow beins training Royal Navy helicopter pilots.
1965: Bristow begins supporting North Sea oil exploration.
1971: A base is established at Aberdeen.
1979: Equipment and personnel evacuated from Iran in Operation Sandstorm.
1991: After being owned briefly by Swedish investors, Bristow undergoes a management buy-out.
1996: Offshore Logistics buys half of Bristow.
2000: BHL is restructured into three divisions.

left Caledonia Investments and Morgan Grenfell Development Capital each owning about 45 percent of shares.

Offshore Logistics, Inc. (OLOG) of Lafayette, Louisiana acquired a 50 percent stake in Bristow Helicopters in December 1996. OLOG had 159 helicopters in its fleet and after the acquisition was second in size only to Norway's Helikopter Service A/S. At the time, Bristow operated 145 aircraft as far abroad as the Falkland Islands, Australia, Nigeria, Trinidad, and Vietnam. *Helicopter News* pointed out that Bristow had become a partner in Irish Helicopters Ltd. with Offshore Logistics rival Petroleum Helicopters, Inc.

Bristow formed a helicopter joint venture with FR Aviation (Flight Refuelling) and Serco Defense Ltd called FBS Ltd. In late 1996, FBS won a 15-year contract to train pilots for Britain's Ministry of Defence.

Restructuring for the 2000s and Beyond

BHL got a new CEO in 1999, former finance director Keith Chanter, who replaced Steve Palframan. Bristow was restructuring, shifting more responsibility from its Surrey headquarters to its European unit at Aberdeen and the International and Technical Services business units based at Redhill. The technical services unit was incorporated as Bristow Technical Services Ltd. in January 2002.

Industry consolidation continued. In 2000, lower oil prices had led to the merger of Bristow's British rivals, Bond and British International Helicopters. CHC Canadian Helicopter had controlling interests in both of these. By this time, Bristow had acquired a 49 percent share in Norsk Helikopter AS.

Around 2003, the Helicopter Operations Monitoring Programme (HOMP) was being developed as a successor to HUMS. HOMP included Flight Data Recorder information as well as data on the aircraft's mechanical components.

As of 2005, the company had a fleet of 120 aircraft. It was the leading operator of the 18-passenger AS 332 Super Puma. The 12-passenger Sikorsky S76A+ was the company's workhorse

for the southern sector of the North Sea. Other helicopter types were used, including a specialized Sikorsky S61N for search and rescue. Bell 212, 412, and 214ST aircraft were also in the fleet.

Principal Subsidiaries

Bristow Technical Services Ltd.; Norsk Helikopter AS (Norway; 49%).

Principal Divisions

European; International; Technical Services.

Principal Competitors

CHC Helicopter Corporation; Petroleum Helicopters, Inc.

Further Reading

"Bristow Eyes Norwegian Offshore Market," *Helicopter News*, November 26, 1993.
"Bristow Helicopters Awarded 'Groundbreaking' Contracts," *Helicopter News*, April 10, 1998.
"Bristow Helicopters CEO Proposes Westland Takeover," *Aviation Week & Space Technology*, May 6, 1985, p. 26.
"Bristow Helicopters Expands Fleet, Facilities," *Aviation Week & Space Technology*, October 29, 1979, p. 59.
Bristow Helicopters Limited, "Bristow History," http://www.bristow helicopters.com/bhl_hist.php.
"Bristow Helicopters; War in the Air," *Economist*, April 23, 1977, p. 115.
"Bristow Looks for New Niche," *Flight International*, November 11, 2003, p. 18.
Buxton, James, "Bristow Sold in £200m Buy-Out; Deal Brings Cayzer Family Back Among Group's Shareholders," *Financial Times* (London), November 9, 1991, p. 24.
"CITIC Plans to Introduce Bristow Helicopters as Investor," *Business Daily Update*, July 26, 2004.
Edwards, Dave, and Tim Collins, "Bristow Helicopters 50th Anniversary Website," http://209.196.171.35.
"Failed BIH Bid Led to Offshore Logistics' Bristow Deal," *Helicopter News*, April 12, 1996.
Healy, Andrew, *Leading from the Front; Bristow Helicopters: The First 50 Years,* Stroud, U.K.: Tempus Publishing Limited, 2003.
"Helicopters Meet New Challenges," *Aviation Week & Space Technology*, September 29, 1975, p. 46.
Mason, Peter, "Skyjack Squadron: Daring Britons Rescue £10m Helicopters from the Ayatollah's Guards," *Daily Express*, May 8, 1979, p. 1.
Morrocco, John D., "FBS Gets Nod to Operate Triservice Helicopter School," *Aviation Week & Space Technology*, October 7, 1996, p. 28.
"Offshore Logistics to Buy Half of UK's Bristow," *Helicopter News*, March 29, 1996.
"UK Increases Civilian-Owned Fleet of Support Helicopters," *Flight International*, September 30, 2003, p. 26.
"US Helicopter Operator Buys into Bristow," *Flight International*, April 3, 1996.
Wastnage, Justin, "Sea Change; The Crisis in the North Sea Oil-Drilling Industry Has Hit Helicopter Operators Who Ferry Workers to Rigs. But Are Prospects Set to Improve?" *Flight International*, October 22, 2002, p. 32.
"Worldwide Transport and Supply Helicopter Survey," *Offshore*, February 1981.

—Frederick C. Ingram

Broadwing Corporation

7015 Albert Einstein Drive
Columbia, Maryland 21046-9400
U.S.A.
Telephone: (443) 259-4000
Toll Free: (877) 926-7847
Fax: (443) 259-4444
Web site: http:www.corvis.com

Public Company
Incorporated: 1997 as Nova Telecommunications, Inc.
Employees: 1,213
Sales: $314.3 million
Stock Exchanges: NASDAQ
Ticker Symbol: BWNG
NAIC: 334210 Telephone Apparatus Manufacturing;
334290 Other Communications Equipment Manufac-
turing; 517110 Wired Telecommunications Carriers;
517310 Telecommunications Resellers; 517910 Other
Telecommunications; 518111 Internet Service Providers;
518210 Data Processing, Hosting, and Related
Services; 519190 All Other Information Services

Broadwing Corporation operates two divisions that serve different segments of the telecommunications industry. The communications division, managed by the Broadwing Communications, LLC subsidiary, is a provider of data, internet, voice, and broadband transport services to carrier and enterprise customers delivered over a nationwide network connecting 137 cities. The communications equipment division, operating under Corvis Equipment Corporation, designs, manufactures, and sells high performance all-optical and electrical/optical communications systems. In response to the severe downturn in the telecommunications industry, the company shifted its focus to become primarily a provider of communications services, which comprises about 99 percent of its revenue.

Origins

Broadwing Corporation is the result of the acquisition by Corvis Corporation of Broadwing Communications Services Inc. and Corvis's subsequent reorganization under the Broadwing name. Corvis was founded in 1997 by David R. Huber, a physicist and technology pioneer. Huber was raised in the small town of Le Grange, Oregon, known for its railroad and lumber. His father was a county agent and ran the local 4-H club. His mother was a school teacher. Huber received a B.S. in physics at Eastern Oregon University and earned his Ph.D. in electrical engineering from Brigham Young University. From 1989 to 1992, he held research and development positions in optical communications at Rockwell International Corporation, Optelecom, Inc., and ITT Industries, Inc.

In 1992, Huber founded Ciena Corporation, an innovator of gear that enabled major telephone companies to increase the capacity of their networks to carry telephone calls and internet messages. Ciena's innovations in fiber optics caused a scramble among major telephone carriers for its products, making the start-up one of the fastest growing firms in American economic history. The company shattered financial records for new start-ups after its February 1997 initial public offering raised $3.4 billion and first-year sales totaled $195 million. With Ciena's rise to international prominence, Huber, the start-up's chief scientist at the time, quarreled with chief executive Patrick H. Nettles and the company's board of directors over the company's future direction. Huber wanted to pursue optical technology, which Ciena's top management and board would not endorse. In a bid for more independence, Huber also wanted to report directly to the board rather than to Nettles. In May 1997, Huber left Ciena with $300 million worth of the company's stock. In June of that year, he founded Nova Technologies, Inc. to develop the world's first all-optical network.

Corvis's Meteoric Rise

By February 1999, Huber had renamed his new firm Corvis Corporation and already had 96 employees, with plans to employ 1,500 by 2001. Corvis also launched a major building spree, constructing a 60,000 square-foot building in Columbia, Maryland in addition to signing a lease on another 100,000 square foot facility. With backing from venture capital firms, Cisco Systems, and his own investment, Huber raised tens of millions to reenter a business that was potentially worth billions for the company that could lower data transmission costs. At the time, major long-distance carriers, including MCI WorldCom and AT&T, were spending huge sums converting data from light to electricity as it passed through switches that directed this traffic to various end points. Because switches were technologically indispensable, the goal was not to eliminate them but to improve their efficiency. In 1999, data traffic exceeded voice transmissions for the first time, threatening revenues as data was less profitable. As a result, lowering transmission costs became increasingly important, especially as the electrical conversion at the switches accounted for about 75 percent of the total cost of transmitting traffic. Huber's innovations eliminated this cost with an all optical network that could carry more powerful optical signals. Although typical optical signals could travel up to 600 kilometers before degrading, Corvis's network could transmit vastly more data up to 3,200 kilometers. Corvis also developed an optical switch, thereby eliminating the need for converting light to electricity. With an eye on competitors that were also developing optical networks, Huber shrouded his company's operations in secrecy. Corvis did not have a Web site until 1999 and investment analysts were required to sign non-disclosure agreements before talking to company officials. In December 1999, Corvis raised another $215 million in venture capital, increasing its total funding to $300 million, to expand manufacturing capacity and hire 200 additional employees over the next year. In addition, although Corvis had yet to generate revenue, four fiber optic networks (Sprint, Quest, Williams, and Broadwing Inc.) began field tests of its all-optical long distance and switching equipment for a total of $35 million to $40 million. The deals offered potentially lucrative follow-up orders.

By the beginning of 2000, Corvis meteoric rise caught the attention of Cisco, Lucent Technologies, and Nortel, each of which wooed the start-up with acquisition offers. In April 2000, Corvis won its first customer in Austin-based Broadwing Communications Inc., a wholly owned subsidiary of Broadwing Inc. of Cincinnati, Ohio, for optical services in the exploding broadband market. After only weeks of testing, Broadwing Communications signed a two-year $200 million deal to deploy Corvis's gear across its nationwide network to offer bandwidth on demand and higher bandwidth capacity to customers at lower costs. Broadwing expected the new gear to increase its network capacity by 400 percent, cut costs by more than 50 percent, and reduce time to install new customer service by up to 70 percent. The agreement made Corvis the first to go to market with an all-optical long distance and routing system, signifying a milestone in the company's development. Corvis quickly landed another $200 million optical equipment deal with Williams Communications Inc., which operated a 33,000-mile nationwide network providing voice, video, and data products and services. In June 2000, Corvis announced a third multi-year deal with Quest Communications International Inc. for its ultra-fast optical networking gear.

In May 2000, Corvis announced it was seeking to raise $400 million in an initial public stock offering to cover sales and marketing costs, as well as expenses related to research and development. By April 2000, the company had raised $346.1 million in venture capital and other funding. At the same time, Corvis began a program of acquisitions, purchasing Algety Telecom, a French telecommunications equipment maker, and Baylight Networks, a designer of optical network access systems. Corvis announced its acquisition of Algety in May 2000 and Baylight one month later. In July 2000, fiber optics rival Ciena filed a patent infringement suit against Corvis, an action that endangered Corvis's plans to go public. In U.S. District Court for the District of Delaware, Ciena accused Corvis of infringing on three technology patents and sought an injunction and damages in the lawsuit. The patent suit nevertheless had no effect on Corvis's July public offering. Originally hoping for a $400 million public offering, Corvis instead raised $1.14 billion after boosting its asking price for its stock from $13 to $36 a share and the size of its offering from 27.5 million to 31.6 million shares. The company increased the price and number of shares in response to the mania surrounding its offering as prospective investors swamped investment bankers with orders. The offering was the largest for a company that had yet to report any revenues. In the first day of trading, shares of Corvis shot up 135 percent despite the broad technology sell-off occurring at the time. The company's shares shot up to $98 before closing at $84.71 on NASDAQ volume of almost 28 million shares, putting Corvis's value on paper at more than $28 billion after one day. Several days later, Corvis boasted a market capitalization of $38 billion, making it more valuable than General Motors. The offering also made company founder David Huber a billionaire, at least on paper, with 22 million common shares worth more than $1.86 billion.

The Collapse of the Telecom Market

In early October 2000, in its first earnings report as a public company, Corvis posted third-quarter revenue of $22.9 million and a net loss of $66.4 million. Wall Street investors anticipated Corvis's sales would rocket to $310 million in 2001, but a sell-off in the shares of Nortel, a market leader, foreshadowed the collapse of the telecom industry. Nortel's shares dived 29 percent when its earnings failed to meet Wall Street's hyper-inflated expectations, sparking reverberations across the industry. In late November 2000, Shares in Corvis sank to $28 from $50 in five days, a far cry from its high of $114.75 in August. By the end of February 2001, Corvis's fortunes were plummeting as investor zeal for optics cooled and its stock sank to $11.88 a share. Shares of all telecom equipment makers were in a free-fall as companies that bought their equipment began cutting back on capital spending. The market value of Corvis's stock dropped more than $4 billion, and the company's total value plunged $30 billion from its peak in the summer of 2000. With its shares faltering in the markets, Corvis needed to conserve cash and backed away from its 100,000 square-foot expansion at a business park in Columbia, Maryland. In addition, in May 2001 Corvis cut 250 positions and later reorganized its Canadian operations, resulting in additional job losses. With the value of its shares collapsing, between May 7 and June 15, 2001, Corvis became the subject of nine class action lawsuits alleging misrepresentation relating to its initial public offering. In the three months ended June 2001, Corvis reported a loss of $821.8 million, and by the end of August its shares closed at $1.97.

Amidst these punishing reversals, Corvis consummated deals with Telefonica SA, a telecommunications firm in Spain and Latin America, and with another, unnamed, major global carrier. In January 2002, Corvis also signed a merger agreement to acquire Dorsal Networks, a privately held provider of transoceanic and regional undersea optical network systems, in a stock transaction for about 40 million shares of Corvis stock, worth approximately $90 million. However, with revenue down 95 percent, all five of its customers in financial trouble, its stock price hovering around $1.00 a share, repeated workforce reductions, and most of the original management gone, David Huber could make little headway in an industry that had glutted the market and set the stage for ruinous price cutting. Nonetheless, by August 2002 Corvis still had $580 million in cash and near cash, enough to operate for five years. In October 2002, Corvis transferred to the NASDAQ Smallcap Market after its stock failed to meet NASDAQ's $1 per share minimum bid price requirement for continued listing on the National Market. In desperate pursuit of revenue, the company formed a subsidiary, Corvis Government Services Inc., to market its services and equipment to the federal government, the only bright spot for information technology amidst the telecom crash. In 2003, Corvis announced several more rounds of lay offs at both its Algety Telecom division in France and its corporate headquarters in Columbia.

Corvis's Desperate Gamble

With few business prospects, Corvis decided to gamble on a major acquisition. In February 2003, the company arranged through C III Communications LLC, a Delaware limited liability company, to acquire Broadwing Communications Services

Inc., the fiber-optic network of Broadwing Inc. Corvis owned 96 percent of C III, which it incorporated specifically to acquire Broadwing Communications, which had been formed in 1999 after Broadwing Inc. purchased IXC Communications for $3.2 billion. Corvis concluded the acquisition in June 2003 for $81 million. Although Corvis owned most of C III, the venture was set up with minority stake holder Cequell III, a St. Louis investment and management firm. Under the terms of the arrangement, Corvis held a 96 percent stake in the acquisition, with Cequel III and former parent company Broadwing Inc. retaining a 1 percent and 3 percent interest respectively. The Austin-based fiber-optic subsidiary with the nation's most advanced communications network built with Corvis's own equipment was once the crown jewel of Broadwing Inc. (later Cincinnati Bell). Under pressure from mounting debt, Broadwing was forced to shed its prized asset built for $4 billion at a fire-sale price. With Broadwing Communications, Corvis acquired an 18,700-mile network that stretched from Seattle to Boston with 150,000 long-distance customers, most of them corporate. Broadwing Communications was also debt free and on track to break even by mid-year 2003.

Nevertheless, Corvis's revenue plunged another 83 percent in the first quarter of 2003, leading it to lay off another 150 employees, almost one-third of its staff. The latest round of lay offs brought Corvis's staff to 350, down from 1,625 employees in 2001. The company took another hit when two different juries found that Corvis violated two patents of its rival Ciena Corporation. Investors also criticized Corvis for buying Broadwing when it was struggling to survive. In September 2003, Corvis initiated a ninth round of layoffs in three years, cutting 200 more jobs and eliminating most of the fiber-optic company's original workforce. In addition, Corvis lost out to Ciena on a lucrative $150 million contract to help expand the federal government's telecommunications networks. With virtually no business and few employees left on the equipment side, Corvis transformed itself from vendor to communications services carrier. However, if Corvis viewed Broadwing as the engine to a more profitable market, the wholesale carrier business looked similarly grim. Although Broadwing retained its customers, it was experiencing reduced traffic and declining sales. With vanishing revenues on all sides, the company seemed to be fast approaching its demise.

Reorganization and Survival

Nevertheless, with the economy on the mend, Corvis began 2004 with brighter prospects. By the end of January, its shares had climbed more than 65 percent from April 2003, when they bottomed out at 48 cents, making it one of the best performers on the major stock exchanges. The company had not said or done anything to cause the rapid rise of its shares, but Corvis became the subject of investment hype as money began returning to the market and its shares rose above one dollar, allowing Corvis's stock to begin trading again on the NASDAQ national market. At the same time, the Broadwing acquisition was beginning to pay off, producing 99 percent of the company's revenue. For the fourth quarter of 2003, Broadwing generated revenue of $142.5 million while the equipment side of the business brought in just $2.1 million. In March 2004, Corvis took another step away from its roots as a maker of fiber-optic gear by purchasing

Focal Communications Corp., a provider of local phone service in twenty-three cities. The purchase was made for $97.7 in acquisition costs and $98.1 million in assumed debt. By combining Broadwing's long-distance network with Focal's local network, Corvis was anticipated to generate revenue approaching $1 billion. The acquisition also was symptomatic of the ongoing turmoil and consolidation in the telecommunications market.

In September 2004, Corvis announced it was changing its name to Broadwing Corporation effective October 8, 2004, reflecting the company's principle focus as a provider of voice, data, and media network services to companies, carriers, as well as federal government agencies. The reorganization under the Broadwing name stemmed from the brand name's visibility and recognition in the marketplace. With the name change, Broadwing Corporation became the holding company for Broadwing Communications, its service provider. In addition, Broadwing Corporation continued to operate its optical communications equipment business under the Corvis name, and founder David Huber remained chairman and chief executive of the renamed firm. The company also initiated a one-for-twenty reverse stock split in which every twenty shares would be the equivalent of one share of stock. Following the stock split, the company offered a one-for-one stock dividend that allowed shareholders to receive one share of stock for each share they owned. As 2004 came to a close, the company had survived the worst of the telecom downturn with a new focus, revenues, rising shares, and a promise of more profitable times ahead in the highly competitive telecommunications market.

Principal Divisions

Broadwing Communications, LLC; Corvis Equipment Corporation.

Principal Competitors

AT&T; Sprint FON.

Further Reading

"Broadwing Inc. to Sell Broadwing Assets to C III Communications," *Business Wire*, February 25, 2003, p. 1.

"Corvis Announces Agreement with Quest Communications," *Business Wire*, June 6, 2000, p. 1.

"Corvis Announces Successful Completion of Field Trial of All-Optical Networking Products with Williams Communications," *Business Wire*, January 2001, p1.

"Corvis Completes Acquisition of Baylight Networks," *Business Wire*, June 14, 2000, p. 1.

"Corvis Corporation to Change Name to Broadwing Corporation," *Business Wire*, September 28, 2004, p. 1.

"Corvis to Acquire Alogety Telecom, Extends Optical Networking Leadership," *Business Wire*, May 5, 2000, p. 1.

Elboghdady, Dina, "Loss Grows, but Corvis Points to Cash On Hand," *Washington Post*, January 26, 2001, p. E5.

Garreston, Rob, "Corvis Shares Surge 135% after IPO," *Washington Post*, July 29, p E1.

Guidera, Mark, "Ciena Sues over Patent; Corvis, a Competitor, Is Accused of Infringement," *Sun*, July 20, 2000, p. 1C.

Hirsh, Stacey, "Corvis Lands a Major Deal; It Will Sell Williams Equipment Worth Up to $200 Million," *Sun*, April 14, 2000, p. 1C.

——, "Corvis, C III Teaming up to Buy Unit of Broadwing; Md Optics Firm Acquiring Long-Distance Division," *Sun*, February 26, 2003, p. 3 C.

Knight, Jerry, "Corvis Raises $1 Billion in IPO; Fiber Optics Firm Has No Revenue," *Washington Post*, July 28, 2000, p. E1.

——, "Muddled Message on the Internet Drives Down the Stock Price of Corvis," *Washington Post*, November 27, 2000.

Landendorf, Kirk, "Broadwing Lit up by All-Optical/Company to Buy $200 Million Worth of Super-Fast Network System from Corvis," *Austin American Statesman*, July 17, 2000, p. D4.

Larkin, Patrick, "Corvis Speeds Fiber-Optic Signals," *Cincinnati Post*, August 5, 2000, p. 7B.

Lemke, Tim, "Corvis Buys Focal to Expand Reach," *Washington Times*, March 9, 2004, p. C 11.

McCarthy, Ellen, "Corvis Will Change Name to Broadwing," *Washington Post*, September 29, 2004, p. E 5.

Menezes, Joaquim, "Optical Network Start-Ups Crop Up," *Computing Canada*, December 17, 1999, p. 21.

Mullaney, Timothy J., "Why Corvis Is Belle of the Telecom Ball," *Business Week*, January 31, 2000, p. 66.

Nee, Eric, "The Upstarts Are Rocking Telecom," *Fortune*, January 24, 2000, p. 104.

Noguchi, Yuki, "Corvis Unit to Market to Government," *Washington Post*, October 8, 2002, p. E5.

——, "Corvis to Downsize Again in Difficult Market," *Washington Post*, January 30, 2003, p. E 5.

——, "Through C III, Corvis is Primary Investor in Broadwing Network," *Washington Post*, March 26, 2003, p. E 5.

"On the Money," *Commercial Appeal*, July 28, 2000, p. C2.

Pappalarado, Denise, "Broadwing/Corvis Union: Year One," *Network World*, February 23, 2004, p. 35.

Patalon, William III, "Corvis Hopeful Despite Big Loss; Telecom Company Says It'll Meet 2001 Predictions," *Sun*, October 20, 2000, p. 1C.

——, "Optical-Networking Stocks Undergo Worrisome Blips," *Sun*, November 5, 2000, p. 1D.

Ribbing, Mark, "Columbia Firm Plans Big Growth: 96 Workers at Corvis Could Rise to 1,500 by 2001," *Sun*, December 1998, p. 9C.

——, "Corvis Raises Needed Funds with a Private IPO; Venture Capital Is Fine When Secrecy Is Golden," *Sun*, December 22, 1999, 1D.

Schafer, Sarah, "Hoping Clients Make the Switch; Columbia-Based Corvis' Technology Could Signal a Change in the Way Large Data Networks Work," *Washington Post*, November 15, 1999, p. F 16.

——, "Md. Telecom Firm Corvis Aims for $400 Million in IPO," *Washington Post*, May 5, 2000, p. E3.

Spinner, Jackie, "Corvis Backs away from Expansion," *Washington Post*, April 2, 2001, p. E 6.

Valdmanis, Thor, and Shawn Young, "Cisco Weighs Buying Upstart Networking Firm; Corvis Would Fill High-Tech Niche," *USA Today*, December 16, p. 1B

—Bruce P. Montgomery

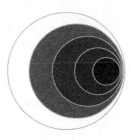

Buckeye Partners, L.P.

5002 Buckeye Road
Emmaus, Pennsylvania 18049-5347
U.S.A.
Telephone: (484) 232-4000
Fax: (484) 232-4543
Web site: http://www.buckeye.com

Public Company
Incorporated: 1986
Employees: 620
Sales: $272.9 million (2003)
Stock Exchanges: New York
Ticker Symbol: BPL
NAIC: 486910 Pipeline Transportation of Refined
 Petroleum Products

Buckeye Partners, L.P., based in Emmaus, Pennsylvania, is a master limited partnership trading on the New York Stock Exchange. The company's main business, conducted through subsidiary Buckeye Pipe Line Company L.P., is a network of pipelines, terminals, and storage facilities serving major oil companies, refineries, and end users of petroleum products. All told, the company owns and operates 4,500 miles of pipelines and more than 100 delivery locations in a ten-state area, as well as operating another 1,200 miles of pipelines on a contract basis. Bulk storage terminals, capable of holding approximately five million barrels of refined petroleum, are located in Illinois, Indiana, Michigan, New York, Ohio, and Pennsylvania. The types of refined products Buckeye transports include gasoline, jet fuel, diesel fuel, heating oil, and kerosene. Since 1996 Buckeye has been majority-owned by management and employees.

Heritage Linked to 1800s Standard Oil

Buckeye was once part of the 19th-century industrial behemoth, Standard Oil Company. The company was launched in 1863 when John D. Rockefeller and a pair of partners bought a Cleveland refinery, at a time when the oil industry was in its infancy, western Pennsylvania fields were center stage, and the major petroleum product was kerosene, used as an illuminant. Rockefeller recognized that Cleveland, because of its links to railroads and Great Lakes shipping and proximity to Pennsylvania crude, was ideally situated to become a major hub for oil refining. In 1870 the business was incorporated and Rockefeller set out to consolidate, if not conquer, the industry—in the process displaying a keen business acumen as well as ruthlessness in getting his way. By the end of the decade Rockefeller and his partner, Henry Flagler, controlled almost all of the oil refining in the United States, but they were not content with Standard Oil as a horizontal monopoly, dominating one aspect of the oil industry. Instead, they began to expand the company's interests to include drilling as well as the sale of petroleum products, transforming Standard Oil into a vertical monopoly as well. In 1882 all of the assets were housed under the first trust in the United States. The Standard Oil Trust controlled 80 percent of the country's oil refineries and 90 percent of the oil pipelines, and was also a dominant player overseas.

By the mid-1880s the only major petroleum deposits were to be found in Pennsylvania and Russia, and with the Pennsylvania fields beginning to play out there was concern at Standard Oil that the company might be little more than a flash in the pan. Then in May 1885 oil was discovered near Lima in northwestern Ohio, a deposit that stretched into Indiana, and within months hundreds of derricks were erected in the area and began pumping crude. But there was one complication: The Ohio crude contained less kerosene than the Pennsylvania deposits, and what kerosene there was contained far too many impurities to make a commercial product. Despite the risk of investing in the Ohio area, Rockefeller forged ahead, putting up money out of his own pocket to finance the business in defiance of the Standard Oil Company board. Thus in March 1886 Standard Oil formed Buckeye Pipe Line Company to transport crude from independent wells through a network of pipelines to storage facilities or railroad terminals. At first Standard Oil sold the Ohio oil as a heating fuel, but it was only after a company scientist found a way to refine the Ohio crude into a marketable kerosene that Rockefeller knew his gamble paid off. It was in Ohio that Standard Oil first became involved in production in a major way, as the company quickly gained complete control of the Lima field, and the trust took a major step in its move toward

---

Company Perspectives:

Buckeye is committed to providing quality transportation service to its customers by continuing to grow and diversify its service offerings.

---

becoming a vertical monopoly. Because the Ohio deposits would be the dominant American play until superseded by discoveries in Kansas and Texas in the early 1900s, Standard Oil was an unchallenged force in the U.S. oil industry for the rest of the 1800s. Although the transport of Ohio crude would not be as important after the Kansas and Texas discoveries, Buckeye Pipe Line remained a viable business because there was still a need to bring crude to the major refining operations established in Lima.

Standard Oil launched the era of the trusts, becoming just one of a number of industry monopolies. The U.S. Congress, fearful of the power these firms wielded, passed the Sherman Anti-Trust Act in 1892. Two years later the Ohio Supreme Court ordered the breakup of Standard Oil, but the firm found a way to skirt the ruling by fleeing to New Jersey, where it was able to reform under a consolidated corporate structure as Standard Oil of New Jersey and continued to operate as a trust. The federal government sued Standard Oil and in 1906 it was declared a monopoly and ordered to dissolve. After the company appealed the decision, the matter was eventually taken up by the U.S. Supreme Court, which in 1911 ruled against Standard Oil and forced its breakup. As a result, Standard Oil was split into several "Baby Standards," and another two dozen smaller subsidiaries also were spun off, including Buckeye Pipe Line, which emerged as an independent, public company.

Moving Toward Refined Products After World War II

Through the end of World War II in 1945, Buckeye was primarily involved in crude oil transportation. Management now decided to expand its ability to move refined products, which were more stable than crude and thus a safer investment. In the 1940s Buckeye established its Midwest Products System, a pipeline that ran from Toledo to Lima, Ohio, and from Indianapolis to southeastern Illinois. Next, Buckeye launched its Eastern Products System in 1952. This unit built pipelines from the New York harbor refining and distribution complex, connecting New Jersey refineries to New York and Pennsylvania marketers. The system became operational in 1954. In the meantime, Buckeye continued to build up its Midwest assets, in 1954 completing construction on an eight-inch refined products pipeline that extended from Lima to Columbus refineries. A year later a link to Toledo's Wolverine Pipe Line Co. was completed as well as a number of other spurs. In addition, some of the crude oil lines were converted to refined products, although the transportation of crude products remained an important part of Buckeye's business. As a result of these changes, Buckeye enjoyed steady growth, improving revenues from $7 million in 1946 to $17 million in 1954.

In 1964 the Pennsylvania Railroad acquired Buckeye, many of whose pipelines paralleled the railroad's right-of-way. Under

Penn Central's ownership, Buckeye expanded its New York City operations, constructing the first pipeline system beneath city streets to serve commercial customers and the area's three major airports: La Guardia, JFK, and Newark. Starting in the mid-1970s Buckeye launched a major capital improvement program, making sizable investments to improve existing service through the addition of modern pumps, control systems, and new storage tanks. The company also extended its pipeline system to new markets. In 1977 Buckeye moved into the New England market by acquiring Jet Lines, Inc., a pipeline network serving the region.

Buckeye's corporate parent in the meantime underwent a number of changes. In 1968 the Pennsylvania Railroad merged with the New York Central Railroad, the largest merger in U.S. history, resulting in the Penn Central Railroad Company. Less than three years later, however, Penn Central was forced into bankruptcy, the largest corporate bankruptcy in history. With the railroad operations turned over to Conrail and Amtrak, the company emerged from bankruptcy in October 1978 as Penn Central Corporation, which had assets in real estate, hotels, oil companies, and pipelines.

To raise cash, Penn Central spun off Buckeye in December 1986. Buckeye Partners, L.P. was incorporated in Delaware as a master limited partnership, and with Goldman Sachs & Co. acting as lead underwriter, 12 million partnership units were then sold at $20 each, raising $240 million. This money, along with $300 million from a private placement of partnership debt securities, was used to purchase Penn Central's interest in Buckeye Pipe Line Co. Penn Central retained a 19 percent stake in Buckeye Partners and also owned another corporation, Buckeye Management Company (BMC), which was formed in 1986 to serve as the general partner of Buckeye Partners. BMC owned a 1 percent interest in Buckeye Partners. Also of note in 1986, Buckeye acquired a controlling interest in Laurel Pipe Line Company, which served Pennsylvania markets from a Philadelphia terminal. The remaining 17 percent interest was then bought in December 1992.

Penn Central sold its 19 percent interest in Buckeye Partners in 1993, but held onto BMC for another three years. Then, in March 1996, Penn Central sold its interests to BMC Acquisition Company, a Delaware corporation created by a management team to acquire BMC. BMC was owned by Glenmoor Partners, an investment group headed by BMC's chairman and CEO Alfred W. Martinelli and including other members of senior management. Also a participating entity in Glenmoor was the BMC Acquisition Company Employees Stock Ownership Plan. The ESOP was funded by a $63 million loan from Glenmoor, which in turn borrowed the money from Prudential Life Insurance Company of America. This $63 million along with $6 million contributed by Glenmoor was used to acquire Penn Central's interest in BMC. It took over the management of a company that in 1995 generated $183.5 million in revenues and posted net income of nearly $50 million.

Late 1990s Expansion

Buckeye Partners, despite its long history, remained little known. To increase its profile with investors, BMC instituted a 2-for-1 split of the partnership's publicly traded units in Febru-

Key Dates:

1886: Buckeye Pipe Line Company is formed by Standard Oil Company.
1911: The breakup of Standard Oil leads to an independent Buckeye.
1964: Pennsylvania Railroad acquires the company.
1986: Buckeye is spun off as a master limited partnership.
1996: Management and employees gain a majority ownership position.
2004: Buckeye acquires 25 terminals from Royal Dutch/Shell.

ary 1998. As a result, the unit price was lower, making it more attractive to individual investors. Buckeye Partners then gained additional recognition by becoming more aggressive in its efforts to expand its operations. In early 1999 it paid $12.6 million to acquire the fuels division of American Refining Group, Inc. (AMG), adding a refined petroleum products terminal and transmix processing plant located in Indianola, Pennsylvania, as well as another transmix processing facility in Hartford, Illinois. Because pipelines carry a variety of products, a certain amount of blending of dissimilar fuels is bound to occur. An undesirable blending of products caused during transport is known as transmix, requiring processing after the product has completed its pipeline journey. The AMG fuels division had been working with Buckeye for a number of years, and with Buckeye's backing it was hoped that the operation, already one of the largest transmix refining operations in the country, could grow even further. Later in 1999 Buckeye also acquired selected assets of Seagull Products Corporation and Seagull Energy Corporation at a cost of $5.75 million. Buckeye added a presence in the Gulf Coast area picking up a 16-mile pipeline, partially leased by a chemical company, as well as six pipeline operating agreements with chemical firms in the area, thereby expanding Buckeye's business in operating pipeline assets for third parties. To house these assets, subsidiary Buckeye Gulf Coast Pipe Piles, LLC was formed. The 1999 acquisition provided an immediate contribution to Buckeye's balance sheet. For the year, revenues totaled $305.8 million, a significant improvement over the $184.5 million recorded the prior year. The addition of refining revenue, accounting for $107.5 million, provided most of the difference. Transportation revenue also grew by nearly $15 million.

Buckeye continued to build on its network in 2000. From BP Amoco it added to its ability to serve the Detroit market by acquiring an area terminal capable of holding 280,000 barrels of petroleum product. Later in the year Buckeye bought another six petroleum product terminals from Agway Energy Products, LLC. Providing a combined capacity of two million barrels of petroleum product, the terminals were located in Macungie, Pennsylvania, and Brewerton, Geneva, Marcy, Rochester, and Vestal, New York. Buckeye also sold some assets in 2000, electing to leave refining operations to others and to concentrate on pipelines and terminals. Kinder Morgan Energy Partners LP bought Buckeye Refining Company, LLC for $37.3 million in cash and $8.3 million in net working capital, taking over Buckeye's transmix processing plants in Indianola, Pennsylvania, and Hartford, Illinois. Buckeye used the money to pay

down debt and provide some operational cash. In 2000 Buckeye also forged an unusual alliance for a pipeline company. It agreed to provide right-of-way access to PetroNet, a fiber-optic network serving 22 northeastern and midwestern cities, in exchange for a stake in PetroNet of nearly 50 percent. Another development of note during 2000 was the appointment of William H. Seas to replace Martinelli as CEO. Martinelli stayed on as chairman. For the year, revenues from continuing operations totaled $208.6 million, and income from continuing operations amounted to $64.5 million.

In 2001 Buckeye completed a pair of deals involving TransMontaigne Pipeline Inc. First, Buckeye bought a 482-mile pipeline and other assets for $62 million. Starting in Hartsdale, Indiana, the pipeline ran east to Toledo, Ohio, and west to Fort Madison, Iowa, plus an 11-mile spur connecting terminals in Hartsdale and East Chicago, Indiana. In addition, Buckeye added the Hartsdale and East Chicago facilities, along with four terminals located in South Bend and Indianapolis, Indiana; Peoria, Illinois; and Bryan, Ohio. The acquisition added significantly to Buckeye's ability to serve the Chicago market while providing flexibility to its Midwest pipeline network. Later in 2001 Buckeye supplemented these assets by acquiring a 18.52 percent stake in West Shore Pipe Line Company, paying TransMontaigne $23.3 million. West Shore owned a pipeline system that originated in the Chicago area and ran to Green Bay, Wisconsin, and Madison, Wisconsin, providing refined petroleum products to markets in northern Illinois and Wisconsin.

The effect of these acquisitions could be readily seen on Buckeye's balance sheet. Revenues increased to $232.4 million in 2001 while income improved to $69.4 million. In 2002 revenues topped $247.3 million and the company recorded net income of $71.9 million. Buckeye completed just one transaction in 2003, paying $28.5 million for a 20 percent interest in West Texas LPG Pipeline Limited Partnership, which owned and operated a 3,000-mile pipeline. But during the course of 2003 Buckeye took steps to raise money to pay off debt, thereby lowering the cost of capital and allowing it to further its growth through acquisitions and capital projects. In February 2003 the Partnership sold 1.75 million units, raising nearly $60 million. Then in July Buckeye netted nearly $300 million through the placement of notes due in 2013. A month later the company raised another $150 million in notes, due in 2033.

Before Buckeye began to use its new financial flexibility to make acquisitions in 2004, Glenmoor, which owned a controlling stake in Buckeye's managing partner, was sold to a private equity fund: Carlyle/Riverstone Global Energy and Power Fund II. The fund was created by Washington, D.C.-based investment firm The Carlyle Group and Riverstone Holdings LLC of New York. There was no plan, however, to change the way Buckeye was run and the company's management team remained virtually unchanged. A few months later, in July 2004, Buckeye returned to acquisition mode in a big way, agreeing to pay $530 million to a unit of Royal Dutch/Shell for 25 terminals and more than 850 miles of pipeline in the Midwest. Early in 2005 Buckeye bought another 478 miles of pipelines and four more terminals, paying $180 million to affiliates of ExxonMobil Corporation. As major oil companies elected to sell off pipeline assets to concentrate on their core businesses, there was every reason to expect that Buckeye would continue to expand.

Principal Subsidiaries

Buckeye Pipe Line Company, L.P.; Laurel Pipe Line Company, L.P.; Buckeye Terminals, LLC; Buckeye Gulf Coast Pipe Lines, L.P.

Principal Competitors

Kinder Morgan, Inc.; TEPPCO Partners, L.P.; The Williams Companies, Inc.

Further Reading

Bary, Andrew, "Happy Returns: Why Pipeline Partnerships Are Creating Rising Interest," *Barron's National Business and Financial Weekly,* August 10, 1992, p. 17.

Blumenau, Kurt, "Lower Milford Township, Pa., Gas Pipeline Firm's Net Income Rises," *Morning Call* (Allentown, Penn.), July 31, 2004.

——, "Parent Sells Controlling Interest in Allentown, Pa.-Area Pipeline Company," *Morning Call* (Allentown, Penn.), March 10, 2004.

"Buckeye Partners LP," *Oil & Gas Investor,* June 2000, p. 4.

"Continuing Program of Expansion Buoys Buckeye Pipe Line Profits," *Barron's National Business and Financial Weekly,* June 27, 1955, p. 34.

Chernow, Ron, *Titan: The Life of John D. Rockefeller,* New York: Random House, 1998.

—Ed Dinger

Caliper Life Sciences, Inc.

68 Elm Street
Hopkinton, Massachusetts 01748-1602
U.S.A.
Telephone: (508) 435-9500
Fax: (508) 435-3439
Web site: http//:www.caliperls.com

Public Company
Incorporated: 1995 as Caliper Technologies Corporation
Employees: 454
Sales: $49.4 million
Stock Exchanges: NASDAQ
Ticker Symbol: CALP
NAIC: 325410 Pharmaceutical and Medicine Manufacturing; 325411 Medicine and Botanical Manufacturing; 325412 Pharmaceutical Preparation Manufacturing; 325413 In-vitro Diagnostic Substance Manufacturing; 325414 Biological Product Manufacturing; 334413 Semiconductor and Related Device Manufacturing; 334516 Analytical Laboratory Instrument Manufacturing; 541710 Research and Development in the Physical, Engineering, and Life Sciences

Caliper Life Sciences, Inc. uses its core technologies of liquid handling, automation, and LabChip microfluidics to produce innovative tools for the life sciences industry. Within the life sciences field, Caliper seeks to address three primary markets: drug discovery and development, genomics and proteomics, and molecular diagnostics. Caliper's customers include leading pharmaceutical and biotechnology customers, universities, government research laboratories, and other research organizations throughout the world.

Origins

Caliper Life Sciences, Inc. was founded in 1995 in Palo Alto, California, by technologist Mike Ramsey and Calvin Y.H. Chow to develop and market the potential of microfluidics, the business of creating new tools for automated bioprocessing and

analysis enabling the controlled movement of minute amounts of fluids on the surface of a microchip. Caliper sought to develop rapid, affordable, and easy-to-use medical test chips to enable basic medical testing at a much cheaper price and without the use of expensive laboratory equipment. The new automated tool for biochemical analysis offered the functional equivalent of a chemistry laboratory on a microchip. By applying advanced microfabrication from the semiconductor industry to the automated handling of fluids, Caliper hoped to fundamentally change the way that chemical, biological, and clinical information was generated and used.

Cofounder and head of development Calvin Chow said he wanted Caliper to be the Intel of the diagnostic testing business. Caliper fashioned its chips with the aim of mimicking what big medical lab machines could do in processing vials of blood. The testing process used a series of simple steps that involved taking a precisely measured quantity of fluid, mixing it with a test solution, adding fluorescent markers that bind to reaction products, and shining a light on the mix in order to compare the test with a color standard. The colors would be identified not by lab technicians but by a miniature photosensor, similar to the millions of photosensors in a home video camera. Microfluidics would perform the job because the channels on the testing chip would admit only a few microdroplets of fluid as several thousands of volts spiked across the intersections and endpoints of the channels in a rolling pattern that governed the flow as needed. The chip moved around molecules in time with electrostatic pulses according to the clock cycles of the operating computer. In addition, the chip could decipher information at any point by sensing how fast a particular droplet moved in response to the electronic stimulus. The chip also kept track by adding fluorescent markers to the fluid, enabling specimens to be identified each time they passed over a photosensor.

Caliper Pursues Corporate Partnerships

In its first year, Caliper raised $6.6 million from private investors and venture capital firms with the expectation that it would have products within 18 months. In March 1997, Caliper signed a collaboration deal with Dow Chemical Company to develop polymers for Caliper's chemical microchips. Under the

Company Perspectives:

Caliper Life Sciences uses its advanced liquid handling and LabChip technologies to create leading edge tools that accelerate drug discovery and enhance the diagnosis of disease.

agreement, Dow would conduct research on the technology at its materials engineering center and make a financial investment in Caliper Technologies. By producing microchips from less expensive polymers rather than from silicon or quartz, Caliper could make the technology feasible for a range of applications requiring disposable chips, including medical, pharmaceutical, industrial, and environmental analysis, as well as potential consumer products.

In May 1997, Caliper announced the appointment of David K. Lam as president and chief executive officer. Lam was the founder of Lam Research Corporation, a pioneer developer of semiconductor process equipment based on plasma etching technology. Immediately before joining Caliper, Lam was president and chief executive officer of ExpertEdge, where he directed software development and marketing from 1989 to 1996. Under Lam's leadership, in May 1998 Caliper signed an agreement with Hewlett-Packard to develop jointly a first-generation, miniature analytical instrument and information system based on Caliper's lab-on-a-chip technology. The deal provided for the companies to invest $20 million for the first year and another $80 million for the following four years to develop and market the technology. In June 1998, the company announced it raised an additional $7.4 million, bringing total financing since its founding to more than $40 million to accelerate the development of its LabChip technology for chemical and biochemical research and analysis.

Caliper earned its revenues primarily from collaborative agreements with corporate partners through a fee-based technology access program. Caliper also sought to use these partnerships to commercialize its technology. As a result, in May 1998 the company signed a deal with Agilent Technologies to create a line of commercial research products based on Caliper's LabChip technologies. The agreement provided Caliper with the scale and expertise of a leading analytical instrumentation firm to bring these novel products to market. Under the agreement, both companies pledged to invest $100 million collectively over a period of five years. The agreement further provided that Caliper focus on developing technology and LabChip applications while Agilent focus on developing instruments and software, manufacturing instruments, and marketing and selling. By December 1998, Caliper also had signed strategic relationships with Dow Chemical, Hewlett-Packard, Hoffman-La Roche, Amgen, and Eli Lilly, and established partnerships with leading academic institutions, including Harvard University, the University of Pennsylvania, Northwestern University, Princeton University, and Oak Ridge National Laboratories, to develop new applications for its LabChip technologies. In addition, in September and October 1998, Caliper received federal grants from the National Cancer Institute and the National Institute of Standards and Technology to adapt its LabChip platform to discover potential anti-cancer agents and to develop a separate DNA diagnostic platform for use in centralized clinical laboratories.

In February 1999, Caliper announced the appointment of Dr. Daniel L. Kisner as its new president and chief executive officer. Kisner came to Caliper from Isis Pharmaceuticals, Inc., where he was president and chief operating officer. With additional prior experience in senior roles at the National Cancer Institute, SmithKline Beckem, and Abbott Laboratories, Kisner arrived with a business background and an understanding of the pharmaceutical industry. His appointment was considered especially important at a time when Caliper was trying to market its LabChip devices and device-based systems that enabled high-throughput experimentation and information access for faster drug discovery, better medical treatment, and more accurate and cost-effective biological and genetic research. Earlier in 1999, Caliper had announced the availability of its new high-throughput screening Technology Access Program (TAP) for pharmaceutical discovery companies. The program attracted Amgen, Hoffman La Roche, and, in August 1999, Eli Lilly to subscribe to Caliper's nanoscale screening systems for biochemical and cellular pharmaceutical targets. Caliper also introduced its proprietary LabChip technology platform, which functioned like a liquid integrated circuit in managing complex laboratory processes on a microchip. The LabChip devices worked by processing fluids containing DNA, proteins, or cells in the same way that semiconductors processed electrons, executing biological tests in seconds. This technology promised applications in a broad range of industries, including pharmaceuticals, agriculture, chemicals, and diagnostics.

In April 1999, Caliper completed the construction of a new 53,000-square-foot corporate and manufacturing facility in Mountain View, California. The facility included an advanced state-of-the-art high throughput drug screening facility, clean room production capabilities, and numerous laboratories for research and development. In late 1999, Caliper's commercial partner, Agilent, introduced the first microfluidic LabChip system, the 2100 Bioanalyzer. Following the introduction of this system, Caliper focused on introducing its own instrument systems while continuing to expand the range of applications for the 2100 Bioanalyzer.

In December 1999, Caliper went public, raising $75 million. After the first day of trading, Caliper's shares rose 145 percent to $39.25, indicating enormous interest in a biochip market that promised $950 million in sales by 2005. For 1999, Caliper reported revenues of $12.1 million compared to $8.2 million in 1998, an increase of 48 percent. Caliper attributed growth in revenue to its collaboration with Agilent Technologies and to its Technology Access Program customers. Nonetheless, the company reported a net loss of $14.4 million, up from $3 million in 1998. The increased loss reflected primarily the company's rise in operating expenses related to the growth of research and development operations.

Caliper Forms a New Company

Caliper's rapid rise in research and development spending stemmed from the potential payoff for drug and bioresearch firms in the emerging genomics revolution. With the mapping of the human genome nearing completion in the summer of 2000, Caliper was in the midst of a race to market miniaturized DNA analyzers and other products to major biotechnology research firms. What once took days or weeks to perform in research labs could now be done in less than twenty minutes.

Caliper's chips could process up to twelve samples, perform sample separation, compare a drug company's collection of molecular compounds against a sample, and find the results of drug and gene interactions.

Caliper also saw opportunity in creating and commercializing a comprehensive database of chemical genomics information. As a result, in September 2001 Caliper formed a new company, Amphora Discovery Corp., to develop the database for use in preclinical drug discovery and to increase the success rate of drugs through clinical development. Amphora was formed as a separate, independent company from Caliper with its own management team and board of directors with Caliper retaining 25 percent ownership. Caliper created Amphora as an independent firm to pursue new opportunities in the rapidly developing field of genomics technology. The database would provide critical information, linking genomics data with chemical structures and information that could produce new medicines at a faster pace for less cost. Because Caliper had scarce resources to pursue these opportunities within the company, the new entity was spun off as an independent firm with separate management that could raise its own venture capital and implement its own corporate strategies. The database would be sold to pharmaceutical companies, biotechnology firms, and academic laboratories involved in preclinical and clinical research in life sciences. In addition, Amphora would rely on Caliper's LabChip high throughput screening systems to develop and expand its chemical genomics database. To lead the new company, Caliper hired Martin Haslanger as chief executive officer. A former president of Sphinx Laboratories of Eli Lilly, Haslanger had more than 25 years experience in pharmaceutical drug discovery with such leading companies as Squibb, Schering Plough, and Eli Lilly. With the backing of $25 million in venture capital, Amphora's set up its headquarters in the Research Triangle Park of North Carolina with offices in Mountain View, California.

During 2001, Caliper also penetrated the Japanese market with an exclusive agreement with Wako Pure Chemical Industries, Ltd. providing Wako with distribution rights to sell the Caliper 250 High Throughput Screening (HTS) system and chips in Japan. The HTS system worked by miniaturizing, integrating, and automating high-throughput screening, the process of testing each component of large chemical compound libraries to discover and characterize compounds with specific biochemical activities. Pharmaceutical companies used these screening methods to uncover compounds of potential therapeutic value. A single high throughput screening project could require critical laboratory analysis of hundreds of thousands of individual chemical compounds. By conducting high throughput screening on a small chip, the Caliper 250 HTP could considerably speed the assay development process, improving data quality and reducing reagent and sample usage. With well-established relationships with major Japanese pharmaceutical companies, Wako offered broad market access to promote Caliper's systems in Japan.

Caliper also introduced four new assays for the Agilent 2100 Bioanalyzer, developed with Caliper's lab chip technology. The assays included the DNA 1000 LabChip kit, the RNA 6000 Nano LabChip kit, the Protein 200 Plus LabChip kit, and the Cell Fluorescence LabChip kit. In addition, Caliper signed an agreement with Bacteria BarCodes, Inc., integrating Caliper's microfluidic technology with Bacteria BarCode's bacterial fingerprinting technology. The company introduced its LabChip Automated Microfluidics System that enabled automated analysis of nucleic acid fragments and began a collaboration with the National Aeronautics and Space Administration to develop macromolecular crystals aboard the International Space Station relying on Caliper's LabChip technology.

As a result of these developments and other continuing operations, Caliper reported that revenue for 2001 increased 59 percent to $29.6 million from $18 million in 2000. Caliper's chief financial officer, Jim Knighton, noted the company had established critical commercial capabilities while maintaining a robust research and development program. In addition, chief executive officer Dan Kisner indicated Caliper's performance was notable considering its transition to a products-based business from a technology access fee company. Previously, Caliper used its automated systems internally to provide screening services to pharmaceutical and biotechnology customers. With the result of Caliper's transition away from a fee-based business to a commercial products strategy, the company no longer offered these fee services to customers.

Key to Caliper's business strategy was the development and protection of an extensive intellectual property portfolio, leading the firm into litigation with Aclara Biosciences for patent infringement. In January 2001, the two companies settled the litigation with Aclara agreeing to pay Caliper $37.5 million over three years with a combination of stock, cash, and committed minimum royalties. Caliper became entangled in additional litigation when three of its officers, Daniel L. Kisner, David V. Milligan, and James L. Knight, were named as defendants in class action lawsuits in the United States District Court for the Southern District of New York. Similar complaints were filed in the same court against hundreds of other public companies that conducted initial public offerings of common stock since the late 1990s. The complaint against Caliper related to the firm's 1999 initial stock offering, alleging that the underwriters charged excessive, undisclosed commissions to investors and entered into improper agreements with investors concerning aftermarket transactions. In October 2002, however, the claims against Kisner, Milligan, and Knight were dismissed without prejudice. In February 2003, the court also granted Caliper's motion to dismiss all other claims against it.

Caliper Confronts an Economic Downdraft

In July 2002, as a result of the broad economic downturn and a reduction in research and development spending by biopharmaceutical companies, Caliper cut its workforce by 10 percent. With the value of its shares falling, in February 2003 Caliper received an acquisitions offer from hedge fund Little Bear Investments, controlled by investment bank WellFleet Partners Inc. of New York. The offer totaled $101.7 million or $4.15 a share, representing a 38 percent premium over Caliper's latest closing price of $3 a share, down from $14 a share one year earlier. After Caliper's board rejected the offer, Little Bear sweetened the bid to $110 million. The hostile bid stirred considerable excitement on Wall Street concerning whether hedge funds would begin buying up struggling biotech firms whose cash reserves and cheap stock prices made them easy targets. At the end of 2002, Caliper reported $154.3 million in cash, but its market capitalization was only $78.6 million. The hedge fund planned to liquidate Caliper for cash, pocketing the $154.3 million and establishing a $5 million trust to hold Caliper's intellectual property, awarding 80 percent to shareholders, 10 percent to employees, and retaining 10 percent for itself. Like other biotech firms, Caliper's shares nosedived during the stock market downturn beginning in spring 2000. Because Caliper's shares had collapsed from $35.00 to $3 in two years, investors believed the acquisition offer provided shareholders with a reasonable out. Despite Caliper's rejection of the takeover offer, the New York-based investment funds of Xmark Fund, L.P and Xmark Fund, Ltd.—all Caliper shareholders—pressed the company to accept the buyout or distribute its excess cash and proceeds from the sale of the firm to shareholders. Xmark also criticized Caliper for what it considered excessive executive compensation in light of the company's weak performance.

Caliper Reorganizes and Looks to the Future

In June 2003, after weathering the reversals of the takeover bid, Caliper purchased competitor Zymark Corporation of Hopkinton, Massachusetts, for $73 million in cash and stock. Under terms of the buyout, Zymark, a provider of laboratory automation, liquid handling, and robotics solutions to the life sciences, biotechnology, and pharmaceutical industries would become fully integrated into the Caliper business. In addition, Zymark's chief executive officer Kevin Hrusovsky was appointed the new president and CEO of the combined firm and joined the board of directors. As a result of the acquisition, Caliper relocated its headquarters to Hopkinton and announced workforce reductions of 9 percent stemming from consolidated operations. Caliper kept its research and development and manufacturing facilities for LabChip devices in Mountain View, California, with direct sales, service, and applications support in numerous locations around the world. In December 2003, Caliper announced another 12 percent workforce reduction, including the elimination of seven vice-president positions, as a result of efforts to reconfigure its operations and to pursue an aggressive commercialization strategy.

In January 2004, the company announced that it was changing its name to Caliper Life Science, Inc. The company's management believed the new name better reflected the firm's position as a leading life sciences company that provided a range of integrated macro- and microfluidics laboratory solutions for the life sciences industry. With the introduction of new products and a more commercially focused management team in place, Caliper appeared well positioned to take advantage of a recovering business climate and continuing rapid technological advancements in the life sciences field.

Principal Competitors

Applera; Beckman Coulter; Molecular Devices.

Further Reading

"Amgen Subscribes to Caliper's TAP Program," *Microtechnology News*, March 1999.

"Biochips to Reach $950 M by 2005," *Drug Discovery & Technology News*," January 2000.

"Caliper and Dow Chemical to Collaborate on Development of Disposable Polymer LabChips," *Business Wire*, March 3, 1997

"Caliper Announces Fourth Quarter and Year-End 1999 Financial Results," *PR Newswire*, February 7, 2000.

"Caliper Announces Fourth Quarter and Year-End 2001 Financial Results," *PR Newswire*, February 6, 2002.

"Caliper Appoints David K. Lam, Lam Research Founder, as President and CEO," *Business Wire*, May 1, 1997.

"Caliper Buys Zymark, Gets New CEO," *Biomolecular Diagnostics News*, August 2003.

"Caliper Forms Amphora to Provide Chemical Genomics Information, Products, and Services to Speed Drug Discovery using LabChip Technology," *PR Newswire*, September 27, 2001.

"Caliper Forms New Company," *Instrument Business Outlook*, September 30, 2001, p. 2.

"Caliper Rejects $102 M Hostile Bid," *Daily Deal*, February 14, 2003.

"Caliper Technologies Announces That Lilly Becomes Third LabChip Technology Access Program Customer," *PR Newswire*, August 18, 1999.

"Caliper Technologies Awarded Grant from the National Cancer Institute to Support Discovery of Anti-Cancer Therapies," *Business Wire*, September 23, 1998.

"Caliper Technologies Cor. Launches New Manufacturing Facility and Corporate Headquarters," *PR Newswire*, April 28, 1999.

"Caliper Technologies Corp. Raises $72 Million in Initial Public Offering of Its Common Stock," *PR Newswire*, December 16, 1999.

"Caliper Technologies Raises $7.4 Million in Financing to Accelerate Core Technology Development," *Business Wire*, June 22, 1998.

"Caliper Technologies to Acquire Zymark," *LC-GC North America*, July 2003.

"Daniel L. Kisner to Join Caliper Technologies Corp. as President and Chief Executive Officer," *PR Newswire*, February 1, 1999.

Delevett, Peter, "Biotech Firms Encouraged by Strong IPO," *Business Journal*, December 31, 1999.

"Diagnostic Instrumentation: Caliper's Lab-on-a-Chip System Acquires a large Development Partner," *Genesis Report-Dx*, May 1, 1998.

"Program Gives Fast Access to LabChip," *High Tech Separations News*, October 1999.

Silverstein, Roberta, "Biochip Makers Race for the Big Payoff," *Business Journal*, June 23, 2000.

"Xmark Votes to Withhold Authority for Election of Caliper Board of Directors Nominees," *PR Newswire*, May 15, 2003.

Young, Jeffrey, "Lab on a Chip," *Forbes*, September 23, 1996, p. 2.

Young, Karen, "Caliper Spin-Off Raises $25 M for Chemical Genomics Program," *BioWorld Today*, September 28, 2001.

—Bruce P. Montgomery

Carter Holt Harvey Ltd.

**640 Great S Road, Manukau City
Auckland 1020
New Zealand
Telephone: (+64) 9 262 6000
Fax: (+64) 9 262 6099
Web site: http://www.chh.com**

Public Company
Incorporated: 1971 as Carter Holt Holdings
Employees: 10,500
Sales: NZD 3.52 billion ($2.53 billion) (2004)
Stock Exchanges: New Zealand Australia
Ticker Symbol: CHH
NAIC: 113110 Timber Tract Operations; 113210 Forest Nurseries and Gathering of Forest Products; 321113 Sawmills; 321211 Hardwood Veneer and Plywood Manufacturing; 321212 Softwood Veneer and Plywood Manufacturing

A leading producer of wood fiber and forestry-based products in New Zealand and Australia, Carter Holt Harvey Ltd. (CHH) is also one of New Zealand's largest corporations. Since 2004, CHH has also begun an effort to expand into the Asia forestry products market, starting with the launch of operations in China. A vertically integrated company, CHH has one of the largest forestry and cutting rights holdings in New Zealand, with some 330,000 hectares under its control. The group operates sawmills, five pulp and paper mills, nearly 70 lumber and wood product manufacturing and distribution facilities, 25 packaging and conversion plants, as well as distribution subsidiaries. CHH has also been developing a number of new businesses, including an IT subsidiary, Oxygen Business Solutions. In the early 2000s, CHH restructured its various holdings into 17 independently operating companies, each with its own CEO. Listed on the New Zealand and Australian Stock Exchanges, CHH's main shareholder is the United States' International Paper, which holds 51 percent of the company's stock. The group's other major shareholder is New Zealand Central Securities Depository Limited, which holds 37 percent of CHH's shares.

Merging Wood Businesses in the 1970s

Carter Holt Harvey, as its name indicates, represented the merger of three prominent New Zealand businesses, each of which had begun operation by the turn of the 20th century. Carter and Holt became leaders in the country's forestry products sector, while Harvey emerged as the country's major packaging company. The development toward the future CHH began in 1971 with the merger of Carter and Holt.

The earliest component of the later CHH was founded by Robert Holt in Napier, who built his first sawmill in 1859. By 1880, Holt had expanded, building a second, steam-powered mill in Port Ahuriri. At the turn of the 20th century, Holt was joined by sons John, James, and Robert, and the company changed its name to Robert Holt & Sons. The firm then expanded by opening a mill in Hastings.

The younger generation showed some flare for innovation and adaptability. In 1920, for example, the Holt company became the first in New Zealand to begin moving logs by truck. The company also fought its way back from a number of setbacks, including fires at its mills in 1922 and 1928 and an earthquake that hit Napier in 1931. The effort to rebuild the town led Holt into lumber products. Later, the demand for lumber during World War II led Holt to become the first in New Zealand to experiment with drying kilns in order to produce seasoned lumber in less time and larger quantities. Holt also began using chemical preservatives, a first in the New Zealand forestry industry.

New Zealand's vast forests encouraged others to enter the lumber business in the late 19th and early 20th centuries. Francis J. Carter had built his first small sawmill in Kaputuroa, near the town of Levin, cutting the white pine found in the forests there. Carter later added another sawmill at Rangataua, close to Waiouru, where he was joined by son Alwyn in the 1920s. The business significantly expanded over the following decades, and by the late 1940s it had developed a network of seven associated companies. Part of Carter's growth came from its decision to expand from its base of lumber into the production of wood products. Carter also began distributing wood products through its own retail network during this time.

Company Perspectives:

Built on Solid Foundations: In the year 2000 Carter Holt Harvey celebrated 100 years in business. Not many companies reach the milestone of a second century, even fewer do so carrying the names of their original founders. Our company today is built on the pioneering history of our founders—Francis Carter, Robert Holt and Alexander Harvey, whose spirit, ingenuity and insight, are still looked to today, as we move forward.

In 1948, Alwyn Carter took over as managing director of the company from his father, who died the following year at the age of 79. Two years later, in 1951, Alwyn Carter led a restructuring of the family's holdings, merging the various companies into the single entity of Carter Consolidated.

The Holt company went public in 1961 as Harold Holt, grandson of the founder, led the company into a new direction. After working in the forest industries in Canada and the United States, he returned to New Zealand with the idea of shifting the company away from its dependence on New Zealand's dwindling natural forests. Instead, Holt encouraged the company to invest in renewable, planted forests. The Holt company began planting exotic hardwood forests while at the same time building a portfolio of cutting rights in such important New Zealand forestry sectors as Hawkes Bay and Lake Waikaremoana.

By early 1960s, New Zealand's timber supply was already running out. Indeed, the dwindling reserves of the North Island led Carter to construct a mill in Jackson Bay on the South Island in the early 1960s. In 1969, Carter touched off considerable controversy when it teamed up with two Japanese companies, Oji Paper and Sanyo Kokusaku, to tender a bid to exploit a concession in the Southern Kaingaroa Forest. The partnership, which called for development of production lines for groundwood pulp and the building of a NZD12.3 million sawmill in Whirinaki, won the bid and construction on the site began in 1971. Under terms of the agreement, Carter's partners consented to purchase all of the mill's production for a 20-year period. Production at the site began in 1973.

Diversified Corporate Powerhouse in the 1980s

By then, however, Carter and Holt had agreed to merge, forming one of New Zealand's top forestry products groups in 1971. The newly enlarged company took on the name of Carter Holt. Into the 1970s, the company faced increasing pressure from conservationist groups, which were alarmed at the country's rapidly diminishing forests. By the late 1970s, the New Zealand government had begun to place severe restrictions on the remaining native timber supply. In the West Coast, in particular, the country's Forest Service announced that it was banning the cutting of native timber starting in 1978. Because of this, Carter Holt was forced to shut down its Jackson Bay mill.

Instead, the company ramped up production at the Kaingaroa site, boosting production to 200,000 tons per year by 1982. That mill also added production of sawn timber, which topped 100,000 cubic meters per year in the early 1980s.

Carter Holt faced pressure of a different sort at the beginning of the 1980s. In 1980, the company faced a hostile takeover attempt from larger rival Fletcher Group. Despite it smaller size, Carter Holt managed to fight off the attempt after a protracted legal battle.

The takeover attempt prompted Carter Holt to seek to gain scale in order to reduce its vulnerability to future unwanted takeover attempts. The opportunity for growth came in 1985, when the New Zealand government brokered a merger between Carter Holt and Alex Harvey Industries, a company that was also under threat of a takeover attempt.

Alexander Harvey came to Auckland in 1886, establishing a company producing machinery and equipment for New Zealand's fast-growing dairy industry. Harvey was joined by sons Alexander, David, and William, and in 1911 the company changed its name to Alex Harvey & Sons. Following World War I, the Harvey company added tin printing capacity and developed a new business in packaging. In 1918, the company opened its first packaging subsidiary in Wellington, where it produced tin containers. This activity led the company into other areas, such as the production of cabinets for washing machines and refrigerators.

Harvey grew rapidly throughout the 1930s and into the late 1940s. In 1948, in order to step up its expansion, Alex Harvey & Sons went public on the New Zealand Stock Exchange. Throughout the 1960s and into the 1970s, Harvey developed into one of New Zealand's largest manufacturers, with diversified packaging capacity in tin, sheet metal, aluminum, and plastics.

In 1984, the New Zealand branch of Australian Consolidated Industries (ACI) proffered a takeover bid to Harvey. With assistance from the New Zealand government, which sought to prevent a foreign company from gaining control of one of the country's largest corporations, Harvey and Carter Holt worked out terms for a merger, creating Carter Holt Harvey in 1985. The company then bought out ACI's stake in the former Carter Holt for NZD300 million.

Expanding International Focus in the 2000s

CHH's new scale gave it the clout to expand rapidly into the 1990s. The stock market collapse of 1987 presented the company with its first growth opportunity, when it bought up struggling Caxton, the New Zealand market leader in toilet paper, tissue paper, paper towels, and related products. CHH found its next acquisition target through Australia's Elders IXL, which had run into its own financial troubles, and in 1990 announced its intention to sell its New Zealand operations, Elders Resources-New Zealand Forest Products (NZFP). Interested only in New Zealand Forest Products itself, CHH agreed to pay as much as AUD682 million, depending on how much it was able to generate through the sell-off of Elders Resources (including mining, gas, and oil interests).

The acquisition of NZFP propelled CHH into a new league, boosting its revenues by more than 60 percent to top NZD7 billion and making CHH the clear leader in the New Zealand forestry sector. Encouraged by its newfound scale, CHH next turned toward international growth, targeting the vast forests of Chile. The company began by forming a joint-venture with Chile's Angelini group to construct a medium-density fiber-

Key Dates:

1859: Robert Holt builds his first sawmill in Napirer.
1880: Holt opens a steam-powered mill in Port Ahuriri.
1886: Alexander Harvey founds a machine business in Auckland.
1948: Alex Harvey & Sons goes public on the New Zealand Stock Exchange.
1951: Alwyn Carter merges seven family forestry and wood products businesses founded by his father Francis, forming Carter Consolidated.
1961: Robert Holt & Sons goes public.
1971: The merger of Carter and Holt forms Carter Holt Holdings.
1985: Carter Holt merges with Harvey, forming Carter Holt Harvey (CHH).
1987: CHH acquires Caxton, a leading producer of tissue papers in New Zealand.
1989: CHH acquires a 50 percent stake in Chile's Codec.
1990: The company acquires New Zealand Forest Products and becomes the largest forestry products group in New Zealand.
1991: International Paper acquires a stake in CHH.
1998: CHH acquires Continental Cup in Australia through a joint venture with International Paper.
1999: CHH begins its exit from Chile to focus on expansion in Australasia.
2001: CHH restructures, creating a network of independent businesses.
2004: CHH acquires a timber business in China and completes its exit from Chile.

board factory in Santiago. From there, CHH joined the Angelini group in the creation of the 50–50 joint venture Los Andes Investment and Development Co., formed to take a controlling stake in one of Chile's largest conglomerates, Copec. The joint venture gave CHH crucial access to Chile's large and fast-growing forestry sector.

CHH's spending spree had weighted the company with debt. The outbreak of the Persian Gulf War caused its bankers to demand repayment of more than $1.3 billion at the beginning of 1992 and another installment before the end of the year. The company stock fell, leaving it vulnerable to takeover. Indeed, Brierley Investments Limited stepped in and succeeded in acquiring a controlling stake in CHH by September 1991. At the end of that year, however, BIL had sold on part of its stake to International Paper of the United States. That company later boosted its shareholding in CHH to 51 percent. The purchase also marked the end of the founding families' involvement in the company.

Under International Paper's control, CHH turned toward the international market in the mid-1990s with the aim of developing an Australasian presence. The company made a series of acquisitions through the 1990s, including Forwood, which was held by the South Australian government, and Raleigh Paper in Melbourne. CHH also expanded its tissue business, buying up the Australian tissue wing of the United Kingdom's Bowater for AUD430 million. In 1998, CHH boosted its packaging wing as

well, forming a joint venture with International Paper to acquire Continental Cup.

CHH's increasing emphasis on the Australasian market led it to exit its shareholding in Copec in 1999, selling its stake to the Angelini group for NZD2.5 billion. The sell-off enabled CHH to pay down nearly all of its debt, setting it up for further growth in the 2000s.

As part of its future strategy, CHH restructured its operations in 2001. Instead of a centralized organization, the company now broke up its operations into 31 smaller-scale businesses. These were later pared down to just 17 businesses, which were then expected to operate independently, with each company appointing its own CEO.

The early 2000s represented a difficult period for the company, as it struggled to cope with an extended economic downturn in New Zealand and elsewhere. In 2003, the company announced its intention sell off its tissue paper business, a move completed in 2004. The company also suggested that it was interested in selling off its consumer products operations and part of its forest holdings as well. Instead, CHH set its sight on expanding into the Asian market. China became the company's first target in that effort, and in June 2004 CHH announced it had reached an agreement to acquire Plantation Timber Products, a manufacturer of MDF and flooring products, for $134 million. Meanwhile, CHH continued expanding in Australia. At the beginning of 2005, the company finalized the purchase of Wadepack Ltd., a carton board packaging manufacturer with plants in Melbourne and Sydney. Such moves served to bolster the prospect that CHH would remain one of New Zealand's leading corporations into the new century.

Principal Subsidiaries

Ace Bag Company Limited; AHI Building Products; AHI Forests (Ngatihine) Limited; AHI Group Limited; AHI Nominees Limited; Carter Holt Equities (No.15) Limited; Carter Holt Forests (Ngatihine) Limited; Carter Holt Group Trustee Limited; Carter Holt Harvey Bonding Technologies Limited; Carter Holt Harvey Climate Coating Limited; Carter Holt Harvey eCargo Limited; Carter Holt Harvey Energy Limited; Carter Holt Harvey Equities (No.12) Limited; Carter Holt Harvey Equities Limited; Carter Holt Harvey Forests Limited; Carter Holt Harvey International; Carter Holt Harvey Loop 1 Limited; Carter Holt Harvey Loop Limited; Carter Holt Harvey New Ventures Limited; Carter Holt Harvey Overseas Limited; Carter Holt Harvey Packaging Pty Limited; Carter Holt Harvey Paper Co. Pty Limited; Carter Holt Harvey Roofing Inc.; Carter Holt Harvey Vortech Limited; Carter Holt Harvey Wood Products Australia Pty Limited; Carter Holt Investments Pokirikiri Farm Limited; Caxton Superannuation Fund Trustee Limited; Crimson Hill Holdings Limited; Dainton Holdings Limited; Delta Nominees Limited; Houpoto Te Pua Forest Limited; Houpoto Whituare Forest Limited; i2B2 Limited Tunapahore 4B Forest Limited; Industry Training Works Limited; Kawerau A1 Forest Limited; Kawerau A6 Forest Limited; NZ Forest Products (Australia) Pty Limited; Oxygen Business Solutions Pty Limited.

Principal Competitors

Weyerhaeuser Co.; Romsilva RA Regia Autonoma a Padurilor; Svenska Cellulosa AB; Metsaliitto Group; Mondi Ltd.; Korindo

Group, PT; Mannesmann S.A.; Xstrata PLC; South African Forestry Company Ltd.; Tenon Ltd; S.C.A. Forest and Timber AB; Société d'Exploitation des Parcs à Bois du Cameroun.

Further Reading

Bayliss, Martin, and John Pearson, ''CHH Rises to International Prominence,'' *Pulp & Paper International*, November 1990, p. 87.

Bromby, Robin, ''Mills Down under Try to Overcome Strife,'' *Pulp & Paper International*, May 1992, p. 143.

''Carter Holt Harvey Earns NZ$ 435m for Year,'' *Asia Africa Intelligence Wire*, January 20, 2005.

''Carter Holt Harvey Running Fast Just to Stand Still,'' *New Zealand Press Association*, October 25, 2002.

''Carter Holt Harvey Sells Last Chilean Business,'' *New Zealand Press Association*, August 3, 2004.

''Carter Holt Harvey to Buy China Timber Maker,'' *Asia Pulse*, June 21, 2004.

''CHH Growth,'' *New Zealand Forest Industries Magazine*, April 2003, p. 5.

''NZ's Carter Holt Harvey Considers Selling Tissue Business,'' *Asia Pulse*, November 19, 2003.

''NZ's Carter Holt Harvey Mulls Sale of Its Forests,'' *Asia Pulse*, January 29, 2004.

''NZ Forestry Products Co. Carter Hold Harvey Back in the Black,'' *Asia Pulse*, January 20, 2005.

—M.L. Cohen

CB Richard Ellis Group, Inc.

865 South Figueroa Street
34th Floor
Los Angeles, California 90071
U.S.A.
Telephone: (213) 438-4880
Fax: (213) 438-4820
Web site: http://www.cbre.com

Public Company
Incorporated: 1906 as Tucker, Lynch & Coldwell
Employees: 17,000
Sales: $1.63 billion (2004)
Stock Exchanges: New York
Ticker Symbol: CBG
NAIC: 522292 Real Estate Credit; 531210 Offices of
Real Estate Agents and Brokers; 531190 Lessors of
Other Real Estate Property; 531312 Nonresidential
Property Managers

CB Richard Ellis Group, Inc., is the world's largest commercial real estate services firm. With 300 offices in 50 countries, it has a truly global reach. The group manages 850 million square feet of commercial property and in 2004 sold $28 billion worth of property in the United States alone. The firm provides brokerage services, property and facilities management, mortgage banking and financial services, appraisal and property tax services, and real estate market research. CB Commercial's history dates to 1906, when Colbert Coldwell established a commercial real estate company in San Francisco. The current entity, however, has operated only since 1989 when investors purchased the commercial real estate operations of the former Coldwell Banker Co. from Sears, Roebuck & Co. The company has been built up into a global leader through a number of mergers since the mid-1990s.

Opportunity from the Ruins in the Early 1900s

In August 1906, with San Francisco only beginning to recover from the devastating earthquake earlier that year, Colbert Coldwell, then 23, and Albert Nion Tucker, 36, left their jobs with the real estate firm of Davidson & Leigh. With the backing of John Conant Lynch, an attorney and socially prominent former California legislator, they formed their own firm, Tucker, Lynch & Coldwell. Lynch was president and Coldwell was vice-president. Tucker, the oldest of the partners at 55, was the least involved in running the business and served as secretary.

From the start, Coldwell insisted that the firm operate solely as a brokerage, acting as the agent for buyers and sellers rather than speculating in real estate itself. That policy also was extended to the firm's partners and salesmen, who were not permitted to buy any real estate except for their personal homes. The firm quickly gained a reputation for honesty and attracted wealthy clients who were grateful for a broker who was not competing with them for the best deals.

By 1912, much of San Francisco had been rebuilt and the city was again flourishing, as was the firm of Tucker, Lynch & Coldwell. Tucker and Lynch decided to reduce their interest and essentially withdrew from the firm, leaving Coldwell to operate the business as a sole proprietorship. The following year, Benjamin Arthur Banker left the prominent San Francisco real estate firm of M.B. McGerry to become a salesman for Coldwell. In 1914, Banker became a partner in the firm.

War broke out in Europe the following year. When the United States entered the conflict in 1917, the firm, still known as Tucker, Lynch & Coldwell, embarked on its first non-real estate business venture—growing rice for the war effort on land it purchased in the Sacramento Valley. The rice farm was a failure, and in 1919, the partners, which then included Albert E. Kerns, vowed never again to invest in a venture outside real estate.

The firm also briefly changed its name to Coldwell, Kern & Banker. However, by 1920, Kern had resigned and was replaced by Bruce Cornwall, the son of a respected San Francisco industrialist and financier, Pierre Barlow Cornwall. The younger Cornwall, then 43, was never active in the business, but Coldwell realized the value of having his name associated with the firm, which became known as Coldwell, Cornwall & Banker.

Coldwell also was becoming a prominent member of the San Francisco community himself, helping to found the Bureau of

Company Perspectives:

CB Richard Ellis exists to serve as an advisor to its clients, helping them seize market opportunities through seamless working relationships and a thorough understanding of their business objectives. Our professionals are motivated not by simply closing transactions, but by working collaboratively with clients to foresee what lies ahead and helping chart which course to follow. We seek to form long-term relationships with our clients—where their success becomes our success. Through CB Richard Ellis, our clients gain the global reach of the world's largest real estate services firm, combined with the in-depth local market knowledge of our professionals. Whether a client has just one property or a portfolio of multi-national locations, the company's offerings can meet individual client needs. No matter how complex that need may be, CB Richard Ellis provides a custom mix of products and services that deliver significant, measurable returns.

Government Research, a citizen's group promoting good government. In 1921, he served as president of the San Francisco Real Estate Board, and in 1923, he was elected president of the San Francisco Chamber of Commerce. The *San Francisco Chronicle* was effusive in its praise: "A man whose activities for twenty years have given convincing evidence of his power to do things in a constructive way and translate vision and high purpose into programs of reality, Mr. Coldwell in the opinion of his associates possesses a touch of that genius which is indispensable to any community leader and city builder." Coldwell and his wife, Johanna, also were members of the most exclusive clubs in San Francisco.

Expanding to Los Angeles in the 1920s

In 1922, Marshall Hale, a San Francisco businessman, purchased the Spring Arcade Building in Los Angeles. He asked Coldwell, Cornwall & Banker to manage the property and invited the firm to open an office in the building. According to Jo Ann Levy in *Behind the Western Skyline,* none of the partners was enthusiastic about property management, and they were even less impressed with Los Angeles. Rather than turn down Hale outright, the partners named what they felt was an excessive fee. Hale, however, accepted. Arthur Hastings, who had been with the firm since 1907, was sent to Los Angeles to open the first Coldwell, Cornwell & Banker office outside of San Francisco. By 1927, the Spring Arcade office was doing so well that Hastings, who had been Coldwell's college fraternity brother at the University of California at Berkeley, was invited to buy into the partnership for $90,000.

By 1928, Coldwell, Cornwell & Banker had opened a second office in Los Angeles. The firm also continued to expand in the San Francisco Bay area, including the company's first office in Oakland, which opened in 1925. The same year, the firm, which had focused almost exclusively on commercial property, opened its first residential sales office in San Francisco. Louis Pfau, another fraternity brother from UC-Berkeley who had joined the firm in 1915, was also made a partner, bringing the number to

five. When the stock market crashed in 1929, plunging the nation into the Great Depression, three of the partners, Coldwell, Cornwall, and Banker, were wealthy men and relatively unaffected. The other partners and the firm's salesmen were not as fortunate. The firm was often forced to accept barter in lieu of commissions and acquired several properties in the process. In 1933, Coldwell, Cornwall & Banker also formed a subsidiary, Home Properties Co., Inc., and purchased 60 acres in the Rancho Santa Anita area of Los Angeles County for $18,000. Home Properties subdivided the land, put in streets and utilities, and even built a few homes to stimulate sale of the lots.

Although not highly profitable, the venture kept the sales force busy during the lean years. Coldwell, Cornwall & Banker also reorganized its property management division to provide a broader range of services, including lease management, to the banks and life insurance companies that suddenly found themselves with an inventory of properties because of foreclosures.

By 1936, the worst of the Depression was over. The following year, Coldwell, Cornwall & Banker opened an office on Wilshire Boulevard, its first residential sales office in Los Angeles, and brokered the sale of Santa Cruz Island to Edwin L. Stanton. In 1939, Coldwell, Cornwall & Banker signed an exclusive agreement to originate and service mortgage loans in California for Aetna Life Insurance Company. The firm also added two more partners, George M. "Dick" Mott, another UC-Berkeley graduate who would become the first corporate president of Coldwell, Banker & Co., and Edward Willingham Arnold.

In 1940, Cornwall, then 63, sold his share of the company to the other partners and the name of the firm was shortened to Coldwell, Banker & Co. A few months later, Hastings died unexpectedly of a heart attack. It was the first death among the partners and began to raise questions about successor provisions of the partnership. Surprisingly, there was no written arrangement, only a verbal agreement that shares in the firm would be purchased by the surviving partners; no heirs or outsiders were allowed to inherit or purchase shares in the business. In 1942, Coldwell's nephew, Charles Detroy, who had joined the firm in 1924, was made a partner in the business, restoring the balance of three partners in San Francisco and three in Los Angeles that was upset by Hastings's death.

Postwar Growth

Coldwell, Banker continued to prosper during World War II, with Arthur Banker serving as a member of the Society of Industrial Realtors, formed to assist the federal government in finding wartime production facilities. When the war ended, the firm began to benefit from California's explosive growth. More than 3.5 million people would move to California between 1940 and 1950, swelling the population by more than half to 10.6 million. By 1960, only seven states would be more populous than Los Angeles County alone. As the firm grew, so did the number of partners, to an even dozen by 1952, when one of the latest, Dan Duggan, finally convinced the others, who ranged in age from 38 to 70, that they needed a written partnership agreement.

In 1952, Coldwell, Banker also opened an office in Sacramento, its first new office in 15 years. Late that year, despite

---

Key Dates:

1906: Tucker, Lynch & Coldwell is established.
1940: Tucker Lynch is renamed Coldwell, Banker & Co.
1969: Coldwell Banker begins trading stock.
1980: Coldwell Banker acquires New York commercial real estate firm Sutton & Towne, Inc.
1981: Sears, Roebuck & Co. acquires Coldwell Banker.
1989: Coldwell Banker Commercial Real Estate Group is spun off.
1995: CB Commercial acquires Westmark Realty Advisors.
1996: CB Commercial acquires L.J. Melody & Company mortgage bankers; the company goes public.
1997: CB Commercial acquires Koll Real Estate Services.
1998: CB Commercial acquires REI Ltd. and becomes CB Richard Ellis (CBRE); Hiller Parker also is acquired.
1999: Japanese operations are merged with Ikoma Corporation; Sweden's Profit Group and Chile's LirAntunez Propiedades are acquired.
2001: CBRE is privatized.
2003: Insignia Financial Group is acquired.
2004: CBRE goes public on the New York Stock Exchange.

Coldwell's reservations, the firm opened an office in Phoenix, its first location outside California. Revenues also topped $2 million for the first time.

Banker, then 75, suffered a heart attack in 1960. Although he recovered, he decided the time had come to retire and urged Coldwell, then 77, and Pfau, then 73, to do likewise. Both decided to stay on. Coldwell, who had no children and whose wife had died, told Banker, "I have nothing else in my life. I don't know what I would do if I couldn't come to the office every day."

The business, however, was changing. Coldwell, Banker then operated 14 offices and employed more than 500 people, and revenues were nearing $3 million, but the company had never reincorporated since Tucker and Lynch withdrew from the business in 1912. In 1961, the Los Angeles partners asked a longtime client, Al Steffey, of Butler Bros. stores, to review the firm's books. His reply was, "Well, you're idiots. You're nice idiots, but you're idiots." Coldwell Banker was incorporated on July 1, 1963.

Banker died two years later, at the age of 80, followed by the passing of Pfau, also 80, and Coldwell, 84, in 1967. Under the articles of incorporation, their shares in Coldwell Banker were purchased by the firm and made available to the other partners and employees. In 1968, Coldwell Banker issued its first publicly traded stock, selling 503,000 shares (about 29 percent of the company) at $25 per share. Each of the former partners kept about 100,000 shares, making their holdings worth about $2.5 million each.

The general partners had continued to manage the business even after incorporation. After Coldwell's death, the company formed its first executive committee, but it was not until 1969

that the committee's powers were fully expanded to "manage the business and affairs of the corporation." By then, Coldwell Banker also had expanded to Nevada and Texas. Wes Poulson, a graduate of the Harvard Business School who had joined Coldwell Banker in 1960, also introduced the company's first-ever organizational chart, based on decentralized, regional management, a concept that would eventually develop into the Coldwell Banker companies.

There were other significant developments in 1969. For more than 40 years, the Coldwell Banker logo incorporated a skyline of whichever city an office represented. But with the firm now involved in residential as well as commercial real estate and offering nonbrokerage appraisal and consulting and financial services, the logo no longer reflected the company. Besides, designing a new logo every time an office opened in a new city was becoming costly, so the firm adopted a unified logo with the Coldwell Banker name surrounded by a blue arch above and below.

Growth Through Acquisitions in the 1970s

In that summer of 1969, after the board of directors declared a first-ever dividend of 20 cents per share, Coldwell Banker also announced its first acquisitions, those of the Seattle-based, residential real estate firm of Henry Broderick, Inc. and Southern California giant Forest E. Olson, Inc. Olson's strength was also in residential sales, especially medium- and low-priced housing, a market then virtually untouched by Coldwell Banker. The acquisitions nearly doubled the number of Coldwell Banker employees, from 800 to more than 1,500, and increased the number of sales offices from 25 to 63.

Coldwell Banker began trading on the New York Stock Exchange in 1971. In the firm's annual report for the following year, Poulson, who was named president in 1970, staked out the company's future: "To establish nationwide full-service real estate offices with some international representation." In 1972, Poulson formed the Coldwell Banker Fund to provide real estate services to institutional investors. The company also authorized a limited partnership, Coldwell Banker Investment Properties, Ltd., as a way for its employees to invest in real estate without violating the longstanding rule against owning property.

By 1973, Coldwell Banker had offices in seven western states and in Atlanta, Georgia. The company formed Coldwell Banker Asset Management Services, later renamed Capital Management Services, to manage commingled real estate funds for institutional investors. In a significant reorganization, the company also split its residential and commercial services into separate divisions and introduced a decentralized management structure, giving greater autonomy to individual offices. Another logo was introduced: interlocking CB initials over each division's name.

In 1975, the Coldwell Banker Commercial Brokerage Co. moved into Chicago, followed in 1977 by the Coldwell Banker Residential Brokerage Co. with the acquisition of Thorsen Realtors. As annual revenues surpassed $100 million, the company purchased Routh Robbins Companies, which operated 14 residential real estate and management services offices in the Maryland and Virginia suburbs of Washington, D.C.

Other acquisitions followed, including Hardin Stockton, the leading real estate brokerage in Kansas City, and Find-A-Home Service, Inc., an Illinois-based referral company with more than 600 affiliated brokers in the United States and Canada, in 1977, and a 50 percent interest in Executrans, Inc., which provided nationwide corporate relocation services, in 1978. In November, *Forbes* magazine took note: "Coldwell Banker has become the strongest force in America's highly fragmented real estate market." Coldwell Banker purchased its interest in Executrans from Allstate Enterprises, Inc., a subsidiary of Sears, Roebuck & Co., establishing a relationship that would prove pivotal to the company's future.

In early 1979, the board of directors approved a ten-year strategic plan that projected 1,000 Coldwell Banker offices nationwide by 1988. Two more acquisitions were approved by the end of the year: Barton & Ludwig, Inc., with 24 residential offices in the Atlanta area, and Spring Co., a leading residential brokerage and mortgage firm in Minneapolis. Coldwell Banker also opened offices in Boston, Philadelphia, Fort Lauderdale, and Colorado Springs. That was followed in 1980 with the acquisition of Previews, Inc., a residential marketing organization that published *Homes International* magazine, and two small insurance agencies, Jenson, Woodward & Lozier, Inc. in Seattle and Wachbrit Insurance Agency in Los Angeles. But the blockbuster announcement was that of the acquisition of Sutton & Towne, Inc., a major player in New York commercial real estate and office leasing. Revenues for fiscal 1980 topped $300 million.

In 1981, the company launched a nationwide advertising campaign to acquaint the general public with the Coldwell Banker name. As Poulson told the stockholders, "Since Coldwell Banker sells more than one percent of the resale homes in the country—and no other company can make that claim—it appears to be time to mass merchandise one of our best-kept secrets." The campaign was accompanied by another new logo, this time emphasizing the full Coldwell Banker name in bold type and replacing the word "corporation" or "company" with the word "services" for its divisions—the Coldwell Banker Commercial Brokerage Company became Coldwell Banker Commercial Real Estate Services, and so on. But before the year ended, it was Coldwell Banker that was sold—to an even better known name, Sears, Roebuck & Co.

Sears, Roebuck & Co. and the 1980s

In the early 1980s, Sears had set out to become the largest consumer financial services company in the United States to shore up sagging sales of its traditional retail merchandise. In 1981, Sears paid $179 million for Coldwell Banker ($42 per share, or 80 percent over the market price) and the real estate company became part of a financial services division that also included Allstate Insurance and, by year's end, the securities firm of Dean Witter Reynolds, Inc.

Sears opened real estate offices in its retail stores in communities that did not already have a Coldwell Banker presence and offered clients discounts on home furnishings and other financial services. With Sears's marketing clout, Coldwell Banker's share of the national residential resale market rocketed to nearly 9 percent by 1987, and *Esquire* noted, "... it's a rare stretch of American roadway that at some point fails to bear a blue-and-white Coldwell

Banker sign." Joe F. Hanauer, then president of the residential real estate group for Sears, whose own Chicago company had been acquired by Coldwell Banker, predicted the demise of the local real estate broker and told *Forbes* that Sears planned to control 20 percent of the market by the end of the decade.

Sears's corporate strategy also appeared to be working. Surveys in 1987 indicated that 30 percent of the public purchased some sort of financial service from the retail giant, compared with 11 percent for American Express. *Esquire* gushed, "Sears, Roebuck has been reconstituted during the 1980s as a powerful, futuristic business machine: a carefully designed material and financial womb fit to supply, service, and protect the American middle class." In 1988, *Forbes* reported "clear signs that Sears really has turned around."

The board of directors at Sears stunned the financial world, however, by voting unanimously to sell off its financial services companies. In one respect, the real estate and financial services strategy had been hugely successful, generating 90 percent of Sears's earnings. But its core merchandise sales continued to fall. *Time* magazine noted, "Rather than help Sears' growth, most analysts believe the financial units only subsidized its failure to compete during the retail revolution that produced such fierce, profit-taking rivals as Wal-Mart, Home Depot, the Gap and Circuit City."

Sears sold its Coldwell Banker commercial real estate operations in 1989 to a management group and outside investors, led by the Washington, D.C.-based Carlyle Group, for $305 million, including the largest amount of cash—$44 million—ever raised from employees in a leveraged buyout. The group paid Sears another $100 million for a five-year noncompete agreement and the temporary use of the Coldwell Banker name. The reconstituted company became the Coldwell Banker Commercial Real Estate Group, with headquarters in Los Angeles. The name was changed to CB Commercial Real Estate Group in 1991, after Sears sold the residential real estate operations to the Fremont Group, a San Francisco-based investment firm, which took the name Coldwell Banker Corp.

The first few years were difficult for CB Commercial, which was forced to close more than a dozen offices because of a weak commercial real estate market. Although it was easily the country's largest commercial broker, it had a negative net worth of $56 million in mid-1991. In 1992, the company was rocked further when a jury in Orlando, Florida awarded $8.5 million to the former owner of an office complex who accused CB Commercial, his leasing agent, of fraud for negotiating a lease for his largest tenant with another office complex. After the verdict, and before a final judgment could be entered, CB Commercial settled out of court in an effort to salvage the company's reputation.

By 1994, CB Commercial had revenues of $452 million and a net profit of barely $4 million. The following year, the firm embarked on an aggressive expansion program, eventually acquiring the Langdon Rieder Corporation, a tenant-representation firm, for $3.4 million. That acquisition was followed by additional acquisitions: Westmark Realty Advisors, a Los Angeles investment management firm, for $37.5 million (1995); the Houston-based mortgage banking firm of L.J. Melody & Co. for $15 million (1996); and Newport Beach,

California-based Koll Real Estate Services (1997), a deal that nearly tripled the amount of property under management. In 1996, the company also formed CB Commercial Partners Inc., a subsidiary that licensed independent commercial real estate offices to use the CB Commercial name and resources.

1996 IPO

CB Commercial went public in 1996 in an $80 million initial public offering (IPO) of stock. Chairman James J. Didion, who had joined the former Coldwell Banker in Sacramento in the early 1970s, told *Commercial Property News* that the move was to provide capital for even more aggressive expansion. In a vision statement adopted in 1997, Didion set forth the company's goal: "To be the industry's preeminent, globally capable, vertically integrated commercial real estate services firm."

One strong challenge was expected to come from Coldwell Banker Corp., purchased in 1996 by HFS, Inc., which also owned Century 21 and several motel and car-rental chains. After the noncompete agreement it inherited from Sears expired, Coldwell Banker Corp. announced that it would enter the commercial market with a subsidiary to be named the Coldwell Banker Commercial Corp.

In an article entitled, "Is This Town Big Enough for Both of Them?," *Today's Realtor* magazine noted the potential confusion and asked, "Does the commercial real estate industry have an identity crisis on its hands?" Thomas Smith, then executive vice-president at CB Commercial, answered: "They (Coldwell Banker) say they're re-entering the commercial business. They're actually entering the business. Their entire commercial business became CB Commercial. Fundamentally, they're now a residential company trying to conduct commercial business. We welcome the competition, but don't see them as a threat to our position in the marketplace."

Going Global in 1998

In 1998 CB Commercial acquired the holdings of REI Ltd., outside the United Kingdom. (The British operations, Richard Ellis Group Ltd., instead chose to merge with Insignia Financial.) The company became CB Richard Ellis Holding, Inc. (CBRE) after the transaction. REI had 1997 revenues of $119 million to CB Commercial's $730 million, and 1,500 employees. The combined company had more than 8,000 employees at more than 200 offices in 29 countries. According to Jim Didion, who remained chairman and CEO at CBRE, the company was "the first commonly owned, commonly managed global real estate services firm."

London-based Hiller Parker May & Rowden was acquired by CBRE later in 1998. The Hiller Parker deal helped extend CBRE's commercial property services throughout the world's major business centers.

In 1999, CBRE's Japanese operations were merged with those of Ikoma Corp. Sweden's Profit Group and Chile's LirAntunez Propiedades S.A. were acquired during the year.

Privatized in 2001

By 2000, CBRE had revenues of $1.3 billion. It had 10,00 employees in nearly 250 office in 44 countries. The company was taken private in July 2001 in an $800 million leveraged buyout. CBRE merged with BLUM CB Corp., which was controlled by BLUM Capital Partners, L.P., in the transaction.

In 2003, CBRE acquired the Insignia Financial Group, Inc., another of the world's top real estate companies. Insignia had been founded in December 1990 by Andrew Farkas, then just 30 years old. *Commercial Property News* noted that Insignia was strong in large cities, including New York and London, where CBRE had lacked a significant presence. The high-profile high-rises it managed complemented CBRE's strengths in industrial buildings and malls. The deal included the Richard Ellis operations that had joined Insignia instead of CBRE in 1998. "We are marking a defining moment in our firm's century-old history: its emergence as the only truly global real estate services firm with a platform built on leadership in every major local market of consequence, and a commitment to the highest degree of client satisfaction," said CBRE president Brett White in a statement.

Revenues were $1.6 billion in 2003; the company posted a net loss of $35 million, after a write-down related to the Insignia buy. By this time, the company had 220 offices in 48 countries. It employed 13,500 people.

Another IPO in 2004

In February 2004 CBRE Holding, Inc., the parent company of CB Richard Ellis Real Estate Services, was renamed CB Richard Ellis Group, Inc. After three years as a private company, CBRE went public on the New York Stock Exchange in 2004. The IPO raised about $138 million, some of which was earmarked for paying down debt. Long-term debt then totaled $815 million.

According to statistics by Real Capital Analytics, in 2004 CBRE led the U.S. market for commercial property sales with a 15.8 percent share. This coincided with a recovery in the market, and an influx of capital into investment property due to low interest rates. It was the fifth consecutive year CBRE led the United States in real estate investment sales. The company sold $28 billion worth of property in the United States alone in 2004.

Principal Subsidiaries

CB Richard Ellis Commercial Ltd. (United Kingdom); CB Richard Ellis, Inc.; CB Richard Ellis Real Estate Services, Inc.; CB Richard Ellis Services, Inc.; CBRE Stewardship Company (United Kingdom); Insignia Financial Group, Inc.; L.J. Melody & Company; L.J. Melody & Company of Texas, L.P.; CB Intermediate Ltd. (United Kingdom); Relam Amsterdam Holdings B.V. (Netherlands); CB Hiller Parker Ltd. (United Kingdom); Insignia Richard Ellis Europe Ltd. (United Kingdom); Insignia B.V. (Netherlands).

Principal Divisions

Asset Services; Brokerage—Tenant & Landlord Representation; Consulting; Corporate Services; Debt & Equity Financing (L.J. Melody & Co.); Facilities Management; Industrial; Investment Brokerage/Agency; Investment Management (CBRE Investors); Project Management; Research & Investment Strategy

(Torto Wheaton Research); Retail; Specialty Services; Valuation/Appraisal Services.

Principal Competitors

CMN Inc.; Cushman & Wakefield Inc.; Grubb & Ellis Co.; Jones Lang LaSalle Inc.; The Staubach Co.; Trammel Crow Company.

Further Reading

Barnfarther, Maurice, "Paying the Piper A Lot," *Forbes,* October 26, 1981.

"CB Commercial Acquires REI Ltd.," *National Mortgage News,* May 18, 1998.

"CB Commercial, Richard Ellis Join Hands to Reach Around the World," *National Real Estate Investor,* May 30, 1998.

CB Richard Ellis Inc., "Background Information," Los Angeles: CB Richard Ellis, Inc., July 2004.

Finkelstein, Alex, "CB Commercial Loses $8.5 Million Lawsuit," *Orlando Business Journal,* June 26, 1992, p. 1.

——, "Settlement 'Hell of a Hit' for CB Commercial," *Orlando Business Journal,* September 11, 1992, p. 1.

Fitzgerald, Therese, "The Insignia Factor," *Commercial Property News,* September 16, 2003, p. 1.

Flynn, Julia, "Smaller But Wiser," *Business Week,* October 12, 1992, p. 28.

Katz, Donald R., "Back from the Brink," *Esquire,* October 1987, p. 177.

King, Danny, "CB Richard Ellis Stock Sale Gives Exit Plan for VC," *Los Angeles Business Journal,* March 8, 2004, p. 1.

Levy, Jo Ann L., *Behind the Western Skyline, Coldwell Banker: The First 75 Years,* Coldwell Banker, 1981.

Maestri, Nicole, "Commercial Real Estate Leader's IPO on Tap," *Reuters News,* June 4, 2004.

Merwin, John, "Go East, Young Man," *Forbes,* November 13, 1978, p. 65.

Much, Marilyn, "Buyout Gives Realtor a New Lease on Life," *Investor's Business Daily,* February 3, 2005.

Parent, Tawn, "Local CB Commercial Office Weathers National Storm," *Indianapolis Business Journal,* September 9, 1991, p. 1.

Patterson, Maureen, "A New Paradigm," *Buildings,* March 1999, pp. 42ff.

Rudnitsky, Howard, "Henry the Magician," *Forbes,* September 9, 1996, p. 98.

——, "National or Bust," *Forbes,* July 30, 1984, p. 136.

"Trimming Frills at the Big Store," *Time,* October 12, 1992, p. 29.

Weiner, Steve, "They Buy Their Stocks Where They Buy Their Socks," *Forbes,* March 7, 1988, p. 60.

Wilcox, Gregory J., "Ellis Gets Set for New IPO; Firm Will Go Public Again to Pay Off Debts," *Los Angeles Daily News,* February 18, 2004, p. B1.

—Dean Boyer
—update: Frederick C. Ingram

Celebrate Express, Inc.

11220 120th Avenue N.E.
Kirkland, Washington 98033
U.S.A.
Telephone: (425) 250-1064
Fax: (425) 828-6252
Web site: http://www.celebrateexpress.com

Public Company
Incorporated: 1994 as Birthday Express
Employees: 293
Sales: $51.9 million (2004)
Stock Exchanges: NASDAQ
Ticker Symbol: BDAY
NAIC: 454111 Mail-Order Houses; 454113 Electronic
    Shopping; 322230 Stationery Product Manufacturing;
    453220 Gift, Novelty, and Souvenir Stores

Celebrate Express, Inc., sells children's party supplies, costumes, and clothing over the Internet and via mail-order catalogs. The company operates through business units called Birthday Express, Storybook Heirlooms, and Costume Express. Four-fifths of its sales come from Birthday Express, which offers a complete range of supplies for children's parties in more than 100 different themes, many of which feature popular characters like SpongeBob, Lil' Bratz, and Harry Potter. Storybook Heirlooms sells holiday and special event clothing for young girls, and Costume Express offers children's and family costumes for Halloween and other dress-up events. Cofounders Mike and Jan Jewell own more than one-third of the company.

Beginnings

Celebrate Express was founded by the husband-and-wife team of Mike and Jan Jewell in Kirkland, Washington. Mike Jewell had gotten his entrepreneurial feet wet in high school by starting a company that sold handmade hotplates to retailers like Neiman Marcus, and after getting an MBA he had worked as an executive for high-tech firms like Credence Systems, Advanced Technology Partners, and Engineering Animation, Inc. By the early 1990s he had become interested in the possibility of selling goods via the World Wide Web, then still in its infancy, and began looking for a product to sell.

The three-months premature birth of the Jewells' third child, in May 1992, proved a pivotal event in their lives both personally and professionally. The boy's birth weight was just one pound, ten ounces, and he required a long period of hospital care before he was healthy enough to take home. Jan Jewell organized a special celebration for his first birthday, and this event gave her the inspiration for their new business: a one-stop source of party supplies for children's birthdays.

After performing market research to determine that consumers were interested in the concept, the new company, dubbed Birthday Express, began operations in June 1994. Initial funding came from $1.5 million in savings the Jewells had accumulated. Although it would start out as a catalog operation, they planned to create a web site when the business was successfully up and running. Two years later, in April of 1996, the company went online as Birthday Express.com. During this time Mike Jewell had continued to work for Engineering Animation, Inc.

Birthday Express offered a full range of party supplies, including invitations, plates, napkins, and decorations. Children's parties were often put together with a specific theme in mind, and the company initially offered customers generic choices like unicorns and dinosaurs. Over time, the firm began to license the rights to children's entertainment properties like the Magic School Bus, Madeline, and Raggedy Ann, as well as buying other licensed items from outside vendors.

In 1995, its first full year of operation, Birthday Express sold 44,000 party packages, and sales nearly doubled the next year, to 80,000. Supplementing the mail-order sales, the company opened a retail outlet in the corner of its printing, manufacturing, and distribution center near Seattle. In April of 1997 the firm bought Great Days Publishing, Inc., a maker of personalized scrolls that listed noteworthy events from a particular date. Its product line would be marketed under the Birthday Express name.

In 1997 the number of packages jumped to 140,000, and it increased again in 1998 to 200,000. By 1999 Mike and Jan Jewell were running the firm as co-CEOs, and employing nearly 200.

1999: Venture Capital Funds Expansion

In August of 1999 the company received $13.1 million in new funding from Arch Venture Partners, Advanced Technology Ventures, and Sigma Partners, which was combined with $12 million in internally generated money to fund a $25.1 million national expansion. In the fall adult-themed party goods were added via the newly created Celebrate Express.com web site. Its party themes included ''Black Tie New Year's Affair'' and ''Autumn Vine Wine Party,'' along with other seasonal and holiday offerings. Packages like the ''Golden Reindeer'' dinner for eight included invitations, disposable dinner and dessert plates, cups, plastic stem glasses, knives, forks, spoons, napkins, confetti, baskets, a table cover, and a papier-mache golden reindeer, all for $64.95.

In December of 1999 Birthday Express leased a 32,000-square-foot distribution center in Greensboro, North Carolina, which tripled its distribution capacity. The new site, which was intended to speed up delivery to East Coast accounts, was located near a U.S. Postal Service bulk mail center and a planned Federal Express cargo hub. Half of the firm's shipments were sent via U.S. mail, with the rest shipped United Parcel Service and Federal Express. One-fifth were expedited for next-day delivery.

The company's online business was now booming, with about a third of its total coming from Internet orders. This category had consisted of less than 2 percent just a year earlier. For 1999 the firm reported sales of $13 million and a loss of $1.1 million.

Since its founding Birthday Express had accumulated a deficit of nearly $5 million, as the cost of building infrastructure and attracting customers consistently exceeded earnings. With a new wave of publicly traded competitors like GreatEntertaining.com and iParty.com nipping at its heels, in January of 2000 the firm announced that it was preparing for its initial public offering (IPO) of stock on the NASDAQ exchange, hoping to raise $40 million. The company also changed its name to CelebrateExpress.com, reflecting the success of its new venture and a desire to brand itself as a source for all types of celebrations.

In March 2000 the company received its one-millionth order, and in July it formed a marketing alliance with Sears Portrait Studio. The company was also busy reaching agreements with a variety of Web-based firms to help bring in customers, giving them a sales commission of up to 18 percent. Nearly 6,000 web sites featured links to the company's sites by mid-summer. The firm now employed 250, and was operating a 24-hour call center out of its Kirkland headquarters.

In August of 2000 CelebrateExpress.com abandoned its plans to go public. The IPO market had turned sour in the spring, and the firm's public competitors had seen their stock prices fall. Over the next year the company instead raised $14 million in new capital from outside sources. During 2000 the firm fulfilled 420,000 orders, which averaged about $70 worth of goods each.

Storybook Heirlooms Acquired in 2001

The first half of 2001 saw Celebrate Express revamp its Birthday Express web site and purchase Storybook, Inc., a retailer of clothing for pre-teen girls via catalogs and the Internet under the Storybook Heirlooms brand name. Its operations were moved to Kirkland. The company also added several new lines of licensed partyware to its offerings, including Curious George, Lego, and Rokenbok.

During 2001 Celebrate Express began a cross-promotional venture with baked goods giant Pillsbury. In January the latter firm placed $5 coupons for Birthday Express in 3.5 million cans of Happy Birthday Cookies, while Birthday Express included coupons for the cookies in its catalogs. In the summer the Pillsbury marketing continued with two Birthday Express contests that were featured on millions of dessert and cake mix packages. Both firms cross-promoted on their web sites, and a Pillsbury coupon appeared in Birthday Express catalogs and in outgoing orders. Pillsbury also created a number of cakes that complemented the firm's party themes. The Birthday Express web site was now recording one million visits per month, while 12 million copies of its quarterly catalogs were being mailed each year.

The company also was continuing to sign new licensing deals, in early 2002 adding popular movie character E.T. The Extraterrestrial to its party theme offerings. In the spring, the Storybook Heirlooms web site was re-launched, after the firm had sorted out problems integrating its operations. The site, and a catalog, offered girls' clothing for celebratory events like weddings and first communions, and holidays like Christmas and Easter. During the year Mike Jewell became the company's sole CEO, while Jan Jewell took the title of chief creative officer.

In 2003 Celebrate Express launched a new brand, Costume Express. Its web site and catalog offered a wide selection of children's costumes and accessories, primarily for Halloween.

IPO Completed in 2004

In 2004 the company again set its sights on a public stock offering. The market for IPOs had rebounded, and Celebrate Express, Inc. (as the firm was now known) had grown substantially since its failed attempt of four years earlier. In the fiscal year ended mid-2004, the company reported sales of $51.9 million and operating income of $300,000. The October stock

Key Dates:

1994: Mike and Jan Jewell found Birthday Express to sell children's party items.
1996: Internet sales begin.
1997: Great Days Publishing is purchased.
1999: The company gets $13.1 million in new funding to expand operations.
1999: Celebrate Express.com is launched with a line of adult party goods.
2000: The company changes its name to Celebrate Express.com; a new distribution center opens; an initial public offering (IPO) is announced, but abandoned after the IPO market turns sour.
2001: Storybook Inc., maker of girls' celebration/holiday clothing, is acquired.
2003: Costume Express is formed to market costumes online and via catalog.
2004: The firm, now known as Celebrate Express, Inc., raises more than $38 million in an IPO.

sale brought in more than $38 million, which was used to pay down $5 million in long-term debt and provide funds for future acquisitions. An additional $18.8 million went to existing shareholders who participated in the offering.

Growth continued in the fall, with the company's sales up 43 percent from a year earlier. Costume Express in particular was doing well, with a wider variety of Halloween costumes boosting sales. The company was still hungry for growth, and with its factory and distribution facilities operating at less than half of capacity, it was well situated for future expansion. It had recently added 24,000 square feet to the Greensboro center.

The company's success was attributable to a variety of factors. Birthday Express maintained a 98 percent in-stock rate and offered as many as 35 different items for each of its 100-plus themes, while allowing customers to order for as many partygoers as they wished. This gave it a distinct advantage over bricks-and-mortar competitors who typically sold in packs of eight, forcing a parent inviting nine children to a party to purchase goods for 16, for example. The company's web site and catalog also offered party planning advice, and informational booklets were shipped with orders. Online and telephone assistance was offered live 24 hours per day, as well.

Celebrate Express now had a database of more than two million customers. The company generated 80 percent of its revenues from Birthday Express, which was logging an average order of $78.03. Storybook Heirlooms orders averaged nearly

$100, while those for Costume Express were closer to $70. Nearly half of the company's orders came from previous customers, and almost three-fifths were made online. The firm also continued to publish catalogs, believing that children used them to pick a party theme or costume, with parents doing the ordering online or over the phone. The firm had by now quietly shut down the CelebrateExpress.com adult party business to focus exclusively on children's items.

In little more than a decade Celebrate Express, Inc. had grown from a small catalog operation into one of the leading mail-order children's party goods suppliers in the United States. Having successfully completed its IPO, the company was preparing for further expansion in the years to come.

Principal Subsidiaries

Birthday Express; Storybook, Inc.; Costume Express.

Principal Competitors

Target Corporation; Wal-Mart Stores, Inc.; Party City Corporation; iParty Corporation; Party America; Hallmark Cards, Inc.

Further Reading

Cook, John, "CelebrateExpress.com Cancels Its IPO," *Seattle Post-Intelligencer,* August 2, 2000, p. C2.
——, "Celebrate Express Has Strong Debut," *Seattle Post-Intelligencer,* October 21, 2004, p. E1.
Duryee, Tricia, "Celebrate Express Files IPO: Proposes Same Plan It Had in 2000," *Seattle Times,* July 17, 2004, p. E1.
——, "Kirkland, Wash. Online Party Supplier Raises Nearly $50 Million in IPO," *Seattle Times,* October 21, 2004.
Ernst, Steve, "Cost-Conscious Mentality Helped Birthday Express.com Survive Market Correction," *Puget Sound Business Journal,* March 2, 2001.
Hill, Cathy Gant, "Birthdays: A Happy Business—West Coast Couple Celebrate Their Business, Which Includes a Greensboro Distribution Center," *Greensboro News & Record,* March 4, 2001, p. E1.
Oldenburg, Don, "Going Online to Create That Perfect Party," *Washington Post,* November 11, 1999, p. C4.
Soto, Monica, "Eastside Business: Online Party Store Plans Public Offering," *Seattle Times,* January 13, 2000, p. C2.
——, "Online and Ready to Party—Couple Turns an Idea for Company into an Internet Bonanza," *Seattle Times,* September 21, 1999, p. B3.
Tice, Carol, "Party Company Aims to Celebrate Public Offering," *Puget Sound Business Journal,* July 23, 2004.
"When IPOs Get Called Off," *Newsweek International,* October 16, 2000.
Wolcott, John, "A 'Jewell' of an Idea: Turnkey Birthday Parties," *Puget Sound Business Journal,* October 31, 1997.

—Frank Uhle

Chr. Hansen Group A/S

Boge Alle 10
Horsholm
DK-2970
Denmark
Telephone: (+45) 45 74 74 74
Fax: (+45) 45 74 88 88
Web site: http://www.chr-hansen.com

Wholly Owned Subsidiary of Chr. Hansen Holding A/S
Incorporated: 1870
Employees: 3,681
Sales: DKK 3.42 billion ($596 million) (2004)
Stock Exchanges: Copenhagen
Ticker Symbol: HHDB
NAIC: 325414 Biological Product (Except Diagnostic)
  Manufacturing

Chr. Hansen Group A/S is one of the world's top food ingredients companies, ranking in the top 15 over all. Chr. Hansen specializes in producing enzymes, bacterial cultures, and related ingredients for the production of cheese and yogurt, as well as for wine and meat. The company also produces natural food colorings, a rising market segment for foods and beverages as manufacturers turn away from artificial colorings. Hansen also develops seasonings, natural flavorings, and organic sweeteners. The company is also an active player in the fast-growing ''neutriceuticals'' market, helping manufacturers produce foods with proven health benefits. For this market, for example, Hansen develops probiotic cultures designed to boost intestinal health and immunity. The company has also developed BioPlus2B, a natural feed additive meant to replace antibiotic growth enhancers. Hansen supports its global reach with research facilities in Denmark, France, and the United States, as well as a globally active subsidiary network. Chr. Hansen Group is part of Chr. Hansen Holding, which also includes allergy preparation and vaccine specialist Alk Abello. Chr. Hansen Holding has announced its intention to split off Chr. Hansen Group into a separate, independent company at the request of its majority shareholder, the Lundbeck Foundation. The breakup is expected to occur in 2005.

Origins

Chr. Hansen Group was founded in 1870 by pharmacist Christian Ditlev Ammentorp Hansen of Denmark. At the age of 22, Hansen began working at the University of Copenhagen, assisting Professor Julius Thomsen, a noted researcher of the time, in his efforts to extract pepsin from cow stomachs. Hansen himself began developing a method for extracting a different substance, the rennet enyzme, an important ingredient in cheese production. Up to that time, rennet remained inconsistent in quality and purity, and the lack of a standardized rennet made it difficult for cheese producers to enter the industrial age. In 1870, however, Hansen succeeded in extracting pure rennet from the stomachs of calves.

Hansen's procedure was to revolutionize the world dairy industry, making it possible to produce cheese in large quantities and of consistent quality. The resulting cheese was also safer for consumers to eat. Recognizing the opportunity to go into business, Hansen formed a company and opened a factory in Copenhagen for producing rennet in 1874.

Hansen next had to convince the dairy industry to adopt his product. While cheese producers in Denmark were relatively quick to adopt the new, standardized rennet, a move that helped the country emerge as a major global cheese producer, other countries proved more reluctant. Hansen began traveling to promote his rennet, even famously drinking a glass of rennet in order to convince observers of the safety of his product.

Any resistance to adopting the new form of rennet vanished soon enough, and in order to meet the growing demand Hansen began establishing a network of international sales offices. Before the end of the 1870s, the company had already opened offices in France, Germany, and the United Kingdom. Hansen also recognized the United States as an important market for his products, and by 1876 the company had already opened its first office there. The long shipping times between Denmark and the United States encouraged Hansen to establish its first production facility there just two years later. In the meantime, Hansen had also begun to branch out from rennet production, adding the development and production of natural colors, used for cheese and butter.

Demand for Hansen's product soon outstripped its supply, and in 1890 the company bought an island on New York's Mohawk River and built a long-scale facility there. That island later became known as Hansen Island. Back in Denmark, the company had begun working with cultures for the production of yogurt and similar dairy products, launching its first cultures in 1893.

Over the next several decades, Hansen added to its string of production facilities. In 1916, the company built a factory in England, followed by a new site in Toronto, Canada, in 1917. The company's U.S. subsidiary moved its production center to Milwaukee in 1930. In 1936, the company had added production facilities in Germany and Italy as well. Hansen later went public.

Diversification and Expansion in the 1970s and 1980s

Hansen's expansion continued following World War II with the opening of a production site in Adelaide, Australia, in 1951, and a new factory for producing rennet in France, another of the world's great cheese capitals, in 1955. By the 1960s, Hansen had begun its expansion into South America, launching a subsidiary in Argentina and building a plant in Quilmes. The company later boosted its South American presence with an entry into Brazil in 1977, as well as establishing operations in Peru.

The rising popularity of yogurt in the west led Hansen to add a new facility for developing and producing cultures in France. The company also became interested in developing cultures for the wine industry, notably in creating new cultures and coagulants used for removing sediment from wine.

A major feature of Hansen's development was its long-standing commitment to the development of natural ingredients for the food and feed industries. Into the mid-1970s, the company began attacking a growing problem within the chicken and meat industries, particularly in the United States, which had turned to the use of antibiotics and growth hormones. In 1975, Hansen launched a research effort into the creation of natural alternatives to these products and for developing bacterial strains to produce more healthful meat.

Hansen also continued to innovate with its dairy cultures. By 1976, the company's research had resulted in the successful launch of its DVS (for Direct Vat Set) procedure. That product was launched in the United States that same year. Hansen had also become interested in the nascent "neutriceuticals" market, that is, developing food products with clinically proven health benefits. By 1987, the company had succeeded in bringing its first probiotic diary supplement, Trevis, to clinical trial.

Toward the end of the 1970s, Hansen opened a number of new production facilities, including a rennet factory in Graasten, Denmark, in 1976 and a plant for producing cultures in Roskilde, Denmark, in 1978. Hansen also expanded its sales and marketing network, launching subsidiaries in Australia and Ireland in 1983 and 1984, respectively. In the meantime, Hansen had diversified into an entirely new sector, buying allergy control and treatment specialist Alk Abello in 1979.

In the mid-1980s, Hansen launched a new expansion strategy based on acquisitions. In 1986, for example, the company bought France's SOCHAL, a specialist in developing ripening cultures and coagulants for the wine industry. That purchase was followed by the acquisition of Extract Oil, a Spanish company which specialized in paprika extracts, in 1990. Also in that year, Hansen added a sales and marketing subsidiary in Spain, buying up its former distributor there. Similarly, the company acquired its Greek and Turkish distributors, then opened sales subsidiaries in the Netherlands, Japan, and Austria that year.

Independence in the New Century?

Hansen's acquisition program continued into the 1990s with the 1991 purchase of Rudolf Muller, based in Germany, which specialized in the development of meat cultures. In that year, Hansen also returned to the United States, acquiring Diversitech, which produced both meat cultures and liquid seasonings. Diversitech was later merged into the company's U.S. subsidiary.

The company made its next acquisition in 1995, buying up Gastronomisk Institut A/S in Denmark. The company then changed its new subsidiary's name to Gourmet Food Ingredients. Also that year, Hansen moved into India, setting up a joint venture, AKAY Flavours and Aromatics.

In 1996, Hansen added another French company, SEFCAL, which focused on the extraction of polyphenols and anthocyanin, and Xantoflor, based in Spain, which specialized in the extraction of carmine, a natural coloring agent. More acquisitions followed through the end of the decade, including the purchase of a fermentation plant in Germany, as well as that country's Stefan Wolf, which focused on meat and poultry seasonings and related products, both in 1997.

The following year, the company went back to the United States to purchase Ingredient Technology Corporation, its largest acquisition to date. Next, Hansen established a manufacturing base in Ireland with the purchase of Quest Natural Color Business, also in 1998. In 1999, Hansen added facilities in Italy through its acquisition of Italiana Ingredienti and Enocanossa.

Hansen had also been building up its marketing network, establishing subsidiaries in Poland, the Czech Republic, Mex-

Key Dates:

1870: Christian D.A. Hansen develops a method for extracting pure, consistent-quality rennet from calves stomachs.

1874: The company sets up its first rennet production plant in Copenhagen, then adds natural coloring agents for cheese and butter.

1876: Subsidiaries are established in the United States, France, and Germany.

1878: Production in the United States begins.

1893: The company begins producing cultures for yogurt and other dairy products.

1916: Production in the United Kingdom is launched.

1918: The company opens a factory in Canada.

1930: A new main production site in Milwaukee, Wisconsin, is opened.

1936: Production subsidiaries in Germany and Italy are established.

1951: The company enters Australia with a production subsidiary.

1955: A rennet production plant in France is opened.

1964: The company enters South America with a plant in Argentina.

1976: DVS dairy culture system is launched.

1979: The company acquires Alk Abello in Denmark, adding pharmaceuticals to its business portfolio.

1986: SOCHAL, in France, is acquired.

1990: Extract Oil, in Spain, is acquired.

1991: Lundbeck Foundation acquires a majority control of Hansen, which is reformed as Chr. Hansen Holding with two core businesses, Chr. Hansen Group and Alk Abello.

1995: AKAY joint venture in India is launched; the company acquires Gastronomisk Institut in Denmark.

1996: SEFCAL, in France, and Xantoflor, in Spain, are acquired.

1998: Ingredient Technology Corporation, in the United States, is acquired.

1999: The company enters Russia and acquires Italiana Ingredienti in Italy.

2000: BioPlus2B receives European Union approval.

2001: A new DKK 100 million facility opens in Denmark for research, development, and testing.

2003: Chr. Hansen enters China with a subsidiary in Hong Kong.

2004: Chr. Hansen Holding announces its plan to split off Chr. Hansen Group as a separate company in 2005.

ico, and Russia in the 1990s. The company moved into Malaysia in 2000 with the launch of a subsidiary in Kuala Lumpur.

Meanwhile, Hansen's new product development had resulted in a number of significant successes. In 1991, the company launched its first chymosin fabricated through fermentation. The following year, Hansen debuted a direct inoculation malolactic culture for the wine industry. The company acquired a global manufacturing and distribution agreement for a promising new probiotic culture, Lactobacillus casei CRL-431 in 1995. Then, in 2000, the company achieved a breakthrough when it received European Union approval for the launch of its probiotic feed additive, BioPlus2B, meant to take the place of artificial antibiotic-based growth stimulants. In that year, also, the company received FOSHU (Food for Specified Health Use) approval for the use of its probiotic culture BB-12 in fermented milk in Japan.

A dip in profits at the beginning of the 2000s encouraged Hansen to restructure its operations, and the company shut down seven plants in order to boost its operating efficiency. Hansen also stepped up its research commitment, opening a research, development, and testing facility in 2001 at a cost of DKK 100 million.

By 2003, Hansen was once again in an expansive mood. In that year, the company moved into the Chinese market for the first time, setting up a subsidiary in Hong Kong. The following year, the company set up new production subsidiaries in India and Ukraine.

Hansen had come under the majority control of the Lundbeck Foundation, which also owned H/S Lundbeck, in 1991. Hansen was then restructured as a holding company, Chr. Hansen Holding, with Alk Abello and Chr. Hansen Group as its two main subsidiaries. At the end of 2004, Lundbeck decided that it preferred to focus its investment interests solely on the scientific research and pharmaceuticals sectors. As such, the Chr. Hansen Group no longer fit within Lundbeck's investment objectives, and the holding company announced its intention to split off Chr. Hansen Group into a separate, independent company before the end of 2005. With a history spanning 135 years, Chr. Hansen was nonetheless expected to remain a leading name in the global food ingredients sector.

Principal Subsidiaries

AKAY Flavours & Aromatics Ltd. (India; 50%); Chr. Hansen A/S (Norway); Chr. Hansen Argentina S.A.I.C.; Chr. Hansen Centroamérica S.A. (Panama); Chr. Hansen Czech Republic, s.r.o.; Chr. Hansen de Mexico S.A. de C.V. (Mexico); Chr. Hansen France S.A; Chr. Hansen GmbH; Chr. Hansen GmbH (Austria); Chr. Hansen Ind. e Com. Ltda. (Brazil); Chr. Hansen Ireland Limited; Chr. Hansen Limited (Canada); Chr. Hansen LLC (Russia); Chr. Hansen Ltd. (United Kingdom); Chr. Hansen Poland Sp. z.o.o.; Chr. Hansen Pty Ltd (Australia); Chr. Hansen S.A. (Peru); Chr. Hansen S.p.A. (Italy); Chr. Hansen, Inc. (United States); Chr. Hansen, S.A. (Spain); Czech Republic; Hansen Hellas ABEE (Greece); Peyma Chr. Hansen's A.S. (Turkey).

Principal Competitors

Danisco A/S; Degussa AG; Kerry Group plc.

Further Reading

"A Blue 'First' for Chr. Hansen," *International Food Ingredients*, February-March 2005, p. 48.

"Chr. Hansen Completes Culture Plant Upgrade," *Feedstuffs*, August 6, 2001, p. 19.

"Chr. Hansen Expands Culture Capacity," *Chemical Market Reporter*, February 14, 2005, p. 10.

"Chr. Hansen Expands Facilities," *Feedstuffs*, June 7, 2004, p. 40.

"Chr. Hansen: 130 Years Old and Evolving," *Nutraceuticals World*, March 2003, p. 117.

"Chr. Hansen (Supplier Spotlight)," *Dairy Foods*, January 2005, p. 58.

"Global Dairy Supplicr: Dedicated Dairy Industry Supplier Positions Itself for the Next Century," *Dairy Foods*, February 1997, p. 39.

Howie, Michael, "Chr. Hansen May Sell Food, Feed Unit," *Feedstuffs*, December 6, 2004, p. 6.

Levitt, Alan. "Hansen's Responds to the Needs of the Marketplace," *Cheese Market News*, August 2, 1991, p. 7.

—M.L. Cohen

Cloetta Fazer AB

Ljungsbro
S-590 69
Sweden
Telephone: +46 13 28 50 00
Fax: +46 13 655 60
Web site: http://www.cloettafazer.se

Public Company
Incorporated: 2000
Employees: 2,090
Sales: SEK 3.03 billion ($438 million) (2004)
Stock Exchanges: Stockholm
Ticker Symbol: CFA
NAIC: 311320 Chocolate and Confectionery Manufacturing from Cacao Beans; 311330 Confectionery Manufacturing from Purchased Chocolate

Cloetta Fazer AB is the Nordic region's leading manufacturer of chocolates and other confectionery. The Ljungsbro, Sweden-based company, a combination of Sweden's Cloetta and Finland's Fazer, commands 20 percent of the Scandinavian market, boasting key brands such as Fazer Blå, Dumle, Kexchoklad, Geisha, Polly, Center, Ässät, Pantteri, Marianne, Fazermint, Bridgeblandning, Tyrkisk Peber, Liqueur Fills, Plopp, and Sportlunch. Sweden and Finland remain Cloetta Fazer's primary markets, and also the site of its largest manufacturing sites in Ljungsbro, Norrköping, Vantaa, and Lappeenranta. These facilities combine for a total annual production of 59,000 tons. Sweden and Finland account for 34 and 31 percent, respectively, of the company's sales, which topped SEK 3 billion ($440 million) in 2004. The company also holds strong positions in the wider Nordic market, including Denmark, Norway, the Baltic States, and Russia, which add more than 10 percent to sales. The company's fastest-growing new market, however, is Poland, where the company has captured a 10 percent market share since its entry in 1995. Cloetta Fazer's Polish operations are supported by a manufacturing plant in Gdansk with a total production capacity of 7,000 tons. At the end of 2004, the company announced its intention to expand its

Polish presence, most likely through acquisitions. Cloetta Fazer is listed on the Stockholm Stock Exchange.

Satisfying the Scandinavian Sweet Tooth in the 19th Century

Cloetta Fazer was formed through the merger of Cloetta, in Sweden, and Fazer Konfektyr, in Finland, in the year 2000. Both companies, however, traced their origins to the 19th century, and had both emerged as the leading confectionery company in their respective markets.

Cloetta's roots also lay in the famed chocolate-making tradition of Switzerland. The company's founders, brothers Christoffer, Bernhard, and Nutin, arrived in Scandinavia from their native Switzerland and set up their first chocolate making studio in 1862. An early success for the brothers came with the company's launch of its Kehlet chocolate in 1867. At first, the Cloetta brothers made chocolate in Copenhagen, then still under Sweden's control. In 1901, however, the company moved to its permanent home, building a new and more modern facility in Ljungsbro, in Sweden.

Cloetta remained in the Cloetta family until after 1917, when it was bought up by the Svenfelt family and placed under the holding, Svenska Chokladfabriks. The company, which by then had emerged as one of Sweden's prominent chocolate and candy makers, launched a new confection, a chocolate-coated wafer in 1921. Originally called the Five O'Clock, the chocolate was renamed as Kexchoklad in 1938. Under its new name, Kexchoklad proved a lasting success—by the mid-1970s, the bar had become Sweden's top-selling chocolate product.

Cloetta used its success in chocolates and confectionery to expand into other businesses, specifically a distribution wing, through subsidiaries Caterman and Cloetta Hushall. At the end of the 1980s, Cloetta expanded this division into one of its core areas of operation. This came about through the purchase of Adaco in 1989. That company had originally been established in 1921 as a pharmaceuticals distribution division of Malmsten & Bergval. Adaco later added a wide range of nonfood items. In 1955, the division was incorporated as a separate company. Originally called Apotekarens Droghandels, but long known as ADA & Co., the company adopted the new name of Adaco.

Company Perspectives:

The company's mission is to create fun and enjoyment. Our vision is to further consolidate Cloetta Fazer's position as the Nordic region's leading confectionery company. Cloetta Fazer will act and be seen as a driving force for development in the industry. Cloetta Fazer, with the market's most attractive portfolio, will create added value for customers, consumers, employees and shareholders.

Two years later, Adaco added food items for the first time, winning the distribution rights to HJ Heinz products. Adaco was acquired by Skane-Gripen in 1983, merged with another Swedish distributor, Saljbolagsgruppen, and placed into a new structure, Interbroker. By the end of the decade, however, Interbroker was restructured, with all of its trading operations merged into a single company, called Adaco.

Cloetta joined in the restructuring of Adaco in 1989, when it acquired a stake in the company—and added its own trading operations to the mix. Cloetta then acquired majority control of Adaco in 1991. Another extension, made the year before, permitted Cloetta to expand its foods production from chocolates to other food items, specifically the growing market for Asian foods, with the purchase of Lecora. Cloetta's interest in expanding the scale and scope of its operations led it to the public market, and in 1994 the company listed its Class B shares on the Stockholm Stock Exchange. The public offering also enabled the company to expand, including through the acquisition of Candelia in 1998. That acquisition enabled Cloetta to claim the undisputed leadership of the Swedish confectionery market.

Finnish Chocolate Leader in the 20th Century

By then, Cloetta had formed a relationship with another leading Scandinavian confectioner, Fazer Konfektry of Finland. In 1990, the two companies, together with Norway's Brynildsen, set up a manufacturing and sales partnership, called Cloetta Fazer Production, which linked the companies' factories in Ljungsbro, Malmo, and Falkoping in Sweden and in Kolding in Denmark.

Karl Fazer originally established a business operating a café in Helsinki in 1891. Fazer began producing chocolates for his customers, and by the middle of the decade demand had grown so strongly that Fazer set up a small factory on Helsinki's Batsmangatan in 1895. Two years later, Fazer decided to enter chocolate making on an industrial scale, opening a new site on Fabriksgatan in 1897. The new plant also enabled Fazer to extend his production into the wider confectionery segment.

Fazer built up its position as Finland's major confectioner with a series of highly successful product launches, starting with the Pihlaja chocolate in 1895. In 1896, Fazer also found success when he released his Mignon Easter egg, borrowing an idea that had already become popular in Germany. The Mignon egg remained a mainstay of the company's product portfolio into the 21st century. Another major product success for Fazer was the launch of its Fazer Blue chocolate in 1922. This was later followed by the launch of the company's Marianne candy in 1949.

Fazer moved to a larger manufacturing site in Fagersta in 1963. The increased production capacity enabled the company to move into the wider Scandinavian market. The company backed up this effort with the creation of a new subsidiary, Karl Fazer AB, in Sweden in 1967.

Fazer's Swedish interests grew again in the mid-1970s with the purchase of Mazetti in 1975. Mazetti had been operating in Sweden since before World War II. In 1945, the company released what was to become its flagship product, a flat lollipop. It was not until 1960, however, that the Mazetti lollipop at last received its brand name. Known as Dumle, the lollipop became one of the Nordic region's best-selling candies. Under Fazer, the Dumle brand later expanded to include Dumle toffees, a chocolate-covered wrapped version. Launched in Sweden in 1987, the new Dumle toffee gained immediate success. By the end of the decade, the candy had been introduced throughout the Scandinavian markets. In the mid-1990s, Fazer successfully launched Dumle in the Baltic states, then extended the brand to Poland in 1999. That country, in fact, emerged as the Dumle brand's single largest market by the mid-2000s.

Although Fazer did not introduce the Dumle brand to Poland until the late 1990s, Fazer itself had staked out a position in that market—which, with 40 million people, was larger than the combined population of the entire Scandinavian market. Poland's emergence from Soviet domination, and the prospect of rapid economic growth into the 21st century, made it an attractive market for Fazer, which set up its Polish subsidiary in 1993.

That subsidiary began producing for the domestic market with the acquisition of a manufacturing plant in Gdansk in 1994. The Gdansk plant had been producing confectionery and other items, including sodas, since 1923, and had become a major Polish candy producer with the launch of its Whips candy in the 1950s. In 1993, the company formed a joint venture with Fazer, known as Whips Chocolate. Afterward Fazer took over control of the joint venture, which was then renamed Fazer Poland. By then, Fazer had made a number of other acquisitions, including Swedish sugar candy confectionery company Chymos, in 1993, and CK Chokolade, a chocolate broker based in Denmark.

Nordic Region Confectionery Leader in the 2000s

In 2000, Cloetta and Fazer decided to take their relationship to the next level, merging to become Cloetta Fazer AB. The company's combined operations gave it a leading position in the extended Nordic market, with a 22 percent market share, compared with primary competitors Kraft Foods (20 percent market share) and Malaco-Leaf (15 percent). Cloetta Fazer maintained its dual Cloetta and Fazer brand families, as well as the production sites from both companies. The company also established a separate wing for its combined trading and distribution operations, called Handel.

In the early 2000s, Cloetta Fazer stepped up its focus on its chocolate and confectionery business. The company began streamlining, selling off Lecora—the only manufacturer grouped under its Handel division—in 2000. In 2001, Cloetta Fazer sold off the Handel division itself, to Switzerland's Valora Holding AG. In this way, Cloetta Fazer became a pure confectionery group.

Key Dates:

1861: Cloetta is established by brothers Christoffer, Bernhard, and Nutin Cloetta in Copenhagen.

1891: Karl Fazer opens a café in Helsinki and begins making chocolates.

1895: Fazer sets up a chocolate making site.

1897: Fazer opens a larger facility for large-scale chocolate production.

1901: Cloetta moves to a larger production site in Ljungsbro, Sweden.

1917: The Svenfelt family acquires majority control of Cloetta.

1921: Cloetta launches the popular Five O'Clock, renamed as Kexchoklad in 1938.

1945: The Mazetti company begins producing a flat lollipop, renamed as Dumle in 1960.

1963: Fazer moves production to a new site in Fagersta.

1967: Fazer enters Sweden.

1975: Fazer acquires Mazetti.

1989: Cloetta acquires a stake in Adaco.

1991: Cloetta acquires control of Adaco; Cloetta enters a production and distribution alliance with Fazer.

1993: Fazer enters Poland, forms Whips Chocolate joint venture.

1994: Cloetta lists shares on the Stockholm Stock Exchange.

1995: Fazer acquires control of Whips Chocolate, renamed as Fazer Poland.

2000: Fazer and Cloetta merge to form Cloetta Fazer AB.

2001: Cloetta Fazer sells the Handel division to Valora of Switzerland.

2004: Cloetta Fazer announces plans to make acquisitions to increase its scale in Poland.

Into the mid-2000s, Cloetta Fazer's sales remained strong in its core Finnish and Swedish markets. Slipping sales elsewhere, particularly in Denmark, Norway, and the Baltic states, led the company to step up its efforts to increase its share of the Polish market—already at 10 percent. At the end of 2004, Cloetta Fazer announced its intention to expand in Poland. With restrictions placed on further expansion of its Gdansk site, the company suggested that it was interested in making acquisitions in Poland. The first of these was expected to come before the end of 2005. With a history of nearly 150 years, Cloetta Fazer remained a major European confectioner in the new century.

Principal Subsidiaries

Chymos AB; Cloetta Fazer Choklad AB; Cloetta Fazer Development AB; Cloetta Fazer Konfektyr AB; Cloetta Fazer Konfektyr AB; Cloetta Fazer Polska Sp. z.o.o.; Cloetta Fazer Produktion AB; Oy NIS - Nordic Industrial Sales AB.

Principal Competitors

Nestle S.A.; Archer Daniels Midland Company; KJ Jacobs AG; Cadbury Schweppes PLC; Orkla ASA; Cargill B.V.; Mars UK Ltd.; Barry Callebaut AG; Koninklijke Wessanen N.V.; Chocoladefabriken Lindt und Sprungli AG; Ferrero S.p.A.; Kronfagel AB; Spoldzielnia Pracy Przemyslu Spozywczego Solidarnosc.

Further Reading

Brown-Humes, Christopher, "The Sweet Taste of Success After Eight Years," *Financial Times,* March 28, 2003, p. 10.

"Cloetta Fazer AB to Close Production Facility in Norrkoping, Sweden," *Nordic Business Report,* September 20, 2004.

"Cloetta Fazer Divests Spring Roll Business," *Nordic Business Report,* March 27, 2001.

"Cloetta Fazer Set to Boost Production Efficiency," *Food and Production Daily.com,* April 18, 2003.

"Cloetta Fazer Signs New Agreement with the Company's Norwegian Distributor," *PrimeZone Media Network,* January 23, 2004.

"Cloetta Fazer Stands Firm," *Food and Drink Europe.com,* October 20, 2003.

"Fazer Eyes Polish Confectionery Market," *Polish News Bulletin,* June 24, 2004.

—M.L. Cohen

Compania Cervecerias Unidas S.A.

Bandera 84
Santiago
Chile
Telephone: (56) (2) 427-3000
Fax: (56) (2) 427-3215
Web site: http://www.ccu-sa.com

Public Company
Incorporated: 1902
Employees: 3,901
Sales: CLP 384.06 billion ($646.76 million) (2003)
Stock Exchanges: Bolsa de Comercio de Santiago
Ticker Symbol: CERVEZAS
NAIC: 312111 Soft Drink Manufacturing; 312112 Bottled
    Water Manufacturing; 312120 Breweries; 312130
    Wineries; 326160 Plastics Bottle Manufacturing

Compania Cervecerias Unidas S.A. (CCU) is the leading beverage company in Chile, where it dominates beer sales and is the leader in mineral water and bottled nectar. It is also the third largest producer of soft drinks and holds the nation's franchise for PepsiCo Inc. beverages. In addition, CCU is Chile's second largest wine producer. The company also produces, distributes, and sells beer in Argentina, where it is the second largest beermaker. CCU makes returnable plastic bottles for its soft drinks.

A Century of Brewing Beer: 1889–1989

Joaquin Plagemann opened one of the first breweries in Chile in Valparaiso in 1850, and Carlos Anwandter established another a year later in Valdivia. In 1889 the Valparaiso brewery merged with another in Umache to form the Fabrica Nacional de Cerveza, which soon after acquired the Gubler y Cousino Cerveceria y Fabrica de Hielo. In 1902 the Fabrica Nacional de Cerveza, acknowledging these predecessors, incorporated itself as Compania Cervecerias Unidas, or United Beer Company. Some years later, CCU acquired the old Anwandter factory, a number of other regional breweries, and two mineral water plants. It also began producing and marketing soft drinks in 1907. By 1916 CCU owned the four largest breweries in Chile. It owned five in 1950.

The bottling and selling of mineral water began in 1960. Until 1978 beer came in only one size of bottle (285 cubic centimeters, or about ten ounces) and was not labeled. Soon, however, the company acquired a brewery whose Pilsener and Malta Dorada brands entered into competition with traditional beers. The only other real competitor was Cervecera del Pacifico, whose Condor brand was introduced around 1980, but this brewery was purchased subsequently by CCU, raising its share of the Chilean beer market to 98 percent.

The Chilean government's one-third share of CCU, dating from 1971, was sold in 1976 for $9.72 million to the Cruzat-Larrain and Edwards groups. In the wake of the extensive privatizations of state-owned enterprises by the government during this period, the Cruzat-Larrain group became Chile's largest conglomerate, with its acquisitions financed by large loans from banks in which the group had become the dominant shareholder. When an economic crisis gripped Chile in the early 1980s, this group's long-term debt swelled to at least $350 million owed to 64 banks. Two sons of Andronico Luksic Abaroa then bought 10 percent of CCU for only $890,000. In 1986 the Luksic family holding company, Quinenco S.A., and Germany's Schorghuber group, producers of Munich-based Paulaner beer, jointly purchased 64 percent of bankrupt CCU for $14 million, or CLP 13 a share, and renegotiated its debt. At this time Chile was still in a recession, and CCU's sales in real terms did not pass the 1980 level until 1987, the year the company began trading its stock on Chilean exchanges. By 1989 CCU was solvent enough to resume paying dividends on its common stock.

Son of a Croatian immigrant to Chile, Andronico Luksic entered the mining business in partnership with French engineers. Their mine attracted the attention of a Japanese company, which accepted their selling price of ''500,000,'' paying not in the pesos that the sellers expected but in dollars. Luksic's shares provided the basis for a far-flung business empire that included copper mining and metals processing, banking, agriculture and food production, railroads, telecommunications, forestry, fisheries, tourism, wineries, and auto distribution. *Forbes* rated him the richest man in Chile in 2004, estimating his fortune at $4.2 billion.

In 1988 CCU radically changed its distribution system, directly supplying its customers by means of a fleet of 859 trucks. In the same year it introduced plastic liter bottles and began promotional pricing. That year, the company ranked third among Chilean enterprises in profit. CCU, directly or indirectly, was, in 1989, producing the beer brands Bavaria, Cristal, Escudo, Morenita, Morenita Especial, Royal Guard, and Schop. By means of an affiliate, CCU was producing the soft drinks Agua Tonica, Bilz, Cachatun, Free, Ginger Ale, Kem Pina, Limon Soda, and Pap as proprietary brands. In 1990 (when it ranked tenth in Chile in sales) the company launched, under license, Paulaner as its high-end beer. This brew dated from 1635, when it was first made by Bavarian monks. By the end of 1990 CCU still held no less than 98 percent of the Chilean beer market, with Cristal composing 57 percent and the Paulaner and Royal Guard brands another 39 percent.

Expansion and Shifting Alliances: 1990–2004

Aided by a credit from Chile's central bank, CCU had greatly reduced its debt by 1991. It began selling the equivalent of shares in the United States in 1992, when it raised $56.5 million in the NASDAQ over-the-counter market and was described in *LatinFinance* as one of the outstanding equity values in Latin America. By late 1995 a share of the company's stock was trading at CLP 2,000 (about $5). Beer was especially profitable for CCU. Its operating profit margin in beer was estimated at more than 25 percent in 1991, when the contribution of beer to total profits was more than 90 percent. Its more than 15 brands of beer were being produced in six facilities along the length of Chile.

Cerveceria y Malteria Quilmes S.A.I.C.A. y G., the dominant beer company in Argentina, entered the Chilean beer market in late 1991 in a joint venture, Cerveceria Chile S.A., with giant Dutch brewer Heineken Brouwerijen N.V. Their Becker beer, positioned to compete with Cristal but priced notably lower, failed to make a large impact in Chile but forced CCU to double its marketing budget and to improve its management and delivery systems. During the next three years the company invested $179 million, the bulk of it on plant improvements.

In 1994 CCU and Buenos Aires Embotelladora S.A. (Baesa), PepsiCo Inc.'s bottler in Chile, established Embotelladoras Chilenas Unidas S.A. (Ecusa) for the production, bottling, distribution, and marketing of soft drinks and mineral water in Chile. Baesa held about 37 percent of the soft drink market at the time. CCU bought Baesa's share of Ecusa in

1999. Also in 1994, CCU entered the Chilean wine market, which was almost as large as the beer market in volume. It took a 48 percent interest in Vina San Pedro S.A., one of the nation's largest wineries. CCU also took an indirect controlling stake in Karlovacka Pivovara d.d., a Croatian brewery.

CCU carried the fight to Quilmes by entering the Argentine beer market (at least four times the Chilean one) in 1995. It paid about $100 million to acquire Cordoba-based Cerveceria Santa Fe S.A. and a majority interest in a smaller northern Argentina brewer, Compania Industrial Cervecera S.A. (CICSA) for its new Argentine subsidiary, Compania Cervecerias Unidas Argentina S.A. These two companies accounted for 8 percent of the Argentine beer market. After buying almost all of the remaining CICSA shares in 1997, CCU Argentina merged the Santa Fe brewery into CICSA. Near the end of 1995 CCU formed an alliance with Anheuser-Busch Companies, Inc. to be the exclusive producer and distributor of Budweiser in Argentina, which it introduced to the market in 1996. Anheuser-Busch took a small stake in CCU Argentina and gradually increased its share to 11 percent. In 1998 CCU added a third regional Argentine brewer, Cerveceria Cordoba, paying $8 million for the acquisition.

CCU sold 22 percent of its shares in a December 1996 public offering in Santiago and New York that raised $89 million as part of a capital expansion program that brought in $107 million more by May 1999. During 2000 the company acquired the Argentine winery Finca La Celia S.A., and made it a subsidiary of Vina San Pedro for the export of high-quality Argentine wines. CCU added to its Chilean beer holdings by purchasing a half-interest in Cerveceria Austral S.A. in 2000 and in Compania Cervecera Kunstmann S.A. in 2002. In 2003 the company began selling pisco, a grape-based spirit. CCU's share in the Croatian brewery was sold in 2003. Also that year, the company raised its share of Vina San Pedro to 60 percent. Anheuser-Busch, in addition to having taken a stake in CCU's Argentine subsidiary, paid $224 million in early 2001 for a 14 percent holding in parent CCU, which it raised to 20 percent by the end of the year.

CCU, in 2001, signed a ten-year pact with Schweppes Holding Ltd. to bottle and distribute, under license, Cadbury Schweppes soft drinks such as Orange Crush, Canada Dry Ginger Ale, Canada Dry Agua Tonica, and Canada Dry Limon Soda. Because Cadbury Schweppes had been acquired by The Coca-Cola Co., PepsiCo Inc. charged that the transaction was a violation of its pact with CCU, but a court ruled for the latter because the soft drinks involved were not colas. An even greater dispute had developed between Quinenco S.A., the Luksic holding company, and Schorghuber, its partner in Inversiones y Rentas S.A. (Irsa), which had held the majority stake in CCU since 1986. Schorghuber, in 2001, sold its interest in Irsa to Heineken, which in view of Heineken's participation in Quilmes' Cerveceria Chile venture, was a competitor of CCU. The transaction led to an extended judicial dispute that ended in 2003, when Schorghuber paid the Luksic group $50 million and CCU's shareholders an extraordinary dividend of $270 million to settle the matter. The major entry of Heineken into CCU's Chilean beer operations apparently upset Anheuser-Busch, for in 2004 it sold its stake in CCU for about $300 million. Before doing so, however, it agreed to allow CCU to continue produc-

Key Dates:

1902: Companias Cervecerias Unidas S.A. (CCU) is incorporated.
1907: CCU introduces its first soft drink.
1916: CCU owns the four largest breweries in Chile.
1960: The company adds mineral water to its line of beverages.
1980: CCU holds 98 percent of the Chilean beer market (and holds the same ten years later).
1986: A Chilean holding company and a German brewer acquire majority control of CCU.
1994: CCU takes a half-share in PepsiCo Inc.'s Chilean affiliate; the company purchases a 48 percent interest in one of Chile's largest wineries.
1995: CCU enters the Argentine beer market by acquiring two regional breweries.
1996: CCU becomes exclusive bottler and distributer of Budweiser in Argentina.
1999: CCU buys out the remaining shares in PepsiCo Inc.'s Chilean affiliate.
2001: CCU becomes exclusive bottler and distributer in Chile for Cadbury Schweppes soft drinks.
2003: Heineken becomes the foreign partner in the joint venture with majority control of CCU.
2004: Budweiser's owner, Anheuser-Busch, sells its 20 percent stake in CCU.

ing and distributing Budweiser in Argentina and continue distributing Budweiser in Chile for 15 years.

CCU in 2003

In 2003 CCU held about 89 percent of the beer market (by volume) in Chile. Cristal alone held 59 percent of this market. Other CCU proprietary brands included Royal Guard, Escudo, Morenita, and Dorado 6.0. The company was producing Austral, Heineken, and Paulaner under license, importing Budweiser, and distributing Kunstmann. It maintained breweries in Santiago and Tenuco and a bottling plant in Antofagasta. In Argentina, CCU held about 14 percent of the beer market. Among its proprietary brands, Schneider was the most popular, accounting for 42 percent of its sales volume. CCU Argentina also was producing Budweiser and Heineken under license and was importing Corona and Guinness under agreements in 1997 and 2001, respectively. The company's Argentine breweries were in Salta and Santa Fe.

CCU held about 23 percent of the market in Chile for soft drinks, about 52 percent of the market for nectars, 100 percent of fruit juices, and about 35 percent of the market for mineral water. Its proprietary soft drink brands were Bilz, Pap, Bilz Light, Pap Light, Kem Pina, Kem Xtreme, and Show. Others were being produced under license from PepsiCo and Schweppes. Glacier was the name of its proprietary mineral water brand; it also was producing Cachentun and Porvenir under license. Its bottled nectar, Watt's, was being produced under a licensing agreement with Watt's Alimentos S.A. dating from 1987. CCU, through Vina San Pedro, had about 18 percent

of the Chilean wine market and about 13 percent of the export market. Vina San Pedro owned eight vineyards (the largest being in Molina) in Chile and one in Argentina.

Of CCU's net sales in 2003, Chilean beer operations accounted for 39 percent and Argentine beer operations for 8 percent. Soft drinks and mineral water accounted for 30 percent and wine for 21.5 percent. The picture was quite different in terms of operating income. Chilean beer operations accounted for 80 percent, soft drinks and mineral water for 19 percent, and wine for 8 percent, whereas Argentine beer operations recorded a deficit of 8 percent. In all, CCU had net income of CLP 54.09 billion ($91.09 million) on total sales of CLP 384.06 billion ($646.76 million) in 2003. Its long-term debt was CLP 104.19 billion ($175.46 million). The company had plants in Antofagasta, Casablanca, Coinco, Santiago, Talcahuano, and Temuco in Chile, and in Rosario de la Frontera, Salta, and Santa Fe in Argentina.

Principal Subsidiaries

Cerveceria CCU Chile Ltda.; Compania Cervecerias Unidas Argentina S.A. (Argentina; 97%); Embotelladoras Chilenas Unidas S.A.; Vina San Pedro S.A. (60%).

Principal Competitors

Cerveceria Chile S.A.; Cerveceria y Malteria Quilmes S.A.I.C.A. y G.; Embotelladora Andina S.A.; Vina Concha y Toro S.A.; Vina Santa Rita S.A.; Vital S.A.

Further Reading

"Andronico Luksic Abaroa: Corazon de Minero," *Gestion,* August 2004, pp. 10–12, 14.
Bickerton, Ian, "Heineken Works on Emerging Markets," *Financial Times,* January 15, 2003, p. 16.
Dolan, Kerry A., "Like Father, Like Sons," *Forbes,* September 21, 1998, pp. 136, 140.
Friedland, Jonathan, "Chile's Luksics: Battle-Tested and on the Prowl," *Wall Street Journal,* December 1, 1995, p. A10.
"Golpe de timon," *Capital,* January 31–February 27, 2003, pp. 48, 50.
"Grandes apuestas," *Capital,* December 19–29, 2003, pp. 52–53.
"Less Filling," *LatinFinance,* November 1992, p. 30.
Manriquez, Rodrigo, "La guerra del pisco," *America economia,* November 7-20, 2003, pp. 40–41.
Mark, Imogen, "Chilean Brewery Prepares for War," *Financial Times,* November 29, 1995, p. 54.
Mora-Mass, Elizabeth, "Espuma continental," *America economia,* February 2002, pp. 25, 27.
Moriaga, Javiera, "El edicto de Kunstmann," *Capital,* September 20–October 7, 2004, pp. 76–79.
Scovin, William, and John Greene, "Compania Cervecerias Unidas," *LatinFinance,* January 1993, pp. 72–73.
Stamborski, Al, "A-B Purchases a 14 Percent Stake in Major Chilean Brewery," *St. Louis Post-Dispatch,* January 5, 2001, p. C1.
"Temblor Grado Heineken Sacudira al Mercado," *Gestion,* May 1990, pp. 31–32.
"El 22% de las Ventas Coirresponde a Productos Lanzados en los Ultimos Tres Anos," *Gestion,* July 2001, pp. 20–21.
Vera, Hector, "Marca a marca," *America economia,* December 2, 1999, pp. 26–27.

—Robert Halasz

Connetics Corporation

3290 West Bayshore Road
Palo Alto, California 94303
U.S.A.
Telephone: (650) 843-2800
Toll Free: (888) 969-2628
Fax: (650) 843-2899
Web site: http://www.connetics.com

Public Company
Incorporated: 1993 as Connective Therapeutics, Inc.
Employees: 218
Sales: $144.35 million (2004)
Stock Exchanges: NASDAQ
Ticker Symbol: CNCT
NAIC: 325412 Pharmaceutical Preparation Manufacturing

Connetics Corporation develops and markets therapeutics for the dermatology market, selling two products, Luxiq and OLUX, both of which use the company's proprietary foam delivery system. Luxiq, the company's first dermatology product, and OLUX treat psoriasis of the scalp. The products are classified as topical steroids; Luxiq competes in the mid-potency category of the topical steroids market and OLUX competes in the high- and super-high potency category of the topical steroids market. Connetics also owns the rights to Soriatane, an oral psoriasis drug originally developed by Switzerland-based La Roche Holding. Connetics follows what it refers to as its "4:2:1" development model, a strategy that calls for the company to have four products in development, two products in final stage trials mandated by the Food and Drug Administration (FDA), and one new, FDA-approved, product every year.

Origins

During its first decade of existence, Connetics was a company trying to find itself. Both its name and its strategic focus were changed during its inaugural decade, as the company's executives worked to find the right niche for their pharmaceutical company. The company began as an enterprise named Connective Therapeutics, Inc., which was spun off in 1993 from another pharmaceutical company, San Francisco-based Genentech, Inc. Connective Therapeutics drew its name from the physiological focus of its business strategy, concentrating on connective tissues, the components of the body that form structural or binding elements such as skin, joints, ligaments, and lining of organs. Connective tissues form the three-dimensional structure that allow cells to function normally; any alteration in the precise framework causes organs to function abnormally, aberrations that Connective Therapeutics sought to eliminate or to treat with its pharmaceutical products.

Connective Therapeutics began business without any marketable products. The company's drugs were under development, still undergoing clinical trials subject to FDA approval. Connective Therapeutics' initial products were obtained through licensing agreements with two companies, its progenitor, Genentech, and Berkeley, California-based XOMA Corporation, a company with a history of collaborating with Genentech. Connective Therapeutics entered into its licensing agreement with Genentech in September 1993, when the company gained the exclusive worldwide rights to relaxin, a natural hormone that helped lessen the hardening of skin and connective tissue and stimulated new blood vessel growth. In June 1994, Connective Therapeutics signed its agreement with XOMA, giving it technology and patent rights to TCR (T-cell Receptor) Peptide, a vaccine product used to treat multiple sclerosis and rheumatoid arthritis.

The one constant during Connective Therapeutics' decade of change was its leader, Thomas G. Wiggans. Although Wiggans was not among the Genentech executives who founded Connective Therapeutics, he arrived soon after the company's formation and guided it through its transformation into Connetics. Wiggans was named president and chief executive officer in July 1994, joining the company one month after it signed its agreement with XOMA. A graduate of the University of Kansas and Southern Methodist University, Wiggans brought nearly 20 years of experience with him to his posts at Connective Therapeutics, beginning his career at Eli Lily & Co. in 1976, where he held several sales and marketing positions during his four-year stay at the giant pharmaceutical company. After Eli Lily, Wig-

Company Perspectives:

There is significant need for improved therapies in the field of dermatology. Connetics focuses on the efficient development of novel therapies using proprietary topical delivery technologies. We believe that our innovative technologies, and competitive advantages, including our development expertise and established sales and marketing infrastructure, drive our success.

gans spent a dozen years serving in various executive capacities at Ares-Serono Group, a pharmaceutical company, leaving in 1992 to serve as president and chief operating officer of CytoTherapeutics. After two years at CytoTherapeutics, Wiggans joined the nascent Connective Therapeutics, where he would become the dominant personality leading the company toward finding its identity.

Public Offering and First Revenues in 1996

During Wiggans' first years in charge, Connective Therapeutics devoted itself to bringing its products through the various stages mandated by the FDA before a drug could be "commercialized." Time and resources were directed toward bringing its drugs to treat scalp psoriasis, multiple sclerosis, and rheumatoid arthritis to market, efforts that yielded no revenue for the company. Connective Therapeutics did not generate revenue during its first three years in business, which is more common than not for a small drug company. Wiggans led Connective Therapeutics through its conversion to public ownership, completing the company's initial public offering of stock in February 1996, when 2.5 million shares were sold for $11 per share. The year included another milestone event for the company. In December 1996, Connective Therapeutics generated its first revenue, a celebratory event that was directly related to an acquisition completed during the month. Connective Therapeutics acquired the exclusive U.S. and Canadian rights to Ridaura from pharmaceutical giant SmithKline Beecham Corporation. Ridaura was an established therapy for rheumatoid arthritis, an autoimmune disease afflicting three million people in the United States. In a transaction that involved cash, stock, a promissory note, and royalty payments, Connective Therapeutics paid $29 million for the rights to Ridaura, gaining its first marketable product. By the end of December 1996, the company was able to post its first sales figure, $428,000. The revenue total was meager, a fraction of the total the company would generate several years later, but it was a start.

The addition of Ridaura forced Connective Therapeutics to mature as a company. With a marketable product, the company needed to establish a sales and marketing dimension to its business. A sales team was formally established in March 1997, when the company decided to change its name to Connetics Corporation, a switch made to aid its newly formed marketing staff. Wiggans explained the reasoning behind the name change in a March 24, 1997 interview with *Business Wire*, stating, "As we begin to establish a commercial presence with our first marketed product, we decided to change the company's name to Connetics,

a name which is shorter, easier to remember, and, we believe, denotes an organization that is energetic and dynamic."

More profound changes followed the company's adoption of a new corporate title, as Wiggans and his team honed their strategic focus and developed what would be Connetics' corporate profile in the 21st century. The company took an important step toward that end in early 1998, when it signed a licensing agreement with Soltec Research Pty Ltd. to develop and bring to market the Australian company's Clobetasol mousse in North America. The significance of the deal was the technology used by Soltec Research to administer its drug. The company's mousse, or foam, technology became the central focus of Connetics' strategy as it entered the 21st century, when the 1998 licensing agreement led to a much deeper relationship between the two companies.

After years of waiting, Connetics began selling the first product it developed in-house, receiving approval from the FDA in March 1999. The product, a topical steroid, was called Luxiq, a foam-based treatment for psoriasis of the scalp, a severely dry and flaky skin condition afflicting 6.4 million Americans. "As soon as I got the letter [of approval from the FDA], I got on the phone and hired 16 dermatology salespeople," Wiggans said in a March 9, 1999 interview with the *San Francisco Chronicle*. Luxiq was first dermatological therapeutic sold by the company, marking its entrance into a market that became the company's sole focus. Annual revenue totals began to swell as Connetics found its commercial footing, leaping from $9.1 million in 1998 to $27 million with the aid of Luxiq in 1999. Profitability, however, continued to elude the company, leading to substantial annual losses. Connetics lost $26.6 million in 1998, a total eclipsed the following year when the company posted a net loss of $27.3 million.

Connetics ended a year in the black for the first time in 2000, a remarkable achievement considering the hefty losses recorded during the preceding years. Part of this financial success was credited to the debut of the company's second dermatological product, OLUX, which entered the market in November. A stronger version of Luxiq, OLUX confirmed Wiggans' commitment to the dermatology market, a commitment that meant Connetics would cut its ties to Ridaura and to developing drugs for treating diseases such as multiple sclerosis and rheumatoid arthritis. In the future, the company would devote itself exclusively to serving the dermatology market, using its foam delivery technology to distinguish it from its competitors.

A New Strategy in 2001

Connetics' conversion to a dermatology-only company was completed in 2001. In April, the company purchased Soltec Research, paying $16.9 million for ownership of the foam delivery technology used in both Luxiq and OLUX. The following month, it sold its rights to Ridaura. The year also marked the establishment of the Connetics Center for Skin Biology, which became a central part of the company's research and development efforts.

The decision to focus solely on dermatology products put Connetics in a market that generated an estimated $1.2 billion worth of business each year. To the company's benefit, many

Key Dates:

1993: Genentech, Inc. spins off Connective Therapeutics, Connetics' predecessor.

1996: Connective Therapeutics acquires the North American rights to market Ridaura.

1997: Connective Therapeutics changes its name to Connetics Corporation.

1998: Connetics signs a licensing agreement with Soltec Research Pty Ltd., giving the company access to Soltec's foam delivery technology.

1999: Connetics is granted FDA approval to market Luxiq, the company's first dermatology product.

2000: Connetics wins FDA approval to market OLUX.

2001: Soltec Research is acquired and the rights to Ridaura are sold.

2004: Connetics acquires the rights to Soriatane.

of the massive pharmaceutical companies were exiting the prescription-skin products market during the first half of the 2000s, creating opportunities for Wiggans to occupy ground vacated by larger rivals and capture market share. A prime example of Connetics benefiting from the decision by larger rivals to abandon the prescription skin products market occurred in 2004, when the company completed an acquisition Wiggans referred to as "a transforming event," according to the February 23, 2004 issue of *Bioworld Financial Watch*.

Roche Holding Ltd., a Switzerland-based pharmaceutical company with $25 billion in annual sales, provided Wiggans with an opportunity to lead Connetics in a new direction. Roche Holding, an affiliate of Genentech, operated in the United States through its New Jersey-based subsidiary, Hoffmann-La Roche Inc., which marketed a drug called Soriatane. In 1997, Hoffmann-La Roche began marketing Soriatane, a once-a-day pill developed to treat psoriasis. The company invested only a modicum of resources into marketing Soriatane, and, consequently, realized only modest financial results in return. "When your sales are in the billions," an analyst remarked in an April 7, 2004 interview with *Investor's Business Daily*, "why pay attention to a potential $100 million drug?" In 2003, Soriatane produced $41 million in sales, a total Hoffman-La Roche's management no longer wanted to try to increase. The company put Soriatane up for sale in early 2004 and Wiggans seized the opportunity, paying $123 million for the rights to market the oral psoriasis drug.

Wiggans termed the acquisition of Soriatane "transforming" because it moved Connetics into the oral systemic area. "We never had a vision we would stay in topicals or

foams," he said in a February 23, 2004 interview with *Bioworld Financial Watch*. Despite Wiggans' assurance that Connetics was not wed to foam delivery technology, the company's strength as it entered the mid-2000s was in the technology it had acquired from Soltec Research. "It takes a tremendous amount of chemistry to make a foam that can hold a drug substance, melt when it hits skin, and turn into a non-greasy, non-staining liquid," John Higgins, Connetics' chief financial officer, said in an April 7, 2004 interview with *Investor's Business Daily*. No other company possessed similar technology, giving Connetics an advantage it intended to keep.

As Connetics plotted its course, the company's success in the immediate future appeared to rest on its proprietary foam technology and the sale of Soriatane. The company planned no further acquisitions and did not intend to expand overseas. "Our plan is to own and commercialize our own products," Higgins said in his interview with *Investor's Business Daily*. "Our focus is on organic growth through our own pipeline." Looking ahead, the company planned to market six products in 2005 and eight products in 2006.

Principal Subsidiaries

Connetics Australia Pty Ltd.

Principal Competitors

Elan Corporation, Plc.; Pfizer Inc.; Schering-Plough Corporation.

Further Reading

Abate, Tom, "FDA Oks Palo Alto Firm's Psoriasis Drug," *San Francisco Chronicle*, March 9, 1999, p. B5.

Benesh, Peter, "Connetics Corp., Palo Alto, California; As Others Exit, It Carves Out a Bigger Share," *Investor's Business Daily*, April 7, 2004, p. A8.

"Connective Therapeutics Changes Name to Connetics Corp.," *Business Wire*, March 24, 1997, p. 03241090.

"Connetics Corp.," *CDA-Investnet Insiders' Chronicle*, February 2, 1998, p. 1.

"Connetics Drops on Setback with Dandruff Drug," *America's Intelligence Wire*, November 24, 2004, p. 31.

"Connetics Reports Net Loss of $27.3 Million for 1999," *Biotech Financial Reports*, March 2000, p. 13.

Haines, Mark, "Connetics Corp.," *America's Intelligence Wire*, June 16, 2004, p. 32.

Osborne, Randall, "Connetics Evolves with Soriatane Purchase," *Bioworld Financial Watch*, February 23, 2004, p. 1.

"Therapeutic IPO," *San Francisco Chronicle*, February 2, 1996, p. C2.

Velshi, Ali, "Stock of the Day: Connetics—President and CEO," *America's Intelligence Wire*, October 18, 2004, p. 54.

—Jeffrey L. Covell

ConsolidatedGraphics

Consolidated Graphics, Inc.

5858 Westheimer, Suite 200
Houston, Texas 77057
U.S.A.
Telephone: (713) 787-0977
Fax: (713) 787-5013
Web site: http://www.consolidatedgraphics.com;
    http://www.cgx.com

Public Company
Incorporated: 1985 as Joe R. Davis, Inc.
Employees: 4,800
Sales: $708.06 million (2004)
Stock Exchanges: New York
Ticker Symbol: CGX
NAIC: 323110 Commercial Lithographic Printing;
    323115 Digital Printing; 323119 Other Commercial
    Printing

Consolidated Graphics, Inc. (CGX) is one of the largest commercial printing groups in the United States, and a leader in the sheet-fed and half-web markets. CGX is a leading consolidator in the United States' commercial printing industry, and has acquired 65 printers in 25 states. CGX seeks out well-run printing companies to acquire. After purchase it usually leaves the existing management in place. The company also grooms its own executives through a unique training program.

Origins

Consolidated Graphics, Inc. was started in Houston in February 1985 by Joe R. Davis. Davis was a veteran of International Paper Company as well as accounting firms Price Waterhouse and Arthur Anderson (where he became partner). He believed the huge, highly fragmented commercial printing industry was ripe for consolidation as it crept through a slow growth period.

Davis told the trade journal *Printing Impressions* that he had picked up a service-driven mentality as a child helping out at his parents' farm and general store in Ogden, Arkansas. He began

stocking shelves with bread at the tender age of six, according to the *Houston Business Journal,* which reported the store was still standing in 1999. According to *Forbes,* his father, J.B. Davis, had over the course of his career managed to parlay a trade as a barber into a small rural business empire.

Davis had studied accounting at the University of Arkansas. He became interested in the printing business in 1981 when he helped find financing for a neighbor's print shop, Superb Printing. Davis received 8 percent of the equity, according to *Printing Impressions;* unfortunately, this enterprise languished due to high costs.

With backing from family and investors, Davis formed Consolidated to acquire Western Lithograph Company in 1985. According to *Forbes,* the cost was $2.6 million. In business since the 1960s, Western had 50 employees and sales of $5 million a year.

A second acquisition, Grover/Houston Litho, followed in 1987. The first out-of-state buy, Tewell's Printing of Denver, came in 1988. Four years later, it was merged with newly acquired Warren Graphics. The neighbor's print shop that had got Davis started in the business also was acquired. Consolidated entered the financial printing market in 1990 by buying the Houston operations of Chas. P. Young.

Launching a Management Training Program in 1991

To recruit and train management talent, CGX started its unique Leadership Development Program in 1991. According to *Graphic Arts Monthly,* the three-year program was similar to those at financial services companies. CGX hired candidates from college, then rotated them around each part of the printing business before bringing them into management. By the end of the 1990s, the program had produced several presidents, under age 30, for CGX's subsidiaries. According to *American Printer,* CGX preferred to recruit liberal arts, business, and engineering graduates.

In the early 1990s, Consolidated bought another Houston printer, Gulf Printing Company, for $30 million to become the area's market leader. Gulf had been founded in 1916. Unlike most of CGX's later acquisitions, Gulf was a web-fed printing operation. It also was losing $5 million a year (on sales of $30 million), according to the *Houston Chronicle*—from then on CGX made it a point to buy thriving companies only.

Gulf had a huge telephone directory contract from Southwestern Bell, its owner, which financed the acquisition, Davis later told *Printing News.* In 1993 Gulf lost the contract and its operations were merged with Western Lithograph two years later. CGX also moved into Gulf's headquarters.

Going Public in 1994

Another half-dozen printing companies were acquired in the early 1990s, extending Consolidated's reach to Colorado. In June 1994, the company went public, raising about $20 million.

Sales were $57 million in fiscal 1995, with a net income of $4.5 million. CGX had about 700 employees. Annualized revenues for the fiscal year ending March 1996 were about $100 million.

The pace of acquisitions stepped up after the initial public offering. A dozen buys in 1995 and 1996 brought Consolidated into Arizona, Iowa, Oklahoma, Virginia, California, Washington, and Oregon. Consolidated bought another ten businesses in 1997 alone.

CGX displayed its buying power in a 1996 order for 210 printing units from Komori America Corp. The deal was potentially worth more than $50 million and was called the largest U.S. purchase of sheetfed presses to date.

On the Big Board in 1997

CGX shares migrated from NASDAQ to the New York Stock Exchange in January 1997. In the 1997 fiscal year, CGX had 1,417 employees, sales of $144 million, and net income of $10 million. The headquarters had just 15 employees, remarked *American Printer,* reflecting on the company's decentralized structure. The 20 operating companies had 93 presses between them.

CGX was the fastest-growing printing company in the United States. More than two dozen companies were acquired in 1998 and 1999, and another 40 deals were still in the pipeline. According to trade journals, CGX was responsible for starting an industry trend toward consolidation, and spawned several copycats.

CGX's more than 50 subsidiaries operated as independent businesses. In 1998, Davis told *Printing News* that of the 37,000 commercial printing companies in the United States, about 7,400 constituted his target market. CGX focused on sheet-fed operations, choosing companies with up to 150 employees and annual sales of $2 million to $25 million. According to *Printing Impressions,* Davis believed that company presidents could have a feel for all departments in operations of this size.

CGX chose well-run businesses to acquire, and typically retained their managers after purchase. The firms benefited from CGX handling administrative tasks. The company also could tap its considerable purchasing power and technological advancement. CGX focused on major metropolitan areas, buying several printers in each city as it expanded across the United States.

Most of the printers CGX bought were about two dozen years old. In 1998, the company acquired one that had been formed in 1885, Wetzel Brothers Inc. The company's owner when it was sold, Arthur Wetzel, told the *Milwaukee Journal Sentinel* that keeping up with technology was a deciding factor in the sale. ''I used to buy a press for $7,000, and now you'll pay $2 million or $3 million,'' said Wetzel. He and his wife had run the business for 60 years. ''They left a great foundation,'' said Davis. Other Consolidated acquisitions had history behind them, such as John C. Otto Co. of East Longmeadow, Massachusetts, which was founded in 1880.

Digital After 2000

Revenues were $625 million in fiscal 2000, while net income was $38.5 million. The company had 5,000 employees. CGX had been investing heavily in digital printing technology. By 2004, all of its companies offered computer-to-plate services. As *Electronic Publishing* noted, CGX also was offering its customers Internet tools.

CGX posted net income of $20 million on sales of $708 million in fiscal 2004. The company had 4,800 employees at the time. A slowing printing industry was working to CGX's advantage by lowering asking prices for acquired companies.

Principal Subsidiaries

AGS Custom Graphics, Inc.; American Lithographers, Inc.; Apple Graphics, Inc.; Austin Printing Company, Inc.; Automated Graphic Imaging/Copy Center, Inc.; Automated Graphic Systems, LLC; Bridgetown Printing Co.; Byrum Lithographing Co.; CGML General Partner, Inc.; CGML, LLC; CGXmedia,

Inc.; Chas. P. Young Company, Inc.; Clear Visions, Inc.; Columbia Color, Inc.; Consolidated Carqueville Printing Company; Consolidated Graphics California; Consolidated Graphics Development Company; Consolidated Graphics Development LLC; Consolidated Graphics Management, Ltd.; Consolidated Graphics Properties II, Inc.; Consolidated Graphics Properties, Inc.; Consolidated Graphics Services, Inc.; Consolidated Paragraphics, Inc.; Copy-Mor, Inc.; Courier Printing Company; Digital Direct, Inc.; Direct Color, Inc.; Eagle Press, Inc.; Eastwood Printing Corporation; Emerald City Graphics, Inc.; Fittje Bros. Printing Co.; Frederic Printing Company; Garner Printing Company; Georges & Shapiro Lithograph, Inc.; Geyer Printing Company, Inc.; Gilliland Printing, Inc.; Graphic Communications, Inc.; Graphic Technology of Maryland, Inc.; Graphion, Inc.; Gritz-Ritter Graphics, Inc.; Grover Printing Company; Gulf Printing Company; H&N Printing & Graphics, Inc.; Heath Printers, Inc.; Heritage Graphics, Inc.; Image Systems, Inc.; Ironwood Lithographers, Inc.; Keys Printing Company; Lincoln Printing Corporation; Maryland Composition.com, Inc.; Maxwell Graphic Arts, Inc.; McKay Press, Inc.; Mercury Printing Company, Inc.; Mercury Web Printing, Inc.; Metropolitan Printing Services, Inc.; Mobility, Inc.; Mount Vernon Printing Company; Multiple Images Printing, Inc.; Piccari Press, Inc.; Precision Litho, Inc.; Pride Printers, Inc.; Printing Corporation of America; Printing, Inc.; Rush Press, Inc.; S & S Graphics, LLC; S & S Graphics Property, LLC; Serco Forms, LLC; StorterChilds Printing Co., Inc.; Superb Printing Company; Superior Colour Graphics, Inc.; Tewell Warren Printing Company; The Etheridge Company; The Graphics Group, Inc.; The Jarvis Press, Inc.; The John C. Otto Company, Inc.; The Printery, Inc.; Theo. Davis Sons, Incorporated; Thousand Oaks Printing and Specialties, Inc.; Tucker Printers, Inc.; Tulsa Litho Company; Tursack Incorporated; Walnut Circle Press, Inc.; Web Graphics, Inc.; Wentworth Corporation; Western Lithograph Company; Westland Printers, Inc.; Wetzel Brothers, LLC; Woodridge Press, Inc.

Principal Competitors

Cenveo, Inc.; Nationwide Graphics, Inc.; Quebecor World; R.R. Donnelley & Sons Company; St Ives US Division.

Further Reading

Appin, Rick, "M&A Colors Commercial Printing Sector: Deal Flow Increasingly Finds Its Way onto the Pages of Fragmented Industry," *Mergers & Acquisitions Report,* September 20, 1999.

Apte, Angela, "Power Behind the Presses: Joe Davis' National Consolidation Efforts Have Changed the Face of Commercial Printing," *Houston Business Journal,* April 30, 1999, pp. 14ff.

Boisseau, Charles, "Printer Trying to Reproduce Strategy of Consolidation," *Houston Chronicle,* Bus. Sec., February 13, 1995, p. 6.

Cross, Lisa, "Chief Consolidators Make Acquisition News," *Graphic Arts Monthly,* April 1, 1999, p. 56.

——, "Grooming Management Talent," *Graphic Arts Monthly,* September 1, 1999, p. 93.

Dresang, Joel, "Nearly 100, Longtime Milwaukee Printer Surveys Changing Industry," *Milwaukee Journal Sentinel,* July 20, 2003.

Greer, Jim, "Printing Powerhouse Acquiring Again," *Houston Business Journal,* April 5, 2002, pp. 1f.

Hamilton, Alex, "A Distinctive Approach; Plans to Acquire Printing Companies and to Build a Group in Major Metropolitan Areas," *Printing Impressions,* February 1, 1995, p. 22.

Hassell, Greg, "On a Roll; Printer Presses Ahead with Acquisitions," *Houston Chronicle,* Bus. Sec., February 4, 1997, p. 1.

Hitchcock, Nancy A., "Top 20 Printing Firms That Inspire the Industry," *Electronic Publishing,* September 2004, pp. 14ff.

Hurtado, Robert, "A Font of Good Fortune for a Business Printer," *New York Times,* Sec. 3, March 8, 1998, p. 5.

——, "Printer Makes Its Mark with Acquisition Strategy," *International Herald Tribune,* March 7, 1998, p. 19.

"A Mentor, An Advisor, A Leader," *Printing Impressions,* October 1, 1998, p. 22.

Palmer, Joel, "A Happy Marriage," *Des Moines Business Record,* February 22, 1999, pp. 12f.

Palmeri, Christopher, and Fleming Meeks, "Better Late Than Never," *Forbes,* November 21, 1994, pp. 192f.

Pybus, Kenneth R., "Printing Entrepreneur Taking Empire Public," *Houston Business Journal,* April 25, 1994, pp. 1f.

Roberts, Ricardo, "M&A Pro Returns to Consolidated After a Stint as a Banker," *Mergers & Acquisitions Report,* March 11, 2002.

Sharples, Hadley, "Progress Starts with People [John C. Otto Co.]," *Graphic Arts Monthly,* January 1998, pp. S2f.

Shelby, Thomas Hart, "The Merger Merchant," *Graphic Arts Monthly,* December 1997, p. 44.

Stapleton, Cy, "The Man With a Plan: Consolidated's Davis Says Full Speed Ahead," *Printing News,* March 9, 1998, p. 1.

Tolliver, Heidi, "Komori Reports a Record Sale of More Than 200 Press Units," *PrintingNews East,* August 5, 1996, p. 6.

"Winning Acquisitions; Consolidated Graphics Leverages Its Buying Power to Stimulate Growth in 20 Partner Companies," *American Printer,* June 1997, p. 44.

—Frederick C. Ingram

DENDRITE ✹

Dendrite International, Inc.

1405/1425 Route 206 South
Bedminster, New Jersey 07921
U.S.A.
Telephone: (908) 443-2000
Fax: (908) 443-2100
Web site: http://www.drte.com

Public Company
Incorporated: 1987
Employees: 2,524
Sales: $321.1 million (2003)
Stock Exchanges: NASDAQ
Ticker Symbol: DRTE
NAIC: 541510 Computer Systems Design and Related
Services; 541511 Custom Computer Programming
Services; 541512 Computer Systems Design Services;
541519 Other Computer Related Services

Dendrite International, Inc., and its subsidiaries are leading providers of a broad array of services and software worldwide that focus on managing and analyzing sales efforts for the pharmaceutical and other life sciences industries. The company's solutions cover the pharmaceutical commercialization process and fit into five primary categories, including clinical development, brand marketing, customer management, sales effectiveness, and compliance management. Dendrite's sales technology and applications enable sales forces to access product information and physician databases, assess competitors, and catalog client and prospect data. With its integrated sales and marketing software, Dendrite allows pharmaceutical companies to tie their sales and marketing strategies together for improved productivity.

Origins

Dendrite International was founded in 1986 by John Baiyle in Sydney, Australia, with $3 million from the sale of a former business he owned and with the help of a partner, an Australian chemical company. Baiyle began the firm by designing the pharmaceutical industry's first management and marketing software for company sales forces. In 1987, Baiyle expanded the

business to New Zealand and moved the company's headquarters to Warren, New Jersey, against the opposition of his corporate partner. As a result, Baiyle began searching for funds to buy out his partner. After a year of considering his options, Baiyle secured venture capital, closing on a deal with lead investor, Edison Venture Fund, for between $7 million and $10 million. The other two investors in Dendrite included a venture fund operated by John Hancock Mutual Life Insurance Company in Boston and Brinson Partners, Inc., of Chicago. With venture capital behind him, Baiyle expanded operations in Japan in 1988 and began opening offices in Europe in the United Kingdom, Belgium, France, Italy, Spain, and Germany. In 1989, Dendrite won its first major U.S. contract with Pfizer, which selected the company's software for its 450-member sales force.

Aggressive Growth in the Early and Mid-1990s

Already by 1993, President and Chief Executive Officer John Baiyle saw Dendrite developing into a $100 million company in the near future and planned a public offering of common stock over the long term. His plans also called for a growth strategy through acquisitions. In June 1995, Dendrite followed through on plans for going public, offering 2.6 million shares in its initial public offering. The company intended to use the proceeds for working capital, including research and development. By 1996, Baiyle's plans for aggressive growth were well underway with Dendrite operating out of eleven offices around the world, providing software and support services that were designed to manage, coordinate, and control large sales forces for the health care and consumer packaged goods industries. Dendrite's client companies included such well known firms as Bristol-Myers Squibb, Johnson & Johnson, Eli Lilly, Hoechst Marion Roussel, L'Oreal, Pfizer, and Rhone-Poulenc Rorer. The company also had offices in Japan, introducing in 1996 a state-of-the-art Windows-based system specifically designed for the Japanese market. With this growing client base, Baiyle boasted that Dendrite had more users of its software and service than its two largest competitors combined.

A Global Reach in the Late 1990s

In May 1996, Dendrite acquired SRCI, the leading provider of custom-designed sales force management systems in France for the over-the-counter drug and cosmetic and consumer packaged goods industries. Dendrite saw SRCI as a springboard for rapidly expanding worldwide into consumer packaged goods. With this aim in mind, Dendrite set up a new consumer business division, which would focus initially on markets in the United States and United Kingdom. The company translated a new system developed by SRCI into English, marketing it under the name ForceOne. Following the SRCI acquisition, by the beginning of 1997 Dendrite's consumer business division had won contracts with several French firms, including Kriter Brut de Brut, Lindt, Martini Bacardi, Moet & Chandon, Panzani, Segafredo, Urgo, Vania, and Varta.

In 1998, with revenue growth increasing at a robust 27.6 percent per annum over several years, Dendrite surpassed the $100 million revenue milestone. The company also made the strategic decision to move beyond its traditional market, which comprised fifty of the largest pharmaceutical companies, by extending its global reach. Although Dendrite already operated offices in countries throughout the world, it launched a more aggressive global strategy with the aim of becoming the only company to offer a complete matrix of solutions in each separate segment of the pharmaceutical industry worldwide. In pursuit of this strategy, Dendrite formed its new SalesPlus Americas division to provide software and services for midrange pharmaceutical companies in the United States, a market it had not served before. In addition, Dendrite accelerated its global reach by signing new agreements with such major firms as Takeda Chemical Industries and Kissei Pharmaceuticals in Japan; Kronenbourg, Evian, and William Pitters in Europe; Pfizer Australia; and Rayovac in the United States. With its new global strategy underway, Dendrite purchased Belgium-based Associated Business Computing in October 1998. By the end of 1998, Dendrite's sales management software tools and services were being used by over 150 corporations in 17 countries, earning revenue of $131 million.

In May 1999, Dendrite announced agreement to buy CorNet International Ltd. for $40 million with the aim of getting one of CorNet's largest worldwide accounts—Bristol-Myers Squibb Co. Like Dendrite, CorNet produced software that helped companies manage their sales and marketing teams. Aside from Bristol-Myers Squibb, Dendrite would assume CorNet's other accounts, including Lifescan and McNeil Consumer Healthcare divisions of Johnson & Johnson, the Wyeth-Ayerst division of American Home Products, and Campbell Soup Company. With a continuing emphasis on its global reach strategy, in July 1999

Dendrite acquired Marketing Management International (MMI), a provider of palmtop software and paper-based solutions and consulting services to subsidiaries of major pharmaceutical companies operating in emerging markets, including Latin America, Eastern Europe, and Southeast Asia. Before the acquisition, Dendrite served as the exclusive distributor of MMI's products in Brazil and the United States. The transaction was structured as an asset purchase for a cost of approximately $10.5 million.

In September 1999, Dendrite's board of directors approved a three-for-two split to be effected as a stock dividend. Under the arrangement, shareholders of record at the close of business of September 23, 1999, would receive one additional share of company common stock for every two shares held on that date. With 1998 sales up 31 percent to $112 million and with a doubling of its stock price and a growing client base that included many of the worlds' leading multinational pharmaceutical firms, Dendrite's stock split represented a robust confidence in its future prospects. The company's business strategy of offering layers of service around its software proved enormously successful in attracting numerous customers around the world. The software enabled pharmaceutical companies to monitor prescription trends against a region's demographics, and use the data to find out which physicians to contact and when. The software also allowed drug firms to track prescription patterns of competitors.

In January 2000, Dendrite acquired Analytika, Inc., a privately-held leader in the emerging sector of marketing automation systems for the pharmaceutical industry. The transaction, valued at $9 million including assumption of debt, was anticipated to be a major link in Dendrite's strategy to combine the emerging, highly analytical field of marketing automation with sales force management. Analytika further enhanced Dendrite's global presence after the acquisitions of CorNet International and MMI. The company also formed a new Clinical Trials and Analytiks division to market its growing software and service offerings.

By the end of 1999, with 150 customers in 57 countries, Dendrite reported another record year for revenue, operating profit, operating margin, and earnings per share. Year end revenue increased 32 percent to $172.7 million with net income rising 56 percent to $22.4 million. Commenting on the 1999 financial results, Chairman and CEO John Baiyle remarked that Dendrite's business remained solid with the company also being selected by Aventis France to be the provider of their next generation SFE solution for Europe's largest sales force. Dendrite also had numerous successes in the mid and emerging markets and in Japan. In the various markets, revenue in the United States reached 78 percent of the total, with Europe accounting for 14 percent, Asia for 6 percent, and Latin America for 1 percent.

The Company Enters the 21st Century

In February 2000, Dendrite announced a mandatory stock ownership plan, requiring its top fifteen executives and five outside directors to own at least 15,000 shares within three to five years. The ownership requirement was intended to serve stockholder interest and provide performance incentives for top management. The company also froze cash salaries for executives and

Key Dates:

1986: Company is founded in Sydney, Australia, by John Baiyle.
1987: Dendrite relocates headquarters to New Jersey.
1988: Dendrite establishes operations in Japan and Europe.
1989: Dendrite secures first major U.S. contract with Pfizer.
1995: Company goes public offering 2.6 million common shares.
1996: Dendrite acquires SRCI of France.
1998: Company surpasses $100 million revenue mark.
2000: Company loses Internet privacy case.
2001: Company appoints Paul Zaffaroni as new president and chief executive officer; company opens branch office in Shanghai, China.
2003: Dendrite outbids rival to acquire Synavant.
2004: Dendrite relocates international headquarters to Bedminster, New Jersey.

eliminated across-the-board raises in favor of earning cash or stock bonuses based on specific performance measures, including revenue and earnings per share. Dendrite aimed to raise the performance level of its executives at a time when the firm was becoming better positioned with the consolidation of drug companies. By August 2000, Dendrite had about a $1 billion market capitalization and was generating over 20 percent operating margins with a large cash flow and a liquid balance sheet.

In September 2000, Dendrite offered new software that for the first time could enable pharmaceutical sales representatives to access information concerning therapy and prescription patterns. With this capacity, drug sales representatives could considerably refine their product marketing to physicians and others in the evolving pharmaceutical industry. In October, Dendrite also announced it would build a new $30 million office complex in Chesapeake, Virginia, to be completed in April 2001. The new office would accommodate 335 employees, including data center operators, project managers, and call-center workers with an average pay of $40,000.

In November 2000, a judge upheld the privacy rights of two people who anonymously posted critical comments of Dendrite on a Yahoo message board. Dendrite filed suit in May in the first case in New Jersey and one of the first in the nation, asking the courts to decide whether a company had the right to learn the identities of pseudonymous on-line critics so that it could purse civil actions against them. The case caught the attention of national privacy rights groups, which argued for protecting anonymity and free expression on the internet. Yahoo's past practice was to divulge names of its members without notifying them when confronted with a subpoena, a policy it changed in April 2000 in favor of protecting member's privacy rights. Critics of Dendrite's case saw it as representing a troubling trend among companies to use lawsuits to silence opinions they find objectionable. In its complaint, Dendrite alleged that four anonymous posters publicized messages that included confidential information and were defamatory in nature. The company also charged that some of the messages were from employees or former employees who violated contracts prohibiting them from making disparaging remarks. The court ruled, however, that there was insufficient evidence that the posters made defamatory comments or did anything unlawful. The court concluded the posters were engaged in a free exchange of views under the protection of anonymity and that to strip away that protection would silence free discussion inherent in the First Amendment.

In December 2000, Dendrite signed its largest ever on-going service agreement in the Japanese market. The agreement provided that Dendrite supply Pfizer Japan K.K. with a comprehensive array of services concerning the implementation and support of its sales force productivity software tools. Dendrite considered the agreement as a milestone in its strategic plan to expand service offerings in both the Japanese and global pharmaceutical markets. Key to the deal was Dendrite's j-forceWeb software tool, which provided sales representatives, field management, and head office personnel with a single, centralized location from which to access product information, analyze sales information, record activity data, and access physician and institution databases. With this and numerous other worldwide marketing agreements, Dendrite reported increased revenues of 28 percent for the year 2000.

Restructuring in the Early 2000s

In October 2001, Dendrite announced the appointment of Paul Zaffaroni as the company's new president and CEO. Zaffaroni, a 20-year IBM veteran, joined Dendrite with an ambitious agenda to grow the company's revenues by more than 20 percent over six years. With this aim in mind, Zaffaroni planned to sharpen the company's commitment to pharmaceutical specialization, expand beyond sales force automation to analytically driven CRM solutions, intensify efforts in clinical trials, and extend relationship with flagship clients while pursuing new partnerships with major pharmaceutical companies. At the same time when Dendrite was appointing a new president and CEO, the company opened a new representative office in Shanghai, China, to provide sales technology and service in that country's growing pharmaceutical industry. With the Chinese pharmaceutical market anticipated to grow between 7 and 10 percent over five years, Dendrite looked forward to providing its services in a market that offered major new opportunities.

Despite its success, Dendrite could not escape the effects of the economic downturn starting in the spring of 2000. As a result, in 2001 Dendrite cut its workforce by about 7 percent as its stock collapsed 75 percent from a high of $35 in early 2000. To boost its share price, Dendrite initiated a stock repurchase program in July 2002 of up to $20 million of its outstanding common stock over a two-year period. With the aim of continued growth, Dendrite also acquired Software Associates International, a provider of consultancy services and specialty software products to the pharmaceutical industry, and Parma Vision, a distributor of data for pharmaceutical representatives in Europe.

In April 2003, Dendrite entered a bidding war with Cegedim S.A. for the assets of Synavant Inc., a global leader in pharmaceutical customer relationship management and integrated marketing services for the biopharmaceutical industry. As part of its acquisitions strategy, Dendrite filed suit in a Delaware court to invalidate a Synavant-Cegedim merger agreement. Dendrite offered to purchase all of the outstanding shares of Synavant at a cash price of $2.50 per share, a 9 percent premium over Cegedim's offer of $2.30 contained in their merger agreement. In response and in accordance with the merger agreement with Cegedim, Synavant's board of directors authorized the company to enter into negotiations with Dendrite. In May 2003, Synavant approved Dendrite's new offer of $2.83 a share, resulting in the termination of the Cegedim merger agreement. Cegedim responded by proposing $3.15 a share, leading Dendrite to up its offer to $3.22, which sealed the acquisition. The merger created the most comprehensive information, software and services company dedicated to the global pharmaceutical industry. The transaction enhanced Dendrite's ability to provide market-leading solutions to the sales, marketing, and clinical operations of pharmaceutical and other life sciences companies.

When Dendrite posted second-quarter 2003 adjusted earnings at 17 cents a share, four cents ahead of estimates by investor analysts, the company's shares rose over 12 percent to hit a 52-week high of $15.29. To accommodate this strong growth, Dendrite relocated its global headquarters from Morristown, New Jersey, to a larger, more modern campus in Bedminster, New Jersey, in 2004. In January 2004, Dendrite through its Japanese subsidiary also completed the purchase of Uto Brain, a provider of pharmaceutical data analysis and a publishing and consulting firm. The agreement together with the signing of new Japanese customers represented Dendrite's strong business momentum in the Japanese market. At the same time, Dendrite continued to expand its European operations, signing new contracts with new and existing customers in Turkey, Greece, and Italy. With an eye on Eastern Europe, Dendrite concluded the acquisition of Medical Data Management (MDM), a privately held group of companies primarily located in Warsaw, Poland. With 2003 sales of $7.5 million, MDM was the leading provider of physician databases, market research, and sales force support services to pharmaceutical companies in Poland, Hungary, Russia, and Ukraine. The transaction was valued at $8 million, comprising $5 million in cash and $3 million in stock.

In July 2004, Dendrite also acquired Schwarzeck-Verlag GmbH, a provider of physician databases, direct marketing services, and sample fulfillment services to pharmaceutical companies in Germany. The acquisition, which further accelerated Dendrites expansion in Europe, created one of the most diversified German-based suppliers of pharmaceutical services, data, and technology to drug manufacturers in one of the world's leading pharmaceutical markets. By the end of 2004 with the pharmaceutical industry continuing to evolve under new market conditions, Dendrite International appeared well-positioned to take advantage of new opportunities in the global marketplace. With a strategy encompassing innovative software development, acquisitions, and strategic alliances, the company had grown into the world's leading provider of sales force technology and other software tools and services for the phar-

maceutical industry. As a result, Dendrite could look to the future with the optimism based on its past successes.

Principal Subsidiaries

Dendrite Andes (Ecuador); Dendrite Australia Pty. Ltd.; Dendrite Belgium S.A.; Dendrite Brasil Ltda. (Brazil); Dendrite Canada Company; Dendrite Columbia Ltda.; Dendrite France S.A.; Dendrite Hungary Software Services, Inc.; Dendrite Interactive Marketing LLC; Dendrite International Services Company; Dendrite Italia, S.R.I. (Italy); Dendrite Japan Corporation; Dendrite Mexico; Dendrite Netherlands, B.V.; Dendrite New Zealand Ltd.; Dendrite Portugal; Dendrite Software India Private Ltd.; Dendrite U.K. Ltd.(United Kingdom); Info-Med Gesellschaft fur Marketing mbH (Germany); Informed Management Ltd. (United Kingdom); Permail Pty. Ltd. (Australia); Pharma Vision BV (Netherlands); Pharma Vision Marketing Services S.A. (Belgium); PMS Pty. Ltd. (Australia); SAI Acquisition LLC; Synavant Australia Pty. Ltd.; Synavant Belgium SA/NV; Synavant Canada Ltd.; Synavant Data GmbH (Austria); Synavant de Brazil Ltda.; Synavant de Mexico S.A.; Synavant Deutschland (Germany); Synavant France S.A.; Synavant Hellas S.A. (Greece); Synavant Italia S.r.L. (Italy); Synavant Nederland B.V.; Synavant Netherlands Finance B.V.; Synavant Singapore (Pte.) Ltd.; Synavant Spain S.A.; Synavant Turkey, Inc.; Synavant UK Holding Ltd. (United Kingdom); Synavant UK, Ltd. (United Kingdom); Uto Brain Co., Ltd. (Japan).

Principal Competitors

Cegedim S.A.; First Consulting Group Inc.; Siebel Systems Inc.; Oracle Corporation; StayinFront Inc.

Further Reading

"Dendrite Acquires Software Associates International," *Telecomworldwire*, September 24, 2002.

"Dendrite's European Success Further Accelerated," *Business Wire*, August 20, 1998.

"Dendrite International, Inc. Announces Stock Repurchase Program," *Business Wire*, January 31, 2001.

"Dendrite Reports Record Revenue & Earnings," *Business Wire*, January 25, 2000.

Jeter, Amy, "Pharmaceutical Services Firm Dendrite to Build Offices in Chesapeake, Va.," *Knight Ridder/Tribune Business News*, October 4, 2000.

Kennedy, Nancy, "Venture Quest," *Business Journal of New Jersey*, July 1993, pp. 34–35.

"Made In New Jersey/Dendrite International Inc.," *Star-Ledger*, July 17, 2002.

"Multimedia Available: Dendrite Announces Plans to Relocate Global Headquarters to Bedminster, N.J., in 2004," *Business Wire*, November 5, 2003.

Perone, Joseph R., "Morristown, N.J.-Based Drug Sales Software Maker Finds Gold in Data Mining," *Knight Ridder/Tribune Business News*, October 4, 1999.

—Bruce P. Montgomery

Double-Cola Co.-USA

537 Market Street, Suite 100
Chattanooga, Tennessee 37402
U.S.A.
Telephone: (423) 267-5691
Fax: (423) 267-0793
Web site: http://www.double-cola.com

Wholly Owned Subsidiary of K.J. International Inc.
Incorporated: 1922 as Good Grape Company
Employees: 20
Sales: $21.1 million (2003 est.)
NAIC: 311930 Flavoring Syrup and Concentrate
    Manufacturing

Double-Cola Co.-USA is a producer and marketer of soft drinks, operating primarily in the cola segment of the industry. The company's products include its signature Double-Cola brand, Diet Double-Cola, eight flavors of Jumbo cola, and Double Dry Ginger Ale. The company also markets its Ski brand of citrus drinks, which includes Diet Ski and Cherry Ski. Double-Cola Co.'s beverages are distributed in the United States primarily east of the Mississippi River. Double-Cola Co. also sells its drinks abroad, doing business in the Middle East, South Asia, and South America. The company is owned by London, England-based K.J. International Inc.

Origins

The late 19th century saw the birth of an industry that became a battleground for dozens of companies, each vying for control of what, a century later, represented a more than $60 billion business. Supremacy in the U.S. soft drink market, particularly the cola segment of the market, involved a decades-long chase that pitted marketing strategy against marketing strategy and distribution might against distribution might, making for one of the classic battles in U.S. business history. Double-Cola Co. played a leading role in what industry observers often referred to as the "cola wars," becoming a fixture in the industry that survived the fiercely fought battle among Coca-Cola, Pepsi-Cola, and their rivals. Double-Cola Co.'s ranking as the fourth largest cola brand

at the dawn of the 21st century was a testament to its success in the 20th century, but for some business analysts the story of Double-Cola was a story of missed opportunities, a tale of what the company might have become had it done things differently. Double-Cola stood as a financially healthy, venerable competitor in the soft drink market at the beginning of the 21st century— overshadowed by Coca-Cola and Pepsi, to be sure—but the natural inclination when examining the company was to determine why a brand that ranked as the fourth bestseller after nearly a century of existence trailed so far behind the market's two leaders. Double-Cola's missteps, and its successes as well, were intertwined into the history of cola itself, a chapter of U.S. business history that began with a pharmacist in Atlanta named John S. Pemberton.

In 1886, the race to capture market share in the soft drink market began. That year, Pemberton developed the Coca-Cola brand, creating a soda fountain drink that he marketed as a "brain tonic and intellectual beverage." His brand and company took advantage of the early start by quickly developing a national distribution system, gaining a lead on the rivals soon to materialize that it maintained for more than the next century. Other cola producers entered the market after Pemberton unveiled his "brain tonic," but the most historically important of the new entrants in the late 19th century was "Brad's Drink." The concoction of another pharmacist, a North Carolina resident named Caleb Bradham, Brad's Drink was renamed later, branded as Pepsi-Cola. Pepsi-Cola, introduced in 1893, never presented much of a threat to Pemberton's Coca-Cola. The brand limped along for more than a half century, not demonstrating any strength nationally until after World War II. Its weakness during the first half of the 20th century was one of the missed opportunities noted by Double-Cola Co.'s critics a century later.

Double-Cola Co. started much later than its two fiercest rivals, joining the soft drink market as a start-up well after Coca-Cola enjoyed national celebrity and Pepsi-Cola was preparing for its 30th anniversary festivities. The brand was started by Charles D. Little, who worked for the Cherco Cola Company. Little left Cherco Cola in 1922, and with the help of a partner, Joe S. Foster, developed his own soft drink brand, Good

Grape. The pair named their company the Good Grape Company, establishing its headquarters in Chattanooga, Tennessee. In 1924, Little developed his first cola drink, Marvel Cola, and changed the name of the company to Seminole Flavor Company. Improvements were made in the formulation of Marvel Cola, changes that warranted the creation of a new, trademarked name, resulting in the introduction of Jumbo Cola, a soft drink packaged in a 7.5-ounce bottle that, with the assistance of Owens Illinois Glass Company, bore the first Applied Color Label in the industry. By 1933, Little believed he had achieved the perfect formulation for a cola, leading him to rename his beverage Double-Cola. The name of the new cola reflected another industry first for the young company, an industry first that would become an industry standard. Double-Cola was packaged in 12-ounce bottles, twice the size of other colas, a novelty that necessitated advertising on six-pack cartons that read: "This carton serves any number from 6 to 12, two glasses in every bottle."

Little's company did well during its second decade in business. Once he was comfortable with the formula for Double-Cola—a formula that remained unaltered throughout the company's existence—he added a range of flavors. By the early 1930s, Seminole Flavor Co. marketed Double-Cola, Double-Orange, Double-Lemon, and Double-Grape. In 1934, the company added Double-Dry Ginger Ale and Tonic Water to its product line. Staying financially solvent during the Great Depression was, by itself, a laudable achievement, but critics pointed to the 1930s as when Little made one of his first mistakes. Vending machines emerged as an important revenue source for soft drink companies during the 1930s, but Little failed to exploit the new market niche. He had a cabinet and refrigeration unit made by Westinghouse, but when the vending mechanism was added, it failed to work, performing horribly in the humidity of textile mills in North Carolina, where Double-Cola enjoyed a strong following. Little refused to invest any capital in developing a working vending machine, not wanting to risk losing the money he had accumulated.

Double-Cola in the 1940s

The 1940s brought difficulties to Seminole Flavor Co. and marked the decade of Little's most glaring miscue. The company's major obstacle during the decade was caused by sugar shortages during World War II, a restriction that affected every soft drink maker in the country. Seminole Flavor Co. was hit doubly hard by the shortages, however, because of the 12-ounce bottles it used, a fate shared by Pepsi-Cola, which had begun using 12-ounce bottles in the late 1930s. Other soft drink companies, Coca-Cola in particular, began using smaller bottles when sugar was rationed, enabling them to meet demand and expand distribution, but executives at Double-Cola and Pepsi-Cola believed the larger bottles were integral to their marketing strategies. Double-Cola marketed its beverages as "Double-Good, Double-Cola," while Pepsi-Cola advertised its drinks as "Twice As Much For A Nickel, Too." Both companies struggled to meet demand during the war years, Pepsi-Cola more than Seminole Flavor Co., an inequity that set the stage for what many industry pundits charged was Little's greatest failure.

By the 1940s, Coca-Cola was far in the lead, making Seminole Flavor Co.'s nearest rival Pepsi-Cola. Both companies were approximately the same size, but unlike Seminole Flavor Co., Pepsi-Cola was suffering mightily, teetering on the brink of bankruptcy on several occasions during the 1940s. Little had a chance to eliminate Pepsi-Cola and gain control of its distribution system, but he failed to pull the trigger. A Marquette University professor, Joyce M. Wolburg, interviewed several Double-Cola Co. executives for a case study published in the Winter 2003 issue of the *Journal of Consumer Affairs,* interviews that revealed the opportunity missed by Little. The company's one-time vice-president of sales, John Kirby, told Wolburg, "He [Little] had a chance to have bought enough stock in the Pepsi-Cola Co. to control it for about a quarter of a million dollars." Kirby continued: "But he told me 'I've got a good cola, I don't need that.' And that's the way he felt. I asked him, 'Could you have done it without jeopardizing the backing you needed to continue to grow the brand as it was?' And he told me, 'In 1946, I was ahead of everyone else.'"

Pepsi-Cola survived the 1940s and went on to mount a serious assault on Coca-Cola. Alfred Steele, appointed as chief executive officer in 1950, was expected to liquidate the company, but instead he made it his goal to pursue Coca-Cola. He introduced new bottle sizes, emphasized supermarket sales, and created new marketing campaigns, realizing a 300 percent increase in sales by the end of the decade. By the mid-1960s, the soft drink market was a two-horse race, with Pepsi-Cola having made up considerable ground and Double-Cola Co. relegated to the tail end of the pack. Coca-Cola controlled 33.4 percent of the market, followed by Pepsi-Cola with 20.4 percent. Seven Up and Royal Crown were tied for third place with 6.9 percent of the market. Dr. Pepper brought up the rear with 2.6 percent. Double-Cola was unranked, not given an industry position until 1980, when the company held onto 0.6 percent of the market.

While Pepsi-Cola galloped ahead during the 1950s, Little's company celebrated its own achievements, although the possibility of gaining a strong market position essentially had disappeared. In 1953, Little changed the name of his company, dropping Seminole Flavor Co. in favor of Double-Cola Co. In 1956, perhaps the most significant development of the second half of the century occurred when Little introduced a new brand. Ski, a citrus soft drink made of natural orange and lemon flavorings, made its debut in 1956, becoming a popular favorite.

For roughly two decades after the introduction of Ski, Little's company endured difficult years—in large part because of

Key Dates:

1922: Charles D. Little and a partner, Joe S. Foster, found Good Grape Company, Double-Cola Co.'s earliest predecessor.
1924: Good Grape Company changes its name to Seminole Flavor Company.
1933: Double-Cola is introduced.
1953: Seminole Flavor Co. changes its name to Double-Cola Co.
1962: Little sells his company to Fairmont Food Company.
1980: K.J. International Inc. acquires Double-Cola Co.
1996: Cherry Ski is introduced.
2001: Caffeine-Free Ski is introduced.

the absence of Little. In 1962, the year a diet version of Double-Cola was introduced, Little sold his company to Fairmont Foods Company, ending his involvement during Double-Cola Co.'s 40th anniversary year. The sale to Fairmont Foods marked the beginning of a series of ownership changes, each negatively influencing the promotion of Double-Cola's line of beverages. Fairmont Foods acquired Little's company for quick gains, draining its cash reserves and refusing to invest in the company's long-term health. In the late 1970s, Fairmont Foods sold Double-Cola Co. to a group of private investors who almost immediately sold the company to a Canadian firm, Pop Shops International. Double-Cola's brands received scant attention under Pop Shops' control, playing a subsidiary role to the Canadian company's other brands. Stability did not come to Double-Cola until London, England-based company K.J. International Inc. acquired the Chattanooga soda operations in 1980. K.J. International remained Double-Cola Co.'s owner into the 21st century, renaming the company Double-Cola Co.-USA.

Staying Alive in the Late 20th Century

As Double-Cola Co. repaired itself under the purview of K.J. International, the company faced a future in which it would have to pay the price for the mistakes that held its growth in check. Little's inability or unwillingness to seize opportunities that might have greatly increased the stature of Double-Cola Co. left the inheritors of his business in a perpetually precarious position. Coca-Cola and Pepsi-Cola were locked in a battle for domination, but small soft drink companies like Double-Cola Co. faced a daily battle for survival. As Double-Cola fought to survive, competition intensified. During the 1980s, Coca-Cola and Pepsi-Cola expanded their product lines, adding an array of flavors that took up more space on retail shelves and left less room for Double-Cola Co.'s brands. Conditions did not im-

prove during the 1990s, as the company fought to hold onto the tiny sliver of the market it held, a percentage that ranged between 0.3 and 0.5.

Double-Cola entered the 21st century successfully waging its battle to stay alive. The company's beverages, once distributed nationally, were sold in the United States primarily east of the Mississippi River. Internationally, the company recorded varying degrees of success in 17 countries, focusing its efforts in South America and South Asia. By this point, as its 80th anniversary neared, the company's share of the $62 billion soft drink market was negligible, pegged at 0.1 percent, but the executives in Chattanooga were mindful of their position and using it to shape their strategies. Two executives explained their feelings to Wolburg in her Winter 2003 *Journal of Consumer Affairs* article, offering a sense of the perspective that Double-Cola Co.'s officials had on the company's future progress. "Coke and Pepsi have financial resources that we will not be able to match," former president L. Edward Shanks said. "If we go into any market . . . and try to do it head to head with either of those companies . . . we will lose. We've got to be selective about the things that we do—be very focused, and show a high degree of flexibility." John Kirby, the former vice-president of sales, added to Shanks's statement, "Unlike Coke and Pepsi, we do not need to own the entire market to be profitable. We are just looking for a fair shot at store space and displays, a good campaign of awareness, and we believe the product will sell on its own."

Principal Competitors

Cadbury Schweppes plc; The Coca-Cola Company; PepsiCo, Inc.

Further Reading

"Chattanooga, Tenn., Drink Company's Executive Assistant Has Long Tenure," *Knight Ridder/Tribune Business News,* March 7, 2003.
Davis, Tim, "Doubled Up; Bad Weather and the Bad Economy," *Beverage World,* March 1993, p. 53.
"Double-Cola Takes a New Direction; New Strategies Make Marketing a Top Priority," *Beverage Industry,* February 1997, p. 15.
Hall, Tony, "Consumerism Russian-Style," *Beverage World,* April 1995, p. 36.
Osterman, Jim, "T.G. Madison Lands Double-Cola," *ADWEEK Southeast,* June 15, 1998, p. 2.
Prince, Greg, "Moving to Another District?," *Beverage World,* October 1991, p. 56.
Wolburg, Joyce M., "Double-Cola and Antitrust Issues: Staying Alive in the Soft Drink Wars," *Journal of Consumer Affairs,* Winter 2003, p. 340.
Wolf, Alan E., "View from the Top," *Beverage World,* March 1992, p. 65.

—Jeffrey L. Covell

The Dreyfus Corporation

200 Park Avenue
New York, New York 10166
U.S.A.
Telephone: (212) 922-6000
Toll Free: (888) 271-4994
Fax: (212) 922-7533
Web site: http://www.dreyfus.com

Wholly Owned Subsidiary of Mellon Financial
Corporation
Incorporated: 1946 as Dreyfus & Co.
Employees: 1,987
Sales: $360 million (1999 est.)
NAIC: 523920 Portfolio Management

A subsidiary of Mellon Financial Corporation, The Dreyfus Corporation is a leading mutual fund company, managing some $158 billion in more than 200 mutual fund portfolios. Products include both load and no-load mutual funds, individual retirement accounts, and variable and fixed annuities. They are sold through brokers, financial advisors, banks, and fund supermarkets. The Dreyfus name, and its corporate symbol of a lion, are well known, the result of an innovative spirit that drove the firm in its early years and played an instrumental role in establishing the mutual fund industry. After falling out of touch with the marketplace in the 1980s, Dreyfus was acquired in 1994 by Mellon, which has struggled to return the firm to its former glory.

Jack Dreyfus: Mediocre 1930s Academic Career

The man behind the Dreyfus name was Jack Jonas Dreyfus, whose life seemed ill suited to prepare him to play such an important role in the development of the mutual fund industry. He was born in 1913 in Montgomery, Alabama, the son of a candy salesman who worked for a family enterprise, The Dreyfus Brothers Candy Manufacturing Company. A middling student more interested in golf than books, Dreyfus ventured north for college, to Pennsylvania's Lehigh University where a cousin was a student. It was an engineering school, a field for which he was hardly suited. Instead he decided to major in Latin

and only switched to Economics because he considered it less demanding. Other than receiving an A in Music Appreciation, Dreyfus maintained that he was a straight C student at Lehigh— as well as captain of the golf team. He wrote in his autobiography that in 1934 he graduated ''Summa Cum Ordinary.''

With no particular career in mind, Dreyfus returned home to live with his family, which was then relocated to New York City because of his father's work. His father suggested he try selling insurance, thinking a gift for playing golf might prove useful. Dreyfus gave it a try, but quit after one embarrassing attempt to sell an annuity to a potential customer, suffering through a dozen rounds of the man's inept golf game. His father next decided the young man should give the candy industry a try, and Dreyfus was sent to learn the ropes at Edgar P. Lewis & Sons, a Massachusetts candy factory. After six months he went on the road with his father to gain some sales training, but after several months of driving the car and carrying the samples, it became obvious that candy was not to be his calling either. Next, an uncle secured a job with an industrial designer, but here too Dreyfus failed to catch on and he quit after a few months.

Another passion of the young Dreyfus was playing bridge. It was while he was spending an evening at a Manhattan bridge club that another player suggested he try the brokerage business and made an appointment for him with the firm of Cohen, Simondson & Co. Hardly keen about the idea of a Wall Street career, Dreyfus, perhaps because he was accompanied by his father, kept the appointment, and to his surprise was hired as a broker's assistant at a salary of $25 a week. Only later would he learn that his father paid 20 weeks of his salary in advance. One of the young man's tasks was to create weekly charts, something that he actually liked and kept him interested in the job. After six months he passed his stock exchange test and became a junior customer's broker. But he was not comfortable as a salesman, drawing most of his business from relatives. After a few years he applied to be a full customer's broker at Bache & Co. and was rejected. Then in 1938 he managed to land a position at E.A. Pierce & Co., which later became Merrill Lynch. The hours suited him, since the stock market at that time opened at 10:00 and closed at 3:00, allowing him to head for his favorite bridge club in the middle of the afternoon.

Founding Dreyfus & Co. After World War II

When the United States entered World War II in late 1941, Dreyfus, despite being classified 4-F by the draft board, volunteered for the Coast Guard. His stay was brief because of a bad back, he was soon discharged, and he returned to his job at Merrill Lynch. A short time later, however, a specialist on the New York Stock Exchange was impressed with the way Dreyfus played gin rummy, and suggested that he might do well on the trading floor. Dreyfus scraped together the money needed to buy an Exchange seat, taking on a friend, Jerry Ohrbach, and his father, Nathan, as limited partners of Dreyfus & Co., formed in 1946. John Behrens also became a partner and took care of business in the office while Dreyfus traded on the floor of the Exchange, executing orders for Bache & Co. and trading on the firm's own small account. Despite a bear market, the new firm with capital of just $100,000 managed to clear $14,000.

At the behest of the Orbachs, Dreyfus acquired a brokerage firm, Lewisohn & Sons, but when the partners soon left Dreyfus was forced to leave the trading floor, where he had been doing well, and return to the office to manage the brokerage firm, for which he was unprepared. Business was so poor that Dreyfus turned to advertising the firm out of necessity. Unhappy with the dull approach of Wall Street advertising agencies, Jack Dreyfus switched to a new and more imaginative shop, Doyle, Dane & Bernbach, and because his budget was so limited he took to writing his own advertising copy. In his attempt to produce ads that he thought would be enjoyable while offering advice, he wrote copy to fit the cartoons his account executive offered to him. For example, a picture of a French poodle sitting like a mistress before a chest of jewels was wedded to a headline, " 'Pets' Can Be Expensive," and copy that read: "Too often investors become sentimentally attached to stocks that have done well for them in the past. These 'pets' can be expensive if they are allowed to prejudice sound judgment."

What Jack Dreyfus did not expect was that his ads, which ran in the business section of the *New York Times,* caught the ideals of customer's brokers, who began to apply for jobs. He made sure to run ads announcing new hires, which not only helped the broker to retain clients but also prompted other brokers to seek employment at Dreyfus & Co., bringing with them a great deal of business and receiving partnerships in return. Although he was just 33, and in many ways not qualified for the post, Jack Dreyfus became the managing partner of a growing firm.

One of the people who sought to become a customer's broker at Dreyfus was John Nesbett, president of a small and struggling mutual fund. Jack Dreyfus had been interested in managing a mutual fund for some time and reached an agreement to take over the fund, which changed its name from the Nesbett Fund to the Dreyfus Fund. It was just a $500,000 fund and took Dreyfus some five years to grow to the $1 million level, costing the firm a good deal of money along the way. To promote the fund, Dreyfus hired Frank Sweetser, who soon suggested that the logo be changed from a DF to a picture of a lion. Later, while lunching with his advertising account executive, Jack Dreyfus suggested the agency make a TV commercial for the fund using a live lion. The resulting spot, featuring a lion emerging from a Wall Street subway stop, was highly successful and ran thousands of times. Jack Dreyfus's iconoclastic ways led to other developments that separated the Dreyfus Fund from the competition. He wrote the nontechnical part of the prospectus, drawing praise from *Barron's.* He then arranged to have the entire prospectus printed as a supplement in the Sunday *New York Times.*

In the beginning, because the management fee of the fund was so small—.5 percent of $500,000, or $2,500—Jack Dreyfus and an assistant ran the fund, and continued in that way for a dozen years. They did well, as the Dreyfus Fund solidly outperformed other mutual funds during this period. Jack Dreyfus believed in being flexible and a willingness to quickly cut losses. The one stock on which he took a long-term approach was Polaroid. His brother-in-law was the head of the company's research department and told him about some 3-D glasses in development. Dreyfus bought the stock because of the glasses but took a large position because of the company's camera. Polaroid became an early major success story for the Dreyfus Fund.

New Leadership in the Mid-1960s

In 1958 Jack Dreyfus began to suffer from bouts of depression that ranged from mild to severe. In 1963, on little more than a hunch, he asked his doctor to prescribe Dilantin, a drug to treat epilepsy. Dreyfus improved dramatically and although he returned to his routine at Dreyfus & Co. and the Dreyfus Fund, an increasing amount of his time and attention was devoted to researching and championing Dilantin. In 1965 he decided to retire from managing the fund in order to establish the Dreyfus Medical Foundation. He hired a recruiter who presented him four candidates, but in the end he decided that someone in his own organization was better suited to the job, Howard Stein, who would head the company for the next 30 years and propel the fund to new heights. Within a few years, Jack Dreyfus retired from his business activities to devote all of his time to his medical interests. In his autobiography, he offered a lighthearted assessment of his business career: "It would appear I had some luck. The Ohrbachs pushed me into the commission business, the Dreyfus Fund walked into the office, and I bought the right stock for the wrong reason. . . . I was an implausible person to have made a lot of money."

Never having gone to college, Stein sought opinions from countless people, but he relied on his own instincts when it came time to make investment decisions. An amateur violinist, he had a sense of counterpoint, bucking the trends to the benefit of the Dreyfus Fund and its investors. The Fund's growth was dramatic: In 1965 assets increased from $800 million to $1.34 billion. In October of that year, Dreyfus Corporation, manager of the Dreyfus Fund, also went public, selling two million

Key Dates:

1946: Jack Dreyfus forms Dreyfus & Co.
1951: The Dreyfus Corporation is formed to manage the Dreyfus fund.
1965: Jack Dreyfus turns over management of the fund to Howard Stein.
1970: Stein is named CEO and chairman.
1974: Dreyfus offers its first no-load mutual fund.
1994: Dreyfus Corp. is sold to Mellon Bank.
1996: Howard Stein retires.
2000: The firm pays $2.95 million to settle SEC charges.

shares at $20 a share, thus becoming one of the first money management firms to turn to the stock market for additional capital. After Jack Dreyfus retired, Stein took over as chief executive officer and chairman of Dreyfus Corporation in 1970.

During the 1970s Stein tried to keep in step with the times. In 1972 Dreyfus introduced The Dreyfus Third Century Fund, pioneering the concept of socially responsible investing. During this period of difficult economic conditions and a bear market, he also sensed that investors were looking for safe, dependable returns. Thus, in 1974, Dreyfus introduced the first direct-marketed, no-load money-market fund. As a result, in just one year Dreyfus saw its assets grow by 50 percent to $3 billion. Even as the stock market began to rebound, Stein became even more focused on money-market and bond funds. Politically connected, Stein, who had been campaign treasurer for Eugene McCarthy's bid for the presidency in 1968, turned his attention to Washington and succeeded in creating tax-free municipal funds, which Dreyfus launched in 1976.

In the 1980s Dreyfus tried its hand at banking. In 1982 it paid $2.8 million to buy Lincoln State Bank in East Orange, New Jersey, creating Dreyfus Consumer Bank to become involved in consumer lending. Because of changes in law that limited the growth of such banks, Dreyfus sold the branch in 1989. On the other hand, it took advantage of changes made by the Tax Reform Act of 1986 to introduce a pair of strategic funds, which made use of hedging with futures and options contracts, sophisticated trading techniques that the law now made available to mutual funds. Also during the mid-1980s, Dreyfus introduced a number of low-expense cash management funds, and the Premier Family of loan funds sold exclusively through banks and broker-dealers. Late in the decade, the firm also launched the Dreyfus WorldWide Dollar Money Market Fund, which offered a chance to invest in foreign money market instruments. Also of note, Dreyfus Corp. completed a secondary stock offering in 1986 that raised $204 million, but instead of using the money to grow through expansion and acquisitions, Stein elected to hold on to the cash. This decision, considered a misstep by many, was compounded by his reluctance to shift from bonds to equities during the post-1987 bull market.

Convinced that stocks were overvalued and would eventually be punished, Stein continued to emphasize bonds, missing out on gains in the stock market during the early 1990s and losing market share in the process. Dreyfus and Stein, its 67-

year-old chairman and CEO, were considered out of step with the times. Nevertheless, the Dreyfus history and brand recognition were strong enough to attract the attention of Pittsburgh-based Mellon Bank Corporation, which like other banks was eager to enter the mutual fund business. The two firms began discussing a sale of Dreyfus to Mellon in 1993. Talks broke off in November when Stein feared that Mellon was going to make wholesale terminations and other changes, but negotiations were revived when Mellon's chairman, Frank V. Cahouet, flew to Stein's California home the day before Thanksgiving to spend time with Stein, a longtime friend. The negotiations were put back on track and culminated in a stock swap valued at $1.7 billion.

Stein stayed on as the chairman of Dreyfus, but the transition to Mellon ownership was far from smooth. The hope was that Mellon would provide a strong retail outlet for Dreyfus products, but it failed to materialize because of a clash between Mellon people and Dreyfus people, resulting in a 15 percent drop in assets in the first year. The bank was not pleased with the firm's continued conservative approach, leading to changes in the top ranks of management, including the retirement of Stein in August 1996. Mellon installed one of its rising stars, Christopher M. Condron, named president and chief operating officer in November 1995, to turn around Dreyfus. He was joined by chief investment officer Stephen Canter and they set about fleshing out the types of funds Dreyfus had to offer. In 1996 it established the Dreyfus Short-Term High-Yield Fund and two years later created the firm's first high-yield closed-end fund. Dreyfus also displayed a new aggressiveness in 1998 when it acquired Denver-based Founders Funds, a $6.8 billion-in-assets manager specializing in growth stocks. Nevertheless, the company remained conservative compared with the competition. From the time Mellon took over until 2001, Dreyfus had more of its funds redeemed than bought, by the tune of $426 million.

To make matters worse, the reputation of the firm was tarnished in 1998 when a portfolio manager of two Dreyfus funds, Michael L. Schonberg, ran afoul of regulators as well as the FBI. He was accused of accepting inexpensive stock or warrants on companies whose share he would later buy for Dreyfus's Aggressive Growth and Premier Aggressive Growth funds. Dreyfus was investigated for the way it advertised the two funds, accused of failing to adequately inform investors about the risks or to note that the fund's initial performance was skewed because it included a large number of initial public offerings. In May 2000 Dreyfus agreed to pay $2.95 million to settle the matter, and Schonberg agreed to pay a $50,000 fine and accept a nine-month suspension from the investment management business. Under terms of the settlement neither party acknowledged any wrongdoing. As a whole, the mutual fund industry, which had enjoyed a clean reputation for many years, was losing some of its luster as New York State Attorney Eliot Spitzer began to look into industry practices that may not have been in the best interest of ordinary investors. Thus Dreyfus faced a number of challenges as it struggled to regain its once lofty status in the marketplace.

Principal Operating Units

Dreyfus Investments; Dreyfus Service Corporation; Founders Asset Management.

Principal Competitors

BlackRock, Inc.; FMR Corporation; The Vanguard Group, Inc.

Further Reading

Belsky, Gary, ''Contrarian's Roar Echoes at Dreyfus,'' *Crain's New York Business,* October 22, 1990, p. 1.

Dreyfus, Jack, *The Lion of Wall Street,* Washington, D.C.: Regnery Publishing, 1996.

Fink, Ronald, ''Cowardly Lion?,'' *Financial World,* March 2, 1993, p. 68.

Fisher, Anne, ''Howard Stein's Rise, Fall, and Exit,'' *Fortune,* September 30, 1996, p. 31.

Frick, Robert, ''The Lion That Wants to Roar,'' *Kiplinger's Personal Finance Magazine,* February 1999, p. 94.

Gandel, Stephen, ''Dreyfus Funds Roar,'' *Crain's New York Business,* April 30, 2001, p. 3.

Hakim, Danny, ''Dreyfus to Pay $2.9 Million After Investigation of Fund,'' *New York Times,* May 11, 2000, p. C11.

Henderson, Barry, and Sandra Ward, ''All-Stars,'' *Barron's,* January 10, 2000, p. F5.

—Ed Dinger

Edwards and Kelcey

---

299 Madison Avenue
Morristown, New Jersey 07962-1936
U.S.A.
Telephone: (973) 267-0555
Fax: (973) 267-3555
Web site: http://www.ekcorp.com

Private Company
Founded: 1946
Employees: 1,016
Sales: $142.3 million (2003)
NAIC: 541330 Engineering Services

Based in Morristown, New Jersey, Edwards and Kelcey is a privately owned engineering and construction firm serving six markets. Originally devoted to the transportation market, Edwards and Kelcey continues to help in the planning and construction of highways, bridges, rail and transit systems, ports and harbors, and airports. The firm has been involved in the communications market since the 1970s and today provides design and construction services for the installation of wireless and fiber optic networks, in-building wireless networks, and integrated security systems, as well as maintenance and inspection services. Another market for Edwards and Kelcey is utilities, providing planning, engineering, and construction services related to generation and storage facilities, transmission and distribution networks, service connections, standby power systems, plant controls, and security systems. The firm serves the institutional and commercial market, designing and constructing facilities for schools, medical centers, and government agencies, as well as commercial projects such as shopping malls, parking garages, warehouses, and industrial plants. Edwards and Kelcey also does work for the federal government, providing civil engineering services to both the military and civilian branches, including agencies such as the U.S. Department of Defense, U.S. Army Corps of Engineers, U.S. Department of Energy, U.S. Department of Justice, U.S. Postal Service, Federal Emergency Management Agency, and U.S. Department of Transportation. Finally, Edwards and Kelcey serves the planning/environment market by helping public and private clients to gain regulatory approval for projects while also gaining public approval by addressing health and safety and economic concerns, and making sure that a community's sense of place is preserved. Edwards and Kelcey maintains more than 20 offices in the United States and one in Puerto Rico.

Founding the Firm Following World War II

The men behind the Edwards and Kelcey name were partners Dean G. Edwards and Guy Kelcey. The longer serving of the pair was Kelcey. Born in Canada in 1889, he moved to Buffalo at the age of ten and became a U.S. citizen in his early 20s. In 1914 he graduated with a degree in civil engineering from the Carnegie Institute of Technology, and during the 1920s made his mark through pioneering work in traffic control, studying ways to control the flow of vehicles by employing devices such as traffic islands. Kelcey was perhaps the first man in the United States to be known as a "traffic engineer." During World War II, he served as the regional director of local transport in the Southeast for the Office of Defense Transportation. In 1945 he became the highway transportation analyst for the Port of New York Authority. A year later, in June 1946, he joined forces with Edwards, who had recently retired as the chief engineer for the Borough of Manhattan, to form the consulting engineering firm of Edwards and Kelcey.

The partnership moved into offices located at 150 Broadway in lower Manhattan and soon won contracts to do location studies and designs for major highways. During the postwar years, automobiles, trucks, and buses were superseding the railroads at an accelerated clip, and for national defense as well as commercial reasons, the U.S. government and the states were willing to fund massive highway building projects that dovetailed nicely with the expertise of Edwards and Kelcey. By the end of the 1940s the firm opened branch offices in Boston and New Jersey after winning major highway projects.

Edwards and Kelcey landed highway contracts throughout the Northeast during the 1950s. Among the projects the firm worked on during this period were sections of the New Jersey and Connecticut Turnpikes, the Garden State Parkway, and the New York Thruway. Edwards and Kelcey also expanded its

> ## Company Perspectives:
>
> *Edwards and Kelcey is a client-focused organization built upon strong and enduring commitment to our clients, our partners, and our employees.*

operations to the Midwest, establishing an office in Minneapolis in 1958 to work with the Minnesota Department of Highways, initially doing design work for I-35 and I-94. During the next 20 years it also designed interchanges and bridges throughout the Twin Cities. In addition, Edwards and Kelcey ventured overseas during the 1950s. Under the auspices of the Technical Cooperation Administration of the Department of State, the firm was involved in the development of Iraq's first highway system.

Changing Leadership and Expanding Services: 1960s–80s

Both Edwards and Kelcey had been approaching retirement age when they formed their partnership, so that a change in the top ranks of leadership soon came. In 1961 Edwards died, and Kelcey, now in his 70s, began to shift increasing levels of responsibility to the eight engineers he and Edwards had hired in the early years of the firm. Kelcey gradually withdrew from active participation, and in August 1972 he died at the age of 84.

During the 1960s Edwards and Kelcey expanded on a number of fronts. To its highway business, the firm added building design contracts, the first of which was a multilevel parking garage for Boston's Logan Airport. It also began to do work involving recreational facilities. After developing ''The New Jersey Comprehensive Outdoor Recreation Plan,'' which determined the minimum amount of public land that should be set aside as open space or dedicated to recreation, the firm designed two major New Jersey State parks: Round Valley Recreation Area and the Spruce Run Reservoir. The firm also added to its international resume during the 1960s, launching a decade of work in Brazil and Columbia, designing highways, bridges, and other transportation projects.

Edwards and Kelcey added greatly to the breadth of its capabilities during the 1970s, as it attempted to remain competitive by keeping up with the growing needs of its clients. Through the acquisition of a pair of small consulting firms, Edwards and Kelcey became involved in airport planning and design and the rail transit business. During this period the firm also established its bridge inspection practice, which started with a contract to assess and rehabilitate the Manhattan Bridge, linking Brooklyn to lower Manhattan. In addition, the firm began doing communications design work, starting out by helping Western Union build its first nationwide microwave communications network. Later, with the advent of new satellite technology, Edwards and Kelcey assisted Western Union in establishing earth stations at key locations in the United States. The firm established a reputation in the planning/environment field during the 1970s by successfully completing one of the first Environmental Impact Statements, regarding the relocation of Maine's 1A highway, as required for federal agencies by the National Environmental Policy Act of 1969. Edwards and

Kelcey also delved into the high-tech area during the 1970s, developing a computerized traffic surveillance system for the New Jersey Turnpike, a forerunner of what would become Intelligent Transportation Systems, or ITS.

During the 1980s Edwards and Kelcey completed a 20-year assignment, providing design and construction supervision services for the Charlestown Urban Renewal Project, which restored the area surrounding the historic Bunker Hill site. The firm's willingness and ability to take a long view on projects also was demonstrated in New Jersey. In 1985 Ronald Wiss, head of the transportation division, urged legislators to build a new rail transfer station in Secaucus, which he contended was necessary if New Jersey was to remain economically competitive. Dozens of different permits would be required, but undaunted, Wiss received approval, tackled the problem, and 13 years later completed the project. Edwards and Kelcey extended its reach to California in the 1980s, winning a contract to design the Hollywood Bowl Station in Los Angeles' new metro rail system. The firm also added other rail transportation capabilities during this period, becoming involved in railroad signals, traction power, and catenary design.

Going Private in the Mid-1990s

In the late 1980s Edwards and Kelcey became employee owned through an employee stock ownership plan (ESOP). The ESOP actually had been established in 1976, but because it was composed of nonvoting stock, it served as little more than a pension plan. When Satashi Oishi took over as chief executive officer in 1987, he wanted to curtail the high turnover rate of key employees and, after getting input from outside consultants, decided to revamp the ESOP. It now consisted of voting stock, giving employees more of a say in the direction of the firm. As Edwards and Kelcey entered the 1990s it was doing about $21 million in annual revenues, operating four branch offices. But after enjoying a major growth spurt in the 1970s, it was clear that Edwards and Kelcey had become stagnant. Then, in the mid-1990s, it began to enjoy something of a rebirth. Wiss took over as president and CEO in 1995, and assumed the chairmanship a year later. He named Kevin McMahon as president, and they along with 18 other employees bought out the company and assessed the firm's situation. The team created a three-pronged business plan that called on the firm to improve profitability, grow geographically, and broaden its services.

In the second half of the 1990s, Edwards opened some 20 offices around the country, either as start-ups or by way of acquisition. The firm established a group dedicated to value engineering, a discipline that attempted to identify and eliminate unnecessary costs, then supplemented the new business with the acquisition of VEI Inc., a Dallas firm specializing in value engineering. Another important purchase was Sypher:Mueller Inc., a Baltimore firm specializing in aviation projects as well as energy conservation and alternative fuel studies and design. Edwards and Kelcey also established alliances with manufacturers to develop products and systems, the purpose of which was to package a product and a service to drum up new business. For instance, the firm worked with Engineered Systems/Datron to develop an arresting material system airports could employ to help decelerate aircrafts making emergency landings; teamed up with Trilon, Inc. to create the IBIIS bridge information system software package;

Key Dates:

1946: Edwards and Kelcey is formed as an engineering partnership.
1961: Dean Edwards dies.
1973: Guy Kelcey dies.
1989: The firm becomes employee owned.
1996: A management team buys out the company.
1999: Kevin J. McMahon is named CEO and chairman.
2005: The firm is ranked 61st among the top 500 U.S. design firms by *Engineering News Record.*

and worked with EnTEch to apply infrared thermography and ground-penetrating radar to analyze the structural integrity of airport runways and bridge decks. Perhaps the fastest growing segment of Edwards and Kelcey's business in the late 1990s was the wireless communications market. After forming a dedicated subsidiary in 1996, two years later communications work contributed 40 percent of the firm's revenues. The group not only did work in the United States but also was involved in a major wireless buildout project in The Netherlands. Another subsidiary formed in the 1990s was EK Technology, dedicated to systems integration work providing construction-at-risk solutions.

In August 1999 the 55-year-old Wiss collapsed while dancing with his wife at a wedding reception and subsequently died, the apparent victim of a heart attack. McMahon replaced Wiss as CEO and chairman and led the firm into the new century, essentially carrying out the business plan put into place by his predecessor, opening new offices, making strategic acquisitions, and adding capabilities. In 2001 a new office was opened in Tarrytown, New York, just north of New York City, an area where many engineers resided, as well as offices in Kittery, Maine; New Haven, Connecticut; and Philadelphia, Pennsylvania. Also in 2001 Edwards and Kelcey bought a Boston company, CID Associates Inc., a full-service engineering and architectural firm that specialized in building facilities, followed by the acquisition of Tighe, Doty, Carrino, a New Jersey firm that also specialized in building facilities as well as site design and development. In addition, in 2001 Edwards and Kelcey formed a Landscape Architecture and Urban Design Group to further the firm's work in landscape architecture, now allowing it to offer a full range of design, planning, engineering, and permitting services for projects of any size and type.

In the spring of 2002 Edwards and Kelcey acquired Aikenhead & Odon, a Jacksonville, Florida design and consulting firm involved in transportation, utilities, private development, and environmental engineering, an important addition because

it strengthened Edwards and Kelcey's presence in Florida and the Southeast, which presented a major opportunity for growth. Later in the year, the firm's presence in the area was further bolstered with the acquisition of Miami-based Kunde Sprecher & Associates, involved in land, sea, and air transportation projects, commercial and industrial facilities, and municipal water and wastewater facilities. The 44-year-old firm was well established, boasting clients such as the Florida Department of Transportation, Miami-Dade County Government, Miami-Dade County Public Schools, City of Miami, and American Airlines. Also in 2002, Edwards and Kelcey acquired Cincinnati, Ohio-based Pflum, Klausmeier & Gehrum Consultants, Inc., a 35-year-old firm providing professional services in traffic engineering, highway engineering, transportation planning, structural engineering, urban planning, and landscape architecture. Next, in February 2005, Edwards and Kelcey acquired Epsilon Engineering, Inc., a consulting and civil engineering services firm with offices in Houston and College Station, Texas. Mostly serving government agencies, it specialized in the design of highways, traffic control, illumination, utility relocations, and storm drainage systems, as well as value engineering services.

Epsilon was Edwards and Kelcey's 15th acquisition in ten years. With more than $140 million in annual sales, the firm was now ranked 61st among the top 500 U.S. design firms by *Engineering News Record.* Given its recent record of strong growth, there was every reason to expect Edwards and Kelcey to move up in the rankings in the coming years.

Principal Operating Units

Transportation; Communications; Federal; Utilities; Institutional/Commercial; Planning/Environmental.

Principal Competitors

HNTB; Parsons Brinckerhoff Inc.; URS Corporation.

Further Reading

Bachelor, Blane, "Revved Up," *American Executive Magazine,* June 2004.
Fairweather, Virginia, "How To Succeed in Business," *Civil Engineering,* October 1998, p. 68.
"Guy Kelcey, Pioneering Engineer on Traffic and Roads, Dies, at 84," *New York Times,* August 10, 1973, p. 34.
Prior, James T., "Edwards & Kelcey Redefines the Engineering Profession," *New Jersey Business,* August 1, 1998, p. 43.
Sundaramoorthy, Geeta, "Edwards and Kelcey, King of the Roads," *NJBIZ,* September 2, 2002, p. 25.

—Ed Dinger

Empresas CMPC S.A.

Agustinas 1343
Santiago
Chile
Telephone: (56) (2) 441-2000
Fax: (56) (2) 671-1957
Web site: http://www.cmpc.cl

Public Company
Incorporated: 1920 as Compania Manufacturera de
    Papeles y Cartones S.A.
Employees: 8,573
Sales: CLP 1.08 trillion ($1.94 billion) (2004)
Stock Exchanges: Bolsa de Comercio de Santiago
Ticker Symbol: CMPC
NAIC: 111421 Nursery and Tree Production; 113110
    Timber Tract Operations; 113310 Logging; 321113
    Sawmills; 322110 Pulp Mills; 322121 Paper (Except
    Newsprint) Mills; 322122 Newsprint Mills; 322130
    Paperboard Mills; 322211 Corrugated and Solid Fiber
    Box Manufacturing; 322212 Folding Paperboard Box
    Manufacturing

Empresas CMPC S.A. is one of the largest companies in Chile. Engaged in the manufacture, sale, and export of cellulose and a broad variety of paper products, it is second only to Empresa Copec S.A. (the nation's largest private enterprise) in the forest products field. CMPC also holds large forest tracts and plantations of fast-growing pine trees. It is the major holding of the Matte group, one of the wealthiest in Chile.

Chile's Paper Tiger: 1920–58

The son of a businessman, Luis Matte Larrain graduated from the University of Chile in 1915 with a degree in civil engineering. Visits to the Panama Canal and the United States gave him valuable contact with the industrial and entrepreneurial practices of North America. With a brother and three friends, he founded Luis Matte y Cia., which engaged in importing goods, principally fuels and lubricants.

But Matte had something more ambitious in mind—using Chile's bountiful forestry resources to manufacture paper products. Toward the end of 1918 he founded the Comunidad Fabrica de Carton Maipu. In 1920 he and Eduardo Morel Herrera merged this factory with that of German Ebbinghaus, who was operating the La Esperanza paper and cardboard factory in Puente Alto, a community on the outskirts of Santiago, to create Compania Manufacturera de Papeles y Cartones. The company had 44 shareholders and the capacity to produce 2,200 metric tons a year of paper and pasteboard. In 1924 it acquired its only meaningful rival, the Santa Victoria factory, also in Puente Alto.

Matte, who was general manager but only a minority stockholder, then presided over the construction of a cellulose (wood pulp) plant in Puente Alto and a hydroelectric power plant in Pirque. He acquired, in 1930, the San Miguel de Chillan hacienda and planted 10,000 hectares (almost 25,000 acres) with pine trees. Following a year of testing which Chilean wood might be most suitable, CMPC in 1931 purchased an industrial plant in Argentina capable of producing 9,000 kilos (about 20,000 pounds) a day of wood pulp. A new cellulose factory was constructed in 1932 to replace the original one. Shortly before Matte died in 1936, he acquired new machinery, expanded the hydroelectric plant, and began work on constructing a new wood-pulp plant to make paper for newspapers and magazines.

Following Luis Matte's death, leadership of the enterprise passed, in 1938, to Jorge Alessandri Rodriguez, an engineer who was brother-in-law of Arturo Matte, Luis's brother. He became general manager. Early in World War II, the German occupation of Norway put an end to CMPC's imports of Scandinavian wood pulp, which still accounted for half of its raw material. Cellulose from North America was more expensive. With an eye to increasing CMPC's cellulose supplies from its own resources, Alessandri, in 1940, purchased a tract of land near Concepcion that contained important reserves of radiata pine. In 1942 the company acquired a Valdivia-based paperboard company. At this point CMPC was supplying nearly all of Chile's demand for printing and packaging paper and, to a large extent, also the nation's supply of newsprint. In the 1950s CMPC built a pulp mill at Laja and a newsprint plant at Bio-

Key Dates:

1918: The company that subsequently becomes Empresas CMPC is founded.
1942: By this point CMPC is providing Chile with almost all of its printing and packaging paper.
1958: CMPC's general manager, Jorge Alessandri, is elected president of Chile.
1971–73: CMPC loses $30 million while fighting off control by Chile's socialist government.
1986: CMPC expands greatly by purchasing debt-ridden Industrias Forestales S.A. (Inforsa).
1995: Empresas CMPC is now Chile's second largest private company.
2003: The company's holdings include 1.75 million acres of forests in Chile and Argentina.

Bio. This was one of the most significant industrial investments by Chilean capital without state support.

The son of a man who was twice president of Chile, Alessandri took time out to serve as Chile's secretary of the treasury (1947–50) and resigned as general manager in 1957 to pursue what proved to be a successful campaign for the presidency of Chile. On his election, the *New York Times* described Alessandri as having been "a brilliant mathematics student and professor. . . . He is identified with Chile's wealthy aristocracy and practices profit-sharing in his company." A bachelor, he was said to have almost no social life, usually dining with Arturo Matte and his wife (Alessandri's sister), who lived in the same apartment building. During his 20-year tenure as general manager, CMPC grew more than fourfold.

Further Expansion: 1958–95

On his election as president, Alessandri was succeeded as general manager of CMPC by Ernesto Ayala. The following year CMPC entered Argentina, Bolivia, Ecuador, Paraguay, Peru, and Uruguay for the first time by selling its newsprint in these countries. Later these nations also began accepting the firm's cellulose, although at first radiata-pine pulp was unheard of. In 1961, Eliodoro Matte Ossa, a grandnephew of the founder, became a CMPC director. A stockbroker who made his fortune on the Bolsa de Comercio de Santiago, Matte Ossa decided that the company's stock was undervalued and, through purchases, raised his share from 2 percent in 1965 to 26 percent in 1972.

By then the left-wing government of President Salvador Allende Gossens had assumed rule over Chile, following the 1970 presidential election, in which Allende narrowly defeated Alessandri, who had returned to CMPC after serving one term as president of the republic. The government already had controlling interests in the other two producers of newsprint and tried, but failed, to win control of CMPC (by far the largest) as well and thereby achieve a monopoly capable of shutting down the opposition press. The government was overthrown in 1973. Writing in *Pulp & Paper* the following year, Albert W. Wilson contended, "The strong paper industry labor unions are credited

with being the decisive factor in Allende's downfall. To save CMPC from going the way of hundreds of other companies, its customers paid bills in advance. Suppliers eased and lengthened credit." Nevertheless, La Papelera, as CMPC was commonly called, lost $30 million in this period.

Matte Ossa bought more shares of CMPC between 1974 and 1978 but left the company in 1976, turning over his role as a director to his son Eliodoro Matte Larrain, who replaced Ayala as general manager in 1981 and executive vice-president in 1986. Alessandri remained president until 1986, when he died and was succeeded by Ayala, who kept the post until he resigned in 2002 at the age of 86. Arturo Mackenna Iniguez, who replaced Matte as general manager, still held this post in 2004. CMPC opened a factory in the 1970s producing molded pulp products for the export of eggs and fruits. In 1979 it transferred most of its forests and timber stands to a subsidiary, Forestal Mininco S.A. In 1982 it purchased full control of Laja Crown S.A., the joint venture it had shared with the U.S. paper company Crown Zellerbach Corp. since 1964. Also that year, the company introduced Austral notebooks, Babysan disposable diapers, and Suave hygienic paper.

In 1986 CMPC purchased 77 percent of debt-ridden Industrias Forestales S.A. (Inforsa) for CLP 6.56 billion ($33.6 million). The purchase included a corrugated-boxboard plant in Buin, a newsprint plant in Nacimiento, 75,000 hectares (185,000 acres) of tree plantations, a sawmill, and 50 percent of wood-pulp producer Papeles Sudamerica S.A. With this purchase CMPC raised its share of national newsprint production to at least 53 percent, wood pulp to 43 percent, corrugated boxboard to 85 percent, and forest plantations in Chile to 17 percent. A government commission, however, fearing a CMPC newsprint monopoly, forced the company to sell (for $123 million) its Bio-Bio mill. As of 1986 CMPC had 18 subsidiaries (including an insurance company fully acquired in 1988) and was involved in eight joint ventures.

CMPC entered Argentina in 1990 by purchasing, in partnership with Procter & Gamble Co., Quimica Estrella San Luis S.A., a manufacturer of sanitary napkins and paper diapers that was renamed Productos Descartables S.A. (Prodesa). By 1996 Prodesa was manufacturing more than half the disposable diapers and paper tissue in that country, and used it to introduce Pampers, Babysan, and Ladysan in Argentina. In 1992 CMPC formed a strategic alliance with Procter & Gamble to develop markets for the aforementioned products in Argentina, Bolivia, Paraguay, Peru, and Uruguay as well as Chile. In 1994 CMPC bought Fabi S.A., an Argentine manufacturer of cement sacks, and Industria Papelera Uruguaya S.A. (Ipusa), the paper-tissue leader in the Uruguayan market. In that year also CMPC established Productos Tissue S.A. for the manufacture, sale, and distribution of hygienic products such as napkins and disposable tissues in Chile. (A similar company had been established in Argentina in 1991.)

New plantings, a higher level of technology, and optimal use of fertilization enabled the company's trees to mature faster, allowing them to be cut down in 18 rather than 23 years. Quality also improved, so that instead of being made into boxes for export to Japan as before, the wood was good enough to be sent to the United States. Reforestation included 20,000 hectares (nearly 50,000 acres) of eroded land in Coyhalque, planted with slower-growing ponderosa pine. In that year (1992) CMPC was the nation's third largest private company in sales and net worth. By 1995 it had reached second place. It was also the leading producer of paper tissues in South America and the sole forestry company making paper tissues in Chile and Argentina. La Papelera was one of the few Chilean enterprises to realize the dream of adding value to its prime materials. By this time the company held 500,000 hectares (nearly 1.25 acres) in Chile planted in radiata pine and eucalyptus, 142,000 hectares more than it held in 1990. It also held 250,000 hectares (nearly 625,000 acres) of pine and 52,000 hectares (128,000 acres) of eucalyptus in Argentina, where it owned Corepa, a wastepaper-collection operation.

Holding Company with Five Affiliates: 1996–2003

CMPC's revenue in 1996 came close to $1.2 billion. In that year the company had 22 affiliates and subsidiaries in Chile and was taking part in 12 joint ventures; it also had six affiliates and subsidiaries abroad. The Puente Alto and Talagante (constructed in 1994–95) plants in Chile were giving it 80 percent of the domestic tissue market. Talagante also was producing toilet paper, paper towels, and folded products such as paper handkerchiefs and napkins. CMPC was investing 70 percent of its profits in new businesses. Projects totaling $500 million were under way. In 1996–97 CMPC purchased La Papelera del Plata S.A. in Argentina for $50 million, raising its share of that tissue market to 40 to 50 percent. In Peru, CMPC was preparing to open paper-tissue and paper-bag plants.

In Chile, CMPC was investing, in 1996, in the modernization of the Laja and Nacimiento plants, and in the new Maule plant for the production of boxboard, or bristol board. With the object of constructing a plant for short-fiber bleached cellulose, the company initiated the planting of trees in the north of Chile and acquired 20,000 hectares (nearly 50,000 acres) of forest property in the provinces of Corrientes and Misiones. By this time the firm had made investments equivalent to $1.3 billion for new plantations and industrial plants over the last five years. On the other hand, CMPC was falling further behind Copec's Celulosa Arauco y Constitucion S.A., the rival cellulose-producing giant owned by the Angelini group, which outbid the Matte interests for Alto Parana S.A., the largest producer of cellulose in Argentina. But, unlike Copec, CMPC regarded wood pulp as only a means to an end. Curiously, the two groups, despite their rivalry, coexisted amicably, with the Matte group actually owning 10 percent of Copec and represented on its board by Bernardo Matte Larrain, Eliodoro's brother. The two companies also shared participation in an investment fund.

At this point CMPC (renamed Empresas CMPC in 1993) was a holding company with five affiliates. CMPC Forestal was responsible for raising the trees from hatchlings until harvesting and sale as doors and tables. CMPC Celulosa was responsible for producing cellulose in bundles for paper production and flat rolls for the manufacture of disposable diapers and sanitary napkins. This subsidiary also was responsible for Forestal e Industrial Santa Fe S.A., in which CMPC had taken a 20 percent share in 1995 and which was raised to 80 percent in 1997 (its properties including a eucalyptus pulp mill), and Celulosa del Pacifico S.A., a giant pulp mill in Mininco that it held as a joint

venture with Simpson Paper Co. from 1989 to 1998, when it bought Simpson out. Simpson also sold its half-interest in a eucalyptus plantation to CMPC. The total cost of the buyout was $476 million.

A third affiliate was CMPC Productos de Papel, consisting of Envases Impresos S.A., a corrugated-boxboard factory; Grafex S.A., producing boxes (estuches) and napkins, but sold the following year; Proyectos Australes S.A., a factory for notebooks, photocopy paper, and flexible packing containers; Propa S.A., a factory making industrial paper bags; Chilena de Moldeados S.A. (Chimolsa), a 40 percent-owned firm producing cardboard trays for the export of fruit; Fabi Argentina, making bags filled with cement; and Fabi Peru S.A. Proyectos Australes later changed its name to Forestal Bosques del Plata S.A. Chimolsa became fully owned by CMPC in 2003.

The major novelties in 1996 were CMPC Tissue and CMPC Papeles. The latter combined the newsprint plants, printing paper, and stationery, and the Maule plant for folding boxboard, in which the parent company was investing $200 million to make it the primary plant of its kind in Chile and to export its product for the production of packing containers. It opened in 1997. But without doubt CMPC Tissue was the major development of this period. In addition to the completion of the $60 million Talagante plant, 1995 saw as well the inauguration of an $80 million Protisa plant in Zarate, Argentina. The subsequent acquisition of Papelera del Plata at a cost of $50 million gave CMPC one of the most famous brands in Argentina and 55 percent of the Argentine market. CMPC Tissue also added Ipusa, in Uruguay, and entered Peru for napkins and hygienic paper. This affiliate also managed Prosan, CMPC's share of the joint venture with Procter & Gamble, turning out Pampers, Babysec disposable diapers, and Ladysoft sanitary pads in Argentina, Bolivia, Chile, Paraguay, and Uruguay until 1998, when CMPC sold its share to Procter & Gamble. CMPC Tissue was producing toilet paper, disposable tissues and diapers, napkins, paper towels, and sanitary napkins in Puente Alto, Talagante, and Zarate, Argentina, and was converting folding products at Naschel, Argentina.

As of 2003, CMPC Forestal (renamed Forestal Mininco S.A.) was administering 709,018 hectares (about 1.75 million acres) of forest. CMPC Celulosa was running the Pacifico, Santa Fe, and Laja mills, which turned out 1.14 million metric tons of wood pulp that year. Much of the timber came from third parties rather than the company's own holdings. CMPC Papeles was responsible for the Nacimiento newsprint plant, the Maule and Valdivia facilities turning out folding boxboard, and the Puente Alto factory producing corrugated container board. CMPC Productos de Papeles was producing boxes in Buin, Quilicara, and Til Til, multiwall sacks in Chillan, and molded trays in Puente Alto. As of 2004, CMPC's projects included a new corrugated board factory in Puente Alto and an expansion of the Pacifico plant to produce 475,000 metric tons of wood pulp per year. In that year the company earned an impressive CLP 219.22 billion ($393.25 million) profit on revenue of CLP 1.08 trillion ($1.94 billion).

Jorge Gabriel Larrain, brother-in-law of Elidorio and Bernardo, was in charge of Minera Valparaiso, the family group's 65 percent-owned major holding outside CMPC. The private port and electric generators used by this company also were being put to use by CMPC. The Matte group owned 55 percent of CMPC.

Principal Subsidiaries

CMPC Celulosa S.A.; CMPC Papeles S.A.; CMPC Productos de Papel S.A.; CMPC Productos Tissue S.A.; Forestal Mininco S.A.

Principal Divisions

Cellulose; Forestry; Paper; Paper Products; Tissue Products.

Principal Competitors

Empresa Copec S.A.

Further Reading

Castillo, Nancy, "La amenaza extranjera," *Capital,* May 18–May 31, 2001, pp. 56–59.

"Chilean Industrialist," *New York Times,* September 6, 1958, p. 8.

Contreras M., Rodolfo, *Mas alla del bosque,* Santiago: Editorial Amerinda, 1989, pp. 117–36.

Garcia de la Huerta, Carolina, "La Papelera va," *Capital,* December 1996, pp. 18–22.

"Gigante Regional," *Gestion,* November 1996, p. 14.

"Hacia una mayor presencia internacional," *Gestion,* January 1987, pp. 14–17.

"Luis Matte Larrain," in *Empresarios en la historia* (2nd ed.), Santiago: Editorial Gestion, 1997, pp. 25–29.

Pappens, Rita, "Chile's Tissue Giant Rolls On," *PPI/Pulp & Paper International,* March 2000, pp. 24, 26.

——, "CMPC Plays at Home and Away," *PPI/Pulp & Paper International,* December 1999, pp. 32–33, 35.

"Las repercusiones de una inversion," *Gestion,* June 1987, pp. 14–17.

"Seremos siempre una empresa forestal," *Gestion,* December 1996, pp. 32–33.

Wilson, Albert W., "How a Paper Firm Survived in Chile," *Pulp & Paper,* October 1974, p. 23.

—Robert Halasz

Eurofins Scientific S.A.

rue Pierre Adolphe Bobierre, BP
Nantes
F-44323 Cedex 3
France
Telephone: (+33) 2 51 83 21 00
Fax: (+33) 2 51 83 21 11
Web site: http://www.eurofins.com

Public Company
Incorporated: 1987
Employees: 2,083
Sales: EUR 175.5 million ($230 million) (2004)
Stock Exchanges: Euronext Paris Frankfurt
Ticker Symbol: 3825
NAIC: 541380 Testing Laboratories; 541710 Research
and Development in the Physical Sciences and
Engineering Sciences; 621511 Medical Laboratories

France's Eurofins Scientific S.A. is a world-leading provider of biotechnology-based testing and analytical support services. The company has developed some 10,000 analytical methods for testing, analyzing, and identifying biochemical components in foods, pharmaceuticals, and other chemicals as well as in fertilizers, pesticides, and the environment. Through analysis, the company is able to prove a substance's authenticity, such as distinguishing between natural and artificial vanillin, and trace its origin. The company's testing methods also permit the identification of various component elements and the presence of bacteria and other health-risk related substances such as dioxins and prions, which have been associated with mad cow disease. In addition to product testing services, the company provides research and development services. Eurofin's client base includes most of the world's largest food, consumer product, and pharmaceutical groups. The company supports its international client base with a network of some 40 laboratories operating in 13 countries. More than 80 percent of the group's sales are generated outside of France. Major markets include Germany at nearly 19 percent of sales, Scandinavia at nearly 18 percent, North America at more than 16 percent, the Benelux countries at 15 percent, and the United Kingdom and Ireland at 8 percent. Founded in 1987, Euronfins has grown rapidly, primarily through a series of acquisitions. In 2004, the company's sales topped EUR 175 million ($230 million). Eurofins is listed on the Euronext Paris and Frankfurt Stock Exchanges. Founder Gilles Martin remains the company's CEO and chairman. The Martin family is also the company's largest shareholder, with more than 55 percent of its stock.

Turning Wine into a Winner in the 1980s

The importance of wine to France's culture, and to its economy, stimulated demands for methods for ensuring the quality and integrity of French wines. The use of certain substances, such as sugar and milk, was therefore outlawed. In the case of sugar, a natural component in the winemaking process, the ban on sugar additives was directed in large part in order to protect the interests of France's grape growers.

Given this context, researchers had developed a variety of analysis methods for testing wines for their purity. Among those working on developing new testing procedures were Maryvonne and Gérard Martin, a husband-and-wife research team at the University of Nantes, close to the Loire Valley wine-growing region. In the mid-1980s, the Martins succeeded in creating and patenting a new and more accurate analysis method. They labeled the method SNIF-NMR, for Site Specific Natural Isotope Fractionation Studied by Nuclear Magnetic Resonance. The use of NMR technology enabled the Martins to examine the chemical composition of wine at a molecular level and thereby determine the nature of its components based on their atomic isotopes.

The patent for the method initially belonged to the University of Nantes. In 1987, however, the Martins' son, Gilles Martin, just then completing a doctorate in mathematics and statistics, decided to establish a company in order to exploit his parents' testing method. Martin bought the patent from the university and set up his business, called Eurofins (in French, SNIF is written as FINS). The company started with just 12 employees. By the end of its first year, Eurofins' sales reached the equivalent of EUR 300,000.

An important turning point for the company came with its successful expansion of the basic SNIF-NMR technique to a wider array of substances. By 1989, the company's range of testing applications included non-alcoholic beverages, fruit juices, and flavorings. The wider array of products the company could test now enabled it to enter the food industry. By 1991, Eurofins's sales had risen to EUR 1.4 million.

While making inroads in France's market for both wine and food analysis, Martin, joined by younger brother Yves-Loic, quickly steered the company's focus to the international market. For this effort, the company at first targeted the creation of a sales and marketing network, setting up subsidiaries in such markets as the United Kingdom, Germany, and the Czech Republic. In 1993, Eurofins entered the United States, establishing Eurofins USA. The company's U.S. presence was boosted in 1996 when the Association of Analytical Communities (AOAC) officially approved SNIF-NMR for use in analyzing fruit juice. By then, the company's sales had climbed to the equivalent of EUR 3.5 million.

Acquiring Scale in the 1990s

Rising food safety concerns buoyed Eurofins in the mid-1990s. The first case of BSE, or "mad cow disease" in the United Kingdom sparked a panic in the food industry across the European continent. Later scandals, including dioxin contamination in Belgium, the presence of benzene in Perrier Water, outbreaks of potentially deadly bacteria such as listeria and E.coli, and the contamination of cans of Coca Cola in France and Belgium, as well as the spread of BSE to the European continent, added to food industry worries. The discovery of genetically modified corn in consumer-oriented foods, as well as the presence of antibiotics and growth hormones, which are banned in Europe, further fueled the demand for sophisticated testing and analysis procedures.

In response to the increasing demand for food and pharmaceutical testing procedures, Eurofins entered a new growth phase. The company now launched a series of acquisitions lasting into the mid-2000s. In 1997, the company made its first acquisition, buying up Nutrition International and Product Safety Labs in the United States. The first purchase whetted Eurofins' appetite for growth, and in October 1997 the company turned to the public market for capital to fuel its expansion, listing on the Euronext Paris Stock Exchange. By the end of that year, the company had expanded again, setting up its own laboratory in the United Kingdom.

Eurofins boosted its U.K. presence in 1998, adding three more companies that were subsequently merged into its existing subsidiary to form Eurofins Scientific Ltd. The company also turned to Germany, soon to become its single largest market, buying its

first laboratory in Berlin-Teltow, then acquiring Institut für Lebensmittel, Wasser und Umweltanalytik, based in Nuremberg, and Labor Dr. Hallermayer GmbH in Augsburg. Before the end of that year, the company had also purchased a major stake in Hamburg's Wiertz Eggert Jörissen GmbH, later boosting its holding to 100 percent. This acquisition also proved significant in expanding Eurofins' range of operations to include testing for contaminants such as pesticides and mycotoxins.

Similarly, in 1999, Eurofins acquired the Alpha Chemical and Biomedical Laboratories, based in California, adding its capacity for analyzing botanicals and nutraceuticals. Back in France, the company added the catering and pharmaceuticals markets to its list of clients with the purchase of Ecobio, near Paris. Another French acquisition, Laboratoire d'Analyses et d'Etudes Industrielles, brought the company to the south of France that year. With two more acquisitions, in Paris and Poitiers, Eurofins became the leading food safety testing and analysis groups in France. By then, the company's sales had soared past EUR 32 million.

Global Leader in the 2000s

In 2000, Eurofins boosted its U.S. position, acquiring Woodson Tenent Laboratories in Memphis, Tennessee. The company also entered Switzerland, acquiring three companies there that were subsequently merged to form Eurofins Scientific AG in that country. Next, the company turned to the Benelux market, buying up Analytico Food BV in Heerenveen, the Netherlands. Another new market opened up to the company with the purchase of 51 percent of Mikjo-Kemi, which operated ten laboratories in Denmark, Norway, and Germany.

The company also acquired a controlling share of Dr. Specht & Partner in Hamburg. Reflecting the group's growing presence in the German market, Eurofins launched a secondary offering on the Frankfurt Stock Exchange that year. By the end of 2000, the company's acquisitions included Celab AG in Switzerland and Gesellschaft für Arbeitsplatz- und Umweltanalytik (GfA) mbH, operating in Munster, Germany, and Orleans, France. This purchase enabled Eurofins to claim the European leadership in analysis of toxic contaminants.

New food tracking regulations encouraged the group to gain expertise in DNA sequencing and genotyping, in part through the acquisition of majority control of Germany's Medigenomix in 2001. In that year, Eurofins carried out a DNA traceability study on more than 14,000 cows in France. The company also met the growing alarm over the potential presence of genetically modified (GMO) components in the food chain with its GMO detection system, GMO Platinum Assay, worldwide. By the end of 2001, the company sales had soared again, topping EUR 127 million. That placed Eurofins as the fourth fastest-growing company among Europe's top 500 in the second half of the 1990s.

Eurofins continued to add to its expertise into the 2000s, buying Okometric in Germany in 2002 and Genescan in 2003. The Genescan purchase, which added operations in Germany, the United States, Hong Kong, and Brazil, placed Eurofins as the world's leader in the GMO testing market.

With the 2003 launch of Aller-Gene, the market's first multi-allergen PCR (polymerase chain reaction) screening test,

Key Dates:

1987: Gilles Martin launches Eurofins Scientific in order to exploit the SNIF-NMR testing procedure developed by his parents; the company's original market was for detection of presence of sugar in wine.

1989: Eurofins expands its technology to include the testing of non-alcoholic beverages and flavorings.

1993: The company creates a sales subsidiary in the United States.

1997: The company lists on the Euronext Paris Stock Exchange and makes its first acquisition when it purchases Nutrition International and Product Safety Labs in the United States.

1998: The company enters Germany, which later becomes company's largest single market.

2000: The company enters the Swiss, Benelux, and Scandinavian markets.

2001: The company launches GMO Platinum Assay for detecting the presence of genetically modified (GMO) food components.

2003: The company acquires Genescan, with laboratories in Germany, United States, Hong Kong, and Brazil.

2005: The company acquires 25 percent of MWG-Biotech Ag in Germany.

Eurofins positioned itself as a "one-stop shop" for testing services and procedures. The company had also begun developing an outsourcing arm, taking over the research, testing, and analysis operations for third parties, including a nutritional assay outsourcing agreement with Glon Sanders reached in 2002.

By the end of 2004, Eurofins had consolidated its position as a global leader in the testing and analysis segment, with more than 10,000 procedures in its portfolio and sales topping EUR 175 million. The company counted most of the world's biggest food and pharmaceutical groups as clients. Meanwhile, Eurofins continued to look for new acquisition opportunities. In January 2005, for example, the company completed its acquisition of a 25 percent stake in Germany's MWG-Biotech. Eurofins had prepared itself to benefit from the rising health and safety concerns focused on the world's food, agro-industrial, chemical, and pharmaceuticals industries.

Principal Subsidiaries

ADME Bioanalyses SAS; Analytico Food BV (Netherlands); Analytico Medinet BV (Netherlands); Analytico Milieu BV (Netherlands); Analytico Milieu NV (Belgium); Dr Specht & Partner GmbH (Germany); ES Développement SAS; Eurofins (NI) Ltd. (Northern Ireland); Eurofins Analytics GmbH (Germany); Eurofins Danmark A/S (Denmark); Eurofins Environnement SAS; Eurofins Scientific (Ireland) Ltd.; Eurofins Scientific AG (Switzerland); Eurofins Scientific Analytics SAS; Eurofins Scientific Biosciences SAS; Eurofins Scientific BV (Netherlands); Eurofins Scientific GmbH (Germany); Eurofins Scientific Inc. (United States); Eurofins Scientific Ltd. (United Kingdom); Eurofins Scientific Ltd.; Eurofins Scientific Test Center SAS; Eurofins Sverige AB (Sweden); Eurofins Ventures BV; Eurofins Ventures BV (Netherlands); GeneScan Analytics GmbH (Germany); GeneScan do Brazil Ltda.; GeneScan Europe AG (Germany); GeneScan Hong Kong Ltd.; GeneScan USA Inc; GfA mbH (Germany); Le Chardonnay Sci; Medigenomix GmbH (Germany); M-Lab AS (Norway).

Principal Competitors

GenTek Inc.; Altera Corporation; IDEXX Laboratories Inc.; Groupe SGS France; RWTUV AG; ENUSA Industrias Avanzadas S.A.; Core Laboratories Inc.

Further Reading

"Eurofins," *Business Week*, October 25, 2004, p. 56.

"Eurofins Buys Majority of GeneScan AG," *Feedstuffs*, July 28, 2003, p. 6.

"Eurofins Maintains Growth with Frankfurt Dual Listing," *Euroweek*, October 13, 2000, p. 17.

"Eurofins Scientific Acquires 51% of Dutch Firm, Analytico Food," *Fund Action*, September 20, 2000.

"Eurofins Scientific a les moyens de sa croissance," *L'Expansion*, December 4, 1997.

"GeneScan do Brazil Gets Ministry Accreditation," *Nutraceuticals International*, July 2003.

Pinaud, Olivier, " 'Nous sommes optimistes pour la suite de l'année.' " *Investir*, August 29, 2001.

—M.L. Cohen

Faurecia S.A.

2 rue Hennape
Nanterre
F-92735 Cedex
France
Telephone: +33 1 72 36 70 00
Fax: +33 1 72 36 70 07
Web site: http://www.faurecia.com

Public Company
Incorporated: 1998
Employees: 52,041
Sales: EUR 10.12 billion ($13.25 billion) (2003)
Stock Exchanges: Euronext Paris
Ticker Symbol: EPED.PA
NAIC: 336399 All Other Motor Vehicle Parts
Manufacturing; 332510 Hardware Manufacturing;
332991 Ball and Roller Bearing Manufacturing;
332999 All Other Miscellaneous Fabricated Metal
Product Manufacturing; 333612 Speed Changer,
Industrial High-Speed Drive, and Gear Manufacturing;
333613 Mechanical Power Transmission Equipment
Manufacturing; 336311 Carburetor, Piston, Piston
Ring and Valve Manufacturing; 337127 Institutional
Furniture Manufacturing

Faurecia S.A. is a leading automotive components supplier focusing on six core products lines: car seats, cockpits, exhaust systems, acoustic package, doors, and front ends. The company is the leading European producer in all but one of these products (it is number two in acoustic packages) and also holds the number two and three position in each of these categories worldwide. Seats account for the largest percentage of Faurecia's sales, which topped EUR 10 billion ($13 billion) in 2003, representing 43 percent of group revenues. Acoustic packages, cockpits, and doors combine to generate 34 percent of group sales, and exhaust systems and front-ends add 16 percent and 7 percent, respectively. Faurecia supplies components to most of the world's major automotive manufacturers, with PSA Peugeot-Citroen and Volkswagen representing its largest customers, at 28 percent and 23.5 percent of sales,

respectively. Other significant customers include Renault Nissan, Ford, General Motors, DaimlerChrysler, and BMW. These seven companies represent nearly 95 percent of group sales. Faurecia supports its operations with a worldwide network of subsidiaries, with production facilities in 27 countries and more than 50,000 employees. Faurecia is listed on the Euronext Paris Stock Exchange; PSA remains the company's majority stockholder, with 71 percent of stock.

French Automotive Origins in the Early 20th Century

Faurecia S.A. was formed in 1998 through the merger of two prominent French automotive component suppliers, Bertrand Faure and ECIA, the former components unit of PSA Peugeot-Citroen. In 2001, Faurecia acquired the automotive division of Sommer Allibert, thereby forming Europe's leading automotive component supplier.

ECIA stemmed from Peugeot's rapid growth in the post-World War II period, when automobile use became commonplace in France. The company began establishing new subsidiaries specialized in the development and production of automotive components and subsystems. Peugeot also diversified into other product areas, such as motorcycles and scooters, power tools, hand tools, lawnmowers and other gardening equipment, and bicycles. Two of the primary subsidiaries to emerge from this period were Aciers et Outillage Peugeot and Peugeot Cycles.

In the mid-1970s, however, these subsidiaries began to refocus around their core automotive components business, launching a long-term divestment program—the last of these noncore activities was sold off only in the late 1990s. In the meantime, both Aciers et Outillage Peugeot and Peugeot Cycles began acquiring scale and competencies in a variety of automotive components. Among the components categories produced by the Peugeot subsidiaries were electric motors (for window mechanisms and sideview mirrors, and other uses), bumpers, hubcaps, steering wheels, and steering columns.

Much of this effort came through a series of acquisitions starting in 1980 and culminating in the purchase of Bertrand Faure in 1998. Among the companies' purchases during this time were the molded plastics company Quillery, and Tubauto, a maker of seat cages and racks. The company became a major producer of exhaust systems through its acquisition of Eli Echappements, and also moved to add a number of foreign operations, including Germany's Leistritz and PCG of Spain.

The refocusing of the two subsidiaries around an automotive components core led to their merger in 1987. The combined company took on the name of ECIA, for Equipements et Composants pour l'Industrie Automobile. ECIA was then listed on the Paris Stock Exchange. Peugeot maintained majority control of ECIA, and remained the company's primary company. Indeed, into the late 1990s, Peugeot continued to account for some 94 percent of ECIA's automotive components-based revenues. Yet the spin-off of ECIA was made in part to improve its efficiency—by enabling it to compete for contracts from automakers other than PSA.

By 1997, ECIA had picked up contracts with a number of other automakers, including Volkswagen and Renault, which represented 18 and 11 percent, respectively, of ECIA's revenues that year, compared with PSA Peugeot-Citroen's 60 percent. Other customers included Daimler Benz, Opel Honda, and Mitsubishi. By then, the company's sales had topped EUR 1.6 billion—double its sales in 1987. The percentage of automotive components in ECIA's total revenues had more than tripled during this time.

By the late 1990s, ECIA had focused its automotive components operations around three primary areas: exhaust systems, cockpits (including acoustic packages), and front ends. The company's merger with Bertrand Faure in 1998 not only doubled its sales again, but also positioned it as a leader in a new automotive component category.

Merging for Scale in the 1990s

Bertrand Faure had its origins in the early 20th century as a seat-maker for France's trams and the Paris Metro. The company established its first workshop in 1914, shortly before the outbreak of World War I. In the 1920s, the company became interested in the growing automobile market. A significant step in this direction came in 1929 when Faure acquired the patents for the Epéda spring system. This spring system enabled the company, later known as Epéda-Bertrand Faure, to begin producing a new generation of more comfortable automobile seats, which in turn allowed the company to emerge as a French leader in this category.

The spring technology also encouraged Faure to begin producing a new type of mattress, and that activity became a major source of the group's revenues as well. In 1973, the company acquired another mattress maker, Mérinos, becoming a leader in this segment in France. In the meantime, Faure had continued building its automotive seating operation, acquiring two French companies, Cousin Frères, which produced seat frame systems, and Autocoussin, which specialized in rear seat designs.

Faure began a diversification drive of its own in the late 1980s. In 1987, for example, the company acquired Delsey, a leading maker of suitcases. That year also saw Bertrand Faure enter the defense industry, when it acquired Luchaire. That company manufactured components for the aerospace industry, but also produced automotive components through subsidiaries Allinquant (shock absorbers) and Eli Echappement (exhaust systems).

Epéda-Bertrand Faure fought off a hostile takeover attempt by another major French automotive components maker, Valeo, in 1988. In order to prevent Valeo, then controlled by Italy's CERUS, from gaining control of its stock, Faure turned to a number of investors, including Peugeot, Michel Thierry, and Michelin. These companies backed a leveraged buyout (LBO) of Faure, which, through a complex financial structure, protected the company from the takeover attempt. Yet the buyout left Faure in an extremely precarious financial system.

The company's difficulties were quickly exacerbated in the early 1990s. In 1991, the company acquired control of Germany's Rentrop, a major seating systems manufacturer in that country. Faure also bought a stake in Italy's Sepi. But the company's bid to establish itself as a major player in Europe's automotive seating sector stumbled on the deepening economic recession in the region in the early 1990s. Adding to the company's problems was a push by its major American competitors, Lear and Johnson Controls, to enter the European automotive components market as well.

Faure began a restructuring effort into the mid-1990s in order to restore its financial balance. As part of that process, the company refocused around a core of automobile seating systems, selling off its bedding operations in 1994 and its aerospace and defense operations in 1996. The company later divested Delsey as well. By 1997, automobile components accounted for more than 91 percent of Faure's sales, which topped EUR 2.4 billion that year.

In 1996, however, the complexity of Faure's LBO package turned against the company, when Michel Thierry decided to sell its 16.6 percent stake in Faure to ECIA. This move precipitated talks between the two companies, leading to a full-scale takeover offer by ECIA for Faure at the end of 1997. The merger, completed in 1998, created a new French and European giant, Faurecia. While Faurecia remained controlled by PSA Peugeot-Citroen, which held more than 70 percent of its shares and remained its primary customer, the new company was established as an independently operating company.

Global Components Leader in the New Century

Faurecia immediately began developing its position as a leading European—and global—automotive components player. The company launched a new strategy to focus on a more limited range

Key Dates:

1914: Bertrand Faure opens a workshop to produce seats for trams and Metro trains.

1929: Faure acquires Epéda spring patent and begins production of seating systems for the automotive market.

1945: Peugeot begins production of automotive components, bicycles, and motorcycles through subsidiaries Aciers et Outillage Peugeot and Peugeot Cycles.

1987: Aciers et Outillage Peugeot and Peugeot Cycles are merged to form ECIA; Faure acquires Delsey and Luchaire.

1988: Bertrand Faure is acquired in a LBO backed by Michelin, Michel Thierry, Peugeot, and others to block a takeover attempt by Valeo.

1991: Faure acquires Rentrop in Germany.

1997: Faure agrees to be acquired by ECIA, forming Faurecia.

1999: Faurecia acquires AP Automotive Systems in the United States.

2001: Faurecia acquires the automotive components operations of Sommer Allibert.

2003: Faurecia wins a $2 billion contract for production of cockpit components for Chrysler in the United States.

of systems, narrowing its operations to a smaller array of core areas in which it was able to establish leadership positions. As part of that process, the company sold off its steering wheel operations in 1999, and also divested noncore operations, such as Peugeot Motorcycles and Delsey, both in 1998.

Instead, Faurecia began expanding its international presence, opening new plants in Brazil and Poland in 1998. The following year, the company turned to North America, acquiring AP Automotive Systems (APAS), that market's third largest producer of exhaust systems. Faurecia's North American presence was boosted that year as well when it was awarded a major production contract for General Motors. The company quickly began extending its production capacity in North America, opening or acquiring factories to reach nearly 30 facilities in that market by 2005.

By then, however, Faurecia had taken a place among Europe's leading automotive components groups and, in its core components areas, had lifted itself to place in the top three worldwide. The most significant step in this growth came in 2001, when the company acquired the automotive division of France's struggling Sommer Allibert. That company's diversified product range included plastic products for bathroom and kitchen; its automotive segment, however, accounted for the largest part of its revenues, some 61.5 percent of sales of nearly EUR 3.5 billion. Sommer Allibert brought a new specialty to Faurecia, that of automotive cockpits, including acoustic packages.

The purchase, which cost nearly EUR 1.5 billion ($1.2 billion), boosted Faurecia into the global top five among automotive components suppliers, with a nearly 7 percent share of the worldwide market. Nonetheless, the acquisition, coupled with the group's other expansion efforts, notably in the United

States, proved difficult to digest. Already losing money at the end of the 20th century, Faurecia's losses continued into the new century, with losses reaching $42 million in 2001 and $59 million in 2002.

Despite these financial difficulties, Faurecia continued making headway in its efforts to expand its geographic base, launching new production joint ventures in China in 2002 and in Korea in 2003, as well as a cockpit production joint venture with Siemens VDO. In that year, the company launched construction of a new manufacturing plant in China, in the city of Wuxi.

Faurecia made headway in its effort to diversify its client base. By 2005, the company had added contracts for a widening range of automakers, including Volvo, DaimlerChrysler, Saab, and BMW. Faurecia also emerged as a major supplier to General Motors at mid-decade. In October 2004, the company began production of cockpits for the new Pontiac G6, beating out usual favorites Johnson Controls and Lear for the contract. Then in November 2004, Faurecia received a contract worth nearly $2 billion to produce instrument panels, door panels, center consoles, and other cockpit components for Chrysler's U.S. automobiles. Faurecia had established itself as a clear and growing force in the global automotive components market.

Principal Subsidiaries

Blériot Investissements; Faurecia Automotive Holdings (formerly Sommer Allibert); Faurecia Automotive Holdings, Inc.; Faurecia Exhaust International; Faurecia Global Purchasing; Faurecia Investments; Faurecia Netherlands Holding B.V. (Netherlands); Faurecia Services Groupe; Faurecia USA Holdings, Inc. (United States); Financière Faurecia; SFEA – Société Foncière pour l'Équipement Automobile; SIP Werwaltungs GmbH Germany; Société Internationale de Participations (SIP) Belgium; United Parts Exhaust Systems AB.

Principal Competitors

ArvinMeritor Inc.; Lear Corporation; Johnson Controls International Inc.; Valeo S.A.; Tyco International Ltd.; Delphi Corporation; Bridgestone Corporation; MAN AG; Siemens VDO Automotive Corporation; Mondragon Corporacion Cooperativa; Valeo S.A.; Valeo GmbH; Magna International Inc.; American Standard Companies Inc.

Further Reading

Beecham, Matthew, ''Faurecia: Company Profile,'' *just-auto.com*, May 2004.

Miel, Rhoda, ''Faurecia Grows Business in N. America,'' *Automotive News Europe*, November 1, 2004, p. 21.

Murphy, Tom, ''Take A Seat,'' *Ward's Auto World*, November 1, 2004.

Saint-Seine, Sylviane de, ''Faurecia Adjusts After Buying Sommer-Allibert,'' *Automotive News*, May 19, 2003, p. 28F.

Schut, Jan H., ''Long-Glass Leader: How Faurecia Helped Put TP Composites in the Driver's Seat,'' *Plastics Technology*, August 2002, p. 44.

Sherefkin, Robert, ''GM Deals Put Faurecia into N.A. Big League,'' *Automotive News*, November 15, 2004, p. 30F.

White, Liz, ''Faurecia Gets Bigger,'' *Urethanes Technology*, December 2000, p. 6.

—M.L. Cohen

Fresh, Fast & Delicious

Fili Enterprises, Inc.

7578 Trade Street
San Diego, California 92121
U.S.A.
Telephone: (858) 831-0334
Toll Free: (888) 414-7335
Fax: (858) 831-0411
Web site: http://daphnesgreekcafe.com

Private Company
Incorporated: 1991
Employees: 500
Sales: $40.0 million (2004)
NAIC: 722211 Limited-Service Eating Restaurants

Fili Enterprises, Inc., operates a chain of more than 50 fast-casual Greek restaurants called Daphne's Greek Café. The restaurants are located in California, offering a selection of kabobs, gyros, pita sandwiches, and spanakopita. The majority of the chain's restaurants are located in southern California and situated in strip malls and shopping centers. Per-person check averages are between $6.50 and $7 during lunch and between $8 and $9 during dinner.

Origins

Daphne's Greek Café's founder, president, and chief executive officer, George Katakalidis, entered the restaurant business to start his second career. He was unemployed, unable to continue with his chosen profession, that of a professional athlete. Born in Greece, but raised in Canada, Katakalidis showed early promise as a soccer player, not only earning a place on Canada's National Youth Team but picked to captain the side. While attending high school in Toronto, Katakalidis attracted the attention of scouts for the New York Arrows, four-time champions of the Major Indoor Soccer League (MISL). Katakalidis joined the professional ranks, playing in two of North America's professional leagues in existence during the 1980s, the North American Soccer League (NASL) and the MISL. He played for the Arrows and the NASL's Golden Bay Earthquakes, ending his career with the MISL's San Diego

Sockers. While playing for the Sockers, Katakalidis broke his toe, an injury that ended his career at the end of the 1980s.

Katakalidis' tour of cities left him in San Diego with nothing to do. He noticed that his new hometown lacked any substantial enclave of Greek culture or cuisine. San Diego, unlike Toronto, could not claim to have a flourishing Greek town. "I thought someone should open a really good Greek place," Katakalidis reflected in a January 31, 2005 interview with *Nation's Restaurant News,* recalling his thoughts at the beginning of the 1990s. "I was unemployed, so maybe that someone was me," he added.

From the start, Katakalidis envisioned a dining destination that the restaurant industry defined as "quick-casual." Quick-casual establishments occupied the middle ground separating full-service restaurants and fast-food restaurants such as Burger King and McDonald's, offering limited service, sit-down dining. Katakalidis came to dominate this niche of the Greek dining market, but his path toward dominance followed a conservative, methodical course. Katakalidis did not begin by opening dozens of restaurants annually; he took his time, carefully honing his concept before considering ambitious expansion plans.

Katakalidis turned to his family for help in starting his career as a restaurateur. He asked for recipes from his aunts and uncles and from his mother, upon whom he conferred the title of executive chef. He used the recipes to develop a menu, but he altered the various recipes in the same way he had while playing soccer professionally. He cut back on the oil and spices used in the traditional Greek dishes, making them less robust—a change he felt was necessary to attract American diners.

For a name for his restaurant, Katakalidis turned to Greek mythology. He, like the Apollo of lore, was attracted to Daphne, a woman whose unrivaled beauty and grace captured the hearts of all who saw her, none more so than Zeus' son, Apollo. Weary of checking Apollo's endless advances, Daphne asked her father, the River God, to intervene. The River God turned Daphne into a laurel tree, which Apollo used to create a wreath in her memory—a wreath that came to symbolize the pursuit of perfection, worn by Olympic athletes and world leaders.

The first Daphne's Greek Café opened north of San Diego, in Del Mar, in 1991. Like his changes with traditional Greek recipes, Katakalidis chose to stray away from convention with the décor of his restaurants. He avoided the typical blue-and-white color scheme of Greek restaurants in favor of designs that lessened the ethnicity of his establishments. The reasoning behind the decision, like the reasoning behind altering his family's recipes, was to broaden the appeal of his restaurants. Katakalidis was compelled to start Daphne's Greek Café because of his love of Greek cuisine and his pride in being Greek, but he discovered that greater success was achieved by toning down the taste of his food and the look of his restaurants. "When we open our units, they have a tough time in the beginning," Katakalidis explained in his January 31, 2005 interview with *Nation's Restaurant News*. "It's still ethnic, and there is still a huge learning curve associated with it. It's not burgers. It's not Mexican food." Accordingly, the décor of Daphne's Greek Cafés, which changed several times during the company's first 15 years in business, tended to project a less distinctive look, designed in a contemporary, European style.

Slow Expansion During the 1990s

The opening of the Del Mar Daphne's Greek Café was followed by the debut of other restaurants, but at a slow pace. Katakalidis' limited cash reserves and the need to accustom each market to Greek cuisine dictated a measured pace of expansion. Katakalidis added no more than several new units annually and never risked a great geographic leap. The company's 2,000-square-foot restaurants, which offered seating for 50 patrons and employed between 15 and 20 workers, slowly crept out of San Diego County during the 1990s. Daphne's Greek Café expanded in neighboring counties, moving north into Los Angeles, Orange, and Riverside counties during the decade.

As Daphne's Greek Café gradually developed into a chain, Katakalidis fine-tuned his concept. Changes were made in the menu and in design, making the company a pioneer in fashioning a quick-casual Greek restaurant chain. What emerged was a popular but small group of restaurants that cultivated a loyal following. Patrons were greeted at the door and asked if they had frequented a Daphne's Greek Café before. If a customer responded in the negative, he or she was offered a brief tutorial on the menu. Orders were placed at a central cash register and the selection, prepared in an open kitchen, was brought to the customer's table. Service was quick, with most patrons finishing their meal within a half-hour of entering one of Katakalidis' establishments.

Once a market was introduced to Daphne's Greek Café food selections, the reception generally was positive—although as Katakalidis pointed out, it often took some time for a new unit to draw in a steady stream of customers. Those patrons who came and returned chose from a menu that included the staples of Greek cooking. Among the offerings on a Daphne's Greek

Café menu were: chicken-and-steak ka-bobs, featuring flame-broiled skewers marinated in lemon, herbs, and spices; gyros; a variety of pita sandwiches; hummus; Greek salads; spanakopita; rice pilaf; avgolemono (egg lemon) soup; and tzatziki sauce. The most distinctive of the items offered was something Katakalidis dubbed "Fire Feta," a creamy feta cheese with four varieties of peppers and 14 seasonings. Fire Feta was offered as a side order and as an addition to salads, sandwiches, and combination plates. The selections on the menu were moderately priced, with the average lunchtime ticket ranging between $6.50 and $7 per person and the average dinnertime ticket ranging between $8 and $9 per person. Most of the chain's restaurants offered a selection of wine and beer. The dessert menu consisted of "Daphne's Baklava," cinnamon and crushed walnuts in layers of fillo.

Expansion Accelerating at the Dawn of the 21st Century

After nearly a decade of moderately paced expansion, Katakalidis shifted into a higher gear in 1999. For the ensuing six years, Daphne's Greek Café recorded annual revenue growth of 30 percent as the chain expanded. By 2002, the chain had developed into a $17 million-in-sales enterprise, a total generated by the nearly 30 restaurants in operation by the year's end. Katakalidis slipped past the 30-unit mark in 2003, but the year's most noteworthy event was the geographic leap completed in the summer. For more than a decade, Katakalidis had restricted his expansion to southern California, fleshing out the presence of the chain in San Diego, Los Angeles, Orange, and Riverside counties. In July 2003, he ventured into the northern reaches of the state, opening a Daphne's Greek Café in Roseville, a suburb of Sacramento. The Roseville restaurant served as a test unit to determine whether additional restaurants would be established outside southern California. Katakalidis monitored the results of the Roseville unit for several months before approving further expansion. Within two years, four additional restaurants were opened in northern California.

The opening of the Roseville restaurant reflected Katakalidis' growing confidence in his concept. At around the time the Roseville unit opened, Katakalidis hired two executives to help him ramp up expansion and fully express his confidence. Ed Huban was hired as director of real estate, bringing with him years of experience gained while working for Pick Up Stix, a chain of Asian restaurants owned by Texas-based Carlson Restaurants Worldwide, Inc. Katakalidis also hired Julie Lanthier Brady, a marketer at Karl Strauss Brewery, as Daphne's Greek Café's senior marketing manager. Together, the trio began expanding the chain at a record pace, opening ten restaurants in 2003 and 17 new units in 2004, more than doubling the size of the company during the two-year period.

As the chain expanded, each unit added close to $1 million in sales to its parent company's revenue volume. To draw in customers, the company usually staged what it called a "Big Fat Greek Fundraiser," an event inspired by the popular motion picture, *My Big Fat Greek Wedding*. Donations from invited guests at such events were given to a local charity in the community in which the restaurant was located. These grand opening celebrations typified the company's marketing strategy, which relied little on paying for advertising. "We market

---

Key Dates:

1991: George Katakalidis opens his first Daphne's Greek Café in Del Mar, California.

1999: The pace of expansion accelerates, fueling an annual growth rate of 30 percent.

2003: A Daphne's Greek Café opens in Roseville, California, the first in the northern half of the state.

2004: The chain is expanded by 17 restaurants, the most grand openings in a single year in the company's history.

2005: Daphne's Greek Café begins construction of a restaurant in Scottsdale, Arizona, the first unit outside California.

---

mostly by reaching out to the community,'' Brady remarked in a January 31, 2005, interview with *Nation's Restaurant News*. When a new store opened, employees frequently visited neighboring businesses, offering free appetizers. Occasionally, the addition of a new unit to the chain was advertised through a direct-mail campaign that targeted residences and businesses near the new restaurant.

With 50 restaurants in operation by the end of 2004, Daphne's Greek Café ranked as the leading quick-casual Greek food chain in the country. Daphne's Greek Café's nearest rivals operated thousands of miles away from the company's stronghold in southern California and operated far fewer restaurants. The chain closest in size to Katakalidis' enterprise was a Calgary, Alberta-based chain called Opa! Souvlaki, which operated 27 restaurants. In the United States, Daphne's Greek Café dwarfed the country's only other contender, a group of four restaurants called Louis Pappas Market Café, which was based in Tarpon Springs, Florida. "Daphne's has no comparable [quick-casual restaurants] to equate them with," the president of a restaurant consulting firm said in the January 31, 2005 issue of *Nation's Restaurant News*. "They are setting the barometer for what quick-casual Greek should be."

As Katakalidis prepared for the future, his expansion plans promised to widen the gap separating his San Diego-based company from others competing in the quick-casual Greek niche. He planned to open at least 20 new restaurants in 2005, the most ambitious undertaking in the company's history. Katakalidis' boldest move of 2005 was his first step outside California's borders, a move that opened up numerous new markets for Daphne's Greek Café. In early 2005, the company was building a restaurant in Scottsdale, Arizona, with its success, like that of the Roseville restaurant, promising the establishment of additional units in surrounding markets. In the future, the evolution of Daphne's Greek Cafe into a southwestern chain appeared likely, provided Katakalidis continued to record success in the quick-casual segment he dominated.

Principal Subsidiaries

Daphne's Greek Café.

Principal Competitors

Garden Fresh Restaurant Corporation; Panera Bread Company; Rubio's Restaurants, Inc.

Further Reading

Berta, Dina, "Daphne's Greek Café: Ex-Pro Soccer Player Scores Points, Gains Fans by Sharing Love of Native Fare with General Public," *Nation's Restaurant News,* January 31, 2005, p. 84.

Chapman, Mary Boltz, "On the Light Side: Fast-Casual Daphne's Updates Greek Food for Its California Customers," *Chain Leader,* May 2003, p. 30.

Choi, Candice, "More Diners Getting in Olympic Mood with Food," *Daily News,* August 21, 2004, p. B1.

"Daphne's Greek Chain Expands to No. Calif.," *Nation's Restaurant News,* July 28, 2003, p. 166.

"Daphne's, a 32-Unit Greek Fast-Casual Chain, Opened Its First Northern California Outlet Here July 18," *Nation's Restaurant News,* July 21, 2003, p. 1.

Lewis, Connie, "Daphne's Opens in Hillcrest," *San Diego Business Journal,* September 13, 2004, p. 34.

Lipson, Larry, "Daphne's Does Greek Quickly," *Daily News,* January 24, 2003, p. U42.

Spector, Amy, "Expanding Fast-Casual Greek Chains Carve Niche in Market," *Nation's Restaurant News,* August 11, 2003, p. 4.

—Jeffrey L. Covell

Gate Gourmet International AG

Balsberg, P.O. Box QV
CH-8058 Zurich-Airport
Switzerland
Telephone: (+41) 43 812 54 80
Fax: (+41) 1 810 91 75
Web site: http://www.gategourmet.com

Private Company
Incorporated: 1992 as Gate Gourmet Management AG
Employees: 22,000
Sales: CHF 2.3 billion ($1.9 billion) (2003)
NAIC: 722110 Full-Service Restaurants; 424820 Wine
    and Distilled Alcoholic Beverage Merchant
    Wholesalers; 541990 All Other Professional, Scientific
    and Technical Services

Gate Gourmet International AG is a leading supplier of in-flight food service for the global airline industry. A spinoff of Swissair, the company has grown to become one of the two largest caterers in the industry. Gate Gourmet's 120 flight kitchens in 30 countries prepare 530,000 meals a day. Gate Gourmet pioneered the direct-to-customer in-flight meal concept after airlines cut back catering services on domestic flights following the September 11, 2001 attacks on the United States. Gate Gourmet also offers supply chain management, inspection and validation services, and in-flight equipment sourcing through its e-gatematrix, Gatesafe, and FiveOceans enterprises.

Early 1990s Origins

Gate Gourmet Group was formed in 1992 as Gate Gourmet Management AG when Swissair made its catering operations, including ICS International Catering Services, a separate company. It was owned by Swissair Associated Companies Ltd. (also Swissair Participations SA or Swissair Beteiligungen AG) along with the much smaller Nuance Trading AG (duty-free sales) and Restorama AG (staff canteens). The company's president and chief executive was Wolfgang Werlé, formerly director of customer service and business development at Deutsche Lufthansa AG's LSG Sky Chefs catering unit.

Gate Gourmet was then the world's eighth largest airline caterer, with 34 locations and 5,300 employees. It had annual revenues of CHF 780 million and supplied almost 130,000 meals per day to 30 airlines. According to *Le Temps,* Gate Gourmet was spun off in an atmosphere of intense competition among caterers due to the global recession. It had to streamline its operations as a result.

The newly independent company grew quickly. Papadacos Catering of Athens was acquired later in 1992. Gate Gourmet ended the eventful year by opening a new $7 million flight kitchen in Johannesburg, South Africa, in a joint venture (called Air Caterers Johannesburg) with the Fedics industrial catering firm.

Gate Gourmet acquired a majority (80 percent) interest in airline catering company AERO-CHEF from Denmark's Sterling Airways in late 1992. This brought Gate Gourmet into the ranks of the world's top five caterers. Turnover was CHF 800 million and the company had 44 units. In March 1993, Gate Gourmet opened a joint venture with Abela at London's Heathrow Airport.

SSP Acquisition in 1994

Gate Gourmet doubled in size through the August 1994 acquisition of the airline and railway catering operations of Sweden's SAS Service Partner (SSP), which had annual sales of SEK 4.8 billion and 32 catering operations in 13 countries. The CHF 250 million buy made Gate Gourmet the third largest caterer in the world, with 13,000 people working at 64 locations in 21 countries. Total sales were about CHF 1 billion a year.

In 1995 and 1996, Gate Gourmet acquired far-flung operations, buying flight kitchens from KLM in Thailand and VARIG in Brazil. Catering operations were also acquired in Portugal. In 1996, the company upgraded its facilities at Heathrow, Geneva, and Amsterdam airports.

In January 1996, company president Wolfgang Werlé moved on to head Swissair Associated Companies (SAC), which included Rail Gourmet, Swissôtel, Nuance, Restorama, and Restosana. Werlé was succeeded as Gate Gourmet president and CEO by Henning Boysen. SAC was renamed the

SAirRelations division in December 1996. Swissair Group was renamed SAir Group at this time.

Two South American acquisitions were made in 1997. Gate Gourmet bought Santiago's La Marmite flight kitchen in July and the Lima-based Aeroservicios Peruanos flight kitchen in March.

In October 1997, Gate Gourmet acquired the Heathrow-based long-haul catering operations of British Airways for £65 million. During the year, Gate Gourmet also entered into a joint venture with Manila Integrated Airport Services and Malaysian Airlines System Berhad for a new facility in the Philippines.

In 1998, Gate Gourmet opened operations in Hong Kong (March) and Manila (December). Its revenues for the year were CHF 1.7 billion ($1.2 billion).

Gate Gourmet entered the Iber-Swiss Catering venture at Barcelona Airport in January 1999. It reached an agreement to buy out the remaining 70 percent of Iber-Swiss it did not own five years later for EUR 23.5 million.

Gate Gourmet bought Australian catering operations from Cathay Pacific Catering Services in March 1999 and Ansett Australia in November 1999. Catering operations were also acquired in Ecuador in March. Italy's Ligabue Catering S.p.A. was acquired in December 1999. The company also obtained catering operations in Mexico.

Dobbs Acquired in 1999

An important buy was the $780 million acquisition of Dobbs International Services, Inc. from Phoenix-based Viad Corp. in July 1999. Memphis-based Dobbs had 1998 revenues of $891 million and 60 flight kitchens, all but five of them in the United States, where Gate Gourmet had been conspicuously absent. It was tops in the U.S. train catering market. The company also had five flight kitchens in Great Britain. Dobbs had been founded in Memphis in 1946 as Dobbs House, a spin-off of the Jack Sprat Corp.

Expanding into the United States was important as more airlines were seeking vendors capable of global support. The Dobbs acquisition brought Gate Gourmet's market share to 25 percent. It was the world's second largest airline catering company, with revenues of more than $2 billion a year and 26,000 employees working at 142 flight kitchens in 27 countries. Following the Dobbs buy, Gate Gourmet was restructured into three geographic divisions: Europe, America, and Asia/Pacific.

Units were opened at Shanghai Pudong International in September of the year and Paris Charles de Gaulle in October 1999. Seven Australian operations were acquired from Ansett in November 1999.

Gate Gourmet acquired in-flight catering equipment supplier Jet Logistics in January 2000. It opened a Latin America office in Miami in 2000.

A new state-of-the-art CHF 128.4 million plant opened in Zurich in 2000. It was designed upon just-in-time principles (production scheduled around aircraft departure times) to reduce refrigeration costs and improve freshness. Many processes were fully automated. In spite of its increased capacity of 48,000 meals per day, the new 32,000-square-meter plant took up 5,000 square meters less space than its predecessor. New flight kitchens were also opened in Paris and Shanghai in 2000.

Around this time, the company was partnering with Dallas-based i2 Technologies Inc. to create a new online marketplace for travel-related catering services. Called e-gatematrix, the new venture aimed to streamline in-flight food service ordering. A single flight could require 40,000 items, ranging from toothpicks to beverage carts. E-gatematrix was based in Atlanta; neighboring Delta Air Lines was first to sign a long-term contract with it.

Retrenching in 2001

By 2001, Gate Gourmet had 30,000 employees in 34 countries. However, ten percent of the workforce (mostly in North America) was laid off soon after the September 11, 2001 terrorist attacks on the United States. While they were flying fewer passengers, airlines were also scaling back their food offerings to cut costs.

Gate Gourmet's Australian operations were dramatically scaled back in 2001 following the failure of Ansett Australia. Ansett folded owing the Gate Gourmet operation AUD$26 million ($13 million).

At the same time, parent company Swissair Group was going through its own bankruptcy. Gate Gourmet was not placed in administration because it was profitable.

The investment firm Texas Pacific Group acquired Gate Gourmet in 2002. The deal had to pass regulatory muster in Switzerland and the United States and was closed in December of the year.

New flight kitchens opened at Port Columbus, Ohio, and San Diego in December 2001, Phoenix Sky Harbor International Airport in January 2002, and New York JFK in January 2003. The flight kitchen at Miami International was replaced in 2003.

A la Carte in 2003

As airlines eliminated meal service on many domestic flights, Gate Gourmet moved to fill the void by offering à la carte food items for sale direct to passengers. A $7–$10 lunch

Key Dates:

1992: A majority interest in Aero-Chef is acquired.
1994: The acquisition of SSP SAS Service Partner doubles Gate Gourmet's size.
1999: The acquisition of Dobbs International Services adds vast U.S. presence.
2001: Ansett collapse and the aftermath of September 11, 2001 attacks on the United States force layoffs.
2002: Texas Pacific Group acquires Gate Gourmet.
2003: Culinary Academy is opened; direct-to-passenger food sales is introduced.
2005: Division Americas HQ is relocated to Virginia.

and snack concept was tested on Northwestern Airlines flights in March 2003. This was followed by a trial of Eli's Cheesecake Co.-branded sandwiches and desserts on one of United Express routes. A similar concept was brought to Delta's Song offshoot and Swiss International Air Lines (SWISS) in October 2003.

United Airlines switched its O'Hare catering business to Gate Gourmet in late 2003. The next year, Gate Gourmet won a bid to supply the new Qantas offshoot, Jetstar, making up some ground it had lost down under in the Ansett collapse.

The operation now employed about 300 chefs around the world. Gate Gourmet opened its Culinary Academy in September 2003. Division Americas CEO George Alvord described to the University of Memphis publication *Business Perspectives* the challenge of retaining employees in a 24/7 flight kitchen environment versus competition from the restaurant industry.

David N. Siegel succeeded Henning Boysen as company chairman and CEO in June 2004. He had guided US Airways through its bankruptcy in 2002 and 2003. Before that, he oversaw Avis-Rent-A-Car's response to the post-9/11 travel slowdown. He also led the operational restructuring of Continental Airlines after Texas Pacific acquired a 40 percent stake in the then-bankrupt carrier during the mid-1990s.

In the winter of 2004–05, Gate Gourmet relocated its Division Americas headquarters to northern Virginia from Memphis, Tennessee.

Principal Subsidiaries

Gate Gourmet, Inc. (USA); Gate Gourmet Norge A.S.; Gate Gourmet Stockholm AB.

Principal Divisions

Americas; e-gatematrix; Europe; FiveOceans; Gate Safe.

Principal Competitors

LSG Sky Chefs; Servair SA.

Further Reading

"Airplane Leftovers Converted into Electricity," *Associated Press State & Local Wire*, July 8, 2001.

Alvord, George, "George Alvord on Customer Service," *Business Perspectives*, June 22, 2000, p. 16.

Ashworth, Jon, "SairGroup Pays £65m for BA's In-Flight Catering," *Times* (London), Bus. Sec., October 9, 1997.

Buffini, Fiona, "Staff Told Caterer's Cupboards Are Bare," *Australian Financial Review*, September 21, 2001, p. 21.

"Contract Caterer of Australia's Ansett in US\$36.77 Mln Collapse," *Asia Pulse*, September 20, 2001.

Cordes, Renee, and Kelly Holman," *Daily Deal,* March 27, 2002.

"Gate Gourmet Zurich Centre Progresses," *Airports International*, April 1, 1999, p. 16.

Grantham, Russell, "Caterer Cuts off Delta in Dispute; Nervous Vendors Uneasy with Threat of Bankruptcy, Say Industry Experts," *Atlanta Journal-Constitution*, September 22, 2004, p. A1.

——, "Caterer Resumes Service to Delta; Gate Gourmet Ordered by Judge to Deliver Food Drink in 50 Cities, Including Atlanta," *Atlanta Journal-Constitution*, September 23, 2004, p. F1.

Higgins, Kelly Jackson, "E-Gatematrix—In-Flight Supply Chain Takes Off," *Network Computing*, October 10, 1992, p. 69.

Hill, Leonard, "Healthy Appetite: Gate Gourmet Continues to Focus on Global Expansion," *Air Transport World*, November 1, 1997, p. 105.

Hutchings, William, "Texas Pacific Seals Gate Gourmet Buy-Out after Nine Months," *efinancialnews.com*, December 20, 2002.

"Iberia Sells Catering Unit Stake to Gate Gourmet Partner for EUR23.5 million," *Pais* (English edition), December 18, 2003, p. 6.

King, Paul, "Chain Operators Vie to 'Fly' Aboard In-Flight Meal Plans," *Nation's Restaurant News*, May 19, 2003, p. 3.

Koppel, Naomi, "Swissair Cuts 3,000 Catering Jobs, Announces Total Restructuring," *Associated Press State & Local Wire*, Bus. Sec., September 24, 2001.

"Meals on Wheels," *Food Manufacture*, February 1, 1999, p. 10.

Nielsen, Peter, "Gate Gourmet Sees Continued Expansion," *Reuters News*, December 15, 1994.

——, "Swissair's Gate Gourmet Boosts 1994 Profit," *Reuters News,* December 15, 1994.

"Outsourcing Airline Services Offers Cost Savings Opportunity," *Airline Financial News*, April 7, 1997.

Reed, Dan, "Food Fight: Airline Caterers Team with Brand Names," *USA Today*, March 31, 2004, p. B4.

——, "Former CEO of US Airways to Lead Big Airline Catering Company," *Charlotte Observer*, June 9, 2004.

Roberts, Jane, "Airline Caterer to Move Division Americas Headquarters to Washington," *Commercial Appeal* (Memphis), November 4, 2004.

——, "Caterer's New Ideas Take Flight," *Commercial Appeal* (Memphis), January 28, 2004, p. C1.

——, "Firm to Test In-Flight Meals to Passenger Purchase," *Commercial Appeal* (Memphis), March 19, 2003, p. C2.

"SAirGroup Catering Unit Builds New Plant at Zurich Airport," *Neue Zuercher Zeitung*, March 26, 1998, p. 31.

"SAirGroup's Gate Gourmet Restructures Into 3 Operating Divisions," *AFX News*, July 16, 1999.

"SAirGroup Unit Gate Gourmet Opens New Plant at Zurich Airport," *Neue Zuercher Zeitung*, September 30, 2000, p. 31.

"SAS Sells Catering Firm to Swissair Unit," *Reuters News*, June 6, 1994.

Studer, Margaret, "Swissair Parent to Buy Airline Caterer; Deal with Dobbs International Responds to Demand for One-Source Service," *Wall Street Journal*, May 20, 1999.

"Swissair Creates Subsidiaries for Catering, Duty-Free Services," *Aviation Daily*, July 31, 1992, p. 189.

"Swissair Hives off Catering Activities," *Neue Zuercher Zeitung*, July 30, 1992, p. 11.

"Swissair In-Flight Catering Unit Seeks to Cut Costs," *Temps*, June 3, 1993, p. 7.

"Swissair Plans New Catering and Baggage Handling Centre at Zurich Airport," *Neue Zuercher Zeitung*, October 29, 1996, p. 29.

"Switzerland's SAirGroup to Buy Viad's Catering Unit for $780 Million," *Dow Jones Business News*, May 18, 1999.

Thompson, Richard, "Merger to Open Gate to Airline E-Catering," *Commercial Appeal* (Memphis), May 3, 2000, p. C1.

Vandyk, Anthony, "So All Might Eat," *Air Transport World*, April 1, 1995, p. 76.

Warburton, Simon, "Dobbs/Gate Gourmet Merger Powers ahead of LSG," *Air Transport Intelligence*, May 19, 1999.

Werner, H.M., "Texas Pacific Serves up Gourmet Deal," *Buyouts*, April 15, 2002.

—Frederick C. Ingram

GEMA (Gesellschaft für musikalische Aufführungs- und mechanische Vervielfältigungsrechte)

Bayreuther Strasse 37
D-10787 Berlin
Germany
Telephone: (49) (30) 21245-00
Fax: (49) (30) 21245-950
Web site: http://www.gema.de

Not-For-Profit Company
Incorporated: 1903 as Anstalt für musikalisches
    Aufführungsrecht (AFMA)
Employees: 1,110
Sales: EUR 813.6 million ($1.2 billion) (2003)
NAIC: 813920 Professional Organizations

GEMA (Gesellschaft für musikalische Aufführungs- und mechanische Vervielfältigungsrechte) is Germany's equivalent of BMI or ASCAP in the United States, an organization that protects and promotes the creative work of composers, songwriters, and lyricists. The nonprofit association educates music users about copyrights, lobbies for a high level of copyright protection in Germany, and collects fees for the public performance of copyright-protected musical works in live settings, through the media, in movie theaters, shopping malls, bars, dance clubs, and even doctor's offices. GEMA also issues licenses for the mechanical reproduction of such works in exchange for a license fee and receives a percentage of the sale price for music copying devices and storage media such as CD-burners, blank CDRs, and cassette tapes. Traveling employees and independent contractors constantly monitor musical activities in Germany and make sure that every public performance of one of the roughly six million GEMA-protected works is properly registered and paid for. The collected fees are distributed to GEMA's 60,000 members in Germany and many thousands of copyright owners abroad with the help of a sophisticated computer system and according to a complex distribution scheme. GEMA cooperates with 117 similar organizations around the world and is overseen by Germany's patent office and antitrust agency.

Difficult Early Years Following Establishment of AFMA in 1903

The 1901 amendment of the German copyright law reestablished the exclusive right of composers to control the public performance of their works. On this legal foundation the collection of royalties for public performances of copyrighted music became possible. In the first half of the 19th century, Ludwig van Beethoven was among the few self-employed German composers to make a decent living. Most composers of classical music achieved a rather modest level of popularity and many of them struggled to make ends meet. As early as 1898, a group of German composers of classical music had established a cooperative to protect and exploit their public performance rights, the Genossenschaft Deutscher Komponisten (GDK), as an answer to a similar organization founded by leading German music publishers and sheet music retailers. Richard Strauss, a popular composer of classical music, together with a handful of composer friends who were knowledgeable in legal matters and driven to secure an economic basis for themselves and their colleagues for the long term, took the lead in setting up their own organization. In 1899 the Genossenschaft held its constituting general meeting and registered about 240 composers as members. Their first task—to boycott the music publisher's organization and to bring the publishers in line with their own ideas—was successfully accomplished. Music publishers entered negotiations and finally agreed to jointly found a new organization in which both parties were represented.

Roughly one year later, on January 14, 1903, Genossenschaft Deutscher Komponisten was transformed into the new Genossenschaft Deutscher Tonsetzer (GDT). On July 1 followed the establishment of the performance fee collection agency, which was named Anstalt für musikalisches Aufführungsrecht (AFMA). Whereas GDT remained a professional association of German composers of mainly classical music, its subsidiary

---

Company Perspectives:

GEMA remains the indestructible bastion of musical creativity, from which the beacon of acceptable compensation for the use of creative works sends out its light. It has achieved this position through more than 100 years of struggle, and it will continue to defend it in the new information age. And it will—in the interest of its members, the composers, lyricists and music publishers—not give up a single piece of the hard-won territory, namely the high level of copyright protection. This, in the end, because the issues always extend far beyond questions of payment rates. In the second century of GEMA's existence, the fundamental issue is still the legal and economic protection of musically creative people, and hence the future of musical culture in Germany and Europe.

AFMA opened membership to lyricists and music publishers. AFMA members had to sign a five-year contract with the agency in which they agreed to transfer the existing and future performance rights to their works to AFMA until they expired or until the agency ceased to exist. Composers received 75 percent of the collected royalties, and music publishers received 25 percent. For musical works that included vocal parts, composers received 50 percent and lyricists were given another quarter of the total. Revenues were distributed according to an evaluation scheme that took into account the kind and complexity of the respective work. A total of 10 percent of AFMA's proceeds went into GDT's pension fund, which supported low-income composers in old age.

AFMA took on the administrative tasks necessary to collect royalties. The agency began to build databases and infrastructure and to educate the public, especially venues, about its existence and purpose. Members registered their works with AFMA, which were then evaluated. For every performance of his or her work the author earned a number of points, which were added up at the end of each year. AFMA employees had to register all the music groups and venues, such as concert halls, theaters, coffeehouses, and cabarets, that were obliged to pay musical performance royalties. Those who were regularly involved with musical performances were issued an annual permit that allowed them to perform all the works on AFMA's list. Every permit was individually negotiated, according to the detailed information venue owners and musical directors submitted. As a rule of thumb, AFMA charged 1 percent of their revenues. Permit owners were obliged to use printed lead sheets and to perform the music in a respectful manner and setting. The agency hired independent traveling salesmen who negotiated contracts and were paid a commission according to their cash value. At the same time these individuals randomly visited musical venues to make sure that they paid their dues and to inform AFMA's Berlin office about any illegal performances.

Convincing the various players in the growing entertainment industry to pay for something for which they did not have to pay before was no easy task. In the beginning, AFMA was confronted with fierce resistance from performers and venues, and even from some composers, who were afraid that charging a fee would prevent venues from performing their works. Many large venues, such as the famous Gewandhaus concert hall in Leipzig, as well as smaller venues and musical groups, declared open opposition to AFMA and refused to pay royalties. A number of successful lawsuits, however, whereby venue owners were fined for illegal performances of copyrighted music, helped AFMA gain acceptance. Large and small venues began to negotiate contracts with the agency. In 1908 the association of German singers *Deutscher Sängerbund* negotiated a general agreement with AFMA. The *Deutsche Gastwirtsverband*, a large association of restaurant, coffeehouse, and bar owners, followed suit.

As the idea of paying composers for the public performance of their works took root in German society, AFMA's member roster and revenues began to grow. The number of AFMA members who were eligible to receive royalties increased from 174 in 1903 to 362 four years later. In 1914 AFMA represented 604 composers and 104 music publishers. The agency's revenues from performance fees grew tenfold between 1904 and 1913. AFMA also entered into mutual agreements with similar organizations in other countries, such as the French SACEM, to execute the rights of their members in their own countries and transfer the collected fees to the respective sister organization.

Competition, Scandals, and Legal Battles Leading to Reorganization in 1930

While AFMA was leaving behind the difficulties of its formative years, a new technological development presented the young organization with a new fundamental challenge. As Europe entered the age of industrialization, music composers witnessed the emergence and growing popularity of the mechanical reproduction of music. In the first decades of the 20th century, the formerly popular *Hausmusik* (playing music together in the home) went into decline and was replaced by the passive consumption of music through mass media, such as juke boxes, movies, and radio broadcasts. While the market for printed music began to shrink, the new market for recorded music boomed. In 1929 there were roughly 30 million records manufactured in Germany. The Bern Convention on international copyrights was revised in 1908, putting the performance of musical works by mechanical instruments under copyright protection. German copyright law followed suit in 1910, ruling that composers had to receive a share in the so-called "mechanical rights." Music publishers, however, resisted the idea of giving up a share of their revenues from this new lucrative source to composers.

In 1909, the association of German musical goods retailers established a new royalty collection agency for mechanical rights called Anstalt für mechanisch-musikalische Rechte (AMMRE). One year later GDT set up its own department for mechanical rights inside AFMA. In 1911 the Austrian agency AKM canceled its cooperation agreement with GDT and began to work with AMMRE instead. In spring 1913, 42 publishers and ten composers canceled their membership agreement with GDT, which allowed its members to transfer no more than a 50 percent share in their mechanical rights to publishers. GDT sued them for breach of contract. While World War I broke out, cutting AFMA's revenues in half, the case went into the German court system. In September 1915 Germany's highest court

---

---

ruled against GDT. In the same year a group of publishers and composers, most of whom created popular music for entertainment, founded their own musical performance rights agency named Genossenschaft zur Verwertung musikalischer Aufführungsrechte (GEMA), which began competing with AFMA. With music publishers taking a leading role in the new organization, GEMA acquired its own catalogue of protected works and demanded that venues pay fees as they did to AFMA.

After the end of World War I in 1918 German composers had the choice between two performance rights organizations. Both of them barely survived the galloping inflation of the early 1920s and suffered financially from the loss of revenue caused by reparation payments. In the mid-1920s, however, AFMA's and GEMA's revenues slowly recovered. Yet, the parallel existence of two agencies with the same purpose increasingly frustrated venues. All parties involved realized that a better solution had to be found. Finding a workable compromise, however, seemed impossible. In addition, financial irregularities were uncovered in both organizations, leading to public protests and loss of members. Only a change in leadership in both agencies eventually made progress possible. After many hours of internal arguments, a number of lawsuits, weeks of public press wars, and many broken-off and re-entered negotiations, they, together with the Austrian AKM, founded a new association for the protection of public performance rights for Germany in 1930. GDT, GEMA, and AKM jointly established a new office for the collection of license fees from movie soundtracks. Long-term contracts were signed with Germany's state-controlled radio station, with the Ufa film studios, and with the German music orchestra association. The new compromise, however, was short-lived.

Nazi Government Taking Control After 1933

Shortly after Adolf Hitler became Germany's new Chancellor in 1933, the collection of musical performance rights (based on new laws) came under government control. A new organization called Staatlich genehmigte Gesellschaft zur Verwertung musikalischer Urheberrechte (Stagma) replaced the existing or-

ganizations, which were dissolved. Immediately, "non-Aryan" directors, committee members, and employees of the old agencies were removed from their positions and replaced by Aryans—often members of the ruling National Socialist Party or similar Nazi organizations. An exception was a number of highly specialized and experienced Jewish copyright lawyers who continued to work for Stagma for a period of time.

Richard Strauss, who had lost faith in democracy during the Weimar Republic, became president of the new Reichsmusikkammer, a department within the Propaganda Ministry that oversaw the musical life of the country. Strauss also headed the new trade organization for German composers. He quickly pushed through organizational changes toward a more authoritarian system. Stagma's board of directors was shrunk from eight to three members, each a representative of the trade associations of German composers, lyricists, and music publishers. If they could not agree on an issue or a decision, Strauss had the final say. After a couple of years, however, mounting protests against his authoritarian leadership finally resulted in Strauss's dismissal in 1935.

The young music publisher and Nazi conformist Leo Ritter, formerly chair of GEMA's advisory board and one of its directors, had become Stagma's executive director. The Nazi government demanded that music publishers publish and perform mainly works of German composers. Due to Germany's growing international isolation, the works of German composers were performed less often in other countries. In addition, many composers had left Germany for racial or political reasons and joined performance rights organizations abroad. Only German citizens whose compositions were not banned (as were the works of most "non-Aryans") were able to become Stagma members and to receive royalties. One prominent example, composer Kurt Weill, was "re-evaluated" in GEMA's distribution scheme from 125 to -5 points, which resulted in a decrease in royalty income from 4,000 marks to 150 marks after 1933. Weill, who compared this procedure with theft or expropriation, fled the hostile country. As many as 315 contracts with mostly Jewish members underwent the same "re-evaluation." Music publishing houses, such as the renowned publisher C.F. Peters based in Leipzig, were Aryanized in a similar fashion.

In 1938 the expansion of the German Reich began with the annexation of Austria. AKM President Bernhard Herzmansky was arrested and AKM as well as AMMRE were merged with Stagma. All occupied areas in Austria, Czechoslovakia, France, and Luxembourg were put under Stagma control. The new income streams from abroad helped offset both the agency's losses from dwindling activities in the entertainment sector and the "trade deficit" with foreign sister organizations. After the official outbreak of World War II in September 1939 Ritter entered active military duty and the number of Stagma employees continuously decreased. In 1940 Goebbels's Ministry of Propaganda abolished the so-called "Serious Third" rule. The rule preferred composers of "serious music"—mostly classical music such as operas, symphonic, choir, and church music—in Stagma's distribution scheme in comparison with composers of "light" or popular music on the grounds that the former was more valuable. After the change, composers of "light music" received more royalty income and the Nazi government began to subsidize composers of "serious music" from state funds.

The year 1944 was the last year in which Stagma members received a regular royalty payment. In February 1945 Stagma's headquarters were bombed to ruins. Leo Ritter died in a Russian prisoner-of-war camp in August 1945.

Luckily, Stagma's card catalogue of members and registered works, as well as the transfer-of-copyright contracts, survived the war, hidden in an old mill where they were brought in 1944. Equipped with these crucial documents Walter Wechsung, a former Stagma accountant, continued the collection agency's work after the war. As had happened after World War I, the victorious Allied Forces seized a great number of copyrights held by German composers as war reparations and forbade Stagma to pay its members any royalties to prevent any payment to former Nazis. In 1947 composers, lyricists, and music publishers met with Stagma leaders to discuss the future of the collection agency. Stagma was renamed Gesellschaft für musikalische Aufführungs- und mechanische Vervielfältingsrechte (GEMA) by Allied control order, and Erich Schulze, one of Stagma's former directors of sales, became the organization's executive director after Wechsung's death in 1949. For the next four decades, Schulze remained in this position, actively engaged in the reestablishment of the organization as a legitimate and intrinsic part of a democratic postwar society in Germany. In 1948 former Stagma employees and German composers went through the obligatory hearings before de-Nazification commissions. The death of Germany's most popular composer of "serious music" for many decades, Richard Strauss, in 1949 marked the end of the Nazi chapter in GEMA's history.

Coexistence and Reunification of Two Agencies After 1950

In 1949 two German states were founded. For the following four decades there were two German musical performance rights organizations—one in each state. In Western Germany GEMA continued to serve musical copyright holders and their heirs. The agency's new bylaws, however, made a minimum amount of royalties a condition for membership. The new commercially oriented concept put a higher emphasis on the market value of a composition than on its artistic aspects. Composers of classical music were still subsidized by revenues derived from popular music, but their relative importance slowly but continuously declined. In 1964 GEMA signed an agreement with its sister organization in Israel and established a fund for descendants of composers who fled Germany for racial or political reasons during the Nazi era.

East Germany's government-controlled musical performance rights agency was founded in April 1951. Based in East Berlin, the agency was named Anstalt zur Wahrung der Aufführungsrechte auf dem Gebiet der Musik (AWA). Composer Max Butting, who had served as GDT's executive director before the Nazis seized political power, became AWA's first chairman. Due to Butting's proposal, the quality of the compositions played a more important role in the distribution of royalties for AWA members. The principle of subsidizing composers of classical music with revenues from popular music was adopted. In 1953 GEMA and AWA signed a cooperation agreement that respected the territory of the respective agency and regulated the mutual exchange of royalties collected there. After East Germany had joined the Bern Convention in 1956 GEMA and AWA worked

together remarkably smoothly through the political ups and downs between the two German states. A new law that obliged East German venues and radio stations to play no less than 60 percent for music by domestic composers in 1958 resulted in significantly less transfers from AWA to GEMA. The West German agency paid the East German "sister" one Deutschmark for one mark and received the same, although the East German currency was worth considerably less.

Beginning in the late 1950s more and more of GEMA's activities were moved to Munich, although the agency's headquarters remained in West Berlin. A new copyright law that protected melodies and parts of published works, extended copyright protection to 70 years after an author's death, and obliged manufacturers and importers of certain recording equipment to pay license fees, passed the West German parliament in 1965. West Germany's music industry participated in the "economic miracle" without having to suffer through any major economic crises afterward. Accordingly, GEMA's revenues roughly doubled every decade. New technologies, however, such as copy machines, cassette tape recorders, computers, and satellite and cable TV presented musical performance rights organizations with new problems during the 1970s and 1980s.

After the two German states were reunited in 1990, GEMA and AWA followed suit. Roughly 7,000 composers and lyricists from former East Germany were integrated into GEMA's membership roster. Erich Schulze was succeeded by Reinhold Kreile, a lawyer who was also a pianist and organist, a member of the German parliament, and a media law professor.

Digital Age Bringing New Challenges in the 1990s

After the two German performance rights organizations were successfully reunited, easy access to copyrighted music, which could be downloaded from the Internet as digital files onto computers and portable players and distributed widely, emerged as a major threat to musical copyright owners at the dawn of the 21st century. Feverishly, the music industry began to search for ways to get a handle on the inexpensive unauthorized copying and downloading of music recordings by hundreds of thousands of computer-savvy teenagers. Free online music exchanges were forbidden, new mechanisms that prevented the illegal copying of music CDs were developed, and an updated German copyright law tightened the rules for making private copies of music recordings. In spring 2003 Kreile told *Süddeutsche Zeitung* that he would dislike seeing GEMA become a sort of "digital police." The agency succeeded against the resistance of digital recording equipment manufacturers, who were obliged to pay license fees to compensate for losses through illegal digital copies.

Despite these serious challenges GEMA's revenues soared during the 1990s and beyond. By that time new technologies also had changed the way popular music was composed. Many contemporary songwriters were knowledgeable computer users, composing on their electronic keyboards without much theoretical and practical musical training. Since GEMA was obliged to represent anyone who registered a musical work and called himself a composer, the number of copyright owners the agency represented exploded. At the same time, more and more of these young composers performed their own music and reported those performances to GEMA. In 2003 the agency served more than 60,000 members and more than one million international copyright owners.

In 2004, GEMA's revenues declined for the first time in six years. Struggling with mounting losses from plunging sales, Germany's record companies demanded that in the future copyright owners should receive only 5.6 percent of the wholesale list price of a CD instead of the 9.009 percent that they had paid to GEMA since 1997—despite the fact that authors already suffered the same losses the music industry was experiencing. For music distributed online, record companies offered to pay GEMA 5.6 percent of the sale price—roughly one third of what GEMA considered a "fair compensation" for composers and lyricists. Although the conflict was brought before a litigation jury of the German patent office, GEMA's lost income from deteriorating CD sales was offset in large part by higher revenues from other sources, including television and radio, and license fees from mobile phone companies. GEMA's executive director of 15 years, Reinhold Kreile, who expected a solution of the conflict between the agency and the recording industry in 2005, was to be succeeded by 47-year-old Harald Heker, CEO of Germany's book publishers association Börsenverein des deutschen Buchhandels, in 2006. Heker's main focus was to convince policy and lawmakers at the European Union's Brussels headquarters of the crucial importance of high-level copyright protection in the digital age and to defend the quasi-monopoly GEMA before its antitrust authorities.

Although the future seemed somewhat uncertain, based on Germany's copyright law effective in 2005, Richard Strauss, the famous composer's grandson, could expect to benefit financially from the public performance of his grandfather's still popular classical works such as the opera *Der Rosenkavalier*, composed in 1911, until the year 2019. At the same time the majority of contemporary German composers of classical music still earned an income far below average standards of living, and about 600 of them received financial support from GEMA Foundation.

Further Reading

100 Jahre GEMA. Festakt 2. Mai 2003 in Berlin, Berlin and Baden-Baden, Germany: GEMA and Nomos Verlagsgesellschaft, 2003.

Brembeck, Reinhard J., "Die Firma zwischen Kunst und Polizei. 100 Jahre Gema II," *Süddeutsche Zeitung,* January 14, 2003, p. 11.

Dümling, Albrecht, *Musik hat ihren Wert: 100 Jahre muskalische Verwertungsgesellschaft in Deutschland,* Regensburg, Germany: ConBrio Verlagsgesellschaft, 2003.

"GEMA. Musik hat ihren Preis," *Focus,* August 28, 1995, p. 198.

Hagedorn, Volker, "Kunst war einmal ideal, Abrechnung trivial," *General-Anzeiger,* June 12, 2003.

Ohler, Arndt, "Gema kämpft mit schrumpfenden Einnahmen," *Financial Times Deutschland,* February 28, 2005, p. 5.

"Private Kabelnetzbetreiber zahlen an die Gema," *Frankfurter Allgemeine Zeitung,* November 3, 1999, p. W6.

Schiller, Maike, "Baden die Autoren nun die Krise der Musikbranche aus?," *Hamburger Abendblatt,* February 14, 2004.

—Evelyn Hauser

Griffin Industries, Inc.

4221 Alexandria Pike
Cold Spring, Kentucky 41076-1821
U.S.A.
Telephone: (859) 781-2010
Fax: (589) 572-2575
Web site: http://www.griffinind.com

Private Company
Founded: 1943 as Falmouth Fertilizer Company
Employees: 1,000 (est.)
Sales: $292.1 million (2003 est.)
NAIC: 311613 Rendering and Meat Byproduct Processing

Privately held and family run, Griffin Industries, Inc., is the second largest independent rendering company in the United States. Griffin collects a variety of waste products, including used restaurant cooking oil; offal, scraps, and hides from slaughterhouses, packing houses, and butchers; poultry feathers; dead farm animals; supermarket discards; and inedible bakery waste from the production of bread, dough, pasta, crackers, cereal, bagels, sweet goods, and snack chips. These materials are transported by a fleet of company trucks to Griffin recycling plants, where they are converted into saleable products. Animal proteins, feeding fats and tallows, and bakery meal are sold as animal feed and converted by other manufacturers into pet food. Bakery waste is converted into Cookie Meal, a corn replacement ingredient used to make animal feed or pet food. The company also makes a biodiesel fuel out of soybean oil and recycled restaurant grease. Griffins' trimmed and cured hides and skins are used as a raw stock in the production of leather goods, including shoes and automobile interiors. Animal proteins are converted into an organic fertilizer product called Nature Safe. Griffin also recycles vegetable oils and animal fats into a methyl ester called VersaGen, which can be used to replace hazardous materials used in such applications as asphalt, cleaners, coatings, compounding, construction, dust control, ink, lubricants, metalworking, personal care products, process oils, and pulp and paper. In addition to its headquarters in Cold Spring, Kentucky, Griffin maintains about 50 rendering plants, bakery plants, hide plants, blending plants, spent cooking oil plants, biodiesel plants, and transfer stations located in a southwest arc from Pennsylvania to Texas. To conduct international business the company also owns and operates ships using Gulf of Mexico ports.

Company Founded in the 1940s

Griffin Industries was founded by John L. Griffin, who was born in Lockland, Ohio, in 1922, and grew up well familiar with the rendering business. As a boy, he often accompanied his father and uncles, employees of the Elmwood Rendering Company in Reading, Ohio. He quit high school to join his father at Elmwood Rendering, and in 1943 moved his wife and newborn son to Falmouth, Kentucky, to start his own business, initially called Falmouth Fertilizer Company. He bought a used furniture truck, left the rocking chairs painted on the doors, and traveled within a 35 mile radius to pick up dead farm animals, which he then sold to Jonathan Smith Rendering in Reading, Ohio. At home, his wife, Rosellen, kept the books and raised the increasing number of children, eventually reaching a dozen. As he began advertising his service, Griffin took on a different company name for each community, supplementing Falmouth Fertilizer with such business names as Brooksville Fertilizer, Maysville Fertilizer, and Williamstown Fertilizer. As these names imply, the focus of the business at this stage was on the production of organic fertilizer.

The early years were difficult for Griffin, especially due to the rise of cheap chemical fertilizers after World War II, which made organic fertilizers too costly. To remain competitive in an expanding rendering industry, he was able to secure a $30,000 Small Business Administration (SEA) loan to buy 40 acres of land and build a plant in 1947. He was now able to skin the deadstock to sell the hides and cut up the rest of the animal for sale to the largest rendering company in the area, Kentucky Chemical. By now, Griffin owned two trucks and employed two men, but he was still operating on a knife's edge. Chicago-based Darling and Company, which had acquired Jonathan Smith Rendering, attempted to buy him out, threatening to ruin him if he did not comply. Griffin refused and, despite missing a payment on his SBA loan in 1948, he persevered. Granted an extension, Griffin took advantage of improving markets to stabilize the business and was soon expanding his routes and building a second processing plant. He invested in a hydraulic press that was used to convert processed materials into 40-pound cakes. These were sold to Kentucky Chemical, which ground them up for animal feed, another area that made up for the loss of the fertilizer business.

A New Name in the Early 1960s

By the early 1950s, Falmouth Fertilizer was picking up deadstock in surrounding counties and as far away as Cincinnati. During this period, the company began servicing its first slaughterhouse, a sausage plant operated by Webber Farms. In addition to the meal cake sold to Kentucky Chemical, the company also sold grease and tallow to Procter and Gamble in Cincinnati. In 1952, Falmouth Fertilizer added chicken feathers to its business after Griffin developed a way to make a meal out of the feathers that could be used to produce organic fertilizer. In the process, he also realized that the meal was extremely high in protein. By accident he found a way to make a meal that he could sell to Ralston Purina for use in animal feeds. Later in the 1950s, Falmouth Fertilizer installed equipment that allowed it to produce ground meal that could be sold directly to feed mills. The company also expanded its sources of raw materials, adding a Kentucky turkey operation and two Cincinnati poultry processors as clients. As business increased, Griffin invested his profits in better equipment, which shortened the company's processing time and prompted it to search out new sources of raw material. By the early 1960s, the company was approaching Cincinnati packing houses and took on a more appropriate sounding name, Griffin Industries, Inc.

Also in the early 1960s, Griffin's eldest son, Dennis, was old enough to join the business, although, in truth, he had been helping since he was a small boy. After a few semesters of college, he quit school and in 1961 became a night foreman at one of his father's plants. In 1966, Griffin Industries completed its first acquisition, paying $75,000 for the Columbus Reduction Company, located in Columbus, Indiana, and 23-year-old Dennis Griffin was dispatched to run it. Less than a month later, the company's chief competitor, Wachtel Company, was hit with a strike, allowing the Columbus operation to take up the slack and pry away a large number of customers in southern Indiana. Wachtel was bought by National-By-Products and was soon back in business, but Griffin Industries had been so successful in raiding Wachtel's customers that Nation-By-Products decided to sell their southern Indiana transfer station in Underwood. Through a third party, Griffin Industries acquired the facility, its first transfer station, and was now able to move into the Louisville, Kentucky, market.

A major turning point in the history of Griffin Industries took place in the summer of 1968. John Griffin was contacted by Martha Jacobshagen, whose husband—the owner of rendering plants in Newberry, Indiana; Henderson, Kentucky; and Jackson, Mississippi—had recently died. She was interested in selling the business, but after the Griffins visited the facilities, they estimated the properties were worth several million dollars, well out of their reach. Nevertheless, they met with Mrs. Jacobshagen, who let them examine the financial records. Poorly run, the plants were losing about $100,000 a month and quickly draining the proceeds of her husband's life insurance policy. While it was not surprising that she would want to unload the assets, the Griffins were nonetheless shocked to hear her asking price, a mere $750,000. Nevertheless, it was still more money than Griffin thought it could raise. Consequently, they convinced her to keep a farm, oil wells, and some other property and finally settled on a price of $550,000. To fund the deal, Griffin Industries took out a loan with Central Trust Bank in Cincinnati, the start of a long-term relationship with the lender.

Griffin Industries completed another acquisition in 1972: Russelville, Kentucky-based Kentucky Animal By Products. The plant had suffered a recent fire, and the owner had just lost a son in an automobile accident and wanted to sell the business. Now operating six plants, Griffin Industries was thriving and outgrew its offices, which were shoe-horned into one of its plants located too remotely to accommodate the number of telephone lines and communication system the company now required. In 1973, the Griffins bought an old road house, the Eight Mile House, located on 5.5 acres of land in Cold Spring, Kentucky. Rather than tear down the historic structure, they remodeled it, adding modern wiring and heating. From this new base of operations, Griffin Industries was well positioned to engineer further growth during the 1970s. In 1974, it acquired West Monroe Rendering Company in northern Louisiana, which now acted as a transfer station for its Jackson, Mississippi, plant, allowing Griffin Industries to service northern Louisiana and southern Arkansas. A year later, a West Virginia operation was purchased, but it never fared well and was sold off a few years later. A more successful venture was launched in 1976, when the company built a facility in Cincinnati to expand its hide and pigskin business, cutting out the middleman to deal directly with tanners. Also in 1978, Griffin Industries opened a steel-fabricating and welding shop called Jay Gee to develop and make the company's own equipment. To close out the decade, Griffin Industries acquired a rendering plant in the Gainesville, Florida, area. In 1979, Dennis Griffin was named president of Griffin Industries and the other roles played by family members were better defined.

Family Difficulties Mar 1980s

The early 1980s brought more growth but misfortune as well. A transfer station was acquired in Alma, Georgia, in 1980, followed a year later by a rendering plant in East Dublin, Georgia, a facility that was destined to cause headaches 20 years later. Also in 1981, Rosellen Griffin was diagnosed with Parkinson's Disease, and her health steadily declined. Then, in 1984, John Griffin suffered a heart attack while attending a rendering convention. Although he recovered, he was left partially paralyzed and his speech impaired. He continued to come into the office but the management of the business now fell squarely on the shoulders of his children. In the meantime, the condition of his wife worsened, and in August 1985 she died at the age of 61. Her husband survived another ten years, dying from a heart attack in April 1995. The Griffin family also suffered another loss in 1988 when one of the brothers, Jim, and his two sons were killed in an automobile accident. (Another son, Ronald Lee Griffin, had died in 1968.) The founder's many offspring would also fall out among themselves over the division of the estate. In 1985, the Griffin children agreed to a redistribution plan that in effect turned over the Griffin Industries stock to the sons who worked in the company, while the sisters were paid in cash for their share. What seemed to be an equitable deal in the mid-1980s, however, was cast in a different light after the business enjoyed tremendous growth a few years later.

Griffin Industries expanded at a rapid clip during the second half of the 1980s. In 1986, it acquired Jacksonville, Florida-based Southern Tallow, doing business from south Georgia to central Florida; Southeast Recycling Corp., located near New Orleans and subsequently linked up with the Jackson, Mississippi, operation; and Tampa Soap and Chemical Company, expanding the central Florida business. Access to the port of Tampa allowed Griffin Industries to directly export tallow and grease to Central and South America rather than rely on New Orleans' brokers. Within a few years, more than one-third of Griffin Industries' sales were the result of direct exports. To accommodate this business, the company bought a 5,500 ton capacity ship in Rotterdam, Holland, and renamed it the "Rosellen" in honor of Rosellen Griffin. In late 1987, the company bought Memphis, Tennessee-based Delta By-Products, and a few weeks later added Texas Rendering Company, located 30 miles southeast of Austin. Duncan Tankage Corporation of Union City, Tennessee, was acquired in September 1988, and a modern plant was built to serve the new slaughter houses that had recently been constructed in western Tennessee and western Kentucky. Also in 1989, Griffin Industries negotiated the package purchase of rendering plants in Marianne, Florida; Atlanta, Georgia; and Shelbyville, Indiana, a deal that was finally closed in July 1990.

The dispute over the disposition of the Griffin estate came to a head in 1990 when sister Betsy Osborn sued Dennis Griffin, executive vice-president John M. Griffin, an executive vice-president, their attorney, his law firm, and Griffin Industries in U.S. District Court. The two brothers had served as co-executors of their mother's estate. Osborn charged in her suit

that they misrepresented their mother's will and estate, made a systematic attempt after her death to accumulate company stock, and among the six brothers realized $43 million in profits from 1986 through 1989, while the five sisters received less than $3 million. Over the next three years, the case worked its way thorough the court system. Just before the trial was set to commence in 1993, the two sides reached a settlement, which according to press accounts awarded some 1,400 shares of Griffin Industry stock to Osborn and nearly 200 shares to each of her two children.

Continued Prosperity in the 1990s and Beyond

Griffin continued to expand in the 1990s. In 1991, the company acquired a pet food operation in Carlisle, Kentucky, and a Dallas-area rendering plant. It was also during the early 1990s that Griffin Industries returned to its roots via the production of organic fertilizer, marketed under the Nature Safe label, a product that once again became viable because of stricter environmental regulations. In addition, the company developed new animal feed products, including BI-PAS, a protein product used to increase milk production, and RUMICAL, a dry fat product used in the dairy industry. In 1993, Griffin Industries acquired a bakery waste recycling company, picking up four southeastern facilities that processed bakery residuals into animal feed, changed the name to Bakery Feeds, Inc., and by the end of the decade added another five plants, spread from Pennsylvania to Texas, in what became a major business for the company. Griffin also moved into the biodiesel market, converting old restaurant vegetable oils and rendered fats from animals into a product that could be blended with petroleum diesel or used as a fuel by itself. Albeit a niche product, it held promise for the future.

Over the years, Griffin Industries had always viewed itself as a good corporate citizen and a company that, in terms of the environment, was part of the solution, not the problem. Nevertheless, during the late 1990s and into the 2000s, the company found itself cast as a polluter in the public arena, and sometimes found itself at odds with local communities. In 1996, Griffin Industries was persuaded, at a cost of $1.3 million to taxpayers, not to open a new plant in the Houston area, after candymaker Russell Stover threatened not to proceed with building a nearby plant, contending that the odors from a rendering plant might contaminate its confections. In 2000, Griffin Industries agreed to move a Bakery Feeds plant from Fayetteville, Arkansas, to Watts, Oklahoma, the result of a settlement connected to complaints by residents alleging odor and noise pollution. The most contentious case involved the East Dublin, Georgia, plant, which converted chicken byproducts into fertilizer and feed. In 1999, area residents complained bitterly about the offensive odors periodically emanating from the plant, leading the district attorney to consider charging Griffin Industries as a public nuisance. The Department of Agriculture stepped in, promising to deal with the problem, but the complaints continued and the matter became a political issue. In 2003, the plant was raided by state and federal officials. Among other things, they investigated whether the company was contaminating the groundwater through Bay Branch Creek, which ran through the plant site. In addition, four residents sued the company, and later in the year a Savannah, Georgia, grand jury indicted the company's five executives on charges that the plant polluted the creek and that company officials falsified environmental records. The criminal charges were settled in November 2004, shortly before a trial was set to begin, when Griffin Industries pleaded guilty and accepted a $50,000 fine. The plant's neighbors, in the meantime, sought to gain class action status for their civil suit on behalf of anyone living within 2.5 miles of the plant, totaling approximately 2,500 people.

Despite the adverse publicity and legal distractions, Griffin Industries remained a healthy and growing business, with annual sales reportedly in the neighborhood of $300 million.

Principal Subsidiaries

Bakery Feeds Inc.

Principal Competitors

Ag Processing Inc.; Darling International Inc.; National By-Products, LLC.

Further Reading

"Cold Spring Firm Accused of Polluting Stream in Ga.," *Kentucky Post*, October 23, 2003, p. A14.

Goldstein, Jerome, "Recycling Food Residuals into Animal Feeds," *BioCycle*, February 1999, p. 60.

Griffin, Dennis B. *A Tradition In Rendering: A Historical Look at Griffin Industries: The Business and the Family Behind It*, Cold Spring, Kentucky: Griffin Industries, 1993.

Hansen, Bruce, "Rendering Business Lives off the Fat of the Land," *Memphis Business Journal*, October 19, 1992, p. 12.

Lim, Serena, "Waste Not, Want Not," *Oils & Fats International*, September 2002.

Peale, Cliff, "Sons and Daughters Fight Over Family Business," *Cincinnati Business Courier*, November 15, 1993, p. 3.

—Ed Dinger

Harry London Candies, Inc.

5353 Lauby Road
North Canton, OH 44720-1572
U.S.A.
Telephone: (330) 494-0833
Toll Free: (800) 321-0444
Fax: (330) 499-6902
Web site: http://www.londoncandies.com

Wholly Owned Subsidiary of Alpine Confections, Inc.
Founded: 1922
Employees: 215
Sales: $51.5 million (2003)
NAIC: 313300 Confectionery Manufacturing from
   Purchased Chocolate

Harry London Candies, Inc. is a North Canton, Ohio-based confectioner primarily known for its high-quality chocolate products. The company also offers caramels, mints, and toffees. A subsidiary of Alpine Confections, Inc., Harry London produces some 2,000 different items in its 200,000-square-foot plant, some sold under the company's own name and others under the label of such major customers as Disney, Universal Studios, May Company department stores, Federated Department Stores, and the Sally Foster fundraising firm. These relationships have helped to even out the seasonal nature of the business, which peaks at Valentines Day and Easter. The Harry London plant is a tourist attraction in the Cleveland-Akron area, attracting school tours and motorcoach groups as well as football fans visiting the Pro Football Hall of Fame in nearby Canton. From behind glass walls, visitors can watch the candy being made and, after the 45-minute guided tour, purchase products from the onsite chocolate store, the largest in the Midwest, offering more than 500 varieties of chocolate and other candies. Harry London also operates a fundraising department to help non-profit groups to make money through candy sales. In addition, the company offers a number of gift items aimed at the corporate market.

An Amateur Chocolate Maker in the Early 1900s

The man who gave his name to Harry London Candies was Harry Alfred London, born in Reynoldsville, Pennsylvania, in August 1900, the eldest of eight children. To help support the family he quit school after fourth grade and went to work for a company that would become part of Republic Steel Corporation. In his spare time, he learned the art of chocolate making from his father, Gilbert London, who knew recipes that had been passed down through generations in the London family, stretching back to the family's European roots. Father and son gained a local reputation for producing handmade chocolates as holiday gifts, and the treats proved so popular that friends offered to buy them. At Gilbert's urging, Harry quit the steel mill and in 1922 launched a small chocolate-making business that would become Harry London Candies. He started out in the basement of his home, and as sales picked up he moved out and over the years relocated to a series of larger Canton, Ohio, locations to keep pace with demand. In addition to possessing skill in chocolate making, London was also something of a tinkerer, building his own equipment to enrobe candy in chocolate. Some of the machines he designed continued to be used several decades later.

Harry London ran the business until his death in March 1969. His first wife had died in 1943, but his adult children from that marriage had no interest in joining the family business. He remarried, taking Iloa Campbell as his wife. After his death in 1969, she ran the company for several years before enlisting the help of her daughter and London's stepdaughter, Bonnie, along with her husband Cedric Waggoner. It was Waggoner's flair for salesmanship that drove the company's success in the 1970s and 1980s. One of the company's most popular products was called the London Mint, a chocolate mint meltaway. It was Waggoner's idea to reproduce the $100 bill for the box cover, as was a giant foil-wrapped chocolate ''kiss'' about as large as a volleyball. In the early 1980s, he took the company international and began exporting Harry London chocolates. Sales grew steadily so that after a dozen years foreign sales accounted for 7 percent of total revenues. The Ohio Department of Agriculture, which maintained a Hong Kong office, was especially helpful in finding Asian distributors for the company. It also organized trade shows in Hong Kong, Singapore, and South Korea that Harry London and other Ohio companies found useful.

Third Generation Takes Charge in the Late 1980s

In the late 1980s, a third generation became involved in the business, as three of London's grandchildren—Mercedes, Joe, and Alison Waggoner—inherited the business. Joe Waggoner was instrumental in modernizing the plant. He grew up in the business, but after a four-year stint in the Army returned in 1988 and recognized that the company could no longer perform so many functions manually and remain competitive. He studied new technologies used around the world and began to incorporate them into Harry London's efforts to automate some of its systems, while retaining the key handmade steps in the chocolate-making process. Many of the technologies were not even designed for candy making. Some of the baking techniques, for example, were originally used by pharmaceutical companies and others were developed for semiconductor manufacturing.

Another key member of the third generation was Mercedes' husband, Peter Young. He held a law degree from the University of Michigan and a master's degree from the London School of Economics and was forging a career at a major glass manufacturer, directing its international business affairs, when the Waggoner family approached him about helping to lead Harry London at a time when Cedric Waggoner began to step away from the business. Young agreed to work at Harry London for a maximum of two years. He eventually stayed seven. Young took advantage of his international sales experience to forge strategic alliances with other gourmet candy makers and initiated a strong marketing push to expand oversea sales. At home he played a key role in moving the company to a new plant. Having made significant upgrades to its technology, Harry London was now looking to increase volume, a goal that could be achieved only by employing larger machines. However, the available equipment, although able to quickly produce large quantities of a product, was not flexible enough to meet the company's needs. A key factor in Harry London's success was that the company could produce a wide variety of items and was willing to complete rush orders for major customers, both of which required the ability to quickly switch over to different product runs. To wed size with adaptability, Harry London had to invest in custom-built equipment that would not only produce a vast array of products but also simultaneously package them in several ways, including boxed, bagged, twist wrapped, and flow wrapped. Although it made a concerted effort to make certain that production lines utilized space efficiently, the company was still in need of more space and a larger facility. However, its North Canton location was not able to accommodate expansion, forcing the company to look elsewhere to locate a new plant. It was Young who spearheaded this move and undertook negotiations with local government agencies to secure the most advantageous terms.

In 1994, Harry London agreed to a property and real estate tax abatement plan offered by Green, Ohio, to build a 100,000-square-foot plant on a site close to the Akron-Canton Regional Airport. The company had hoped for a ten-year, 10 percent tax break that would have resulted in savings of more than $850,000 but settled for a plan that saved $644,000 over ten years. It was also a good deal for Green, which would receive more than $200,000 in taxes on undeveloped land owned by the airport and not previously subject to taxes. Moreover, the community expected to collect another $1.8 million in income tax during that period. Harry London also received help from Stark County, receiving further tax abatements and millions of dollars in industrial revenue bonds to aid with construction costs.

In 1995, Harry London moved into its new facility, the most modern chocolate manufacturing plant in the country. Situated in a more visible and accessible location, it was also built with tourism in mind. While the former plant was simply too small to host large groups and tours, the new factory was designed to cater to motor coaches, including an entrance portico to allow tour-bus visitors to enter and exit the building while shielded from the elements, additional women's restrooms, and parking spaces large enough for motor coaches. A tour program was also devised, featuring a documentary on the history of chocolate, a tour of the plant, and a visit to the "Chocolate Hall of Fame" and a retail store selling Harry London products. In the first six months after opening the new plant, the company conducted more than 400 tours, accommodating some 20,000 people. Although the Harry London factory was not a target destination in itself, it served to compliment the other tourist attractions in the area, such as Canton's Pro Football Hall of Fame, Akron's McKinley Museum, and Cleveland's Rock 'N Roll Hall of Fame, making the entire area more of a desirable destination.

Late 1990s Bring Rapid Expansion

Despite the major addition of space, Harry London quickly outgrew its new location as the company enjoyed rapid growth in the second half of the 1990s. It took advantage of its new equipment to add items, giving the company a competitive advantage in private label work. The major customers, such as Disney and Universal Studios, preferred to do one-stop shopping with a trusted vendor like Harry London rather than contract their business to a dozen smaller specialty chocolate companies. Aside from growing the wholesale business, Harry London also opened six retail stores in Ohio to move even more candy. In July 1999, the company opened an addition that more than doubled the plant's original floor space to 220,000 square feet, allowing it to increase efficiency, which was crucial in its efforts to be the low-cost producer in each of the 2,000 items it made while at the same time maintaining high quality. For a relatively small company—generating revenues anywhere from $20 million to $40 million, according to what company officials reluctantly told the press—Harry London's success was balanced on a knife's edge, simultaneously attempting to match variety and quality with low prices. Previously, the company had to warehouse raw materials and finished products in the same space, but with the extra room it could now install dedicated systems to provide better inventory control of both raw materials and finished goods, thus leading to lower overhead costs and an increased ability to competitively price its merchandise.

Key Dates:

1922: Harry London launches a chocolate-making business.
1969: Harry London dies.
1994: The company opens a state-of-the-art plant.
1999: HLC Holdings LLC acquires a controlling interest.
2003: Alpine Confections acquires the company.

In 1999, Cedric Waggoner retired and Young replaced him as CEO. A majority interest in the company was sold to HLC Holdings LLC, an affiliate of private equity fund Lombard North America Partners. Harry London's sale mix at this stage was 50 percent branded wholesale products, 30 percent private label contract business, and 20 percent retail margin sales. It was also during this period that the company was contacted by Home Shopping Network about hawking Harry London products on television. In early 2000, Young signed a deal to develop and produce some exclusive HSN items and recruited his 33-year-old sister-in-law, Allison Waggoner, to serve as the Harry London pitchwoman. As director of marketing, she had recorded some radio commercials but had never appeared on camera. Nevertheless, in March 2000 she was dispatched to HSN's Tampa, Florida, studios with a five-pound box of assorted chocolates. The first appearance lasted just eight minutes but proved successful enough to warrant return visits; as sales increased, Harry London graduated to hour-long shows. Within two years, HSN sales were accounting for about 10 percent of the company's total revenues.

In December 2000, Young finally left Harry London and moved his family to Washington, D.C., to resume his international law career. His replacement as CEO was Rex Mason, a former general manager of Bristol-Myers Squibb subsidiary, hair-care products manufacturer Matrix Essentials. His primary focus when he took over was to improve Harry London's systems and customer service operations, which had lagged behind the company's ability to produce massive quantities of high-quality chocolates. Although customers were pleased with the products, they were never certain that the items they ordered would arrive on time. Mason also began to lessen the focus on private label work, looking instead to build up the Harry London brand name.

The growth Harry London achieved during the 1990s came with a cost, however. Although it remained profitable, it carried too much debt for a company its size and rate of growth, the result of spending $13 million to build and expand its plant and the cost of opening seven specialty retail stores in Ohio in the late 1990s. Unable to refinance its debt, the company then breached its credit agreements. In January 2003, Harry London filed for Chapter 11 bankruptcy protection, listing $34 million in assets and $33 million in liabilities. With the cooperation of its primary secured creditors, KeyCorp and BankOne, Harry London continued to operate normally as it took steps to complete a financial restructuring. In the meantime, in an effort to focus on its core business, the company closed seven of its eight retail stores, keeping only the one that was part of the plant tour.

Although several companies inquired about entering into a financial arrangement with the company, Harry London found a more suitable partner in Alpine Confections Inc. and signed a letter of intent to have the Salt Lake City, Utah-based company fund and implement its reorganization plan. After an amendment of the plan, Alpine received court approval to acquire Harry London at a cost of $10 million to $15 million. The privately owned Alpine was founded in 1994 by partners R. Taz Murray and David Taiclet, who entered the candy industry after earning their Harvard MBAs. Over the next decade, they acquired three candy companies: Kencraft Candy of Alpine, Utah, makers of specialty hard candies; Salt Lake City's Maxfield Candy, makers of chocolate candies; and Vancouver, Canada-based Dynamic Chocolates. Along the way, Alpine lined up deals to produce chocolate products under the Mrs. Field's and Hallmark names.

Although Harry London was no longer a family-run business, with Alpine bringing in its own management team, installing senior vice-president Terry Mitchell as the company's new president, there was no threat that the Harry London name would suddenly vanish. Alpine recognized the brand's strength and was eager to grow it even more. The workers' jobs were also secure, as the new owners looked to take advantage of Harry London's excess production capacity to produce other confections, which would likely result in even more employment opportunities. Alpine was also committed to producing quality products, in keeping with the tradition passed down by Harry London himself. Moreover, Harry London was now part of a larger company that was continuing to grow. In 2004, Alpine acquired the venerable Fannie May and Fannie Farmer brands and retail stores from Archibald Candy Corporation.

Principal Competitors

Cadbury Schweppes plc; Godiva Chocolatier, Inc.; Hershey Foods Corporation; Nestle S.A.

Further Reading

Fuhrman, Elizabeth, "Alpine Wins Court's Blessing for Harry London Purchase," *Candy Industry*, August 2003, p. 14.

Harrow, Victoria Reynolds, "Diverse & Efficient," *SBN Akron*, September 1, 1999, p. 18.

Snook, Debbi, "Chocolate Factory a Sweet Tour," *Plain Dealer*, December 23, 1995, p. 3E.

Thompson, Lynne, "The Taste of Success," *SBN Stark*, February 1, 2002, p. 14.

Whitehouse, Tammy, "1999 Northeastern Ohio Entrepreneur of the Year: Going for a Sweet Ride," *SBN Cleveland*, July 1, 1999, p. S13.

—Ed Dinger

Henderson Land Development Company Ltd.

6/F World-Wide House, 19 Des Voe
Hong Kong
Hong Kong
Telephone: +852 2908 8888
Fax: +852 2908 8838
Web site: http://www/hld.com

Public Company
Incorporated: 1976
Employees: 4,900
Sales: HKD 6.72 billion ($860 million) (2003)
Stock Exchanges: Hong Kong
Ticker Symbol: HLDC
NAIC: 531210 Offices of Real Estate Agents and
    Brokers; 551112 Offices of Other Holding
    Companies; 236116 New Multi-Family Housing
    Construction (Except Operative Builders); 237210
    Land Subdivision; 523999 Miscellaneous Financial
    Investment Activities; 531120 Lessors of
    Nonresidential Buildings (Except Miniwarehouses);
    541512 Computer Systems Design Services; 721110
    Hotels (Except Casino Hotels) and Motels

Henderson Land Development Company Ltd. is one of Hong Kong's leading real estate development companies. Henderson's primary operations include property development, property investment, and management of the group's land bank—including a portfolio of some 21 million square feet of total attributable floor area, encompassing the company's developments, hotels, investments, and subsidiary properties. In addition, Henderson controls 23 million square feet of agricultural land, a majority of which is slated for conversion toward property development in the early part of the century. Henderson is committed to maintaining a large land bank, and replenishes its holdings as it completes developments. Less than 25 percent of the group's properties is located in the city of Hong Kong. Instead the group has focused the majority of its portfolio on the Kowloon market, which accounts for 36 percent of Henderson's land bank, and especially the fast-growing New Territories, representing 41 percent of the group's portfolio. Through publicly listed subsidiary Henderson China Holdings, Henderson has ventured onto the Chinese mainland as well. While Henderson Land remains a pure-play development group, it controls 75 percent of Henderson Investment Limited, also a publicly listed company. Henderson Investment was developed as the holding company for Henderson's diversified investments, which include the development and management of two hotels in Kowloon, the five-store chain of Citistore department stores, control of the Hong Kong Ferry, Miramar, and The Hong Kong and China Gas Company Limited. Henderson itself, listed on the Hong Kong Stock Exchange, remains controlled at more than 65 percent by founder Lee Shau Kee, who generally features near the top of the world's wealthiest people. Lee has surrounded himself with family members, including his two sons, at Henderson, many of whom occupy top-level management positions with the company. Day-to-day operations are carried out under the direction of deputy chairman and Lee protegé Colin Lam.

Building Hong Kong in the 1970s

Lee Shau Kee's rise to become one of the world's wealthiest people began during the Communist Revolution of 1948. Lee's father, Lee Kai-po, owned a business exchanging currency and trading gold in Guangzhou. As the Communist troops were approaching, Lee divided the family's assets between his two sons, sending one to Macau, and Lee Shau Kee to Hong Kong.

Lee Shau Kee arrived in Hong Kong with just HKD 1,000 and began working for a foreign currency trader in Hong Kong into the 1950s. Lee tried his hand at other businesses, including selling hardware and operating an import-export business. In 1958, however, Lee decided to enter the real estate market, and together with several investors founded the Eternal Enterprise Company.

Lee's timing was perfect. As Hong Kong rose in prominence to become one of the major financial centers of the Asian region, real estate prices skyrocketed. In 1963, Lee set up a new business, this time with brothers Kok Tek Seng and Fung King Hey. The new company, Sun Hung Kai Properties, quickly emerged as one of Hong Kong's most prominent real estate companies.

Company Perspectives:

The Group's business strategy is to: build on its leading position in the small and medium sized residential units development segment; increase recurring income from growing rental property portfolio; maintain strategic investments to strengthen income and asset base; generate significant future cashflow from diversifying businesses.

By the early 1970s, Lee had established himself as one of Hong Kong's growing number of self-made real estate legends. In 1972, Lee decided to leave the real estate business and concentrate his activities on the still more promising property development center. In 1973, Lee founded Henderson Land Development.

Joining Lee were several members of his family, including his brother, Lee Tat Man, and sister Lee Woon King, who became company directors, as well as first wife Lau Wai-kuen. In 1975, Lee took control of a second company, Wing Tai, which had been publicly listed in 1972. That business later developed into Henderson Investment. Another business launched by Lee during this period was the Hang Yick Property Management Company, an extension of the company's property development operations founded in 1974.

Lee formally incorporated his company in 1976, and then took Henderson Land Development public in 1981. At the time, the company's land bank remained relatively small, at less than eight million square feet. Yet Lee had already begun to inspire others with his shrewd eye for the property development market. An avid dealmaker, Lee became known for the rapidity of his business decisions. He was also a canny businessman, insisting on maximum floor space efficiencies in the properties under his development. More important was Lee's ability to spot the diamonds in the rough of Hong Kong's building booming sector, leading him to venture into developments others chose to avoid. Lee's knack at picking winners quickly raised him to legendary status among the growing class of Hong Kong real estate billionaires.

Henderson's relatively restrained portfolio at the beginning of the 1980s helped shield it from the worst effects of the island's dramatic real estate crash that lasted into mid-decade. When Lee recognized signs that the market was going to pick up, he led Henderson on an aggressive acquisition drive. Among Henderson's targets were the New Territories then in the beginning phases of their development. Henderson emerged as a major developer in the region, which accounted for more than 60 percent of the group's land bank into the 1990s. By 1988, the company had built up a portfolio of more than 20 million square feet. Of importance, the company's average land bank cost during this period stood at just HKD 200 per square foot—compared with an average selling price of HKD 1,800 per square foot at the beginning of the 1990s.

Property Giant in the 1990s

Henderson acquired control of Wing Tai in 1985. That company was then renamed as Henderson Investment. In 1988, Henderson Land restructured in order to redevelop itself as a

Key Dates:

1948: Lee Shau Kee arrives in Hong Kong from mainland China and begins working with a foreign currency agent.

1958: Lee sets up his first real estate business, Eternal Enterprise.

1963: Lee founds Sung Hung Kai Properties, which grows into a major Hong Kong real estate firm.

1973: Lee leaves Sung Hung Kai in order to launch a property development company, Henderson Land.

1976: Henderson Land Development is incorporated.

1981: Henderson Land Development goes public on the Hong Kong Stock Exchange.

1985: The company acquires Wing Tai, owned by Lee Shau Kee, renamed as Henderson Investment.

1988: The company restructures, spinning off property not related to property development to Henderson Investment.

1989: The Citistore department store chain is launched.

1992: The company enters the hotel business with two hotels in Kowloon.

1995: Megastrength Security Services Company is founded.

2000: The company begins restructuring, placing certain assets under direct control.

2003: An attempt to acquire full control of Henderson Investments is blocked by minority investors.

2004: The Lee family establishes a private investment company for high-risk investments.

pure-play real estate company. The company spun off its other holdings and investments, which were placed into Henderson Investment. Henderson Land nonetheless retained a 75 percent stake in Henderson Investment.

In the 1990s, Henderson Investment began developing a wider range of activities. In 1992, for example, Lee entered the hotel business through Henderson Investment, developing and managing two Kowloon hotels. The company then acquired a controlling stake in the 525-room Miramar Hotel, also in Kowloon. The company's foray into hotel management came after its entry into the retail sector, in 1989, through the launch of its Citistore department store chain. By 2004, the company operated five department stores in Kowloon and in the New Territories.

The New Territories set the stage for the launch of another Henderson subsidiary, Well Born Real Estate Management, founded in 1996 to oversee the real estate management operations at eight company properties under development in the late 1990s. In another entry into the services sector, Henderson set up Megastrength Security Services Company, which hired former elite Hong Kong Police special security officers to provide security management and related services. That business began in 1995. Into the mid-2000s, Henderson's investment portfolio also included stakes in Hong Kong Ferry Company and The Hong Kong and China Gas Company. The company also moved into the telecommunications and technology sectors through a new subsidiary, Henderson Cyber, set up in 2000.

Restructuring in the 2000s

Like the rest of the Hong Kong real estate and property development market, Henderson was hit hard by the weak real estate market on the island in the late 1990s. The transfer of Hong Kong to the Chinese government's control made investors wary, while the economic crisis that swept most of the Asian region in the later part of the decade further eroded confidence in Hong Kong's property market. By 1998, Hong Kong real estate prices had been slashed in half.

Henderson came under shareholder pressure to restructure. One move the company made was to place Hong Kong and China Gas and a number of other cash-generating businesses directly under the control of Henderson Land Development. In this way, the company was able to generate additional revenues to compensate for its dwindling property development business. In 2003, Henderson Land attempted to take full control of Henderson Investment as well. But minority shareholders blocked the move, complaining that the offered share price was too low. Instead, Lee himself set up a new investment business, fully controlled by his family, for the purpose of pursuing riskier investments than were possible through Henderson Investment. One possible market for the new company, which began with HKD 500 million in December 2004, was said to be Macau.

As the real estate market began to pick up again toward mid-decade, Henderson had once again emerged from the down-cycle with a strong property portfolio. By the end of 2004, the company held more than 21 million square feet of development land; the company's land bank also included more than 24 million square feet of agricultural land, which the company planned to convert little by little to development properties over the next decade. Lee Shau Kee, one of the world's richest people, maintained tight control of the company he had founded more than two decades earlier.

Principal Subsidiaries

Henderson Land Development Company Ltd.; Henderson Investment Ltd.; Henderson China Holdings Ltd.; The Hong Kong and China Gas Company Ltd.; Hong Kong Ferry (Holdings) Company Ltd.; Miramar Hotel and Investment Company, Ltd.; Henderson Cyber Limited.

Principal Competitors

Cheung Kong (Holdings) Ltd.; New World Development Company Ltd.; Sino Land Company Ltd.

Further Reading

Leahy, Joe, "Henderson Revamp Lifts HK Sector," *Financial Times,* November 7, 2002, p. 31.
——, "Henderson's Offer for Key Arm 'Too Low,' " *Financial Times,* November 12, 2002, p. 28.
Lau, Eli, "Higher Risks for Private Lee Firm," *Standard,* December 8, 2004.
"Li & Lee: Miramar," *Economist* (US), July 24, 1993, p. 78.
Wang, Raymond, "Henderson Eyes $10b in Flat Sales," *Standard,* July 28, 2004.
——, "Henderson to Increase Share Capital," *Standard,* October 29, 2004.

—M.L. Cohen

Henry Schein, Inc.

135 Duryea Road
Melville, New York 11747
U.S.A.
Telephone: (516) 843-5500
Fax: (516) 843-5658
Web site: http://www.henryschein.com

Public Company
Incorporated: 1992
Employees: 8,000
Sales: $4.1 billion (2004)
Stock Exchanges: NASDAQ
Ticker Symbol: HSIC
NAIC: 423500 Medical, Dental and Hospital Equipment and Supplies Merchant Wholesalers; 423990 Other Miscellaneous Durable Goods Merchant Wholesalers; 511210 Software Publishers

Henry Schein, Inc., is the largest distributor of health care products and services to office-based health care practitioners, mostly in the markets of North America, Europe, New Zealand, and Australia. These health care customers include physician practices, dental practices and laboratories, veterinary clinics, and government and other institutions. Henry Schein performs its operations through four groups: Medical, Dental, International, and Technology. Its dental and medical products are categorized into: medical products; consumable dental products and equipment; large dental equipment; dental laboratory products; and veterinary products. Technology products are divided into software and related products including Henry Schein's practice management software products. These products are offered under the Company's brand names including Henry Schein, AVImark, Dentrix, ProRepair, Easy Dental, and Digital Dental Office.

Origins

Henry Schein, a pharmacist, and his wife Esther founded the eponymous company in 1932 as a corner drugstore in the Woodside community of New York City's borough of Queens. By the 1950s Schein had also began offering supplies to doctors via a mail order catalog. In 1962 Schein moved the store to a larger location in Flushing, Queens.

Controversy characterized the mid-1960s. In 1964 a federal prosecutor filed a criminal complaint against Schein, who was charged with selling bottles containing counterfeit Dexedrine capsules to three out-of-state pharmacies. Schein also was charged with illegally selling amphetamine, barbiturate, and penicillin tablets to an undercover federal agent.

The mail order operation, which was intended to address a need not met by sales representatives, apparently suffered no such problems. "It was in the 1970s that things really took off," Chief Executive Officer Stanley Bergman told Susan Konig of the *New York Times* in 1996. "That's when the Schein family discovered the dental market. There were around 3,000 dental distributors back then. But they sold products at relatively high prices and with relatively poor service. So the Scheins decided to put together catalogs which would offer them at lower prices and have them ready for immediate delivery. That was a pretty new concept at the time."

Henry Schein sold his retail store in the mid-1970s to become a full-time distributor of medical and dental supplies and generic drugs. By the late 1970s his company had annual sales of about $40 million. Within a decade, the company was dominant in its field and by 1988 controlled more than 40 percent of the mail order market for dental supplies. The firm moved in 1979 from Queens to a 100,000-square-foot facility in suburban Port Washington, Long Island.

After Schein's son Jacob, a Wall Street attorney, joined the company in 1980, it began automating distribution. In the mid-1980s the firm introduced two interactive methods to enable dentists to file orders for supplies at any time of day or night, either by telephone or computer. It also issued one of the first affinity credit cards and, in 1988, developed a frequent-buyer program at a time when such incentives were confined to airlines.

During this period Schein, which had purchased a Connecticut pill producer in 1970, also became an important manufacturer and distributor of generic drugs. In 1985 it formed a subsidiary, Schein Pharmaceutical, Inc., to serve retail and hospital pharmacies. This company was offering more than 1,500 prescription and over-the-counter drugs and vitamin products through a network of franchised wholesalers. The prescription drugs were being produced for the most part by another Schein subsidiary, Danbury Phamacal Inc., and the over-the-counter drugs and vitamins were being supplied by a number of vendors. In 1992 Schein Holdings, Inc., the parent of Henry Schein, Inc. and Schein Pharmaceutical, spun off the latter as an independent company.

By this time Schein was being run by Bergman, who became chief executive officer after Jacob Schein's premature death from cancer in 1989. Henry Schein had died in 1987. (Esther Schein, who also had been active in management, died in 1992. Jacob's brother Marvin became head of the company's dental equipment division in 1995, after it purchased Schein Dental Equipment Corporation, a separate company that had been founded by Marvin Schein.)

Broadening Scope in the Early 1990s

According to Bergman, Henry Schein was barely profitable when he took charge. "In the early 80's, our competitors started copying us," he recalled to Konig. "They came out with catalogues, they started discounting their products and improving their service, and the bottom line was we started looking just like them. We had to differentiate ourselves again in the dental world, and we did it with value-added services." These services included selling computer products to dentists and offering them financial products.

Another way that Henry Schein differentiated itself from its competitors was to start focusing on European markets in 1990, when it opened its first foreign subsidiary, in The Netherlands. By mid-1991 the company had established three more such foreign operations—in England, Germany, and Spain. It also had begun selling through a distributor to Mexico and it launched its first catalog directed to the Canadian market. Schein was now receiving orders from 70 countries.

In the United States, some 160 telemarketing representatives at Schein's Woodbury, Long Island office, were responding to more than 1.5 million calls a year from doctors, dentists, and veterinarians. Computer-telephone integration, installed in 1992, allowed agents to send a computer profile, simultaneously with the call, to the first available agent. This enabled the company to cut an average of 17 seconds each from incoming calls—a significant saving when considering the volume of calls. By collecting data on the items ordered by a particular account, as well as the frequency of the orders, the profile enabled Schein representatives to anticipate which products the customer might need and to make further suggestions.

Schein's reliance on catalogs and telemarketing rather than salespeople was allowing it to price its products 5 to 10 percent lower than its competitors, according to a securities analyst, but in 1993 the company added 200 field sales consultants to take face-to-face orders from health professionals. In 1996 the company opened a 25,000-square-foot retail outlet near Miami International Airport to cater to the Caribbean and Latin American health care markets. Some 5,000 to 6,000 of its more than 50,000 items were available for purchase on the spot.

Schein's annual sales grew from $236.3 million in 1990 to $415.7 million in 1993. Of this total, the North American Dental Group accounted for 40 percent (and 20 percent of the total U.S. dental supplies market). The Diversified Healthcare Group, established in the 1980s to market products to general practitioners, pediatricians, podiatrists, and other nondentist health care professionals, accounted for almost one-third. The International Group accounted for less than 20 percent of company revenues. The Professional Services Group, Schein's newest division, had developed the leading software package for dental office management and another program for complying with safety regulations. This group also was selling and configuring computer hardware, repairing dental equipment, conducting continuing education, and providing some financial services to dentists.

By late 1994 Schein was selling products in more than 140 countries. The firm also was forming alliances with professional organizations and some other companies. The Diversified Healthcare Group, for example, had taken a 50.1 percent share of Universal Footcare Products Inc., a joint venture with Chicago Medical Equipment Co. to market products to health maintenance organizations and more than 9,500 podiatrists. An agreement with the American Medical Association enabled the group's member physicians to receive discounts on Schein's catalog roster of 18,000 medical supply products. Schein then formed a partnership with the U.S. Army under which it became the prime vendor for the army's more than 100 dental clinics in the United States.

Acquisition-Fueled Growth in the Late 1990s

Schein went public in November 1995, raising $72.5 million from its initial public offering at $16 a share. In July 1996 it raised an additional $124.1 million by selling more stock at $35 a share. Some of the proceeds were used to retire debt, but much of it was reserved for the company's continuing acquisitions program. By the fall of 1996 Schein had acquired 40 regional dental, medical, and veterinarian supply companies over the past five years, including 14 in 1996 alone with combined annual revenue of $100 million. Schein's strategy for integrating its acquisitions—usually made for stock rather than cash—was to deploy a team that spent 10 to 12 weeks evaluating the new company's products and shedding those that did not fit with Schein's own goods, plus integrating the acquired company's customer list with Schein's own and contacting new customers with marketing materials. Schein often retained the acquired firm's sales force but generally eliminated its warehouse operations.

In March 1997 Schein purchased Micro Bio-Medics Inc., a company with $150 million in annual revenues that was expected to double Schein's sales to physicians. Three months later it entered into a joint venture by acquiring a majority interest in the dental division of a regional health care group with operations in Australia and Auckland, New Zealand. In the United States, 65 percent of all dentists and 30 percent of all physicians were Schein customers, according to an investment analyst firm.

Later in 1997 the company, which had ranked second in the U.S. dental distribution industry, became the world's largest distributor of dental equipment and supplies by purchasing the third largest U.S. firm in its field, Sullivan Dental Products Inc., for stock valued at $318 million. Tim Sullivan stayed on as president of the Wisconsin-based company, which was renamed Sullivan-Schein Dental Products Inc. In all, Schein's 24 acquisitions in 1997 had aggregate net sales of about $558.6 million in 1996 and enabled it to reach net sales of $1.52 billion in 1997. The company lost $1 million, however.

In 1998 Schein acquired five more companies. The biggest of these was H. Meer Dental Supply Company, a Michigan-based dental distributor with 1997 sales of about $180 million that was purchased for stock valued at $145.5 million. During the same year, however, Schein sold Marus Dental International, its dental equipment manufacturing operation. In early 1999 the company acquired General Injectibles and Vaccines, Inc., a direct marketer of vaccines and other injectible products with 1998 sales of about $120 million. It also purchased the international dental, medical, and veterinary health care distribution businesses of German-based Heiland Holding GmbH, which had 1998 sales of about $130 million.

Schein had, in 1994, moved its headquarters and telemarketing office to a three-story leased building in Melville, accepting financial and tax incentives from the state of New York, Suffolk County, and Long Island Lighting Company to remain on the island. The company sold its Port Washington warehouse in 1998, with the intention of moving the operation to a larger leased space in Denver, Pennsylvania. Of its eight warehouses, three were in the United States and five in Europe. Schein also was leasing space in nine other countries.

Including its acquisitions, Schein had net sales of $1.92 billion in 1998 and net income of $16.3 million. The dental group accounted for 56 percent of the total; medical, for 27 percent; international, for 12 percent; and the veterinary and technology groups for about equal shares of the remaining 5 percent. Sales under the Henry Schein private label (manufactured by third parties or affiliated HS Pharmaceutical, Inc.) accounted for 8.6 percent of the total. The company's total debt

at the end of the year was $209.5 million. In April 1999 Bergman held or controlled more than 15 percent of the stock.

Schein was selling products to more than 75 percent of the estimated 100,000 dental practitioners in the United States in 1998. It distributed more than 12.5 million pieces of direct marketing materials, such as catalogs, flyers, and order stuffers to about 600,000 office-based health care practitioners. The number of its stock-keeping units now exceeded 60,000 in North America and came to about 55,000 in Europe and about 22,000 in Australia. The company also sold more than 28,000 dental practice management software systems, more than any of its competitors. It estimated that about 99 percent of all orders in the United States and Canada received before 7:00 p.m. and 4:00 p.m., respectively, were shipped on the same day the order was received and that about 99 percent were received within two days. The number of its telesales personnel had reached about 700 and its field sales consultants amounted to about 1,100.

Restructuring in the 2000s

Schein announced in August 2000 a restructuring plan targeted to improve customer service, increase profit efficiency, and deal with pending changes in the healthcare industry. The plan included the closing or reduction of specific facilities, and the elimination of about 5 percent of the total workforce. In the fall of 2000, the company sold its half interest in dental anesthetic manufacturer HS Pharmaceutical Inc. The company also finalized the acquisition of one technology business and two healthcare distribution businesses. Henry Schein used four major U.S. distribution centers and over 10 foreign distribution centers to ship over 49 million items as it grew more than 60 percent. In all, Henry Schein posted record sales in 2000, despite the negative impact on its overseas operations of a strong U.S. dollar with respect to the Euro.

In January 2001, the company introduced its new website www.henryschein.com for the use of all of its customers. The company also opened its website www.sullivanschein.com for its office-based dental practitioner customers. After completing its five-year restructuring plan, Henry Schein implemented a three-year strategy plan to improve sales growth, cash flow, and operating margins. As a result, the company posted record financial results. Specifically, medical net sales increased mostly due to improvements in the core physicians' office and alternative care markets. Increases in dental net sales were caused by entry into new markets. Net sales in the international market increased due to improved methods to enter new markets, especially in France, Germany, and the United Kingdom but were offset somewhat by unfavorable international exchange rates to the U.S. dollar. Decreases in net sales in the veterinary market were due to a loss of a product line. Increases in net sales within technology were due to strong sales of products and related services. During the year, Henry Schein completed the acquisition of two healthcare distribution businesses.

The year 2002 was another good year for Henry Schein, mostly due to its wide diversity of products and services, number of markets that it served, and number of geographic areas where it operated. During the year, 43 percent of its revenues came from the Dental Group, 39 percent from the Medical

Group, 16 percent from the International Group, and 2 percent from the Technology Group.

During 2003, Henry Schein posted another year of record net sales. As a result, the company debuted on the 2004 *Fortune* 500 list of largest companies in the United States, being listed at 487. After a four-year departure from major acquisitions, Henry Schein completed several important purchases in 2003, including Colonial Surgical, Hager Dental, Damer & Cartwright, and American Medical Services. The company also began the process of buying three of Europe's leading dental distributors: KRUGG S.p.A., demedis GmbH, and DentalMV GmbH (Muller & Weygandt).

Schein's four groups were all leaders within their particular sectors. Its Medical Group served over 45 percent of the estimated 230,000 U.S. office-based physician practices and had about 16 percent of the estimated $7.1 billion market. It offered over 30,000 products to physicians through three primary brands: Henry Schein Medical, Caligor, and General Injectables and Vaccines (GIV).

The Dental Group had about 30 percent share of the estimated $4.4 billion U.S. and Canadian dental distribution market. The group served over 75 percent of the about 135,000 U.S. and Canadian dental practices, and approximate 15,000 dental laboratories. It is also a major supplier to large group practices, schools, and government and other institutions. The group included Sullivan-Schein Dental in the United States, Henry Schein Arcona in Canada, and the Zahn Dental laboratory supply business.

The International Group had about a 9 percent share of the Western European dental, medical and veterinary markets. It offered more than 75,000 products to 170,000 customers located in 14 countries outside of North America, those countries being Austria, Australia, Belgium, the Czech Republic, France, Germany, Iceland, Ireland, Israel, the Netherlands, New Zealand, Portugal, Spain, and the United Kingdom.

In 2004, Henry Schein expanded its corporate headquarters in Melville, New York; and at the same time increased the number of jobs by 800 at its headquarters and other office locations on Long Island. The company is expected to invest about $30 million for this expansion and renovation.

For over 70 years, Schein had developed unique sales and marketing expertise, a global centralized operating structure, and a broad product offering at competitive prices. In all, the company served medicine professionals in more than 125 countries worldwide and sold about 90,000 products and various services to more than 425,000 global customers. In addition, Henry Schein had an integrated marketing and sales program with more than 1,550 field sales consultants and specialists; about 875 telesales representatives, along with 110 equipment sales and service centers; and more than 550 equipment service technicians. The company also maintained a direct marketing program with more than 31 million materials distributed each year, including such materials as catalogs, flyers, order stuffers, e-mails, and newsletters.

Principal Subsidiaries

Henry Schein UK Holdings Ltd.; Henry Schein Van den Braak, B.V. (Netherlands); Zahn Holdings, Inc.

Principal Operating Units

Dental; Medical; International; Technology and Value Added Services.

Principal Competitors

Allegiance Corporation; Darby Group Companies, Inc.; DENTSPLY International Inc.; Owens & Minor Inc.; Patterson Companies, Inc.; World Med Inc.

Further Reading

Anderson, David, "Millions of Fake Dexedrine Pills Sold," *New York Times*, August 29, 1964, p. 11.

Anderson, Jim, "CTI Enhances Customer Service for Healthcare Marketer," *Telemarketing*, May 1993, pp. 74–75.

Bernstein, James, "Nassau Loses Big Employer to Suffolk," *Newsday*, November 5, 1993, p. 61.

Chevan, Harry, "Henry Schein," *Catalog Age*, April 1994, p. 63.

Gallun, Alby, "Sullivan Dental Acquisition Shines Through," *Business Journal-Milwaukee*, October 30, 1998, p. 7.

"Henry Schein Celebrates 70 Years of Innovation and Dedication to Excellence in Customer Service by Opening Nasdaq Trading," *Business Wire*, March 7, 2002.

"Henry Schein Inc. Acquires 2 Specialty Drug Distributors," *Long Island Business News*, November 21, 2003, p. NA.

"Henry Schein to Create 800 New Jobs," Long Island Business News, May 14, 2004.

Joshi, Pradnya, "Shopping Spree," *Newsday*, July 7, 1997, pp. C6–C7.

Kiley, Kathleen, "A Healthy Schein," *Catalog Age*, October 15, 1996, p. 5.

Konig, Susan, "From Small Beginnings to a Company with Millions in Sales," *New York Times*, June 30, 1996, Sec. 13, p. 2.

LaFemina, Lorraine, "Henry Schein Shines as New IPO," *LI Business News*, February 26, 1996, p. 3.

Miller, Susan R., "Filling a Medical Cavity," *South Florida Business Journal*, October 4, 1996, p. 3.

"New Schein Subsidiary To Serve Pharmacies," *Drug Topics*, June 17, 1985, p. 40.

Oberndorf, Shannon, "Associating with Strategic Partners," *Catalog Age*, March 1995, p. 65.

" 'Scheining' Overseas," *Catalog Age*, July 1991, p. 8.

Solnik, Claude, "Back on the Prowl," *Long Island Business News*, November 16, 2001, v. 48, I. 47, p. 5A(2).

Somerville, Janice, "Pair of Foot Care Companies Merges into Universal Force," *Crain's Chicago Business*, October 31, 1994, p. 28.

Unger, Michael, "Schein's Biggest Buy Yet," *Newsday*, August 5, 1997, p. A36.

Wax, Alan J., "Henry Schein, That Is . . . ," *Catalog Age*, March 1997, p. 72.

——, "Melville Firm Plans Warehouse Closing," *Newsday*, December 19, 1997, p. A64.

—Robert Halasz
—update: William Arthur Atkins

Hibbett Sporting Goods, Inc.

451 Industrial Lane
Birmingham, Alabama 35211
U.S.A.
Telephone: (205) 942-4292
Fax: (205) 912-7290
Web site: http://www.hibbett.com

Public Company
Incorporated: 1945 as Dixie Supply Company, Inc.
Employees: 3,400
Sales: $320.9 million (2003)
Stock Exchanges: NASDAQ
Ticker Symbol: HIBB
NAIC: 451110 Sporting Goods Stores

Hibbett Sporting Goods, Inc., is a leading operator of retail stores for a full line of sporting goods. Founded in 1945, the company targets small to mid-sized markets located mostly in the southeastern United States. In early 2005 Hibbett had 488 stores located in 23 states. These stores consist of the company's flagship Hibbett Sports, Inc. stores, Sports & Co., Inc. superstores, and smaller-format Sports Additions, Inc. stores. The stores offer a broad assortment of quality athletic equipment, footwear, and apparel at competitive prices. They feature a core selection of brand-name merchandise for team and individual sports and localized apparel and accessories designed to appeal to customers within each market. About 90 percent of Hibbett's retail outlets are located in large enclosed malls, but the stores also operate profitably in strip-center locations. More than 80 percent of the company's stores are in county markets with a population of less than 250,000. Company subsidiary Hibbett Team Sales, Inc. specializes in customized athletic apparel, equipment, and footwear, selling directly to school, athletic, and youth associations in Alabama. Team Sales has its own warehouse and distribution center from which it manages its operations independently from those of the company's other divisions. When the company went public in 1996, Hibbett stock traded for $16 a share; in 2005, shares of Hibbett stock were in the $25 to $28 range.

Founding and Early Years

In 1945 Rufus Hibbett, a high school coach and teacher in Florence, Alabama, founded Dixie Supply Company, a retailer of athletic, marine, and aviation equipment. When his two sons joined the business in 1952, Rufus changed the company's name to Hibbett & Sons and focused operating strategy on merchandise for team sports. In the mid-1960s, the company further refined its retail strategy and changed its name to Hibbett Sporting Goods, Inc.

In 1980 the Anderson family of Florence, Alabama, purchased Hibbett, invested in professional management and systems, and continued to expand the company's store base at a moderate pace. Hibbett's unique operating strategy was to target small to mid-sized markets ranging in population from 30,000 to 250,000. By focusing on markets of this size, the company achieved significant strategic advantages, including numerous expansion opportunities, comparatively low operating costs, and a more limited competitive environment than generally would have prevailed in larger markets. Hibbett also was able to establish greater customer and vendor recognition as the leading retailer of a full line of sporting goods in a local community. Furthermore, the company's regional focus enabled it to achieve significant cost benefits, including lower corporate expenses, reduced distribution costs, and increased economies of scale.

Rapid Expansion in the 1990s

By the early 1990s Hibbett's primary retail format was that of its flagship Hibbett Sports, Inc. stores: 5,000-square-foot stores located predominantly in enclosed malls. The company tailored this Hibbett Sports concept to the size, demographics, and competitive conditions of its small to mid-sized markets. Hibbett also established Sports Additions, Inc. stores, which were smaller units of 1,500 square feet. About 90 percent of the Sports Additions merchandise was footwear, with the remainder consisting of caps and limited apparel. These stores offered a broader assortment of athletic footwear and emphasized a more fashionable footwear assortment than could be found in Hibbett Sports stores. All Sports Additions stores were located in the same malls as Hibbett Sports stores. By the end of fiscal 1993, Hibbett recorded combined sales of $32.03 million from

Company Perspectives:

Hibbett Sporting Goods, Inc.'s stores offer a high level of customer service and competitive prices for an extensive assortment of quality athletic equipment, footwear, and apparel for team and individual sports.

34 Hibbett Sports stores and four Sports Additions stores. By the end of fiscal 1994, company sales had grown to $40.12 million from the operation of 41 Hibbett Sports and eight Sports Additions stores. The company grew from 38 stores at the end of fiscal 1993 to 60 stores at the end of fiscal 1995.

The market for sporting goods remained highly fragmented; large retailers of sporting goods competed for market share by using a variety of store sizes, including larger-format stores, called superstores. Although several retailers of sporting goods— namely, Foot Locker and Foot Action—were already present in most of Hibbett Sports' mall locations, the company believed that the Hibbett Sports store format could be adjusted effectively to a superstore format focused on a full line of quality sporting merchandise that included products for individual and team sports and a localized mix of apparel and accessories.

From a Private to a Public Company in 1996

In 1995 the Anderson family sold control of the company to Saunders Karp & Co., an investment firm. During the spring of the same year, Hibbett opened its first 25,000-square-foot superstore, dubbed Sports & Co., in Huntsville, Alabama. Athletic equipment and apparel represented a higher percentage of the overall merchandise mix at the Sports & Co. superstore than they did at Hibbett Sports stores. The superstore was designed to project the same atmosphere as that of Hibbett Sports stores, but on a larger scale. For example, the superstore included space for customer-participation areas, such as putting greens and basketball-hoop shoots. Periodically, the superstore featured special events with appearances by well-known athletes.

The need for expanded inventory and larger operating quarters led Hibbett to build a state-of-the-art office/warehouse in Birmingham's Oxmoor Industrial Park. In January 1996 the company relocated to this 130,000-square-foot center, which had significant expansion potential to support Hibbett's growth for the foreseeable future, and centralized the distribution process from its corporate headquarters located in the same building. The company saw strong distribution support for its stores as critical to its expansion strategy and central to maintaining a low-cost operating structure. Hibbett received substantially all of its merchandise at the Birmingham distribution center, where it maintained back stock of key products allocated and distributed to stores through an automatic replenishment program based on items sold during the prior week.

In October 1996 Hibbett completed an initial public offering (IPO) of its shares of common stock for $16 per share and traded on the NASDAQ under the symbol HIBB. The company accelerated its rate of new store openings to take advantage of the growth opportunities in its target markets. Hibbett's clustered expansion program, which called for opening new stores

within a two-hour driving radius of another company location, made for greater efficiency in distribution, marketing, and regional management. In evaluating potential markets, the company considered population, economic conditions, local competitive dynamics, and availability of suitable real estate. Although the core merchandise assortment tended to be similar for each Hibbett Sports store, the company recognized important local or regional differences by regularly offering products that reflected particular sporting activities in a particular community, local college, or professional sports team. Thus Hibbett Stores was able to react quickly to emerging trends or special events, such as college or professional championships.

During fiscal 1996, sales from Hibbett's 67 stores increased 28.3 percent to $67.1 million. This gain was attributable to the opening of four Hibbett Sports stores and three Sports & Co. superstores. Hibbett's leading product categories, ranked according to sales, were athletic footwear, apparel, and sporting equipment. Although aggressive about expansion, Hibbett continued to emphasize the sale of quality brand-name merchandise at competitive prices. The breadth and depth of the company's merchandise selection generally exceeded that of local independent competitors. Among the brand names that Hibbett offered, the top 25 (based on sales) included adidas, Asics, Champion, Converse, Columbia, Dodger, Easton, Everlast, Fila, Louisville Slugger, K-Swiss, Mizuno, New Era, New Balance, Nike, Pro Line, Rawlings, Reebok, Rollerblade, Russell, Spalding, Starter, The Game, Umbro, and Wilson.

Because many of these branded products were highly technical and required considerable customer assistance, Hibbett coordinated with its vendors to educate the store-level sales staff about new products and trends. The merchandise staff analyzed current sporting goods trends by monitoring sales at competing stores; communicating with customers, store managers, and personnel; maintaining close relationships with the company's multiple vendors; and reviewing industry trade publications. The staff also worked closely with store personnel to assure availability of sufficient quantities of products at individual stores.

During 1997, the company further accelerated its store-opening rate by taking advantage of the growth opportunities in its target markets. Hibbett opened 21 Hibbett Sports stores and one Sports & Co. superstore, thereby making the company the operator of 77 stores at the end of fiscal 1997; sales peaked at $86.4 million. Hibbett's increase in sales was attributable to the opening of 22 new stores and to increased footwear sales. The company's largest vendor, Nike, represented approximately 40 percent of its total purchases. Based on its performance in the full-line sporting goods category, Hibbett received the Nike Retailer Excellence Award for the Southeast region for the ninth consecutive year.

Toward the 21st Century

Thirty years of profitable retailing in small to mid-sized markets validated Hibbett's adherence to the Hibbett Stores format for competing effectively against both the general and the specialty retailers in its industry. Compared with discounters and department stores that generally offered limited assortments of sporting goods, Hibbett carried a wide selection of branded products. Compared with national specialty retailers that typically focused on a single category, such as footwear, or on a specific activity, such as golf or tennis, Hibbett differentiated itself by its breadth of quality merchandise geared to local sporting and community interests. Although some competitors carried product lines and national brands similar to those found at Hibbett's stores, Hibbett Sports stores were usually the primary retailers of a full line of sporting goods in their markets. In the company's 1998 annual report Hibbett President Michael J. Newsome commented that there were three options open to retailers in the sporting goods industry: "Stand idly on the sidelines and let the world pass you by; 'slug it out' for incremental market share; or cater to a genuine need. We prefer the latter." The strength of Hibbett's niche, Newsome pointed out, was that the company "offers a full line of sporting goods with superior customer service. Concentration on smaller markets generally limits our competition to small, independent sporting goods operators and national footwear chains and allows us to better serve a broader customer base."

The company targeted special publicity opportunities in its markets to increase the effectiveness of its advertising budget. To further differentiate itself from national chain competitors, Hibbett preferred promotional spending in local media. Advertising in the sports pages of local newspapers served as the foundation of its promotional program; in 1997 the major portion of the company's publicity budget was spent in this way. Hibbett also used local radio, television, and outdoor billboards to reinforce name recognition and brand awareness in the community.

Hibbett's primary retail format and growth vehicle remained that of the Hibbett Sports 5,000-square-foot store located predominantly in enclosed malls. The company used relevant design, in-store atmosphere, and eye-catching signage to channel mall traffic into the stores. Hibbett's management information systems tracked different retail prices for the same item at different stores, thereby enabling more competitive pricing by location. Furthermore, the purchasing staff regularly reviewed and analyzed the company's point-of-sale computer system in order to make appropriate merchandise allocation and markdown decisions.

During 1998 Hibbett opened 31 Hibbett Sports stores and two Sports Additions stores; sales increased 31.4 percent to

$113.6 million. The increase was due to the addition of 33 new stores, to larger sales for ladies' and children's footwear and apparel, and to higher equipment sales. Higher earnings also reflected lower store operating and selling expenses as a percentage of sales due to improved leveraging of administrative costs. At the end of fiscal 1998, Hibbett operated 120 stores in 14 southeastern states. Hibbett expanded its geographic reach when it opened its first store in eastern Oklahoma and five stores in Arkansas, but the majority of the new stores were in states where Hibbett already operated. To keep pace with the company's rapid expansion, Hibbett continually evaluated and improved the capacity and effectiveness of its Birmingham distribution center. The addition of radio frequency technology reduced labor costs and increased accuracy. The installation of additional conveyors and of other equipment decreased processing time and improved inventory turns.

During the first six months of fiscal 1999, Hibbett surpassed all its previous records for increases in net income, net sales, and number of store openings. Net sales increased 25.3 percent to $65.86 million, compared with $52.56 million for the same period in fiscal 1998. Net income increased 33.2 percent to $3.2 million, compared with net income of $2.4 million for the first six months of fiscal 1998. During the first quarter, Hibbett opened a record 15 stores, making a total of 135 Hibbett stores operating in 16 southeastern states. During the second quarter, the company opened 20 additional stores, including 18 Hibbett Sports stores and two Sports Additions stores. Hibbett acquired two of the stores from W.C. Bradley Company and five of the stores from Olympia Sports. Five of the seven stores were converted to Hibbett Sports stores and two were converted to Sports Additions stores.

New Stores for a New Century

As the new century opened, Hibbett continued to follow its business plan of opening 5,000-square-foot stores in small to mid-sized towns throughout the South. The company also opened stores as far west as New Mexico and Colorado and as far north as Illinois, Indiana, and Ohio. Primary competitors in the small communities served by Hibbett continued to be the Wal-Mart chain and local mom-and-pop stores. But although Wal-Mart sold sports equipment, Hibbett offered a much larger range of equipment, including the high-price products not carried by Wal-Mart. For this reason, Hibbett often opened stores in strip malls where a Wal-Mart store was the anchor. Speaking to Hilary Cassidy of *Sporting Goods Business,* Hibbett CEO Mickey Newsome explained his company's impact on local small mom-and-pop stores: "The mom-and-pop usually specializes in the team and school business. Because we're retail athletics, we don't necessarily put anybody out of business, we don't really bother the mom-and-pops in regard to their team and school business—that's not what we do. We do the retail, so we coexist very well with the mom-and-pops, but that's typically our number-one competitor."

Between 2000 and mid-2002, the company expanded the number of its stores by 48 percent. In 2003 the company added 57 stores and opened an additional 60 new stores in 2004, including two stores in New Mexico, the first to be built in that state. By early 2005 the company had a total of 488 stores in 23 states. Hibbett planned to increase the number of its stores by 15 percent a year over the next few years. The company identified some 400 potential sites for future growth. The states of Florida (with 15 stores) and Texas (with 14 stores) showed the most potential for future expansion.

Sales and profits during this period also rose at a steady pace. Hibbett reported profits of $63.6 million on sales of $209.6 million in 2000; by 2003, profits had risen to $102.3 million on sales of $320.9 million. Sales for 2004 were expected to be about $375 million, setting a new record. Third-quarter sales for 2004 increased by 17.5 percent over the previous year, and for the busy holiday season, sales increased 17.2 percent over the previous year. The solid gain was attributed by company officials to increased sales in footwear and team equipment. Speaking of Hibbett's recent performance, company CFO Gary Smith told Marianne Bhonslay of *Sporting Goods Business,* "We have a good growth record with a simple model. But it works."

Principal Subsidiaries

Hibbett Sports, Inc.; Hibbett Team Sales, Inc.; Sports Additions, Inc.; Sports & Co., Inc.

Principal Competitors

Sport Chalet; Shoe Carnival; Sports Authority Inc.; Foot Locker Inc.

Further Reading

"Baseball Comes Out Swinging at Stores," *Daily News Record,* April 9, 1996, p. 1.

Bhonslay, Marianne, "Sweet Home, Alabama," *Sporting Goods Business,* June 2002, p. 47.

Cassidy, Hilary, "Mickey Newsome" (interview), *Sporting Goods Business,* September 15, 2000, p. 28.

Clark, Ken, "Bigger Isn't Always Better," *Chain Store Age Magazine,* September 2003.

Evans, Chuck, "New Book Claims to Hold Keys to Retailing Secrets," *Birmingham Business Journal,* June 1, 1998.

Fickes, Michael, "Hibbett Grows By Staying Small," *Sporting Goods Business,* February 12, 2001, p. 46.

"Hibbett Sporting Goods Reports Record Holiday Sales," *Globe and Mail,* January 6, 2005.

"Hibbett's Team Spirit Leads to Big Profits," *Chain Store Age Magazine,* November, 1998, p. 80.

Leand, Judy, "Masters of Invention," *SportStyle,* February, 1995, pp. 88–89.

Linecker, Adelia Cellini, "Birmingham, Alabama, Retailer Eyes a Southern-Fried Lift from NCAA," *Investor's Business Daily,* December 12, 2003, p. A6.

Lloyd, Brenda, "Hibbett Plays By Its Own Rules; Cost-Conscious Sporting Goods Chain Targets Small Markets," *Daily News Record,* December 23, 2002, p. 53.

Longo, Don, "Hibbett's Sticks to Small," *Retail Merchandiser,* May 2004, p. 12.

Milazzo, Don, "Hibbett to Relocate HQ and Warehouse to Oxmoor," *Birmingham Business Journal,* February 20, 1995, p. 6.

Parr, Karen, "Driving Ambition," *SportStyle,* July 1995, p. 62.

Reeves, Amy, "Birmingham, Ala. Retailer Learns Lesson After a Slight Misstep," *Investor's Business Daily,* March 11, 2002, p. A12.

Ryan, Thomas J., "Piece of Cake: As Sales Gradually Begin to Increase, Retailers Seek Growth," *Sporting Goods Business,* February 2004, p. 8.

Schaefer, Kayleen, "Hibbett Thinks Small to Think Big," *Footwear News,* June 24, 2002, p. 10.

"Sporting Goods Executives Share Outlook at NSGA Show," *Discount Store News,* August 4, 1997.

Troy, Mike, "Soft Economy Can't Stop Hibbett," *DSN Retailing Today,* May 5, 2003, p. 5.

—Gloria A. Lemieux
—update: Thomas Wiloch

The Hockey Company

3500 Boulevard de Maisonneuve, Suite 800
Montreal, Quebec H3Z 3C1
Canada
Telephone: (514) 932-1118
Fax: (514) 932-6043
Web site: http://www.thehockeycompany.com

Wholly Owned Subsidiary of Reebok International Ltd.
Incorporated: 1991 as SLM International, Inc.
Employees: 1,303
Sales: $239.9 million (2003)
NAIC: 339920 Sporting and Athletic Goods
    Manufacturing

As its name suggests, Montreal-based The Hockey Company is devoted to the sport of ice hockey. The company manufactures and markets equipment and apparel under some of the best known brands involved in the sport: CCM, JOFA, and KOHO. Primarily known for skates, CCM is a major North American brand that also makes equipment and jerseys. JOFA, founded in Sweden, is famous for its helmets and other high-quality equipment. Finnish brand KOHO started out in the 1950s as a stick manufacturer but has since added skates, protective equipment, and apparel to its product lines. In addition, The Hockey Company owns smaller sub-brands, including Canadien, Titan, and Heaton. While the Hockey Company is very much involved with professional hockey, providing equipment and official National Hockey League uniforms, its business is more reliant on equipment sales to young people as well as NHL-licensed apparel. To a much smaller degree, the company also sells in-line skates and ski and equestrian helmets. The Hockey Company is a subsidiary of Reebok International Ltd., the result of a 2004 acquisition.

Origins

The man behind the creation of The Hockey Company was a Montreal businessman named David Zunenshine, who first made his mark in the 1950s with the launch of a commercial real estate company, Belcourt Inc. In the 1970s, he took advantage of a tax-loss credit to diversify by acquiring a small Montreal knitting factory that produced athletic uniforms. With this toehold in the sporting goods industry, Zunenshine took a major step in 1983 when he purchased the hockey equipment business of CCM Inc. By acquiring CCM, an icon brand in North America, Zunenshine instantly made himself a player in the hockey equipment industry.

The history of CCM dates back to 1899 and the launch of Canada Cycle & Motor Company Limited in Weston, Ontario, Canada. CCM grew out of the bicycle industry, the result of five Canadian manufacturers—Massy-Harris, H.A. Lozier, Welland Vale, Goold, and Gendron—banding together to fend off U.S. competition in the form of the American Bicycle Company, which was looking to invade the Canadian market. As had been the case in the United States, the market for bicycles quickly became saturated, so that within a few years CCM looked for other sources of income. An attempt to become involved in the automobile business failed, prompting the company to turn its attention to ice hockey, a sport that had been gaining in popularity in Canada since the introduction of the Stanley Cup, a silver bowl awarded to the winning amateur hockey team in an annual tournament. Interest in the Stanley Cup led to the creation of professional leagues and eventually the creation of the National Hockey League in 1917. The first hockey product CCM introduced in the early years of the new century was the Automobile Skate. The new product line proved so successful that by the 1930s more than 90 percent of all NHL players used CCM skates, a fact that carried great weight in the sales to amateur players. Over the years, CCM reinforced its dominant position by enlisting major NHL stars as official spokesmen. CCM also remained Canada's leading bicycle manufacturer but began to falter in the early 1980s. Despite a government bailout, the company was forced into bankruptcy in 1983, resulting in Zunenshine picking up the hockey division and the bicycle assets sold elsewhere.

Company Adds Toy Assets in Late 1980s

Zunenshine's next move in diversification, two years later, was to acquire another struggling business, St. Lawrence Manufacturing Company Inc., a skate blade maker. Taking advantage of the company's plastic injection molding equity, he had the plant turn out plastic sleds as well. To add some summer sales to the mix, in 1988 he acquired the children's pool division of bankrupt Coleco Industries, a company that had enjoyed tremendous success with Cabbage Patch dolls in the mid-1980s but had failed to deliver a follow-up hit, posted massive losses, and was forced to shed assets as it spiraled into bankruptcy. Zuzenshine made further inroads into toys in 1990 through another distress sale, picking up the remains of U.S. toy truck maker Buddy L Corporation.

To take charge of his assorted toy and sporting goods interests, Zunenshine brought in Earl Takefman, a veteran of the toy industry. After earning his MBA, Takefman started his career in the school supply business, where he had success in licensing television and sports names to everyday items, such as NHL rulers and Kermit the Frog erasers. He moved into the toy industry, becoming president of Charan Industries, which succeeded nicely as the Canadian distributor of the fad doll Teddy Ruxpin. Unfortunately, when the U.S. supplier began to falter, it dumped merchandise into the marketplace, leaving Charan with overpriced inventory. The offer of employment from Zunenshine came just in time for Takefman, who now took over Zunenshine's collection of castoff assets. In addition, Zunenshine controlled a money-losing chain of Canadian fitness centers, which he began to shut down. Because he still owned the rights to market some exercise products, such as Heavy Hands weights, he placed that on Takefman's plate as well.

To turn around this assortment of money-losing companies, Zunenshine needed to raise funds and looked to the equity markets. When Canadian underwriters showed no interest, he turned to the United States, and in September 1991 he formed a Delaware corporation called SLM International, Inc., drawing on the initials of St. Lawrence Manufacturing for the company name. Now based in New York City, SLM made a public offering of stock at $10.50 a share in November 1991. Zunenshine's son, David Zunenshine, served as co-chief executive officer of the company, heading the sporting goods division in Montreal, while his counterpart, Takefman, handled the toy business from New York City offices.

After the infusion of cash, SLM enjoyed a successful run for the next few years. Takefman replicated his success in school supplies by licensing names for its pools and sleds, such as Big Bird for pools and Harley-Davidson for sleds. He supplemented this business in 1992 by acquiring Montreal-based Norca Industries Inc., maker of children's swimming pools and sleds, as well as sandboxes, some of which bore the Batman and Playskool licenses. To fill out the exercise equipment he inherited, Takefman acquired the licenses for other products, and began moving the merchandise with infomercials. Takefman was also adept at cutting ad budgets to lower prices and spur sales. Another

way he grew sales was by adding extras along with a lower price, such as integrating voice recognition into Buddy L trucks to give them an edge over more heavily promoted Tonka trucks.

The licensing idea was also taken up by the sporting goods division, which applied Reebok's "The Pump" cushion technology and logo to hockey skates. Sporting goods took another page from the toy side of the company by acquiring Innova-Dex Sports, maker of bicycle helmets, to provide seasonal balance to SLM's hockey helmet business. Also in 1992, SLM found a way to combine its toy and sporting goods aspirations by acquiring Kevin Sports Toys International, an Alberta, Canada-based company that produced the official Wayne Gretzky National Hockey League rod-driven table hockey game. As a result of these endeavors, SLM's balance sheet now showed a marked improvement. After the toy and sporting good assets combined for an operating loss of $2.2 million in 1990, the newly constituted SLM experienced records sales and earnings for several consecutive quarters, resulting in a soaring stock price.

SLM continued to expand in 1993. In May, it acquired The Toy Factory, Inc., a New Jersey maker of children's games. Later in the year it acquired #1 Apparel, a K-Products Inc. subsidiary that produced baseball caps and jackets. However, SLM's high-flying days soon came to an end, as rising advertising costs, especially the infomercials, and large debt soon overshadowed sales increases. Starting in the fourth quarter of 1993, the company began losing money. The situation was only exacerbated by the problems Zunenshine now endured with his Canadian real estate business, Belcourt, which was forced to file for bankruptcy in September 1994. SLM's stock, priced over $30 in November 1993, plummeted to less than $7 a year later. By this point, Takefman was already gone, having resigned in August 1994 because of philosophic differences over the company's future direction. Howard Zunenshine attempted to right the ship by emphasizing products that did not require much in the way of promotion, such as perennial models of trucks and swimming pools, but the change in strategy provided little relief.

From Bankruptcy to New Ownership: Mid-1990s and Beyond

In 1995, SLM began to discard assets. Buddy L. was sold to Empire of Carolina Inc. in January, followed a few months later by the sale of SLM Fitness assets to Madison Group Assets. Nevertheless, these moves could not halt the company's plunging stock price. The shares were delisted by the NASDAQ, and in October 1995 SLM filed for Chapter 11 protection in U.S. Bankruptcy Court in New York. The company's most valuable remaining asset was CCM, a traditionally profitable business that had been long neglected by the Zunenshines and Takefman. An example of mismanagement was the jersey division producing thousands of Quebec Nordiques jerseys well after the team had taken steps to relocate the franchise to Colorado. Many investors recognized CCM's underlying strength and began jockeying to gain control as SLM developed a plan of reorganization in 1996. The man that a reported 19 investment groups contacted to help take over was Gerald Wasserman, a former NHL back-up goalie now retired in California. A chartered accountant, Wasserman was a seasoned executive as well as an experienced hockey man. During his career he helped turn around Melchers Distilleries Ltd. and Bellevue Home Enter-

---

Key Dates:

1983: David Zunenshine acquires CCM Inc.
1991: Zunenshine forms SLM International, Inc.
1995: SLM files for Chapter 11 bankruptcy protection.
1997: SLM emerges from bankruptcy protection.
1998: Sports Holdings Corporation is acquired.
2000: SLM changes its name to The Hockey Company.
2004: Reebok acquires the company.

---

tainment Inc. In the late 1980s, he took over struggling Canstar Sports Inc., a company that made such non-hockey products as ski boots and appliances. Under Wasserman, Canstar focused on hockey, straying only as far afield as in-line skates. Having resurrected Canstar, Wasserman left in 1993 to become president of Weider Health and Fitness. Canstar was acquired in 1995 for CAD546 million by Nike, Inc., the U.S. athletic footwear company that had its sights set on hockey. Canstar subsequently changed its name to Bauer Inc.

In September 1996, Wasserman signed a five-year agreement to succeed Howard Zunenshine as SLM's CEO at the behest of a creditor's committee comprised of representatives from six insurance companies and several banks. With Wasserman in the fold, the New York investment firm Wellspring Holdings agreed to pay approximately $30 million to acquire a controlling stake, slightly over 50 percent, in SLM. The insurance companies took the rest, while Wasserman held stock options contingent upon the company's performance. Thus, early in 1997 SLM was able to emerge from bankruptcy protection and lost no time in introducing new products into the marketplace. This action was in keeping with Wasserman's strategy of spending money on research and development to position SLM as a leader in innovation.

SLM greatly expanded its hockey assets in the fall of 1998 when it acquired privately held Sports Holdings Corporation. During the mid-1990s, SHC had been involved in a number of sporting goods areas in addition to hockey, such as footwear, cross-country skis, and snowboards. By 1998, however, the company shed these assets to become a hockey-focused company, looking to exploit its stable of hockey brands, including Titan, Jofa, Canadien, Heathon, and Koho. Jofa and Koho were both venerable European brands doing business for half a century. In October 1998, SLM bought all the outstanding shares of SHC, thereby bringing all of the world's major hockey equipment brands under one roof. In keeping with the addition of these brands, which made it the largest manufacturer of ice and roller hockey equipment and apparel in the world, SLM in March 1999 changed its name to The Hockey Company, its headquarters now located in Montreal.

From a marketing perspective, The Hockey Company viewed itself as three separate companies operating as one. Thus, when in 2000 it won the licensing rights to manufacture and market jerseys for all 30 NHL teams as well as the uniforms for officials, the company parceled the business to the different brands. CCM and Koho would each supply 15 teams with official game jerseys, as well as manufacture replica and official

jerseys. Jofa, on the other hand, was tapped to provide the practice jerseys for all 30 teams as well as linesman jerseys. The other brands—Heaton, Canadien, and Titan—became sub-brands under the main three, with CCM associated with Heaton, Titan with Jofa, and Koho with Canadien. The Hockey Company supplemented its NHL apparel business in 2003 with the acquisition of Roger Edwards Sports, a company that produced vintage hockey apparel as well as other sports apparel items.

In June 2003, The Hockey Company completed an initial public offering, netting CAD72 million, and its shares began trading on the Toronto Stock Exchange. The company's days as a publicly traded company would be limited, however, as less than a year later, in April 2004, Reebok agreed to pay $204 million in cash and assume $125 million in debt to acquire The Hockey Company. It was an important deal for Reebok, ranked second behind Nike in almost every sports category. With the addition of The Hockey Company, however, Reebok dominated Nike and its Bauer subsidiary in the hockey market, with a 30 percent market share compared to Nike's 15. Moreover, NHL jerseys were doing well with young men, a demographic that Reebok hoped to target, as well as young girls, who were turning to hockey as a participatory sport in growing numbers. Across the board, participation in youth hockey leagues, high school teams, and college teams had been on the rise for the past decade. Moreover, sales of NHL-licensed apparel was growing, and that business dovetailed nicely with Reebok's successful apparel business, which already included providing uniforms for the National Football League and National Basketball Association.

Labor problems that resulted in the cancellation of the 2004–05 NHL season may have had an adverse impact on The Hockey Company in the short run, but its main business was in fact youth sales, and here the demographics—the continued rise of the echo generation of Baby Boomers—favored the company's long-term prospects.

Principal Subsidiaries

Sport Maska Inc.; Sport Holdings Corporation; JOFA AB; KHF Finland Oy.

Principal Competitors

Bauer Nike Hockey Inc.; Easton Sports, Inc.; K2 Inc.

Further Reading

Gatlin, Greg, "Reebok Skates into Hockey Big Time," *Boston Herald*, April 9, 2004, p. 33.
Klems, Brian, "The Hockey Company Sharpens Its Marketing Platforms," *Sporting Goods Business*, September 15, 2000, p. 13.
Millan, Luis, "Ice Follies," *Canadian Business*, June 1997, p. 126.
Reguly, Eric, "Toymaker SLM Playing with Big Boys," *Financial Post*, June 26, 1993, p. 14.
Sanford, Jeff, "The Ice Age: Will the Echo Generation Swap Their Toys for Hockey Sticks?" *Canadian Business*, May 12, 2003.
"SLM International"—A Buy in Toyland," *Financial World*, July 21, 1992, p. 16.
Weinberg, Neil, "One Thing Led to Another," *Forbes,* October 25, 1993, p. 206.
——, "Back to Basics," *Forbes*, November 7, 1994, p. 16.

—Ed Dinger

IINDUS

Indus International Inc.

3301 Windy Ridge Parkway S.E.
Atlanta, Georgia 30339-5618
U.S.A.
Telephone: (770) 952-8444
Toll Free: (800) 868-0497
Fax: (770) 955-2977
Web site: http://www.indus.com

Public Company
Incorporated: 1997
Employees: 850
Sales: $146.4 million (2004)
Stock Exchanges: NASDAQ
Ticker Symbol: IINT
NAIC: 511210 Software Publishers; 518210 Data
    Processing, Hosting, and Related Services; 54151
    Computer Systems Design and Related Services;
    541511 Custom Computer Programming Services;
    541512 Computer Systems Design Services; 541519
    Other Computer Related Services; 611420 Computer
    Training

Based in Atlanta, Georgia, Indus International Inc. is a leading provider of enterprise asset management (EAM) and service delivery management (SDM) products to some 300,000 customers in 40 countries. The company offers software and services in the areas of asset management, workforce management, customer relationship management, supply chain management, product lifecycle management, business process management, and maintenance/calibration management. It also provides custom training, return-on-investment analysis, financial and business analytics, complex billing, hosting, professional consulting, extended enterprise resource planning, post implementation optimization, and staff augmentation services. According to Indus, its offerings ''enable companies to optimize the management of their customers, workforce, spare parts inventory, tools, and documentation—empowering organizations to maximize efficiencies in their equipment, facilities, workforce, and field service operations.'' The company's customer base includes large

and small organizations in 20 major industries including chemicals, communications, complex industrial equipment, defense/aerospace, discrete manufacturing, energy delivery, facilities, forest products, healthcare, higher education, managed service provision, metals and mining, oil and gas, power generation, process manufacturing, the public sector, telecommunications, transportation, utilities, and water/wastewater. As of 2005, Indus had 56 strategic partnerships in place across the globe. More than 85 percent of the world's utility and energy firms used the company's products to manage their assets. Additionally, Indus was an industry leader in research and development, devoting some 30 percent of its revenues to this area.

Origins

Although Indus International was officially formed in 1997, its roots stretch back about 20 years earlier. One of the company's predecessors, The System Works International Inc. (TSW), was founded in 1976. TSW developed and distributed an asset management software suite called EMPAC. In its third year of operation, TSW was chosen by one of the world's most efficient aluminum smelting facilities to implement a computerized maintenance management system. According to Indus, this system was the first of its kind.

Indus International's other predecessor, the Indus Group Inc., was established in 1988. With operations based at 60 Spear Street in San Francisco, Indus Group operated as a sole proprietorship until it was incorporated in 1990. The company's first product was an asset management software suite called PassPort that helped companies in so-called process industries— namely the petrochemical and electric utility sectors— effectively comply with regulatory issues and maximize performance in a variety of areas.

By August 1993 PassPort's capabilities included work management, document management, purchasing, fugitive emissions management, inventory control, engineering change control, personnel qualifications data, and equipment tag-out. PassPort's software modules ranged in price from $50,000 to as much as $350,000, and were available across IBM's CICS family of products.

In October 1993, the Indus Group ranked third (first in California) on *Inc.*'s list of America's 500 fastest growing privately held companies. The average company on *Inc.*'s 500 list experienced annual growth of 1,761 percent that year, while Indus grew at a rate of 19,499 percent. This phenomenal growth translated into strong performance. From the time it incorporated in 1990 through 1994, Indus Group was a profitable company. By 1995 its sales totaled $53 million, up from $30.5 million the previous year and $27.5 million in 1993.

In 1994 Indus formed a consulting arm called the Reengineering Services Group that operated from its San Francisco headquarters, and from offices in Pittsburgh; Portland, Oregon; Stamford, Connecticut; Monterey, Mexico; and London. At the time, many of Indus Group's petrochemical and electric utility clients were reengineering their business processes and utilizing new technology to deal with a more complicated operating environment. Indus Group sought to provide its customers with meaningful guidance in translating conceptual strategies into new business practices.

In a January 27, 1994, *Business Wire* release, Indus Group President and CEO Robert Felton said: "We have learned through on-site experience, the 'best practices' of our customers and our packaged software products contain those solutions which serve as the catalyst for change. The expertise, tools and methodologies that made us an industry leader in the enterprise software solutions business will be made available to our reengineering customers. ... We distinguish ourselves from the consulting firms who write endless recommendations because acting as our customer's mechanic, we are the hands-on guys who get things done."

In 1995 Indus recorded its first net loss due to a one-time compensation charge. By this time the company had two product lines: PassPort and Abacus, and its clients included the likes of Pacific Gas & Electric Company and Chevron USA. Of its 320 employees, about one-third were involved in research and development initiatives. That year, a strategic alliance was formed with Computer Sciences Corporation to provide the utility industry with information technology services on an outsourced basis. In addition, the company employed a direct sales force that covered the United States, the United Kingdom, and the Middle East. Less than a decade after it was established, The Indus Group went public with an initial public offering on February 29, 1996.

A Powerhouse Is Born in the Late 1990s

On August 25, 1997, Indus Group merged with TSW International to form Indus International Inc., the largest enterprise asset management (EAM) software company in the world. By the time of the merger, TSW had developed into a leader in the asset care software market. Its Enterprise MPAC software included modules for asset maintenance, procurement, inventory, electronic document management, workflow, and workforce management.

Based in Atlanta, TSW had service centers in Australia, France, and the United Kingdom. It served more than 900 customer sites in 48 countries. These customers included discrete manufacturers, utilities, hospitals, process companies, transportation authorities, educational systems, and government agencies.

Indus Group CEO Robert W. Felton became the chairman and CEO of Indus International, while TSW International President and CEO Christopher R. Lane was named vice-chairman and president of strategy and product development. The newly formed enterprise had an expanded sales force of 120 people, and continued on its previous strategic course of supporting business segments within vertical markets. PassPort and Enterprise MPAC software became Indus International's two main product lines.

Building on the international presence that Indus Group and TSW already had prior to the merger, Indus International continued global expansion efforts with the formation of a wholly owned subsidiary called Indus International Canada Inc. in February 1998. At this time, a new office also was added in Buenos Aires, Argentina, to support Latin American/Caribbean customers. A third Australian office was added in May. Located in Melbourne, the new site joined existing offices in Brisbane and Sydney. Other developments in 1998 included the incorporation of Indus International's EAM system into Oracle Corporation's Oracle Energy business software suite, as well as $2 million in new education sector contracts, including one with the Yale University School of Medicine. Indus' revenues reached $195.5 million, up from $177 million in 1997. Net income for 1998 reached $13.4 million, up from $990,000 the previous year.

In 1999 Indus International benefited from a three-year, $60 million deal with British Energy. In addition to providing software and services to British Energy, Indus stood to improve its offerings by learning about the company's best practices and using that information to improve its software products. It also was in 1999 that Indus announced the publication of a new quarterly magazine called *Indus Insight*. Developed for the company's EAM customers, the new magazine contained best practices, tips, articles from customers and users, and information about industry trends.

Challenges in the Early 2000s

Indus International started the new millennium with the January appointment of Kent O. Hudson as president and CEO. Hudson, who served as a consultant to Indus during 1999 when the company designed its myindus.com Web portal, was the former president and CEO of Carolina Power and Light subsidiary Strategic Resource Solutions. Hudson replaced William Grabske, who had served an 11-month term as CEO. Indus credited Grabske with bolstering the company's internal processes and bringing discipline to its global operations. However, following his departure, Grabske sued Indus over the

Key Dates:

1976: The System Works International Inc. (TSW) is founded.

1988: The Indus Group Inc. is established.

1993: The Indus Group ranks third (first in California) on the *Inc.* list of America's 500 fastest growing private companies.

1997: Indus merges with TSW to form Indus International, the world's largest enterprise asset management software company.

1998: Company continues global expansion efforts with new offices in Canada, Argentina, and Australia.

2001: Indus relocates its headquarters to Atlanta. Employees number 1,000 in 18 offices throughout the world.

2002: Indus expands in Japan and China.

2003: Indus acquires Global Energy and Utilities Solutions for $37.8 million.

2004: Indus acquires Wishbone Systems Inc., a provider of workforce management and optimization software.

reimbursement of more than $100,000 in expenses and severance pay matters.

Shortly after this leadership change, a group of shareholders filed a class action lawsuit against Indus when the company's auditors indicated that third quarter 1999 revenues had been overstated. According to an April 7, 2000, *Business Wire* release, the lawsuit specifically charged "Indus International and certain of its officers and directors with issuing false and misleading statements concerning the Company's business and prospects."

By January 2001 the U.S. District Court for Northern California had approved a $4.3 million settlement between Indus and its shareholders. While this brought an end to the matter for the company, in September 2001 the Securities and Exchange Commission filed criminal and civil charges against Grabske and another former Indus executive, alleging that they had engaged in fraudulent accounting activity.

Amidst these challenges, Indus continued to introduce new offerings for its customers in 2000. The company integrated e-procurement software called IndusBuyDemand with its asset management offerings. This allowed Indus clients to take advantage of Internet exchanges and marketplaces. The company also unveiled a line of integration tools called IndusConnect, which enabled its clients to link software from other vendors to Indus applications. Initially, the company released tools pertaining to document control, GIS, and financial services. It also was in 2000 that Indus expanded its Canadian operations. In addition to more Canadian staff and office locations, Indus sought to increase strategic partnerships with other firms, increase its share of the application service provider market, and focus on small and medium-sized businesses.

By the beginning of 2001 Indus had moved beyond difficult legal challenges, as well as a number of management changes

that included key leadership. However, the company was faced with falling revenues and declining market share. In 2000 the company's revenues totaled $145.7 million, with a net loss of $58.8 million. This compared to revenues of $178.5 million and net income of $23.8 million in 1999.

In the January 19, 2001 issue of the *San Francisco Business Times*, META Group Vice-President Hollis Bischoff offered his view on Indus' predicament, commenting: "They were in the middle of their troubles when e-business took off . . . and by the time they figured out how to get on the e-train, that one had passed. They've suffered from bad timing and bad organization and it's going to take a while to get back in place, if there's a place for them to get back to."

Indus relocated its headquarters in May 2001. The company, which then employed some 1,000 workers in 18 offices throughout the world, moved from 60 Spear Street in San Francisco to a 107,200-square-foot facility at 3301 Windy Ridge Parkway in Atlanta. CEO Kent Hudson indicated that the more affordable real estate market in Atlanta would help the company in its effort to reduce expenses and increase shareholder value. The move included Indus' marketing, finance, and accounting operations, among others.

In 2001 Indus introduced a new PassPort software module called IndusAnyWare, which it developed in conjunction with IBM. In a January 10, 2001, *PR Newswire* release, the company said the module, which was part of its Indus Solution Series, offered: "the mobile computing architecture, mobile server and client application to extend the core asset management capabilities of PassPort's Work Management product to field personnel." Indus also released version 9.0 of its PassPort software, which was easier to use than past versions and included improvements related to safety and compliance, supply chain, and work management functions.

Indus' clients credited the company with improving its customer service during 2001. In the September 17, 2001, issue of *Computerworld*, Indus International User Group President Steve Thomas said that customers were very frustrated with the management team Indus had in place prior to CEO Kent Hudson, but that Hudson was more receptive to the needs of users and had even established a channel through which functionality upgrade requests could be submitted.

Indus ended 2001 with revenues of $176 million, up from $145.7 million in 2000. After reporting losses for seven consecutive quarters, the company reported a quarterly profit in October. While Indus once again experienced an annual net loss, at $11.5 million its losses were down from $58.8 million the previous year.

Indus expanded its Asian presence during 2002. In April, the company announced that it had enhanced its Tokyo office, formed a partnership with Kaihatsu Computing Service Center Ltd., and contracted with Japan's Electric Power Development Company Ltd. In December, *China Business News* reported that Indus had formed a partnership with Yao De Computer Software—an arm of A3 Systems Ltd.—to market its EAM Solutions in mainland China.

A number of significant leadership changes occurred at Indus in 2002. In January Thomas R. Madison was named chairman. That July, Madison assumed the additional role of CEO, replacing Kent Hudson. At that time, Chief Operating Officer Richard H. Beatty also parted ways with Indus after his position was eliminated as part of a larger effort to cut costs, restructure operations, and achieve profitability. Faced with weak IT spending in the utility and mining sectors, the company also planned to cut staff within its professional services group. Revenues for 2002 fell to $117.2 million, with a net loss of $33.8 million.

Indus started off 2003 by joining the Nuclear Energy Institute (NEI), the policy organization for the nuclear energy industry. The company announced that it would collaborate with the NEI and its members to develop standards and share best practices. In April Indus continued its Asian expansion efforts by inking a deal to provide software to Tokyo Electric Power Company., the world's largest private electric power company and the largest electrical utility in Japan.

In June 2003 Indus finalized its acquisition of Systems & Computer Technology Corporation's subsidiary Global Energy and Utilities Solutions (GEUS). The $37.8 million acquisition was expected to generate $60 million in annual revenues for Indus from licenses, maintenance, and service. GEUS eventually was renamed Indus Utility Systems. The deal prompted Indus to change its fiscal year-end from December 31 to March 31 in order to make it easier to compare the financial performance of the combined companies.

Approximately two months after the GEUS deal was finalized, Indus Executive Vice President Gregory J. Dukat was promoted to president and chief operating officer. That November, the company announced a new strategic initiative that aimed to help long-term revenue growth. Called Service Delivery Management (SDM), it essentially involved expanding Indus' market outside of the utility sector to include original equipment manufacturers and third-party service providers.

Indus began 2004 by acquiring Wishbone Systems Inc., a provider of workforce management and optimization software. In February, Indus President and COO Gregory Dukat assumed the additional role of CEO from Thomas Madison, who remained company chairman. The transition came at a positive time for the company, as it celebrated its third consecutive quarter of profitability. In addition, Indus announced a customer loyalty initiative called Indus Service Select that involved a corporate reorganization effort. According to a February 2, 2004, *Business Wire* release, Indus "combined its separate product development teams into a single organization and merged that group with the Customer Service Division to form the Global Development and Client Services (GDCS) group. Furthermore, the company has placed the responsibility for

developing strategy and vision for these products into a separate and independent Product Strategy organization."

Although Indus reported a fiscal year 2004 net loss of $12 million on revenues of $146.4 million, the company appeared to be on the road to recovery after a series of profitable quarters and a broadening client base. In August Indus announced that it has signed SDM deals with three new customers in France in the areas of facilities management, healthcare, and transportation.

Principal Competitors

AXS-One Inc.; Datastream Systems Inc.; GE Capital IT Solutions; i2 Technologies Inc.; IBM Corporation; Invensys plc; LogicaCMG plc; Microsoft Corporation; MRO Software Inc.; Oracle Corporation; SAP AG.

Further Reading

Alvey, Jennifer, "Indus Absorbs SCT Unit," *Public Utilities Fortnightly*, June 1, 2003.

"British Energy and Indus International Sign Ground-Breaking Enterprise Asset Management Partnership Deal," *European Report*, June 9, 1999.

Brown, Jennifer, "Indus Arming for Expansion Bid: More Staff, New President Marks Second Anniversary in Canada," *Computing Canada*, July 7, 2000.

Fried, Rinat, "The Indus Group Inc. Targets Industrial Niche," *Recorder*, March 13, 1996.

"Indus Announces Reengineering Services for Electric Utilities & Petrochemical Industries," *Business Wire*, January 27, 1994.

"Indus International Relocates Corporate Headquarters to Atlanta," *Business Wire*, May 25, 2001.

"Indus International Teams with IBM to Develop Mobile Computing Solution—IndusAnyWare," *PR Newswire*, January 10, 2001.

"Indus Opens New Office," *Computergram International*, May 21, 1998.

"Indus Reorganizes to Support Customer Loyalty Initiative," *Business Wire*, February 2, 2004.

Liedtke, Michael, "Feds File Charges of High-tech Fraud, Say More Cases in Works," *Associated Press State & Local Wire*, September 6, 2001.

"Lionbridge and Indus Expand into China in Partnership with Chinasoft and Yao De, Respectively," *China Business News*, December 12, 2002.

"Shareholder Class Action Filed Against Indus International, Inc. by the Law Firm of Schiffrin & Barroway, LLP," *PR Newswire*, April 7, 2000.

Songini, Marc L., "Indus Replaces CEO, Plans Cuts in New Turnaround Bid," *Computerworld*, July 8, 2002.

——, "Users Credit Indus with Changing," *Computerworld*, September 17, 2001.

Temple, James, "Cost-Conscious Indus Shops Around Sublease Space," *San Francisco Business Times*, January 19, 2001.

—Paul R. Greenland

Interbrand Corporation

130 Fifth Avenue
New York, New York 10011
U.S.A.
Telephone: (212) 798-7500
Fax: (212) 798-7501
Web site: http://www.interbrand.com

Wholly Owned Subsidiary of Omnicom Group Inc.
Founded: 1974 as Novamark
Employees: 1,000
Sales: $140 million (2003)
NAIC: 541611 Administrative Management and General Management

Interbrand Corporation is a subsidiary of Omnicom Group Inc., the world's largest advertising conglomerate. Interbrand is devoted to all aspects of branding, helping clients to develop new brand names or reposition existing ones through proprietary research methodologies. The company also designs the necessary graphics, and offers assistance in introducing brands across markets, protecting them, and determining their market value. In addition to its headquarters in New York City, Interbrand maintains more than 40 offices in 25 countries around the world.

Founder Becoming Involved in Branding in the 1970s

Interbrand was founded by John Murphy, a native of Essex in the United Kingdom. In 1962 he received a degree in geography at the University of Manchester, then turned his attention to business, becoming a marketing manager at Lessona Corporation. He returned to school at Brunel University, where he earned a technical degree in business management in 1966. Murphy's interest in branding began during his tenure at Dunlop Corporation, a longtime leader in the tire industry. Murphy joined Dunlop's corporate planning and marketing department in 1970 just after the company made the ill-fated decision to merge with Italian tire manufacturer Pirelli. The Italians were worried about conditions in their country, where the Mafia held sway and the Communist Party was making strides politically, and management looked to British control as a harbor in the storm. As for Dunlop, its chairman was bent on creating a global empire but his management team and the board of directors were not up to the task. Murphy, serving in his role as corporate planner, had an up-close view over the next four years of the unfolding disaster at Dunlop, watching—as he told *Brand Strategy in 2001*—"a great old British brand destroyed by incompetence. Decisions were made on the old-boy network, and nobody ever took any blame. I couldn't bear it." Murphy offered an even harsher assessment of Dunlop to *Marketing* in 1994: "The management there were complete idiots." But his work at Dunlop provided him with experience in branding when he was assigned the task of naming a new product.

Murphy found that naming a product, while difficult, was gratifying work. In 1974, at a time when his wife had completed her own education and was beginning to earn an income, Murphy decided to leave Dunlop and launch a product-naming consultancy, which he named Novamark. Initially working out of his London apartment, Murphy was soon joined by another disgruntled Dunlop employee: Mike Grant, Dunlop's trademark agent. The two divided the workload, with Grant handling the legal searching and trademark registration, while Murphy was in charge of sales and marketing. One of Novamark's important early clients was the Post Office, for which the firm created the Prestel brand name for a new teletext service. When the British government then decided to break off the telecommunications aspect of the Post Office, Novamark was hired to handle the naming of the new organization and created the British Telecom name. Moreover, the firm was asked to serve as British Telecom's trademark attorney, thereby adding legal work to Novamark's capabilities. It was a natural progression for clients to ask Novamark to take on the graphic work as well. Murphy was reluctant to move that far afield from his original plan—to serve as a wordsmith. In addition, he did not want to offend the design studios with which he worked. His opinion began to change, however, when he discovered that some of the design groups to whom he referred clients were charging five times as much as Novamark, which was doing the more important work. The final straw came when two of these studios announced they were launching their own brand naming companies. As a result,

---

Company Perspectives:

Since our founding in 1974, we have challenged our own ideas of what a brand can be, pioneering new ground in branding and growing through the diversity that surrounds us.

Murphy no longer felt any compunction about adding design capabilities to Novamark.

Murphy's major break came in 1979 when struggling auto-maker British Leyland hired Novamark at the last minute to help in the naming of a new vehicle, which represented a make-or-break moment for both Leyland and the British automobile industry, struggling to compete against European and Japanese imports. Leyland was satisfied with the car it designed but could not decide among the thousands of possible names they collected. Novamark narrowed down the possibilities to three: Match, Maestro, and Metro. The idea was to create some marketing continuity over a range of cars and the Metro name was ultimately chosen to serve that purpose. The first car in this line, the Mini Metro, was introduced in 1980, became an instant success, and ultimately gained the distinction as the United Kingdom's bestselling small car, with more than two million produced over the next 18 years.

A New York Office and a New Name in the Late 1970s

It was also in 1979 that at the behest of its clients, in particular the Mars candy company, Novamark decided to open a New York office, but under a new name, Interbrand, reflecting a shift in emphasis for the firm. No longer focused on naming and registering trademarks, the company was now involved in the more encompassing activity of branding, a seldom used word at the time. It was still a very small operation as it entered the 1980s, employing ten in London and just three in New York. The U.S. branch struggled in the early years and depended on funding from the London office. In 1986 Murphy hired Charles E. Brymer, an advertising veteran from the Batten Barton Durstine & Osborn agency, to serve as president, and he was instrumental in making the New York operation a success.

During the 1980s other international offices were opened—including Tokyo and Frankfurt in 1983, Milan in 1987, and Los Angeles and Melbourne in 1988—all of them offering a full range of branding services: naming, legal searches, and graphic design. By going global, Interbrand, almost out of necessity, developed abilities to deal with cross-language and cross-cultural branding. In many respects Interbrand remained a small company, but it had become increasingly difficult to run, given the wide range of talent employed: from lawyers to linguists to marketers to graphic designers to computer programmers. Murphy grew less comfortable with the operational responsibilities, preferring instead to concentrate on the more creative aspects, developing brands and pitching for business. To handle the day-to-day chores of making the firm work, he hired Michael Birkin, who had a law degree and was a trained accountant, to serve as managing director in London. Another important role player during the 1980s was finance director Paul Stobart.

During the 1980s Interbrand enjoyed a number of noteworthy achievements, including the 1984 naming of Prozac as well as Hobnobs, a popular English biscuit. A year later Interbrand coined the Slice name for Pepsi's new lemon-lime drink. The firm developed new award-winning packaging for the Boots United Kingdom drugstore chain in 1988, the same year that it named Land Rover's Discovery sport-utility vehicle. It was also during the 1980s that Interbrand developed the important concept of brand evaluation. Murphy explained to *Brand Strategy* in 2001 that the need for such a methodology arose because there was "a huge buying and selling of branded-goods businesses where what was essentially being bought and sold was brands. But nobody knew how to value brands." Sensing an opportunity, Interbrand proclaimed itself an expert in the field, despite never having attempted before to place a monetary value on a brand. In 1987 it announced that it had developed a proprietary methodology for brand evaluation and a year later completed its first project, valuing 50 brands for Ranks Hovis McDougall, one of the United Kingdom's largest flour millers. Then in 1989 Interbrand conducted the evaluation of the Pillsbury brand for the Grand Metropolitan PLC acquisition of Pillsbury Co., a milestone achievement in the branding industry. According to *Brand Strategy,* Interbrand's approach to brand evaluation consisted of three steps: "First, analysis of the brand's market, its management and its strength. Second: analysis of the brand's earnings, isolating those attributable to the brand rather than its parent company. . . . Third: a multiple is applied to brand earnings, based on the quality of the brand."

Surrounded by talented executives, Murphy entered the 1990s as the head of a small company facing a difficult decision in how to suitably award its chief lieutenants, given that he was not interested in giving up his job to any of them. They thought about taking the company public, but rejected that idea. In the meantime, the firm continued to take assignments from high-profile clients, including the design of packaging for Breyers ice cream, creating a new corporate identity for Compaq Computers, developing brand names for new SmithKline Beecham drugs, providing a global valuation of the IBM brand, and creating the Zeneca brand name for the life sciences business spun off from Imperial Chemical Industries PLC.

New Ownership in the Early 1990s

In late 1993 Murphy agreed to sell Interbrand to Omnicom, a deal that rewarded all ranks of the firm's staff, which now numbered about 600. Murphy agreed to stay on for two years to help in the transition, during which time he developed a new business interest: running a brewery. He resigned as Interbrand's chairman in April 1996. During the transition phase, the company opened a branch office in Seoul, South Korea, in 1994 and expanded by way of acquisition, adding Schechter Group, a New York brand consultancy and packaging design firm. Its founder, Alvin H. Schecter, would succeed Murphy as Interbrand's chairman, a post he held until retiring in 1999. Interbrand also gained a presence in Singapore by acquiring Design Counsel. The two companies previously had landed a contract together for the Singapore Broadcasting Corporation, which was undergoing privatization, and had worked well together. Interbrand bought a 40 percent stake in Design Counsel, then in 1996 bought the rest of the company. Also in 1996

Key Dates:

1974: The company is founded in London by John Murphy as Novamark.
1979: The name is changed to Interbrand, and an office opens in New York.
1984: The firm develops the Prozac name.
1994: Omnicom acquires Intercom.
1996: Murphy retires.
2001: A Shanghai office opens.
2004: A Moscow office opens.

Interbrand opened an office in Osaka, Japan; added a branch in Zurich, Switzerland, through the purchase of identity group Zintzmeyer & Lux; and acquired the New York design firm of Gertsman & Meyers. Some of the noteworthy work conducted by Interbrand during this transitional period included the positioning of the Deutsche Telekom brand, and the valuation of the Guinness brand.

Following Murphy's departure, Brymer as CEO carried on the task of growing Interbrand, adding the chairmanship after Schecter's retirement. In 1997 the firm opened offices in Jakarta, Indonesia, and Mexico City. It also acquired another firm, London-based Newell and Sorell. Interbrand opened an office in Johannesburg, South Africa, in 1998, and added a branch in Buenos Aires, Argentina, by acquiring the design firm of Avalos and Bourse. Interbrand closed out the 1990s by opening an office in Santiago, Chile. Some of the important work the firm completed in the final years of the decade included the creation of new corporate identities for insurer Nationwide and the accounting firm of PricewaterhouseCoopers; redesigning new looks for Quilmes, a popular South American beer, and Grupo Financiero Bancomer, one of Mexico's major banks; and creating the Imation brand for a 3M spin-off. Interbrand also became involved in publishing, offering several titles: *Trademarks,* a book on brand protection; *Brands: The New Wealth Creators; Brand Valuation; Co-Branding;* and *The Future of Brands.*

In the early years of the 21st century, Interbrand continued its worldwide expansion. In 2000 it opened offices in Sao Paulo, Brazil, and Munich, Germany, and moved into Toronto, Canada, by acquiring Tudhope Associates, a design consultancy. Also in 2000 Interbrand acquired Cincinnati-based Hulefeld Associates, a 70-year-old design firm boasting major Midwest clients such as Procter and Gamble and the Kroger supermarket chain. Interbrand established a presence in China in 2001, opening a Shanghai office. In that year it also completed a pair of acquisitions: New York-based Wood Worldwide, involved in pharmaceutical brand name development, and the Paris-based design group Gerard Barrau. In 2002 Interbrand acquired Dayton, Ohio-based Design Forum, a firm specializing in branding through store design. An office in Bangkok was added in 2003 and Moscow in 2004. The firm continued to do work for some of the most high-profile brands in the world, including Heinz ketchup, the Subway sandwich chain, the Cooper Mini automobile, Samsung, and Nikon. Interbrand also did work for notable clients such as the Girl Scouts of America, redesigning its look and packaging, and the 2002 FIFA World Cup soccer tournament in Japan and Korea.

Although many product category leading brands were developed in the United States—the likes of Kodak, Wrigley, Kellogg's, Nabisco, Del Monte, Singer, Campbell's, and Gillette—and had been at the top since 1920s, there was reason to believe that other parts of the world, in particular Asia, were developing equally strong brands. Regardless of any shift in branding power from the West to the East, Interbrand was well positioned to retain its role as the leading brand consultancy for years to come.

Principal Competitors

FutureBrand Worldwide; Landor Associates; Wolff Olins.

Further Reading

"John Murphy Walks Out on the Retreads," *Brand Strategy,* May 1, 2001, p. 3.
Lewis, Colin, "Murphy's Law Is Art of Measuring Brands," *Birmingham Post,* February 26, 2001, p. 13.
Meller, Paul, "It's All in a Name for Metro Man," *Marketing,* May 26, 1994, p. 25.
Simmonds, John, "It's Branding, But Not As You Know It," *Observer* (London, U.K.), October 17, 2004, p. 12.

—Ed Dinger

JanSport, Inc.

N850 County Road CB
Appleton, Wisconsin 54912-1817
U.S.A.
Telephone: (920) 734-5708
Fax: (920) 831-7779
Web site: http://www.jansport.com

Wholly Owned Subsidiary of VF Corporation
Founded: 1967
Employees: 800 (est.)
Sales: $300 million (2004 est.)
NAIC: 315999 Other Apparel Accessories and Other
   Apparel Manufacturing

JanSport, Inc., is the leading designer and maker of backpacks, shoulder bags, luggage, and laptop bags. The company is a subsidiary of VF Corporation, better known for its blue jeans lines, including Lee, Rustler, Wrangler, and Rider. JanSport also offers apparel, designed by another VF subsidiary, San Francisco-based The North Face. The lines of traditional and snowsports outerwear and accessories were launched in the fall of 2004, with plans to add sleeping bags and tents.

Company's Founding in the Late 1960s

JanSport grew out of a design contest sponsored by the Alcoa aluminum company. Seattle native Murray Pletz won the competition with his design for an aluminum flexible-frame backpack. Using his winnings, he joined forces with his cousin, Skip Yowell, to launch a company to make backpacks. Although they managed to find a temporary home for the business above the Seattle transmission shop owned by Pletz's father, the young entrepreneurs faced an additional problem. Neither one knew how to sew. Pletz appealed for help from his girlfriend, Jan Lewis, who knew how to sew, and made an unusual offer to induce her to join the fledgling business. Not only would he name the company after her, Pletz promised to marry Lewis. As a result the new backpack company took the name JanSport, and two of the company's three founders were wed. The marriage would end in the 1970s, but the company carried on, with

Pletz leaving and Lewis and Yowell staying to help JanSport to grow into a very successful company.

Early on JanSport made its mark with a panel-loading daypack, offering a different approach to traditional top-loading packs. The company received its first patent on this design in 1970. A year later Yowell further demonstrated his creative abilities by applying the concept of the Eskimo Igloo to create the first dome tent, a revolutionary design concept that unfortunately he did not patent. Another major innovation credited to the company during this period was the 1972 introduction of the first D-2 technical pack, designed for a Himalayas' expedition, featuring an adjustable hip arm. It was also in 1972 that the ownership of JanSport changed hands for the first time, with the business sold to ski-maker K2 Corporation.

K2 was launched in 1967 by brothers William and Don Kirschner and grew out of a Seattle company started by their father, Kirschner Manufacturing, which in the years following World War II was involved in making fiberglass animal splints and, later, chew-proof fiberglass dog crates. In the late 1950s William Kirschner decided to use fiberglass to make skis, which only recently had graduated from hickory wood as a raw material. Kirschner owed a debt of gratitude to a failed-writer-turned-aircraft engineer named Howard Head, who gave skiing a try in the mid-1940s. Faring poorly, Head blamed his wooden skis, which he concluded too easily lost their shape and resulted in an unstable ride. He decided to develop his own skis using metal and aircraft manufacturing techniques, resulting in the first composite ski, combining two layers of aluminum bonded to plywood sidewalls. By the mid-1950s Head was the leading brand of skis in the United States and Europe, and within a few more years Hickory skis were all but forgotten. Kirschner revolutionized the industry further with the introduction of fiberglass skis, which Kirschner Manufacturing first offered in 1964. The demand for the product was so strong that the Kirschner brothers formed a separate company devoted to skis, K2, named for the founding brothers as well as the second largest mountain in the world. In 1970 the company was sold to Indiana-based Cummins Engine Company, which at the time was branching out in a number of directions, including leisure goods. JanSport was one of its acquisitions in this category. Six years later, however, William Kirschner and some partners regained control of K2 Corporation, and along with it JanSport. But when disappointing snowfalls in the early 1980s hurt business, K2's ski business suffered, forcing the company to sell off noncore assets, eventually leading to the sale of K2 to Anthony Industries.

Mid-1970s: A Period of Innovation

During the K2 years, JanSport, now based in Everett, Washington, made strides on a number of fronts. In 1975 the company introduced the first convertible travel pack, a concept that was ahead of its time and only found a market about a decade later. JanSport introduced its signature product, the daypack, in 1975. It became such a classic, used by countless students to transport books and binders from home to school, that the company never felt the need to change the design. Also of note during this period was the 1978 climb of K2 by mountaineer Jim Whittaker using a JanSport pack called the Alpine Phantom, which Whittaker helped to design. This endeavor was in keeping with Yowell's tradition of testing JanSport equipment in the grueling conditions of mountain climbs. In addition to backpacks, the company by this time was manufacturing tents and sleeping bags.

K2 sold JanSport to Appleton, Wisconsin-based Downers, a college sweatshirt company in April 1982. Downers was started by a high school student named Kim Vanderhyden, who made silk-screen T-shirts for friends in the basement of his parents' home. In 1967 he formed Downers—referring to another basement location for the business, this beneath an Appleton movie theater. In 1975 Dan Spalding took over running the business, which made T-shirts with school logos sold to sporting goods stores and college bookstores. Spalding began mailing a catalog and assembled a sales staff, and in just five years he improved sales from less than $200,000 to $20 million. The $5 million acquisition of JanSport represented a major step for Downers. Spalding, with his knowledge of the college market, coveted JanSports' backpacks, which he knew were highly popular with high school and college students. He dropped the tent and sleeping bag product lines and shifted the marketing focus from sporting goods stores to mass merchants. He also brought in a new advertising agency to make a concerted effort to target a younger demographic. He elected to take advantage of JanSport's brand recognition and in December 1982 Downers changed its name to JanSport, Inc.

Less than two years after Spalding took over, however, the company again changed owners, as the new JanSport was acquired by Jantzen, Inc., a swimwear subsidiary of Blue Bell, Inc., maker of Wrangler jeans, western wear, uniforms, and work clothes. The hope was that Jantzen's greater resources, both in terms of money and production capabilities, would help JanSport to accelerate its growth, but another major factor in

agreeing to sell the business was that Spalding received an offer that he felt exceeded the worth of the company. In truth, Blue Bell was saddled with debt because of this and other acquisitions, and JanSport's ownership carousel continued. The company again changed hands in 1986 when Blue Bell was acquired by VF Corporation in a deal worth $775 million.

The roots of VF date back to 1899 and the founding of the Reading Glove and Mitten Manufacturing Company. In 1919 the company added undergarments to the product mix and took the name Vanity Fair Silk Mills. The company then went public in 1951, and in 1969 acquired its first jeans company, H.D. Lee Company, and also changed its name to VF Corporation. The addition of Blue Bell was important because its doubled the company's size and provided VF with a 25 percent market share in the $6 billion jeans industry. Moreover, VF achieved a level of diversification by adding the likes of Red Nap workwear, Jantzen swimwear, and JanSport backpacks.

Despite the change in ownership, Spalding stayed on to run JanSport. In 1985 the company reached a pair of milestones, selling its millionth daypack and reaching sales of $25 million for the year. Spalding stayed until 1988, when he left to take over another Wisconsin business, Valley School Supply, at the behest of his father, who was a part-owner of the failing school supply business. Spalding would achieve spectacular results, transforming Valley School Supply into School Specialty, Inc., a $1 billion company. Before leaving JanSport, Spalding organized the company under a strategic business unit model, whereby separate sales and marketing teams were created to concentrate on the apparel and backpack divisions. The company also launched a merchandising program named JS 2000, the thrust of which was to further move backpacks out of retailers' camping departments and cross-merchandise them with other products. During the Back-To-School season, for instance, JanSport urged retailers to make backpacks available where parents and children bought clothes and footwear. Moreover, the JS 2000 program also sought to make backpacks available in stores and showed retailers how to best present the product. As a result, JanSport sales began to grow at a steady clip. In 1987 the company controlled about 5.2 percent of the daypack market, a number that reached 10 percent a year later. Sales were spurred by clever use of television advertising, with spots running on MTV, ESPN, and other programming. The sale of daypacks then surged with the start of the 1990s, so that by 1994 the company controlled 27 percent of the market and had a virtual lock on the college bookstore channel.

With the departure of Spalding, JanSport was headed by President Dan Delorey, who had become friends with Vanderhyden in 1977. A psychology major, Delorey had no ambitions for a business career, although he had worked in a bookstore at Eastern Michigan University. Vanderhyden eventually convinced Delorey to come to work for Downers, and he accepted, taking charge of assembling the company's first college sales force. He successfully carried out what Spalding had begun, although the company suffered a misstep in 1990 when it had to discontinue an apparel line that got off to a poor start. But a year later the company launched JanSport Apparel, offering pants, jeans, sweatshirts, jackets, and other products in keeping with a rugged outdoor image. Aside from daypacks, JanSport also was enjoying strong growth in the backpack and briefcase divisions, leading to expansions in the company's production and distribution capabilities. In December 1993 the company moved its international headquarters from Everett, Wisconsin, to a new 212,000-square-foot facility near Appleton, twice as large as the former Downers plant.

Shift in Strategy in the Mid-1990s

For years JanSport successfully sold daypacks into the mass merchants, full-line, and specialty channels, but by the mid-1990s the company had to revisit its distribution policy, which had been tilted too much in favor of selling to mass merchants. It also faced increased competition from Wolverine and The North Face, both of which made strong bids in the daypack category. To protect the value of its brand, JanSport in 1995 launched a replacement brand for the mass merchandise market, Wolf Creek, and began to restrict which retailers would be able to carry the JanSport lines. The company also entered the rugged footwear business in 1995, but the timing proved poor. The market for such products was soft, and JanSport decided that despite having a quality product to sell it was better served by making a quick exit from the business and not devoting resources to an area that required a long-term commitment.

In the second half of the 1990s JanSport added to its lines of packs, or what the company referred to as "convenience bags," as sales grew to the $150 million to $200 million range. In 1996 it introduced waterproof rubber-bottom packs. A year later it brought out a technical equipment line, offering specialty packs suited for laptop computers and CD players, as well as bags designed for biking, hiking, skating, and skateboarding. In 1999 JanSport invented the innovative Airlift and Loadlift backpacks. The company also began to offer transparent packs in response to the shootings at Columbine High School and violence on other school campuses.

Innovation continued into the new century. In 2002 JanSport introduced a collection of business casual luggage, as well as the Lifestyle line of shoulder bags and crossover packs. A year later the company brought out its first technical product de-

signed with women in mind. Also in 2002 it added an Active travel line of bags. Aside from internal growth, JanSport grew by way of acquisitions. In 2000 it bought its largest competitor, Eastpak, which had a 6 percent market share, doing about $90 million in sales, mostly in Europe. The company was formed in the 1960s as Eastern Canvas Products, maker of duffel bags and backpacks for the U.S. Army. In 1977 it entered the daypack market under the Eastpak label, selling into the college market.

At the end of 2001 Delorey, who was just 50, chose to retire, citing a desire to spend more time with his family and to pursue volunteer work after countless long hours working for JanSport. He was replaced as president by Michael P. Cisler, a 24-year veteran of the company who had spearheaded the Eastpak acquisition and was well familiar with virtually the entire operation, having held positions in operations, information systems, marketing, finance, and strategic planning. During his two-year tenure as president, Cisler oversaw the launch of a line of outerwear and accessories, to be designed by a recent VF acquisition, The North Face. VF brought the supply chain expertise and other resources. JanSport also looked to bring back some of its original products, tents and sleeping bags, and possibly make another attempt at footwear. In the fall of 2004 JanSport decided to move its equipment division to The North Face facilities in San Francisco, leaving the customer apparel business—the licensed clothing business created by Downers for the college bookstore and sporting goods stores—to remain in Appleton. A few weeks later, Cisler left JanSport, replaced by Mike Corvino, the vice-president of sales and merchandising at VF Imagewear.

Principal Divisions

Eastpak.

Principal Competitors

L.L. Bean, Inc.; Samsonite Corporation; The Timberland Company.

Further Reading

Dougherty, Terri, "A Business Made Up of Several Businesses," *Marketplace Magazine,* September 13, 1994, p. 37.
——, " 'We Invest in our employees,' JanSport's New Corporate Headquarters Was Built with the Company's Workers—and Their Children—in Mind," *Marketplace Magazine,* March 1, 1994, p. 6.
McEvoy, Christopher, "Paul Delorey," *Sporting Good Business,* March 1999, p. 55.
Prinzing, Debra, "Bulging at the Seams, JanSport Plans Expansion," *Puget Sound Business Journal,* July 31, 1989, p. 3.
Zuhl, Joanne, "Greenville, Wis.-Based Backpack Maker to Acquire Lowell, Mass.-Based Rival," *Post-Crescent,* March 23, 2000.

—Ed Dinger

John Frieda Professional Hair Care Inc.

57 Danbury Road
Wilton, Connecticut 06897
U.S.A.
Telephone: (203) 762-1233
Fax: (203) 762-2262
Web site: http://www.johnfrieda.com

Wholly Owned Subsidiary of Kao Brands Company
Incorporated: 1989
Employees: 130
Sales: $200 million (2004 est.)
NAIC: 325620 Toilet Preparation Manufacturing

John Frieda Professional Hair Care Inc. sells a wide variety of hair care products and shampoos through drugstores, supermarkets, and mass merchants. The company's signature product is Frizz-Ease, developed by British celebrity hair stylist John Frieda in the 1980s. Since then, he has worked with chemists to develop products to address specific needs of virtually all hair types (from frizzy to limp) and colors, which are addressed in the Sheer Blonde, Brilliant Brunette, and Radiant Red product lines. Although Frieda remains very much involved in the company, it is now a subsidiary of Kao Brands Company (formerly Andrew Jergens Company), which in turn is owned by Kao Corporation, Japan's leading manufacturer of personal care, laundry, and cleaning products. John Frieda Professional is based in Wilton, Connecticut.

Launch of a Hairstyling Career in the 1970s

Grooming hair was already a family tradition when John Frieda was born in England in 1951. His grandfather, a Polish immigrant, was a Fleet Street barber whose customers included newspaper mogul Lord Beaverton. Frieda's father switched to women's hairstyling, his clientele including the likes of movie star Ava Gardner, Eleanor Roosevelt, and Clementine Churchill, wife of Winston Churchill. He also dabbled in real estate. Frieda, along with his three siblings, enjoyed visiting his father's shop, in large measure because it was conveniently located behind a candy store. Early on, Frieda did not intend to

follow in the footsteps of his father and grandfather, dreaming instead of becoming a doctor. But as a teenager he was distracted from his private school education by—in his own words—a combination of "girls, cars and fun." After failing all of his exams, Frieda asked his father for a job, primarily to avoid schoolwork. While trying to convince the youngster to resume his studies, the elder Frieda allowed him to work in the salon on Saturdays. When he concluded that John was determined to become a hairdresser, he decided to make the best of the situation and found him an apprenticeship at one of London's major salons: the House of Leonard, headed by Vidal Sassoon protégé Leonard Lewis. After a month Frieda became Lewis's top assistant, a position that suddenly thrust him—albeit a bit player—onto the stage of London's fashion and celebrity world of the late 1960s. He now found himself catering to supermodels and celebrities. Soon he began to do some styling on his own, taking on clients such as singer Diana Ross and Jacqueline Kennedy Onassis. He also displayed something of his father's entrepreneurial spirit, investing in real estate, so that by the age of 20 he owned three houses.

Having started out as a hairdresser at such an early age, Frieda was bored with his position at the House of Leonard by the time he was 25 and even considered quitting the business. Instead, he decided to fulfill his need for a challenge by opening his own salon in 1976, a move he had earlier resisted, fearful that taking on managerial responsibilities might hamper his creativity. He joined forces with another Leonard stylist, Nicky Clarke, to open a salon in London. It was here that Frieda made a name for himself by creating the "Purdey" cut, a bowl-shaped bob that graced actress Joanna Lumley, who is best known today for her role in the "Absolutely Fabulous" television comedy, but at the time was playing the character of Purdey in the 1976–78 revival of "The Avengers," a popular 1960s British television series. The Purdey cut was much imitated and helped Frieda to open the first salon that featured his name.

Frieda began building up his own roster of celebrity clientele, one of whom was not yet well known but would emerge as one of the most famous and admired women in history. In 1980 he received a call from someone at British *Vogue* asking him to come to Lord Snowdon's home. Here he met a 19-year-old girl,

Lady Diana Spencer, who would soon become known to the world simply as Lady Di. Although she became his most famous client, Frieda did not lack for celebrity clients, a situation aided by having married one in 1976: singer Lulu. But even owning and operating a successful salon failed to challenge Frieda for very long. He dismissed the idea of opening more salons, instead deciding to become involved in hair care products. At the time, creating a professional line bearing the name of a stylist was still a novel idea, the only example being the Vidal Sassoon label, which had been introduced in 1973.

Developing Hair Care Products in the Mid-1980s

Frieda used his experience working on fashion-shoots, day-long affairs during which models' elaborate hairstyles had to be changed often, hold, then rinse out easily. He had learned a number of tricks to control hair and decided to find a way to make them into viable products. Working with a chemist, Frieda developed a thickening lotion, which along with some other signature products he began using in his salon and selling to clients. The line proved so popular that women were soon visiting the shop simply to buy the lotions. Frieda sensed that his products had retail potential but he knew he lacked the necessary knowledge about marketing and distribution needed to launch the line properly. The need for a seasoned business partner increased when British drugstore chain Boots, which was interested in trying upscale designer-brand products, became aware of Frieda's product and wrote a letter to him requesting a meeting to discuss the possibility of retailing the product in its stores.

A thickening lotion was taken on by Boots on a trial basis in 1988 and performed well enough that the chain placed a 20,000-bottle order. For Frieda it was a major step up, since he had been ordering only a few hundred bottles a month from his supplier. It was around this time that he met the woman who would become his business partner and play a major role in the success of the fledgling products business. Her name was Gail Federici, vice-president of advertising and marketing at Zotos, a U.S.-based hair care company. She was in London working on a video for Zotos and also recruiting a guest artist for a trade show in Milan. She watched about 20 presentations at an Alternative Hair Show, and was impressed by Frieda, who stood out from the rest. She met with him and they hit it off, deciding to work on a styling book together, an idea that was then approved by Zotos. While they worked together on the project, Frieda was attempting to run his new products business out of the basement of his salon. His line of Signature products would include a thickening lotion, bodifying mousse, and a nonsticky hair spray. Frieda's life became even more hectic after making an appearance on television to perform a ''before and after'' demonstration of his thickening product. The response was immediate, as the television station's

switchboard was flooded with inquiries about where to buy the product. Frieda's line, which had started out in 40 Boots stores, was to be found in more than 1,000 within six months. Suddenly he was hit with an order for 1.2 million bottles of thickening lotion. At this important juncture, just when he needed help the most, Federici was on the verge of quitting her job, looking for a change of pace and thinking about launching her own advertising agency. Frieda suggested she do some consulting work for him, to help him get a handle on his new business. They decided in the end to become partners, and in 1989 formed John Frieda Professional Hair Care Inc., with Federici serving as president and each owning half of the business.

John Frieda Professional wasted little time in taking on the U.S. market. In 1990 Frieda opened a New York salon, which provided a platform to launch a newly developed product, Frizz-Ease Serum, into the U.S. market. The product grew out of complaints he fielded from salon clients who were frustrated about their uncontrollable frizzy hair. Because the marketing budget was a miniscule $30,000, Frieda had to hawk Frizz-Ease at personal appearances and on television talk shows, this before makeover programs became a staple of daytime television. The hard work paid off, leading to a major break when the hair care buyer for the Eckerd Drugstore chain, Richard Hakel, took a gamble and decided to stock Frizz-Ease, a rarity for a single-product company. It proved to be a shrewd move. Not only did Frizz-Ease find a ready market in the United States, its high price of $9.99—at a time when $5 was the threshold for hairstyling products—did not drive away customers. Instead, it provided retailers with a healthy profit margin of 40 percent. Those numbers caught the attention of other drugstore chains and retailers, who soon began to stock Frizz-Ease as well. To the original product, John Frieda Professional systematically added another dozen products to the line, including shampoos and conditioners.

Frizz-Ease was launched in the United Kingdom in 1992, while the original John Frieda Signature line of products sold by Boots was launched in the United States in 1994. The collection of six products debuted in three drugstore chains: Eckerd's, CVS, and Walgreen's. A year later the number of locations grew fourfold, as Signature was picked up by retailers such as Perry, Revco, Thrifty, Arbor, and Target. John Frieda's name, despite his many successful American television appearances, did not carry the same clout as it did in England, however. The line struggled to find its place in the market, leading in 1996 to a change in name to Ready To Wear, an allusion to the fashion industry as well as connoting speed and ease of use.

Successes in the Late 1990s

John Frieda Professional enjoyed greater success in October 1998 when it launched Sheer Blonde, a line of seven hair care products aimed to address specific problems encountered with pale hair. Sheer Blonde helped to drive company growth, and within a year three more styling products were added to the line. It also elevated John Frieda to household name status, due in large part to television commercials in which he appeared pitching the product line. Meanwhile, sales of Frizz-Ease remained strong, but Ready to Wear, while generating an acceptable level of sales, continued to fall short of expectations. The line was designed for fine-limp hair, but unlike Frizz-Ease and Sheer

Key Dates:

1976: John Frieda opens his first hairstyling salon in London.
1988: The Boots drugstore chain begins selling the John Frieda Signature line of products in the United Kingdom.
1989: John Frieda Professional Hair Care Inc. is formed.
1990: Frizz-Ease is launched in the United States.
1998: The Sheer Blonde line is launched.
2002: Kao Corporation acquires the company.
2004: The Brilliant Brunette line is launched.
2005: The Radiant Red line is launched.

Blonde, there was nothing in the name that immediately communicated the mission to the consumer. Unable to coin a more suitable name, the company tweaked the line, dropping the price of the shampoo from $4.99 to $3.99, and adding a pair of new styling products. On another front, in 1999 John Frieda opened a Los Angeles salon with stylist Sally Hershberger, known for the much copied style she created for actress Meg Ryan. The posh Melrose Avenue salon was called Sally Hershberger at John Frieda. By now he ran five salons, including three in London and one in Paris.

John Frieda Professional expanded into new and usual distribution channels in 2000, targeting the teenage market by offering exclusives to the Tower Records music and video chain in the United States. The items included Summer Shimmer, a shine-building kit that came in four different versions, essentially repackaging products from the company's three main lines; and Sparkle and Shine, which packaged Frizz-Ease with the company's Shine Serum and an assortment of hair jewels. Tower also sold the company's four Hot Hollywood Hair kits, which combined a booklet of Hershberger styling tips with Sheer Blonde, Frizz Ease, and Ready to Wear products. The Top Shop apparel chain, which catered to the teen market in the United Kingdom, also agreed to distribute the kits. In 2001 John Frieda Professional launched a new product line, but again it was a variation on one of the three major lines. Frizz-Ease Relax was a nine-product line targeting women with relaxed hair, especially African-American women.

In August 2002 Frieda and Federici agreed to sell John Frieda Professional to Kao Corporation's subsidiary, The Andrew Jergens Company, for $450 million. John Frieda's salons were not part of the deal. Kao derived about 30 percent of its $6.3 billion in annual revenues from beauty products and had set a goal to become the leading marketer of premium personal care products in North America. In 2001 Kao almost acquired Clairol from Bristol Myers Squibb for $4.5 billion in an auction, but at the eleventh hour was outbid by Procter & Gamble Company, which took the prize after upping its offer to almost $5 billion. Although Kao acquired John Frieda Professional only because it lost out on Clairol, it was an acquisition that proved beneficial to both sides. Federici and Frieda were able to cash out, while

Frieda also stayed on to serve as CEO and was well supported by Jergens' management, based in Cincinnati. Within a matter of weeks accounting, human resources, information technology, and other support services were transferred from the Wilton, Connecticut, headquarters to Cincinnati. The European operation also was reorganized, with a centralized management system replaced by a set of country managers in the United Kingdom, Germany, France, Holland, Denmark, Norway, and Sweden, each charged with marketing the products to their individual countries. In addition, Kao had deep enough pockets to promote the Frieda product lines, which possessed a great deal of untapped potential. The company had spent only $5 million in advertising in the United States in 2002, but that amount increased dramatically, to about $30 million in 2003.

The increased promotion budget would be put to good use as John Frieda Professional began launching a number of new product lines. In 2004 the company brought out Volume, a line of seven cleansers and styling products, as well as the Brilliant Brunette line that played to the success of Sheer Blonde. The 12-product collection was designed to add shine and draw out the color of brown hair. On another front in 2004, John Frieda succeeded in recruiting French hairstylist Serge Normant to headline a New York salon. Furthermore, Normant became John Frieda Professional's first creative director, and the first dual appointment with the salon business and the Kao-owned hair products company.

In early 2005 John Frieda Professional completed its trilogy of hair care product lines with the launch of Radiant Red, products geared primarily to prevent color shifting. Because so much red hair was achieved through dyes, redheads had to contend with colors that either turned too brown or too orange. The new line included shampoos, conditioners, sealers, and hairsprays. The company now believed it was able to address the concerns of 95 percent of the population, thus reaching critical mass. Having exceeded the $200 million mark in revenues in 2004 and sales growing at a fast clip, there was every reason to expect John Frieda Professional to continue to prosper for the foreseeable future.

Principal Competitors

P&G-Clairol, Inc.; L'Oreal S.A.; Revlon, Inc.

Further Reading

"Frieda Makes Mark on Hair Care Category," *Chain Drug Review*, December 5, 1994, p. 58.
Grossman, Andrea M., "KAO Corp. Snares John Frieda Hair Care Brand for $450 Million," *WWD*, August 2, 2002, p. 1.
Lague, Louise, "Wigged Out? Worry Not! A British Hairstylist, John Frieda, Has a Formula to Take the Fight Out of Frizz," *People Weekly*, May 10, 1993, p. 57.
Oldfield, Claire, "Grooming Guru Takes on the Industry's Giants," *Sunday Times*, June 27, 1999, p. 15.
Thackray, Rachelle, "Me and My Partner: John Frieda and Gail Federici," *Independent* (London, U.K.), November 24, 1999, p. 8.

—Ed Dinger

The Jordan Company LP

767 Fifth Avenue, 48th Floor
New York, New York 10153
U.S.A.
Telephone: (212) 572-0800
Fax: (212) 755-5263
Web site: http://www.thejordancompany.com

Private Company
Founded: 1982
Employees: 25
Operating Revenues: $4 billion (2004)
NAIC: 522339 Miscellaneous Financial Investment
   Activities

The Jordan Company LP is a New York City-based private investment firm. Although formed in the 1980s and a practitioner of leveraged buyouts, TJC has never adopted the corporate raider approach of that era, selling assets and slashing costs as a way to realize a quick profit, however harmful to the long-term health of the acquisition. Instead, the management team, led by partners John "Jay" Jordan and David Zalaznick, prides itself on being "patient money" and taking steps to insure an acquired company is positioned for future growth. TJC targets well-run companies, enlisting management as partners by offering an equity stake in the business. TJC also makes sure the company is not overburdened with debt, then provides the capital necessary for internal growth and acquisitions. All told, TJC has completed approximately 100 major acquisitions, supplemented by the purchase of another 200 companies serving as tuck-ins. Middle market companies, worth from $50 million to $1 billion, are TJC's primary interest. The current slate of companies are involved in such industries as women's swimwear, home healthcare mobility products, electric motors and gearboxes, lubrication pumps, precision metal stamping, property and casual insurance, outsourced direct marketing, maritime containers, and private post-secondary education. A separate company, Jordan Industries, concentrates on smaller companies, owning about 20, and is essentially run by the same management team at TJC. Jordan and Zalaznick also make investments in Europe through a fund, JZ Equity Partners plc.

Jordan and Zalaznick Partner in the 1970s

The more senior of TJC's founding partners was Jay Jordan. He grew up in Kansas City and attended Pembroke Country Day School, where, according to *Forbes,* he dreamed of buying companies. He then earned a degree in business administration at the University of Norte Dame and took a job in the trust department at First National Bank of Kansas City, working as a stock specialist. There he met another Norte Dame alumnus, G. Robert Fisher, who helped him put together an investment group which bought stock in a trucking outfit for $3 a share and later sold it at $67 a share, reaping a hefty profit. Jordan now moved to New York where in 1972 he enrolled in the Columbia Business School to earn an MBA. However, he would never complete his degree, as he became increasingly involved at Carl Marks & Co., a bond firm where he had originally taken part-time work. At Carl Marks, Jordan carved a niche for himself as a venture capitalist at a time when few Wall Street firms operated mergers and acquisitions departments. By employing typical real estate financing techniques, he became a pioneer in the leveraged buyout. Over the course of the 1970s, he acquired a number of small companies for Carl Marks Capital, including PCI Group Inc. and Pressed Steel Tank. He was joined in 1980 by Zalaznick. Born in 1954, Zalaznick earned a bachelor's degree from Cornell University in 1976, followed by an MBA from Columbia in 1978. He then went to work as an associate in investment banking at Merrill Lynch White Weld Capital Markets Group before becoming a vice-president at Carl Marks.

In 1982, Jordan elected to strike out on his own, forming The Jordan Company, and taking with him Zalaznick as well as interests in 20 buyouts he accomplished at Carl Marks. TJC began searching out little heralded companies in the heartland of the United States, ones that were profitable yet could be acquired inexpensively. Jordan once told the *Chicago Tribune,*" We're masters of the mundane, the prosaic. . . . We look for old-line, historically profitable, well-managed companies that have a market niche, a proprietary product that's withstood the test of time where we can minimize our business risk."

Many of those companies were family owned, launched in the years after World War II, and were now facing succession issues. To assuage fears that the New York LBO firm would strip the business of assets and fire employees, TJC made a point of keeping younger management talent and motivating them through the offer of equity stakes. Just as important was Jordan's willingness to personally close a deal. According to a competitor quoted by *Forbes* in a 1986 profile, "Jay comes in. His suits are wrinkled, and they can't help but like the guy. With Jay it's not really a financial transaction. The essence of Jay is that he knows what makes people tick. He doesn't play an adversarial game."

TJC was also selective about the companies it sought to buy. According to *Forbes,* Jordan, Zalaznick, and their associates considered about 500 annual prospects presented to them by a network of business brokers. About 100 warranted further research, and about half of those were paid a visit. In the end, TJC acquired four or five of these candidates. An early success story for the firm was the $22.5 million purchase in 1982 of Piece Goods Shops, a family-owned North Carolina-based chain of 90 home-sewing stores. After adding another 40 stores and paying off the debt taken on to make the acquisition, TJC sold the business for $65 million, representing a tidy profit on the $1 million cash TJC laid out originally.

By 1988, TJC owned controlling interests in 30 companies. As the cost of acquiring the types of companies TJC targeted began to increase, however, the firm began to diversify somewhat. In 1986, it moved into real estate and money management through the acquisition of Penn Square Management Corp., a Reading, Pennsylvania-based real estate firm that ran the $200 million Penn Square Mutual Fund. Jordan and Zalaznick also looked overseas, setting up JZ Equity Partners in 1987 and raising a pool of investment money on the London Stock Exchange.

Late 1980s Creation of Jordan Industries

Several of the companies TJC had acquired in the first six years were not achieving the kind of growth rate management had hoped for, however. Jordan believed they needed to make some strategic acquisitions in order to boost their performance, but he and Zalaznick were already stretched too thin. Thus, he formed Jordan Industries, a holding company to house six of the companies. He also enlisted the help of Thomas H. Quinn, a former roommate and fellow member of the football team at Notre Dame. Quinn had 15 years of experience at American Hospital Supply Corporation, rising to the rank of Group Vice-President, and stayed on when the company was acquired by Baxter Travenol Laboratories Inc. in 1985. He welcomed the opportunity to head Jordan Industries, telling *Venture* magazine in February 1989 that he had been "a highfalutin hired hand for a long time," adding, "I wanted to build something for my-self." The headquarters for the company was located in Deerfield, Illinois, a Chicago suburb where Quinn lived. In some sense, this new conglomerate was as diverse as many of the old ones, which had proven inefficient and bloated and fell out of favor with businessmen and investors. Jordan Industries was involved in such far flung industries as Venetian blinds and plastic pipe products. However, the operation was kept lean and retained an entrepreneurial spirit. In a matter of months, the company acquired seven more companies. The main benefit of putting this baker's dozen of companies together on the same balance sheet was that Jordan Industries was able to raise additional capital at better terms, thereby allowing the parts to command the financial power of the whole to make acquisitions and achieve the kind of growth that eluded them as standalone operations.

TJC and Jordan Industries shared some of the same management team, with Jordan serving as managing partner of the one and chairman of the board of the other, while Zalaznick and Quinn were sometimes named officers to new acquisitions. As a result, the two companies were often confused for one another. As they grew into the 1990s, however, the two staked out their own territories. TJC tended to focus on better-known consumer brands and franchised food operations, while Jordan Industries concentrated on products with industrial or business applications.

One of the largest acquisitions TJC completed during its first decade was American Safety Razor Company, which was bought for $140 million in cash in 1989. The Virginia-based company made shaving blades and industrial/surgical blades for the global market, controlling such tradenames as Personna, Gem, and Flicker. It was also a major custom bar soap manufacturer through a Dayton, Ohio-based subsidiary, Hewitt Soap Subsidiary.

In the early 1990s, TJC enjoyed a number of successes. It scored a hit with an investment in Georgia-based Carmike Cinemas Inc., which enjoyed success in fielding movie screens in second-tier cities, mostly in the South. In 1991, TJC became involved in the candy industry, acquiring Fannie May Candy Shops Inc. and its manufacturing branch, Archibald candy. A year later, the business was bolstered with the acquisition of Fanny Farmer Candy Shops, thereby merging two of America's oldest candy chains. Fannie May was founded in 1915 and Fanny Farmer in 1919. TJC entered the fast food business in 1994, forming National Restaurant Enterprises Inc. to become a Burger King franchisee. It teamed up with Larry Jaro, who owned 11 Chicago Burger King restaurants, and Bill Osborne, who owned another three stores. Former Burger King executive Gary Hubert was then recruited to help run National Restaurant Enterprises. Within three months, the new company purchased 68 Chicago stores from Burger King, as well as 14 units in the West, and bought another 29 Chicago-area stores from several franchisees. As a result, National Restaurant Enterprises was the third-largest Burger King franchisee. Doing business as AmeriKing, the company topped the 200-unit mark in 1997, and by the end of the decade approached the 400 level, with restaurants located in 12 states, ultimately emerging as Burger King's largest franchisee.

By the end of 1995, the TJC stable of companies combined for sales in excess of $500 million, drawn from such diverse products and services as specialty advertising products, watches, pressure-sensitive labels, electronic hardware, crystal and glassware, bicycle reflectors, security locks, electronics connectors and switches, precision machined parts, religious musical recordings, and Bibles. One of the major deals engineered by TJC in the second half of the 1990s was the $240 million LBO of sports apparel manufacturer Winning Ways Inc. in 1996. The deal had been originally broached nearly a decade earlier, a clear reflection of the long-term approach Jordan and his associates took in doing business. Founded in 1974 by chairman Bob Wolff, Winning Ways started out designing and selling tennis warmup suits. It expanded into other sportswear in 1979 when it signed a licensing agreement with Wilson Sporting Goods Co., selling the apparel in Sears stores. Winning Ways then scored a major success in 1985 with the creation of its GEAR for Sports division, selling activewear featuring school graphics in the college bookstore market. Annual sales grew to around $185 million when TJC acquired the company. As was the case with previous LBOs, Winning Ways' management team was kept on and received equity stakes in the business.

According to *Venture Capital Journal*, TJC invested some $600 million from 1997 to 2001, "but had to slough off approximately $125 million more on other equity sponsors because of capital constraints. Such frustrations helped lead the firm toward the realization that it needed to up its own ante." In 2002, the firm launched its first private equity fund, although in truth Jordan and Zalaznick had experience in this area through JZ Equity Partners. Helping to attract investors in the new $1.5 billion fund, named The Resolute Fund, was Greenwich, Connecticut-based Atlantic-Pacific Capital Inc. serving as placement agent. The fund came at a time when the economy was struggling, and it was difficult to raise capital for further acquisitions. Despite less than ideal conditions, the fund met its target, due in large measure to the firm's 20-year reputation for making smart acquisitions and building value.

Challenges in the 2000s

Jordan Industries did not fare as well during the early 2000s, dependent as it was on high-yield bonds to raise new funds. With investors worried about federal deficits, higher oil prices,

and a weak dollar, however, the junk bond market tightened considerably and investors turned instead to safer corporate securities and U.S. Treasury bonds. Although there was talk in the press that Jordan Industries was on the verge of default, Jordan downplayed the idea, noting that he and three other shareholders held $145 million of the company's debt. As he told *Crain's Chicago Business* in March 2004, "If there was any problem, we just wouldn't pay ourselves interest, and the world would be wonderful. . . . [The firm is] highly leveraged. We keep it purposefully highly leveraged."

TJC also endured other struggles. AmeriKing and Archibald Candy were both forced into bankruptcy and emerged under new ownership. Nevertheless, TJC was able to continue making acquisitions. In October 2004, Professional Paint, a company it formed in 2000 to become involved in the paint industry, acquired a subsidiary of Consocio Comex S.A. de C.V., picking up the leading architectural paint brand in Mexico. Also in 2004, TJC formed TTS, LLC to acquire Tolin Mechanical Systems Company, a $50 million deal funded by The Resolute Fund. Tolin provided facilities maintenance programs and formed the foundation for what was planned to become a national, contractually based technical facilities services business. TJC also divested some assets during this period, including the sale of Acadia Elastomers Corporation and special-chemicals products company Permatex Inc. Given TJC's successful 20-plus years of deal making and ability to retain key partners, there was every reason to expect the firm to continue to find a way to grow no matter what the economic conditions.

Principal Subsidiaries

Apparel Ventures, Inc.; Healthcare Products Holdings, Inc.; Kinetek, Inc.; Lincoln Industrial Corporation; Precision Engineered Products, Inc.; Safety Insurance Group, Inc.; Tolin Mechanical Systems Company; Universal Technical Institute, Inc.

Principal Competitors

Clayton, Dubilier, & Rice, Inc.; Haas Wheat & Partners; Heico Companies LLC.

Further Reading

Andrews, Edmund L., "LBO Firms Meet Their Maker," *Venture*, February 1989, p. 47.

Gallun, Alby, "A Difficult 3-Point Shot for Jordan," *Crain's Chicago Business*, January 28, 2002, p. 3.

Kosman, Josh, "PE Pioneer Jordan Raises First Fund," *Daily Deal*, February 12, 2002.

Leonard, Burr, "Make Mine Private," *Forbes*, December 1, 1986, p. 56.

Palmer, Ann Therese, "LBS Are Forever at Jordan Industries," *Chicago Tribune*, December 1, 1991, p. 3.

Primack, Dan, "Jordan Nabs $1.5B," *Venture Capital Journal*, November 1, 2002, p. 1.

Ryan, Nancy, "Jordan CO., Officer Buy Fannie May," *Chicago Tribune*, November 5, 1991, p. 1.

—Ed Dinger

Kemıra

Kemira Oyj

Porkkalankatu 3
PO Box 330
Helsinki
FIN-00101
Finland
Telephone: 108611
Fax: 108621119

Public Company
Incorporated: 1920 as Valtion Rikkihappo-ja
    Superfosfaattitehtaat Oy
Employees: 10,537
Sales: EUR 1.69 billion ($2.1 billion) (2004)
Stock Exchanges: Helsinki
Ticker Symbol: KRA
NAIC: 325131 Inorganic Dye and Pigment Manufacturing;
    325188 All Other Inorganic Chemical Manufacturing;
    325131 Inorganic Dye and Pigment Manufacturing;
    325510 Paint and Coating Manufacturing

Finland's Kemira Oyj is a leading industrial chemicals manufacturer focused on four primary areas: Paints and Coatings; Pulp and Paper Chemicals; Industrial Chemicals; and coagulants and other chemicals for water treatment processes. Pulp and Paper Chemicals represents the group's largest division, generating 33 percent of the group's revenues of EUR 1.69 billion ($2.1 billion) in 2004. This division produces chemicals for bleaching, coating, and processing pulp and paper, as well as pigments and inks used in printing. Kemira's next largest division is its Paints and Coatings division, the Nordic region's largest producer of paints and related products, and one of the top paint manufacturers in Europe. The company's main brands, including Tikkurila, Alcro, and Beckers, combine to generate 25 percent of Kemira's total sales. Under Industrial Chemicals, which adds 19 percent to group revenues, Kemira includes titanium dioxide, formic acid and derivatives, and bleaching agents for detergents. Kemwater is the company's division dedicated to the production of coagulants and other chemicals for water treatment, and generates 17 percent of total

sales. In 2004, Kemira spun off its then-largest division, Kemira GrowHow, as an independent, publicly listed company. GrowHow was the holding company for Kemira's agrochemicals division. The company intends to develop its remaining subsidiaries into world leaders in their categories, through both organic growth and an ongoing acquisition program. In February 2005, for example, the company acquired Finnish Chemicals Oy, a producer of chemicals for pulp and paper, water treatment, and other industries; and Verdugt, based in The Netherlands, and the world's top producer of organic salts. Kemira, formerly controlled by the Finnish government, is listed on the Helsinki Stock Exchange.

Finnish Phosphate Start-up in the 1920s

Finland's independence from Russian domination following World War I presented new challenges for the country. In particular, the new Finnish government sought to establish self-sufficiency for the country's agricultural and industrial sectors. In order to supply the raw materials needed for the development of these sectors, the government targeted the creation of a domestic industrial chemicals industry. Among the earliest components of this strategy was Valtion Rikkihappo-ja Superfosfaattitehtaat Oy, or the State Sulfuric Acid and Superphosphate Plants, established in 1920. One of the new plant's first and largest customers was the state-owned gunpowder production plant in Vihtavuori.

Construction began on a sulfuric acid plant in Lappeenranta, and, in Kotka, a production facility for superphosphates. Both factories were completed in 1922, and before the end of the decade had achieved production levels of 20,000 tons of sulfuric acid and as much as 40,000 tons of superphosphates per year. While producing for a variety of industries, the two plants targeted especially the country's agricultural sector, with a particular focus on the production of fertilizers. In 1931, the two plants were incorporated into a single limited company. Nevertheless, the new company remained under government ownership, placed under the Ministry of Agriculture.

The strong growth in the demand for superphosphates at the end of the 1930s led the company to build two new plants into

Company Perspectives:

We aim to be: the leading chemical and integrated service provider for the pulp & paper industry; the world leader in chemical water purification; a leading European paint and coatings company; a world-class performer in industrial chemicals.

the 1940s. The first of these was built in Kokkola in 1945, and produced sulfuric acid as well as superphosphates. Construction began on the second in Harjavalta in 1947, with production launched in 1949. In the meantime, the company had made its first acquisition, of the Vihtavuori plant, in 1945. This facility was then merged with a Vaasa-based company that produced gas masks and other protective equipment.

Into the 1950s, the company expanded its focus to include more complex products, such as granulated fertilizers. The company also began an expansion into industrial chemicals as well, later emerging as a leading producer of formic acid and derivatives, and titanium dioxide, an important paint component. In the meantime, new sulfuric acid capacity was added at the Harjavalta site, with two new plants built in 1955 and 1957. The company's Vihtavuori subsidiary in the meantime expanded its explosive operations with the completion of a new plant for manufacturing dynamite in 1957.

The state-owned company simplified its name, to Rikkihappo, in 1961. The following year, the company added a new sulfuric acid facility in Kokkola, which enabled it to shut down its original Lappeenranta site in 1963. The company continued to expand its production of sulfuric acid through the 1960s and into the 1970s, with major extensions accomplished in 1967 and 1974 at Kokkola, and in 1970 and 1975 at Harjavalta.

Harjavalta and Kokkola were also central to Rikkihappo's extension into the production of heavy industrial chemicals. The company first built an aluminum sulphate plant in 1960 in Harjavalta, which was followed by the addition of a calcium chloride and sodium sulfate production facility in Kokkola in 1962. During the 1960s, the company also began producing concentrated granular fertilizers, at a new purpose-built plant in Uusikaupunki, starting in 1963. The new plant also featured its own harbor, becoming part of the group's move onto the international market.

Exports of fertilizers were launched toward the late 1960s, backed by the addition of several new plants in Siiklinjarvi. The first of these, a sulfuric acid plant, was completed in 1967. By 1972, the company had added a phosphoric acid factory, and new factories for producing ammonium phosphate, nitric acid, and complex fertilizers. The company also built a new inland waterway harbor linking its Siiklinjarvi site to the coast. The development of this new capacity enabled the company to shut down its original Kotka plant in 1973.

Diversified Agro-Chemicals Leader in the 1980s

The adoption of a new acquisition-driven growth strategy, starting in the 1960s, transformed the company into one of

Finland's largest corporations and into a leading chemicals group in the Nordic region. One of the group's earliest acquisitions was that of Vuorikemia, which produced titanium dioxide-based pigments. That purchase, made in 1968, permitted the group to extend itself into finished paint and dye products and also became one of its earliest avenues to the export market. Another significant acquisition came in 1971, when the company acquired Typpi Oy. Founded in Oulu in 1952, this company added the production of nitrogen-based chemicals to the company's list.

The addition of Typpi's business also led to the adoption of a new name for the increasingly diversified chemicals group. In 1972, the company changed its name to Kemira—using the initial letters of the Finnish words for its three main areas of operation, Ke (chemicals), Mi (minerals), and Ra (fertilizers).

Through the end of the 1970s, Kemira continued to add to its domestic operations. In 1972, the company acquired a paint manufacturing plant from Oy Schildt & Hallberg AB. The new subsidiary, Tikkurilan Varitehtaat Oy, gave Kemira the Tikkurila brand, one of the leading paint brands in the Nordic region. The addition of the brand and a developing focus on the export market led Kemira to begin establishing a network of foreign sales subsidiaries starting in the late 1970s.

Through the 1980s, Kemira continued to expand domestically. In 1980, the company opened an apatite mine in Siilinjarvi. The company expanded into formic acid production with the construction of a plant in Oulu, and then added an ammonia plant, and a factory for the production of hydrogen peroxide, in 1988. The company also branched out into fine chemicals with the launch of a new plant at its Kokkola site.

Yet international growth became a company priority during the 1980s as well. For this effort, Kemira focused especially on developing its fertilizer and agricultural chemicals operations—which continued to account for more than 50 percent of company revenues into the 1990s. One of the group's first acquisitions came in 1982, when it purchased a fertilizer factory in the United Kingdom. In 1984, the company moved into The Netherlands, buying a fertilizer plant there, then increased its presence on the European continent the following year with the acquisition of the Gechem fertilizer factory, in Belgium. In 1987, the company added Denmark's Superfos Godning, followed by Pernis, in The Netherlands, and Ince, in the United Kingdom, in 1988. By the end of the decade, Kemira's fertilizer operations were the second largest in Europe.

Other Kemira operations expanded internationally during this time, notably with the 1984 acquisition of the Donald Macpherson Group, in the United States. The following year, Kemira returned to the United States in order to acquire a titanium dioxide production facility. In 1989, the company's chemicals division quadrupled in size with the acquisition of Boliden Kemi, based in Sweden. Also that year, Kemira entered the Far East, setting up a hydrogen peroxide production joint venture with Japan's UBE Industries. By then, the company also had developed a growing specialty in producing chemicals for the water treatment sector. In 1991 and 1992, the company boosted that business area with the addition of Aliada Quimica, in Portugal, and Kemira Iberica in Spain.

<table>
<tr><td colspan="2">

Key Dates:

</td></tr>
<tr><td>1920:</td><td>The Finnish government establishes Valtion Rikkihappo-ja Superfosfaattitehtaat Oy (the State Sulfuric Acid and Superphosphate Plants) and constructs two factories.</td></tr>
<tr><td>1931:</td><td>Control of the two factories is placed under a single company.</td></tr>
<tr><td>1945:</td><td>The company acquires the state gunpowder plants at Vihtavuori.</td></tr>
<tr><td>1961:</td><td>The company name is changed to Rikkihappo as the company expands into industrial chemicals production.</td></tr>
<tr><td>1971:</td><td>The company changes its name to Kemira and enters pigment and paint chemicals production.</td></tr>
<tr><td>1982:</td><td>The company begins international expansion with the acquisition of a fertilizer plant in the United Kingdom.</td></tr>
<tr><td>1989:</td><td>Kemira acquires Boliden Kemi AB in Sweden, quadrupling its chemicals business and entering the water chemicals market.</td></tr>
<tr><td>1991:</td><td>The company launches a restructuring of its operations, shedding 28 percent of its payroll.</td></tr>
<tr><td>1994:</td><td>Kemira shares are listed on the Helsinki Stock Exchange.</td></tr>
<tr><td>1999:</td><td>The company announces a decision to refocus around a core of pulp and paper chemicals, paints and pigments, and water chemicals.</td></tr>
<tr><td>2004:</td><td>The fertilizer business Kemira GrowHow is spun off as a separate publicly listed company.</td></tr>
<tr><td>2005:</td><td>The company acquires Finnish Chemicals Oy and Verdugt of The Netherlands.</td></tr>
</table>

Kemira's rapid expansion during the 1980s had come at the cost of taking on a high debt load, however. Kemira's status as a state-owned company restricted it from turning to the stock market for capital; instead, the company was forced to turn to banks to finance its expansion. The company originally requested that it be allowed to go public in 1984. That request was denied. By 1989, however, the Finnish government had agreed to an offering—yet a dramatic slump in the global chemicals industry forced Kemira to put its public offering on hold. The company's fertilizer division was particularly hard hit, and entered a protracted period of losses in the early 1990s. Nonetheless, Kemira made a new attempt at growth, launching a takeover offer for the fertilizer division of troubled British company ICI. Kemira's offer was blocked by the United Kingdom's monopolies commission, however.

Refocused for a New Century

By 1991, Kemira was forced to restructure its operations. In that year, the company reformed its operations into a number of wholly owned subsidiaries, including Kemira Agro, Kemira Chemicals, Kemira Fibres, Kemira Pigments, Kemira Metalkat, Kemira Safety, Kemira Engineering, and the Tikkurila paint operations. As part of the company's restructuring effort, it shed some 28 percent of its payroll. The restructuring took place ahead of Kemira's public offering, which at last came off in

1994. Kemira's listing came as part of a wider Finnish government privatization plan that also resulted in the public offering for telecommunications giant Nokia.

Kemira's appetite for acquisitions remained strong through the 1990s and into the next decade. The company's target turned especially toward its chemicals and pigments divisions. During this period, Kemira emerged as a world leader in water treatment chemicals, with the 1992 acquisition of Ferriklor AB of Sweden, and the creation of joint ventures in Romania, The Netherlands, Poland, the Czech Republic in 1994, Thailand in 1995, and Brazil in 1996.

Meanwhile, Kemira's pigment division grew in 1993 through the purchases of a 20 percent stake in the Nord Kaolin Company, in the United States, and of TCF Tiofine, a titanium dioxide producer in The Netherlands. The company also expanded its paints and pigment operations into Latvia, Russia, Estonia, Brazil, and, with the creation of Tikkurila Inc. in 1996, the United States. That year also marked the group's entry into the Australian pigments industry.

Kemira launched a new strategic review at the end of the 1990s and in 1999 announced its decision to refocus itself around three core businesses—pulp and paper chemicals, paints and pigments, and water treatment chemicals. By 2001, the company had launched an active divestment program, cutting out some one-third of its operating revenues. As part of its new strategy, Kemira once again began seeking acquisitions. In 2001, the company boosted its paints operations with the acquisition of Sweden's Alcro Beckers, originally founded in Sweden in 1865. That purchase made Kemira the Scandinavian region's largest paint manufacturer.

Kemira's independence appeared in doubt later that year when Industri Kapital, behind the creation of Nordic chemicals giant Dynea, approached Kemira with a takeover offer that would have created a global chemicals giant with sales of more than EUR 25 billion. That offer failed, however. Instead, Kemira announced its intention to find a buyer for its Kemira Agro division. Yet the difficult economic situation at the beginning of the century put that effort on hold as well. Kemira Agro was then renamed as Kemira GrowHow.

The spinoff of GrowHow came at the end of 2004, when the newly independent company was listed on the Helsinki Stock Exchange. Kemira had in the meantime continued to boost its other operations through a series of acquisitions. Nonetheless, the spinoff of GrowHow shaved off some EUR 1 billion from Kemira's annual revenues.

The streamlined Kemira entered 2005 off and running. In February of that year the company made two significant acquisitions. The first of these was of rival Finnish Chemicals, which presented an operation portfolio similar to Kemira's own. The second was of The Netherlands' Verdugt, one of the world's top producers of formic acid and other organic salts. Lean and mean, Kemira turned toward the challenges of the new century.

Principal Subsidiaries

A/S Ammonia (Denmark); Alcro-Beckers Barvy Tjeckien (Czech Republic); Aluminum Sulphate Co. of Egypt, S.A.E.

(Egypt); Biolchim Tunisie; CPS Color Group Oy; DA Kemikaalide AS (Estonia); Farmit Website Oy; Färgsam AB (Sweden); Haapaveden Puhdistamo Oy; Indkoebsselskabet for Kali I/S (Denmark); KemMaq L.L.C. (United States); Kemax B.V. (Netherlands); Kemira Arab Potash Company (Jordan); Kemira Compound Fertiliser (Zhanjiang) Co. Ltd. (China); Kemira Emirates Fertilizers Company (Kefco) (United Arab Emirates); Kay Fertilizer Sdn. Bhd. (Malaysia); Kemira GrowHow (Thailand) Ltd.; Kemwater Phil. Corporation (Philippines); Movere Oy; Pharmatory Oy; PK Düngerhandels-gesellschaft GmbH (Germany); Scanspac & Co. AB (Sweden); Scanspac AB (Sweden); SECO Fertilisants S.A. (France); Superstar Fertilizers Co. Ltd. (Thailand); Swede Pavimenta S.a.s di Carazza & Co. (Italy); Swedish Water Corporation AB; Union Kemira Company L.L.C. (United Arab Emirates).

Principal Competitors

BASF AG; Dow Chemical Company; BP Amoco Chemical Company; Bayer AG; E.I. du Pont de Nemours and Company; Norsk Hydro ASA; ATOFINA; Merck KGaA; Shell Nederland B.V.; Mitsubishi Chemical Corporation; CEPSA.

Further Reading

Alperowicz, Natasha, "Kemira Makes Two Acquisitions," *Chemical Week,* February 16, 2005, p. 13.

——, "Kemira Narrows Its Focus," *Chemical Week,* July 18, 2001, p. 35.

"Kemira Faces a Challenge," *Fertilizer International,* September-October 1997, p. 38.

"Kemira Oyj, 2004: Year of Major Restructuring," *Hugin,* February 8, 2005.

"Kemira Reorganizes, Retains Agro," *Chemical Market Reporter,* December 24, 2001, p. 2.

"Kemira to Buy Vinings for $138 Million," *Chemical Market Reporter,* December 24, 2001, p. 2.

"Kemira Unveils GrowHow Plans," *Chemical Market Reporter,* September 20, 2004, p. 6.

Lerner, Ivan, "Kemira Expands in US Water Treatment Chemicals," *Chemical Market Reporter,* November 15, 2004, p. 16.

"25bn Giant on the Way," *Chemistry and Industry,* September 17, 2001, p. 59.

—M.L. Cohen

Knight Trading Group, Inc.

Newport Tower
525 Washington Boulevard
Jersey City, New Jersey 07310
U.S.A.
Telephone: (201) 222-9400
Toll Free: (800) 544-7508
Web site: http://www.knighttradinggroup.com

Public Company
Incorporated: 1995 as Roundtable Partners LLC
Employees: 933
Sales: $670 million (2003)
Stock Exchanges: NASDAQ
Ticker Symbol: NITE
NAIC: 523120 Securities Brokerage

Based in Jersey City, New Jersey, Knight Trading Group, Inc. is a trade execution specialist, primarily handling stock trading for securities listed on the NASDAQ, OTC Bulletin Board, and Pink Sheets, but also New York Stock Exchange and American Stock Exchange listed securities as well. Knight "makes a market," a function that has been at the heart of stock trading since 1792 when the open auction concept for each stock trade was introduced. Specialists make a market by matching up sellers and buyers at a fixed price, a service for which they receive a commission. Specialists like Knight also step in to buy or sell stocks from their own accounts when there is an imbalance between sellers and buyers. Because of this unique position in the stock market, possessing advance knowledge about the intentions of buyers and sellers, specialists are in a highly advantageous position, one that has been open to abuse. Knight's conduct has come under scrutiny in recent years, leading to National Association of Securities Dealers (NASD) fines for trading violations and Securities and Exchange Commission (SEC) charges that led to a settlement agreement in 2004. In addition to its Equity Markets business segment, Knight also provides asset management services for individuals and institutions. Knight is a public company trading on the NASDAQ.

Cofounder Learning Market Making in the Late 1970s

Although Knight Trading was cofounded by Walter Raquet and Kenneth Pasternak, it was the latter who was the driving force behind the company's growth. In 1976 Pasternak earned an undergraduate degree at the State University of New York, New Paltz, intending to become a teacher. After one semester, however, he realized that he was not cut out for the teaching profession, and went to work with his father in the car trading business. Then, in 1979, he landed a job with the Troster Singer unit of stock specialist Spear, Leeds & Kellogg, which during the 1970s acquired a number of smaller firms, including Troster Singer, to emerge as one of Wall Street's top specialists. Pasternak displayed a knack for trading, as well as a truculent personality, and quickly moved up the ranks, eventually managing the trading room at Troster Singer, where Raquet also worked.

With the rise of discount brokers and online stock purchasing, the securities industry was undergoing significant changes by the early 1990s, leading some, like Pasternak and Raquet, to believe that traditional market makers were losing touch with the times. According to a 1999 company profile in *Institutional Investor,* the two men got the idea to start Knight "from Lawrence Waterhouse, chairman of discount brokerage firm Waterhouse Securities. 'He worried that he would eventually lose control over the execution quality as the result of brokerage mergers,' recalls Raquet. 'He was too small to support a dedicated market-making operation. But five firms together could provide enough order flow.' " In 1994 Pasternak and Raquet decided to put the idea to the test, founding what was originally called Roundtable Partners. The pair made a simple but effective pitch to convince brokers to take a stake in the venture. By sending their orders to the new market maker for execution, they would be compensated directly for "order flow," and indirectly by their ownership of the firm. Everybody won, especially Pasternak and Raquet. Thus, instead of lining up five partners, they signed up 25 firms, some of which were of the new online variety. These online operators, in the words of *Institutional Investor,* were "the rocket fuel for Knight's business."

Success for Roundtable was predicated on a large trading volume and the use of the most advanced technology available. To achieve that volume, the firm engaged in what many consid-

147

Company Perspectives:

Knight was founded with an entrepreneurial spirit that is woven into our culture and engenders innovation at every turn. We have a strong corporate culture that's based on firmly held beliefs. We believe that our commitment to the interests of our clients proves our value to them. We believe that marketplace leadership is earned, and not given. We believe that integrity is demonstrated by daily actions and that collaboration is the key to successful, long-term partnerships.

ered an ethically questionable, albeit legal, practice of paying for order flow. While advantageous to both broker and market maker, such arrangements invariably cost investors money. Keeping costs in line was also of importance, hence the decision to set up shop in Jersey City, where the rents were much lower than on Wall Street. Roundtable then began making online trades and acquiring a number of small specialty brokers to fill out its business. It formed subsidiary Knight Securities to make markets for stocks listed on NASDAQ and the OTC Bulletin Board, and in 1995 acquired Trimark Securities, L.P., which then served as market maker for New York Stock Exchange and American Stock Exchange equities. By the end of the year, Roundtable was only the 88th largest market maker of the NASDAQ, but it was growing quickly.

Aside from shrewd moves, Roundtable was the beneficiary of good timing. According to *Business News New Jersey*, "The company's start meshed neatly with changes in the way Nasdaq operated. The Securities and Exchange Commission all but shut down a long-time income source for Nasdaq brokers in 1997 when it blocked them from setting artificially wide spreads between the selling and purchase prices of stocks. When that changed, Nasdaq's wholesale business became less fragmented as market makers like Knight stepped into a void the new regulations created."

Going Public in the Late 1990s

The firm got off to such a strong start that in April 1998 it incorporated Knight/Trimark Group Inc. in Delaware, a preliminary step to making a public offering of stock. But even as the company began to pitch its offering, it came under a cloud when it was revealed that Pasternak faced disciplinary action from the SEC from his days at Troster Singer, the result of a SEC probe into the conduct of NASDAQ market makers, charged with colluding to keep spreads artificially wide. All told, 24 firms, including Spear, Leeds, had faced antitrust charges and reached a $1 billion settlement with the Justice Department in 1996. But the SEC continued to look into the matter. Knight had not been a target of the Justice Department investigation, instead benefiting from the situation. Although Pasternak now faced a possible civil penalty and suspension from trading for a failure to adequately supervise the activities of some Troster Singer traders, he was never charged with any violation. Moreover, the suspicion did little to hinder Knight's initial public offering (IPO), which was not met with much institutional excitement but still managed to sell. In July the IPO was completed, raising $145 million, at which point Roundtable Partners became a wholly owned subsidiary of Knight/Trimark Group.

Knight was riding high early in 1999, as the stock market surged and suitors like Goldman Sachs and Lehman Brothers approached Pasternak about selling the firm. Because he insisted on receiving a top post the deals fell through, but he could afford to be demanding, given Knight's strong growth. It was now the NASDAQ's top market maker, a meteoric rise achieved in just five years. According to a *Fortune* magazine profile published at the time, Knight "executes some 40% of all online trades and controls almost one-fifth of the trading in Nasdaq/OTC stocks. That's more than Merrill Lynch, Morgan Stanley Dean Witter, Goldman Sachs, and Salomon Smith Barney combined, and almost twice as much as the No. 2 firm. . . . Ranked by volume in U.S. equities, Knight/Trimark is $5\frac{1}{2}$ times bigger than the American Stock Exchange."

By May 1999, when Knight's stock made a 2-for-1 split, Pasternak's stake was worth about $610 million. The little known firm looked to upgrade its image, hiring Omnicom Group's specialist in financial advertising to put together the firm's first national advertising campaign. In addition, Pasternak looked to beef up his executive talent pool to prepare for expansion. He hired John Hewitt, a Goldman Sachs vice-president in the electronic trading group, to become the president of the Knight Securities unit. Hewitt was expected to help the firm become involved in other kinds of securities, including options, as well as to spearhead international expansion. Weeks earlier, Knight announced that it was investing in the Easdaq Stock Market, a wannabe European version of the NASDAQ. In addition, Pasternak harbored dreams of convincing mutual funds, pension plans, and other large institutional investors to trade through Knight. In some respects, however, Knight's ambition was borne out of necessity. Its core business was coming under pressure from new computerized trading technologies, in particular electronic communications networks (ECNs), which had the potential to diminish the need for market makers. ECNs did not buy stocks, but merely coordinated buy and sell orders electronically for a fee. They were more matchmakers than market makers, but they were still very much a threat to Knight's business.

Knight clearly had benefited from a bull market, and as the stock market began to recede, investors questioned whether Knight could sustain revenues under normal trading conditions, since its business model was very much dependent on volume. As soon as the firm failed to maintain its growth rate, investors punished the stock. After reaching a high of $78 in May 1999, it dipped below $25 in October. Moreover, Knight's prospects were dimmed by the upcoming move by the NASDAQ to begin using a decimal pricing system, a change that would tighten the spreads between the price at which Knight bought and sold stocks, resulting in smaller profits.

New Name for the 2000s

In 2000 Knight changed its name to Knight Trading Group, Inc. and took a number of steps in an attempt to diversify and secure its independent position, which was further jeopardized by a consolidation trend that saw a number of major Wall Street firms acquiring NASDAQ market makers and taking in house business that might have been directed to Knight. In January it entered the options-trading business by acquiring Arbitrade Holdings, LLC, a little known Minnesota firm that relied on computers to identify trading opportunities. Arbitrade was renamed Knight Financials and business quickly surged, providing the parent company with a welcome source of revenue as NASDAQ trading volumes appeared to have crested. Knight also continued to pursue diversification by applying its model internationally. The firm became a member of the London Stock Exchange, Deutsche Borse, and Euronext Paris, with the goal of becoming a market maker in each. It also established an alliance with Japan's Nikko Securities.

The independent directors on Knight's board and major shareholders, however, were not pleased with the firm's performance, as Knight became a possible takeover candidate because of its low stock price. The board began to pressure Pasternak to step down. In July he made a partial concession, turning over the presidency to Peter Hajas, the head of Knight Financial Products. But Pasternak's position was untenable and by late December he decided to retire, giving up the chairmanship and the CEO post as well, some six months before his contract was set to expire.

Knight settled on Pasternak's replacement in May 2002, hiring Thomas M. Joyce, an experienced trader known for his work ethic and upstanding reputation. A Harvard graduate in economics in 1977, Joyce started out as a stockbroker but did not fare well working with individual investors. It was only after he moved to Merrill Lynch and began doing block trades with other traders that he found his niche, and within four years became the head of the block trading desk. In the mid-1990s he took over the firm's U.S. equities unit, where he was credited with producing record results. When it became apparent that he was not likely to ascend to Merrill's top posts, Joyce in 2001 quit and took a job at Sanford C. Bernstein, where he established a NASDAQ trading department, his last stop before succeeding Pasternak at Knight.

Several months before Joyce took over, in January 2002, the NASD fined Knight $700,000 and ordered the firm to pay $800,000 to clients because of a number of market making and trading violations. One of Joyce's strengths was his clean reputation, but its value to the firm was undermined as Knight faced further investigations into its conduct during the Pasternak years, initiated by a whistleblower, the former head of Knight's institutional trading desk, Robert Stellato. He accused Knight of engaging in "front running," a practice in which the firm used knowledge of client orders to buy or sell stock before placing the client's order. The *Wall Street Journal* offered an example: "If an investor wanted to buy, say, 1,000 shares of Intel Corp., that person would call their stockbroker, who would arrange to have Knight place the order. But before doing that, Knight's trader allegedly would at times buy Intel stock for his own Knight account, presumably getting in at a cheaper level than what the price would be when the customer order was finally

filled. In some cases, the trader's buying could even drive up the stock price, making it yet more expensive for the customer who placed the order in the first place."

Despite the legal distractions, Joyce took steps to turn around Knight. In 2002 Knight lost $43.2 million on revenues of $527.4 million, but a year later sales improved to $670 million and the firm returned to the black, posting net income of $38.5 million. To reorganize the firm, he added to Knight's ability to serve institutional customers by acquiring Atlanta-based Donaldson & Company, which provided research and other services. He also closed down Knight's American Stock Exchange equity options desk, then in 2004 sold the firm's derivatives business to Citigroup Inc. for approximately $225 million. Not only did this business provide a low return, it was capital-intensive, so that its sale allowed Knight to focus more resources on its remaining business segments, Equity Markets and Asset Management.

In 2004 Knight began to come out from under the cloud of litigation when it reached a settlement with the SEC and NASD, agreeing to pay $79 million in penalties, interests, and trading profits. A whistleblower suit also was settled in 2004 when a NASD-overseen arbitration panel ruled against Stellato, who had maintained that he had been wrongfully fired because he exposed Knight's trading practice. The firm's counterclaims also were dismissed. With the legal issues now behind the firm, Joyce could fully concentrate on growing Knight, which continued to face challenges in a highly competitive and changing marketplace.

Principal Subsidiaries

Knight Capital Markets LLC; Knight Equity Markets, L.P.; Knight Equity Markets International.

Principal Competitors

The Charles Schwab Corporation; Instinet Group Incorporation; Spear, Leeds & Kellogg.

Further Reading

Alpert, Bill, "Plugged In," *Barron's,* March 8, 1999, p. 49.
Davis, Ann, "Stock-Trading Cheats Are in the Cross Hairs," *Wall Street Journal,* July 8, 2004, p. C1.
Ip, Greg, "Catbird Seat," *Wall Street Journal,* March 3, 2000, p. A1.
Kelly, Kate, "Knight Trading's Chief Executive Steps Down," *Wall Street Journal,* December 19, 2001, p. C1.
——, "Regulators Are Investigating a Big Nasdaq Trade—Knight Trading Faces Allegations That It Violated Rules and Cost Investors Millions of Dollars," *Wall Street Journal,* June 4, 2002, p. C2.
McKnight, Marshall, "Champions of the Day Trader," *Business News New Jersey,* September 26, 2000, p. 6.
——, "Trying to Put the Past Behind It," *NJBIZ,* March 15, 2004, p. 5.
McLean, Bethany, "The Stealth Superstar Online Trading," *Fortune,* September 27, 1999, p. 184.
Rosato, Donna, "A Mild-Mannered Mr. Fix-It," *New York Times,* December 8, 2002, p. 3.
Willoughby, Jack, "Day Traders' Knight," *Institutional Investor,* February 1999, p. 52.

—Ed Dinger

Lamar Advertising Company

5551 Corporate Boulevard
Baton Rouge, Louisiana 70808
U.S.A.
Telephone: (225) 926-1000
Fax: (225) 923-0658
Web site: http://www.lamar.com

Public Company
Founded: 1902
Employees: 3,000
Sales: $810.1 million (2003)
Stock Exchanges: NASDAQ
Ticker Symbol: LAMR
NAIC: 541850 Display Advertising

Lamar Advertising Company is the third-largest outdoor advertising company in the United States, ranking behind Outdoor Systems, Inc. and Clear Channel Communications, Inc., both of which have more assets and larger networks than Lamar. Lamar has closed the gap with its recent acquisitions, however, and now operates the most outdoor displays in the United States and ranks third in outdoor advertising companies. Through two of its subsidiaries, Lamar Outdoor Advertising and Lamar Transit Advertising, it manages approximately 149,000 billboards in 43 states. The company operates 34 transit advertising franchises in 12 states with displays posted on buses, bus shelters, and benches. Through a third subsidiary, Interstate Logos, Inc., it provides 97,500 logo displays for limited access highways, including federal Interstates. These are green highway exit signs that post logo information about nearby restaurants, gas stations, and motels. Lamar has also secured contracts in Ontario, Canada, and in 20 of the 25 states that allow private contractors to fabricate the signs. It is the primary provider of such services in the United States. In addition, the company offers graphic design and production services for its customers. In total, Lamar operates 152 outdoor advertising companies through its subsidiary network. Although its central management offices are housed in its 53,500-square-foot headquarters in downtown Baton Rouge, Louisiana,

much local autonomy is allowed the managers of each of these companies, and they remain in charge of day-to-day company operations. Even though it is a public company, Lamar remains a family business under the control of third and fourth generation members of the Lamar and Reilly families. Robert Switzer, the great-grandson of Charles Lamar, Sr., serves as vice-president of operations. CEO and president Kevin Reilly, Jr. owns approximately 40 percent of the business, and Charles Lamar III and his sister, Mary Lee Lamar Dixon, great-grandchildren of the company's founder, own about 27 percent.

Origins and Development: 1902–58

Lamar's history goes back to 1902, when J.M. Coe created the Pensacola Advertising Co., a small poster company involved in promoting the coming attractions of the Opera House in Pensacola, Florida. In 1905, Charles W. Lamar, Sr., president of the American National Bank of Pensacola, became Coe's partner in the business. The two men owned the opera house as well as the poster business. When the partners decided to break up in 1908, they used a coin toss to decide who would get what part of their mutual business. Coe won the more lucrative opera house and Lamar, who lost the coin toss, got the poster business. He named the new firm Lamar Advertising.

The poster business was a relatively new industry. Just a decade earlier, in 1891, poster makers had created the Associated Bill Posters' Association, generally credited with being the nation's first association of advertisers. At the time, posters were used to advertise on what were called billboards but were nothing like the large, steel-frame structures used today. Then they were nothing more than town and city wall spaces used to advertise businesses or, just as often, upcoming public events. Posters could be stripped away or covered up when it was necessary to replace them with new ones.

It proved to be a timely venture, however, for although Lamar's business was the design and fabricating of wall displays, it placed him in a position to finance expansion into a new realm of advertising just as modern technology created a need for it. Before the company's first decade of business ended, it became clear that the auto would soon replace the horse and buggy and that roads would be needed to accommodate it. By

Company Perspectives:

Lamar's strategy is to be the leading provider of outdoor advertising in each of the markets it serves, with an emphasis on markets with a media industry ranking based on population between 50 and 250. Important elements of this strategy are Lamar's decentralized management structure and its focus on providing high quality local sales and service.

1912, when Henry Ford introduced the Model-T, the nation had begun its love affair with the car, and Ford's assembly-line method of manufacturing enabled it to be priced within the reach of middle-class Americans. Lamar's response was to move into the new area of outdoor, roadside advertising. In 1926, Lamar and his two sons, Charles Lamar, Jr. and L.V. Lamar, purchased the Baton Rouge Poster Advertising Co., renaming it Lamar Advertising Co. of Baton Rouge.

Despite the Great Depression and the fact that Lamar's markets were in states with few paved roads, the company soon turned roadside advertising into its primary business. Like others in the industry, Lamar was aided by Outdoor Advertising Inc., an organization formed in 1931 to promote billboard sales nationwide. During the 1930s Lamar slowly expanded the business, purchasing five outdoor advertising companies in Louisiana and Florida, areas where a paved road infrastructure was, like the company, rather slow to develop. Lamar died in 1944, leaving the business to his son Charles, Jr. and his two daughters. The three siblings took over the management of the Louisiana and Florida operations of the now prosperous and growing family business.

Although it was a growth industry, the billboard advertising business was a tough one. In the industry's early years, many billboards had to be hand-painted on the actual display surfaces, a tedious process. Eventually that method gave way to printing the billboard displays on sheets and assembling them at the "plant" (the site of the billboard). Today, most billboard advertisements are prefabricated as computer-designed and precision cut vinyl pieces and can be assembled with an efficiency far beyond what the technology of Charles Lamar's day allowed.

Obstacles to the growth of billboard advertising companies arose in the form of state and local zoning regulations that did everything from imposing permit requirements to specifying the allowed locations and size and shape of the displays. Nevertheless, the industry steadily prospered, especially after World War II, when the average American family could again afford to buy an automobile. Between 1940 and 1960, industry-wide yearly revenues increased from $44.7 million to more than $200 million.

New Expansion and New Directions: 1958–89

A new period of expansion for Lamar began in 1958 under the leadership of president and CEO Kevin Reilly, Sr. Reilly represented a third generation of family management of Lamar Advertising through his marriage to Charles Lamar, Sr.'s granddaughter, Ann Switzer Reilly. Under Reilly's leadership over the next 15 years, Lamar purchased an additional eight companies in Florida, Alabama, and Louisiana. Growth was abetted by the fact that Florida had become a tourist and retirement mecca, and its roads were improving quickly.

However, Reilly also faced serious problems, some of which were industry-wide, including growing public resistance to billboard advertising. Critics felt that the industry was cluttering American highways with eyesores, blocking out the natural beauty of the landscape. They also offered proof that billboards were dangerous distractions for drivers and caused unnecessary accidents. By the late 1950s, the federal government began paying attention to critics of billboard advertising, thus threatening the strong possibility of additional regulation. The rumbling prompted some important efforts by the industry to govern itself, particularly through the agency of the Outdoor Advertising Association of America and the Institute of Outdoor Advertising. Nevertheless, the critics prevailed. Enlisting the aid of Lady Bird Johnson, the industry's opponents prompted a milestone piece of legislation. The Highway Beautification Act of 1965, a law designed to limit and govern outdoor advertising along 300,000 plus miles of federal highways. The act, strongly opposed in southern oil-producing states, ended the indiscriminate erection of billboards on the right-of-ways along all federally funded roads. It was a heavy blow to the outdoor advertising industry.

However, while this development initially had an adverse effect on Lamar's business, in the long run the company may have benefitted from the setback. Although the Highway Beautification Act brought unit growth of billboard displays to a virtual standstill, it forced Lamar to develop adequate contingency planning and to diversify.

In 1973, the original company and its acquired companies, totaling 13, were organized into the Lamar Corporation, a network of affiliates created to provide a central and more efficient system of accounting and management. Ten years later, Lamar gained total ownership of all of its 15 affiliated partnerships. It also acquired Creative Displays, Inc., which added another ten billboard markets to the company's total.

Additional Expansion in the 1990s

In February 1989, Kevin Reilly, Jr. became Lamar's president and CEO. He had first joined the company in 1978, the year after he earned a B.A. from Harvard University. Until assuming the presidency, he had served as president of Lamar's Outdoor Division, starting in 1984. Under his leadership, Lamar greatly expanded its operations. Kevin Reilly's brother Wendell Reilly served as chief financial officer from 1985 to 1989, while brother Sean became the vice-president of mergers and acquisitions. Charles Lamar III was the company's first general counsel, acting in this capacity from 1982 until 1998.

In 1988, just before Reilly took over the company's reins, Lamar entered the business of fabricating interstate logo signs, winning a contract from the State of Nebraska in Reilly's initial year and eventually expanding to become the principal provider of logo signs in the United States. Thanks to the burgeoning super-highway infrastructure, the need for signs on public rights-of-way for approved franchises continued to grow, and Lamar's logo sign business, through competitive bids, won contracts from 18 states.

Key Dates:

1902: J.M. Coe creates the Pensacola Advertising Company in Pensacola, Florida.
1905: Charles W. Lamar, Sr., enters into a partnership with Coe.
1908: Lamar and Coe dissolve their partnership and the company is renamed Lamar Advertising.
1926: Lamar and his two sons, Charles Lamar, Jr., and L.V. Lamar, purchase the Baton Rouge Poster Advertising Co., renaming it Lamar Advertising Co. of Baton Rouge.
1944: Charles Lamar, Jr., becomes company president.
1958: Kevin Reilly, Sr., becomes president and CEO.
1973: The Lamar Corporation is formed to facilitate management of the operating companies.
1979: Corporate headquarters is moves to its present site in Baton Rouge, Louisiana.
1989: Kevin Reilly, Jr., becomes president and CEO.
1991: Lamar Advertising Company is formed.
1996: Lamar Advertising goes public.
1999: The company acquires the outdoor advertising division of Chancellor Media.
2004: Obie Media Corporation is acquired.

Through the 1990s, Lamar expanded its operations into other important areas, including transit advertising and wireless communications. It started creating and maintaining advertising displays on buses, bus shelters, and commuter benches in 14 of its primary markets as well as three other states: South Carolina, Utah, and Georgia. It also began contractual negotiations with electronic communications providers to allow them to attach receiving and transmitting devices to billboards on properties they owned. To date, it has made agreements with four of the principal providers of such services in the United States.

The company also went public, making an initial stock offering in August 1996. Although Lamar became a public company, to a large extent it was still a family-owned and operated business that prided itself on its friendliness and the experience and loyalty of its managerial personnel. On average, its regional managers had been with the company for 25 years.

Lamar undertook a vigorous acquisitions program in the 1990s, despite the fact that it faced some problems. A major, industry-wide setback was the steady decline in the billboard advertising of tobacco products, which had begun in 1992. Leading tobacco companies, yielding to both governmental mandates and societal pressures, began a drastic reduction in their outdoor advertising, a policy that continued over the next several years. This development cut fairly deep into the billboard advertising business and left many billboards blank. Recovery was slow. Not until 1996 did the industry, with 396,000 operating displays, come close to the 400,000 of its peak year, 1985. In 1992, tobacco advertising accounted for 12 percent of Lamar's net revenue, and although it had dropped only by 3 percent by 1997, Lamar was faced with the prospect that settlements in suits against the tobacco industry would lead to a total ban of outdoor advertising of tobacco products. The company responded by planning the total elimination of tobacco advertising by April 1999.

Lamar easily weathered the end of its tobacco accounts, however. Many non-tobacco advertisers had been waiting for billboard locations to free up. In any case, most of Lamar's real growth in outdoor advertising now derived from its transit and logo displays, areas in which Lamar had put major efforts. This proved to be a fruitful strategy. In 1996, Lamar purchased FKM Advertising. In the next year, its revenue increased by 61 percent over the previous year and its earnings rose by 74 percent, reaching $92.3 million.

During 1997, Lamar continued to expand through important acquisitions. In fact, it was a year of tremendous growth, accounting for 24 of the 106 acquisitions the company made between 1983 and 1997. Lamar also increased its total number of outdoor displays by a hefty 47 percent. In April, it purchased Penn Advertising, gaining close to 7,000 displays in New York and Pennsylvania, and in June it bought Headrick Outdoor, adding close to 3,200 bulletin displays and providing entry into four new states: Arkansas, Illinois, Kansas, and Missouri. It also bought McWhorter Advertising and some markets from National Advertising Company (3M), owned by Outdoor Systems, Inc., and made several smaller acquisitions. These resulted in expanded markets plus a significant increase in the total number of outdoor bulletin displays operated by Lamar.

Acquisitions continued in 1998. By July, Lamar had completed the purchase of an additional 24 concerns, and by October it had five more. Early in the year, after purchasing Ragan Outdoor in Iowa and Illinois, Derby Outdoor in South Dakota, and Pioneer Outdoor in Missouri and Arkansas, Lamar also signed an agreement to buy Northwest Outdoor, which, in addition to adding about 4,000 displays, allowed the company to enter markets in Washington, Montana, Oregon, Idaho, Wyoming, Nebraska, Nevada, and Utah. In May, Lamar acquired two more companies: Sun Media and Odegard Outdoor Advertising, L.L.C. A major acquisition followed in October, when, for $385 million and a debt assumption of about $105 million, Lamar purchased Outdoor Communications, Inc., adding 14,700 displays in 12 southeastern states.

In a major acquisition in June 1999, Lamar purchased the outdoor advertising division of Chancellor Media Corp., ranked number five in the billboard advertising business, for $1.6 billion. The deal involved Lamar paying $700 million in cash and the remainder in stock. With this purchase, Lamar became number one in total number of display signs operated in the United States.

Continued Growth in the 2000s

In the early 2000s, Lamar continued to expand through acquisition. Much of the expansion was in the western and southern United States. In October 2000, the company bought Bowlin Outdoor Advertising & Travel Centers Inc. in a $27.2 million stock trade. Bowlin operated displays throughout New Mexico, Arizona, and Texas. In December, it acquired PNE Media L.L.C. and Victory Outdoor Advertising L.L.C., both based in Georgia. In August 2001, Lamar announced a trade with its competitor, the Viacom Outdoor Group, in which the two firms would swap outdoor displays. Viacom traded 144 displays in Birmingham, Alabama, for Lamar signs in California, Florida, and Missouri. In 2002, Lamar purchased American Outdoor Advertising from Landmark Communications of Virginia. The firm operated 960 displays in 11 southeastern states. In July 2004, Lamar purchased 611 displays in 19 states from Olympus Advertising. Later in that same year, it purchased Oregon-based Obie Media Corp., which sold advertising space on 38 transit systems and operated more than 1,100 billboards. Under the terms of the agreement, Lamar bought Obie's stock for $43 million and assumed some $23 million in outstanding debt. Writing in *AdWeek Southwest,* Richard Williamson quoted Lamar's chief financial officer Keith Istre as stating that, between 1996, when the company went public, and 2004, Lamar had spent about $5 billion in acquiring other companies.

Due to Lamar's aggressive campaign of acquisitions, it experienced losses in the early 2000s. However, throughout this period it also showed continued growth, with sales revenue rising from $687.3 million in 2000 to $810.1 million in 2003. Company finances turned around in 2004, with the first reported profit in several years.

Lamar's future continued to look bright. Among it strategies for growth, the company planned to firm up its position as the largest logo sign operator by adding new state franchises and, possibly, new acquisitions. In an industry that is highly fragmented at best, Lamar continued to work toward consolidation of its various operations without sacrificing its local identity in the various communities served by its individual companies. It remained a major player among the 600 companies in the outdoor advertising business, successfully competing with both rival display concerns as well as media advertisers vying for the same market share.

Principal Subsidiaries

Lamar Outdoor Advertising; Interstate Logos, Inc.; Lamar Graphics; Lamar Advertising of Penn Inc.; Lamar Advertising of Oklahoma Inc.; Lamar Advertising of Youngstown Inc.; Lamar Advertising of Michigan Inc.

Principal Competitors

Infinity Broadcasting, Inc.; Clear Channel Communications, Inc.; Omnicom Group Inc.; Viacom Outdoor Group.

Further Reading

Atlas, Riva, "Billboard Mania," *Forbes*, November 4, 1996, p. 371.

Beatty, Sally Goll, "Billboard Firms Ease into Smokeless Era," *Wall Street Journal*, October 30, 1997, p. B6.

Brownlee, Lisa, "Sign of the Times: Billboards IPOs Catch Eye with Oversize Gains," *Wall Street Journal*, September 12, 1996, p. B6.

Dinsmore, Christopher, "Lamar Advertising Acquires Billboard Firm American Outdoor Advertising," *Virginian-Pilot* (Norfolk, Virginia), June 5, 2002.

Harrison, Joan, "A Face Lift for a Drab Industry," *Mergers and Acquisitions*, May–June 1997, pp. 46–47.

"Lamar Advertising Company Announces Third Quarter 2004 Operating Results," *Business Wire*, November 15, 2004.

"Lamar Advertising to Buy Obie Media," *UPI NewsTrack*, September 20, 2004.

"Lamar Spends $1.6 Bil for Chancellor Outdoor Biz," *Advertising Age*, June 7, 1999, p. 44.

Lovel, Jim, "Lamar Profits Fall Short of Projections," *AdWeek Southeast*, August 5, 2004.

Nicholson, Gilbert, "Lamar Boosts Its Dominance Over Billboards," *Birmingham Business Journal*, August 31, 2001, p. 1.

Sparks, Debra, "Musical Billboards Are the Hottest Advertising Medium. Then Why Is the Smart Money Bailing Out?," *Financial World*, February 18, 1997, pp. 48–51.

Williamson, Eric, "Louisiana-Based Advertising Company Expands with Augusta, Ga.-Area Purchase," *Augusta Chronicle*, December 9, 2000.

Williamson, Richard, "Lamar to Buy Outdoor Firm in $43 Mil. Deal," *AdWeek Southwest*, September 24, 2004.

—John W. Fiero
—update: Thomas Wiloch

Landmark Theatre Corporation

2222 South Barrington Avenue
Los Angeles, California 90064
U.S.A.
Telephone: (310) 473-6701
Fax: (310) 473-8622
Web site: http://wwwlandmarktheatres.com

Wholly Owned Subsidiary of 2929 Entertainment
Incorporated: 1974
Employees: 280
Sales: $26 million (2003)
NAIC: 512131 Motion Picture Theaters (Except Drive-Ins)

Landmark Theatre Corporation operates the largest chain of movie theaters in the United States that exhibit specialty films, that is, first-run independent films and foreign films that are often referred to as "art" films. Landmark, as an art-house operator, exhibits films that mainstream movie theater chains do not show, presenting its features in nearly 60 theaters in 14 states and the District of Columbia. Landmark is owned by 2929 Entertainment, an entertainment holding company co-founded and co-owned by Mark Cuban, the high-profile owner of the National Basketball Association's Dallas Mavericks.

Origins

Landmark changed its business orientation once during its first 30 years in business. Ownership of Landmark changed considerably more frequently, as one company after another sought control of the largest art-house theater chain, or "circuit," in the United States. Landmark began operating in 1974, when the acquisition of Los Angeles's Nuart Theatre was completed. Located on Santa Monica Boulevard in the heart of Los Angeles's Westside, the Nuart Theatre, which later become a favorite venue for staging world premiere events, served as the flagship theater for the soon-to-develop Landmark circuit. Landmark was led by Stephen Gilula, who co-founded the company and would preside over its operation through many of the changes that lay ahead. After acquiring the Nuart Theatre, Gilula and his management team acquired the Ken Cinema, a theater built in 1946 that exhibited the first high-quality foreign films in San Diego. Landmark acquired the Ken Cinema in 1975, adding another theater the following year when the company purchased the Rialto Theatre, located in Pasadena. Built in 1925, the Rialto Theatre was nearly razed by a wrecking ball shortly after Gilula completed its acquisition, but its addition to the National Register of Historic Places in 1978 spared the building from destruction. In addition to these venues, Landmark also opened a theater near the University of California at Berkeley and in other markets, all of which followed the company's operating strategy.

During their first years in business, Gilula and his co-founders followed a repertory-style format, one that differed from the operating strategy later used by Landmark. During the 1970s, Landmark's theaters showed old, "classic" films, foreign films, and cult features, presenting a different lineup of films every night. In an age when video cassette recorders (VCRs) had yet to become ubiquitous, Landmark's format thrived, drawing college students and others who delighted in watching films such as *Harold and Maude, King of Hearts,* and *Pink Flamingos*. Landmark attracted long lines of film watchers by distributing free monthly calendars of its schedules and by staging promotional events, tactics that enabled it to develop quickly into the nation's largest repertory film circuit.

Gilula's business strategy began to lose its effectiveness as the 1980s began. The decade saw the rise of the home-video market, as the proliferation of VCRs and the emergence of video rental businesses sounded the death knell for many repertory-style circuits. Gilula and his team responded to the changing market dynamics by adopting the operating strategy that would underpin its success into the 21st century. Thus, Landmark theaters began to show high-quality independent films and first-run foreign films, offering film goers a chance to see what the mainstream theaters were not showing. The plan worked well, attracting queues of film aficionados and encouraging Gilula to expand further. In 1982, Landmark was merged with a Sante Fe, New Mexico-based company named Movies, Inc., a transaction that gave Gilula 12 new screens in eight new cities in the southern and southwestern United States. At the end of the decade, Landmark merged with Seattle-based

Company Perspectives:

Landmark Theatres, the nation's largest art-house chain, features first-run independent and foreign films, restored classics and non-traditional studio fare in 58 theaters representing 209 screens in 14 states and the District of Columbia. In exhibiting indie hits such as Garden State, Monster, The Pianist, Memento, Fast Runner, Monsoon Wedding, Bowling for Columbine, The Blair Witch Project, Run Lola Run *and* Crouching Tiger, Hidden Dragon, *Landmark has never veered from its commitment to present cutting edge entertainment or shied away from controversial films, such as* Fahrenheit 9/11, Y Tu Mamá También, Kids, Romance *or* The Last Temptation of Christ.

Seven Gables, which added another 33 screens. The Seven Gables merger was completed in 1989, by which time Gilula's company had begun to experience the numerous ownership changes that provided the backdrop for Landmark's second 15 years in business.

Ownership Changes in the 1980s and 1990s

While Gilula fashioned Landmark into one of the premier art-house chains in the country, an entertainment executive in Hollywood was transforming the nature of his company. Arthur Steloff ran Heritage Entertainment Inc., a company he took public in 1969. Until Steloff began to seek greater prominence for his venture, Heritage survived by licensing film and television series to other companies. Starting in 1982, however, Steloff began producing content for both television and movies houses, aggressively transforming Heritage into a production company. In 1985, he acquired New York-based IFEX, an importer and exporter of films that for the previous decade had acted as an agent for Soviet-bloc countries to acquire Western programming. By acquiring IFEX, Steloff gained control of more than 1,800 feature films and other programs made by Eastern-bloc countries, filling his library with art-house classics such as *Closely Watched Trains*, a film made in Czechoslovakia, and *Moscow Does Not Believe in Tears*, a Soviet-made film that won an Academy award for Best Foreign Film. The acquisition of IFEX, combined with other acquisitions and Heritage's internally produced content, gave Steloff a voluminous collection of films that were ideally suited for exhibition in specialty movie theaters. Steloff completed the vertically integrated connection between owning content and owning the venues to showcase the content when he acquired Landmark in 1989, the same year Gilula's company's merged with Seven Gables.

However, Steloff's bid to create an entertainment empire failed not long after his acquisition of Landmark. While Heritage declared bankruptcy in December 1990, the purchase of Landmark was not considered to be the cause for the company's rapid collapse. The art-house circuit, in fact, had drawn the attention of another suitor in the months leading up to Heritage's demise. Samuel Goldwyn, Jr., the son of famed movie mogul Samuel Goldwyn, had attempted to acquire Heritage in the fall of 1990, but negotiations with Steloff stalled before Heritage filed for Chapter 11. Goldwyn, who started his own

company, Samuel Goldwyn Co., in 1979, began acquiring movie houses in 1985 as an outlet for films produced by his company, a move that gave him the four-screen Samuel Goldwyn Pavilion Cinemas. His interest in Heritage stemmed from the company's Landmark subsidiary, which was regarded as the jewel of Steloff's holdings. The collapse of Heritage breathed new life into Goldwyn's attempt to acquire Landmark, resulting in a reorganization plan for Heritage that was designed to make Steloff's company a subsidiary of Samuel Goldwyn Co. The deal was concluded in late 1991, making privately held Samuel Goldwyn Co. a public company because of Heritage's status as a publicly traded concern. The merger gave Goldwyn control over Landmark, which by this point operated theaters in 17 cities, all of which operated under the Landmark name except in Seattle, where the Seven Gables name was retained. Gilula, who had remained in charge of the company under Steloff's rule, was named president of the Samuel Goldwyn Theatre Group, the Samuel Goldwyn Co. subsidiary that counted Landmark as its primary asset.

Backed by the financial resources and stability of its new parent company, Landmark blossomed during the 1990s. The chain expanded by acquiring theaters, building theaters, and improving its existing properties. In 1994, Landmark was midway through an expansion program whose aim was to increase the number of its screens by 30 percent. By November, the company had acquired two theaters in Houston and six theaters in Berkeley, giving it a total of 100 screens in 42 theaters. The company was also using the roughly $20 million set aside for the expansion program to build its own, architecturally distinct, movie theaters. In 1995, two of Landmark's own creations opened, the five-screen Embarcadero Center Cinema in San Francisco and the nine-screen Kendall Square Cinema in Cambridge, Massachusetts, the largest art house in the country. Gilula and executives at Samuel Goldwyn Co., who helped pay for the expansion program, were encouraged by the success of speciality films such as *The Piano*, *The Crying Game*, and *Like Water for Chocolate*. "There are many differing special interests out there for movie-going audiences besides just the mass market," Gilula said in a November 7, 1994 interview with the *Los Angeles Business Journal*, "and we feel that we've helped to develop that. The distinction between a true specialized film and a mass-market film has blurred," he added. "The public is more open-minded, and the exhibitors are more open-minded too."

By the mid-1990s, Landmark ranked as the largest and most profitable art-house circuit in the country. Its parent company, however, could not boast the same level of success. Samuel Golden Co. began to struggle financially as it entered the late 1990s, suffering annual losses that prompted Goldwyn to diversify and reposition his company. Landmark, for the second time in a decade, found its ownership changing hands, resulting in its acquisition in 1998 by Silver Cinemas Inc. Silver Cinemas, based in Dallas, ranked as one of the largest second-run film exhibitors in the country. When Silver Cinema acquired Landmark, the art-house chain operated 54 theaters with 156 screens. Its theaters were located along the West Coast and in Dallas, Houston, Denver, Minneapolis, Milwaukee, Boston, Detroit, New Orleans, among other cities.

New ownership of Landmark once again triggered an expansion program, helping the company increase its stature as a specialty film exhibitor. The most notable aspects of the circuit's growth were the theaters constructed by Landmark, the first of which was the Plaza Frontenac Cinema in St. Louis. The six-screen Plaza Frontenac Cinema opened in 1998, the same year the company completed construction of the six-screen Embassy Cinema in Waltham, Massachusetts. In 2000, construction of a third theater was completed, the seven-screen Century Centre Cinema, a property that marked Landmark's return to the Chicago market.

Landmark in the 2000s

Expansion of the Landmark circuit stopped after the opening of the Century Centre Cinema. For the third time in a decade, the financial difficulties of the circuit's parent company led to a change in ownership. Silver Cinemas declared bankruptcy in 2000, making its two divisions, Landmark and a chain of 21 discount theaters, available for purchase by any interested party. Landmark, in mid-2001, was acquired by Silver Cinema's leading unsecured creditor, a Los Angeles-based investment management company named Oaktree Capital Management LLC. Oaktree paid $40 for Landmark and installed Paul Richardson and Bert Manzari as its two senior executives. Richardson, who was named president and chief executive officer, and Manzari, who was appointed executive vice-president, had helped manage Landmark since the company began its transformation from a repertory movie chain into an art-house chain. The pair left Landmark when Silver Cinemas acquired the company and marked their return by vowing to re-establish "Landmark's traditional core values," according to Richardson in a May 26, 2001 interview with *The Dallas Morning News*. Those values, according to Richardson, included exhibiting quality films in architecturally distinct theaters and employing a "film savvy" staff.

As Landmark neared its 30th anniversary, a familiar refrain from its history provided a new perspective on its future. Ownership of the company changed hands again. Oaktree, whose investment strategy meant it generally held onto a company for only a short time, sold Landmark in 2003 to an entertainment holding company named 2929 Entertainment. The company was founded by Dallas entrepreneur Todd Wagner and Mark Cuban, the owner of the National Basketball Association's Dallas Mavericks. Wagner and Cuban had founded a company named Broadcast.com, which they sold to Yahoo! for $5.7 billion in 1999. 2929 Entertainment was one of the ventures the pair founded with their enormous personal fortunes, a company that owned Rysher Entertainment, a film and television library, Magnolia Pictures Distribution, an independent distribution company, and stakes in HDNet (a high definition television network) and Lions Gate Entertainment, a creator, producer, and distributor of films. The acquisition of Landmark presented 2929 Entertainment with the same opportunity for vertical integration that it had afforded its previous owners, giving Wagner and Cuban the ability to control various steps of content creation, distribution, and exhibition. "What that adds up to," Wagner remarked in a September 24, 2003 interview with *The Dallas Morning News*, "is now being able to control your own destiny. All of a sudden, I can actually make a movie, play it on television, and release it theatrically."

Under the ownership of 2929 Entertainment, Landmark celebrated its 30th anniversary and prepared for the years ahead. The company added 11 screens in 2003, including the five-screen Magnolia Theatre in Dallas. In 2004, construction of the circuit's newest addition, the eight-screen E Street Cinema in Washington, D.C., was completed. Aside from the further expansion of the chain, 2929 Entertainment's plans for the future included remodeling Landmark's existing theaters, developing non-traditional concession items, launching a retail arm of the chain to sell DVDs, soundtracks, and other merchandise, and installing liquid crystal display and digital projectors into its network of theaters.

Principal Competitors

AMC Entertainment Inc.; Reading Entertainment, Inc.; Regal Entertainment Group.

Further Reading

Block, Alex Ben, "When the Enemy Zigs, Zag!," *Forbes*, November 17, 1986, p. 128.
Burton, Jonathan, "Samuel Goldwyn, Jr.," *Chief Executive (U.S.)*, June 1995, p. 26.
Glover, Kara, "Goldwyn, Heritage Entertainment Merging," *Los Angeles Business Journal*, September 23, 1991, p. 50.
Godinez, Victor, "Dallas Firm to Purchase Art-House Theater Chain," *Dallas Morning News*, September 24, 2003, p. B3.
Harris, Kathryn, "Like Father, Like Son," *Forbes*, October 28, 1991, p. 174.
Kirkpatrick, John, "Los Angeles-Based Investment Group Buys Dallas-Based Movie Theater Chain," *Dallas Morning News*, May 26, 2001, p. B2.
Simon, Bernard, "Quick Collector of Silver Screens," *New York Times*, June 30, 2002, p. 2L.
Spring, Greg, "Goldwyn Envisions Movie Theater Chain Expansion," *Los Angeles Business Journal*, November 7, 1994, p. 12.
Walter, Bob, "Sacramento, Calif., Tower Theatre Gets New Management," *Knight Ridder/Tribune Business News*, August 14, 1998, p. OKRB982260BD.
Williams, Norman D., "Sacramento, Calif., Specialty Movie Theater to Close," *Knight Ridder/Tribune Business News*, April 8, 1999, p. ORB9909810C.

—Jeffrey L. Covell

Lilly Endowment Inc.

2801 North Meridian Street
Indianapolis, Indiana 46208-0068
U.S.A.
Telephone: (317) 924-5471
Fax: (317) 926-4431
Web site: http://www.lillyendowment.org

Not-for-Profit Corporation
Incorporated: 1937
Total Assets: $8.6 billion (2004)
NAIC: 813211 Grantmaking Foundations

Operating out of Indianapolis, Indiana, Lilly Endowment Inc. is a private family endowment established by members of the Lilly family through gifts of stock in the giant pharmaceutical firm of Eli Lilly and Company. With some $10 billion in assets, the endowment distributes about $500 million in charitable contributions each year, about 60 to 70 percent of which, in keeping with the founders' wishes, remains in Indiana. In addition, the endowment, as directed by its founders, focuses its attention on three areas—religion, education, and community development—with a special emphasis on benefiting young people. Lilly Endowment has played a crucial role in the rebirth of downtown Indianapolis. All told, since its founding in 1937, Lilly Endowment has issued more than $5 billion in grants.

Lilly Family Business Dates to 1870s

The fortune that would one day form the financial backbone for the Lilly Endowment may be traced to 1876, when Colonel Eli Lilly (he served for the Union Army during the Civil War) opened a small pharmaceutical laboratory in Indianapolis to manufacture drugs. Lilly was a civic-minded man, a devotion he passed on to his descendants. Not only did he become the head of the Commercial Club to spur development of Indianapolis, he offered help to the masses devastated by the financial panic on 1893 and funded the building of a children's hospital. His son, Josiah Lilly, and grandson, also named Eli Lilly, proved adept at business and shared the colonel's philanthropic spirit. The younger Lilly, after earning a degree from the Philadelphia College of

Pharmacy, joined the firm in 1907. He was instrumental in the development of a blueprinting process that could produce multiple copies of a manufacturing process, thus allowing for a significant increase in production. As head of the manufacturing division, he modernized the firm's overall approach to production, bringing in efficiency experts as well as instituting other changes, such as a guaranteed wage and a bonus system to create worker incentives. With the advent of World War I, the firm, dependent on European sources for drugs, was forced to engage in pharmaceutical research to develop substitutes. Following the war, Lilly headed the scientific unit which during the 1920s developed the first commercially available insulin for diabetics. This product initiated a series of blockbuster drugs that made the Lilly family immensely wealthy.

Eli Lilly succeeded his father as president of the family business in 1932. He also took on his grandfather's mantle as the family philanthropist. He began campaigning for the creation of a family endowment, and in 1937 he and his father and brother, Josiah Lilly, Jr., created an endowment through gifts of 17,500 shares of stock in Eli Lilly and Company worth $280,000. During Eli Lilly's time as president, the firm's revenues grew from $13 million to $117 million in 1948, when he became chairman after his father's death and his brother assumed executive responsibility. The value of the endowment's stock was growing steadily and now Eli Lilly had more time to devote to the foundation's activities.

During the first 40 years of its existence, the Lilly Endowment was essentially run by Eli Lilly out of his desk drawer. Board members were his friends and business associates, and there was no systematic approach to the endowment's charitable contributions. Some $5 million worth of rare books was donated to Indiana University, and a $5.5 million coin collection was donated to the Smithsonian Institution, to name a few of the foundation's diverse acts. Sharing an interest in archaeology and popular religious literature that held up the New Testament as a guidebook for character development in the modern era, Lilly supported archaeologists researching Indiana's ancient history as well as religious writers. During the early decades of the endowment, however, the contributions it made were to tried-and-true charities, including the Community

Chest and the Red Cross. It was not until after Eli Lilly died in 1977 and the endowment became more of a formal foundation that it began to expand its activities and take advantage of its rising financial resources. Moreover, because of a change in federal tax laws in 1969, the endowment was required to spend more of its money.

In the late 1970s, the endowment decided to concentrate its activities in Indianapolis and began to play a crucial role in the city's development. At the time, the city was known for the annual Indianapolis 500 motor race and little more. Far from having no image, the city was in danger of developing a poor one, for, like many Midwest cities, it had begun to hemorrhage manufacturing jobs, becoming part of what was known as the Rust Belt. In a 1999 article, James Dunaway of *Mediaweek* offered a bleak picture of Indianapolis 20 years earlier: "In the center of the city, storefronts were empty or boarded up. There was a single, down-at-the-heels, 70-year-old hotel, with fewer than 200 rooms. The few downtown restaurants did most of their business at lunchtime. Even the well-known St. Elmo Steakhouse shut down every evening at 7:30. The heart of Indianapolis was a ghost town, and scheduling a convention in the city was like booking into a cemetery." In short, Indianapolis was a dying city. In 1979, a group of business leaders conducted research that recommended five areas in which the city could build a positive reputation that help launch a rebirth: arts and culture, education, health and medicine, food and nutrition, and sports. Given Indianapolis's association with the annual Memorial Day automobile race, it was not surprising that the leaders decided to focus their resources on sports, especially amateur sports. As a result, a non-profit organization, Indiana Sports Corp., was formed, the first in the nation dedicated to the identification, solicitation, and hosting of sporting events.

Indianapolis Enjoys Growth in Amateur Sports in the 1980s

Sports Corp. started out with no office, no money, and just one employee, Sandy Knapp, a former cheerleader for the Indiana Pacers professional basketball team. Lily Endowment provided a six-figure grant that got Sports Corp. started, and in 1980 the organization made its first major move, bidding on the 1982 National Sports Festival, later renamed the U.S. Olympic Festival. Despite its lack of suitable facilities, such as a track-and-field stadium, competitive swimming facilities, a velodrome, or a softball complex, Indianapolis won the bid. According to Knapp, "We used a lot of smoke and mirrors." In addition to the city and state and other private donors, Lilly Endowment made major contributions to the construction of the necessary facilities. It provided $10.7 million of the $21.5 million needed to build swimming pools, and $4 million out of the $5.9 million needed for the track and field stadium. Thou-

sands of volunteers were also instrumental in making a major success out of the festival, which set attendance and ticket sales records and allowed Indianapolis to become the self-proclaimed "Amateur Sports Capital of the United States." Indianapolis also looked to boost its image through professional sports. In 1981, the endowment contributed $25 million of the $77.5 million needed to convert the downtown convention center into a 61,000-seat football stadium. It was a risky maneuver, given that the city had no prospects of receiving a new National Football League franchise, but it paid off when in 1984 Indianapolis was able to lure away the Baltimore Colts. The Hoosier Dome, later renamed the RCA Dome, was also used to secure three NCAA basketball Final Four tournaments.

In 1984, Lilly endowment named James T. Morris president. A former chief of staff for Indianapolis mayor Richard Lugar (who went on to become a U.S. Senator), Morris had joined the endowment in 1973 as the director of community development, then worked his way up through the ranks as vice-president and executive vice-president. He was also a founding member of the Indiana Sports Corp. During his five-year tenure at the helm, the endowment was actively involved in Indianapolis's efforts to secure the 1987 Pan American Games and made sizeable contributions to the construction of new facilities. The games were very successful, drawing more than one million spectators to the city and generating an estimated $175 million in business. All told, during the 1980s Lilly endowment contributed more than $300 million to Indianapolis, which included funding for such sports facilities as the Hoosier Dome, Market Square Arena, William F. Kuntz Memorial Soccer Stadium, the Indiana University Natatorium, the National Institute of Fitness and Sport, and the American College of Sports Medicine, as well as other venues used for bicycling, track and field, and skating activities and events. With Indianapolis's reputation vastly improved and the downtown area revitalized, Lilly Endowment in the late 1980s shifted its focus from athletics to education, another area of need in the city and state. In the long-term, education had accounted for 29 percent of the endowment's spending but had declined to 19 percent during the 1980s when there was a special emphasis on community development. Spending on religion during this period remained relatively stable, slipping from 17 percent to 15 percent. It was religious funding that gave the endowment a national reach, however. Lilly Endowment was, in fact, the largest foundation in the country that placed a significant emphasis on religion.

In 1989, Lilly Endowment named a new president, John M. Mutz, who had served as Indiana's lieutenant governor from 1981 to 1986. After failing to secure the Republican nomination for governor in 1988, Mutz elected to remain in public service by taking the helm at Lilly Endowment. He took charge of a foundation with $2.1 billion in assets, one of the five largest philanthropies in America. Among his greatest achievements during his five-year tenure was the establishment of the GIFT initiative (Giving Indiana Funds for Tomorrow), which set up community foundations in each of Indiana's 92 counties. With the endowment's seed money, the individual foundations then launched their own fundraising activities to develop even more charitable funding for Indiana, while getting more people involved at the community level. Also during Mutz's time in charge, Lilly Endowment reached the $1 billion mark in total contributions in its history, 70 percent of which had been given away in the previous ten years. Because Elli Lilly prospered, spurred by the sales of the antidepressant drug Prozac, the firm's stock grew by 95 percent from 1989 to 1991 and the asset base of the endowment soared, reaching $3.9 billion. As the economy soured, however, Eli Lilly stock plummeted, resulting in a $1 billion loss to the endowment. Lilly Endowment now received some criticism in the press about its dependence on Elli Lilly stock rather than on developing a more diversified investment approach usually followed by such organizations, which placed about 38 percent of its assets in stocks, 35 percent in bonds, and the rest in other investments. For confidential reasons, this was not case with the Lilly Endowment. Possibly the founders had stipulated that investments be kept in Lilly stock. Moreover, having about 16 percent of its outstanding shares in the hands of the endowment benefited Eli Lilly in some ways, bolstering the company's stock price and providing some protection from a hostile takeover bid. Whatever its rationale, the endowment did not change its investment practice, electing to view what transpired in the early 1990s as little more than a paper loss. Nevertheless, the endowment had to cut back on its contributions to avoid selling off stock.

In 1994, Mutz was replaced as president by N. Clay Robbins, an Indianapolis attorney whose practice had specialized in laws relating to tax-exempt organizations. A Sunday school teacher, he was especially interested in the endowment's contributions to religious programs but was also dedicated to improving the educational attainment of Indiana citizens. The state ranked a disappointing 47th in the percentage of adults holding an undergraduate college degree. In the mid-1990s, the endowment began making sizeable contributions to Indiana institutions of higher learning to improve that ranking, then in 1998 launched the Lily Endowment Community Scholarship program to provide four-year, full-tuition scholarships to Indiana colleges. In addition, it contributed funds to organizations already involved in efforts to prepare young people for college.

Asset Base Soars in 1990s

While Wall Street enjoyed one of its longest bull markets in history, the price of Eli Lilly stock soared in the 1990s, resulting in a massive increase in the endowment's assets, growing from $5.3 billion in 1995 to $12.7 billion in 1997. Lilly Endowment now became the largest private foundation in the country, eclipsing the Ford foundation, which had taken a diverse portfolio approach and now had $9.4 billion in assets. As a result of this windfall, the amount of money Lilly Endowment had to distribute grew from $253 million in 1997 to more than $400 million in 1998. What's more, the organization was required by law to give away 5 percent of its investment assets each year, based on an average value over the course of the year. Rather than search out new charities, Lilly Endowment elected to make larger general grants to organizations to which it already contributed, essentially trusting them to make wise use of the funds. For instance, the United Way of Central Indiana, received $50 million, the largest single grant ever made to a community United Way organization. In 1997, it had received $5.4 million from the endowment. Other large grants included $42 million to the United Negro College Fund, $25 million to the National Urban League, and $25 million to the GIFT program.

In the late 1990s, Lilly Endowment began to contribute money to Indiana colleges and universities in an effort to stem the flow of college graduates leaving the state to seek work elsewhere. According to a study partially funded by the endowment, more than 36 percent of Indiana residents and more than 89 percent of non-residents left the state after graduation. To address the "brain drain" problem, Lilly Endowment made sizeable contributions to several Indiana universities to help them develop marquee departments that would attract students, with the hope that this program would elevate the educational standing and thereby attract employers in search of a talented workforce. Much of the money was also earmarked for high technology projects, which might lead to start-up companies and a new source of jobs, thus making up for the loss of traditional manufacturing jobs in Indiana.

As the stock market continued to flourish, Lilly Endowment steadily increased the amount of money it gave each year, distributing a record $594.1 million in 2001. In 2002, as the price of Lilly stock declined, the endowment cut back to $563 million. Also during 2002, the $10.1 billion foundation was surpassed by the Bill & Melinda Gates Foundation, with more than $24 billion in assets, as the largest private foundation in the country. The fortunes of Lilly Endowment remained closely tied to the price of Lilly stock, which performed well in 2003 but dipped somewhat in 2004. Nevertheless, the board showed no inclination to change the endowment's investment strategy, content to adjust the amount it gave away from year to year. In the long-run, holding onto Lilly stock had proven an effective strategy, allowing the endowment to make more than $5 billion in grants since its foundation in 1937.

Further Reading

Andrews, Greg, "Endowment's Focus on Lilly Stock Stirs Debate, Concern," *Indianapolis Business Journal*, March 15, 1993, p. 1A.

Dafforn, Erik, "What Things in Life Are Truly Important," *Wabash Magazine*, Winter 1998.

Davis, Andrea Muirragui, "Lilly Endowment Uses Cash to Plug Brain Drain," *Indianapolis Business Journal*, October 1, 2001, p. A9.

Dunaway, James, "Indianapolis," *Mediaweek*, November 1, 1999, p. 20.

"Larger Small Cities: Salvation through Sport," *Economist*, June 10, 1989, p. 29.

Thomas, John, "A Quiet Giant," *Indianapolis Business Journal*, April 10, 1989, p. 1A.

—Ed Dinger

London Scottish Bank plc

London Scottish House, Mount Street
Manchester
M2 3LS
United Kingdom
Telephone: +44 161 834 2861
Fax: +44 161 834 2536
Web site: http://www.london-scottish.com

Public Company
Incorporated: 1936 as Refuge Lending Society Ltd.
Employees: 1,278
Sales: £312.6 million ($500 million) (2004)
Stock Exchanges: London
Ticker Symbol: LSB
NAIC: 522110 Commercial Banking

London Scottish Bank plc (LSB) is one of the United Kingdom's leading providers of credit to the "sub-prime" market—that is, to consumers typically denied credit at other financial institutions. LSB's core operations revolve around its traditional base in the so-called doorstep lending sector, in which loans are made and collected in door-to-door fashion. In this segment, LSB's loans are typically small, at an average of £420 and ranging up to £1,000, and for older customers, as high as £3,000. Loans are also typically short-term, usually no more than six months, with interest rates at 20 percent APR and higher, and payments are made weekly. LSB customers, primarily working class and low-income, generally begin with small loans, which are gradually replaced with larger loans as the customer establishes a credit history. Consumer Credit remains LSB's largest division, representing more than 70 percent of annual revenues of nearly £313 million in 2004. Debt collection, principally through the company's Robinson Way subsidiary, is the company's main profit generator. The company not only supports its own operations, but also provides debt collection and related services—including meter reading—to a variety of customers. Since the early 2000s, London Scottish Bank has made an effort to diversify its lending portfolio away from a reliance on doorstep lending. The company has made a number of acquisitions, including Call-4-Cash, Sterling Direct, Pacific Homeloans, and Personal Loan Centre, boosting its direct lending business. This operation also has been extended to LSB's national network of more than 100 branches. In 2004, the Manchester-based company also launched its first retail deposit offering to the public. In another move, LSB has stepped up its efforts to win commercial lending customers, a division that adds some 15 percent to group turnover. Listed on the London Stock Exchange, LSB is led by CEO Roy Reece. Chairman of the board is Jack Livingstone, grandson of the company's founder.

Turn of the 20th Century Lender

London Scottish Bank traced its roots back to turn of the 20th century England, when Lewis Livingstone set up a small money-lending business in Wigan, Lancashire. By providing small, short-term loans to the area's large, low-income working class—which tended to be shunned by larger lenders—Livingstone's business grew quickly. By 1903, Livingstone opened an office in Manchester. That city then became the company's headquarters, as well as its major market.

Livingstone's company became a family affair in 1918 when son Harry Livingstone, just 15 years old at the time, joined his father's business. Together the pair expanded the company's base of operations. By the mid-1930s, the company operated seven branches, all within the Lancashire region. In 1936, the Livingstones incorporated the company as Refuge Lending Society Limited. Harry Livingstone's son Jack Livingstone joined the company in 1958.

Lancashire remained Refuge's focus through the 1950s, and by the beginning of the 1960s, there were 15 Refuge branches throughout the region. In 1961, however, the company, then led by Harry Livingstone, decided to expand beyond its home base for the first time. Adopting a strategy of organic expansion and acquisition, Refuge added 18 new branches by 1962, including the acquisition of Reliance Guarantee Company. The company also established new regional subsidiaries, Refuge Lending Company (Northern) Ltd. and Refuge Lending Company (Midlands) Ltd. in 1962.

Refuge's earlier expansion targeted primarily England's North and Midlands regions. In the second half of the 1960s,

Company Perspectives:

London Scottish Bank is a Specialist Financial Services Company. It has been Established for over a century. Over 2000 staff provide services to the Public and Private sectors, as well as the consumer, through a nationwide network of over 100 Branches and a state of the art Call Centre. Its High Power Systems are without equal.

Refuge began extending further across the country. By the end of the decade, the company operated 38 branches, including two in London, first established in 1968.

Public Offering in 1970

Concurrent with its geographic expansion, the company began to expand its range of financial services as well. Into the 1970s, Refuge's client base topped 18,000 customers, the majority of whom were regular customers. Average loan amounts ranged from £40 to £200, and regular customers tended to arrange advances twice per year. A distinguishing feature of Refuge was its low bad debt ratio. By conducting thorough investigations of its potential clients, the company was able to maintain its defaulted loan rate at just 2 percent of total turnover.

This success led the company to extend its loan services into longer-term categories in 1966, with the creation of a new subsidiary, Sameday Re-Mortgage Company Limited. Refuge then began providing loans for up to three years, as compared with its main business's average of just six months. Through the 1970s, the company continued to shift its balance of business toward the longer term, in part by targeting council tenants, seen as better risks, with one- to three-year loans.

Refuge restructured at the beginning of 1970 in preparation for its public offering. In July 1970, the company listed its shares on the London Stock Exchange, and prepared to step up its expansion. A major milestone in the company's growth came in 1975, when it acquired debt collection agency Robinson Way. That business, like Refuge itself, conducted a great part of its debt collection services through door-to-door visits. In this way, Robinson Way proved a strong complement for Refuge's core business. It also proved to be one of the most profitable areas of the company's operations, eventually responsible for some 30 percent of group profits.

During the 1980s, the company added a small commercial debt collection operation as well, as an add-on to Robinson Way's focus on the consumer market. This diversification of the company's activities, coupled with a liberalization of the British banking sector, led Refuge to change its name in 1986, when it adopted its new moniker, London Scottish Bank (LSB).

LSB continued to seek growth opportunities through the end of the 1980s. In 1988, for example, the company acquired Manchester-based James Stewart Group. That purchase boosted LSB's consumer finance and retail credit operations. The company also continued to expand its debt collection operations, both through organic growth and through a number of smaller acquisitions. Another acquisition, of Commercial Credit Con-

sultants in 1990, helped establish the group's commercial debt collection operations as a major part of its overall business.

Diversified Financial Group for the New Century

Despite the lean economic times of the early 1990s, especially in the United Kingdom, which only slowly pulled out of a national recession toward the latter half of the decade, LSB remained in relatively good health. This was due in large part to its focus on the low-income sector. LSB's clientele relied heavily on relief benefits, or, in the case of working clients, wages that barely climbed above the relief level—because of this, these populations tended to be much less affected by economic downturns. As a result, LSB came through the worst of the recession with more or less stable bad debt levels.

Nonetheless, LSB's core market was seen as relatively mature as the company approached the new century. In response, LSB began preparations to diversify its operations beyond its reliance on doorstep lending and, to a lesser extent, debt collection.

Acquisitions played a prominent role in LSB's new diversification strategy. In 1997, the company established a new direct lending wing, with the acquisition of Personal Loan Centre. This was followed in 1998 by the addition of another area of operation, factoring—that is, providing billing services for smaller companies—when it acquired Isis Factors, paying £6 million.

Acquisitions continued into the next decade. In 2000, the company added telephone-based direct lending specialist Call-4-Cash. By 2001, the company's direct lending activities accounted for some 15 percent of total turnover.

LSB continued looking for acquisitions in order to expand into the new century. In 2002, the company acquired Stirling Direct Finance Ltd. This purchase enabled LSB to establish a mortgage-secured lending wing. LSB returned to the acquisition trail and, in June 2003, purchased Prime Finance, a sub-prime lender and loan packager.

By 2003, LSB's customer base had topped 180,000. With the sub-prime market estimated to be as much as eight million people in the United Kingdom, the company was considered to have strong potential for future growth. In that year, the company took a new approach toward attracting customers, launching its first retail deposit account for the first time. The fund, offering rates as high as 5.85 percent, quickly attracted nearly £29 million from more than 1,700 customers.

By then, LSB also had boosted its secured loans division. In February 2003, the company announced its acquisition of Pacific Home Loans, based in Leigh, Essex. LSB paid an initial price of £3.2 million for the purchase. LSB did not neglect its core doorstep lending business, however. In August 2004, the company boosted that division through the acquisition of the debt portfolio of Morse's Ltd. The purchase, for £10 million, added Morse's more than 123,000 customers to LSB's books. The acquisition also provided LSB with Morse's 500 staff, including 200 collectors employed directly by Morse's. In addition, the purchase gave LSB the option to hire more than 300 self-employed collectors who had worked with Morse's.

Key Dates:

1895: Lewis Livingstone opens a money-lending business in Wigan.

1903: Livingstone opens an office in Manchester and moves headquarters there.

1918: Son Harry Livingstone joins the business.

1936: With seven branch offices, the company incorporates as Refuge Lending Society Ltd.

1958: Jack Livingstone, grandson of the founder, joins the business.

1962: The company launches expansion beyond the Lancashire region.

1966: The company founds Sameday Re-Mortgage Company Ltd. as part of a shift in focus to longer-term loans.

1975: The company acquires Robinson Way in diversification into debt collection.

1986: The company changes its name to London Scottish Bank.

1988: The James Stewart Group, in Manchester, is acquired.

1990: Commercial Credit Consultants is acquired, boosting commercial lending operations.

1997: Personal Loan Centre is acquired, adding direct lending operations.

1998: The company acquires Isis Factors and enters factoring (invoicing) services.

2000: Call-4-Cash is acquired, adding telephone-based direct lending services.

2002: The company buys Stirling Direct Finance Ltd., adding secured lending operations.

2004: The company acquires the doorstep loan portfolio of Morse's Ltd.

Yet, LSB faced uncertainty at the beginning of 2005. The company's low stock valuation exposed it to a potential takeover and breakup—indeed, in September 2004, the company was rumored to have faced down just such a threat. More troubling, however, came the news in January 2005 that the British Competition Commission had launched an inquiry into the doorstep credit market. With some members of the sector reportedly collecting as much as 170 percent APR on loans to the United Kingdom's poorest households, observers feared a shakeup of the industry upon the inquiry's completion in 2006. LSB's reliance on doorstep lending, despite its diversified operations, left it vulnerable to any measures enacted by the Competition Commission.

Principal Subsidiaries

Pacific Homeloans; Personal Loan Centre; Robinson Way; Sterling Direct.

Principal Competitors

Provident Financial plc; Cattles plc.

Further Reading

Brignall, Miles, "Anatomy of a Specialist Lender," *Guardian,* October 30, 2004, p. 13.

Eastlake, Elizabeth, "Strong Growth at London Scottish," *Financial Times,* June 11, 2003, p. 26.

Hall, William, "Debt Collection Arm Lifts London Scottish," *Financial Times,* January 20, 2005, p. 25.

——, "London Scottish in 14th Year of Growth," *Financial Times,* November 13, 2004, p. 4.

Jivkov, Michael, "Bid Approach Rumours Lift London Scottish Bank," *Independent,* September 8, 2004, p. 48.

"LONDON SCOTTISH BANK (LSB)," *Investors Chronicle,* January 28, 2005.

Mackintosh, James, "London Scottish Bank Expects Continued Growth," *Financial Times,* June 13, 2001, p. 24.

Moore, Sheryl, "London Scottish Profits Rise on Soaring Demand," *Manchester Evening News,* June 10, 2003.

Shah, Saeed, "London Scottish Too Costly to Bank On," *Independent,* January 15, 2004, p. 25.

—M.L. Cohen

märklín

Märklin Holding GmbH

Stuttgarter Strasse 55-57
D-73033 Göppingen
Germany
Telephone: (+49) 7161 608-0
Fax: (+49) 7161 608-550
Web site: http://www.maerklin.com

Private Company
Incorporated: 1888 as Gebr. Märklin
Employees: 1,460 (2004)
Sales: EUR164.4 million ($206.4 million)
NAIC: 339932 Game, Toy, and Children's Vehicle
  Manufacturing

Märklin Holding GmbH is the management company of Germany's number one model train manufacturer. From the imperial train of German emperor Wilhelm II to modern high-speed Intercity Express trains, Märklin has built a true-to-life model of the most famous locomotives and the most mundane wagons imaginable. The company makes the whole range of locomotives and rolling stock for all common gauge sizes. The detail-rich, all-metal historical and modern trains of the upscale and expensive Märklin brand have found a loyal following among mainly male railroad enthusiasts in Germany and abroad. Nuremberg-based subsidiary Trix makes gauge N-sized mini-trains which are marketed under the "Trix" brand name. Märklin also makes a small number of limited edition models of cars, ships, and vintage toys. Märklin puts out about 300 new products each year, ranging from $175 two-train starter kits to limited editions of collector's items made of precious metal that cost tens of thousands of dollars. Headquartered in Göppingen near Stuttgart, the company has manufacturing plants in Germany and Hungary and sales subsidiaries in Switzerland, the Netherlands, Belgium, France, and the United States. Exports account for almost 30 percent of total sales. Märklin is still owned by descendants of company founder Friedrich Wilhelm Märklin and his later business partners who established the firm in the second half of the 19th century.

Toys for Boys and Girls in the Late 19th Century

In 1859, tinsmith Theodor Friedrich Wilhelm Märklin started a toy making business in Göppingen, a city in the German state of Württemberg, where he had lived and worked since 1840. His product line consisted of miniature cooking utensils and other accessories for dollhouses made of lacquered tinplate. His second wife Caroline Hettich, whom he had married in the same year, played a crucial part in the business. While Friedrich Wilhelm skillfully crafted the toys, Caroline took on the role of the traveling saleswoman, a rare task for a woman at the time. She traveled extensively through southern Germany and Switzerland and brought in so many orders that only a few years after its foundation the business had to move to larger premises. However, her husband's sudden death after an accident in 1866 left Caroline running the family business just by herself for the next twenty years. Although she remarried two years after Friedrich Wilhelm's death, her new husband did not lend her the support she had hoped for. Despite her determination, high energy, and organizational talent, it took continued hard work and extreme hardship to keep the business going until her three sons were old enough to take it over.

When her sons reached the critical age, none of them—it seemed—was interested in the family business. After her second husband had died in the 1880s, Eugen Märklin, one of her sons who had a well-paid position in another business, decided to take over the toy workshop as a side line. In 1888, he and his brother Karl established the unlimited trading company Gebr. Märklin & Co., which included their mother's business. Three years later, Märklin took the opportunity to acquire the Ludwig Lutz toy factory in Ellwangen, which had gained a reputation for beautifully crafted technical tinplate toys. Many of the factory's highly skilled workers accepted Märklin's offer of continued employment if they moved to Göppingen. Besides miniature kitchen utensils for doll houses and toy ovens, the company's product range now included tiny merry-go-rounds, doll carriages, wagons, carts, and boats. However, it was a model train Märklin introduced at the 1891 Leipzig Spring Fair as a novelty that determined the company's fate for the next century. Caroline Märklin died three years after this fateful decision that put the business she had run for over two decades on the track to lasting success and worldwide fame.

Company Perspectives:

True-to-Life and Practical Modeling. *With our models we strive to achieve an optimal synthesis between original details and practical robustness, taking the model size into account. This is not a rigid process, but it always results in more sophisticated models, due to improved materials and refined production techniques.*

Model trains were nothing new at the time. However, Märklin's clockwork-driven wind-up train ran on a sectional track whose shape could be changed. The company was also the first manufacturer to introduce a standardized gauge size that made it possible to continuously add pieces such as additional wagons or track to an expanding system. Märklin's train was a major attraction at the fair and positioned the company as a leading manufacturer in the evolving model train market, which proved relatively stable even after the heyday of the railroad had long passed. While the Märklin brothers worked on finding the right balance between detail-rich handmade models and low-cost mechanical mass production, the company's range of technical toys for boys expanded at the cost of the traditional line of toys for girls. As with the latter, the company emphasized a wide variety of accessories. In 1892, another business partner, Emil Fritz of Plochingen, joined the firm. Three years later, the business moved to a new location, which it outgrew within five years.

Märklin's clockwork-driven model trains were followed by methylated spirit-fueled steam locomotives. The latter ran longer than clockwork-driven models which started off at a great speed but got slower and slower with every round until they stopped when the spring had lost its tension. Spirit-fueled steam locomotives, however, heated up quickly and could not be controlled in any way. They ran very fast until all the fuel was burned and sometimes tipped over in curves. Spilled fuel could then break into flames when it touched the hot body of the locomotive, a security risk that was not appropriate for children's toys. The solution was to build models that could run on electric power. Even before Göppingen's first power station began to generate electricity, Märklin introduced toys that were powered by electricity. In 1895, the company launched the first electric model tram, followed by a number of electric model trains.

Focus on Model Trains: 1920s and 1930s

At the turn of the 20th century, Märklin moved into a brand-new 6,000-square-meter factory building in Göttingen's Stuttgarter Strasse. Around the same time, the dimensions Märklin had used for gauges and model scales were adopted as international standards. To finance the next stage of growth, the company owners decided to invite another partner, Richard Safft, into the business in 1907. One year later, it was renamed Gebr. Märklin & Cie. In 1911, a new office building six-storeys high was added to the factory. By 1914, the company employed about 600 workers.

The early years of the 20th century saw Märklin's range of products expand very rapidly. Eugen Märklin's business partner

Emil Friz, who was driven to make the company the world's largest toy manufacturer, added ever more articles to Märklin's range of products. Toy-sized models of the latest technical innovations took a prominent place in Märklin's output. For example, by 1909 the company manufactured as many as 90 different models of steam engines. Märklin also began to put out large catalogues which were mailed to various toy dealers. In 1914, the company launched the first metal construction set for boys, which remained a popular item until the 1960s. The kits were often used to build bridges, cranes, and ramps for their model trains. Because of the cyclical nature of the toy market, the company complemented its extensive range of toys with various household goods and "summer articles." The beginning of World War I in 1914 suddenly interrupted Märklin's growth. The company was cut off from export markets. Many employees were drafted into the military, and the firm was ordered to produce war goods.

The postwar years brought organizational changes. After Emil Friz' death in 1922, Märklin was transformed from an unlimited trading company into a limited liability company. One year later, Eugen Märklin's son Fritz Märklin entered the family business. In 1926, the son-in-law of Emil Friz, Max Scheerer, joined the executive management team. Nine years later, Eugen Märklin retired and was succeeded by his son Fritz.

Because of Märklin's solid position in the domestic market, the company came out of the difficult postwar years fairly well despite hyperinflation, low consumer budgets, and mass bankruptcies. However, to make better use of limited resources, Märklin's range of products was slimmed down. In regards to model trains, the number of gauge sizes was reduced. The company also focused more and more on model trains that were based on actual locomotives and wagons. The new German state-owned railway company Deutsche Reichsbahn, which had been founded in 1920, was Märklin's main source of inspiration. In 1926, the company switched power supplies for electric model locomotives from the German household current of 220 Volts to a 20-Volt system, which was much safer for children. In 1929, the growing popularity of Märklin products was reflected in the size of the company's workforce which—with 900 workers—had greatly exceeded pre-war levels.

At the beginning of the 1930s, one of Märklin's major competitors in Germany, the Bing company, withdrew from the toy business. When the new Nazi government tightened raw material supplies for manufacturers of consumer products, Märklin's reaction was a stroke of genius. In 1935, the company launched a new line of electric table top model railroads that were half the size of common models, creating the so-called H0 gauge measuring just 16.5 millimeters. The new H0 series not only cut the raw material needed for production in half but also became an instant bestseller. One of the reasons might have been that the H0-sized model trains could easily be set up on table tops and did not require as much space in a child's bedroom. In 1938, Märklin introduced a remote control that made it possible to reverse the direction in which a model train was running. During this time, models made to gauge 1 size, as well as many products not related to model trains, were phased out. With the beginning of World War II in 1939, the production of civil goods was again replaced by war goods.

"mini club" train managed to run 720 kilometers in 1,219 hours. In the late 1970s, Märklin boosted its international marketing and distribution network by establishing subsidiaries in Switzerland, Belgium, France, and the United States. At the end of the decade, the company launched a solar powered "mini-club" train. In the 1980s, Märklin trains entered the electronic age. Launched in 1984, the electronic control system "Märklin Digital" enabled independent multi-train operation with or without the help of a computer. Theoretically, the new system was able to manage up to 80 locomotives and 256 switches within one circuit. Three years later, the company put out a prototype of a locomotive with an inbuilt video camera that beamed pictures onto a monitor. Innovations notwithstanding, in the second half of the 1980s Märklin's sales stagnated and profits vanished, partly due to the company's single-minded focus on adult railroad hobbyists.

Expansion and New Marketing Strategies in the 1990s and 2000s

In the early 1990s Märklin was able to overcome the stagnation of the late 1980s. The company acquired three new production sites and launched a comprehensive marketing campaign. The 1990s began with an unexpected expansion of Märklin's domestic market when East Germany was reunited with the western part of the country. Märklin acquired a toy factory in Sonneberg in the eastern German state of Thuringia and moved its production of rolling stock there. Another production subsidiary was established in Györ, Hungary, where 100 employees assembled small parts, railroad tracks, and switches. Later in the decade, in 1997, the newly established management holding company Märklin Holding GmbH took over Nuremberg-based model train maker Trix Modelleisenbahn GmbH & Co. KG. It took three years of major investments and modernization until the manufacturer that had carved out a market niche with gauge N-sized mini-trains, and with which Märklin had cooperated in special projects since 1978, broke even in 2000. In addition, the company launched a joint marketing initiative with specialized toy retailers, the Märklin Student's Club for children, and the Märklin Insider Club for adult customers who received a club magazine and were able to buy exclusive models. The company even opened its own model railroad museum in Göppingen. A new advertizing campaign featured fathers and sons playing together with Märklin model trains. The combined effect of all these measures was a period of dynamic growth that lasted until the second half of the 1990s, when sales began to stagnate again.

At the end of the 1990s, Märklin found itself in the middle of a crisis that was partly self-made. Old-fashioned production methods and long waiting times for electronic parts caused a backlog of orders, some of which were not filled until months after the promised delivery date. About 10 percent of them were not filled at all. In 2000, Märklin produced losses for the first time in many years. The company eliminated 400 products from its catalogue, cut the time for new product development, and updated production technologies. The Trix production was moved to a new site, the tool-making workshop spun off, and the workforce cut in half. However, the company had to face additional problems, including decreasing interest of Germany's specialized toy retailers in model trains, lower consumption spending, and competition from electronic toys and video games. To win back the interest of teenage boys, Märklin

---

Key Dates:

1859: Tinsmith Friedrich Wilhelm Märklin and his wife Carolyn start a toy making business.

1888: Two of the founder's sons take over the business and name it Gebr. Märklin.

1891: The company presents the first standardized wind-up train running on sectional track.

1935: Märklin introduces electric table top model railroads half the size of common models.

1972: The company launches the smallest mass-produced electric model train system under the "mini-club" brand.

1984: The electronic control system "Märklin Digital" enables independent multi-train operation.

1994: Management company Märklin Holding GmbH is established.

1997: Märklin takes over German competitor Trix Modelleisenbahn.

2003: The company launches a model of Harry Potter's Hogwarts Express train.

Innovations Drive Growth after World War II

Märklin's factory was left untouched by World War II. Soon after the war had ended, model train production was taken up again in Göppingen. With many German cities in ruins and buying power severely reduced, the first batches of model trains were shipped abroad. Managing director Richard Safft died in 1945 and was succeeded by his son Herbert. Two years later, the last managing partner of the second family generation, Eugen Märklin, died. His son Fritz continued as managing director until his death in 1961. In the postwar years, the company followed a dual strategy based on the fact that there were different kinds of customers: adult collectors who put their model trans on display rather than in a "model train landscape," adult model train enthusiasts who were involved in building and expanding their own "living room railroad," and boys who just wanted to have fun playing with Märklin's locomotives and wagons. While sticking with the idea of making true-to-life model trains, the company also wanted them to be easier to handle as toys. Märklin focused on expanding the range of products for the 00 and H0 gauges and dropped the entire gauge 0 program. Production methods switched from lacquered tinplate modeling to zinc and plastics die casting, which allowed even more detailed models. As the postwar reconstruction period gave way to the German "economic miracle," Märklin's sales exploded. At the end of the 1960s, the company relaunched a model train series in the traditional gauge 1 size.

The 1970s and 1980s saw Märklin launch a number of major product innovations and expand into new geographical markets. In 1972, the company introduced the world's smallest mass produced electric model train system under the "mini-club" brand at the Nuremberg Toy Fair. The fully functional mini-train, which was 220 times smaller than the original and ran on 6.5 millimeter-wide gauges, was included in the *Guinness Book of World Records* not only for its small size but also for breaking the world record in uninterrupted operation. A Märklin

put out models of high-speed Intercity Express (ICE) trains along with historical product lines. The company's model of the bright red Hogwarts Express train that the title hero of the popular Harry Potter novels took to school became a bestseller in the 2003 Christmas shopping season. Märklin made about 60 percent of its annual sales during this period each year.

By 2004, Märklin was back on track. More than 110 years after the first Märklin model trains were sold, they had become collector's items. The various Märklin fan clubs counted over 120,000 members and roughly two-thirds of the company's output was purchased by collectors. Confronted with a stagnating domestic market, further expansion into the world's biggest market for model trains—the United States, where Märklin's market share was lower than 2 percent—was declared one of the company's major goals at the beginning of the 21st century. Fred Gates, president of the company's U.S. subsidiary in New Berlin, Milwaukee, summed up his take on Märklin's future when he told *Playthings* in November 2002 that there will be model trains as long as there are trains in the real world.

Principal Subsidiaries

Gebrüder Märklin & Cie; Trix Modelleisenbahn GmbH & Co. KG; Märklin-Vertriebs AG (Switzerland); Märklin B.V. (Netherlands); Märklin S.A.R.L. (France); S.A. Märklin N.V. (Belgium); Märklin, Inc. (United States).

Principal Competitors

Gebr. FLEISCHMANN GmbH & Co. KG; ROCO Modellspielwaren Ges.m.b.H.; Tillig Modellbahnen GmbH & Co. KG; Lionel LLC; Bachmann Industries; Kato USA, Inc.

Further Reading

"An der Modelleisenbahn wird nicht gespart," *Frankfurter Allgemeine Zeitung*, September 28, 1994, p. 27.
"Märklin rutscht erstmals seit vielen Jahren in die Verlustzone," *Frankfurter Allgemeine Zeitung*, October 17, 2001, p. 25.
"Märklin verkleinert Sortiment und organisiert sich neu," *Frankfurter Allgemeine Zeitung*, October 8, 1999, p. 20.
Rovito, Rich, "Local motives," *Business Journal-Milwaukee*, December 8, 2000, p. 3.
Wassener, Bettina, "Big Boys Put Marklin on Track," *Financial Times*, February 12, 2004, p. 8.
Weiskott, Maria, "Successful Training: Marklin Wind-up Train Launches Company on Fast Track," *Playthings*, November 2002, p. 7.

—Evelyn Hauser

The Marmon Group, Inc.

225 West Washington Street
Chicago, Illinois 60606-3418
U.S.A.
Telephone: (312) 372-9500
Fax: (312) 845-5305
Web site: http://www.marmon.com

Private Company
Incorporated: 1953 as The Colson Company
Employees: 22,000
Sales: $6 billion (2004)
NAIC: 315211 Men's and Boys' Cut and Sew Apparel
    Contractors; 316999 All Other Leather Good
    Manufacturing; 331421 Copper Rolling, Drawing, and
    Extruding; 331316 Aluminum Extruded Product
    Manufacturing; 332611 Spring (Heavy Gauge)
    Manufacturing; 332722 Bolt, Nut, Screw, Rivet, and
    Washer Manufacturing; 332913 Plumbing Fixture
    Fitting and Trim Manufacturing; 332919 Other Metal
    Valve and Pipe Fitting Manufacturing; 333111 Farm
    Machinery and Equipment Manufacturing; 334412 Bare
    Printed Circuit Board Manufacturing; 336510 Railroad
    Rolling Stock Manufacturing; 339112 Surgical and
    Medical Instrument Manufacturing; 421510 Metals
    Service Centers and Offices; 532411 Commercial Air,
    Rail, and Water Transportation Equipment Rental and
    Leasing; 532490 Other Commercial and Industrial
    Machinery and Equipment Rental and Leasing; 551112
    Offices of Other Holding Companies

The Marmon Group, Inc., one of the largest privately owned organizations in the United States, is in essence a holding company for more than 100 autonomously operated manufacturing and service companies, many of which are leaders in their respective industries. A small central office in Chicago (with about 70 employees) manages and invests the financial resources of member companies, and aids and advises them on accounting, legal, tax, finance, personnel, and other matters.

Marmon companies consistently achieve high returns from low-technology, low-glamour industries. Marmon has repeatedly bought and turned around troubled ''smokestack'' companies. With about 300 facilities in 20 countries, the Marmon Group today earns about half of its revenues from service companies and about half from manufacturers. The major sectors represented by Marmon companies are agricultural, industrial, and medical equipment; automotive equipment; building and commercial products; consumer and health care products; industrial materials and components; marketing, finance, and information services; mining equipment; railway equipment; and water treatment products. The Marmon Group has been built up and managed by members of the Pritzker family, which was dividing its holdings among eleven heirs.

Origins

Marmon's history as a corporate entity dates from 1953, but the Pritzker family, who built and control the massive conglomerate, has been active significantly longer. In the late 19th century, the Pritzkers immigrated to the United States from the Ukraine. Patriarch Nicholas Pritzker led them to Chicago, and in 1902 he founded Pritzker & Pritzker, the law firm that was to evolve into a management company and the center of the Pritzkers' many and varied investments.

Pritzker & Pritzker grew, and by the late 1920s it had become a respected local firm. At that time, the Pritzkers' best client was Goldblatt Brothers, the low-priced Chicago department store chain. Through the Goldblatts, Abram (A. N.) Pritzker, Nicholas Pritzker's son, met Walter M. Heymann, then a leading Chicago commercial banker and an officer at the First National Bank of Chicago. In succeeding years, A.N. Pritzker and Walter Heymann became business associates, and the powerful First National Bank of Chicago became the financial cornerstone of the Pritzker family empire.

Using a line of credit from the First National Bank, A.N. Pritzker began acquiring real estate, something he already knew about from Pritzker & Pritzker's concentration on real estate reorganization. As his and the family's investments grew, the law practice shrank, and in 1940 Pritzker & Pritzker stopped accepting outside clients, concentrating solely on Pritzker fam-

---

Company Perspectives:

The member companies of The Marmon Group operate independently under their own management. Through service agreements with each member company, a small professional organization in Chicago, Illinois—The Marmon Group, Inc.—provides consulting and administrative services, including tax and accounting services, legal counsel and management consulting, to member companies of The Marmon Group.

---

ily investments. At the same time, A.N. Pritzker initiated the family practice of sheltering his holdings within a dizzying array of interrelated family trusts.

The story of Marmon, however, begins with the generation of Pritzkers following that of A.N. Pritzker. By the early 1950s, Pritzker's oldest son, Jay, had become active in the family business. Something of a prodigy, Jay Pritzker had graduated high school at the age of 14. He finished college soon thereafter and then took a law degree from Northwestern University. During World War II, he worked first as a flight instructor and later for the U.S. government agency that managed German-owned companies. In that position, he sat on corporate boards with men many years his senior. An accomplished deal-maker, even in his earliest years, Jay would later become well known for his quickness at sizing up balance sheets and offering deals.

While Pritzker was beginning his career as a deal-maker, his younger brother Robert Pritzker was finishing advanced training in industrial engineering at the Illinois Institute of Technology in Chicago. Robert Pritzker, A.N.'s second son, was the family's only engineer. Beginning in the 1950s, his interest in industrial processes, both theoretical and practical, led the family into manufacturing and later enabled him to turn around a staggering array of troubled companies.

The relationship between Jay Pritzker, the lawyer/deal-maker, and Robert Pritzker, the engineer/manager, became the basis for the continuing operations of The Marmon Group. (Their youngest brother, Donald Pritzker, would later become the force behind Hyatt Hotels before dying suddenly at the age of 39 in 1972.) Jay would buy troubled companies, usually for less than 80 percent of their book value, then Robert would nurse the companies back to health, finding their real profit-making potentials and with Jay's help exploiting any tax advantages a company's previous losses might produce.

Early Activities: 1950s–60s

Jay and Robert Pritzker's first venture was the acquisition of Colson Company in 1953. Colson, a money-loser, was a small, $8 million in sales, manufacturer of casters, bicycles, navy rockets, and wheelchairs. In Colson, Jay Pritzker saw a company that had some profit-making potential but whose assets could nevertheless be liquidated at a price higher than what the family had paid for it.

After Jay completed the deal, Robert Pritzker went to Ohio and took over the running of Colson. He began by eliminating unprofitable lines. Bicycles went first. He knew he could not compete with cheaper European bikes, so he dropped them. To improve production of U.S. Navy rockets, Pritzker instituted modern statistical quality controls. Cost-cutting steps paid for most of Colson. When the program ended, he discontinued military production. This left him with casters and wheelchairs, products he was able to promote and sell successfully.

Over the next several years, the Pritzkers acquired several more manufactures of small metal products. Chief among these was the L.A. Darling Company of Bronson, Michigan, a maker of merchandising display equipment and retail fixtures; it also operated a plastics division and a foundry division. To achieve economies of scale, the Pritzkers combined and affiliated their new companies with Colson and, in a typically adept financial move, made Colson a subsidiary of L.A. Darling.

It was not until ten years after acquiring Colson that the Pritzker brothers made their next major acquisition. In 1963, the Pritzkers acquired the Marmon-Herrington Company, successor to the Marmon Motor Car Company. According to the manner in which Jay Pritzker structured the deal, the L.A. Darling Company, which was headed by Robert Pritzker, paid approximately $2.7 million for 260,000 shares of Marmon-Herrington's 580,000 outstanding shares of stock. This acquisition gave the Pritzkers's industrial holdings their permanent name, The Marmon Group. Marmon discontinued the company's production of heavy-duty tractors, transit vehicles, and bus chassis. The most significant addition to the Pritzker holdings was the Long-Airdox Company, a division of Marmon-Herrington that added a broad range of coal mining equipment to Darling's display equipment and fixtures, along with foundry operations, as well as augmenting Colson's caster business with institutional housekeeping trucks and hospital equipment. The acquisition was also indicative of the complex, interlocking ways that the Pritzkers owned their companies. Sales grew quickly, and in 1965 Marmon topped $51.8 million in total revenues.

In 1966, Marmon merged with publicly held Fenestra Incorporated, a maker of architectural steel doors and leaf springs for trucks. As the deal was structured as a stock swap, Marmon itself became a public company, The Marmon Group, Inc., and for the first time, the Pritzkers' industrial empire was exposed to the scrutiny of shareholders.

Shy of the public eye and jealous of their controlling interest, the Pritzkers soon moved to take greater control of The Marmon Group. In a complicated stock transaction of October 1967, Jay Pritzker had Fenestra, which was technically controlled by a subsidiary of The Marmon Group, Inc., acquire both The Marmon Group, Inc. and Boykin Enterprises, another newly acquired Pritzker company, which produced and exported agricultural equipment. At the end of the deal, the Pritzkers owned more than 84.3 percent of the voting stock of Fenestra and had changed Fenestra's name to The Marmon Group, Inc.

In 1968, Marmon acquired Triangle Auto Springs Company, a manufacturer of flat-leaf truck springs for the replacement market. Triangle's line of springs fit in well with the products Marmon was already making at Fenestra's Detroit Steel Products subsidiary.

In 1969, Marmon further consolidated its role in the parts replacement business by buying Lowell Bearing Company, a

Key Dates:

1953: Pritzker family begins acquiring metal goods manu-facturers, starting with the Colson Company.

1960: L.A. Darling Company and Midwest Foundry Company are acquired.

1963: Marmon-Herrington Company, a maker of heavy vehicles, is acquired for $2.7 million.

1966: Marmon merges with Fenestra Incorporated, a publicly held maker of steel doors and springs.

1967: Fenestra is renamed The Marmon Group, Inc.

1968: Triangle Auto Springs Company is acquired.

1969: Lowell Bearing Company is acquired.

1970: Revenues exceed $100 million.

1973: Marmon begins acquisition of Cerro Corporation conglomerate.

1977: Organ manufacturer Hammond Corporation and subsidiary Wells Lamont (work gloves) acquired.

1978: Seat-belt manufacturer American Safety Equipment Corporation is bought for $27 million.

1980: Revenues approach $2 billion.

1981: The $1 billion conglomerate Trans Union Corporation is acquired.

1984: Altamil Corporation is acquired.

1989: Revenues approach $4 billion.

1995: Fenestra Corp. is closed.

1998: Total revenues exceed $6 billion.

2002: Robert Pritzker retires as Marmon CEO and acquires control of Colson companies.

2005: Trans Union credit bureau is spun off.

distributor of replacement parts to truck, bus, and trolley fleets in the United States and around the world. The same year, the L.A. Darling plant was moved from Michigan to Paragould, Arkansas. Also in 1969, the company acquired the rights to the Universal Track Machine, a machine that Marmon had previously manufactured under contract. It performed mechanized maintenance on the nation's railroad tracks and railroad rights-of-way. Rising labor costs had made this robotic maintenance device a highly desirable product.

By the end of 1969, Marmon had become a diversified industrial company supplying low-tech goods in noncompetitive fields not vulnerable to changes in consumer tastes. About 39 percent of sales derived from automotive replacement parts, with another 30 percent coming from building materials, hardware, and retail fixtures, much of which was sold by the L.A. Darling Fixture division. Mining equipment supplied by Long-Airdox and Pickrose & Co., of England, accounted for 25 percent of sales, and agricultural, irrigation, and animal husbandry equipment by Jamesway Company Limited, later Jamesway Incubator Corporation, of Canada, and the AMISA export arm accounted for the remaining 6 percent of sales.

Acquisition of Cerro Corporation in the 1970s

The year 1970 was a time of internal investment and growth for Marmon. Sales climbed from $77 million to $87 million. Triangle Auto Springs and Jamesway each made additions to its physical plant. The Darling Store Fixtures division was in the process of building a new plant in Corning, Arkansas. New plant equipment was bought for Fenestra, Detroit Steel Products, and Darling. Finally, in December of 1970, Marmon paid $6 million for Keystone Pipe and Supply Company, a nationwide supplier of pipes and tubes based in Butler, Pennsylvania. In succeeding years, Great Lakes Corporation, which was owned by Marmon Holdings, which was itself owned by the Pritzkers, bought up outstanding shares and converted preferred stock to voting stock. In 1970, sales topped $100 million, and by 1971 The Marmon Group was again private.

Marmon's largest and most successful acquisition of the 1970s was Cerro Corporation, with $800 million in sales, a company that the Pritzkers gradually acquired between 1973 and 1976. Cerro's operations included mining, manufacturing, trucking, and real estate. Like many Marmon acquisitions, the Cerro deal was financed through the First National Bank of Chicago. The relationship between the Pritzkers and First Chicago had remained strong since their initial contacts in the late 1920s.

Cerro was a typical acquisition, albeit a much larger one than those it had made previously. It was rich in assets and selling at far below book value. In fact, Cerro was atypical only in that it was publicly held and that the Pritzkers ousted the current management and installed Jay Pritzker as chief executive officer and Robert Pritzker as president.

Soon after taking a controlling interest in Cerro, Robert Pritzker began commuting to Cerro's New York headquarters, where he oversaw its industrial processes and worked at freeing up the somewhat tense corporate culture. Robert Pritzker told the *Wall Street Journal* for March 27, 1975 that "Cerro is one of those typical, highly structured big companies. . . . We think that loosening it up will make people there feel better and perform better, too." By 1977, Marmon had the Cerro acquisition under control. It sold Cerro's trucking subsidiary, ICX, for $22.6 million, and it was also dealing with Cerro's troubled Florida real estate venture, Leadership Housing Incorporated.

During the same period in which Marmon was acquiring Cerro, it bought the Hammond Corporation. Completed in 1977, the acquisition of the organ manufacturer was neither as successful nor as canny as the Cerro acquisition had been. The Pritzkers bought Hammond just as a recession struck and the decline in the economy caused a slump in organ sales. The one bright spot of the deal was Hammond's work gloves subsidiary, Wells Lamont. Using these facilities as a basis, Marmon has gone on to become a leading manufacturer of gloves and other apparel items.

In 1978, Marmon paid $27.3 million for American Safety Equipment Corporation, a maker of seat-belt systems for cars and aircraft, with $48.1 million in sales and owner of Kangol Limited, a British headwear manufacturer. Also in 1978, Marmon divested itself of Leadership Housing by distributing as dividends its investments in the company.

Between 1970 and 1980, Marmon's sales grew from $103 million to $1.9 billion, and during the same period profits rocketed from $5 million to $79 million. Marmon had expanded from five basic product groups to a much larger cluster of companies making pipe and tubing, wire and cable, automotive products, other metal products, apparel accessories, mining and agricultural equipment, and musical instruments. Moreover, services such as metals trading and coal mining were becoming increasingly important elements of the business.

Some of Marmon's successes of the 1970s can be attributed to the advantages of a privately owned company whose owners get on well. In a March 27, 1975 interview with the *Wall Street Journal*, J. Ira Harris, then a Chicago-based partner of Salomon Brothers, said that the Pritzkers' ability to work together "gives them the kind of flexibility that doesn't exist elsewhere at their level of operations. They've closed a lot of important deals because they were able to move faster than the competition."

The ability to move fast also helped Robert Pritzker deal effectively with Marmon's divisions. Normally a manager who allowed Marmon's component companies substantial autonomy, he was able to make necessary decisions on a person-to-person basis without expensive and time-consuming studies. The Marmon Group's board of directors, headed by Jay Pritzker, rarely met, and the corporate office was sparsely staffed. The divisions themselves spent little on advertising and less on their offices.

While Robert Pritzker ceded authority to managers, he kept the accounting tight. Divisional controllers reported not only to their general managers but also to a corporate controller in Chicago. Robert Pritzker often left final decisions to local managers. Marmon's commitment to capital investment and drive to be the low-cost producer in its various business sectors allowed local managers to make the large investments that stand-alone companies could never make. After buying Midwest Foundry Company in 1960, for example, Marmon's capital commitment led the company to expand tenfold in 20 years. During the same period, 40 percent of all gray-iron foundries in the United States shut down. In the early years of the 1980s, Midwest Foundry was returning 40 percent on Marmon's investment.

Further Growth in the 1980s

In September 1980, Marmon announced the proposed acquisition of Illinois-based Trans Union Corporation for $688 million. Trans Union was a $1.1 billion conglomerate whose businesses included rail car and general-equipment leasing by its Union Tank Car Company subsidiary, credit information services, international trading by the subsidiary Getz Corporation, and the manufacture of waste and water treatment equipment.

Completed in 1981, the Trans Union acquisition was unusual in that it was both huge and expensive. Jay Pritzker had been attracted by Trans Union's large accumulation of investment tax credits and federal tax deferrals, which Marmon could use to offset taxable income. Furthermore, once bought, Robert Pritzker found a series of unexpectedly profitable components within the larger Trans Union. A case in point is the Getz Corporation, a San Francisco-based Pacific trading company that grossed over $600 million in 1989. When Marmon acquired Trans Union, Getz was failing. Within a few years, Robert Pritzker had solidified Getz's management and was exploiting Getz's untapped potential as a travel agency and its experience as a player in the expanding market of the Pacific Rim. Getz deals in a wide array of automotive, industrial, and food products, from farm tractors in Thailand to powdered milk in Taiwan.

In January 1984, Marmon purchased Altamil Corporation and thereby acquired the Fontaine Trucking Company, a manufacturer of truck and trailer couplers, trailers, and special purpose truck bodies; Aluminum Forge Company, a producer of precision aluminum forging for aerospace industries; and American Box Company, a maker of wirebound boxes and crates, which later was sold.

Between 1980 and 1989, revenues jumped from $1.9 billion to $3.9 billion. During the same time, earnings swelled from $84 million to $205 million. At the start of the decade, Marmon's average return on equity, profits as a percentage of the company's total worth, ran 19.1 percent, a full five points higher than the median of the Fortune 500, and in 1989 that proportion reached 26.3 percent, more than ten points higher than the median of the Fortune 500.

Struggles in the 1990s

Starting in the late 1980s and into the early 1990s, much of Marmon's expansion came through member companies that were themselves making acquisitions, such as the early 1990 acquisition of the medical products division of the National Standard Corporation by Marmon's Microware Surgical Instruments Corporation. The same was also true of Marmon's increasing growth outside the United States. Marmon/Keystone Corporation, a Pennsylvania-based distributor of steel pipes and tubing, was particularly active outside the United States, with a 1993 acquisition of the Canadian distributor Lyman Tubeco; the 1994 purchase of Specialty Steels, another Canadian distributor; the establishment of a sales office in Mexico in 1994; and the acquisition in 1995 of The Anbuma Group, a tubing distributor based in Belgium.

During the late 1980s, Marmon had grown to such an extent that some observers had begun to question the ability of its corporate structure to handle its holdings, which were becoming increasingly diverse, both technically and geographically. An example of a high-tech firm that failed under Marmon leadership was Accutronics Inc., a maker of printed circuit boards, which Marmon shut down in 1994, selling its assets. The president of Accutronics, while praising Marmon's financial and management skills, blamed the inability of Marmon to deal with a non-low-tech business for the failure.

Marmon also struggled to turn around some of the low-tech firms on which it had made its name. For example, in early 1995 it closed Fenestra Corp., a manufacturer of steel and fiberglass doors and door frames, which had lost money for the previous four years. Robert Pritzker blamed the closure on Marmon's own "lousy management" of the company as well as the difficulties of strained relations between management and the unionized workers at Fenestra's plants.

Such failures, however, seem inevitable for a company that had taken on as many troubled firms as Marmon had. Through 1995, Marmon continued to grow to record levels, with revenues increasing from $3.85 billion in 1990 to $6.08 billion in 1995. Meanwhile, earnings jumped from $125.1 million to $306.9 million.

Marmon Group continued to invest in metal industries. Its subsidiary Marmon/Keystone Corporation acquired Fort Lauderdale, Florida-based Future Metals in the fall of 1996. Future Metals supplied tubing to the aerospace industry. Wheeler Group, a distributor of tubing, was acquired the next year.

Marmon saw a future in medical equipment, an industry that was bringing in revenues of $350 million a year. In 1997, Marmon acquired B.G. Sulzle Inc., a family-run maker of surgical needles in North Syracuse, New York. Sulzle had been formed in 1945 and employed 550 people. Manan Medical Products of Northbrook, Illinois, was also acquired during the year. Among other acquisitions at the same time was the purchase of UK-based cable and wire manufacturer General Cable Industries Ltd. Wire and cable accounted for more than $400 million of Marmon's revenue. Marmon sold British headwear maker Kangol Ltd. to its management for $48.7 million (£30 million).

Total sales exceeded $6 billion in 1998. However, manufacturing in general was experiencing a persistent slump that would cut into earnings. The group opened an office in Beijing during the year.

Marmon continued to acquire companies, buying 30 in 1998 and another 35 in 1999. The group spent $500 million on acquisitions in 1999, buying medical-related companies OsteoMed and Bridport and power cable supplier Kerite.

By 2000, the group had 40,000 employees. Revenues grew 4 percent in 2000 to $6.8 billion, though earnings dropped 14 percent to $300.8 million in a difficult manufacturing environment. Revenues slipped to $6.5 billion in 2001. The group made more than 20 acquisitions in 2000, at a cost of another $500 million, while two mining equipment businesses were sold off the next year.

One of these was Long-Airdox, once central to Marmon's holdings, which was bought by RAG Coal International. Long-Airdox had expanded throughout the 1990s and was focusing on the Asian market via its unit in Australia. It had about 2,000 employees and sales of $600 million a year, according to *Australia's Mining Monthly.*

New Leadership in the 2000s

Company chairman Jay Pritzker passed away in 1999. Robert A. Pritzker retired in January 2002 at the age of 75. John D. Nichols, the retired head of Illinois Tool Works Inc. (ITW), became Marmon's new CEO, while Pritzker's nephew Thomas J. Pritzker, aged 51, took over the role of chairman. According to *Crain's Chicago Business,* Nichols intended to apply cost-cutting and efficiency techniques he had used effectively at ITW.

When Robert A. Pritzker retired as CEO of Marmon Group, he also acquired a majority interest in its caster companies through a new firm, Colson Associates. Robert Pritzker had started the Marmon Group four dozen years earlier with the small Colson caster business. Since then, Colson Caster Corp.'s product line had grown to 35,000 different models, from small casters for chairs to huge industrial ones, noted *Arkansas Business.*

Marmon Group companies saw pre-tax earnings rise 32 percent in 2003, to $573 million. Total revenues were up slightly at $5.56 billion. Marmon sold off the British brass manufacturer Cerro Extruded Metals Limited to Boliden MKM Limited for £5 million.

Marmon spun off TranUnion LLC in early 2005. It was reorganized as TransUnion Corp. Pritzker Realty Group head Penny Pritzker was named its new chairman. The reasoning behind the spinoff was to separate the technology-oriented business from Marmon's core manufacturing activities. TransUnion had revenues of more than $1 billion a year.

The Pritzker clan was planning to divide its $15 billion in holdings, including the Marmon Group, among 11 heirs. A lawsuit by two other heirs was settled in January 2005. The breakup of the Pritzker holdings was to be completed around 2015.

Principal Subsidiaries

Aetna Insulated Wire; Alamo Water Refiners, Inc.; Amarillo Gear Company; Anderson Copper and Brass Company; Atlas Bolt & Screw Company; Cable USA, Inc.; Catequip S.A.; Cat'Serv S.a.r.l.; Cerro E.M.S. Limited; Cerro Flow Products, Inc.; Cerro Manganese Bronze Limited; Cerro Metal Products Company; Cerro Wire & Cable Co., Inc.; Comtran Corporation; Dekoron Wire and Cable; Dekoron/Unitherm; Detroit Steel Products Co., Inc.; Ecodyne Limited; EcoWater Systems, Inc.; Eden Industries (UK) Limited; Enersul Inc.; EXSIF Worldwide, Inc.; Fontaine Fleetline Products; Fontaine International Inc.; Fontaine Modification Company; Fontaine Trailer Company; General Cable Industries Ltd.; Graver Technologies, Inc.; Harbour Industries, Inc.; Hendrix Wire & Cable, Inc.; IMPulse NC, Inc.; Koehler-Bright Star, Inc.; L.A. Darling Company; Leader Metal Industry Co., Ltd.; MarCap Corporation; Marmon/Keystone Corporation; McKenzie Valve & Machining Company; Meyer Material Company; NHD Group Limited; NYLOK Corporation; Owl Wire and Cable, Inc.; Pan American Screw, Inc.; Penn Aluminum International, Inc.; Penn Machine Company; Perfection Clutch Company; Prince Castle, Inc.; Procor Limited; Railserve, Inc.; Robertson Inc.; Rockbestos-Surprenant Cable Corporation; Silver King Refrigeration, Inc.; Sloane Group Ltd.; Sterling Crane; Store Opening Solutions, Inc.; Streater, Inc.; The Kerite Company; Thorco Industries, Inc.; Trackmobile, Inc.; Triangle Suspension Systems Inc.; Unarco Industries, Inc.; Uni-Form Components Co.; Union Tank Car Company; Webb Wheel Products, Inc.; Wells Lamont Corporation.

Principal Competitors

Ebara Corporation; General Electric Company; Ingersoll-Rand Company; ITT Industries, Inc; Molex Incorporated; Raytheon Company.

Further Reading

Arndorfer, James B., ''Curtain Falls on Solo Act at Marmon; Outsider Vows to Beef up Management,'' *Crain's Chicago Business,* January 21, 2002, p. 4.

''Boliden Acquires British Brass Company,'' *Waymaker,* June 30, 2003.

Cuff, Daniel F., ''A Pritzker 'Hobby' Is Expanding Abroad,'' *New York Times,* September 1, 1989, pp. C3, D3.

Elstrom, Peter J.W., ''How Bob Pritzker Does It: At Marmon, A Light Touch Yields Profits,'' *Crain's Chicago Business*, May 22, 1995.

Hannagan, Charley, ''N. Syracuse Surgical Needle Maker Sold,'' *Post-Standard* (Syracuse, N.Y.), December 9, 1997, p. D9.

''The Hustling Pritzkers,'' *Business Week*, May 5, 1975.

Klein, Frederic C., ''Family Business: The Pritzkers Are an Acquisitive Bunch Which Pays off Well,'' *Wall Street Journal*, March 27, 1975.

''Management Buys Kangol from Owners,'' *WWD*, May 5, 1997, p. 9.

Mulder, James T., ''Chicago Firm Buys Owl Wire and Cable,'' *Post-Standard* (Syracuse, N.Y.), February 24, 1999, p. B7.

Neubart, Dave, ''The Rich List: Robert Alan Pritzker, 74,'' *Chicago Sun-Times*, October 29, 2000, p. 2.

''RAG Coal to Buy Long-Airdox,'' *Mining Journal*, April 13, 2001, p. 275.

Roberts, Richard, ''Australia New Base for Longwall Equipment Leader,'' *Australia's Mining Monthly*, December 19, 1997.

''TransUnion Spun off from Marmon Holdings Conglomerate,'' *Associated Press State & Local Wire*, January 19, 2005, Bus. News.

Waldon, George, ''Marmon's Losses Are Prtzker's Gains,'' *Arkansas Business*, January 27, 2003, p. 18.

Worthy, Ford S., ''The Pritzkers: Unveiling A Private Family,'' *Fortune*, April 25, 1988, pp. 164–82.

—Jordan Wankoff
—updates: David E. Salamie; Frederick C. Ingram

Matt Prentice Restaurant Group

30100 Telegraph Road, Suite 251
Bingham Farms, Michigan 48025
U.S.A.
Telephone: (248) 646-0370
Fax: (248) 646-0379
Web site: http://www.mattprenticerg.com

Private Company
Incorporated: 1980 as Deli Unique
Employees: 753
Sales: $42 million (2004)
NAIC: 722110 Full-Service Restaurants; 722320 Caterers;
    722211 Limited-Service Restaurants; 311812
    Commercial Bakeries

The Matt Prentice Restaurant Group runs more than a dozen eateries in the metropolitan area of Detroit, Michigan, and also operates one of the largest catering businesses in the state. The firm's concepts range from the low-key Deli Unique and Flying Fish Tavern to the upscale Morels: A Michigan Bistro, Shiraz, and Coach Insignia, located on the 71st floor of Detroit's landmark Renaissance Center. The company's catering business serves a number of hotels, temples, and senior citizen residences, as well as special events throughout the area.

Beginnings

The namesake and founder of the Matt Prentice Restaurant Group grew up in Royal Oak, a suburb of Detroit, where he set his sights on becoming a professional chef. He entered the Culinary Institute of America to learn the trade but quit one year into the two-year program because of financial difficulties and family health problems, returning home to take a job with a local restaurant.

Prentice's cooking and management skills soon impressed his boss, and he was given the job of running a grungy delicatessen in nearby Oak Park. He worked hard to improve it, spending many nights painting and repairing equipment, but after a year the owner announced it would be closed. Rather than let his hard work go to waste, the 20-year old Prentice decided to buy

it, and after securing funds from investors and settling the former owner's debts, he reopened it as Deli Unique. The reasonably priced menu featured gourmet dishes like Beef Wellington and Flaming Duck, which Prentice would cook tableside with the lights lowered for effect.

The revived restaurant soon proved a success, and its business grew with the addition of carryout deli trays and a catering service. One assignment, for a lawyer in the wealthy suburb of West Bloomfield, led to Prentice's recommendation to Sam Frankel, owner of Somerset Mall, who was seeking to replace a failing restaurant in the middle of his shopping center.

In 1984, with funding from Frankel, Prentice opened Le Café Jardin and a gourmet take-out operation, La Cuisine Jardin, in the mall. It did well, and two years later he convinced the developer to let him open another restaurant, Sebastian's, in the space where a now-closed competitor had stood. Prentice's first attempt at a formal dining establishment was a relative disappointment, however, and he subsequently worked at improving his ability to manage multiple businesses at once. In 1986, the company formed a wholesale produce unit, GW Produce, and 1987 saw the opening of a second Deli Unique in West Bloomfield. In 1989, Prentice took over management of the Plaza Deli in Southfield, Michigan, which he later bought.

Morels Debuts in 1990

In 1990, Prentice took another shot at fine dining, and this time he hit a home run. Morels: A Michigan Bistro, located in the Detroit suburb of Bingham Farms, featured regional cuisine, and it garnered rave reviews from local restaurant critics. Prentice also opened a Deli Unique next door and Unique Restaurant Corporation (URC), as the firm was now known, installed its headquarters there.

The year 1991 saw Sebastian's reworked into the more casual Sebastian's Grill, and the opening of Tavern on 13 in Birmingham, which took the place of a failed restaurant in the same space. By now the firm had 500 employees.

In 1992, URC sold the original Deli Unique in Oak Park, and in 1993 the company opened an 11,000-square-foot bakery called the Sourdough Bread Factory in Pontiac and bought a

Company Perspectives:

Matt Prentice Restaurant Group (MPRG) offers fine dining, unique atmosphere and impeccable service within an array of fine dining, casual and deli restaurants located in southeastern Michigan. MPRG is also Michigan's largest privately owned caterer, with a variety of facilities accommodating events for several hundred guests.

20,000-square-foot plant for its growing produce unit. That same year, the family-oriented Table Tavern debuted in Sterling Heights, but it was not a hit and closed after less than a year. Also in 1993, Bruschetta Café opened in Oakland Mall, and the upscale Italian restaurant Trattoria Bruschetta debuted in the Hotel Baronette in Novi. Like Prentice's other restaurants, they had been acquired after failing under different management, and he was able to take control with minimal investment.

In mid-1994, URC's bakery began selling its bread through retail outlets, having already begun supplying the firm's restaurants and Northwest Airlines dinner flights originating in Detroit. The company's Unique Catering unit was growing at this time as well. It serviced banquet facilities at Morel's (120 seats), Hotel Baronette (300 seats), Temple Israel in West Bloomfield (600 seats), and was preparing to add Temple Shir Shalom in West Bloomfield. For 1994, the company's restaurants and catering division took in $18.8 million, the produce unit $4.4 million, and the bakery $1 million.

In February 1995, the firm opened a new restaurant called America, which replaced a failed diner in Royal Oak. Located on Woodward Avenue, it was URC's highest-profile site to date. A few months later, Relish was opened in Farmington Hills, and in December the Sourdough Café, featuring bread and rolls from the firm's bakery, debuted in the Summit Place Mall. The company also scored a coup during the year when it hired wine expert Madeline Triffon away from rival restaurateur Jimmy Schmidt. Triffon was the first American woman certified as a Master Sommelier by the British Court of Master Sommeliers and one of fewer than 50 people so designated in the United States.

The combination of a less-than-ideal location and a too-progressive menu led to the closing of America in November 1996, and its staff members were transferred to Relish. Early the next year, URC opened Northern Lakes Seafood Co. and a new Deli Unique in the upscale Detroit suburb of Birmingham. Both were located in a renovated hotel, the Kingsley Inn. Northern Lakes seated 260 and included an oyster and vodka bar, while the delicatessen seated 80, with most of its business consisting of takeout and catering tray orders. Also during 1996, the firm spent $500,000 renovating the banquet rooms of Relish and creating an atrium and garden there. By this time, URC had a full-time horticulturalist on staff to tend this and several other plant-filled spaces in its restaurants.

The company's ongoing expansion left it chronically short of qualified staff, and to attract new employees and reduce turnover the firm provided numerous perks, including paid vacations, health insurance, and a 401(k) pension plan. In September 1997, URC added a $2 per hour day-care supplement payment for full-time employees with children. Prentice also gave ownership stakes in his restaurants to their top managers, increasing their commitment to the success of each operation.

Multiple Restaurants Opened in 1998

The year 1998 was a busy one for URC. In January, the firm paid $205,000 for a West Bloomfield restaurant called Memphis Smoke, which became the casual seafood restaurant Flying Fish Tavern several months later. Tavern on 13 was soon converted into a second Flying Fish Tavern as well. In the spring, Sebastian's Grill was moved to a new location in Somerset Mall and reopened as Portabella, serving Italian fare. The company's first location in downtown Detroit, Duet, opened in late May near historic Orchestra Hall. Its menu offered pairings ("duets") of dishes such as seafood and steak. A new Deli Unique was later opened next door.

Also in 1998, URC converted Trattoria Bruschetta at the Hotel Baronette into the No. VI Chop House and Lobster Bar. It was soon a popular destination for business executives, many of whom were in town for meetings related to the auto industry. Within a short period, the restaurant was averaging $4 million in annual sales, four times what the previous concept had done.

In December 1998, the company opened an Asian-style noodle restaurant, Fusion, to replace the unsuccessful Relish. URC also sued the owners of the Summit Place Mall over their unfulfilled promise to perform renovations. The firm's Sourdough Café, which had been losing money there since opening, had closed. For 1998, the company had $38 million in revenues, and its employee ranks stood at 1,000.

In August 1999, URC licensed the Deli Unique name to the MotorCity Casino, which would open a round-the-clock delicatessen that seated 150. Fall saw the sale of the underperforming Flying Fish Tavern in West Bloomfield and the conversion of Fusion into an all-catering operation.

In January 2000, the company ordered all 250 of its cooks and dishwashers to be vaccinated against the Hepatitis A virus, with new hires to be vaccinated in the future. Matt Prentice had had the illness as a child, and it was a recurring problem in the foodservice business, especially in the Detroit area, where one person had recently died from a food-borne infection. The move, which would cost the company $30,000, was made to protect both the workers and the firm's clientele.

In March 2000, URC took over management of four restaurants at the Star Southfield movie theater complex from Ark Restaurant Corp. of New York, which had spent $14 million on renovations before pulling out. In May, the Mexican restaurant Volcano Grill was reopened, but business was slow, and the debut of Mash, which would feature only potato-based dishes, was delayed. A brewpub that would make beer on-site and a pizza-by-the-slice restaurant were slated to round out the offerings, but in late February 2001 Prentice abandoned these projects along with Mash, which never opened.

In 2001, URC was chosen by Ford Motor Company as a branding consultant for its auto shows throughout the United States. During the year, the firm catered the North American International Auto Show in Detroit and the New York Auto Show.

Key Dates:

1980: Matt Prentice founds Deli Unique in Royal Oak, Michigan.

1984: Prentice opens Café Jardin in Somerset Mall with help from owner Sam Frankel.

1986: Sebastian's opens at Somerset; the company forms a wholesale produce operation.

1990: Morels: A Michigan Bistro opens in Bingham Farms.

1993: Sourdough Bread Factory opens in Pontiac.

1998: New restaurant openings include Portabella, No. VI Chop House, Duet, Flying Fish Tavern.

2001: The firm begins catering auto shows for the Ford Motor Company.

2002: Kosher restaurant Milk & Honey opens.

2004: Coach Insignia, located atop Detroit's Renaissance Center, opens.

2005: The company becomes known as Matt Prentice Restaurant Group.

The year 2001 also saw a lobbying effort spearheaded by Prentice to cause the state of Michigan to change an archaic law prohibiting staff from sampling wine on the job. He had prompted the state restaurant association to take action after learning that it was illegal for his employees to sample wine at work, which he considered essential for them to properly advise their customers. The bill was signed in July by Michigan Governor John Engler.

In addition to running his restaurants, Prentice also found time to work with several charitable organizations. In October 2000, he had formed the Variety Produce Resource Program, which distributed surplus food to the hungry, and had also worked with Share our Strength, Forgotten Harvest, the Food Bank of Oakland County, and Gleaners.

In the weeks after the September 11, 2001 terrorist attacks, the company's business fell off dramatically as fearful Americans stayed home. Sales had already been declining due to a recent economic downturn, which hit the firm's catering business particularly hard. Due to the rising unemployment rate, URC was able for the first time in its history to have all of its restaurants fully staffed with qualified personnel.

Dairy Restaurant Added in 2002

In February 2002, the company opened a kosher dairy restaurant, Milk & Honey, in the Jewish Community Center in West Bloomfield Township, where it had been providing catering services since 2000. The restaurant's kitchen followed strict Jewish dietary laws, and a special inspector was employed to certify compliance. Milk & Honey was pitched partly at vegetarians, and half of its business was estimated to come from outside the Jewish community. Later, the restaurant began catering meals to the Meer and Hecht apartments for senior citizens.

In July 2002, the firm closed the Deli Unique next door to Morel's. It was replaced in October by an upscale steakhouse called Shiraz, which featured wines made from the grape the restaurant was named after.

In early 2003, URC, still hurting from the economic downturn, cut its employees' health benefits. Both dental and prescription drug coverage were cancelled, and hourly workers were asked to pay a third of their healthcare premiums. The move would affect only about 200 of the company's now 800 employees, as many already had coverage from their spouse's employers, had not worked long enough to earn these benefits, or did not work full time. Despite the cuts, URC's benefits program was still more generous than the industry average.

May 2003 saw the closure of both of the firm's downtown Detroit restaurants, the Deli Unique and Duet. They had been doomed by the lack of foot traffic in the city, with business largely tied to special events in the area like concerts and ball games. A massive power outage in August also caused the firm to lose tens of thousands of dollars worth of food, though Prentice and his staff worked many extra hours to make sure all scheduled catering events went off without a hitch.

In the fall, an agreement was reached with General Motors to take over a closed restaurant at the corporation's headquarters in the 72-story Renaissance Center in downtown Detroit. After months of negotiations, GM had agreed to cover most of the renovation costs, which were more expensive due to the restaurant's elevated location, as well as basing the rent on a percentage of revenues.

Prentice's new concept was called Coach Insignia, whose name was taken from a type of wine made by Fisher Vineyards, run by the grandson of the founder of one-time GM division Fisher Body. Fisher's wines would be featured in the restaurant's $250,000 wine cellar, which was overseen by Madeline Triffon. The dinner-only menu would include steak, seafood, and chicken dishes. Coach Insignia's circular space had once rotated slowly to give diners a panoramic view of Detroit and environs, but Prentice decided to abandon this feature to allow for more tables and better food service. In addition to 220 seats on two floors, the space also offered banquet seating for 110 and private dining rooms.

In February 2004, URC closed Café Jardin, and in April of the same year the firm opened its first brewpub, Thunder Bay Brewing Co., in Great Lakes Crossing Mall in Auburn Hills. It replaced the shuttered Alcatraz Brewing Co. In the summer, Coach Insignia started operations, earning four-star reviews from both the *Detroit News* and the *Detroit Free Press*.

The year 2005 saw the firm begin operating as the Matt Prentice Restaurant Group in order to reflect its owner's high visibility in the community as well as to distinguish it from other companies with "Unique" in their names. Plans were also underway for the Portabella restaurant to close in late spring, with a new brewpub featuring soul food and live jazz music, Etouffe, set to open in the summer at the Star Southfield Entertainment Complex.

After a quarter-century, the Matt Prentice Restaurant Group had grown from a single delicatessen into one of the Detroit area's largest restaurant management and catering firms. With offerings that ranged from unpretentious deli fare to some of the city's most highly acclaimed food and wine, the firm had established itself as one of the most respected organizations of its type in the Midwest.

Principal Subsidiaries

MPRG Off Premise Catering; Sourdough Bread Factory.

Principal Competitors

Cameron Mitchell Restaurants; Epoch Restaurant Group; Andiamo Restaurant Group; Forte Belanger Catering.

Further Reading

Anglebrandt, Gary, "Thinking Like a Chef: Restaurateur Prentice Helps Soup Kitchens Get Most from Budgets," *Crain's Detroit Business*, November 25, 2002, p. 1.

Blassingame, Kelley M., "Serving a Benefits Buffet. Prentice Offers Unparalleled Benefits Smorgasbord for Restaurant Staff," *Employee Benefit News*, October 1, 2003.

Bohy, Ric, " 'MMMMM' Is for Morels," *Detroit Monthly*, May 1, 1996, p. 73.

Boldt, Ethan, "Unique Restaurant Corp.," *Restaurant Business*, April 15, 1999, p. 24.

Kosdrosky, Terry, "Milk & Honey Has Unique Approach," *Crain's Detroit Business*, February 4, 2002, p. 19.

——, "Prentice to Sell One Eatery, Convert Another," *Crain's Detroit Business*, October 18, 1999, p. 3.

"Matt Prentice Restaurant Group History," Matt Prentice Restaurant Group, 2005.

Norris, Kim, and Sylvia Rector, "Unique Restaurant Corp. Trims Health Benefits," *Detroit Free Press*, February 12, 2003.

Perlik, Allison, "Unique Restaurant Corp.," *Restaurants & Institutions*, November 1, 2002, p. 66.

Rector, Sylvia, Mark Stryker, and John Gallagher, "Restaurateur Says Deal Near for Detroit Renaissance Center," *Detroit Free Press*, May 23, 2003.

Snavely, Brent, "Restaurant Events Help to Fill Charities' Plates," *Crain's Detroit Business*, November 1, 2004, p. 24.

Stopa, Marsha, " 'Roadkill' Restaurateur: Prentice Has Way with Leftovers," *Crain's Detroit Business*, February 27, 1995, p. 3.

Strong, Michael, "Prentice Reaches for New Heights," *Crain's Detroit Business*, October 6, 2003, p. 21.

Van Houten, Ben, "Rescue Operation," *Restaurant Business*, October 15, 2000, p. 29.

Ytuarte, Chris, "Food Chain to Require Hepatitis A Vaccinations," *Supermarket News*, January 31, 2000, p. 29.

—Frank Uhle

::::MediaNews Group

MediaNews Group, Inc.

1560 Broadway, Suite 2100
Denver, Colorado 80202
U.S.A.
Telephone: (303) 563-6360
Fax: (303) 894-9327
Web site: http://www.medianewsgroup.com

Private Company
Incorporated: 1985
Employees: 10,000
Sales: $754 million (2004)
NAIC: 511110 Newspaper Publishers; 513112 Radio
  Stations; 513120 Television Broadcasters

MediaNews Group, Inc., is the seventh largest newspaper company in the United States. The company owns and operates 40 daily newspapers and about 65 non-dailies. The company owns newspapers in Alaska, Colorado, Connecticut, Massachusetts, Pennsylvania, Texas, Utah, Vermont, and in both northern and southern California. Many of its properties are clustered in suburban areas. For example, MediaNews owns 17 papers in the Los Angeles area, including the *Los Angeles Daily News* and smaller papers such as the *Long Beach Press Telegram,* the *Pasadena Star News,* and the *Whittier Daily News.* MediaNews owns 11 papers in Massachusetts and nine in Texas, similarly clustered in suburban markets. Its larger papers include the *Denver Post* and the *Salt Lake Tribune.* The combined circulation of MediaNews Group's daily papers is 1.7 million, with circulation of 2.3 million for Sunday papers. The company operates several regional divisions as well as a web site division called MediaNews Interactive. MediaNews also owns four radio stations and an Alaska television station. The company's principals are Richard B. Scudder and William Dean Singleton.

Company Origins Steeped in Ink

The MediaNews Group was founded in 1985, but its chairman, Richard B. Scudder, already had a long career in the newspaper industry by that time. The company's vice-chairman and chief executive officer, William Dean Singleton, though many years younger than Scudder, also had done much in the newspaper world before forming MediaNews. Richard B. Scudder was born into the newspaper business, as his grandfather had founded the *Newark (New Jersey) News* in 1882. Scudder fought in World War II, then returned home to run the family paper, which was New Jersey's largest and most prominent. A big problem in the newspaper industry in the postwar years was lack of newsprint. By the early 1950s, there was such a shortage of newsprint that one newspaper in Philadelphia went to print on brown wrapping paper. Scudder met an inventor who claimed that he could remove the ink from old newspapers so they could be recycled. This inventor turned out to be wrong— he could not do what he promised—but Scudder nevertheless continued to investigate newspaper recycling. Working with various industry experts and in his own kitchen with a blender, Scudder eventually came up with a workable process for recycling newspapers. Although the paper industry was extremely skeptical, Scudder managed to get financial backing for a newspaper recycling plant. He founded Garden State Paper Company in 1961, the first company in the nation to make 100 percent recycled newsprint. Garden State Paper continued to operate through the early 2000s, but Scudder sold it, and his family newspaper, in 1970. The buyer was a Virginia firm, Media General. Scudder continued to work as the *Newark News'* publisher until 1972, when the paper closed, and he was chairman of Garden State Paper until 1994.

William Dean Singleton was born in 1951 and grew up in a small town in west Texas. Singleton was keen on business from an early age, earning money by selling greeting cards and raising livestock. He became a reporter for his hometown paper when he was 15, and then founded his own weekly paper a few years later, after dropping out of college. In his 20s, Singleton worked for Texas financier Joe Albritton. By the time he was 27, Singleton was president of Albritton Communications, the newspaper arm of Albritton's empire. He had finessed the purchase of the *Fort Worth Press,* that Texas city's second place newspaper, in 1975, and then folded it within months when it did not prove financially viable. By 1977, Singleton had put together several groups of dailies for Albritton Communications, and he was busy running a new purchase, the *Paterson (New Jersey) News.* The New Jersey connection brought Singleton and Scudder together. In fact, the *Paterson News* owed Scudder's Garden State Paper some $400,000, and Scudder called on Singleton to collect the debt. Although Scudder was old enough to be Singleton's grandfather, the two men found they had much in common. Within a few years, they began investing together, as MediaNews Group.

Assembling Chains in the 1980s

Singleton and Scudder made their first purchase in 1983, when they picked up the *Gloucester County (New Jersey) Times* for $3 million. The pair founded MediaNews Group in 1985, and soon controlled strings of newspapers in several states. Scudder's role in the partnership was mostly to put up the money, while Singleton's expertise was in handling the day-to-day operations of the newspaper business. The company that bought out Scudder's family paper, Media General, also provided much financial backing to MediaNews. Singleton, as the hands-on manager, quickly acquired a reputation as a ruthless cost-cutter. The papers his company bought were mostly small town dailies, often family-owned businesses. Singleton closed papers that did not thrive, but he also managed to bring many of his acquisitions back to life. Some of the papers Media General purchased might not have survived without his management. Yet his was apparently a thankless task, as Singleton practiced what *Time* magazine (September 28, 1987) called "radical budget surgery," laying off personnel and making editorial and format changes in order to make the papers more profitable.

By 1987, MediaNews Group owned 56 newspapers. At one point, the company was growing so fast that it was buying on average one paper every ten days. It had become the eleventh largest newspaper conglomerate in the United States by 1987. All of its papers were relatively small in circulation, and followed a pattern whereby the company bought in clusters in particular markets. An exception was the *Dallas Times Herald,* a large urban newspaper with a circulation of 247,000. MediaNews bought it for $110 million in 1986. The next year, the company bought another large Texas paper, the *Houston Post,* for $150 million. That paper, with a circulation of 309,000, was the number-two paper in the Houston market, notably less profitable than the leading *Houston Chronicle.* After these two uncharacteristic buys, MediaNews bought one more large paper, the *Denver Post.* Like the *Houston Post,* the *Denver Post* was the number-two paper in its market, and it was locked in a competitive battle with the market leader, the *Rocky Mountain News.*

By 1988, MediaNews Group had spent more than $700 million on its acquisitions. Much of the cash had been put up by Media General, and MediaNews was highly leveraged, meaning it skated along with a high degree of debt. Aside from Media General, the company had another significant backer, the media company Times Mirror. Times Mirror loaned MediaNews $60 million in 1986 for the purchase of the *Dallas Times Herald,* and then loaned the company another $70 million in 1987 for the *Denver Post.* MediaNews, which was privately owned and did not give out financial information, seemed to be doing well off its investments for the most part. Scudder claimed to have recouped ten times his initial $3 million investment. Yet not all of the company's purchases became profitable. MediaNews sold the *Houston Post* and the *Dallas Times Herald* within a few years of buying them, and both papers soon folded. The *Denver Post,* on the other hand, did turn into a profitable paper. It continued to do well through the 1990s, while competition weakened its rival, the *Rocky Mountain News.*

Going Coast to Coast in the 1990s

While the *Denver Post* became the flagship paper of the MediaNews Group, the company continued its original strategy of focusing on small-market dailies and weeklies. The company built up a presence in New Jersey in the 1990s. It owned many small papers, such as the *North Jersey Herald News* in Passaic and *Today's Sunbeam* in Salem, and weekly papers in the counties of Bergen, Passaic, Union, and Warren. In 1997 MediaNews bought a group of 14 New Jersey weekly papers and four buying guides from Forbes, Inc. The papers had a combined circulation of about 86,000, and 130 employees. Two years later, MediaNews made another big transaction, bringing the number of California dailies it controlled up from 12 to 22. This deal was a merger between a MediaNews subsidiary, Garden State Newspapers, and an Arkansas-based newspaper group called Donrey Media. The merger gave MediaNews management control of a cluster of small papers in the Los Angeles area with a combined circulation of 500,000. By 1998, MediaNews had clusters of newspapers in 13 states, with Western properties in Texas, Utah, New Mexico, Arizona, Colorado, and California, and Eastern groups in Connecticut, New Jersey, Pennsylvania, Massachusetts, and Vermont. By 1999, company revenue had grown to more than $800 million.

Competition at the End of the 20th Century

By 1999, MediaNews had only one atypical paper in its stable. Amidst its many small-town and suburban newspapers, the *Denver Post* was a large-circulation, urban daily. When MediaNews bought the *Denver Post* in 1987, *Time* magazine (September 28, 1987) characterized the paper as "ailing," and it was considered the junior newspaper, behind the more successful *Rocky Mountain News.* Yet a dozen years after the purchase, the *Denver Post* was evidently in fine financial shape, in spite of cutthroat competition with its rival paper. Singleton told a reporter from the *Rocky Mountain News* (May 22, 1999) that the *Post* had "been profitable every quarter since the 1980s." On the other hand, the *News* had lost at least $120 million over the past ten years. In 1999, MediaNews bought out half of Media General's 40 percent stake in the *Denver Post,* and agreed to purchase the rest of Media General's stake over the next five years.

Key Dates:

1983: Scudder and Singleton make their first newspaper purchase.
1985: The company is founded.
1987: MediaNews buys the *Denver Post.*
1997: The company buys a cluster of New Jersey papers.
2000: The *Denver Post* and *Rocky Mountain News* begin joint operation.

The next year, the parent company of the *Rocky Mountain News,* E.W. Scripps Co., announced that it had invested some $250 million in the paper over the past 15 years, and never seen a profit. The two papers had battled for subscribers and advertisers, until both businesses were practically giving subscriptions away. While the *Post* had remained profitable, the *News* found itself in dire financial straits by 2000, and the two papers announced a joint operating agreement. The new arrangement combined the two papers' business offices, though each paper continued to publish its own daily paper. The deal, which cost E.W. Scripps $60 million, was supposed to end the detrimental competition and assure the continuance of both papers for the next 50 years. Singleton told the *New York Times* (September 2, 2002) that he had decided in 1999 to build the *Denver Post* into a strong newspaper. Singleton's reputation was founded on his cost-cutting management style rather than on his fostering of fine writing, but he told the *Times* that he "wanted to build a great newspaper." He made executive changes at the *Post* to facilitate improvements in the paper's regional and national coverage, and he increased the paper's budget in 2001 in order to send 15 reporters to the Middle East. Also in 2001, Singleton took the title of publisher of the *Denver Post,* in addition to his role as vice-chairman and chief financial officer of MediaNews Group.

Another Urban Market in the 2000s

Meanwhile, MediaNews continued to buy small-market papers, and to sell them. The company unloaded its New Jersey papers in 2000, claiming its collection of papers there did not have enough impact on the total market. It also bought a group of Connecticut papers, including that state's largest, the *Connecticut Post.* By 2000, MediaNews owned 130 newspapers in 13 states. MediaNews Group's most notable purchase, however, was its acquisition in 2000 of Utah's *Salt Lake Tribune* for $200 million. The *Tribune,* with a circulation of 135,000, was, like the *Denver Post,* an urban paper on a much larger scale than the typical MediaNews property.

Its financial situation was complicated on several fronts. The paper had long been family-owned, but the McCarthey family had sold it in 1997, while staying on as managers. The *Tribune* went through several owners, until MediaNews bought it from AT&T Broadband. The *Tribune* had a longstanding joint operating agreement with Salt Lake City's rival paper, the *Deseret News,* which was owned by the city's dominant political and religious force, the Mormon (Latter Day Saints) Church. The two papers had shared their business operations since 1952, but their newsrooms had become increasingly antagonistic in the late 1990s, with the *Deseret News* accusing the *Tribune* of overly aggressive reporting on church affairs. When MediaNews unexpectedly bought the *Tribune,* the McCarthey family felt sideswiped, as they had hoped to buy the paper back themselves. Rumors raged that Singleton had made some kind of deal with Mormon Church officials regarding news coverage in order to continue the joint operating agreement.

This situation led to a lawsuit by the McCarthey family. In a decision in 2003, a federal appeals court upheld the family's option to buy the newspaper back. The family declared victory. But MediaNews also announced that it had won the appeal on all counts. So this decision seemed to do little to resolve the conflict between the parties. The McCartheys had only won an option to buy, and they still disputed the appraised price of the *Tribune,* set by a third party at $352.5 million. This seemed $100 million too high to the McCarthey family. As of early 2005, the *Salt Lake Tribune* was still part of the MediaNews stable.

Other Developments in the 2000s

In July 2000, MediaNews Group sold its New Jersey papers, including the *Gloucester County Times,* which was the first newspaper the company bought when it got its start in the early 1980s. Singleton told *Editor & Publisher* (April 30, 2001), "It broke my heart to turn over our first paper," yet his company seemed to be turning in a new direction. MediaNews Group's revenue was close to $1 billion by 2000, but it had passed up acquiring several newspapers that had come up for sale recently. Instead, MediaNews spent $7 million to acquire the number-two television station in Anchorage, Alaska, KTVA-TV. The company declared it was actively looking for more radio and television opportunities. The company made an arrangement with a Denver television station, KWGN-TV, in which the *Denver Post* and KWGN collaborated on a subscription news service on the Internet. MediaNews opened a new division to handle Internet business, called MediaNews Interactive, in 1995. By 2005, the Interactive division provided web-based versions of the reporting from 49 of the company's daily papers, often in partnership with area radio and television broadcasting. Singleton explained his strategy to *Forbes* (July 3, 2000): "If all I had was a newspaper in Podunk City, over the next ten years I would deteriorate. But if I had a newspaper in Podunk City and full Internet technology and a radio and TV station, the combined entity would survive."

Nevertheless, growth into new media did not come quickly. Until June 2, 2003, the Federal Communication Commission (FCC) prohibited the owner of a newspaper from also owning a television or radio station in the same market. When the rule was relaxed, MediaNews was quick to announce its intentions to increase its so-called "cross-ownership." Yet by 2005, the company still had only the one television station in Alaska, in addition to four radio stations in Texas. And MediaNews continued to buy plain old newspapers. It strengthened its hold on the Los Angeles area in 2004, buying two weeklies, the *Grunion Gazette* and *Downtown Gazette,* with a combined circulation of 65,000. Around the same time, the company lost a bid to buy the *Orange County Register,* a leading area paper with a circulation of more than 360,000. The company's revenue in the early 2000s dropped off from its peak in 2000.

Principal Divisions

MediaNews Interactive; West Coast MediaNews LLC.

Principal Competitors

E.W. Scripps Company; Gannett Company, Inc.; Tribune Company.

Further Reading

Accola, John, "Post Parent Buys Salt Lake City Paper But Tribune Executives Seek Injunction on Sale by AT&T," *Rocky Mountain News,* December 2, 2000, p. 3B.

Barrett, Beth, "Daily News Won't Be Sold to L.A. Times, Owner Says," *Los Angeles Daily News,* May 19, 2000, p. N1.

Barringer, Felicity, "Businessman vs. Newsman, All in One Person," *New York Times,* September 2, 2002, p. C1.

Booth, Michael, and Don Knox, "$250 Million Was Poured into News," *Denver Post,* May 21, 2000.

Caulk, Steve, and Kevin Flynn, "Papers' Owners Tell Story of Deal," *Rocky Mountain News,* May 21, 2000, p. 5A.

DeMarrais, Kevin G., "Founder of Garfield, N.J. Firm Wrote the Book on Newspaper Recycling," *Hackensack (NJ) Record,* November 4, 2001.

"Denver Post's Chairman Becomes Publisher," *Denver Post,* January 23, 2001.

Fitzgerald, Mark, "Survival of the Fittest," *Editor & Publisher,* April 30, 2001, p. SR10.

"Former Owner of the Salt Lake Tribune Addresses Staff, Vows to Return," *Knight Ridder/Tribune Business News,* July 31, 2002.

Garneau, George, "Scudder Sues Media General," *Editor & Publisher,* February 11, 1995, p. 18.

Herszenhorn, David M., "The Connecticut Post Is Sold Along with 5 Smaller Papers," *New York Times,* July 13, 2000, p. B5.

Lacter, Mark, "Where's Dean?," *Forbes,* July 3, 2000, p. 76.

Lewis, Al, "Media General Sells Stake in Post," *Rocky Mountain News,* May 22, 1999, p. 3B.

Martin, Claire, "Scudder Helped Wayward Teens," *Denver Post,* May 19, 2004, p. C-10.

"MediaNews Adds Group of Papers," *Los Angeles Daily News,* January 13, 1999, p. B1.

Moulton, Kristen, "Managers of Salt Lake City Newspaper Win Crucial Legal Battle," *Knight Ridder/Tribune Business News,* February 22, 2001.

"News Mogul Wants 7th Paper," *San Francisco Examiner,* September 9, 2000, p. C1.

Palmeri, Christopher, "Press Lord Redux," *Forbes,* October 24, 1988, p. 398.

Sanchez, Felix, "MediaNews Buys Gazette Newspapers," *Knight Ridder/Tribune Business News,* January 7, 2004.

Simon, Ellen, "Forbes Sells Off Newspapers," *Newark (NJ) Star-Ledger,* February 13, 1997, p. 43.

Vigh, Michael, "Former Owners of the Salt Lake Tribune See Way to Buy Back Paper," *Knight Ridder/Tribune Business News,* February 27, 2003.

——, "Salt Lake City Tribune Owner Says Former Managers Knew Sale Was Risky," *Knight Ridder/Tribune Business News,* September 12, 2002.

"Weak Sales in Bay Area Contribute to Drop in MediaNews' Net Income," *Denver Post,* February 22, 2004, p. K-04.

Zuckerman, Laurence, "Forget About Art and Cars, William Dean Singleton Keeps Collecting Papers," *Time,* September 28, 1987, p. 55.

—A. Woodward

Mercury Drug Corporation

7 Mercury Avenue, corner E. Rodrigu
Quezon City
PH-1110
Philippines
Telephone: +63 2 911 5071
Fax: +63 2 911 6673
Web site: http://www.mercurydrug.com

Wholly Owned Subsidiary of Mercury Group of
*   Companies, Inc.*
Incorporated: 1945
Employees: 7,000
Sales: PHP 42.98 billion ($8.8 billion) (2003 est.)
NAIC: 446110 Pharmacies and Drug Stores

Mercury Drug Corporation is the Philippines' dominant pharmacy group. The Quezon City-based company operates a national chain of more than 450 drugstores, including company-owned and franchised stores. Mercury Drug is estimated to sell as much as 60 percent of all medicines sold each year in the Philippines (the country's hospitals sell about 12 percent of medicines). Mercury Drug's pharmacies follow the American model, combining drug and medical equipment sales with over-the-counter medicines, personal care items, basic household needs, cosmetics and other beauty products, and the like. Most of the company's stores also are equipped to store and sell serums, blood plasma, albumin, and similar biologically active medical products. In addition to its drugstores, Mercury operates a chain of Mercury Drug Superstores. Generally attached to the company's pharmacies, the Mercury Drug Superstores extend the group's assortment to include convenience store and fast-food items. By the mid-2000s, Mercury Drug Corporation operated more than 150 Mercury Drug Superstores. Founded by Mariano Que, who first sold pills from a pushcart in the 1940s, Mercury Drug Corporation remains a privately held company. Leadership of the company also remains in the family: The company's president is Mariano Que's daughter, Vivian Que-Ascona. Mercury Drug is a subsidiary of the Mercury Group of Companies, which governs other Que family interests, including the 10*Q convenience store chain and the Tropical Hut fast-food group. In 2003, Mercury Drug's revenues amounted to nearly PHP 43 billion ($8.8 billion).

Founding a Filipino Pharmacy Giant in the 1940s

Mariano Que started his career working in a Manila drugstore in prewar Philippines. There he came into contact with many medications, including the newly discovered class of sulfa drugs, including sulfathiazole. These new drugs, developed by German scientists in the early 1930s, were quickly hailed as new "miracle" drugs. Indeed, the sulfa drugs enabled the treatment of many illnesses, such as pneumonia, gonorrhea, and other bacterial infections, that previously had been difficult, if impossible, to treat. Despite the fact that the sulfa drugs later were shown to have a number of undesirable side effects (they formed deposits in the kidneys, and bacteria quickly became resistant), they were credited with saving millions of lives around the world through World War II.

The end of the war and the liberation of the Philippines by U.S. forces brought new business opportunities in the country. During the occupation, supplies of medicines had become scarce, and the immediate postwar period saw a surge in demand for sulfa drugs, and sulfathiazole, considered by many to be a virtual cure-all. With most of the country's businesses, including its pharmacies, destroyed during the war, much of the country's trade shifted to its busy marketplaces. Mariano Que, inspired by the new entrepreneurial spirit, used his drugstore experience to launch his own business.

At first, Que bought and sold medical vials and capsules. After he had generated sufficient savings, however, he took PHP 100 (worth about $1.50 at the time) and bought a bottle of sulfathiazole tablets. Que brought the sulfathiazole bottle to Manila's busy Banbang market and sold the pills—in single doses. The method of selling, known as "Tingi-tingi," became extremely popular in the poverty-stricken Philippines, bringing life-saving medications within financial reach of many more people than before.

Que invested his profits in purchasing more pills, and before long he had generated enough revenue to buy a pushcart, which he filled with an expanding assortment of pharmaceuticals. The unregulated nature of the country's drug market, especially its pharmaceutical black market, led to abuses by sellers, who sometimes peddled fake or dangerous formulations, or sold medications long out of date, often at extortionist prices.

Que, however, built a reputation for the quality and freshness of his products, and also for the fairness of his prices. Before too long, he had built up a steady clientele, and in March 1945, Que opened his first store. Que named the Bambang-located store Mercury Drug, after the Roman god and bearer of the caduceus, the symbol of the medical profession.

Branching Out in the 1970s

Mercury Drug remained a one-store operation into the 1960s. In the meantime, Que continued to drive innovations in the Filipino pharmacy sector. In 1948, for example, Que began a drug delivery service, becoming the first to use motorized vehicles for swifter delivery times. In the 1950s, Que expanded his store hours, introducing a 17-hour-per-day, seven-days-per-week opening schedule. Part of the motivation behind the move came in recognition of a Filipino tendency to auto-medicate their illnesses. By remaining open longer, Mercury Drug responded to its clients' demands for increased access to pharmaceutical products. Launched in 1952, the new opening schedule was expanded to 24 hours per day in 1965.

Mercury Drug began its drive to become the Philippines' dominant drugstore group in the next decade. At the beginning of the 1960s, the company was contacted by the Ayala Corporation, which was building a shopping center in Makati. Ayala offered to lease space to Mercury, in order to include drugstore services at the center. Mercury agreed, and once again revealed its penchant for innovation, opening the country's first self-service pharmacy in 1963.

Two years later, Mercury opened its third drugstore, in Quiapo, which became the company's flagship and set the model for its further development. In 1967, the company opened a centralized warehouse to serve its growing store chain, introducing computer-guided temperature controls to safeguard its products. Then, in 1969, the company became the first to introduce biological refrigerators in its stores. This permitted the company to assure the quality of its life-saving medicines.

Mercury Drug began building out its network of drugstores, staying close to the Manila market for much of the early 1970s. The company also began branching out beyond pharmaceutical sales. A significant early purchase was that of Medical Center Drug Corporation (MCDC). Founded in 1946, MCDC focused on sales of pharmaceutical supplies, equipment, and basic surgical instruments.

The purchase of MCDC, complementary to its existing drugstore business, led Mercury Drug to change its structure. In 1972, Que created the Mercury Group of Companies, Inc., which in turn oversaw Mercury Drug and MCDC. Both companies remained independent of the other; in 1980, MCDC changed its name, to Medical Center Trading Corporation (MCTC), in order to highlight its difference from Mercury Drug. MCTC then grew into the Philippines' leading importer and distributor of medical, hospital, laboratory, and related equipment, with branches throughout the Metro Manila and surrounding region.

MCTC was not the only venture by Que (who was joined by daughter Vivian Que-Ascona, later president of Mercury Drug) to expand beyond his drugstore empire. The introduction of the convenience store concept in the Philippines in the early 1980s represented both a new source of competition for Mercury Drug and a new opportunity. Mercury developed its own convenience format in response to the growth of competitors such as 7-11. Typically located next to its drugstores, the Mercury Drug Superstores expanded the company's range of goods beyond drugs and into wider consumer categories, such as beauty and personal care products, fast-foods, and the like.

Separately, the Que family added other interests, including the Q*10 convenience store format and the Tropical Hut fast-food restaurant chain. Nonetheless, Mercury Drug Corporation remained the focus of the family's holdings.

"Oligopoly" in the New Century

Mercury Drug, meanwhile, continued to grow strongly. In 1976, the company expanded beyond the Metro Manila market for the first time, and over the next decades added locations in the Luzon, Visayas, and Mindanao regions of the Philippines as well. Supporting this network was the implementation of a fully computerized warehousing, inventory, and order processing system, installed in 1985.

Mercury Drug's growth was impressive: By 1995, the company operated more than 270 stores. Less than ten years later, Mercury had expanded its number of branches to more than 450, giving it a near monopoly grip on the country's drug sales. By 2004, Mercury controlled as much as 60 percent of all drug sales in the Philippines.

Ironically, Mercury's dominant position led the group, which had achieved its early growth based on its low prices, to be criticized for what many considered as its restrictively high prices. Indeed, as some critics pointed out, similar drugs could be purchased in India and other markets for as much as one-third the price Mercury Drug charged.

In the early 2000s, the government began taking action to force the Philippines' drug industry, including Mercury Drug, to lower prices on many life-saving medicines. As part of that effort, the country's Trade and Industry and Health departments began encouraging the parallel importation of pharmaceutical generics from India, which had earned worldwide recognition for the quality of its generic equivalents.

In 2004, the government stepped up its pressure. In September of the year, the government passed legislation expanding drug discounts for the country's senior citizens. The country's smaller independent drugstore owners protested the decision, in

Key Dates:

1945: Mariano Que begins selling sulfathiozone out of a cart, then opens a store in Manila and founds Mercury Drug Corporation.
1963: Mercury Drug opens its second store, in a shopping center built by the Ayala Group.
1965: Mercury Drug opens a third, flagship branch in Quiapo.
1970: The company acquires Medical Center Drug Corporation (MCDC).
1972: Mercury Group of Companies, Inc. is set up as a holding company for MCDC and Mercury Drug.
1976: Mercury begins expanding beyond the Manila market.
1985: The company sets up fully computerized warehousing, inventory, and ordering systems.
1995: Mercury celebrates its 50th anniversary with more than 270 stores.
2004: Mercury operates more than 450 stores, with annual sales of nearly PHP 43 billion ($8.8 billion).

part because it was expected to serve only to increase Mercury's dominance over the market—as the country's largest retailer of pharmaceutical products, Mercury was easily able to negotiate discounted prices from its supplies. Also in that year, President Arroyo established the lowering of drug prices as one of the government's priorities.

In December 2004, the Filipino government announced a new plan to break what some were calling Mercury's "oligopoly" on the country's retail market. The Philippine International Trading Corp. (PICT), owned and run by the Filipino government, announced its intention to organize up to 300 of the country's independent pharmacies into a new network of privately owned and operated drugstores, dubbed "Botika ng Bayan." The new network would then sell drugs, sourced by PICT directly from drug companies, at prices as much as six times less expensive than "market"—i.e., Mercury's—rates.

Despite these pressures, Mercury Drug Corporation remained a fixture on the Philippines pharmacy market. The company also remained one of the Philippines' largest corporations, ranking in eighth place among the country's largest corporations and third place among the corporations in the high-quality services/products bracket. Mercury Drug appeared to have discovered its own "miracle drug" for success.

Principal Subsidiaries

Mercury Drug Superstore.

Principal Competitors

Caltex; I-Mart International Corporation; Phils. Corporation; Easy Mart; Petron Corporation; Philippine Seven Corporation; Robinsons Convenience Store Inc.; Seaoil Philippines Inc.; Shell Philippines Inc.; Philippines Corporation.

Further Reading

Aning, Jerome, "City Hall Clarifies Mercury Contract," *Philippine Daily Inquirer,* July 11, 2002.
Balabo, Dino, "Pagdanganan Vows to Break Oligopoly in Pharma Industry," *ABS-CBN.com,* December 17, 2004.
Flores, Shirley, "Mercury Drug Not Planning to List in Stock Exchange Yet," *Corporate News,* December 7, 1999.
Jiminez, Cher, "Drugstores Protest Discounts," *ABS-CBN.com,* November 23, 2004.
"Mercury Drug Corporation Honored by the Philippines," *Stamps,* November 11, 1995, p. 13.
"MSD, Mercury Renew Deal to Increase Access to Drugs," *Business World,* September 17, 2003.

—M.L. Cohen

Merisant Worldwide, Inc.

10 South Riverside Plaza, Suite 850
Chicago, Illinois 60606
U.S.A.
Telephone: (312) 840-6000
Fax: (312) 840-5146
Web site: http://www.merisant.com

Private Company
Incorporated: 2000
Employees: 700
Sales: $352 million (2003)
NAIC: 325199 Synthetic Sweeteners Manufacturing

Merisant Worldwide, Inc., of Chicago, Illinois, is a privately-held company that markets more than 20 brands of aspartame-based artificial sweeteners in over 100 countries. The company's flagship brands Equal and Canderel occupy one-third of the world's tabletop sweetener market. Aspartame was discovered in 1965 by James Schlatter, a research scientist at the pharmaceutical company G.D. Searle, while he was combining amino acids in search of an ulcer drug. When Schlatter licked his finger to pick up a piece of paper, he found that one of the amino acid combinations, a mixture of aspartic acid and phenylalanine, tasted like sugar. Unlike such artificial sweeteners as cyclamate and saccharin, aspartame had no bitter or metallic aftertaste. The new sweetener was found to be 180 times sweeter than sugar.

Establishing a New Sweetener

While Merisant was founded in 2000, the history of its primary product, aspartame, may be traced to the 1970s. Searle branded its discovery NutraSweet and sought approval to market aspartame in the United States and Europe. The U.S. Food and Drug Administration (FDA) initally approved the substance for use in foodstuffs in 1974, but withdrew approval the following year because of concerns that the sweetener might cause brain damage in animals. After thorough retesting, approval was granted in France in 1979 and in the United States in 1981. By 1983, aspartame was an approved food additive in nearly all

of Europe. Although anecdotal claims of adverse effects caused by aspartame still lingered, there was no scientific evidence that the substance caused harm. Studies by the French Food Safety Agency (2002) and the European Union Commission Health & Consumer Protection Directorate-General's Scientific Committee on Food (2002) reaffirmed the safety of the sweetener. Aspartame was one of the most thoroughly tested food additives ever to be approved for market.

Searle initially marketed aspartame to the food service industry as a tabletop sweetener. In France the product appeared in tablet form under the name Canderel. In the United States, the product was packaged in single-serving packets under the name Equal. Aspartame was subsequently marketed to food and drug manufacturers under the NutraSweet brand for use in such preparations as medications, cereals, and desserts. In 1983 aspartame was approved for use in carbonated beverages, and NutraSweet came to dominate the artificial sweetener market as an ingredient in low-calorie drinks. By 1985, aspartame sales topped $700 million.

That year, the agricultural products giant Monsanto purchased G.D. Searle and combined the tabletop sweetener and NutraSweet operations into a single unit, the NutraSweet Company. With the company's patent on aspartame, essentially its sole product, due to expire in 1992, and competitors including saccharin-based Sweet'N Low and Johnson & Johnson's sucralose-based sweetener gaining greater and greater market shares, the company began advertising campaigns designed to lure manufacturers using aspartame/saccharin blends into using aspartame exclusively by raising consumer awareness of the sweetener's presence in products, especially low-calorie drinks. The NutraSweet Co. also launched research programs to develop a new sweetener, sweetener blends, and a fat substitute in order to diversify its product base.

The Birth of Merisant

In March 2000, Monsanto merged with two other companies to form the Pharmacia Corporation. The NutraSweet Company was divided and sold. The company's tabletop sweetener division, comprised of the Equal and Canderel brands, was purchased by Tabletop Holdings, an investment group formed by Pegasus Capital Advisors, computer mogul Michael Dell's MSD Capital, and Brener International. The new company was formally launched under the name Merisant on March 20, 2000. At that time, the company's 19 brands earned about $400 million in sales, approximately one-third of the world's tabletop artificial sweetener market. According to Brandon Copple of *Forbes,* the new company faced stiff challenges: "Sure, it had the industry's top brand, Equal, and a dominant 30% market share. But the sugar substitute business hadn't grown for ten years. And Johnson & Johnson, the $30 billion (sales) consumer products Goliath had just announced its plan to crash the category with a product called Splenda, the granular version of sucralose, already used in some 400 products like Diet Rite, Ocean Spray and Swiss Miss. Its biggest plus: "It tastes more like sugar than aspartame-based Equal."

In addition, aspartame had significant limitations in product stability and use in cookery that were not shared by its rival. Aspartame was heat-sensitive, and if it were stored for six months in warm conditions, the product would lose its sweetness. Likewise, in applications that called for heat, such as baking, aspartame broke down, not only losing its sweetness but also destroying the texture normally imparted by sugar. Splenda, however, had an indefinite shelf life and could be used in baking.

Merisant responded to these challenges by recasting its brands and aiming its advertising at different market segments than those addressed by Johnson & Johnson's Splenda advertising. Where Splenda was marketed to health-conscious younger people, especially women, Equal was pitched to an older market whose concerns included existing health problems that precluded the use of sugar almost entirely. Advertisments for Equal appeared in *Country Living, O, Diabetes Digest, Voice of the Diabetic,* and editions of *TV Guide* and *Reader's Digest* produced specifically for older consumers. This audience, comprised of the baby boomers and their elders, were likely to use Equal for more than just sweetening coffee and tea. People managing such conditions as diabetes and obesity required a sweetener that could be used in cookery as well as drinks, so Merisant set about developing recipes in order to promote Equal as a household staple. Arnold Donald, Merisant's chief, explained, "People who don't even use ketchup have ketchup in their homes. Why? For friends who visit, for guests" (*St. Louis Post-Dispatch,* June 11, 2002). The advertising focused on the idea that Equal could be used to boost flavor in a broad range of foods. Over 130 recipes, including many for baked goods, were posted to the company's website http://www.equal.com.

Merisant also closed deals with manufacturers of candies and desserts, the Blockbuster video store chain, donut maker Krispy Kreme, Panera Bread, and McDonald's, among others. Television advertising featuring TV host and restaurateur B. Smith and a recipe contest judged by Gladys Knight increased nationwide exposure for Equal. In 2004, following a market trend toward the use of blended sweeteners that exploit the benefits of different sweetening agents, a technique long in use in Europe, Merisant launched Sugar Lite, a mixture of sugar and other sweeteners that could be used cup for cup like sugar in recipes. The new product was stable for baking and would brown and provide volume in baked goods. Other new products released in 2004 focused on packaging innovations that would carry Equal out of the home. One such product, the ergonomically designed Easy Squeeze Travel Pack, harkened back to the early days of Canderel by presenting Equal in tablet form. The new product was packaged in a convenient, palm-sized dispenser that held 100 tablets, each equivalent to a teaspoonful of sugar in sweetness.

Nevertheless, competition from Splenda and Sweet'N Low remained intense. Equal's market share fell five percent in 2003 to 25.6 percent of U.S. sales to mass merchandisers, supermarkets, and drugstores. Splenda grew 99 percent and secured 37.3 percent of those markets during 2003; Sweet'N Low held 17.8 percent. By the fourth quarter of 2004, Splenda's retail sales amounted to $141 million, double those of Equal. In 2003 Merisant attempted a $320 million recapitalization by offering an unusual stock-and-bond hybrid to the public, but buyers were scarce enough to cause Merisant to withdraw the offer in November 2004. Chief financial officer Donald Hotz opined that market conditions and the newness of the hybrid instruments were the cause of the offering's poor reception. The *Chicago Tribune* quoted him as saying, "It is similar to the real estate investment trusts, which initially were not widely accepted. It is just a matter of understanding." At the end of the third quarter of 2004, Merisant reported net sales of $251, 577, 000, down slightly from the previous year, and posted an estimated loss of $2.2 million. By the end of the fourth quarter of 2004, the company's efforts remained directed at advertising and packaging its products to expand their use among existing customers and reach new customers worldwide.

Principal Subsidiaries

Merisant Manufacturing Australia Pty. Ltd.; Merisant Company 2 SARL (Switzerland); Merisant México S. de R.L. de C.V.

Principal Competitors

The NutraSweet Company; Cumberland Packing Corporation; Johnson & Johnson; Tate & Lyle plc; American Crystal Sugar Company.

Further Reading

Arndorfer, James N., "People: NutraSweet CEO Blending New Sweetener Strategy," *Crain's Chicago Business*, April 5, 2004, p. 12.

Christensen, Dan, "NutraSweet Maker's Suit against Small S. Florida Wholesaler Tossed Out," Legal Review, *Miami Daily Business Review,* June 14, 2002, p. A10.

Copple, Brandon, "Bake Off," *Forbes,* April 16, 2001, p. 305.

Kirsche, Michelle L., "Merisant Worldwide," *Drug Store News,* August 23, 2004, p. 47.

Lee, Thomas, "Rival's Success Doesn't Sour Chairman of Clayton, Mo., Sweetener Maker," *Knight Ridder/Tribune Business News,* August 1, 2003.

——, "St. Louis-Based Equal Manufacturer Launches Campaign to Recast Brand," *Knight Ridder/Tribune Business News,* June 11, 2002.

Schmeltzer, John, "Chicago-Based Artificial Sweetener Company Cancels Stock, Debt Offering," *Chicago Tribune,* November 2, 2004.

—Jennifer Gariepy

Merriam-Webster Inc.

47 Federal Street
Springfield, Massachusetts 01102
U.S.A.
Telephone: 413-734-3134
Fax: 413-731-5979
Web site: http://www.merriam-webster.com

Wholly Owned Subsidiary of Encyclopaedia Britannica Holding
Founded: 1831 as G. & C. Merriam Company
Employees: 90
Sales: $26.5 million (2003 est.)
NAIC: 511130 Book Publishers; 511210 Software Publishers; 511199 All Other Publishers

Merriam-Webster Inc. is among the world's leading publishers of dictionaries. With its flagship products, *Webster's Third International Dictionary* and *Merriam-Webster's Collegiate Dictionary,* Merriam-Webster boasts a tradition in dictionary-making that extends back in a direct line to the great American lexicographer Noah Webster. Merriam-Webster also publishes an array of other reference books, including *Merriam-Webster's Dictionary of English Usage, Merriam-Webster's Geographical Dictionary, Merriam-Webster's Collegiate Encyclopedia, Merriam-Webster's Manual for Writers and Editors,* a full range of dictionaries and thesauruses for students, and Spanish-English and French-English dictionaries in various sizes and formats. The Merriam-Webster editorial department, which is responsible for collecting the words and revising the Springfield, Massachusetts-based firm's dictionaries, is the largest group of lexicographers employed by any publisher in North America. With more than 16 million examples of word usage in context, the Merriam-Webster citation file may be the largest resource of its kind anywhere. Merriam-Webster publications are available in many electronic formats, including editions for the World Wide Web and for a variety of handheld devices. The *Merriam-Webster Online Dictionary* can be consulted free-of-charge at www.Merriam-Webster.com; the unabridged *International* and the popular *Collegiate* are both available by subscription online. Merriam-Webster Inc. is a subsidiary of Encyclopaedia Britannica Holding.

Noah Webster Compiling the First American Dictionary in the Early 1800s

The history of Merriam-Webster dictionaries begins in the 18th century with Noah Webster, the compiler of the first dictionary of the American language. Born in 1758, Webster established his reputation with the 1783 publication of *A Grammatical Institute of the English Language.* The *Blue-Backed Speller,* as it was popularly known because of its blue paper cover, was the book that more than five generations of American schoolchildren used from the end of the 18th century to the beginning of the 20th when learning to read and write. With more than 100 million copies sold, Webster's *Blue-Backed Speller* is likely the best-selling book in the history of American publishing.

In 1806 Webster published *A Compendious Dictionary of the English Language.* With 30,000 entries, the *Compendious Dictionary* was not much larger than a modern-day paperback dictionary, but it was a ground-breaking book, the first to describe English as it was being spoken in North America. He then set to work on a much larger book, *An American Dictionary of the English Language by Noah Webster L.L.D.,* which was published in 1828 when he was 70 years old.

The appearance of *An American Dictionary* was a revolutionary event in American history. It boldly staked the claim for the existence of a uniquely American form of English, as evidenced by words such as ''skunk'' and ''chowder'' that had never appeared in any British dictionary, as well as vocabulary of the still-new American political experiment, like ''Senate'' and ''Congress.'' Webster introduced other innovations as well. His book advocated the use of new, simpler forms of spelling—he altered ''musick'' to ''music'' and ''centre'' to ''center,'' to name but two examples. *An American Dictionary* won almost immediate acceptance by public institutions in the United States, including legislatures, courts, and universities. However, selling for $20 a copy, an enormous sum of money at the time, the two-volume set was unlikely to be purchased in large numbers by the country's middle class.

The Merriam Brothers Revolutionizing Dictionary Publishing in the 1840s

In 1841, 82-year-old Webster published a revised and expanded edition of his lexicographical masterpiece. In 1843 he died. Not long afterward brothers George and Charles Merriam entered the dictionary business. Since 1831 their printing company in Springfield, Massachusetts, the G. & C. Merriam Co., had been producing everything from wallpaper and calendars to bibles and a series of law books. The Merriams negotiated a contract with Webster's heirs. It gave them the right to sell the remaining copies of the 1841 dictionary and, more important, to produce their own revisions of the book. The dictionary provided the company with a clear focus. In 1847 with the editorial assistance of Webster's son-in-law and literary executor, Professor Chauncey Goodrich of Yale University, the Merriam company published the third edition of *An American Dictionary*.

The Merriam brothers' shrewd business sense made their revision as revolutionary as Webster's first dictionary had been. Using smaller type and eliminating most of the generous margins, the Merriams reduced the physical size of the dictionary from two volumes to one. Their production savings were so considerable that they were able to lower the retail price of the dictionary from $20 to $6. Webster's family was shocked. But the G. & C. Merriam Co. had published a book that was, in its way, the first mass-market dictionary. Middle class Americans could afford it, as could most schools. The Merriams' marketing campaign, targeted aggressively at educational sales, went a long way toward establishing Webster's as the definitive dictionary. Having first encountered the dictionary in school and having regularly used it there, many people later bought one for use at home. In 1859 the G. & C. Merriam Co. brought out another revision. In addition to including sections on new words and synonyms, it was the first American dictionary to use illustrations.

By then the innovations of the Merriam Company's dictionaries had unleashed a wave of traditionalist backlash, the first that would occur periodically during the company's history. Objecting to the Merriams' innovations as reflecting the deterioration of the language and hoping to restore its purity, in 1860 Joseph Worcester brought out *A Dictionary of the English Language,* a book that for nearly a half-century would be the Merriam Company's primary competition. Even as the 1859 edition of *An American Dictionary* was being released, however, G. & C. Merriam had begun work on yet another revision. The company would labor over the new book for five years, as the Civil War raged in the nation. In 1864 *An American Dictionary of the English Language, Royal Quarto Edition, Unabridged,* under the editorship of Noah Porter, was published. It had an entry count three times larger than Noah Webster's 1828 edition. Popularly known as *Webster's Unabridged,* the dictionary was used in schools and universities, and in state and federal government up to the Supreme Court. It soon established itself as the standard dictionary in the country.

Moving Editorial Work In-House in the 1870s

After Noah Webster's death, work on the dictionary was conducted under the supervision of various professors at Yale University. By the 1870s, to guarantee stylistic and editorial consistency in their dictionaries, the Merriam brothers had assembled an in-house editorial department. The most important task of the department was oversight of the ongoing growth of the unabridged dictionary. Its 1878 printing included a new biographical section; the 1884 edition introduced a dictionary of place names.

The company's editorial department also began assembling the Merriam-Webster citation file. The file was originally a collection of index cards, each containing a single citation, that is, an example of a word as it had been used in a published source. The quotations were collected first from textbooks and later from newspapers, magazines, and other reputable sources by Merriam's editors. Citations were subsequently used by Merriam editors to infer the meaning of words. By the late 20th century the computerized citation file consisted of more than 80 citation words of searchable text, but they continued to be recorded on index cards as well. In 2005 the citation file contained more than 16 million examples of English usage, possibly the largest such collection in the world.

A New Title and a New Product in the 1890s

In 1890 G. & C. Merriam made ready to release the latest revision of *An American Dictionary of the English Language.* Much had transpired, however, in the years since Noah Webster published his early editions. By 1889, however, the copyrights on all of Webster's books had long expired; that very year the copyright on the Merriam Company's own 1847 edition expired as well. Some publishers began selling their own editions of these books once they were in the public domain. Others were calling their own books "Webster's Dictionary." To distinguish its dictionary—the direct descendent of Noah Webster—G. & C. Merriam gave its 1890 edition a new title: *Webster's International Dictionary of the English Language.* The new title was the first time that the Merriam Company had used the "Webster" name directly in the book's title; it also reflected the growing status of English as a global language and the United States' growing awareness of itself as a world power. The new book had grown since the 1864 edition, from 56,000 entries to more than 175,000.

Specialized editions of the dictionary had been common since Noah Webster's time. He had published a one-volume version of *An American Dictionary* and had created a dictionary for children from his *Compendious Dictionary.* In their time the Merriam brothers published *The Counting-House Dictionary* and a variety of other specialized dictionaries. In 1898 they created what would prove to be their most successful spinoff of all. *Webster's Collegiate Dictionary* was based on *The National Illustrated Dictionary,* an earlier and only modestly successful abridgement of the *International.* A great part of the *Collegiate*'s eventual success was due to its size. Unlike the burgeoning *International,* the *Collegiate* was compact enough to fit easily on the average bookshelf or desktop. It could without much effort be quickly consulted on the sort of language questions most college students or educated adult readers might have. The *Collegiate* also reflected the extent to which English

Key Dates:

1806: Noah Webster publishes *A Compendious Dictionary of the English Language.*

1828: Webster publishes *An American Dictionary of the English Language.*

1831: G. & C. Merriam is founded in Springfield, Massachusetts.

1841: The revised edition of *An American Dictionary* is published.

1843: Noah Webster dies.

1843: G. & C. Merriam obtains the rights to unsold copies of *An American Dictionary* and to create revisions of the work.

1847: G. & C. Merriam publishes its first revision of *An American Dictionary.*

1870: The editing of the dictionary moves from Yale University to company headquarters in Springfield.

1877: Charles Merriam sells his interest in the company.

1880: George Merriam dies.

1890: *Webster's International Dictionary* is published.

1898: *Webster's Collegiate Dictionary* is first published.

1917: G. & C. Merriam sues Saalfield Publishing Company

over the use of the name "Webster" in the dictionary title.

1942: *Dictionary of Synonyms* is first published.

1943: G. & C. Merriam publishes its first biographical dictionary.

1947: The first paperback dictionary is published.

1949: G. & C. Merriam publishes its first geographical dictionary.

1961: Publication of the *Third New International Dictionary* unleashes a storm of controversy over "permissive" lexicography.

1982: The company changes its name to Merriam-Webster Inc.

1995: *Merriam-Webster's Collegiater Dictionary, Deluxe Electronic Edition for CD-ROM* is the first in a line of Merriam-Webster CD-ROM products.

1996: The company web site, Merriam-Webster OnLine, is launched.

2002: *Webster's Third International Dictionary* is put online in a subscription web site.

2003: *Merriam-Webster's Collegiate Dictionary, 11th edition* is published.

vocabulary had grown. It boasted a wealth of new words from the fields of education, social science, and sports, and in particular from the tremendous scientific and technological revolution the country was going through, from which inventions and concepts, such as the telephone, the automobile, the phonograph, and the light bulb, emerged almost daily. *Collegiate* sales would grow steadily through the 20th century until by 2004 Merriam-Webster had sold more than 55 million copies, making it one of the best-selling hardcover books in American publishing history, second only to the Bible.

Establishment of the Merriam-Webster Brand in the Early 20th Century

By the end of the first decade of the 20th century, G. & C. Merriam had firmly established its Webster's dictionaries as North America's preeminent language reference, as evidenced by the adoption of the book as the dictionary of choice by a steadily growing number of educational and governmental institutions and the constantly increasing sales of Merriam products. The leadership of the company entered a new phase at the beginning of the 20th century. Charles Merriam sold his interest in the firm in 1877. When George Merriam died in 1880, the presidency passed to their younger brother, Homer Merriam. Homer remained at the helm—in name, at least—until 1904, when at the age of 91 he was replaced by Orlando Baker, who had in fact long been responsible for the company's oversight.

G. & C. Merriam's position as the market leader also was underscored by the continued use of the Webster name by dictionary publishers who had no relationship to Noah Webster or his work. For much of the early 20th century, the Merriam company struggled in the courts and before the Federal Trade Commission to block the sale of these so-called "fake Websters." Despite efforts that extended into the 1940s, the courts

would uphold the right of other publishers to call their books "Webster's Dictionary." By the 1950s the Merriam Company had given up trying to control the use of the name.

Expanding Dictionaries and Facilities in the 1930s

Competition with other publishers to produce the best and biggest unabridged dictionary continued apace through the early years of the century. New editions of the unabridged dictionary appeared regularly. *Webster's New International Dictionary* was published in 1909. Twenty-five years later, after working through the hardest years of the Great Depression, Merriam published *Webster's New International Dictionary, Second Edition.* Including expanded front and back matter, color plates, maps, and geographical and biographical sections, it was an enormous book that had been as difficult to manufacture as it was unwieldy to use. It nonetheless maintained Merriam's exacting attention to lexicographical accuracy.

While the dictionary grew in size, the G. & C. Merriam facilities in Springfield were becoming more and more crowded. In the early 1930s planning was begun for a new building. It was completed in 1939 with an entire floor given over to the editorial department. The building continued to serve as Merriam-Webster's headquarters in 2005.

The publication of the mammoth *Second International Dictionary* in 1934 led to the realization that certain sections had grown large enough to be published as separate books. In 1943 Merriam published the first *Webster's Biographical Dictionary* and in 1949 the first *Webster's Geographical Dictionary.* Their status as independent volumes in the Merriam backlist was established in 1961 when a new revision of the *International* appeared without any geographical or biographical sections. The 1940s also saw the first appearance of the *Dictionary of*

Synonyms, a book that formed the basis for the *Merriam-Webster Thesaurus,* which was first published in 1976.

Controversy Around the Third International in the 1960s and 1970s

After World War II Merriam saw its most important task as a new revision of the *International Dictionary.* Revisions had appeared approximately once a generation since the mid-1800s, and it was felt that since the 1930s the language had grown to such an extent that a new unabridged dictionary was needed. The result was *Webster's Third New International Dictionary, Unabridged,* a book that polarized lexicographers, writers, and readers alike. The controversy focused on Merriam's fundamental philosophy of dictionary making, which is so-called descriptivism. Descriptivist dictionaries attempt to accurately record how language *is* used by educated speakers rather than to dictate how language *should* be used (the approach taken by prescriptivist dictionaries). Merriam used its citation file, culled from publications such as the *New York Times, Wall Street Journal, Harper's,* and *Atlantic Monthly,* to document the evolving nature of English. Prescriptivist critics were appalled by the barbarisms they perceived in the *Third International.* Wilson Follett, the author of a well-known text on American English usage, was angered by the inclusion of words and phrases such as "wise up," "ants in one's pants," "one for the books," "center around," and "due to." Follett complained that "to convert the language into a confusion of unchanneled, incalculable williwaws, a capricious wind blowing whithersoever it listeth . . . is exactly what is wanted by the patient and dedicated saboteurs in Springfield." So outraged was one individual that he attempted to buy the G. & C. Merriam Company in order to do the book all over again from the ground up. The purchase bid was unsuccessful. The would-be buyer, however, was able to persuade Houghton Mifflin to publish its own book, the *American Heritage Dictionary,* a prescriptivist antidote to the *Third International,* which came out in 1969.

That was the first shot in a dictionary war, the likes of which G. & C. Merriam had not experienced since the days of Joseph Worcester. Other major publishers began releasing dictionaries of their own to great public fanfare. Random House published its own unabridged dictionary, the *Random House Dictionary of the English Language* in 1968, while in 1980 Simon & Schuster acquired the rights to *Webster's New World Dictionary,* a competitor that had first appeared in the 1940s. In the words of Merriam-Webster President John Morse, by the early 1980s dictionary publishing was, "a bare-knuckles business, with very bloody fights for market share." Merriam's situation was complicated further by the consolidation of retail book-selling in the same period. Publishers endeavored to offer big chains like B. Dalton, Crown Books, Barnes & Noble, and Borders deals that would sell thousands of books, guarantee their product would be promoted in hundreds of stores across the country, and possibly close their competitors out of those same retail locations. As a result, by the beginning of the 1990s the Merriam company—which in 1982 changed its name to Merriam-Webster Inc.—had seen its share of the dictionary market drop noticeably.

Electronic Products and Recovery in the 1990s

Merriam-Webster sold its first electronic products in the 1960s when it leased its typesetting tapes to linguists for re-search purposes. Its first true electronic consumer products had to wait until the 1980s. Then, in conjunction with Franklin Electronic Publishers, Merriam-Webster produced handheld electronic spellcheckers and, later, handheld dictionaries that looked like calculators, except they had miniature typewriter keyboards instead of numeric pads. In 1995 Merriam-Webster introduced the first electronic product of its own, the *Merriam-Webster's Collegiate Dictionary, Deluxe Electronic Edition for CD-ROM.* That same year the company established its first online presence at America Online under the AOL keyword MERRIAM.

By then work had already begun on the company's own web site. Launched in 1996 under the name Merriam Webster Online, the site took the bold step of offering visitors unlimited free access to the *Merriam-Webster Collegiate Dictionary.* There were several reasons for the move. First, the company saw the online dictionary as a tremendous vehicle to promote the Merriam-Webster brand. For decades the company had struggled to link the names "Merriam" and "Webster" in the public consciousness. By the late 1990s the site was getting more than ten million page views every month—a number that had grown to more than 100 million monthly page views by the 2000s—and every visitor saw plainly they were using a Merriam-Webster dictionary. The strengthened brand awareness carried over to the sale of print dictionaries, which by 2003 had increased 17 percent.

Moreover, the company was convinced that while dictionaries in various electronic formats, especially Web-based, might never fully replace print dictionaries, they would be an important means of dictionary use in the future. Finally, Merriam-Webster realized that to keep hold of its leadership in dictionary publishing, its dictionaries had to be accepted as the standard by which dictionaries were measured. To prevail as the country's standard it *had* to be online as well as in print. To surrender the Internet to another dictionary was to concede that Merriam-Webster's product was not the standard there.

In 2000 Merriam-Webster released the *Third International Dictionary* on CD-ROM. In 2002 the book was integrated into a newly designed subscription web site, Merriam-WebsterUnabridged. The site's subscribers are, naturally, individuals with a strong interest in language, people who perhaps grew up with the big unabridged dictionary in their home or local library, but who have come to appreciate the convenience and features of the online version. The company's most popular electronic products by the mid-2000s were its free web site and the handheld version of the *Collegiate* produced by Franklin Electronic Publishers.

In 2001 Merriam-Webster's owner parent company, Encyclopaedia Britannica, put out feelers in the publishing world about interest in buying the dictionary maker. The two firms declined comment on the possibility of a sale, but Merriam-Webster's market value was estimated in the business press between $20 million to $40 million. Encyclopaedia Britannica was trimming costs with drastic cuts in its workforce and in its presence online. In the end, however, no sale was made.

Moving into the latter half of the 2000s, Merriam-Webster anticipated increased use of its products electronically, not only online, but also in PDAs, cell phones, e-book readers, and other devices. Coupled as it is with the ongoing promotion of the Merriam-Webster brand, the company expected use of the electronic products to lead to further growth in sales of the print products as well. The company also anticipated an expansion into the world market, with dictionaries for individuals learning English as a second language. By 2000 English had become the *lingua franca* of world commerce and education. Approximately one billion people were learning the language every day, a fact British dictionary publishers had long known. A successful entry into this market would bode well for Merriam-Webster in the coming decades.

Principal Competitors

Houghton Mifflin Company; Oxford University Press; Simon & Schuster, Inc.; Random House, Inc.

Further Reading

Aucoin, Don, ''A Defining Moment: Updating the Dictionary Calls for a Way with Words,'' *Boston Globe,* October 7, 2003, p. E1.

Barlas, Pete, ''His Perseverance Defined Success; Innovate: Noah Webster's Love for American Language Made His Dictionary Tops,'' *Investor's Business Daily,* November 29, 2002, p. A03.

Czach, Elaine, ''Turning Trademarks into Slang,'' *American Journalism Review,* April-May 2004, p. 58.

Dahlin, Robert, ''Word to the Wise: Merriam-Webster Weds Print, Disc and Web in a New Dictionary Edition,'' *Publishers Weekly,* May 12, 2003, p. 22.

Evans, Rory, ''Picturing a New Webster's,'' *New York Times,* August 3, 2003, p. F13.

Fiske, Robert Hartwell, ''Don't Look It Up! The Decline of the Dictionary,'' *Weekly Standard,* August 18, 2003.

Kiben, David, ''Sure, the Dictionary Got 'Phat,' But It Also Trimmed the Fat,'' *San Francisco Chronicle,* September 24, 2003, p. D1.

Kirkpatrick, David D., ''Dictionary Publishers Going Digital,'' *New York Times,* August 21, 2000, p. C1.

Rollins, Richard M., *The Long Journey of Noah Webster,* Philadelphia: University of Pennsylvania Press, 1980.

Roncevic, Mirela, ''The Making of a Tradition,'' *Library Journal,* June 15, 2003, p. 62.

Unger, Harlow Giles, *Noah Webster: The Life and Times of an American Patriot,* New York: John Wiley & Sons, 1998.

Weeks, Linton, ''Dueling Dictionaries,'' *Washington Post,* June 28, 2001, p. C01.

—Gerald E. Brennan

MOL Rt

Oktober huszonharmadika u 18
Budapest
H-1117
Hungary
Telephone: (+36) 1 209 0000
Fax: (+36) 1 464 1997
Web site: http://www.mol.hu

Public Company
Incorporated: 1992
Employees: 16,000
Sales: $7.9 billion (2004)
Stock Exchanges: Budapest Luxembourg
Ticker Symbol: MOL
NAIC: 213111 Drilling Oil and Gas Wells; 211111 Crude
Petroleum and Natural Gas Extraction; 213112
Support Activities for Oil and Gas Field Exploration;
221210 Natural Gas Distribution; 447110 Gasoline
Stations with Convenience Stores; 486210 Pipeline
Transportation of Natural Gas

Hungary's largest company, MOL Rt (formerly MOL Magyar Olaj- es Gazipari Rt) is also the leading integrated oil company in Eastern and Central Europe, beating out Austria's OMV and Poland's PKN Orlen. MOL is active in crude oil exploration and production, largely through a joint-venture in Siberia, as well as refining, transportation, storage, and retail and wholesale distribution. The company operates Hungary's largest service station network, through which it sells its own branded gasoline. In Hungary, MOL operates 400 stations. The company also operates service stations in Croatia and Slovenia. Romania is the group's largest foreign retail market with 130 stations, including 60 stations purchased from Shell at the end of 2004. MOL also operated a natural gas production and distribution business through 2004. In December of that year, however, the company sold most of its money-losing gas business to Germany's E.On for EUR2.1 billion. MOL is listed on the Budapest and Luxembourg Stock Exchanges. The Hungarian government retains a 23 percent stake in MOL. In 2004, the company posted sales of $7.9 million.

First Refinery Operations in the 19th Century

The first efforts to develop an oil industry in Hungary came toward the mid-19th century, with the processing of the crude oil found in shallow deposits in the Transylvania and Mura regions. These supplies were limited, however, and production levels were unable to support and fund the development of a full-scale refinery. The rising demand for oil, in particular for lighting paraffin lamps, forced the region to import oil from other parts of the Austro-Hungarian empire and beyond.

New tax and tariff legislation passed in 1882 provided a more favorable environment for the development of a domestic oil industry. By the end of that year, the country saw its first refinery, built in Fiume. The newly established Hungarian Petroleum Industry Co. began construction on a second refinery in Budapest in 1883. That plant began operations the following year.

Other plants followed, including another refinery in Budapest built by the Budapest Mineral Oil Company in 1891. The number of refineries continued to increase in what was then Hungary, a larger geographic territory than the later modern Hungarian state. By the turn of the 20th century, as many as 13 refineries were in operation.

Hungary's oil sector had further been stimulated by new government policy adopted in 1893 that provided subsidies and other incentives for both domestic and international companies willing to undertake exploration efforts in the region. A number of exploration initiatives were undertaken, while production at the existing shallow oil fields continued. Yet the effort to produce a domestic supply of oil was hampered by a lack of expertise, aging equipment, outmoded technology, and, most importantly, a reluctance to invest capital. By 1905, the total production of crude oil in Hungary remained below 55,000 tons.

In the meantime, demand for oil and oil products rose strongly. The build-up of the empire's army, an ongoing effort launched in the later part of the 19th century, played a major part in stimulating demand for petroleum. By the beginning of

World War I, the country's refineries had neared a total production of nearly 600,000 tons. The empire's reliance on imports left its crude oil supply highly vulnerable.

In 1911, the government adopted a proposal made five years earlier according to which the state would take charge of exploration in the region. The passage of a new Mining Act gave the government a monopoly on oil exploration and production as well as the right to award concessions to both domestic and foreign companies. The government itself set up its own exploration wing, the Treasury Exploration Company, and began exploiting the existing gas fields in Transylvania. A second field, in Egbell, yielded oil in 1914. At the same time, the government awarded the first exploration concession to the United Kingdom's Anglo-Persian Oil Company, for the Mura and Izaszacsal region.

Postempire Production

Hungary's oil exploration and production effort was largely severely undermined by the advent of World War I, although production of natural gas continued at a new site in Transylvania during the war. However, following the breakup of the Austrian-Hungarian empire at the end of World War I, the borders of Hungary were redrawn. All of the country's former oil and gas fields now lay outside of the new country. Meanwhile, the new Hungarian government lacked the funding needed to launch its own exploration operations. Instead, the government turned to the Anglo-Persian Oil Company, which, in 1920, was awarded the exploration concession for a region spanning some 60,000 square kilometers. Anglo-Persian established a new subsidiary, Hungarian Oil Syndicate Ltd., in 1921. After several years of fruitless searching for petroleum deposits, the British company abandoned its concession.

Another company, The European Gas and Electric Company, or EUROGASCO, was granted an exploration concession to the area of Hungary west of the Danube river in 1933. EUROGASCO, initially a joint venture between British and American interests that later came under the control of the Standard Oil Company, launched exploratory drilling in 1934. By 1937, the company had succeeded in located a field in the Budafapuszta and established the Hungarian-American Oil Industry, or MAORT, to exploit the site in 1938.

The Treasury Exploration Company by then had relaunched its own exploration program, searching in the Great Hungarian Plain and in the region around Bukkszek. The exploration of the Great Hungarian Plain was unsuccessful; in Bukkszek, the state-run company drilled some 50 exploratory wells through the 1930s. In 1937, company finally discovered an exploitable site in Bukkszek.

By 1939, MAORT, supplemented by production at the state-run Bukkszek field, was capable of supplying some 90 percent of Hungary's oil needs, and by 1940 nearly 100 percent of the country's oil supply demand was met with its domestic production.

In the meantime, the country had rebuilt its refining industry, since the breakup of the Austro-Hungarian empire had also placed most of the larger refineries outside of Hungary's borders. Only six refineries remained, including the Hungarian Petroleum Industry Co. and the Budapest Mineral Oil company. Following the empire's breakup, the country's smaller refineries were merged into a single company, Fanto Works Co. in 1924. In 1933, Fanto was merged with Hungarian Petroleum Industry and the Budapest Mineral Oil, forming Fanto United Hungarian Mineral Oil Factories Co. Several other refineries were built in the post-World War I period, including Nyirbogdany Petroleum Factory in 1922 and the Szoreg Petroleum Factory in 1931. In 1930, the Anglo-Dutch Shell Company constructed a refinery on Csepel island in Budapest. With a production capacity of 130,000 tons per year, that facility was then Hungary's largest and most modern.

Post-World War II Reconstruction

Hungary's oil industry was temporarily boosted during World War II with the restoration of its former borders. By 1943, the country's refining capacity had topped 800,000 tons. The MAORT production operation, which, along with the Anglo-Dutch Shell refinery and other Allied-owned facilities, was requisitioned by the Hungarian government during the war, continued to supply all of the country's crude oil needs. Other production facilities in the country's reacquired territories boosted production, which neared 850,000 tons per year by 1943.

By the end of the war, however, most of Hungary's oil industry lay in ruins. Whatever had survived the bombing of the country had been stripped clean of equipment by the retreating German army. The restoration of Hungary's borders to their pre-war limits placed a number of refineries and oil fields out of its reach once again. The Soviet Union took over those parts of the country's oil industry that had fallen under German ownership during the war. In 1948 and 1949, the Soviet-dominated Hungarian government carried out a nationalization of the country's oil refinery sector. As part of that process, a number of companies, including Fanto United Hungarian Mineral Oil Factories Co., were shut down.

Under Soviet domination, Hungary set up a new oil company in 1946, called the Hungarian Soviet Crude Oil Co., or MASZOVOL. That company began drilling for oil in Berkboszormeny, on the Great Hungarian Plain. That site was followed by a second drilling site, at Biharnagybajom. The latter site proved more successful, and in 1947 the first oil field was opened in the Great Hungarian Plain. MASZOVOL also began production at a natural gas field in Kaba in 1949.

Exploration and production operations continued into the 1950s. MASZOVOL became MASZOLAJ (the Hungarian Soviet Oil Co.) in 1949, then took over the former MAORT operations in 1952. Exploration operations continued throughout the 1950s, focusing on existing wells in the Trans-Danubian

Key Dates:

1882: The first Hungarian oil refinery is established in Fiume.

1933: Fanto United Hungarian Mineral Oil Factories Co. is created.

1938: MOART oil exploration and production company is established.

1948: The Hungarian oil and gas industry is nationalized.

1957: OKGT, National Crude Oil and Gas Trust is created.

1991: Seven OKGT companies merged to form Magyar Olaj- es Gazipari Rt (MOL).

1995: MOL is privatized with a listing on the Budapest Stock Exchange.

1998: MOL adopts a regional expansion strategy.

1999: The company launches an oil production joint venture with Yukos in Russia.

2000: The company acquires a 36 percent of Slovnaft oil refinery in Slovakia.

2002: Full control of Slovnaft is acquired.

2003: MOL acquires a stake in Croatia's INA.

2004: The company acquires Shell's service station network in Rumania and sells a majority of its natural gas business to E.On.

2005: MOL launches its bid for a stake in Bosnia's Energopetrol.

region and on the potential of the Great Hungarian Plain. A number of successful wells were established, such as at Nagylengyel, which produced some 1.2 million tons of crude oil in 1955. A number of natural gas reserves had been discovered as well, notably in Nadudvar and Rakoczifalva in 1953.

During the 1950s, the Hungarian government exerted increasing control over the country's oil industry. In 1957, the state combined much of the country's crude oil operations into a single, government-owned company, the Orszagos Koolaj-es Gazipari Troszt (OKGT) or the National Crude Oil and Gas Trust. The OKGT also took over the country's natural gas industry in 1960.

Hungary's industrialization in the postwar period stimulated the country's refinery sector. A new atmospheric distillation plant was constructed in 1961, followed by the reconstruction of the Szony refinery in 1962. That year, a new refinery was built at Szazhalombatta in order to refine crude oil from the Soviet Union. The Danube Oil Company was established in 1965, with an initial capacity of one million tons per year, which was then doubled by 1968. Another refinery, in Tisza was established in the early 1970s, becoming the country's largest, with a capacity of three million tons per year.

Eastern and Central European Leader in the 2000s

Throughout the 1980s, the OKGT grew into Hungary's largest corporation, with more than 43,000 employees, and operations stretching beyond oil exploration, refining, and distribution to include machinery manufacture and a variety of other businesses. The OKGT was unusual among other Eastern and Central European oil companies in that it remained a single entity in control of the entire domestic petrochemicals market. Nonetheless, Hungary remained the most open of the Soviet bloc countries and even allowed a level of investment in the domestic industry. Shell, for example, had launched operations in the country in the early 1970s. By the end of the 1980s, a number of other oil industry players, including British Petroleum, Total, Agip, and Aral had been allowed to establish operations in Hungary.

The collapse of Soviet domination in 1989 opened new prospects for the country's oil industry. The Hungarian government quickly opted for a free market economy and began plans to open up the oil industry for competition. As a preparation for this, the OKGT was restructured. Many of the group's unrelated businesses were stripped away, and by 1992 the company's payroll had been cut in half. Seven of the former OKGT-controlled companies were merged together, forming Magyar Olaj- es Gazipari Rt, more popularly known as MOL.

MOL's privatization took place over several stages in the early 1990s. In 1995, the Hungarian government passed a new Privatization Act. MOL reincorporated as a limited liability company and listed its shares on the Budapest Stock Exchange that year, with a float of some 67 percent of its shares. The Hungarian government retained control of the remainder.

In 1998, MOL, now facing competition at home, launched a new strategy to become a regional powerhouse. The company began expanding its network of service stations into neighboring markets such as Croatia, Slovenia, and Rumania. MOL also began looking for acquisition targets among the slowly privatizing markets in Eastern and Central Europe. In 1999, the company reached an agreement with the Croatian government to acquire a large stake in that country's INA oil company. However, the deal fell through.

In 2000, MOL moved into Slovakia, acquiring a 36 percent stake in its Slovnaft refinery. MOL boosted its stake in Slovnaft to full control in 2002. MOL also moved to secure its future oil production, forming a joint venture with Russia's then fast-rising Yukos to win a major concession in Malobalyk, in Siberia, in 1999. MOL's share of the joint venture surpassed its domestic production levels by 2003. In that same year, MOL finally succeeded in buying a 25 percent stake in INA.

MOL's empire building continued throughout 2004. The company added to its network of service stations, notably through the purchase of some 60 stations in Rumania from Royal Dutch Shell in November of that year. One month later, MOL took a step toward focusing itself as a pure oil company player. In December 2004, the company sold off most of its money-losing natural gas business to Germany's E.On for EUR2.1 billion (US$2.7 billion). The sale provided MOL with a war chest for further expansion. In January 2005, the company announced that it was entering the bidding for a stake in Energopetrol, the largest oil company in Bosnia, which went up for sale in March 2005. All evidence suggested that MOL planned to hold on to its position as the top oil company in Central and Eastern Europe into the 21st century.

Principal Subsidiaries

Balatongáz Kft. (Ltd); Geofizikai Szolgáltató Kft. (GES Kft.); GEOINFORM Mélyfúrási Információ Szolgáltató Kft.; KUNPETROL Kiskunhalasi Szolgáltató Kft.; MOL Austria Handels GmbH; MOL Földgáztároló Rt.; MOL INVEST Vagyonkezelo és Értékesíto Részvénytársaság; MOL Natural Gas Supply Plc.; MOL Natural Gas Transmission Plc.; MOL Romania Petroleum Products Srl; MOL Slovensko spol. s.r.o.; MOL-LUB Lubricant Production Distribution and Service Ltd; MOLTRADE-Mineralimpex Kereskedelmi Rt.; MOLTRANS Tankautós Fuvarozó Kft.; Petrolszolg Karbantartó és Szolgáltató Kft.; Terméktároló Rt.

Principal Competitors

Shell Nederland B.V.; Total SA; Crosco doo; OMV Aktiengesellschaft; Polski Koncern Naftowy Orlen S.A.

Further Reading

"All for One, and One for All?," *Economist*, June 30, 2001, p. 2.

Harvan, Rob, "MOL—A Force to Be Reckoned With," *World Refining*, March 2004, p. 6.

Higginson, Matthew, "MOL Buys Stations," *Budapest Business Journal*, November 29, 2004.

"Hungary: Mol Sells Gas Interests to E.On," *Petroleum Economist*, December 2004, p. 39.

"Hungary's New Empire Builder," *Economist*, July 19, 2003, p. 55.

"Mol Has Submitted a Bid with Its Croatian Affiliate, Ina, to Buy a Stake in Bosnia's Largest Oil Firm, Energopetrol, Which Is Majority Owned by the State," *Petroleum Economist*, January 2005, p. 42.

"MOL Looks toward a Regional Role," *Euromoney*, April 2002, p. 60.

"MOL Opens the Door for Gas Sale," *FSU Energy*, September 5, 2003, p.11.

"MOL, OMV Battle for Downstream Supremacy in Eastern Europe," *International Petroleum Finance*, January 2003, p. 9.

"Oil in Eastern Europe—MOL's milestone," *Economist*, April 8, 2000, p. 72.

"State Oil Firm Gears up for Competition," *Petroleum Economist*, September 1992, p. 20.

—M.L. Cohen

Monrovia Nursery Company

18331 East Foothill Boulevard
Azusa, California 91702
U.S.A.
Telephone: (626) 334-9321
Fax: (626) 334-3126
Web site: http://www.monrovia.com

Private Company
Founded: 1926
Employees: 2,000
Sales: $145 million (2002)
NAIC: 111421 Nursery and Tree Production

Operating as Monrovia Growers, privately owned Monrovia Nursery Company is one of the leading nurseries in the United States, supplying more than 5,000 garden centers with approximately 22 million plants in over 2,000 varieties. Plant offerings include more than 45 varieties of camellias; citrus, including limes, lemons, grapefruit, tangerines, and an assortment of oranges; conifers in all shapes and sizes, including pines, fir, cypress redwoods, and spruce; ferns, grasses, and bamboo; perennials such as geranium, lavender, peony, sage, and periwinkle; rhododendrons; shrubs; topiaries (plants trained and trimmed to form ornamental shapes); trees in varieties found around the world; and vines and vine-like shrubs. Monrovia is constantly introducing new plants, relying on its own researchers as well as professional plant hunters who scour the globe for exciting new plants. Monrovia operates nurseries in Dayton, Oregon; Visalia, California; Springfield, Ohio; La Grange, North Carolina; and Cairo, Georgia. All told, Monrovia's operations cover more than 4,700 acres. The plants are shipped in refrigerated trucks, either in a container or as ball-and-burlap. Since the mid-1950s Monrovia has maintained its headquarters in Azusa, California, close to Los Angeles, where most of its growing operations were once conducted. Since 2004, however, Monrovia has begun the process of transferring most of the work to its largest operation in Visalia.

1920s Origins

Monrovia was founded in 1926 by Danish immigrant Harry Rosedale. He started his nursery on ten acres of land in Monrovia, California, and named his business after the town. Rosedale was a visionary in the nursery field. He played a pivotal role in developing the practice of growing plants in containers, thus avoiding the stress involved in uprooting a plant for sale. His revolutionary method resulted in more successful transplants for his customers. He also established the Monrovia tradition for continually searching for new ways to improve production and provide customers with healthier plants. Rosedale also made significant innovations in the way nurseries did business. In the 1940s, Monrovia became the first nursery to follow a set schedule for truck delivery of its plants throughout California and Arizona. Monrovia was the first grower to forego brokers in favor of hiring its own sale force to negotiate directly with garden centers. Then, in the 1950s, Monrovia became the first nursery to begin successfully shipping its container plants across the country, another practice that revolutionized the nursery industry.

Rosedale's innovations resulted in a thriving business, one that by the mid-1950s outgrew its acreage in Monrovia. In 1956, he transferred his operations to Azusa in the lush San Gabriel Valley, although he retained the Monrovia name. Ultimately, he would acquire some 450 acres and become the largest nursery in America. Throughout the 1950s, he continued to build on his record of innovation. Monrovia became the first nursery to establish a research department, which then pioneered the creation of special soil mixes, containing blends of minerals and fertilizers, that helped plants to put down roots quicker and adapt to a new landscape. During the 1950s, Monrovia became the first nursery to replace clay pots with plastic pots in liner production. Monrovia also made news on the business side. It became the first nursery to maintain a sales force in more than one state, and it created a reservation system, allowing retailers to order plants in advance. In this way, Monrovia was better able to match production with demand, and customers were better served as a result. Furthermore, Monrovia became involved in retail, opening a string of Rosedale Garden Centers.

A Trendsetter in the 1960s

Monrovia remained an industry trendsetter in the 1960s. Company researchers continued their work on soil mixes, incorporating time-release fertilizers that extended the shelf life of plants in garden centers, keeping them healthy and flourishing even after they left the controlled conditions of the nursery. Monrovia replaced hand pumps with an automated watering system that included liquid feed, an idea that was then transferred to the nursery irrigation system. In this way, plants received nutrients as they were being watered. In the greenhouses, Monrovia developed a system to spray a mist of water on plants, a practice that helped cuttings to resist disease and resulted in stronger growth. This idea was taken outdoors, leading to the creation of heated outdoor mist beds and a significant increase in the number of rootings that took place.

By 1970, Monrovia had to face up to the environmental impact of its operations. Containerized plants required twice as much irrigation as regular plants, because extra water was used to remove excess salt from the soil mix. However, this practice led to an increasing level of nitrates in the groundwater. Moreover, the nursery knew that it would also be facing a future water shortage. To address these problems, Monrovia became the first nursery to develop a water recycling system, so that runoff water was captured, purified, and reused. It took eight years to create and implement a viable water recycling system. In the system's final form, water flowed into sedimentation pits located at the lower ends of the nursery. Here, gravel, sand, and silt particles settled. Next, flocculating and coagulating agents were introduced to bind fine clay particles, which could then settle out quickly. The water was then pumped through a tall clarifier tank, so that the clay could settle while the clarified water emerged at the top and could then be filtered through a thick layer of anthracite coal, followed by a layer of sand and gravel. Finally, the recycled water was mixed with an equal measure of new water and pumped into the nursery's 1.6 million gallon reservoir. In addition to tainted water, Monrovia also produced a great deal of refuse, such as discarded plants and packaging, prunings, and scrap lumber. These items were subjected to composting, resulting in an organic material that was in many ways superior to peat as a growing medium. For example, it had the ability to suppress plant disease, something peat did not do.

Monrovia pioneered advances on other fronts in the 1970s. It completely replaced traditional metal containers with new plastic pots. Instead of using rubbing alcohol to disinfect pruning shears, the nursery was the first in the industry to rely on the more environmentally compatible monochloramine, which would also play a part in Monrovia's water recycling system. Another first that took place in the 1970s was the introduction of new propagation mist beds. Instead of gravel on dirt, they were crowned with concrete and used copper tubing. Because of the even transfer of heat, the new beds significantly increased the levels of propagation. During the 1970s, Monrovia also became the first nursery to be certified as snail free by the State of California. As a result, the nursery was able to ship its products to many areas of the country where California plants had previously been banned. Also of note, Monrovia shut down its Rosedale Garden Centers in 1971 to concentrate on its thriving wholesale business.

In 1981, Harry Rosedale's son, Miles, joined the company on a full-time basis. Heading the nursery at this stage was Martin Usrey, who had been with Monrovia since 1931 when he started out as a water boy. It was Usrey along with colleague Clifton Comstock who took the lead in expanding the market for container-grown plants during the late 1940s and early 1950s, a time other nurseries had not yet adopted the practice. Usrey was also the one responsible for establishing the first research department in a nursery, which he staffed with trained horticulturists. Moreover, he personally held the patent on 18 plants, such as Mint Julep and Gold Coast Juniper. In 1988, he retired at the age of 76 and was replaced by Miles Rosedale.

Monrovia continued to maintain its reputation as an industry innovator during the 1980s and 1990s. It was the first to use citric acid as a pH water conditioner to replace more caustic inorganic substances. It was also the first to employ a wind tunnel to test the effects of high winds on container plants, information not only useful to garden centers in providing wind protection but also helpful to Monrovia in its selection of new nursery sites. During the 1980s, Monrovia developed natural ways to control weeds such as Liverworts, which plagued Camellias. Researchers discovered that pecan shells included in the mulch of container plants killed Liverworts. Eucalyptus waste was also introduced into container soils to eliminate other weeds. In terms of marketing, Monrovia introduced a number of changes. It provided garden centers with color posters that educated customers about the bloom varieties of a number of plant categories. Monrovia also began to include an information label with its plants that informed customers of the best way to care for their purchase.

Under the leadership of Miles Rosedale, Monrovia expanded its operations, opening wholesale nurseries in Visalia, California, and Dayton, Oregon. The younger Rosedale took over the company during a time of significant change in the nursery industry, which became increasingly driven by the retail side, as big-box retailers like Home Depot, Lowe's, and Wal-Mart gained an increasing share of retail plant sales. To satisfy the needs of these giant customers, who insisted on better service from suppliers, nurseries began to diversify and broaden their plant offerings. Because growing plants required specific expertise, it was understandable that nurseries would begin to consolidate their operations to get a handle on the new status quo. One manager and one nursery could oversee the growing of 100 varieties, but the amount of expertise needed to take on 1000 varieties was beyond the scope of a small grower. The nurseries had to combine to survive, and even a giant like Monrovia had to adapt. In 2001, it merged with Wight Nurseries, a 113-year-old nursery based in Cairo, Georgia, with additional operations in La Grange, North Carolina. Wight also brought with it Berryhill Nursery, located in Springfield, Ohio.

Wight was founded in Cairo in 1887 by J. Byran Wight, a minister who needed to supplement his income. He started out growing fruit trees and nut trees and his descendants grew the business from there. It was run by two succeeding generations, then in 1982 was sold to Weyerhaeuser Co. Nevertheless, a family connection remained in the form of Richard VanLandingham, whose uncle, John B. Wight, Jr. had been the head of the nursery when Weyerhaeuser took over. VanLandingham stayed on as vice-president of operations. He first started working for the nursery in 1965 when he was just 14 years old. After attending Georgia Tech University, dropping out, and moving to California, he returned to Wight in 1972. He became president of Wight Nurseries in 1990 and a year later put together a management-led buyout of the business. In 1995, he oversaw the acquisition of Berryhill Nursery, founded in 1915.

By acquiring the Wight and Berryhill operations, Monrovia was able to bolster its position east of the Mississippi. Moreover, Monrovia broadened its product line by adding Wight and Berryhill's selection of large trees and shrubs. While Monrovia and Wight combined their sales and marketing forces, Wight and Berryhill continued to operate as separate entities. All the growing locations, however, began to offer the same expanded product line. Because Monrovia had operations spread across the country, it was now able to better serve customers, offering greater availability of plants, faster and cheaper delivery, and smaller minimums. Monrovia also reorganized its production approach, establishing two product lines, one to meet the needs of retailers and another for landscape contractors.

New Century Brings New Leadership

VanLandingham was named president of Monrovia's new East Coast operations, and in 2003 he became Monrovia's chief executive officer. He reorganized the business, creating two separate divisions. The Monrovia Nursery Division, which included the California, Oregon, and North Carolina operations, focused on Monrovia's branded products, while the new Wight Nurseries Division used the Georgia and Ohio facilities to produce non-branded products for retail, wholesale, and landscape customers. When VanLandingham took over, he was also charged with selling the Azusa operation, which was now surrounded by suburban sprawl. For several years, the nursery had been attempting to sell a major portion of the property for a housing development, but the plan met with community opposition. As the matter came to a vote in a special election held in May 2004, VanLandingham had to deal with a problem of a different sort, one that potentially threatened the very existence of the company.

In February 2003, it was revealed that camellias at the Azusa nursery had tested positive for *Phytophthora ramorum,* the sud-

den oak death pathogen that had killed tens of thousands of trees along the California and Oregon coasts since it was first discovered in 1995. Although scientists knew that the pathogen had hosts beyond oaks, it was not believed to be able to survive in the hotter climate of Southern California. Some scientists predicted that if it spread, *P. ramorum* could rival the large-scale devastation caused by Dutch elm disease a century earlier. Its appearance in Monrovia camellias, therefore, took the industry by surprise and caused some panic. A few state departments of agriculture took the extreme measure of banning all plants from California. VanLandingham and his staff responded quickly, destroying some 200,000 camellias, many of which were not infected but were merely located within ten meters of an infected plant. Monrovia also assured its customers that it would give full credit for any of its plants that had to be quarantined and would pay for any cleanup costs. Despite a rash of negative publicity, the episode passed without the pathogen spreading. According to VanLandingham, the company's open and decisive reaction to the problem actually served to improve its reputation. Moreover, Monrovia was now the most tested nursery in the country and had put in place preventive fungicide rotations, so that blocks of host plants were kept separate. In this way, the number of plants that would have to be put on hold were limited. Employees also became extremely vigilant about keeping an eye out for symptoms. In truth, no one knew how *P. ramorum* showed up in Azusa in the first place, so there was no assurance that it might not make another appearance in the future.

In May 2004, Azusa voters approved a development plan for the 300 acres Monrovia wanted to sell for a housing development, and the company could now begin transferring workers and operations to the 1,000-acre Visalia nursery. The company retained 100 acres and planned to keep its headquarters in Azusa, where it would also continue to cultivate a handful of varieties that benefited from Southern California's milder winters. Monrovia was well positioned to enjoy ongoing growth and maintain its well earned reputation as an industry leader.

Principal Subsidiaries

Wight Nurseries; Berryhill Nursery.

Principal Competitors

Color Spot Nurseries, Inc.; Griffin Land & Nurseries, Inc.; Hines Horticulture, Inc.

Further Reading

Blizzard, Peggy, "Monrovia Nursery Co. . . . U.S. Biggest," *Southern California Business,* July 1, 1986, p. 7.
Dardick, Karen, "Harry Rosedale Pioneered the Concept of Growing Plants," *Pasadena Star-News,* October 12, 2001.
"Grower of the Year," *Nursery Management & Production,* November 2004, p. 29.
Logsdon, Gene, "Where's the Waste at This Nursery?," *BioCycle,* May 1993, p. 64.

—Ed Dinger

N.F. Smith & Associates LP

5306 Hollister Road
Houston, Texas 77040
U.S.A.
Telephone: (713) 430-3000
Toll Free: (800) 468-7866
Fax: (713) 430-3099
Web site: http://www.smithweb.com

Private Company
Incorporated: 1984
Employees: 300
Sales: $500 million (2004 est.)
NAIC: 423430 Computer and Computer Peripheral
Equipment and Software Merchant Wholesalers;
423690 Other Electronic Parts and Equipment
Merchant Wholesalers

Based in Houston, N.F. Smith & Associates LP is a leading independent distributor of computer components and semiconductors. The company's offerings include everything from inductors, capacitors, resistors, and switches to memory chips, microprocessors, sound cards, monitors, CD-ROM drives, and motherboards. In addition to marketing components and products, Smith & Associates also provides an array of testing services specific to microprocessors, CPUs, memory, CD-ROM drives, floppy drives, and more. Other services include bar code labeling, dry packing and packaging, and component programming. Smith & Associates is a global enterprise, conducting business in more than 20 different languages from office locations throughout the world. In addition to its ISO 9001:2000 certified headquarters in the United States, the company has branches in Spain, South Korea, the Netherlands, Mexico, Hong Kong, and China. Though geographically dispersed, these sites are connected in real time to trading systems and international market information that enable Smith to quickly locate parts for its customer base, which includes both computer equipment resellers and leading manufacturers. One key focus for Smith & Associates has been to smooth out supply chain volatility for its customers. By analyzing and understanding the component market, Smith attempts to forecast upcoming part shortages and surpluses so that manufacturers can bolster or liquidate their inventories accordingly.

A Successful Start in the 1980s

Smith & Associates got its start in 1984, the same year that Apple Computer unveiled its Macintosh and IBM introduced the PC. As the popularity of personal computing exploded, a component shortage soon followed. When manufacturers began searching high and low for parts, brothers Robert and Leland Ackerley were inspired to form their own distribution business. "We got our start helping companies get parts at a time when many parts were allocated," explained Robert Ackerley in the October 30, 2000, issue of *Electronic Buyers' News (EBN)*.

Armed with a $51,000 investment, which included contributions from friends and family, the Ackerley brothers teamed with their wives and established a fledgling home-based distribution enterprise. The new business immediately benefited from a strong market, and the Ackerleys closed their first deal before their start-up even had a name. In fact, they were forced to invoice the sale through a real estate company owned by Robert's wife, Nora Ackerley, called Smith & Associates. The name stuck, and by year's end Smith & Associates was operating from a leased office with a staff of ten employees.

Growth continued at a strong clip throughout the remainder of the 1980s. The company's small staff worked around the clock to serve international markets. "We were a fairly small company, with about 15 or 16 people, but we were working with some of the bigger manufacturers to try and augment their purchasing departments and help them locate product, specifically allocated semiconductors," Ackerley said in the same issue of *EBN*. "The first evolution of our business came in 1988 and 1989, [when] you had the new generation of 386 PCs. We got heavily into importing memory chips from the Far East to supply American manufacturers with DRAMs and augment their existing supply channels."

As the Ackerleys diligently reinvested their profits back into the business, Smith & Associates prospered. By 1991 the company's staff numbered 35 and it had moved to a 15,000-square-

Company Perspectives:

Founded in 1984, Smith & Associates pioneered the Independent Distribution business with a focused, 'can-do' approach. This customer-oriented approach requires a certain passion for getting the job done and it's what has earned us the reputation with our customers as the one to turn to in time of need.

foot facility at 10440 Westoffice Drive in Houston. By this time Smith & Associates had developed a pioneer status among independent American distributors for its emphasis on buying and selling in the international market.

Smith & Associates' sales reached $30 million in 1992. Two years later sales reached $150 million and the company established its Express Components division to concentrate on broker and distributor sales. That same year Smith was recognized as one of 100 privately-owned companies making a significant impact on Houston, Texas, and was listed on the "Houston 100."

National and international recognition soon followed. In 1995 Smith & Associates was named to the "World Trade 100" and also ranked 219 on *Inc.*'s list of the 500 fastest growing companies. That year, the company established a contract manufacturing business called Assembletech. Sales skyrocketed to $367 million in 1995, and employees exceeded 100.

A Distribution Leader: Mid-1990s and Beyond

Heading into the mid-1990s, Smith & Associates had established a leadership position within the independent distribution market. Industry publications frequently listed the company on their lists of top distributors. In 1996 Smith again made *Inc.*'s list of the 500 fastest-growing companies. Fueled by a five-year growth rate of 3,109 percent, Smith rose in the publication's rankings from 219 to 49.

The independent distribution market struggled in 1996. As computer memory prices dropped significantly, a number of independent distributors either folded or downsized. Although its unit sales increased from 1995, Smith saw revenues drop from $376 million to $154.5 million. Even still, the company remained focused on future growth. It formed its ExStock division to buy and resell surplus products on behalf of its manufacturing customers and also created a value-added services division called Reel Technology.

By 1997 Smith & Associates obtained more than half of its revenues from the international market, up from 10 to 20 percent during the company's early years. By this time the company had established offices in Limerick, Ireland; Hong Kong; and Los Angeles.

An exciting development occurred when Smith moved from a two-building, 40,000-square-foot facility to new, 60,000-square-foot headquarters in Houston. In addition to a new purchasing and sales floor and additional space for offices and meeting rooms, the new structure included a state-of-the-art shipping and receiving area, and allowed the company to expand its warehouse and reel and tape operations.

In the January 6, 1997, issue of *EBN*, President Robert Ackerley commented on the move, stating: "The opening of our new headquarters marks a milestone in the history of our company. It serves as a focal point for our commitment to the international market and our ability to meet the challenges of a global industry."

It also was in 1997 that Smith & Associates forged an agreement with Houston-based EnterpriseWorks to handle its IT functions on an outsourced basis. According to a November 18, 1997, *PR Newswire* release, the multi-million dollar deal included help desk setup and support, Web site development, network integration and planning, and software development.

Another development in 1997 was the launch of Smith & Associates' Web site, which included Smith Market Watch, a free service that provided daily prices for microprocessors and computer memory, as well as a channel to request online price quotes. On the heels of these developments, sales improved to $343 million.

In 1998 Smith & Associates created an in-house training program called Smith University. Established with an investment of approximately $1 million, the month-long program sought to reduce learning time for component traders. According to the July 20, 1998, issue of *EBN*, the program involved the construction of a classroom at Smith headquarters, with dedicated training center staff and 26 workstations.

Industry recognition continued in 1998. That year, Smith was named as the leading independent distributor by *Electronic Business*, and as the top non-franchised distributor by *EBN*. Regionally, the company was included in *Current Technology*'s Texas Top 100, along with the likes of computer industry heavyweights Dell and Compaq. Revenues grew significantly over 1997 levels, reaching a record $470 million.

Smith & Associates ended the 1990s by celebrating 15 years of successful operations. In 1999 the company continued to expand internationally with a new office in Amsterdam, the Netherlands. *Purchasing* magazine ranked Smith as the industry's leading independent distributor, and *EBN* once again named the company as the top non-franchised distributor. It also was in 1999 that Smith's Reel Technology division was assimilated into the company's renovated operations facility, and warehouse facilities were expanded. Smith ended the decade with a staff of approximately 137 employees and annual revenue of $282 million.

Several developments took place at Smith & Associates in 2000. That year the company established a new domestic office in Silicon Valley, as well as international locations in Barcelona, Spain; Guadalajara, Mexico; and Seoul, South Korea. Smith also dedicated a 15,000-square-foot warehouse to handle excess inventory and consignment items for its customers.

In addition, Smith combined its ExStock and Express Components divisions under the name SmithMart. A related move was the formation of a new business-to-business Web site called Smithmart.com that enabled real-time component trad-

Key Dates:

1984: Brothers Robert and Leland Ackerley establish a home-based distribution enterprise; by year's end, Smith & Associates operates from a leased office and has ten employees.

1988: Smith begins heavily importing memory chips from the Far East for American manufacturers.

1995: Smith & Associates ranks 219 on *Inc.* magazine's list of the 500 fastest growing companies.

1996: The company forms its ExStock division to buy and resell its customers surplus, and also creates a value-added services division called Reel Technology.

2000: The company establishes a new domestic office in Silicon Valley, as well as international locations in Barcelona, Spain; Guadalajara, Mexico; and Seoul, South Korea.

2003: A New York sales and purchasing office is opened, completing North American expansion efforts.

2004: An office in Shanghai is opened; the Ackerleys appoint Senior Vice President of Corporate Development Doug Kelly as CEO; Smith celebrates its 20th year of successful operations with revenues of $500 million and 300 employees.

ing, instantaneous communications with Smith & Associates representatives, and hundreds of simultaneous real-time excess/surplus auctions. The auction tools, which included short "ultra" auctions and reverse auctions, were mainly intended for other brokers and distributors.

By late 2000 Smith & Associates continued to improve its understanding of component market trends. In addition to insight from years of experience, the company's analyses also involved the use of special tools. In the October 30, 2000, issue of *EBN*, Robert Ackerley explained: "Over the years, we've developed proprietary software that gives us a view of what's happening at the component level in the semiconductor market, so we see trends, what people are buying, what they're looking for. It helps us see a part, something that no one has been asking for, coming from southern Europe or the Far East. It can also tell us that suddenly certain parts are becoming more available, which alerts us that there'll be issues with pricing on those parts."

In 2001 Smith & Associates continued to garner third-party recognition. In addition being named a Top Global Importer by the U.S. Government, *EBN* once again placed the company at the top of its list of leading non-franchised distributors.

In the wake of an economic slowdown and the aftermath of the September 11 terrorist attacks, the tech industry faced tough times in 2001. In addition to massive layoffs, the industry was marked by oversupply and slack demand. In the May 13, 2002, issue of *EBN*, Smith & Associates Executive Vice-President Lee Ackerley indicated that 2001 had been the most difficult year in the company's history.

On the heels of rapid growth and expansion during the latter half of the 1990s, Smith saw its sales drop from $464 million in 2000 to $324.4 million in 2001. Nevertheless, the company did better than the industry as a whole and managed to emerge on solid footing. In the same *EBN* article, Lee Ackerley said: "The downturn in 2001 allowed us to finc-tune the advancements made in the proceeding years, and in spite of the market slump, there were no layoffs or offices closed."

In particular, during 2001 Smith & Associates was able to expand warehouse space at its Houston headquarters, relocate its Amsterdam office to a larger and more technologically advanced site, and also move its Spain office to larger quarters. In addition, the company formed its Corporate Security division and made $100,000 in enhancements to the Smithweb.com site, including a new design; increased browser/platform compatibility; and translations into Chinese, Dutch, German, Japanese, Korean, and Spanish.

In 2002 Smith & Associates was once again recognized by a number of trade publications, including *EBN* and *Purchasing* magazine, for its industry leadership position. Another major accomplishment came when the company was awarded ISO 9001:2000 Certification, after an extensive assessment of its procedures and processes.

In a February 18, 2002, news release, Smith's Vice President of Operations Gary Morrissey said: "Quality is such a fundamental process for Smith & Associates—it's not a standard, it's an obligation. This certification is not about 'bragging rights,' it's a reflection of a company-wide commitment and an essential part of our continual pursuit for a quality operation. All of our offices worldwide are fully dedicated to surpassing customer expectations, increasing management involvement, and continual quality improvements."

In 2002 Smith also completed a $300,000 expansion of its Amsterdam consignment warehouse, which was used to house its customers' excess inventory. The project, which involved the addition of 100,000 square feet in security and racking systems, resulted in overall consignment inventory capacity of 150,000 square feet. Other noteworthy developments in 2002 included business expansion efforts in both Asia and Europe. These initiatives included the appointment of new business operations directors for both regions.

In 2003 Smith & Associates' sales reached $319.2 million, up from $295 million in 2002. That year, the company was one of only 16 U.S. firms to qualify for the U.S. Custom Service's elite Importer Self Assessment (ISA) program. The opening of a New York sales and purchasing office in April completed Smith's North American expansion efforts. From its new Park Avenue location, the company was able to better serve customers on the East Coast. Customers in the central states were served by Smith's Houston headquarters, while its Silicon Valley site—which relocated in 2003 as part of an expansion effort—provided support for clients on the West Coast.

A special accomplishment was realized in 2004 when Smith & Associates was named as North America's leading independent electronic component distributor, as well as one of the top ten distributors in all of North America, by *Electronic Business*.

That year, the company positioned itself to capitalize on the burgeoning Asian market with the formation of a Chinese office in Shanghai. In a March 22, 2004, news release, Leland

Ackerley explained: ''Shanghai is the epicenter of the expanding electronics manufacturing industry in the People's Republic of China. By opening an office here, we are acknowledging the importance of China in our global sourcing network, and we are giving the many OEM and EMS providers in China greater access to our unique suite of technological, financial and logistical resources.''

In June 2004 the Ackerleys appointed Senior Vice-President of Corporate Development Doug Kelly as CEO. Kelly, who assumed responsibility for day-to-day operations, had joined the company in 1995 as chief financial officer. According to the founding brothers, this move was necessary so that they could focus solely on growing the business. As Smith celebrated its 20th year of successful operations, the Ackerleys were halfway to a goal of $1 billion in annual sales. In 2004 revenues reached $500 million and the company's workforce reached 300 employees.

Principal Competitors

TTI Inc.; Richardson Electronics Ltd.; MA Laboratories Inc.; Bell Microproducts Inc.; Avnet Inc.; Arrow Electronics Inc.; America II Inc.; All American Semiconductor Inc.; Advanced MP Technology Inc.

Further Reading

''Co. Moves into New Facility,'' *Electronic Buyers' News*, January 6, 1997.

Cohodas, Marilyn, ''Smith Sinks $1M into Training,'' *Electronic Buyers' News*, July 20, 1998.

Darwin, Jennifer, ''When the Chips Are Down,'' *Houston Business Journal*, August 8, 1997.

''EnterpriseWorks Garners Multi-Million Dollar Contract with Leading High-Tech Company,'' *PR Newswire*, November 18, 1997.

''Graceland Receives $2 Million Gift from the Ackerley Families,'' *Graceland Horizons*, Spring 2003.

''Optimism Reigns at Smith & Associates,'' *Electronic Buyers' News*, October 30, 2000.

Sheerin, Matthew, ''Smith & Associates Upgrades Site,'' *Electronic Buyers' News*, March 20, 2000.

''Smith & Associates Celebrates 20th Anniversary,'' Houston, Texas: N.F. Smith & Associates LP, June 15, 2004.

''Smith & Associates Expands Asian Presence with New Sales and Purchasing Office in Shanghai,'' Houston, Texas: N.F. Smith & Associates LP, March 22, 2004.

''Smith & Associates Expands Warehouse in Amsterdam,'' *Houston Business Journal,* June 3, 2002.

''Smith & Associates Launches Business-to-Business E-Commerce Website,'' *Canada NewsWire Ltd.*, April 11, 2000.

''The 2002 Top 10 Nonfranchised Distributors,'' *Electronic Buyers' News,* May 13, 2002.

—Paul R. Greenland

Nichirei Corporation

6-19-20 Tsukiji, Chuo-ku
Tokyo
104-8402
Japan
Telephone: (+81) 3 3248 2235
Fax: (+81) 3 3248 2119
Web site: http://www.nichirei.co.jp

Public Company
Incorporated: 1942 as Teikoku Marine Products Control
    Company
Employees: 5,770
Sales: ¥496 billion ($4.8 billion) (2004)
Stock Exchanges: Tokyo
Ticker Symbol: 2871
NAIC: 493120 Refrigerated Storage Facilities; 311412
    Frozen Specialty Food Manufacturing; 311612 Meat
    Processed From Carcasses; 311712 Fresh and Frozen
    Seafood Processing; 325412 Pharmaceutical
    Preparation Manufacturing; 333415 Air Conditioning
    and Warm Air Heating Equipment and Commercial
    and Industrial Refrigeration Equipment
    Manufacturing; 424210 Drugs and Druggists'
    Sundries Merchant Wholesalers; 424420 Packaged
    Frozen Food Merchant Wholesalers; 484110 General
    Freight Trucking, Local; 484121 General Freight
    Trucking, Long-Distance, Truckload; 531210 Offices
    of Real Estate Agents and Brokers

Nichirei Corporation has developed a two-pronged leadership strategy in two core markets: processed foods, on the one hand, and, on the other, refrigerated and frozen food warehousing and logistics. The company is one of Japan's leading producers of frozen and canned processed foods, as well as a leading domestic importer and processor of fresh fish and shellfish. Nichirei has also developed a line of drinks and health foods based on acerola berries and has begun extracting cosmetic ingredients from acerola seeds. Nichirei also processes beef and poultry for use in soups, fried chicken recipes, and the like. The company's Temperature Controlled Logistics division, operating through subsidiary Nippon Teion Ryutsu Co. Ltd., is Japan's leading providers of refrigerated and frozen food transport and warehousing services and is also one of the top five frozen foods logistics groups in the world. These operations are carried out in more than 70 logistics centers throughout Japan and the Asian region, as well as in Europe and North America. In addition to food processing and logistics, Nichirei has interests in residential and commercial property developments, including the operation of a parking garage in Osaka. Nichirei's Biosciences division develops antibiotics, cell culture reagents, and active ingredients for cosmetics. The company also develops orchids and other flowers. Nichirei is listed on the Tokyo Stock Exchange. In 2004, the company's sales topped ¥496 billion ($4.8 billion).

Beginnings in the 1940s

Nichirei Corporation was launched in 1942 in order to coordinate the processing, freezing, warehousing, and distribution of the ocean-netted fish and shellfish of some 18 Japanese fishing companies. The new company, originally called Teikoku Marine Products Control Co., operated under legislation enacted that year, the Fisheries Control Ordinance, which regulated the seafood market during the wartime years. With the end of the war, and the lapsing of the control ordinance, Teikoku Marine Products incorporated as a privately held company, changing its name to Nippon Reizon Co. in 1945.

As Nippon Reizon, the company began to branch out, adding a foods wholesaling operation in 1946. That business later became known as Yukiwa Co. Ltd., and remained an important part of the group's activities into the late 1990s. Nippon Reizon's entry into food wholesaling soon led the company to deepen its operations in the foods sector. In 1948, the company expanded its foodstuffs business to including the import and export of a range of products, including canned foods, fertilizers, oils and fats, and animal feed. The company also began processing and selling its own canned goods at this time.

In order to expand, Nippon Reizon listed its stock on the Tokyo Stock Exchange in 1949. The public offering enabled the company to begin investing in expanding its production, notably with the construction of a canning factory in 1951. This marked the company's full-scale entry into the food processing business. One year later, Nippon Reizon launched its first branded line of frozen fish products. By the end of the decade, it added a livestock program in order to insure the supply and quality of fish for its growing food processing business. The company became known for its quality standards, including its insistence on hormone-free and antibiotic-free fish, shellfish, and meats.

Diversifying in the Late 1970s and 1980s

Nippon Reizon changed its name to Nichirei Corporation in 1985. Through this period and into the 1990s, food processing, as well as food import and export operations, remained the major part of the company's business. As late as 1992, foodstuffs still accounted for 83 percent of the company's sales. This segment of Nichirei's operations was boosted in the late 1970s with an expansion into the United States. In 1979, the company established a U.S. subsidiary, Nichirei Foods Inc., which began purchasing food products, including meats, fish, and shellfish, as well as agricultural products, for import into Japan.

The late 1970s and 1980s marked a period of the diversification for the company. In 1977, for example, the company launched a dedicated subsidiary for its transportation and logistics operations. That subsidiary became known as Nippon Teion Ryutsu and grew quickly into Japan's leading refrigerated and frozen foods logistics group. An important step in Teion Ryutsu's development came with the opening in 1986 of a freight-handling refrigerated warehouse. The company also acquired a number of other refrigerated transport specialists, notably in Tokyo and Osaka.

Another area of diversification for the company came in 1982, when the company established its own biotechnology wing. That operation focused on producing antibiotics but was also concerned with the development of other products, including health foods. This latter activity led to the company's commercialization of its first acerola-based product, an acerola beverage, in 1988. Another offshoot of the company's bioscience interests was its entry into the production, wholesaling, and marketing of pharmaceuticals and reagents in 1984. The company also began trading and developing seeds and seedlings at this time.

Nichirei added two more business lines in the 1980s. The company's seed interest led it into the cultivation of flowers, with an emphasis on developing new flower varieties. (Orchids

became a particular specialty for the company.) Nichirei also entered the real estate development market, beginning with such projects as the construction of office buildings, residential apartments, and parking garages.

Reorganization in the 2000s

By the early 1990s, Nichirei had added another wing to its growing empire, that of a network of distribution and service centers. By 1992, the company operated 68 centers in Japan. Nichirei had also boosted its logistics business, merging its three existing businesses into a single, national giant, Nippon Teion Ryutsu, in 1990. In 1992, that business opened a new Kansai logistics terminal, reinforcing its leadership status in Japan's refrigerated and frozen foods logistics sector.

At the same time, Nichirei had launched an international expansion drive as well. The company boosted its presence in the United States, adding six new operations in that market, including a meat processing subsidiary known as Sun Husker Foods and a Seattle-based branch for expanding its frozen fish exports. Nichirei also added a subsidiary in Australia before turning its attention to the European market in the late 1980s.

Nichirei's expertise in frozen and refrigerated foods logistics provided the group's entry into Europe. With the purchase of Eurofrigo in 1988, the Netherlands became the company's first target market in the region. Nichirei next turned to Germany, acquiring Thermotraffic in 1989. The following year, Nichirei boosted its presence in the region with the addition of Holland International Warehousing, known as HIWA. Into the late 1990s, Nichirei's logistics business was primarily directed toward supporting the company's own food processing activities. In 1998, however, Nichirei began providing its frozen and refrigerated foods logistics services to third parties.

In 2000, the company acquired more than 15 percent of Bangalore, India's Snowman Frozen Foods Ltd., becoming the second-largest shareholder in that company after majority shareholder Mitsubishi. Having entered the Chinese market in the 1990s, Nichirei quickly became a major supplier of shrimp and other seafood to that country and opened a subsidiary in Shanghai. In 2004, the company added a second subsidiary in that city in order to market pouch-packed soaps and other products.

Nichirei opened a central research and development facility in Chiba in 1997. By then, the company had developed a number of products and technologies, including a line of special purpose foods for diabetics in the late 1980s and early 1990s. Nichirei also continued working on the development of products from the acerola fruit. These efforts led to the launch of a new cosmetics ingredient extracted from acerola seeds—previously a waste byproduct—in 2004. In the same year, the company unveiled its newly developed frozen fish with edible bones.

The shift of Japan's demographics, accompanied by a zero population growth and the loss of the country's financial luster at the turn of the 21st century, introduced new challenges for the company. In the early 2000s, Nichirei undertook a new Medium-Term Plan that restructured the company around a dual core of food processing and logistics. The company's restructuring continued into the mid-2000s with the launch of

Key Dates:

1942: Teikoku Marine Products Control Company is formed by 18 fishery companies in response to new legislation governing the Japanese fishing market.
1945: The company incorporates as a private corporation under name Nippon Reizo Co. Ltd.
1946: Nippon Reizo begins food wholesaling.
1949: The company makes a public offering on the Tokyo Stock Exchange.
1951: Nippon Reizo establishes a cannery and a food processing business.
1977: A dedicated transportation and logistics subsidiary is formed.
1979: Nippon Reizo opens offices in New York.
1984: The company diversifies into biosciences, pharmaceuticals, and seed and seedling production.
1988: Expansion into the European market begins with the acquisition of Eurofrigo BV in the Netherlands.
1989: The company Germany with its purchase of Thermotraffic.
1990: The company expands its presence in the Netherlands with purchase of HIWA.
1997: A central research and development facility in is opened in Chiba.
2004: A second subsidiary is opened in Shanghai.
2005: The company reorganizes as a holding company for five independent businesses.

a company-wide reorganization at the beginning of 2005. Under this reorganization, Nichirei established itself as a holding company. The company then planned to merge businesses within each of its five primary divisions, which were then to be reincorporated as five independently operated businesses. In this way, Nichirei expected to prepare itself for the coming challenges in Japan's food and food logistics industries.

Principal Subsidiaries

Nichirei Foods Inc.; Nichirei Australia Proprietary Ltd.; Nichirei Carib Corporation N.V.; Nichirei do Brasil Agricola Ltda.; Nichirei Europe S.A.; Nichirei Holding Holland B.V.; Shandong Nichirei Foods Company Ltd.; Shanghai Nichirei Foods Company Ltd.; Surapon Nichirei Foods Company Ltd.

Principal Competitors

Maruha Group Inc.; Agricola International S.A.; John Swire and Sons Ltd.; Christian Salvesen plc; Senko Company Ltd.; Komatsu Forklift Company Ltd.; Mitsui-Soko Company Ltd.; CJ Food System.

Further Reading

"Nichirei Launches New Marketing Unit in Shanghai," *Jiji*, October 1, 2004.
"Japan's Nichirei Develops Acerola Seed Extract for Use in Cosmetics," *Asia Pulse*, March 31, 2004.
"Nichirei Develops Frozen Fish product with Edible Bones," *Japan Food Products & Service Journal*, June 25, 2004.
"Nichirei's Net Profit up but Slumping Sales Cut Full-yr Outlook," *Japan Weekly Monitor*, November 10, 2003.
"Nichirei Found to Have Secretly Recalled Imported Prawns," *Jiji*, October 2, 2003.
"Japan's Nichirei to Take Stake in Mitsubishi Unit in India," *AsiaPulse News*, April 4, 2003.

—M.L. Cohen

NVR Inc.

7601 Lewinsville Road, Suite 300
McLean, Virginia 22102
U.S.A.
Telephone: (703) 761-2000
Fax: (703) 761-2030
Web site: http://www.nvrinc.com

Public Company
Incorporated: 1980 as NVHomes, Inc.
Employees: 3,852
Sales: $4.3 billion (2004)
Stock Exchanges: American
Ticker Symbol: NVR
NAIC: 236110 Residential Building Construction; 236115
    New Single-Family Housing Construction; 522310
    Mortgage and Nonmortgage Loan Brokers

NVR Inc., is one of the largest homebuilders in the United States, with operations in 11 states, primarily in the East, and a large share of that business in the Washington, D.C., area. The company builds, sells, and finances new homes. Its homebuilding unit sells and constructs homes under the trade names Ryan Homes, NVHomes, Fox Ridge Homes, and Rymarc, while NVR Mortgage oversees a variety of financing programs as well as settlement and title services for buyers. Having weathered a rough patch in the 1990s that culminated in a bankruptcy filing, NVR had fully restructured and reemerged by the early 2000s. In 2004, the company reported solid gains that included revenues of $4.3 billion, a 17 percent increase over the previous year.

1980s Origins

NVR's history is relatively short and tumultuous. The company was founded in 1980 as NVHomes, Inc., by Dwight C. Schar. Between 1973 and 1977 Schar served as vice-president and group manager of Ryan Homes, Inc.'s Washington, D.C., operations. From 1969 to 1973 Schar headed Ryan Homes's land acquisition and development efforts in Ohio, Kentucky, and Indiana. Like Ryan Homes, which was founded in 1948,

NVHomes specialized in the construction of single-family homes primarily in the Washington, D.C., area.

By 1983 NVHomes achieved income in excess of $1 million from homebuilding operations on the East Coast. The company continued to grow quickly throughout the early 1980s, doubling its net income each year to nearly $14 million in 1986. In that year, concurrent with its initial public offering, NVHomes was reorganized into a limited partnership and was renamed NVH L.P.

A few months after becoming a limited partnership, NVH acquired a controlling interest in Ryan Homes, Inc. Before the end of 1987 NVH had acquired all of Ryan, making it a subsidiary of the newly formed NVRyan L.P. holding company. Profits continued to skyrocket in 1987 and 1988, with net incomes exceeding $21.5 and $33.5 million respectively. In 1989 the company shortened its name to NVR L.P.

As the company expanded in the 1980s, an organization evolved that was comprised of nearly 100 subsidiaries. By acquiring and establishing new subsidiaries, NVR was able to provide services relating to construction, land acquisition, home finance, investment advice, and other real estate development activities. Through its network of companies, NVR generated profits from almost every phase of the homebuilding and financing process. The company also branched out regionally, entering markets in Florida, California, Indiana, Kentucky, North Carolina, Ohio, Pennsylvania, and Virginia.

Contributing to the success of NVR and its subsidiaries in the 1980s were several factors that prompted housing industry growth in the early part of the decade. For instance, the demand for new homes in the United States rose significantly in the early and mid-1980s, bolstered by a generally strong U.S. economy. In addition, favorable tax laws pertaining to real estate investments, particularly limited partnerships, were enacted by the presidential administration of Ronald Reagan. These laws made it possible, for example, for limited partners to write off losses incurred from real estate investments against personal income. These developments, in concurrence with the deregulation of some lending institutions in the early 1980s, made it easy for NVR to obtain capital for expansion.

Company Perspectives:

As a corporate entity NVR, Inc. provides various support functions for each of its sub-entities. These include essential managerial structures, vital human resource specialists, and an advanced information technology department, which all intertwine to provide a network of resources utilized by NVR, Inc. holdings.

Challenges in the Late 1980s and Early 1990s

Despite strong growth and healthy profits through 1988, NVR began experiencing severe financial difficulties in 1989. By this time, the demand for new housing was beginning to decrease significantly as the economy fell into recession. In addition, changes in the tax code were making it more difficult for companies like NVR to obtain capital. For example, the Tax Reform of 1986 reduced, over time, the benefits derived from investing in real estate and limited partnerships. The result was over-built housing markets in many regions and the subsequent decrease in demand for new homes that continued through 1991.

Although NVR showed a net income of more than $30 million in 1989, the company was severely distressed going into 1990. The company's homebuilding and land development inventory grew from about $400 million in 1988 to over $600 million at the start of 1990. At the same time, revenues from NVR's construction and development activities plummeted from $1.15 billion in 1988 to about $0.9 billion in 1990 and $0.6 billion in 1991. In addition, as the development industry slowed, NVR's assets lost much of their market value. As a result of reduced asset values and operating revenues, NVR posted a net income loss of over $260 million in 1990.

In response to the dire market conditions of 1989 and 1990, NVR adopted a comprehensive business reorganization plan in 1990 that was designed to streamline its operations and reduce further losses. The major goals of the plan, which was implemented in 1990 and 1991, were to: restructure homebuilding operations into two product lines—moderately priced and upscale; reduce homebuilding activity and place all development companies under one management structure; exit all markets except those in the eight mid-Atlantic states in which NVR operated profitably; close several home manufacturing plants; consolidate some finance operations and increase mortgage offerings to customers other than NVR home buyers; and exit speculative land development businesses.

By 1991, NVR maintained two principal business segments: construction and marketing of homes, and financial services, which included both a mortgage and a savings bank. Home construction and marketing activities, NVR's chief source of revenue, was handled through its two primary development companies, Ryan Homes and NVHomes. Ryan Homes, which developed moderately priced single-family units, was responsible for most of NVR's construction activity. NVHomes, on the other hand, concentrated on move-up buyers that were able to purchase relatively high-priced homes yet could not afford custom-built units.

Ryan Homes offered a variety of basic home designs for condominiums, townhomes, and detached houses. In 1992, for instance, it built detached homes ranging from 1,000 to 3,350 square feet in size and from $54,000 to $479,000 in price. The largest homes, which were part of the "Ryan Classics" line, offered amenities such as libraries, sun rooms, cathedral ceilings, hardwood floors, and hot tubs. Although 55 percent of the homes Ryan built in 1992 were detached houses, 35 percent of its dwellings were townhomes. These units ranged from 900 to 2,300 square feet and averaged $127,000 in price. The few condominiums that Ryan built averaged about 1,000 square feet in size and cost an average of $88,200. Although most of its homes were built in the Washington, D.C., area, Ryan also operated in Pennsylvania, New York, North Carolina, and Delaware.

NVHomes developed significantly fewer homes than Ryan, although at a much greater price. For example, the average price of a NVHomes unit in 1992 was $289,100, compared to $137,600 for a Ryan Home development. Because NVHomes catered more heavily to move-up buyers, its homes usually offered four or more bedrooms and at least two and one-half bathrooms. Its larger homes, some priced at more than $600,000, offered luxury amenities such as extra fireplaces and bedrooms, finished basements, and garden rooms. About 30 percent and 12 percent of NVHomes units were townhomes and condominiums, respectively. The company built almost exclusively in the Washington, D.C., metropolitan area.

Both NVHomes and Ryan Homes employed innovative marketing and product delivery techniques to survive in the increasingly competitive market of the early 1990s. For instance, the operations began building homes as they were ordered, rather than by speculation. This was accomplished by first developing a model home in each community being developed. Customers could visit the model home, which also served as a sales center, and choose the floor plan and options that they would like to see integrated into their home. Customers also selected a site within the community. After the neighborhood was fully developed, the model home was also sold. In the case of townhomes and condominiums, construction began only after a significant number of the units in each building had been sold.

Besides building homes as they were ordered, NVR also began to reduce its exposure to risk by not actually purchasing home sites until a customer chose to build on the lot. Instead, after its reorganization, NVR purchased individual options to buy land that were exercised only after home buyers qualified for their mortgages. After the customer qualified, NVR would construct the house using on-site contractors. NVR was able to minimize costs, increase quality, and speed product delivery through its subsidiaries that premanufactured segments of the home in off-site facilities. The ready-made panels were delivered to the site where contractors, under the supervision of NVR representatives, assembled and finished the home. In 1992 NVR completed detached homes in an average of 86 days.

NVR's second principal business activity, financial services, allowed the company to extract greater profits from its homebuilding operations and to generate revenues from unrelated activities. Financial services operations were divided into two functions: thrifts and mortgage banking. In accordance with its goal of streamlining operations and consolidating its finance operations, NVR established NVR Finance in August 1991. NVR Finance assumed all of the mortgage origination and servicing activities that were formerly conducted by several different divisions. In 1992 NVR Finance arranged financing for approximately 75 percent of NVR's home sales. While NVR's construction activities shrunk regionally, NVR Finance expanded its operations to serve several western states. It also sought to diversify by increasing its share of the retail mortgage market. NVR Finance also provided broker title insurance and title search services for NVR's homebuilding services as well as for third parties.

In the early 1990s NVR continued to operate a thrift institution that it acquired through RFS, one of its subsidiaries. RFS acquired Mclean Federal Savings and Loan Association by merger to form a wholly owned subsidiary called NVRSB. NVRSB provided checking, savings, and lending services, and concentrated on lending for home and automobile purchases as well as other consumer finance loans.

In addition to its thrift and mortgage banking operation, NVR was active in real estate investment trusts and mortgage backed securities operations in the late 1980s. These activities were curtailed following the reorganization plan of 1990.

Despite NVR's attempts to minimize losses by reorganizing and streamlining its operations, falling home prices combined with the continued low demand for new construction proceeded to place the company under severe financial stress in 1991 and 1992. In 1991 NVR built just 3,831 housing units, down almost 27 percent from 5,240 in 1990. Furthermore, total company assets continued to decline, from a peak of $2.4 billion in 1988 to less than $1.6 billion by 1991. Although net income losses decreased in 1991 to –$36.7 from –$260.5 million in 1990, NVR's cash flow was still insufficient to meet its obligations to creditors.

In 1992 NVR developed 10.4 percent more homes than it built in 1991. This increase resulted from an increase in new orders in late 1991 and 1992. The increase in orders, however, was partially offset by a further reduction in the average price of NVR's new homes, which fell from $200,000 in 1991 to $189,000 in 1992. NVR realized a jump in revenue of about 5.8 percent, or about $37 million. Even an improvement in sales and income in

1992 was not enough to buoy the company, however. Net income remained negative in 1992, at –$3 million, despite a 26 percent jump in gross revenue over 1991 to $818 million.

Bankruptcy and Recovery in the 1990s

On April 6, 1992, NVR and some of its homebuilding subsidiaries filed for Chapter 11 bankruptcy. NVR Finance's mortgage banking subsidiaries also filed for bankruptcy later in the year. Moreover, the CFO of financial operations fled the country after embezzling funds from the company. Pursuant to its petition for bankruptcy, as well as its default on mostly all of its debts, NVR filed a joint plan of reorganization. The plan was designed to allow NVR to emerge from bankruptcy intact while minimizing losses incurred by NVR creditors.

In addition to problems related to bankruptcy, including claims and suits filed against NVR as a result of default, NVR was also burdened by litigation related to its homebuilding activities. During the 1980s NVR built about 20,000 townhomes and 2,500 condominiums that may have contained faulty fire retardant plywood in their roofs. In an effort to rectify the situation, NVR spent, as of 1993, about $10.8 million. It also planned to spend an additional $9.4 million in the future. As a result, NVR sued both the supplier of the plywood and NVR's insurer to recover these losses.

Despite bankruptcy proceedings in 1993, NVR continued to develop homes in the Northeast and to expand its financial services subsidiaries throughout selected regions in the United States. The company was ranked as the sixth-largest developer of single-family homes by *Builder* magazine.

By the late 1990s NVR had pulled itself out of bankruptcy, had new leadership and ownership, and was taking advantage of the huge economic upturn to develop its strengths. In March 2001 *Forbes* ranked NVR 11th among its Platinum 400 list of strong performers. Since 1996, the magazine reported, the builder had made huge gains in capital growth—in particular a massive 833 percent stock appreciation since 1996. The listing marked a change in Wall Street attitudes toward builders in general and NVR in particular. Construction had traditionally been regarded as too volatile an industry for its stocks to perform strongly over time. The building market was regarded as a place where maverick, risk-taking entrepreneurs worked in an environment too unsettled for long-term investment. NVR's performance on the *Forbes* list—which excluded such high-profile companies as Hewlett-Packard and IBM—changed that attitude almost overnight.

In 1997, NVR acquired Fox Ridge Homes, adding that competitor's name to its roster of brands and thereby establishing a presence in Nashville, Tennessee. Two years later the company added to its mortgage unit with the acquisition of First Republic Mortgage, which it retooled to exclusively serve NVR customers. Despite predictions of gloom from investment analysts anticipating a downturn in the construction market to parallel the downward slide of the rest of the economy in 2001, the housing boom continued into the 21st century. In 2001 the housing construction industry outperformed all other sectors of the economy in Dow Jones and Standard & Poor's industry groupings. In all lists NVR emerged as an industry leader. Gross revenue in 2001 topped $2.6 billion, with net income ROE coming to 79 percent, and the company's price to earnings ratio stood at 11.7. By 2003, revenues had reached $3.7 billion. At the same time, the company's compensation for its top officers tripled, making it the industry leader in payouts to executives as well. Company founder Dwight Schar remained NVR's chairman and retained a small interest in the company.

Principal Subsidiaries

Ryan Homes, Inc.; NVHomes L.P.; NVR Mortgage Finance, Inc.; NVR Savings Bank; Ryan Mortgage Acceptance Corporation (RYMAC).

Principal Operating Units

Homebuilding; Mortgage Banking.

Principal Competitors

Pulte Homes, Inc.; The Ryland Group Inc.; Beazer Homes USA Inc.; Champion Enterprises Inc.; Centex Corporation.

Further Reading

Lurz, Bill, "Builders Shine in Forbes Ranking," *Professional Builder*, March, 2001, p. 26.

Marcial, Gene, "A Low Ceiling at NVR?," *Business Week*, December 9, 2002, p. 138.

Richmond, Iris, "The Producers: A Bullish, High-Profile Performance by the Public Builders Positions Them to Pull Away from the Pack," *Builder*, May, 2002, p. 33.

Serwer, Andy, "A Balloon Bound to Burst," *Fortune*, June 10, 2002, p. 197.

—Dave Mote
—update: Kenneth R. Shepherd

Old Navy, Inc.

1 Harrison Street
San Francisco, California 94105
U.S.A.
Telephone: (650) 952-4400
Toll Free: (800) 333-7899
Fax: (415) 427-2553
Web site: http://www.oldnavy.com

Wholly Owned Subsidiary of The Gap, Inc.
Incorporated: 1994
Employees: 7,000 (est.)
Sales: $6.5 billion (2004)
NAIC: 448140 Family Clothing Stores

Old Navy, Inc., a subsidiary of The Gap, Inc., operates a chain of approximately 850 clothing stores, marketing itself as a low-priced provider of apparel to women, men, children, and infants. The chain operates throughout the United States and in Canada, home to more than 30 stores. Old Navy accounts for approximately 40 percent of The Gap, Inc.'s $15.8 billion in sales.

Origins

The Gap, Inc. represented one of the most impressive success stories in the history of the U.S. retail business. The clothing chain was founded by Donald G. Fisher, whose frustration at finding a pair of jeans that fit led him to open his own clothing store in 1969. Fisher, a successful real estate developer, was 40 years old when he opened the first Gap store near San Francisco State University and attracted crowds of customers a generation his junior. Featuring a broad selection of low-priced blue jeans and records, Fisher's store was the first of what would become a massive chain of stores. After fine-tuning his concept, Fisher expanded remarkably quickly, creating a $100 million, 200-store chain spread across more than 20 states by the mid-1970s. By the end of the decade, the publicly traded chain, which was growing by as many as 80 stores each year, was generating more than $300 million in sales.

The Gap's stunning success during its first decade of existence was eclipsed by its achievements during the 1980s. The company recorded another decade of phenomenal growth, with much of the success credited to Fisher's successor, Millard Drexler, who was appointed president in 1983. A Bronx native, Drexler joined The Gap after serving as president of apparel retailer AnnTaylor. Under Drexler's guidance, The Gap revamped its image, honed its merchandising strategy, and expanded internationally. The company also diversified its interests by either acquiring or starting other retail chains. Drexler achieved mixed results when he branched out, but the successes by far outweighed the failures. In 1983, the company acquired a two-store retailer named Banana Republic, which it tailored as an upscale version of The Gap. In 1986, Drexler started opening a chain of GapKids stores, followed by the establishment of the babyGap chain in 1990. All three, Banana Republic in particular, proved to be highly successful. Failures included Hemisphere, an upscale sportswear chain created in 1987 that was sold two years later, and Pottery Barn, a furnishings retailer that struggled under The Gap's ownership, but flourished under the stewardship of Williams-Sonoma, Inc., which bought the company in 1986 after Drexler and his team cut their losses and liquidated the chain.

After Drexler spent a decade experimenting with different retail concepts, Old Navy became his next creation. The idea for the chain came from Drexler, and his inspiration was drawn from an article in a trade publication. In the early 1990s, Drexler learned that Dayton Hudson Corp., the operator of the Target and Mervyn's retail chains, was planning to introduce a new chain of stores, describing its new entry, Everyday Hero, as a cheaper version of Gap. "I thought, they must know something that we don't," Drexler remembered in a February 29, 2004 interview with the *San Francisco Chronicle*. Drexler sprang to action, ordering assistants to fan out and purchase merchandise in the $10 range at other retail chains. The buyers returned with an assortment of apparel from retailers such as J.C. Penney, Target, and Wal-Mart, and Drexler directed that the clothes be put on a boardroom table at company headquarters. Drexler assembled about a dozen of his advisors and the group surveyed the sampling, trying to assess if The Gap could produce a markdown version of itself. Calls were made to see if overseas garment factories could produce a lower-priced line using less expensive fabrics and finishes. The decision was made to press forward with the concept, and in August 1993, the company converted some of its Gap outlets into the new format, which initially operated under the banner "Gap Warehouse."

The idea was immediately successful. The sales recorded during the first few weeks convinced Drexler and fellow executives that the lower-priced concept deserved its own identity and a format designed specifically for catering to the new demographic. After dismissing suggestions such as "Forklift," Drexler chose the name "Old Navy," having seen an identically named bar while taking a walk in Paris. The first store designed specifically to be an Old Navy store opened in 1994 in a shopping center in Colma, California. At the grand opening, actress/model Cindy Crawford was on hand to sign autographs amid a flurry of media interviews and merchandise giveaways.

With the enormous financial resources of The Gap supporting its growth, Old Navy expanded at a feverish pace. By the end of its first year in business, the chain had 59 stores opened, generating $120 million in sales. In 1995, when the company opened its flagship store in Manhattan, it more than doubled its store count, ending the year with 131 stores and $420 million in sales. The success of the chain surprised even its most optimistic supporters, attracting a broader, more upscale clientele than its creators had targeted. A study conducted by NPD Group at the end of the decade found that more than 70 percent of Old Navy's sales was to households earning at least $50,000 a year. "I don't think any of us in the company ever thought Old Navy would be what it was, and what it became," Drexler said in his February 29, 2004 interview with the *San Francisco Chronicle*. "That's the truth," he added.

Customers flocked to the ever-expanding number of Old Navy stores, creating a retail phenomenon that rivaled The Gap's storied success in the 1970s and 1980s. Inside Old Navy units, which were roughly twice the size of The Gap units, customers could buy $22 jeans ($12 cheaper than a pair from The Gap) and $7 T-shirts in a setting designed to look "industrial chic," with exposed pipes, cement floors, and chrome fixtures. Drexler added to the excitement surrounding the chain by launching the first of a series of quirky television advertisements in 1997, when celebrities from past decades such as Morgan Fairchild and the Smothers Brothers (referred to as "retro-celebrities" by some members of the press) began hawking hugely popular lines of Old Navy apparel. The public's embrace of the Old Navy concept enabled the chain to make business history in 1997 when it became the first retail brand to reach $1 billion in sales in less than four years. The company ended the year with 282 stores and $1.3 billion in sales, a sales volume that represented nearly 20 percent of The Gap's total revenue.

Ming Taking Command in 1999

Old Navy represented the driving force behind The Gap during the late 1990s. More than 100 stores were opened each year in 1998 and 1999, giving the company a total of 513 stores by the decade's end. The company intended to continue expanding at more than 100 units a year for the next several years, a pace mandated by the chain's new president. Jenny Ming was appointed Old Navy's president in April 1999, but she was no newcomer to the company. Ming was there from the start, one of the dozen executives Drexler gathered around the boardroom table to assess the viability of the chain. It was Ming who made the calls to overseas garment factories to determine whether a less expensive line of clothing could be made. A native of a Portuguese colony near Hong Kong named Macao, Ming moved to San Francisco at age nine. After earning a degree from San Jose State University, Ming was working as a buyer in linens and junior wear at Mervyn's when Drexler recruited her in 1986.

Under Ming's stewardship, Old Navy continued to expand, with its success playing an increasingly important role in the health of The Gap. Old Navy accounted for 16 percent of the total number of stores operated by its parent company, but accounted for nearly 30 percent of its sales volume, a ratio that placed enormous pressure on Ming. To strengthen Old Navy's position as The Gap's growth vehicle, Ming intended to expand aggressively, relying on her widely praised ability to predict emerging apparel trends and greatly widen their appeal by filling Old Navy units with hip-looking merchandise. "She gets very excited about the merchandise," a colleague explained in a November 8, 1999 interview with *Business Week*. "She's definitely a toucher and feeler. When she sees something she likes, she winks, claps her hands, and says, 'I love that'."

Ming's tenure began strongly and then faltered, resulting in Old Navy's first setback. Within months of her appointment, speculation circulated throughout the apparel industry that Old Navy was plotting its first international expansion. The Gap's chief financial officer confirmed analysts' theories, announcing in August 1999 that Old Navy was close to establishing its first foreign store, a move that was going to be made in either Japan, the United Kingdom, or Canada. While senior executives mulled over their decision, Ming presided over the opening of the largest Old Navy store in the five-year history of the company. In November 1999, a massive, four-level store was opened in San Francisco, the fourth flagship store opened by the company (New York, Chicago, and Seattle were home to the other three flagships).

Old Navy stumbled for the first meaningful time in 2000, and the timing could not have been worse for The Gap. The sprawling retailer began recording declining sales, guilty, according to critics, of pursuing fickle teenage customers and alienating its over-30 customers. By October 2000, the company had posted five consecutive months of same-store sales declines, while its stock value plummeted 57 percent. The downward spiral dragged on, culminating in a $7.7 million loss in 2001—two years after the company had recorded $1.1 billion in net income. Old Navy, which for several years had helped to compensate for The Gap's miscues, offered little help. Plans for the company's international expansion were derailed by distribution problems that bogged the chain with excess inventory. "Right now," an analyst commented to the *San Francisco Chronicle* in August 11, 2000, "Old Navy is driving in reverse."

International Debut in 2001

Although The Gap continued to suffer during the beginning of the new century, Old Navy managed to recover from its choked-up distribution system. In 2001, the chain made its international debut, compensating for the delay with a forceful entry into Canada. In April 2001, Old Navy opened 12 stores in the province of Ontario, orchestrating the maneuver on the same day early in the month, the first multiple store openings executed by the company on the same day. "We really wanted to be able to have a strong presence from the start," Old Navy's director of public relations explained to the *San Francisco Chronicle* on April 10, 2001.

As Old Navy closed in on its tenth anniversary, its pace of adding at least 100 new stores annually began to slow. By the end of 2002, the chain consisted of 842 stores, having added 44 units during the year. In 2003, the company increased its store count by only one store. The same was true of 2004, as Old Navy ended the year with 844 stores. The majority of the expansion during these years took place in Canada, where Old Navy operated 33 stores in 2004.

Despite the negligible expansion achieved in the years leading up to its tenth anniversary, Old Navy represented a powerful retailing force. After only a decade, the chain accounted for approximately 40 percent of The Gap's nearly $16 billion in revenue, figuring as an incredibly important business to its parent company. As Old Navy prepared for its second decade of business, the chain promised to remain the lifeblood of The Gap and a popular choice among bargain hunters for years to come.

Principal Subsidiaries

Old Navy (Apparel), LLC; Old Navy (Canada) Inc.; Old Navy (East) L.P.; Old Navy (Holdings), LLC; Old Navy (ITM) Inc.; Old Navy (Puerto Rico) Inc.; Old Navy, LLC.

Principal Competitors

Wal-Mart Stores, Inc.; Target Corporation; J.C. Penney Corporation, Inc.

Further Reading

Devaney, Polly, "Now Gap Has Something to Sing and Dance About," *Marketing Week,* February 27, 2003, p. 32.

Emert, Carol, "Old Navy Brings Gap Earnings Down," *San Francisco Chronicle,* August 3, 2000, p. C7.

Jones, Adam, "Gap May Start Old Navy Roll-Out in UK," *The Times,* August 13, 1999, p. 31.

Kingston, Anne, "Bridging the Gap," *National Post,* May 4, 2002, p. 13.

"Old Navy Crosses Canadian Border," *San Francisco Chronicle,* April 10, 2001, p. C4.

Ozzard, Janet, "Analysts Await Gap Comeback," *WWD,* October 27, 2000, p. 2.

Rozhon, Tracie, "Not Enough New at Old Navy?," *New York Times,* December 8, 2004, p. C2.

"A Savvy Captain for Old Navy," *Business Week,* November 8, 1999, p. 130.

Strasburg, Jenny, "Retailer's Cheap Thrills; Gap Inc. Fights to Keep Young at Old Navy," *San Francisco Chronicle,* February 29, 2004, p. I1.

Walkup, Carolyn, "Torpedo Joe's to Open in Four Old Navy Stores," *Nation's Restaurant News,* August 17, 1998, p. 8.

—Jeffrey L. Covell

Overhead Door Corporation

1900 Crown Drive
Farmers Branch, Texas 75234-6028
U.S.A.
Telephone: (972) 233-6611
Toll Free: (800) 275-3290
Fax: (972) 233-0367
Web site: http://www.overheaddoor.com

Wholly Owned Subsidiary of Sanwa USA Inc.
Founded: 1921
Employees: 3,000
Sales: $675 million (2003)
NAIC: 332321 Metals Window and Door Manufacturing

A subsidiary of Japanese-owned Sanwa USA Inc., Overhead Door Corporation is primarily involved in the garage door business. The Farmers Branch, Texas-based company is comprised of three operating divisions: Access Systems, Horton Automatics, and TODCO. The largest division is Access Systems, operating out of Dallas, Texas. It offers the Overhead Door and Genie lines of garage doors and openers, as well as wet/dry vacuums. In addition to garage doors and openers, Hudson, New York-based subsidiary W.B. McGuire manufactures commercial sectional door systems, rolling steel door systems, high-speed traffic doors, and loading dock equipment. Horton Automatics, operating out of Corpus Christi, Texas, concentrates on the automatic entrance market, manufacturing such products as automatic doors, revolving doors, security access doors, and automatic sliding windows. Horton serves a number of commercial customers, including airports, casinos, convenience stores, government buildings, hospitals, hotels, nursing homes, office buildings, and supermarkets. TODCO, an acronym for the Overhead Door Corporation, is based in Marion, Ohio, and makes overhead and swinging truck and trailer doors.

Company Founded in 1920s

Overhead Door was founded in Detroit, Michigan, by C.G. Johnson, who early on in the history of the automobile recognized that the growing number of automobile owners would want to store their vehicles indoors and out of the elements. The obvious answer was to use or build a shed with swinging doors, but such doors tended to sag and were easily blocked. Some had tried a window blind approach to making an overhead door, but these attempts were bulky and prone to jamming. Johnson conceived of a sectional garage door that could be lifted straight up and over the vehicle. Moreover, by making it counterbalanced it would require little strength to use and be easy to operate. Johnson is credited with inventing the first upward-acting overhead garage door in 1921. His concept was both elegant and functional, and only required a simple demonstration to sell it. In 1921 Johnson and Detroit attorney Forest E. McKee formed a company to manufacture and market the invention, A year later, McKee's brother, Paul W. McKee, a bank cashier, joined the company as well.

At first the business hand built one door a day in a two-story barn located on Rohns Avenue in Detroit. The company began efforts to promote its product, first demonstrating it at the 1923 New York automobile show. Johnson then built a miniature garage with one of his upward acting doors, mounted it on the back of his Model T Ford, and along with his wife, visited county fairs throughout the Midwest to drum up sales. He was so successful that he was unable to build and install overhead doors for such a large area. Instead, he franchised the territorial rights to manufacture and sell the doors to independent operators across the country. It was at a demonstration in 1923 at the Indiana State Fair in Indianapolis that members of the Hartford City, Indiana, Chamber of Commerce saw Johnson's door and invited him to make an appearance at Hartford City's annual fall fair. When it was shown there, the people of Hartford City were so enthusiastic that they convinced Overhead Door, which was looking for a new home, to move its operation there. The town boosters lined up shareholders to provide the funding the company needed to build a manufacturing plant in the small town. It was an offer the young company could not refuse, and in 1923 the headquarters were moved to Hartford City and the business was incorporated in Indiana as the Overhead Door Corporation. In April 1924 the 1,000-square-foot facility was completed and Overhead Door relocated its primary manufacturing operation from Detroit to Hartford City.

During the first few years at Hartford City, Johnson made constant improvements to his overhead door: adding new hinges, rollers, a channel track and a patented wedge closure system to create a weather-tight seal. In 1926 the company introduced the first electric opener for commercial doors. The technology would be extended to residential doors in 1950. In addition to providing his mechanical skills Johnson also served as president of the company until 1935, when Forest McKee succeeded him. McKee saw the company through the remaining years of the Depression and World War II, during which Overhead Door installed many units for the Army and Navy and also made parts for Crosley Corporation, Sylvania, Packard Motor Car Company, and the Dodge division of Chrysler Corporation. Business was so strong during this period that in addition to its franchised manufacturing operations the company opened plants across the country, including in Dallas, Texas. Following the death of Forest McKee in 1951, his brother Paul assumed the presidency. In 1956 the company transferred its expertise in making upward-acting sectional garage doors to trucks and trailers, forming TODCO. Increasing demand for the new product line led to the unit relocating to a new plant in Marion, Ohio.

The 1960s–70s Bring Steady Growth

In the 1960s Overhead Door began to buy out the franchised operations that had served the company so well in the early years. It also remodeled existing facilities and opened new door manufacturing plants in Athens, Georgia, and Shelbyville, Indiana, and a hardware and electric operating plant in Covington, Kentucky. In 1964 the company, which at this point was generating more than $25 million in annual sales, was taken public and its stock began trading on the American Stock Exchange. Because of its new status, management felt that the company needed to establish its headquarters in a larger city. Thus, with the retirement of Paul McKee in 1965, the company relocated to Dallas, where Overhead Door continued its expansion program. In 1966 the company acquired a West Coast manufacturer that added rolling metal doors to its slate of products. This business was then supplemented by an expansion in the Dallas operation and the 1967 acquisition of New York-based Caltron Industries, a Flushing, New York, company that made rolling, fire doors, and counter doors, as well as decorative grills. Moreover, Caltron gave Overhead Door an East Coast manufacturing base. Also in 1967 Overhead Door opened a plant in Covington, Kentucky, to produce all of the company's hardware and electric door operators. The decade closed with the purchase of Philadelphia, Pennsylvania-based Snyder Doors Inc. and its subsidiary, New Hampshire Doors, Inc., and a Fort Worth, Texas, company, McLeland-Harris Door. Co. Also in 1968 Overhead Door added hydraulic lift gates for trucks and trailers by acquiring Watson-Atlas Co. In addition, Overhead Door expanded its core residential door business by making use of

new materials: fiberglass, aluminum, and steel. Overhead Door closed the 1960s with sales growing well beyond the $50 million mark.

In 1970, Overhead Door moved into the automatic sliding door and sliding window markets by acquiring Horton Automatics. The company was founded in Corpus Christi, Texas, by Lew Hewitt and Dee Horton. They invented the automatic sliding door in 1954 and essentially started a new industry. Their inspiration was the gusty South Texas winds that had a tendency to cause conventional push-pull doors to fly open or slam shut, resulting in countless panes of shattered glass and sometime personal injury. The two men knew the problem firsthand because they worked for Horton Glass Company and spent a good deal of their time repairing damaged glass doors. They developed an automatic sliding door that initially relied on a mat actuator, a device that was not subject to the vagaries of the wind, and installed their first unit for free at the city's utilities department. They began to sell their automatic doors in 1960, installing the first one in a hotel restaurant in Corpus Christi. They patented the invention in 1964. Hewitt would also invent the automatic sliding window, and after Overhead Door bought the business he stayed on as general manager, later becoming president.

In the 1980s, Overhead Door launched an aggressive effort to diversify in answer to the cyclical nature of the garage door industry, due to its close ties to housing starts. The company completed a number of acquisitions in the early part of the 1980s to add other product lines, spending $37 million from 1980 to 1984 on capital expenditures. In 1984, for instance, it acquired Veach-May-Wilson Inc., a Tennessee company that manufactured hardwood flooring for trucks and trailers. At the same time, Overhead Door bought Insoport Industries Inc., a Williamsport, Pennsylvania-based maker of laminated foam panels. It also bought eight sawmills located in Virginia, West Virginia, and Kentucky. In addition, Overhead Door added such items to its product mix as sliding patio doors, revolving doors, aluminum windows, and fireplaces. Because of this expansion, the company posted record results in 1984, with revenues of $381 million and profits of $16.6 million. The goal was to become a Fortune 500 company by the end of 1985. To emphasize the changing nature of the business, management elected in January 1985 to change the name from Overhead Door, which was considered too limiting, to Dallas Corporation. The company was also reorganized into three divisions: the original Overhead Door business, vehicular equipment, and specialty products.

Dallas Corporation introduced more than 20 new products in 1985, but the company appeared to have attempted to grow too quickly and was left vulnerable when housing starts declined and the truck and trailer industry fell into a slump. Moreover, the price of hardwood lumber dropped, causing problems for the company's sawmill operations, which became a particular drain on resources. Dallas Corporation quickly moved to sell the sawmills. It also cut back production at some of its plants, including the original operation at Hartford City.

Challenges in the Late 1980s

In the second half of the 1980s, Dallas Corporation struggled to find a new identity. It also suffered from some unforeseen problems. A Pennsylvania unit, Heritage Door Co., was partially damaged by a fire, which halted production. The plant was subsequently closed and adversely impacted the company's earnings. Dallas Corporation was also hit with an antitrust case concerning conduct that dated back to the early 1970s. A Florida company, Telectron Inc., manufacturer of radio-operated garage door openers, charged that Overhead Door tied the sale of its garage doors to its radio control units, thus making it difficult for Telectron to compete. The two companies reached a settlement in 1987, costing Dallas $5.9 million and cutting into earnings for the year.

Dallas completed one significant acquisition during this period, purchasing Hudson, New York-based W.B. McQuire Company in 1987, a move that added loading dock traffics doors and other loading dock equipment, including mechanical or hydraulic dock levelers, seals or shelters, and safety truck restraints. The move into loading dock products, however, was one of the few successes Dallas had in its diversification drive. In late 1988, the company decided to return its focus on the garage-door business and took steps to sell off four units that made hardwood flooring and other residential building products. In 1989, the company was taken private when a management team in concert with New York securities firm Bessemer Capital Partners engineered a $180 million leveraged buyout. As part of a succession plan, there was also a change in leadership. The company's CEO, Robert C. Haugh, who had held the post for 23 years, stepped aside in favor of Brian J. Bolton, who had worked for the company from 1973 to 1979, then left to become president and chief operating officer at Aircondex, Inc., involved in air conditioning and refrigeration. He returned to what had become Dallas Corporation as chief operating officer and director in 1987 and prepared to succeed Haugh. Under Bolton, the company discarded the Dallas name and reverted back to Overhead Door.

Buyout and Reorganizations: 1990s and Beyond

Overhead Door struggled during the recession years of the early 1990s, posting net losses in 1990 and 1991. Part of the problem was that the company had taken on too much debt during the diversification push a decade earlier. To reduce its debt load of some $120 million, Overhead Door proposed a $90 million bond offering in the fall of 1992. The company then took steps to make a stock offering in hopes of raising as much as $125 million by selling a 49.7 percent stake in the company. However, both offerings were put on hold. In the meantime, Overhead Door took on even more debt by acquiring rival

garage door manufacturer GMI Holdings, better known as the Genie Company, from Brynwood Partners II LP for $184 million. The money was cobbled together from a $145 million loan and a $75 million revolving credit line provided by Chemical Bank. In addition, Bessemer helped to finance the deal by making an equity investment of $42.3 million. Although Overhead Door was already burdened by debt, it was an acquisition that all parties believed was necessary to remain competitive in a mature industry that had been undergoing consolidation in recent years. It was also a very good fit, given that Genie was the market leader in residential garage door openers and Overhead Door was the leading maker of residential and commercial garage doors. Genie also produced home and shop vacuums, which Overhead Door elected to retain, in keeping with its history of allowing acquisitions to operate as stand-alone businesses. Genie's management team also remained in place.

The history of Genie dated back to 1923 and the founding of Alliance Manufacturing Company, named after the city its was based in—Alliance, Ohio. The company possessed strong electrical engineering capabilities which it used to produce a wide variety of consumer, industrial, and military products. In 1954, to take advantage of the post-World War II housing boom, Alliance entered the garage door market by producing the first mass-produced, radio-controlled residential garage door opener. It called the product Genie. Within a year, Genie became the company's principal product line, although during the 1960s the company continued to make such items as electric toothbrushes, kitchen appliances, and rotating television antennas. Genie also continued to be an innovator in the garage door industry. In 1958, it introduced the first screw-drive opener, and later in the 1970s it produced a split rail garage door that could be shipped unassembled for the do-it-yourself market. Along the way, Genie also replaced chain drives with quieter screw mechanisms and developed security features. In 1983, the company diversified by adding home and shop vacuums and two years later introduced a trash compactor. The Genie assets were sold to GMA Holdings in 1990.

Overhead Door never completed its proposed stock offering. Instead, the company was sold to Sanwa Shutter Corporation, a Japanese company that paid $470 million for the business. The assets were then assigned to a newly formed subsidiary incorporated in Delaware, Sanwa USA Inc. Sanwa was founded in Hyogo, Japan, in 1956. Its relationship to Overhead Door dated back to 1974, when the two companies forged a technical alliance. Bolton stayed on to run Overhead Door for the new owners, serving as CEO and chairman.

While Sanwa opted to pull out of the U.S. market on some fronts, closing down its investment banking unit, it appeared committed to growing Overhead Door. However, information about the health of the business was now hard to pry free from new ownership. In 2000 Overhead Door restructured its operations but did not explain the reasons behind the move. In any event, the company laid off nearly 400 employees. Plants in Salem, Oregon, and Muncie, Indiana, were closed as well as the facility in Hartford City. It was a difficult blow for the small town of Hartford City, where Overhead Door had made its home some 80 years earlier and where many residents had worked for 20 or 30 years. Overhead Door retained 17 other plants and was also in the process of building two dozen warehouses across the country. In addition, there were changes at the top at Overhead Door in 2000. Bolton announced his retirement. He was replaced as chief executive by director Masat Izu, whose tenure would be brief. He was replaced by Howard Simmons, and then in February 2001 Dennis Stone was hired as president of the Door Group and was subsequently named CEO. Stone had worked for 20 years at Intotek Corporation and during the previous five years served as president and led a successful turnaround of the distribution and service organization.

As Overhead Door entered the 2000s it clearly had global ambitions. Already holding a strong market share in the United States and Japan, it staked out a position in Europe in 2003 by acquiring Novoferm group, the second largest door and shutter manufacturer in Europe. Despite a scarcity of information, there was every reason to believe that Overhead Door was doing well under Japanese ownership and that it was ready to enjoy even greater growth in the years to come.

Principal Divisions

Access Systems Division; Horton; TODCO.

Principal Competitors

General American Door Company; Griffon Corporation; NCI Building Systems, Inc.

Further Reading

Bounds, Jeff, "About 300 Layoffs Set at Five Rea Companies," *Dallas Business Journal*, March 10, 2000, p. 24.

Campanella, Frank W., "Growth at Overhead Door Hinges on Aggressive Sales and Know-How," *Barron's National Business and Financial Weekly*, April 7, 1969, p. 40.

Simnacher, Joe, "Dallas Corp. Returning to Old Name," *Dallas Morning News*, March 16, 1990, p. 2D.

Zuckerman, Steve, "With a New Name, Dallas Corp. Begins to Diversify Operations," *Dallas Business Journal*, September 30, 1985, p. 8.

—Ed Dinger

Peter Piper, Inc.

6263 North Scottsdale Road, Suite 100
Scottsdale, Arizona 85250
U.S.A.
Telephone: (480) 609-6400
Fax: (480) 609-6520
Web site: http://www.peterpiperpiza.com

Private Company
Founded: 1973
Employees: 50
Sales: $39 million (2003)
NAIC: 722110 Full Service Restaurants

Peter Piper, Inc. is the Southwest's leading family pizza and entertainment restaurant chain. The company and its franchises operate more than 150 pizza parlors throughout the southwestern United States and the Republic of Mexico. Its facilities range in size from 8,500 to 10,000 or more square feet and provide an abundance of seating and entertainment options, including big screen televisions, video games for teens and live-wire games, prizes, and play areas for small children. The restaurants serve a variety of pizza styles and toppings along with other items, including bread sticks, chicken wings, and salads. Most Peter Piper locations offer delivery service as well as dine-in seating. The company is backed by investment firms Venture West Group and Madison Dearborn Partners.

Origins

Peter Piper Pizza was founded in 1973 by New York native Tony Cavolo, a colorful owner and television pitchman whose thick New York accent made the chain's early TV campaigns memorable. Cavolo opened his first pizza parlor in Glendale, Arizona, with three guiding principles in mind: provide a quality pizza, sell it at a reasonable price, and make dining in his restaurant fun for kids of all ages. The operation first started out primarily as a pizza restaurant but slowly grew into the gaming business, from three to five games in the beginning to forty to sixty games later on. The formula proved to be a success, and by 1992 Peter Piper had established a regional chain of 100 dine-in/ delivery/carry-out restaurants operated through ownership and franchise. The restaurants were located in Arizona, California, Colorado, New Mexico, Oklahoma, Texas, as well as Mexico.

Investors Buy Peter Piper in the Early 1990s

In November 1992, The Venture West Group, Inc., an Arizona investment company, acquired a majority and controlling interest in the Peter Piper. Venture West recruited new senior management and implemented a revitalization program to update and revitalize the Peter Piper concept. In July 1995, Peter Piper received a $12.8 million cash investment from Madison Dearborn Capital Partners P.P., a $1 billion Chicago-based investment firm that specialized in funding privately held companies. Mushtak Kahatri, the Madison Dearborn analyst overseeing the investor's stake in Peter Piper, refused to comment on future plans for the company. In August 1995, however, Peter Piper applied part of the financing to acquire its hometown and regional competitor, the 30-restaurant Pistol Pete's Pizza, and planned a program of conversion, renovation, and expansion to comport with the Peter Piper concept. The acquisition fit into the company's strategy of expanding its brand and updating its units, following a Phoenix prototype that was larger than its existing pizza parlors and featured brighter colors, games, and a menu of moderately priced counter-service pizzas. Peter Piper president Joseph R. Pederson said it was not the company's intention to expand the Pistol Pete concept but instead to convert all company-owned restaurants to the Peter Piper banner. The conversions would boost the company's business to 40 owned and 85 franchised stores.

Both Peter Piper and Pistol Pete's had similar business concepts in that they combined pizza and entertainment. However, Pistol Pete restaurants tended to be larger than those of Peter Piper, averaging 13,000 square feet to Peter Piper's new prototype size of 8,000 to 10,000 square feet, which seated around 300 patrons and allotted more than a quarter of its space to video games and other such machines. According to Pederson, the goal was to take a sleepy concept with a definable niche and take it national. With the acquisition, the company anticipated combined sales to exceed $100 million versus its previous annual sales of about $75 million.

On September 23, 1996, Rick Campbell, owner of the last two remaining Pistol Pete outlets, filed suit against Peter Piper, claiming that the company was attempting to monopolize the El Paso, Texas, pizza-restaurant market. Campbell alleged that Peter Piper and other parties had conspired to restrict his expansion in the market, had violated his franchise agreement, and had prevented him from converting his restaurants to the Peter Piper concept as other franchisees had done. The company, however, claimed that it had been supportive of Campbell's operations and denied violating any state or federal laws.

Peter Piper Rapidly Expands in the Mid- to Late 1990s

In November 1996, the company named C. Ronald Petty, the former president and chief executive officer of Denny's Inc., as its new chairman, president, and chief executive officer. After successfully turning around the 1,600-unit family restaurant chain over the previous three years, Petty took the helm of Peter Piper, a $100 million company ranked among the top-ten pizza-restaurant chains in the United States, in the middle of an aggressive expansion plan. Before joining Denny's, Petty spent twelve years at Burger King Corp., where he was president and chief operating officer for the chain's domestic division. He succeeded Joseph R. Pederson, who successfully positioned Peter Piper for growth and who returned to Michigan to become principal owner of a multi-unit restaurant company and real estate concern. At the time of Petty's recruitment, the company had 125 restaurants in seven southwestern states and Mexico with projected growth of 30 percent for the next three years.

The company focused on a basic pizza at a modest price of $6.59 for a large one-topping pie and attracted families with a combination of pizza and entertainment, including about 30 to 50 video and virtual-reality games, but not playgrounds like those at Chuck E. Cheese restaurants. Half of its sales were from take-out orders. The chain did not own the games but had an agreement with a supplier that rotated fresh games and split the revenue with the restaurants. The age appeal of the games presented a critical difference between the company and much of its fun-centered competition, which focused more on small children. Unlike its competitors, Peter Piper had gaming attractions that appealed to 17-year-olds as well as to five-year-olds. In the prizes linked to the games, the company enhanced value by offering coupons that could be saved up and redeemed for brand-name merchandise, including audio equipment, sporting goods, mountain bikes, and, in some markets, washers, dryers, and refrigerators. Under Petty, the company planned to augment its franchise growth by opening between 15 and 35 restaurants a year.

By July 1998, Peter Piper had signed eight franchise development agreements to open 137 new restaurants in three to five years. The restaurants were planned for California, Texas, Oklahoma, and Mexico. The company also planned expansion in the Midwest and on the East Coast. The company withdrew efforts to move into the Florida market due to cost but opened its first Michigan restaurant in June 1998 and one month later entered the Austin, Texas, market. The Austin market was targeted after the company conducted national demographic research, looking for households with 3.8 to 4 people. In 1999, citing favorable demographics, Peter Piper announced plans to open 80 branches of the pizza-and-games chain in the Los Angeles and San Diego areas over the next seven years. Southern California had long been an expansion target for the company, which had a large following among the Hispanic community. Ronald Petty, who left the company in 1998 to head a 340-unit Del Taco Inc. in Laguna Hills, California, observed that Los Angeles and Riverside counties included areas that were about 60 to 70 percent Hispanic. After Petty's departure, the company was run by interim president Neil R. Simon and executive director of operations Greg Barton.

Despite its rapid growth, the Peter Piper chain, was still dwarfed by such leading competitors as Domino's and Pizza Hut. It was therefore anticipated that Peter Piper would face stiff competition in the Southern California market, where national chains had a strong presence and western regional chains such as Round Table Pizza, based in the northern California city of Walnut Creek, had a loyal consumer base. Round Table alone had 540 restaurants, with about 100 in Southern California, and had plans to add another ten company-owned and franchised units in the area in 1999. In addition, Papa John's International out of Louisville, Kentucky, which ran the country's fourth largest chain with 2,061 restaurants, planned to add 200 units in Southern California by 2004. Nevertheless, approximately half of pizza chain customers in Southern California had children less than 18 years old, a group that Peter Piper directly appealed to with its game arcades.

In the vanguard of establishing the Southern California restaurants was Ron Stillwell, Peter Piper's former vice-president of entertainment in Scottsdale, Arizona, and now one of its new California franchisees. Stillwell began signing development agreements in 1998 in an effort to expand the chain beyond the company's concentration of restaurants in Arizona and Texas. Stillwell's group of Peter Piper franchises operated under the company name Southern California Pizza, which was one of two such enterprises in the Los Angeles region. He and partner Terry Davis obtained franchise development rights for their Chino Hills, California-based company and opened the first of 25 planned restaurants in Colton, California. Southern California Pizza acquired the rights for the eastern halves of Los Angeles and Orange counties as well as for inland Riverside and San Bernardino counties. Another franchisee, Mike Storm, gained rights to develop ten Peter Piper Pizza stores in Puerto Rico and began construction of a 12,000-square-foot Los Angeles restaurant in the predominately Spanish-speaking community of Huntington Park in southern Los Angeles County. Storm, who was president and chief executive of Santa Monica-based Stormin' California Family Entertainment, also signed a seven-year deal in 1998 to build 45 restaurants from north of the San Diego County line to Santa Barbara, as well as in the

San Francisco Bay area. Peter Piper was Storm's second choice for a franchising vehicle behind Chuck E. Cheese's, owned by CEC Enterprises of Irving, Texas, which could not offer him a development agreement. A third leading franchisee was Sunroad Restaurant Concepts, a joint venture between managing partner Patricia Cohen's U.S.-based business, Food & Fun LLC, and Sunroad Enterprises, a San Diego-based car dealer and real-estate developer. Cohen's family began franchising Peter Piper Pizza outlets internationally in 1994, when its Tijuana, Mexico-based company, Alimentos Y Diversiones, acquired the master franchise agreement for Baja, California. Sunroad obtained the rights to develop 14 outlets by 2003 in San Diego County, where it already operated one restaurant in the southern San Diego suburb of National City.

Change of Leadership in the 2000s

In August 2000, Frank Sbordone, Jr., Peter Piper's vice-president and chief financial officer since 1997, was named president and chief operating officer, succeeding Neil R. Simon, who remained chief executive and a board member. Tim Flynn, formerly the company's controller, replaced Simon as vice-president and chief financial officer. Both Simon and Flynn were veterans of Ruby Tuesday. Flynn came to Peter Piper after being controller of Ruby Tuesday's Tia's Tex-Mex division, and Sbordone was a senior vice-president at Ruby Tuesday before joining Peter Piper. Sbordone's goal was to expand both company-owned and franchised locations of the family-oriented chain, which then operated 51 company units and 97 franchises sites. Sbordone planned to move forward in a more deliberate manner, opening up a new concept in Chandler, Arizona, that it intended to use as a prototype for expansion. While in the past, Peter Piper focused on placing restaurants in

neighborhoods, the company began building its newer restaurants, such as in Chandler, in high-traffic strip-mall locations with a large proportion of families. In addition, the company secured from Fleet National Bank an $18 million line of credit to pay off debt and provide new funds for expansion and the remodeling of existing restaurants.

By 2003, the Peter Piper chain had 48 company-owned and 97 franchised restaurants with an average unit volume of $1 million for food and beverages. Each outlet had 35 to 50 games, which accounted for approximately 35 percent of revenue. Pepperoni pizza was the most popular with children, although the seven-topping Works and the Chicago Classic were strong sellers as well. The company also introduced a hand-tossed crust version. Peter Piper continued opening up new restaurants throughout 2003, operating more than 150 company-owned and franchised outlets by 2004. Although increasingly operating within a crowded market, the company appeared well positioned to continue its profitability into the future.

Principal Competitors

Domino's Pizza, Inc.; Mr. Gatti's Inc.; Pizza Hut, Inc.

Further Reading

Campbell, Rick, "Pistol Pete's Operator Sues Peter Piper," *Nation's Restaurant News*, September 23, 1996, p. 4.
Gin, Calvin, "Retailer Uses Pizza to Whet the Appetite for Video Rentals," *Merchandising*, May 1985, p. 24.
Magruder, Janie, "Tony's ADS Made Many 'Come on Over' For Pizza," *Arizona Business Gazette*, May 1, 1997, p. 39.
Mull, Angela, "Peter Piper Cooking up Expansion Plans," *Business Journal*, July 24, 1998, p. 7.
Rubin, Daniel, "Venture West Group Acquires Majority and Controlling Interest in Peter Piper," *Business Wire*, November 20, 1992, p. 1.
Ruggless, Ron, "Peter Piper Mum over Replacement of Chief Exec Petty," *Nation's Restaurant News*, October 19, 1998, p. 1.
——, "Peter Piper Picks Smith to Oversee Franchise Development," June 16, 1997, p. 6.
——, "Peter Piper Purchases Pistol Pete's," *Nation's Restaurant News*, August 21, 1995, p. 3.
——, "Peter Piper's Simon Hands Prexy Post to Sbordone; Flynn is CFO," *Nation's Restaurant News*, August 21, 2000, p. 8.
Shonna, James, "Former Chief Executive Officer and President of Denny's to Take Helm of Peter Piper Pizza," *Business Wire*, November 4, 1996.
Speck, Amy, "Peter Piper Franchises Peck S. Calif. Pizza Market, Plan 80 Units," *Nation's Restaurant News*, August 2, 1999, p. 22.

—Bruce P. Montgomery

PHOENIX

Phoenix Footwear Group, Inc.

5759 Fleet Street
Carlsbad, California 92008
U.S.A.
Telephone: (760) 602-9688
Toll Free: (800) 341-1550
Fax: (760) 602-9684
Web site: http://www.phoenixfootwear.com

Public Company
Incorporated: 1882 as Daniel Green & Company
Employees: 130
Sales: $39.08 million (2003)
Stock Exchanges: American
Ticker Symbol: PXG
NAIC: 316210 Footwear Manufacturing; 316213 Men's
    Footwear (Except Athletic) Manufacturing; 316214
    Women's Footwear (Except Athletic) Manufacturing;
    422320 Men's and Boys' Clothing and Furnishings
    Wholesalers; 422330 Women's, Children's, and
    Infants' Clothing and Accessories Wholesalers;
    422340 Footwear Wholesalers

Phoenix Footwear Group, Inc., markets a number of leading brands of footwear and apparel. Brands include Trotters, SoftWalk, H.S. Trask, and Ducks Unlimited footwear, and Royal Robbins and Audubon apparel. These brands tend to feature conservative styling, shielding them somewhat from the fickle nature of the fashion industry. Phoenix is headquartered in Carlsbad, California, and has an operations center in Old Town, Maine. Most of its footwear is produced in Brazil, and clothing is sourced in South America and Asia. Phoenix was formerly known as the Daniel Green Company; however, the Daniel Green slipper brand is now owned by an entirely separate company.

Origins

The origins of Phoenix Footwear Group, Inc., begin with the Daniel Green Company of Dolgeville, New York, located 60 miles northwest of Albany. Daniel Green was a shoe salesman in 1881 when he found that a company manufacturing felt for pianos had also fashioned some slippers that factory workers used to keep their feet warm. Green and his brother gained the license to market the felt slippers and set up shop at their home in Canastota, New York. Billed as the "Original Comfy Slipper Company," the Daniel Green Company flourished, eventually moving operations and incorporating in New York City. The company was advertising nationally by the late 1920s in such publications as *Ladies Home Journal*, and by the 1960s, the company was manufacturing a wider variety of slippers and shoes for women and men.

Big changes ensued in the 1990s. James Riedman joined the Daniel Green Company in 1987, and in 1996 he became chairman and chief executive officer, having acquired an initial 35 percent interest in the company under the auspices of his insurance brokerage, the Riedman Corporation. Under Riedman's leadership, Daniel Green pursued a strategy of developing and complementing its brands while cutting costs.

By 1998, according to the *Business Journal* of Syracuse, New York, Daniel Green employed only 300 people. In June 1999, the company shut down its plant in upper New York State. About 125 people were laid off, while another 35 remained at the distribution center. In the mid-1980s, the company had as many as 700 employees.

By June 1999, all of the company's footwear manufacturing had been outsourced overseas. Its suppliers at the time were in Spain, China, and Mexico. The company earned $1.5 million on sales of $15 million in 1999.

The issue was not merely lower wages. As one of the last shoe manufacturers in the United States, the company was having problems sourcing materials and machinery, company president Greg Tunney lamented to the *Business Journal*.

New Brands in 2000

Daniel Green acquired a number of brands from the L.B. Evans & Son Company Limited Partnership in February 2000. Evans, based in Fitchburg, Massachusetts, was the oldest footwear manufacturer in the United States, established in 1804. It had been a serious competitor for Daniel Green for 100 years and was a leader in the men's slipper business.

Another important acquisition was made in April 2000, the purchase of the Penobscot Shoe Company, a publicly traded importer of women's footwear and owner of the Trotters brand. The company paid $17.8 million for Penobscot, which had been founded in 1935 as Philco Shoe Company by Max Kagan and Philip W. Lown. Penobscot originally made moccasins. When acquired by Daniel Green, it was publicly traded on the American Stock Exchange and had sales of about $20 million a year.

In May 2000, Green relocated its headquarters and distribution center to the Penobscot site in Old Town, Maine. Penobscot had been producing women's shoes for more than six decades, and had outsourced its production five years earlier.

Revenues more than doubled in 2000 to $33 million, and the company narrowed its net loss from $1.5 million to $682,000. The company was profitable again in 2001, posting net income of $1.4 million on sales of $46.9 million. The Riedman family sold Riedman Corporation to Brown & Brown Inc. for $62 million in January 2001.

Shedding Slippers in 2001

The company was producing slippers under the Daniel Green, L.B. Evans, and Woolrich names, but sold these lines to St. Louis-based Elan-Polo, Inc. in December 2001 to focus on the fast-growing Trotters and SoftWalk brands (the latter was new). Shoes were also a less seasonal business than slippers.

This was the end of the company's involvement with its original brand name, Daniel Green. The company changed its name to Phoenix Footwear Group, Inc. in May 2002 (while the brand's new owner Elan-Polo formed Daniel Green Enterprises, LLC). In the same month, the company's shares migrated from the NASDAQ (ticker symbol: DAGR) to the American Stock Exchange under the symbol PXG.

Trotters footwear sold for up to $99 a pair and featured a wide variety of sizes and widths. After acquiring the brand, Phoenix updated it to appeal to a younger audience, Greg Tunney, company president since 1998, told *FN*. SoftWalk shoes, priced up to $129, were designed as "comfort" footwear and boasted a patented, extra depth footbed. This brand debuted in fall 2000 with a line of sandals and clogs.

Tunney also told *FN* the company's recent turnaround was greatly helped by diversifying distribution beyond major department stores to catalogs and independent stores.

Moving to California in 2003

The company relocated its headquarters to Carlsbad, California in fiscal 2003. During the year, the company added two new footwear brands to its line-up and also acquired a leading apparel brand.

Phoenix acquired H.S. Trask & Co. in August 2003. Trask, based in Bozeman, Montana, was known for producing Western-style boots using exotic materials such as bison, longhorn, and elk leather. It had been founded in 1993 by John Brewer and Harrison Trask, a former regional sales manager for Reebok who had begun his career at the Brown Shoe Co. in St. Louis. By 1997, H.S. Trask & Co. had estimated revenues of $12 million, according to *Forbes,* and was selling almost 200,000 pairs of shoes a year. After the acquisition, Phoenix soon won rights to distribute footwear under the Ducks Unlimited brand; this was assigned to the H.S. Trask unit.

By this time, almost all of Phoenix's production was coming from Brazil. Starting with spring 2003, the company had begun to use some of this capacity to supply private-label customers like the Mason Shoe Comfort Footwear catalog, reported *FN*.

The Royal Robbins brand was acquired in October 2003 in a deal worth up to $11.5 million, depending on performance. Royal Robbins produced comfortable, conservatively styled apparel designed for traveling and outdoor recreation. It was a well-developed line with more than 250 styles.

Royal Robbins had been founded in 1968 as a mountaineering equipment store by climber and adventurer Royal Robbins. His wife Liz introduced the clothing aspect in 1975 with the Billy Goat Shorts of her own design. Entrepreneur Dan Costa acquired control of the company in 1999.

Phoenix was also developing a men's comfort footwear line called Strol, to reach stores in October 2004. It featured the same patented footbed technology as the SoftWalk line. Strol shoes were more expensive, in the $160 to $180 range. The H.S. Trask brand was also extended into a women's line, something that had been tried unsuccessfully by Trask's previous owners ten years earlier.

The company had net income of $941,000 on sales of $39 million in 2003. A weak economy benefited Phoenix by keeping companies' asking prices down. Nevertheless, an attempted acquisition of Antigua Enterprises Inc., an Arizona-based man-

Key Dates:

1882: The Daniel Green Company is founded.
1996: James Riedman becomes CEO and chairman after acquiring ownership position.
1999: The Group begins outsourcing all footwear production.
2000: Penobscot Shoe (Trotters) and several brands from L.B. Evans are acquired.
2001: The men's and women's slipper business is sold off.
2002: The original Daniel Green Company is renamed Phoenix Footwear Group, Inc.
2003: Phoenix headquarters are relocated to Carlsbad, California; H.S. Trask and Royal Robbins are acquired.
2004: Army boot manufacturer Altama Delta Corporation is acquired.

ufacturer of golf apparel, did not go through. Former Cole Haan executive Richard White was hired as chief executive officer in June 2004, taking over the position from James Riedman, who remained chairman.

Phoenix acquired army boot manufacturer Altama Delta Corporation in July 2004. Altama, based in Atlanta, produced combat boots for the U.S. military and others, and had sales of $40 million a year. It had been supplying the U.S. Department of Defense for 35 years and began a commercial business in 1991.

According to an April 2004 story in the *New York Times,* footwear prices had remained fairly stagnant for the previous decade. "If anything, prices are going downward," said Riedman. The only way for Phoenix to reach new price points was to introduce new and improved shoes. The company redesigned the entire H.S. Trask line in 2004. In 2005, the company also was revamping its Trotters brand.

Principal Subsidiaries

H.S. Trask & Company; Penobscot Shoe Company; Royal Robbins, Inc.

Principal Divisions

Altama Footwear; H.S. Trask; Trotters.

Principal Competitors

Brown Shoe Company; C&J Clark International Ltd.; Cole Haan Ltd.; Columbia Sportswear, Inc.; ECCO Sko A/S; R.G. Barry Corporation.

Further Reading

"2004 Forty Under 40: James Riedman," *Rochester Business Journal,* November 12, 2004, p. S39.

Dougherty, Conor, "Carlsbad, Calif.-Based Phoenix Footwear Will Acquire Shoe Brand H.S. Trask," *San Diego Union-Tribune,* May 23, 2003.

——, "Footwear Firm Joins Others Seeking Good Life in San Diego Area," *San Diego Union-Tribune,* May 2, 2003.

Ebeling, Ashlea, "The Three Icons of the Old West," *Forbes,* November 17, 1997, pp. 152f.

Interview with James Riedman, CEO of Daniel Green Company, *Wall Street Transcript,* Apparel & Fashion Issue, April 23, 2001.

Lenetz, Dana, "Daniel Green Co. Exits Slipper Biz," *FN,* December 10, 2001, p. 2.

——, "Reinventing Daniel Green: New Name, New Product," *FN,* May 6, 2002, p. 4.

Malin, Patricia J., "Daniel Green Departs," *Business Journal—Central New York,* April 30, 1999, p. 1.

Moran, Tim, "Modesto, Calif.-Based Outdoor Clothing Company Changes Hands," *Modesto Bee,* July 2, 2001.

Niemi, Wayne, "Phoenix Names New CEO, Buys Boot Firm," *FN,* June 21, 2004, p. 4.

——, "Phoenix Sets Sights on Altama Footwear," *FN,* May 31, 2004, p. 2.

——, "Phoenix to Pursue Acquisition Plan After Scoring Two Deals in 2000 and 2003; The $39-Million Firm Says Time Is Right to Consider Further Buyouts," *FN,* May 17, 2004, p. 6.

Pankratz, Howard, "If That Rugged, Bison-Leather Shoe Fits, Sell It," *Denver Post,* September 29, 1997, p. E1.

"Phoenix Footwear Makes Play to Acquire Lifestyle Apparel Maker," *FN,* January 20, 2003, p. 2.

Porter, Eduardo, "A Corporate Quandary Over Raising Prices," *New York Times,* April 16, 2004, p. C1.

Schneider-Levy, Barbara, "Sound Footing; In the Wake of Its Successful SoftWalk Women's Collection, Phoenix Footwear Group Is Venturing into the Men's Comfort Category with Its New Strol Line," *FN,* July 26, 2004, p. 94.

"Spreading Its Wings; About to Close Its Deal to Buy H.S. Trask, Phoenix Footwear Is Looking for More Brands to Add to Its Nest," *FN,* July 28, 2003, p. 84.

Stamborski, Al, "St. Louis Store Sells Buffalo-Hide Shoes," *St. Louis Post-Dispatch,* October 27, 1999.

—Frederick C. Ingram

PLIVA d.d.

Ulica Grada Vukovara 49
10000 Zagreb
Croatia
Telephone: +385-161-20-999
Fax: +385 1 61 11 011
Web site: http://www.pliva.com

Public Company
Incorporated: 1921 as Kastel d.d.
Employees: 6,654
Sales: HRK 6.80 billion ($1.13 billion) (2004)
Stock Exchanges: Zagreb London
Ticker Symbol: PLVA-R-A; PLVD
NAIC: 325411 Medicinal and Botanical Manufacturing;
325412 Pharmaceutical Preparation Manufacturing;
325413 In-Vitro Diagnostic Substance Manufacturing;
325414 Biological Product (Except Diagnostic)
Manufacturing

PLIVA d.d. is Central and Eastern Europe's leading pharmaceutical company. Through much of its history it produced vitamins and generic drugs for Soviet states. The company attained global prominence in the 1980s on the strength of Azithromycin, an antibiotic of its own design, marketed under license in the West as Zithromax and in Eastern and Central Europe as Sumamed.

Eighty percent of revenues came from outside Croatia in 2003. In a dramatic shift from its Soviet Bloc origins, its largest markets were the United States and Western Europe. PLIVA has invested heavily in research and development, aiming to bring new proprietary drugs to market following the lapse of Azithromycin's patent protection beginning in 2006. The company has evolved into a multinational corporation, with subsidiaries throughout Europe and the United States.

Origins

PLIVA d.d.'s origins date back to the 1921 founding of predecessor company Kastel d.d. Kastel (or Kashtel) was formed as a joint venture of Budapest-based Chinoin and Isis of Zagreb, Croatia.

A research program was begun in 1935 under the direction of Dr. Vladimir Prelog, who would go on to win the Nobel Prize in chemistry 40 years later. Kastel was taken over by the state in the early 1940s. In 1941, it was given the name PLIVA, an acronym for the State Institute for Production of Medicines and Vaccines.

PLIVA began producing vitamin C in bulk in 1953. Vitamin B6 production began six years later. In 1959, the company also began producing oxytetracycline, an antibiotic.

Introducing Azithromycin in the 1980s

PLIVA researchers patented a new fast-acting macrolide antibiotic dubbed Azithromycin in 1980. U.S.-based Pfizer began licensing production of the drug for sale in Europe and the United States in 1986, where it became a bestseller under the name Zithromax. PLIVA sold it in the Soviet bloc under the name Sumamed.

Economic crisis affected the Soviet Union, the company's main export market at the time. The local workforce of 7,000 was cut in half during the lean times. As staffing levels were rebuilt, the company became more international, reported the *Financial Times,* with many foreign employees joining and many being based overseas. English became the language of the company's meetings and memos.

PLIVA's longtime president and CEO Zeljko Covic left the company for two years beginning in 1991. He was frustrated at its conservative response to industry globalization, said Britain's *Financial Times.* After he returned in 1993, Covic had the food and cosmetics divisions divested, although they were profitable, in order to focus on the core business.

PLIVA became a joint stock company in 1993. Revenues were $300 million in 1994, with more than 40 percent from exports. Former Soviet satellites made up its largest market, and PLIVA was the largest pharmaceutical company by sales in

Central and Eastern Europe. Revenues were about $400 million in 1995.

Another big product was vitamin C, for which it was the world's fifth leading producer. Other products included agricultural products, food items, and health and beauty supplies.

Croatian army advances and the signing of the Dayton Peace Accord in December 1995 brought more security to investing in the country.

Public in 1996

The Croatian government privatized PLIVA in 1996, selling 31 percent of shares. The company was valued between $415 million and $510 million. After being listed in Zagreb, PLIVA shares began trading publicly on the London Stock Exchange on April 11, 1996, a first for an East European industrial company, according to the *Financial Times*. Part of the $140 million in proceeds from the highly successful initial public offering (IPO) were earmarked for building a new $100 million azithromycin factory in Savski Marof, near Zagreb. A research plant was being built nearby, at a cost of $80 million. Designed by British architectural firm Sheppard Robson, it opened in 2002.

After the IPO, PLIVA also invested in export marketing. Sales to Russia more than doubled in 1997. Total sales rose 23 percent to HRK 2.9 billion and net profit grew 32 percent to HRK 604 million ($92.3 million).

In 1997, PLIVA acquired a 70 percent stake in a leading Polish pharmaceutical company, Polfa Krakow, for $102.5 million. This holding was soon raised to 81.5 percent through a $38 million infusion of new capital. It was renamed PLIVA Krakow.

The Croatian government sold off the last of its directly owned, 14 percent shareholding in 1998. The European Bank for Reconstruction and Development reduced its stake from 11 percent to 8 percent. Together this raised $238 million.

PLIVA used its Polish subsidiary, PLIVA Krakow, to acquire control of Lachema, a leading Czech pharmaceutical company, in December 1999. Lachema had revenues of $30.5 million in 1999. Two other companies were acquired during the year: FARMACOM and MIXIS Genetics.

R&D a Priority After 2000

The company was diversifying and investing in research to prepare for a drop in revenues when its top seller came off patent. In 2000, worldwide azithromycin sales accounted for nearly a quarter, or HRK 854 million ($107 million), of PLIVA's total revenues.

PLIVA was developing both new and generic drugs, reported Britain's *Financial Times*. It was teaming with Glaxo

Wellcome (later Glaxo-SmithKline) to test a successor to azithromycin. Glaxo, a British firm, had a laboratory four hours from Zagreb in Verona, Italy.

German pharmaceutical company AWD.pharma GmbH & Co. KG was acquired from the Degussa chemicals group for Euro 50 million in August 2001. AWD specialized in generics and was approaching Euro 115 million in annual revenues.

Sobel Holdings, Inc., PLIVA's first U.S. purchase, was acquired in June 2002 for $212 million. It included Sidmak Laboratories, Inc. and its subsidiary Odyssey Pharmaceuticals, Inc. PLIVA had acquired ten companies in the previous ten years.

By this time, PLIVA was testing three products to treat digestive disorders, fungal infections, and blood clots. Another half-dozen drugs were in earlier stages of development. PLIVA also had a presence in the world's largest generic markets (the United States, Germany, the United Kingdom, Spain, and Italy) chief executive Zeljko Covic told the *Financial Times,* and it was shifting to a strategy of organic growth through them rather than acquisitions.

Revenues rose 32 percent in 2003 to HRK 7.22 billion ($1.1 billion). Pre-tax profit was HRK 1.1 billion. Eighty percent of revenues came from outside Croatia. The company's largest export markets were now Western Europe and North America. During the year, PLIVA sold off a plant in Trogir, Croatia for HRK 31 million.

PLIVA adopted a new, streamlined organizational structure in January 2004. Around the same time, the company began licensing an array of technologies from Louisiana State University. These included potential treatments for type 2 diabetes, obesity, and cardiovascular problems.

A new overactive bladder treatment, Sanctura, was launched in the United States in August 2004. PLIVA was marketing it with Odyssey Pharmaceuticals, Inc. and Indevus Pharmaceuticals, Inc., which had obtained U.S. rights for the drug from Germany's Madaus AG five years earlier.

Revenues rose 5 percent to $1.1 billion (HRK 6.8 billion) in 2004. Western Europe was the strongest region of growth, with sales rising 25 percent to $159 million. Italy and the United Kingdom were the fastest-growing markets. Sales in Central and Eastern Europe rose 7 percent to $365 million. The U.S.

market fell 6 percent to $210 million due in large part to new generic competition for PLIVA's Urecholine, a bladder control product. Pharma Chemicals sales rose 11 percent on the strength of Azithromycin orders. Research revenues slipped 7 percent to $170 million. The Non-Core division contributed another $54 million, up 6 percent. Finally, other income rose 28 percent to $42 million.

Principal Subsidiaries

PLIVA HRVATSKA d.o.o.; PLIVA—ISTRAZIVACKI INSTITUT d.o.o.; PLIVA ISTRAZIVANJE I RAZVOJ d.o.o.; Globalni Poslovni Servisi—IT d.o.o.; Pharmaing d.o.o.; PLIVA ESOP d.o.o.; Pliva Zdravlje d.o.o.; Velaris d.o.o.; VETERINA d.o.o.; PLIVA Ljubljana d.o.o. (Slovenia); PLIVA Sarajevo d.o.o. (Bosnia and Herzegovina); Pliva Skopje d.o.o.e.l. (Macedonia); Pharmazug AG (Switzerland); Mixis Genetics Ltd. (Great Britain); PLIVA Pharma UK Ltd.; PLIVA, Inc. (U.S.A.); PLIVA Pharma Holding B.V. (Netherlands); PLIVA London Ltd. (Great Britain); PLIVA Research India Private Ltd.; PLIVA Global Finance AG (Switzerland).

Principal Divisions

Pharmaceuticals; Pharma Chemicals; Research; Non-Core.

Principal Competitors

Barr Pharmaceuticals, Inc.; Johnson & Johnson; Mylan Labs Inc.; Par Pharmaceutical, Inc.; Sanofi-Aventis S.A.

Further Reading

Boland, Vincent, "Croatia Begins Sale of Rump of Pliva Stake," *Financial Times* (London), April 27, 1998, p. 26.

——, "Croatia Completes Sale of Remaining Stake in Pliva," *Financial Times* (London), May 14, 1998, p. 44.

"Croatia's Pliva Acquires AWD.pharma (Kroatische Pliva Kauft AWD.pharma), *Frankfurter Allgemeine Zeitung,* August 23, 2001, p. 18.

Done, Kevin, "A Formula for European Expansion," *Financial Times* (London), Survey—Croatia 98, July 7, 1998, p. 3.

Gray, Gavin, "Croatia Prepares Historic DM150m Drugs Group Offer," *Financial Times* (London), September 29, 1995, p. 28.

——, "Pliva Aims to Put Croatia on Investors' Maps—Zagreb Hopes Drug Group's Issue Will Lift Country's Profile Abroad," *Financial Times* (London), March 13, 1996, p. 31.

Jenkins, Patrick, "Pliva to Acquire US Drugs Group," *Financial Times* (London), June 12, 2002, p. 30.

"Louisiana State University: College Licenses Metabolic Drug to Croatian Company," *Cardiovascular Business Week,* January 12, 2004, p. 35.

"Pliva's Flotation Success Exceeds Expectations," *Pharmaceutical Business News,* April 11, 1996.

Smy, Lucy, and Robert Wright, "Antibiotic Cash Fuels Growth," *Financial Times* (London), Survey—Croatia, June 22, 2000, p. 5.

Warner, Melanie, "The Ultimate Turnaround: It's Hard Enough to Woo Investors Who Have Never Heard of Your Company. Imagine If They've Never Heard of Your Country," *Business 2.0,* October 2004, pp. 124ff.

Wright, Robert, "Pliva Stresses Independence," *Financial Times* (London), U.S.A. ed., September 26, 2002, p. 20.

Whitaker, Daniel, "Pliva's R&D Edge in Eastern Europe; The Croatian Group Has a Successful Formula in a Difficult Region," *Financial Times* (London), U.S.A. ed., June 9, 2003, p. 10.

—Frederick C. Ingram

NY WATERWAY®

Port Imperial Ferry Corporation

Pershing Road
Weehawken, New Jersey 078087
U.S.A.
Telephone: (201) 902-8700
Toll Free: (800) 533-3779
Fax: (201) 348-9384
Web site: http://www.nywaterway.com

Wholly Owned Subsidiary of Arcorp Properties
Incorporated: 1984
Sales: $73 million (2002)
NAIC: 483212 Inland Water Passenger Transportation

The largest ferry operation in North America, Port Imperial Ferry Corporation serves the New York City metropolitan area, operating under the name of NY Waterway. The company is a subsidiary of privately owned Arcorp Properties, which also operates The Port Imperial Marina in Weehawken, New Jersey, Imperatore Landscaping, and a pair of restaurants located on the New Jersey side of the Hudson River across from Manhattan. NY Waterway provides commuter service from New Jersey communities to Midtown Manhattan and the financial district of Lower Manhattan. In addition, it offers sightseeing cruises that tour the New York harbor as well as venturing upriver to visit Hudson Valley sites, including trips to Army football games at West Point. NY Waterway ships also transport baseball fans to Yankee Stadium and Shea Stadium, as well as offering dinner and theater excursions and chartered parties that use Manhattan as a backdrop. Following the September 11, 2001, terrorist attacks that leveled the World Trade Center towers and destroyed the underlying PATH train station, NY Waterway enjoyed a sudden surge in business. As business receded to pre-9/11 levels, however, the company found itself saddled with too much debt caused by overexpansion and on the verge of a collapse. NY Waterway has negotiated a rescue plan, but its future remains uncertain.

Starting Out in Trucking in the 1940s

The man behind the birth of NY Waterway was Arthur Edward Imperatore. He was born in West New York, New Jersey, in 1925, one of ten children born to Italian immigrants. After serving in the United States Army from 1945 to 1947, he joined his brothers, who had launched a small trucking operation. What started out as two brothers and a single truck soon became an enterprise known as A & P Trucking (later becoming A-P-A Trucking Corp.), which included two surplus Army trucks and all five of the Imperatore brothers. Although Arthur was the youngest of the boys, he quickly emerged as the leader. He started out in sales, driving only as a substitute, but also became the company's planner and deal maker—and a workaholic who took only a single week's vacation in 20 years. Trucking in the post-World War II era was a rough and tumble, and thriving, industry. Unlike many area shippers, who concentrated on the major hauling business between Newark and Manhattan, A-P-A took on junk freight and small shipments and recognized that the outer boroughs of Brooklyn, Queens, and the Bronx offered an opportunity for growth. In 1958, A-P-A opened a second terminal in Reading, Pennsylvania, a move that transformed the company from a local trucker into a regional operation.

At this stage Arthur grew disenchanted with the business and thought about quitting. He then experienced an epiphany of sorts during a 1960 snowstorm, when he and a new driver were shoveling the Reading lot. The employee complained bitterly about shoveling not being a part of his job description, infuriating Imperatore, who suddenly realized that A-P-A was to blame for having hired the man in the first place. During the 1950s, when labor was scarce, he had trawled area bars in search of new drivers, who would later become permanent employees and because of union rules were difficult to dismiss, causing him no end of headaches. Imperatore decided that as a two-terminal operation, A-P-A had to exert greater control over its hiring. As a result he instituted a strict and thorough hiring process that included polygraphs and security checks. Imperatore renewed his commitment to the business and formalized its organization on other fronts as well. As a result, revenues grew rapidly and A-P-A expanded its geographic reach, eventually including some 30 terminals.

Imperatore reached another turning point in his life in 1975 when the company helicopter crashed, killing his brother Arnold, vice-president of operations along with the pilot. Arthur was grieving over the loss of his brother when two weeks later his mother also died. He was 51 years old. He had succeeded in

Company Perspectives:

NY Waterway has the largest ferry and excursion fleet in the NY Harbor, but it is still a family business with all the personal attention to service and amenities that it had when it was just Arthur's ferry.

building A-P-A into one of the leading trucking firms in the country, and did not relish the prospect of taking over the day-to-day managerial responsibilities of his brother. He decided to groom his 32-year-old stepson, Armand Pohan, a lawyer, as a successor. A longtime company lieutenant handled daily affairs while Armand learned the ropes and Arthur looked for new challenges.

Imperatore bought a pair of Virginia coal mines and acquired the Colorado Rockies National Hockey League franchise, which he relocated to New Jersey as the Devils. He also dabbled in real estate. Eventually he found a project that would completely capture his imagination. On a Friday evening in September 1981 he learned that an old railyard, a 2½-mile section of crumbling waterfront landfill property located in his old West New York neighborhood and Weehawken, was being put up for sale by the bankrupt Penn Central railroad. It was one of the few large tracts of undeveloped real estate located within 25 miles of Midtown Manhattan. Over the weekend he arranged a Monday meeting with Penn Central executives, then in a matter of 20 minutes was able to knock down the $14 million asking price to $7.5 million in cash, and the two sides had a deal. What Imperatore purchased for that money included a network of rusted rails, abandoned railcars and barges, hundreds of old automobiles, and assorted squatters' shacks. But Imperatore's vision for the property was grand and ambitious: he wanted to build a new, privately managed Venetian city, complete with townhouses, hotels, banks, schools, and churches, as well as an observation tower inspired by Leonardo da Vinci. He would call it Port Imperial, and it became his obsession. The estimated price tag was $5 billion.

A Ferry Service in the Mid-1980s

While Imperatore met with scores of architects, planners, and consultants, and visited waterfront developments around the world, he had the property cleaned up. Over the next few years, Imperatore launched a few businesses on the site as he worked on realizing his vision for Port Imperial. He opened a marina, a golf driving range, and an upscale restaurant called Arthur's Landing. Another venture grew out of a trip he took one day in a company yacht crossing the Hudson river. He timed the trip at less than four minutes, about the same amount of time he estimated someone in a car might expect to wait at a single Manhattan intersection. Imperatore envisioned that one day residents of Port Imperial could commute by ferry to Manhattan, but on the cliffs behind his Weehawken landing, the famous Palisades, were towns already filled with potential customers. He decided that there was no reason to wait for Port Imperial and that he could start a ferry service now.

Ferries had a long history in New York City, and in fact Imperatore as a child used to ride the Weehawken ferry. To save

50 cents, A-P-A would later rely on the ferry instead of using the Lincoln tunnel. As early as 1650 the Raritan Indians ferried Dutch settlers in canoes across the Arthur Kill to Staten Island. Twenty-five years later the Dutch established a ferry to cross the Harlem and Hudson rivers. With the advent of steamboats in the early 1820s, ferries increased in popularity, so that by the end of the century there were 50 steam ferries operating in the metropolitan area. But with the opening of the Brooklyn Bridge in 1883, followed by other bridges spanning New York's waterways, or tunnels that burrowed beneath the rivers, the need for ferries began to fade. The Weehawken Ferry went out of business in 1959, and in 1967 the last operator to cross the Hudson, the Hoboken ferry, shut down, leaving only the venerable Staten Island ferry to continue the tradition in New York City. But as the bridges, tunnels, and mass transit links to the city became strained, the idea of bringing back ferry service gained credence in the early 1980s, as Imperatore was not alone in sensing an opportunity to reintroduce ferry service to New York. Around the same time that Imperatore launched NY Waterway to run a ferry between Weehawken and midtown Manhattan—to a ramshackle railroad pier acquired on West 38th Street—Tradebase International began running a ferry between Fort Lee, New Jersey, and Wall Street.

It took 27 months and $1 million for Imperatore to start his new ferry service, which some nicknamed "Arthur's Folly." Unfortunately, the idea of taking the ferry to work was not readily embraced by commuters. The Fort Lee operation went out of business after only four months, attracting less than 100 riders a week. NY Waterway began service on December 3, 1986, with just two dozen passengers, and they were riding for free. In an attempt to establish a customer base, the ferry was offered free for the first month. But Imperatore was undeterred and continued to pour money into the venture, likely drawn from the coffers of A-P-A, to the detriment of the family trucking line. What Imperatore realized, unlike other ferry operators before him, was that a ferry was not an attractive option to commuters if they were simply dumped on the river's edge in Manhattan and had to find a way to get to their office buildings. He added free shuttle buses that transported passengers to and from work and the ferry. It was the idea that made NY Waterway a viable business.

Imperatore, from his days as a trucking executive, knew the importance of political connections in the transportation industry. He began courting politicians on both sides of the Hudson—in New Jersey, in New York City, and in New York's capital of Albany. In 1988 he received a major break when the Port Authority of New York and New Jersey hired NY Waterway to run a ferry between Hoboken and the World Financial Center to help ease overcrowding on the Authority's PATH trains that linked New Jersey with Manhattan's financial district. After a few years of operating at a loss, NY Waterway finally became profitable in the early 1990s. Other ferry companies sprang up to emulate Imperatore's success, but NY Waterway was well entrenched, and so politically connected, so that it controlled about 90 percent of the city's ferry business.

NY Waterway also expanded beyond the commuter trade in the early 1990s, using ships during off-peak ferry hours to conduct excursions, touring the New York harbor and venturing up the Hudson River in conjunction with chartered buses to visit historic Hudson Valley towns such as Sleepy Hollow, as well as the Rockefeller family home in Pocantico Hills. By 1993 NY Waterway had cobbled together a profitable little venture, the bulk of the business coming from the four routes the company's 12 boats traveled across the Hudson, carrying 11,000 passengers a day. The same could not be said, however, for Port Imperial. Imperatore was unable to convince nearby communities to grant permission to build high-rise structures taller than the Palisades. In 1994 a bank foreclosed on a $50 million loan and Imperatore lost half of the Penn Central property, essentially leaving him with the restaurant, marina, and NY Waterway.

Imperatore and NY Waterway, however, were more successful in their efforts to curry political favor. The company hired lobbyists in New York City, Albany, Trenton, and Washington, D.C. Imperatore held fundraising dinners at his restaurant for New York's governor, George Pataki, and New York City Mayor Rudolph Giuliani. He named ferries after New Jersey Senator Frank Lautenberg and New Jersey Representative Robert A. Roe. On his yacht Imperatore also wined and dined New Jersey mayors and Port Authority executives. In 1995 New York Waterway offered a job to Donald J. Liloia, the Port Authority's supervisor of the ferry industry. Three months later, he went to work for the company, then helped to draft NY Waterway's winning bid for a Port Authority contract. Unlike other transit companies that relied on government subsidiaries, NY Waterway was privately financed. Where it did receive help was in the building of new terminals, which NY Waterway would then lease, generally based on the number of passengers it served.

In 1996 Arthur Imperatore turned over the presidency to his son, Arthur E. Imperatore, Jr. Unlike his father, the younger Imperatore did not grow up under hardscrabble conditions. After prep school in New Hampshire, he studied at both Yale and Harvard, and after giving consideration to a teaching career became an attorney specializing in real estate before succeeding his father. Although his father failed to build his dream city, he was instrumental in the ferry resuming its place, albeit small, in the New York City area transportation network. During the 1990s there was talk of launching ferry service to La Guardia and Kennedy airports, but the plans never materialized, so that by 2001 NY Waterway was still very much a Hudson River ferry operation, with 15 routes, serving 33,000 passengers each day—and only a modicum of competition. Rounding out the business were the baseball and theater excursions and sightseeing cruises.

Then on September 11, 2001, a pair of hijacked airliners were crashed by terrorists into the twin towers of the World Trade Centers, bringing down both structures and destroying the Path Station and tubes below ground. That day, NY Waterway ferries repeatedly crossed the Hudson, ultimately evacuating some 160,000 people from Lower Manhattan. With the PATH train running to lower Manhattan out of commission, and subway traffic altered as well, there was some concern that the economy of Lower Manhattan was in jeopardy. The ferries were called on to fill the void in transportation, with the Federal Emergency Management Agency providing funds through the Port Authority to subsidize four new ferry routes and increase service on another. Three of the contracts were awarded to NY Waterway without public bidding, and the company won the other two as well, much to the displeasure of its competitors. The Port Authority maintained that NY Waterway was simply the best suited company for the task, given its size and the emergency situation.

Post-September 11 Surge in Business

In the months following September 11, NY Waterway saw its ridership almost double, prompting the company to add several more routes, lease more boats, and hire more workers. Revenues and profits grew quickly, due in large part to the government contracts, which guaranteed a 20 percent profit. But the company came under fire, accused of running empty ferries at night simply to reap more of the available subsidy. The company maintained, however, that it was just providing the level of frequent service for which the government had contracted, in essence replicating the lost PATH service, which had always run its share of empty passenger cars late at night.

In 2002 A-P-A, once the envy of the trucking world, went out of business, due in large part to the recession, but according to a number of employees, Arthur Imperatore, Sr., had to shoulder some of the blame. Not only was the firm not as well managed after he left, it also was crippled by the money that was siphoned off to fund Port Imperial, NY Waterway, and Imperatore's other ventures. With the collapse of A-P-A, NY Waterway now found itself the subject of lawsuits involving at least six pension funds for an estimated obligation of $8.2 million.

But paying off A-P-A pension funds was just one of several problems facing NY Waterway. In November 2003 PATH service was restored to Lower Manhattan and ridership on the ferry dropped off dramatically. Moreover, Lower Manhattan had never recovered all of the jobs lost from the destruction of the Twin Towers, meaning fewer commuters to transport by train or ferry. A spike in gasoline prices also served to exacerbate the situation, as did a harsh winter that led to icy conditions on the Hudson and resulted in ferry service being shut down for two weeks in January 2004. The company also had taken on too much debt, electing to buy five boats at the cost of $10 million rather than to continue leasing them for as much as $5,000 a day. NY Waterway quickly found itself in a death spiral that even fare increases, the cutting of routes, and the sale of assets could not stop.

It was in the interest of the community to retain the ferry service, but none of the plans meant to rescue NY Waterway could find traction. Then at the eleventh hour, in late December

2004, the Port Authority, working behind the scenes, engineered a deal with Manhattan attorney William Wachtel in which Wachtel would take over half of the NY Waterway routes, while NY Waterway would retain the rest. Most of the financial consideration was Wachtel's assumption of NY Waterway debt. Ferry service continued uninterrupted while the two parties had 60 days to iron out the details, which included gaining approval from lender J.P. Morgan Chase, the federal Maritime Administration, and the Port Authority. For the time being at least, the ferries would continue to be the province of private enterprise, but whether they would remain so remained very much an open question.

Principal Competitors

New York Water Taxi; SeaStreak America, Inc.

Further Reading

Bagli, Charles V., and Kevin Flynn, ''Ferry Operator's Dominance Draws Rivals Anger,'' *New York Times,* July 22, 2003, p. A1.

Brodsky, Sascha, ''Many Routes to Ferry King's Success,'' *Downtown Express,* July 12, 2002.

Orgill, Roxana, ''Ferries Resurface All Over New York Harbor,'' *Wall Street Journal,* August 7, 1990, p. A14.

''The Return of the Native,'' *Inc.,* November 1983, p. 104.

Richardson, Lynda, ''On the Busy Ferries, It's Steady As He Goes,'' *New York Times,* December 19, 2001, p. D2.

Rounds, David, *Perfecting a Piece of the World: Arthur Imperatore and the Blue-Collar Aristocrats of A-P-A,* Reading, Mass.: Addison-Wesley, 1993.

Sforza, Daniel, ''Investor and New York Ferry Line Work Out Rescue Deal,'' *Record* (Hackensack, N.J.), December 23, 2004.

—Ed Dinger

Posterscope Worldwide

Cardinal Tower
12 Farringdon Road
London EC1M 3HS
United Kingdom
Telephone: (+44) 20 7336 6363
Fax: (+44) 20 7490 4030
Web site: http://www.posterscope.co.uk

Wholly Owned Subsidiary of Aegis Group Plc
Incorporated: 1982 as Harrison Salinson
Sales: £800 million ($1.5 billion) (2004)
NAIC: 541850 Display Advertising

Posterscope Worldwide is the world's leading player in the outdoor (also known as the "out of home," or OOH) advertising media sector. The company provides campaign planning and purchasing services to clients (typically advertising agencies but also direct advertising clients) for the world's billboards, posters, in-transit advertising (such as in buses and trains), and related venues. Posterscope is the leader in most of the markets it serves; in the United Kingdom, for example, the company controls some 42 percent of the country's outdoor market. Originally focused on the United Kingdom, with additional offices representing northern England and Ireland, Posterscope has expanded in the 2000s and is now present in more than 16 countries worldwide, including the United States, France, Germany and other European countries, China, India, and elsewhere in the Asian region. Much of this expansion comes through the restructuring of parent company Carat, itself the main media buying subsidiary of Aegis Group Plc. Under that restructuring, Carat has re-branded many of the outdoor operations of its own globally operating subsidiary network under the single Posterscope name. The company has also grown through acquisition, notably that of airport media specialist PSI in 2003. In 2004, Posterscope posted worldwide revenues of approximatly £800 million ($1.5 billion). The company is led by CEO Anne Rickards and managing director Steve Bond.

Filling a Vacuum in the 1980s

Billboard advertising was a highly fragmented business in the United Kingdom into the 1970s. For the most part, the nation's billboards and other public poster locations, a market collectively known as "outdoor" or "out of home" in the trade, were owned by a large number of companies. Coordinating a billboard advertising campaign, considered part of an advertising agency's responsibility, was a time-consuming effort. This was particularly true for short-term campaigns, which generally remained in place for just days or weeks.

In the early 1970s, three of the largest billboard owners, Mills & Allen, Provincial Poster Group, and More O'Ferrall, joined together to create a new, centralized operation to take over their outdoor media buying needs. In 1971, the partners launched a new company, British Posters. David Harrison and Judith Salinson took charge of the new business and began seeking clients among the country's advertising agencies.

The agencies greeted the idea warmly, and British Posters took off, building up a large clientele across the United Kingdom. Meanwhile, other billboard owners recognized British Posters' successful formula and signed on. By 1974, the British Posters controlled some 80 percent of the United Kingdom's billboards. At the end of the decade, ten of the country's largest billboard owners had pooled their holdings in British Posters. By then, both Harrison and Salinson had left the company. Harrison went to work as a marketing director at a furniture company, while Salinson took charge of outdoor and local media buying for the Leo Burnett advertising agency.

British Posters' control over the outdoor market came under attack in the late 1970s. A number of voices began to criticize the company's control of the market and accused the company of hoarding billboard space. In the early 1980s, the company came under the scrutiny of the British Mergers and Monopolies Commission. In 1981, the commission called for British Posters to be broken up, despite opposition to the move both from the billboard operators and from the advertising agencies themselves.

British Posters was shut down in 1982, marking the first time a company had ever been closed down at the behest of the country's Mergers and Monopolies oversight body. The end of British Posters, however, represented an opportunity to create a new style of media buying and planning business, and a number of companies appeared to fill the vacuum. Many of these companies were launched by advertising groups.

In 1982, Harrison and Salinson came together again, and, joined by fellow ex-British Posters executives Anne Rickard and John Scurfield, launched their own outdoor media planning group, Harrison Salinson. The new partners went to work in much the same way they had under British Posters. The main difference, however, was that, rather than representing the billboard owners, Harrison Salinson now found their clients among the country's advertising agencies.

Harrison Salinson was not alone in the field. The company was joined, and even in some cases preceded, by several major competitors, including Concord, Poster Publicity Limited, and Portland, the latter set up by another former British Posters executive. Nonetheless, the new companies, like Harrison Salinson, filled a definite need in the advertising industry.

With the demise of British Posters, advertising agencies were once again faced with the task of organizing outdoor campaigns for their clients. The task involved a great deal of planning and, more and more, market research in order to provide for effective and appropriate placement. However, because an agency's clients did not always require outdoor campaigns, agencies were reluctant to devote full-time staff to this area. Instead, they preferred to turn over this business to the new specialist companies, which, at the beginning at least, remained independent of agency affiliation. This gave the specialist companies the appearance of remaining impartial in their outdoor placement strategies.

Joining Aegis in the 1990s

By the end of the 1980s, specialist companies like Harrison Salinson had begun to recognize the limitations inherent in their independent status. Linking up with a major advertising agency, or one of the newly appearing media buying companies, provided an opportunity for gaining scale and market share. At the same time, the specialist was guaranteed a client base through the agency's own clients, which also provided an opportunity to include outdoor placement strategy during the planning stages of an advertising campaign. Meanwhile, the specialist was able to continue to seek clients from other agencies.

Harrison Salinson chose this route when, in 1989, it agreed to be purchased by Carat Espace, the media-buying wing of fast-rising advertising agency WCRS, soon to be known as Aegis Group. WCRS had been founded in 1979 in London by several partners, including Peter Scott. The agency grew quickly and by 1984 had listed its stock on the London Stock Exchange. The public offering enabled WCRS to step up its growth, notably through a series of acquisitions in the United Kingdom, the United States, and France.

By the late 1980s, WCRS had branched out from its original advertising base to include public relations, design, and, through its purchase of Carat Espace, media buying. Carat Espace had been founded by Francis Gross in Paris in the late 1960s. Gross had recognized the potential in buying up media space—for example, in newspapers, magazines, and on billboards—in bulk at reduced prices. In turn, he was able to sell the space on to advertising agencies and corporations with their own advertising staff, while retaining profit margins as high as 15 percent or more. Gross also profited from year-end ''rebates'' that media sellers paid to the company, a legal practice at the time. Gross's idea took off, and revolutionized the European advertising industry before being imported into the United States in the 1990s. In the meantime, Carat quickly dominated France's media buying market.

WCRS paid Gross £64 million for a 50 percent stake in Carat Espace in the early 1980s. In 1984, WCRS acquired full control of Carat Espace. Gross, joined by his brother, and WCRS's Scott, then launched Carat on a massive expansion drive in the 1980s, buying up market-leading media planning and buying companies throughout Europe. By the end of the decade, Carat had moved into some 18 different markets and had a leading 11 percent share of the total media market. Carat counted some 4,000 clients, including such major accounts as Coca-Cola, BMW, Kodak, Walt Disney, Guinness, and Fiat.

Carat's rise, coupled with an advertising industry slump in the late 1980s, encouraged WCRS to exit its other businesses, including advertising, to refocus itself around its core media planning and buying activities. The company then changed its name to Aegis Group in 1990, later complementing its media operations with a market research arm.

Harrison Salinson's decision to join Carat was seen as a delicate choice. On the one hand, the company viewed the move as a means of catching up to outdoor leaders Concord and Portland. On the other, Harrison Salinson risked losing clients. In the end, however, most of the company's clients remained, and Harrison Salinson continued to win new clients independent of Carat. Into the early 1990s, the outdoor group claimed that less than ten percent of its revenues were generated through Carat.

Global Network in the 2000s

Harrison Salinson moved into the U.K. outdoor big leagues by 1993 when it won the coveted United Distillers contract, which was previously held by Portland. From there, Harrison

Key Dates:

1971: David Harrison and Judith Salinson lead the launch of British Posters.

1982: British Posters is dismantled; Harrison and Salinson form Harrison Salinson and are joined by Anne Rickard.

1989: Harrison Salinson is acquired by Carat Group, by then part of Aegis.

1996: Harrison Salinson becomes Posterscope.

2000: Aegis acquires Outdoor Vision in the United States, which becomes part of a new global outdoor strategy centered on the Posterscope model.

2001: Lord Media, based in Poland, is acquired; the re-branding of Carat's outdoor media operations under the Posterscope name is launched.

2002: Posterscope sets up its first office in China.

2003: Posterscope Hyperspace, specializing in digital out-of-home media, is created.

2004: Airport media specialist PSI is acquired, giving Posterscope the global lead in this market.

2005: Posterscope enters India through the purchase of 51 percent of Percept.

Salinson never looked back, and, even after its name change to Posterscope in the mid-1990s, remained the United Kingdom's leading outdoor buying and planning group. Part of the reason behind the company's name change was the departure of David Harrison and Judith Salinson. At that time, Anne Rickard became Posterscope's CEO, a position she continued to hold into the mid-2000s.

Posterscope remained focused on the U.K. market into the early 2000s, becoming the dominant outdoor specialist with a market share of more than 40 percent. The company claimed a client base of more than 130 media agencies, including the top three players, Carat, ZenithOptimedia, and Mediacom. Posterscope's revenues had grown strongly during the 1990s as well, rising from around £20 million in the early 1990s to top £210 million by 2001. In that year, the company named Steve Bond, who joined the company in 1992, to the newly created managing director position.

CEO Rickard was now free to focus her efforts on developing Posterscope's new strategy: that of becoming the global outdoor media champion. At the beginning of the decade, Aegis and Carat decided to launch Posterscope as its international outdoor brand, built on the British agency's model. Posterscope then took over the outdoor operations of Carat's own global subsidiary network.

Posterscope at first focused on building its European network, integrating the former Carat's operations. Posterscope also benefited from acquisitions, such as Aegis's purchase of Outdoor Vision in the United States in 2000, and of HMS in Germany and Lord Media in Poland in 2001. Posterscope also expanded through new development, launching a subsidiary in Italy in 2001, for example. In 2002, the company entered China, and within a year Posterscope had built up a staff operating out of offices in Hong Kong, Beijing, Shanghai, Guangzhou, Chengdu, and Xian.

Posterscope continued its expansion in the mid-2000s. Taking advantage of the development of a new generation of digital outdoor media platforms, the company created a new division, Posterscope Hyperspace, in 2003. The company also adapted to a shift in the outdoor industry towards the broader out-of-home market, which targeted not only the traditional outdoor markets but also other public locations such as airports, buses, and trains. Boosting its business in this area, Posterscope acquired the United Kingdom's PSI in 2004. This move enabled Posterscope to become the world leader in the airport media segment as well.

Posterscope remained in expansion mode into 2005. At the beginning of that year, the company announced that it was entering India by purchasing a 51 percent stake in Percept. Through this acquisition, the company gained access to one of the world's largest populations. By then, Posterscope had become an important element in Aegis's media buying division, posting revenues of more than $1.5 billion.

Principal Competitors

Clear Channel Outdoor; JCDecaux SA; Zenith Optimedia.

Further Reading

"Aegis Acquires PSI," *Marketing*, October 23, 2003, p. 9.

Barrett, Lucy, "Alban Reels as Rival Wins Briefs." *Marketing Week*, November 14, 2002, p. 15.

Griffiths, Ana, "Demonstrating How Effective Outdoor Advertising Really Is," *Campaign*, June 1, 2001, p. 15.

Krishnakumar, Aparna, "Pushing Outdoor," *Business Standard*, January 19, 2005.

Krishnakumar, Aparna, and Reeba Zachariah, "Percept Group to Re-enter Market Research," *Business Standard*, January 12, 2005.

Lam, Vincent, "A Year in China," *PS Posterscope*, October 2003.

"Posterscope Snares PSI," *Aegis Media Globe*, January 2004.

"Posterscope Wins Outdoor Account for Estee Lauder," *Campaign*, April 4, 2003, p. 3.

"Poster Specialists: The Independence Question," *Marketing*, April 29, 1993.

Sames, Claire, "Posterscope Lures Starcom Head," *Media Business*, November 19, 2001, p. 6.

—M.L. Cohen

Pranda Jewelry plc

333 Soi Rungsang, Bangna-Trad Rd
Bangkok 10260
Thailand
Telephone: (+66) 2 393 8428
Fax: (+66) 2 398 2143
Web site: http://www.pranda.co.th

Public Company
Incorporated: 1973
Employees: 6,000
Sales: $75 million
Stock Exchanges: Thailand
Ticker Symbol: PRANDA
NAIC: 339911 Jewelry (Including Precious Metal)
    Manufacturing; 339914 Costume Jewelry and Novelty
    Manufacturing

Pranda Jewelry plc is one of Thailand's leading manufacturers of jewelry, producing principally gold and gemstone jewelry, as well as costume jewelry. Pranda is also one of the country's most internationally oriented jewelry groups, generating more than 84 percent of its revenues outside of Thailand. These sales are supported by a network of manufacturing plants, including its main plant in Bangkok, with a production capacity of 3.4 million pieces per year, and foreign plants in Vietnam, Indonesia, and China. The company also has a number of international sales and distribution subsidiaries, including in the United States and the United Kingdom. Pranda also owns French jeweler H. Grinoire. The company markets its jewelry under a number of brand names, including Prima Gold, Prima Diamond, Cristalina, Esse, and Batik. Prima Gold is also the name of the company's growing retail network, which includes more than 70 stores in Thailand and across Asia and into the Middle East. Originally an original equipment manufacturer (OEM), Pranda has repositioned itself as an original design manufacturer (ODM) in the 2000s. The company expects nearly all of its production to be based on its own designs before the end of the decade. Pranda is listed on the Thai Stock Exchange and is led by the Tiasuwan family, including chairman Prida Tiasuwan.

Jewelry Maker in the 1970s

The Pranda jewelry group was founded in 1973 as Pranda Design Ltd. From the start, the company focused on the export market, shipping gemstones and jewelry designs. The company's initial target was the European market but later expanded to include the United States as well. By the early 1980s, Pranda had begun to export its own jewelry designs, establishing such brand names as Esse and Batik.

Pranda made the leap from design and export to production in the mid-1980s. In 1984, the company built its own factory, in Bangkok, employing some 300 artisans. While Pranda produced and marketed its own jewelry designs, the bulk of its business came from the OEM market, with the company producing designs for third parties. The shift toward production led the company to change its name that year, to Pranda Jewelry Ltd.

Pranda also adopted stricter quality control standards, enabling it to build a strong reputation on the international market. The company also added a second Thai operation, the Crystaline Company, which focused on the costume jewelry segment. By the end of the 1980s, the company's success encouraged it to launch an ambitious international expansion program. In order to fund this effort, Pranda went public, listing on the Thai Stock Exchange in 1990. The company then adopted a new name, Pranda Jewelry Public Company Limited.

The public offering gave Pranda the capital backing to expand its distribution and production capacity. In 1990, the company moved into North America, establishing its Crystaline North America subsidiary. That operation was joined by a second U.S. business, Pranda North America, in 1992.

Pranda also targeted growth in Europe, acquiring H. Grinoire, a Paris-based jeweler originally established in 1880. The addition of Grinoire gave Pranda another strong brand, adding high-end gold jewelry designs to the company's more usual focus on the costume and mid-range gold and gemstones sectors. After moving into France, Pranda sought a new Euro-

Company Perspectives:

Our commitment to customers: "Our prices will be competitive, our quality exceptional, and the services that we extend to facilitate your business transactions with the Pranda Group will be unexcelled."

pean opportunity, and in 1994 the company established its subsidiary in the United Kingdom. Germany also became a major European market for the company in the mid-1990s.

International Jewelry Group in the Late 1990s and 2000s

With more than 20 years of experience in the international jewelry export market, and with a decade of its own production under its belt, Pranda targeted a new area for the next phase of its expansion. In 1992, Pranda launched a new type of gold, called Prima Gold, which was 99.99 percent pure gold. The company's success in developing designs based on Prima Gold led it to enter the retail market, opening two Prima Gold stores in Bangkok in 1993. The concept caught on, and, after expanding into the rest of Thailand, the company began exporting its store format. By the mid-2000s, Pranda counted nearly 30 company-owned stores throughout Thailand and another 80 franchised stores throughout Asia and in the Middle East.

In order to stock its retail stores with its own merchandise, Pranda inaugurated a dedicated New Product Design and Development center in 1993. Pranda also expanded its production capacity. Pranda's main Bangkok site built up a capacity of some 3.4 million pieces per year, crafted by an employee base of more than 2,100 people. The company's Crystaline facility added an addition 80,000 piece-per-year capacity, produced by 400 workers. The company then built a new facility in Korat, Thailand, in 1994.

Pranda's international growth, and the expansion of the Prima Gold chain overseas, led it to begin developing an international production network as well. One of the group's first efforts in this direction was the creation of a joint-venture manufacturing plant in Jakarta, Indonesia. That facility grew into the group's second-largest, with a production capacity of more than 1.2 million pieces per year.

In 1998, Pranda moved into Vietnam, building a small facility there. Into the early 2000s, the Vietnam site's capacity remained at just 400,000 pieces per year. In 2002, however, Pranda launched an expansion of the site's capacity. The relatively low wages in Vietnam made it a particularly promising location for Pranda, which already exported some 90 percent of its Vietnamese production.

Pranda's attention turned to China in the early 2000s. In 2002, the company launched construction of a new production facility in Guanzhou. The plant was expected to support Pranda's entry into the Chinese retail sector as well, as the company made plans to open some 15 shops in China by mid-decade. Yet the effort hit a snag when the outbreak of the SARS virus, then the launch of war in Iraq, forced the company to put a temporary freeze on new expansion efforts.

Key Dates:

1982: Established in Bangkok, Pranda Design Limited begins operating as a jewelry design and export business.
1984: Pranda opens its own production facility and changes its name to Pranda Jewelry.
1990: Pranda goes public with a listing on the Thai Stock Exchange; the company's first U.S. subsidiary is launched.
1992: The company launches its Prima Gold brand and establishes the subsidiary Pranda North America.
1993: A Prima Gold retail network is launched.
1994: A new production plant in Thailand is added.
1997: The company opens a production facility in Vietnam.
2002: Pranda enters the Chinese market.
2003: Construction of a Guanzhou, China, production facility begins.
2004: A second production plant in Vietnam is constructed.
2005: The company announces a 200 million baht investment program in order to boost production past six million pieces per year.

Instead, Pranda approached the Chinese retail market in a different way. In 2003, Pranda signed a deal with Home Shopping Shanghai Ltd. to begin distributing its Esse jewelry brand in China. By the end of the year, however, the company's fortunes in China had changed. The drop-off in jewelry trade following the outbreak of the SARS virus led the Chinese government to loosen its gold trading rules. The new suppleness in the market encouraged Pranda to relaunch construction of its Guangzhou site, backed by an investment of some 60 million baht. At the end of 2003, the company also announced the opening of the first Prima Gold stores in China.

At the beginning of 2004, Pranda announced its plans to phase out its OEM operations and its intention to become a full-fledged original design manufacturer. As part of that effort, the company stepped up investment in its Prima Gold International subsidiary in order to boost its branded sales. Pranda also launched an expansion of its production capacity, adding some ten percent by 2005. A major beneficiary of the company's expansion program was its Vietnamese subsidiary, which began construction of a new factory in Danang that year.

Pranda's expansion continued into 2005 with the announcement of an additional 200 million baht in investments. This program aimed at increasing the company's total capacity to more than six million pieces per year. The production boost was expected to support not only Pranda's growing Chinese sales but also its move into Eastern Europe. In January 2005, the company announced that it was close to reaching an agreement with a German distributor in order to introduce its brands into Eastern European markets. After 30 years, Pranda had become Thailand's leading jewelry exporter.

Principal Subsidiaries

Crystaline Company Limited; Crystaline North America Inc.; H. Gringoire S.A.R.L.; LG-Pranda Co., Ltd.; P.T. GOLD Martindo; P.T. Pranda SCL Indonesia; Pranda (Guangzhou) Company Limited; Pranda Jewelry Public Company Limited; Pranda North America Inc.; Pranda U.K. Limited; Pranda Vietnam Company Limited; Prima Gold International Company Limited.

Principal Competitors

Chow Sang Sang Holdings International Ltd; LLD Diamonds Ltd; Beauty Gems Factory Company Ltd; EganaGoldpfeil Holdings Ltd; Royal Selangor International Sdn Bhd; Tasaki Shinju Company Ltd; Hang Fung Gold Technology Ltd.

Further Reading

Costello, Carol, and Becky Anderson, "Jewellery-maker Opens Plant in China," *Worldsources*, January 16, 2004.

Hemtasilpa, Sujintana, "Pranda Continues to Expand," *Bangkok Post*, January 26, 2005.

Pongvutitham, Achara, "Pranda Plans JV in Germany," *Nation*, January 26, 2005.

"Pranda Jewelry Stays on Sales Growth Path," *Thai Press Reports*, January 28, 2005.

"Pranda Ranked First in Export of Genuine Jewelry," *Thai Press Reports*, September 24, 2004.

"Pranda Ready for China Free Trade," *Bangkok Post*, March 10, 2004.

"Pranda Sets Goal to Work Only on Its Original Designs," *Bangkok Post*, January 17, 2004.

"Solid Growth Likely Despite Challenge from China and India," *Bangkok Post*, January 26, 2005.

Wiriyapong, Nareerat, "Thai Jeweler Set to Strike Gold Early in China," *Bangkok Post*, April 23, 2003.

——, "Pranda Sees Flat Sales Ahead as Sars Impact Starts to Bite," *Bangkok Post*, May 24, 2003.

——, "Vietnam a 'Gold Mine' for Pranda," *Bangkok Post*, March 30, 2004.

—M.L. Cohen

Price Pfister, Inc.

19701 Da Vinci
Foothill Ranch, California 92610
U.S.A.
Telephone: (949) 672-4000
Toll Free: (800) 732-8238
Fax: (800) 713-7080
Web site: http:www.pricepfister.com

Wholly Owned Subsidiary of Black & Decker
  Corporation
Incorporated: 1910
Employees: 2,300 (2003 est.)
Sales: $218.7 million (2003)
NAIC: 332913 Plumbing Fixture Fitting and Trim
  Manufacturing

Price Pfister, Inc. is a leading manufacturer of plumbing fixtures. Best known for its stylish faucets, the company also makes other kitchen and bath accessories. Price Pfister produces a number of different lines, ranging from the budget-priced Contempra to the higher-end Parisa, Marielle, and Catalina. The firm's innovations include the first faucet with a built-in water filter, created in association with Water Pik, and TwistPfit, an easy-to-install replacement faucet.

Beginnings

Price Pfister was founded in 1910 by Emil Price and William Pfister in Los Angeles, California. The company's first product was a gasoline powered generator that was marketed to farmers who did not have electrical service. Several years later the firm began to make garden faucets, and during World War I Price Pfister produced items for the U.S. military.

In the 1920s, the company's product line was expanded to include other types of faucets, valves, and hose nozzles for indoor sinks and bathtubs. More new products were added in the 1930s, including the ''Make-A-Shower'' fixture, which could convert an existing bathtub into a shower.

In 1941, Price Pfister was sold to Isadore Familian, and during World War II the firm again turned to military production, hiring women to replace men who had left for military service. The company manufactured aircraft fittings and hand grenade shells until the end of the war. With the postwar housing boom, Price Pfister began to specialize in producing residential faucets. This led to the introduction of color-coordinated fixtures in hues like cotton candy pink and sea green, which were designed to coordinate with the colored tile bathrooms popular during that era.

In the 1950s, Price Pfister introduced designs evocative of the atomic age, with swooping curves and rocket-like shapes. The company was growing at this time, and in 1960 a new plant was constructed on 25 acres in Pacoima, California, near Los Angeles. During the 1960s, more new products were introduced, including the Flowmatic Shower Handle, which featured a fingertip control lever to adjust water volume and temperature.

Sale to Norris Industries in 1969

In 1969, the company was purchased by Norris Industries, Inc., a maker of military, commercial, and household products. At this time, the company, known as Price Pfister Brass Manufacturing Company, had annual sales of approximately $27 million. In 1971, the firm's new automated foundry began operations at its Pacoima complex. It was the largest foundry in the western United States.

In 1972, Price Pfister opened warehouses in Georgia and Texas. The company was making 1,500 faucets per day. In 1974, Peter Gold, who had started with the firm as a salesman in 1956, was named president. The 1970s saw the addition of new translucent faucet handles with bronze fittings in a variety of colors, among other items.

In 1981, parent firm Norris was purchased in a leveraged buyout by Kravis, Roberts & Company and became known as NI Industries. When NI found itself strapped for cash two years later, Price Pfister was sold to company president Peter Gold and two partners for $35 million. To finance the deal, Gold had turned to childhood friend Sydney Irmas, then a well-known Los Angeles attorney, and David Rousso, a former partner at accounting firm Touche & Ross & Co. With their established credentials, the partners were able to borrow enough money to finance the deal. The interest rates at this time were high, however, and Price Pfister would have to increase its revenues in order to service the debt.

Focusing on Retail in Mid-1980s

Up to this time, most of Price Pfister's products had been sold directly to the construction and plumbing industries, and there was little awareness among the general public of the firm's name. Noting the growing popularity of stylish, expensive plumbing fixtures imported from Europe, Gold decided to introduce a new line for retail sale under the Society Finishes brand name. The firm used European crystal, porcelain, polished brass, antiqued bronze, black nickel, and hardwoods to create a line of striking faucets and accessories. The company focused on producing these quality products at an attractive price, typically 60 to 200 percent lower than the imports.

This move coincided with a growing trend among homeowners to do more of their own plumbing work, which was facilitated by the rise of retail chains like Home Depot and Builder's Square, outfits that offered discount prices and assistance with projects. The company soon launched a television advertising campaign that used the tagline, "The Pfabulous Pfaucet with the Pfunny Name," which was devised by L.A. ad agency Eisaman, Johns and Laws. The 30-second spots were run regionally at first, then given national exposure beginning in 1987.

By the latter half of the 1980s, Price Pfister was deriving 60 percent of its sales from the so-called "aftermarket," which was largely comprised of do-it-yourself remodelers. The firm's ability to sell quality fixtures at a reasonable price was made possible by its vertically integrated manufacturing process. At its 525,000 square foot Pacoima plant, the company had a brass casting foundry; die-casting, stamping, and injection molding machinery; automatic screw machines; machine and finishing shops; and tool-building, testing, and research and development facilities. Some 55,000 faucets were now being built each day.

Under Gold, the company grew from $50 million in annual sales to $117 million in 1987, and captured 14 percent of the U.S. faucet market. It also began exporting its wares to South America and Asia. Products introduced during the 1980s included the lower-priced Genesis line and a new ceramic-cartridge faucet, the Pforever Seal, which was guaranteed for life against leaks.

In April 1987, the firm, which now employed 1,600, went public on the NASDAQ, selling 18 percent of its stock for $34.5 million. Peter Gold and his partners retained a majority stake. A year later, in April 1988, Farmington, Connecticut-based Emhart Corp. reached an agreement to acquire the company for $215 million. Emhart was a maker of industrial, high-tech, and consumer products.

Black & Decker Buys Company in 1989

Just a year after the sale to Emhart, Price Pfister's new owner was acquired by Black & Decker Corp. of Towson, Maryland for $2.8 billion. Black & Decker, founded in 1910, was one of America's leading makers of power tools and appliances, and was seeking to broaden its offerings.

In December 1992, a lawsuit was filed against Price Pfister and more than a dozen other manufacturers of faucets by California's attorney general, which alleged that the firms had violated Proposition 65, the so-called "anti-toxics" law enacted in 1986. The companies' brass fixtures were manufactured with lead, which over time leached from the brass and entered the water supply. A similar suit was also filed by the Natural Resources Defense Council and the Environmental Law Foundation. Price Pfister and the other named companies countered that the method of measuring the lead had been flawed, as it was based on new faucets only, and noted that lead levels decreased significantly after a faucet had been in use for several months.

In the summer of 1994, the California attorney general's suit was decided in favor of Price Pfister, but a short time later competitor Delta Faucet's parent Masco Corp. filed suit against the company, alleging patent infringement on a new faucet in its Genesis line. Delta won the suit, and the judge blocked Price Pfister from making or selling the infringing faucet.

At about this time, the firm redesigned its packaging to reduce the number of faucets that were received in damaged condition or with missing parts. These sometimes amounted to as much as 30 percent of the total items shipped. The 1990s also saw the firm introduce the Pforever Warranty, which covered finish and function for life.

Environmental Lawsuit Settled and Foundry Closed

In January 1996, Price Pfister agreed to settle the lawsuit of the two environmental groups for $2.4 million and to decrease the amount of lead in its faucets to levels that complied with the law. This meant that the firm would have to change its manufacturing process from sand casting to machining, which was more expensive. The company had already begun reducing lead use and had spent a reported $40 million toward this end in recent years. At this time, Price Pfister's annual sales stood at approximately $200 million.

After the lawsuit was settled, the company announced that it would move its foundry operations out of the country, blaming the high cost of doing business in the United States. Price Pfister soon began laying off workers at the Pacoima facility and

Key Dates:

1910: Emil Price and William Pfister begin manufacturing generators in Los Angeles.

1910s: Garden faucet is the company's first plumbing offering.

1920s: The company expands its product line to include valves and hose nozzles.

1941: The company is sold to Isadore Familian.

1940s: The company begins to focus on residential faucet production.

1960: A new plant is built in Pacoima, California.

1969: The company is sold to Norris Industries, Inc.

1983: Peter Gold acquires the firm and remakes it as a supplier to the retail market.

1988: Emhart Corp. purchases Price Pfister for $215 million.

1989: Black & Decker buys the company through the acquisition of Emhart.

1996: Price Pfister pays $2.4 million to settle a lawsuit over lead in its faucets.

1997: The company's Pacoima foundry is closed and its operations shifted to Mexico.

1999: The firm becomes part of Black & Decker's new B&D Hardware and Home Improvement division.

moved their jobs to a plant in Mexicali, Mexico. Another 750 workers in manufacturing, marketing, and administrative positions would remain in Pacoima for the time being. A number of protests by laid-off workers followed, including a November hunger strike over their severance pay, but Price Pfister officially closed its foundry in January 1997.

In late 1997, the company reached an agreement with CheckOLite International, a maker of lighting, fans, and lamps, to create complementary lines of faucets and light fixtures under the Matchmakers brand name. Also in 1997, Price Pfister began working with oral care and water filtration products maker Water Pik to create a kitchen faucet with a built-in water filter. The resultant "Pfilter Pfaucet" was introduced the next year and priced at between $150 and $170. The year 1998 saw the company double its bathroom faucet offerings with three new collections that were affordable yet stylish.

TwistPfit Debuts in 1999

In 1999, Price Pfister introduced TwistPfit, a new replacement faucet and valve assembly that was easy to install. Unlike a typical faucet, it could be installed above, rather than below, the sink using only an Allen wrench. The first model, dubbed the Georgetown, was available in October for a suggested retail price of $227. Also in 1999, the firm also combined with Black & Decker's Kwickset security hardware unit to form the new Black & Decker Hardware and Home Improvement Group. The two companies' administrative operations were subsequently moved to a new building in Lake Forest, California.

In 2000, the firm awarded $20,000 in scholarship money to three industrial design students and their schools in its "Pfaucet

of the Pfuture" contest, part of the company's 90th birthday celebration. Also during that year, Price Pfister received International Organization for Standardization (ISO) certification for ISO 14001 and ISO 9002 compliance.

In early 2001, Price Pfister eliminated 60 administrative jobs and moved 60 to Lake Forest. Its Pacoima office space was closed, though 350 manufacturing jobs remained in place there. During the year, the company's sales dipped as the U.S. economy tightened. In 2002, the firm suffered a further sales decline when Home Depot decided to stop selling its products east of the Rocky Mountains. The company bounced back the following year, however, when Home Depot rival Lowe's agreed to boost its offerings.

In 2003, Price Pfister moved the last of its Pacoima staff to Lake Forest, and a year later it put the now-closed plant up for sale. The site required significant decontamination, as high levels of industrial chemicals and metals such as lead were left behind in the soil. It was later sold to a developer who planned to build a shopping center there which would, ironically, feature a Lowe's store that sold Price Pfister products.

In 2004, the company introduced the Catalina pullout faucet, the industry's first such faucet for the bathroom. Customers had the option of using it like a regular faucet or pulling out the 55-inch braided stainless steel hose for tasks like hair washing. It featured an aerator that gave either a standard stream or a spray of water. Price Pfister had earlier introduced pullout kitchen faucets in its Marielle and Parisa lines. The year 2005 saw the company regain some of the shelf space that it had previously lost at Home Depot.

In nearly 100 years of operation, Price Pfister, Inc. had grown into one of the leading manufacturers of faucets and other plumbing fixtures in the United States. It continued to offer products that were both innovative and stylish under the stewardship of owner Black & Decker.

Principal Competitors

Moen Inc.; Masco Corporation; American Standard Companies, Inc.; Kohler Company; Eljer Plumbingware, Inc.; Elkay Manufacturing Company.

Further Reading

Adamson, Deborah, "Ex-Workers Plan Hunger Strike at Price Pfister Plant," *Los Angeles Daily News*, November 21, 1996, p. N3.

——, "Outpouring of Job Insecurity; Plant Workers Protest Layoffs," *Los Angeles Daily News*, October 5, 1996, p. N1.

Beatty, Gerry, "Price Pfister's Pfilter Pfaucet Finds an Audience," *HFN*, August 10, 1998, p. 40.

"Black & Decker Profit Rises but Stock Falls," *Reuters News*, January 26, 2005.

Blizzard, Peggy, "Price Pfister . . . Pfabulous Pfaucets," *Southern California Business*, March 1, 1988, p. 7.

Cavanaugh, Kerry, and Rachel Uranga, "Retail Complex to Bring Jobs Back to Former Pacoima, Calif. Plant Site," *Los Angeles Daily News*, July 19, 2004.

"Emhart, Black & Decker Announce Merger," *Dallas Morning News*, March 21, 1989, p. 15D.

"Faucet-Makers Defend Work," *Dallas Morning News*, December 17, 1992, p. 9A.

Ference, Jeff, "Delta Says Price Pfister Copied Faucet," *Contractor*, August 1, 1994, p. 3.

Finz, Stanley, "Price Pfister to Close Foundry in Pacoima Today; City Officials Seeking Tenant for Site," *Los Angeles Daily News*, January 31, 1997, p. N4.

Garcia, Shelly, "Pacoima Site of Price Pfister Plant Put up for Sale," *San Fernando Valley Business Journal*, March 1, 2004.

Hack, Roxanne, "Stylish Faucets Won't Soak You," *Orange County Register*, December 11, 2004, p. 1D.

Hooper, Larry R., "Faucet Mfrs. Stunned by Calif. Suits," *Contractor*, January 1, 1993, p. 1.

Miondonski, Bob, "Faucet Makers Win One," *Contractor*, June 1, 1994, p. 1.

"New Box Cushioning Helps Faucets Arrive Safely," *Packaging*, October 1, 1993, p. 27.

"Price Pfister Offers Builders Style, Great Features and Value Projects," *Builder*, October 1, 2001, p. 204.

"Tap Water Lead Suits Pose Problem for Price Pfister," *Associated Press*, January 27, 1993.

Weber, Joseph, "The Corporation: Black & Decker Cuts a Neat Dovetail Joint," *Business Week*, July 31, 1989, p. 52.

Wilcox, Gregory J., "Faucet Firm Settles in Lead Suit," *Los Angeles Daily News*, January 31, 1996, p. B1.

—Frank Uhle

Punch Taverns plc

Jubilee House, 2nd Avenue
Burton-upon-Trent
Staffordshire DE14 2WF
United Kingdom
Telephone: (+44) 1283 501600
Fax: (+44) 1283 501601
Web site: http://www.punchtaverns.com

Public Company
Incorporated: 1997
Employees: 550
Sales: £638 million ($1.1 billion) (2004)
Stock Exchanges: London
Ticker Symbol: PUB
NAIC: 722410 Drinking Places (Alcoholic Beverages);
424820 Wine and Distilled Alcoholic Beverage
Merchant Wholesalers; 531190 Lessors of Other Real
Estate Property

Punch Taverns plc has worked its way to the top of the United Kingdom's pub market. Based in Burton-upon-Trent, Punch owns a portfolio of more than 7,800 pubs located throughout England, Wales, and Scotland, making it the country's number two pubs operator, trailing Japan's Nomura. Punch specializes in leased and tenanted pubs. Under this arrangement, the company owns the pubs, which are then rented to pub operators. The company provides marketing, design, training, and other support services to its pub operators, who in turn agree to purchase beers and ales exclusively from Punch. Punch also operates a Machines division that takes charge of vending and amusement machines located in the group's pubs. Formed in 1997 in order to acquire Bass Plc's pubs estate, Punch has grown through a series of massive acquisitions. In 1999, for example, the company acquired more than 2,000 pubs from Allied Domecq. Another major acquisition came in 2003, with the purchase of the Pubmaster group of nearly 3,000 pubs. The company is led by Giles Thorley and listed on the London Stock Exchange. In 2004, the group's sales topped £638 million ($1.1 billion).

Beginnings in the 1990s

The pub remained an enduring British tradition in the late 1980s, supported by another tradition, the "tied" system, in which pub owners and operators were bound by contract to purchase their beverages and other supplies exclusively from one of the country's brewers. Often, the brewers themselves owned the pubs outright. In this way, a large majority of the country's more than 50,000 pubs were owned by the brewers.

The British government decided to dismantle this system in the 1980s in order to introduce a more competitive market. In 1989, the government passed the so-called "Beer Orders," which limited brewers to the ownership of no more than 2,500 pubs each. Forced to sell off large portions of their pub portfolios, brewers were also faced with additional restrictions on the operation of the pubs they retained. Among these was a provision that obliged brewers to offer "guest beers" in their pubs. Guest beers tended to be sourced from local and regional brewers.

The legislation put into play a vast number of pubs, most of which were hived off into large-scale portfolios. The Beer Orders also created a new and highly vibrant industry in the United Kingdom, as a number of new companies appeared specializing in the ownership and management of pubs, bars, and other drinking establishments.

The loss of captive outlets for their beer sales in turn encouraged the brewers to focus on developing and expanding their beverage portfolios, spurring a massive restructuring of the drinks industries, not only in the United Kingdom but on a global scale. As companies such as Bass, Allied Domecq, Whitbread, and others grew into giant beverage groups, their pub operations were reduced to minor operations within their overall business. The limits on the size of their pub portfolios also made it difficult for the brewers to compete effectively against the growing number of large-scale pub owners. A new industry trend appeared in the mid-1990s as an increasing number of brewers now began to sell off their pub operations entirely.

Bass Plc decided to take this route in the mid-1990s and began taking bids for a portfolio of 1,428 pubs. In 1997, two successful British entrepreneurs, Hugh Osmond, a director and founder of

Company Perspectives:

Mission Statement: *Helping retailers build better businesses.* Goals and strategy: *In order to develop our business further, our goals are to: Maximise the overall profitability of every site; Optimise our share of the available profit; Grow through selective acquisitions.*

Key Dates:

1997: Hugh Osmond and Roger Myers found Punch Taverns in order to acquire Bass Plc pubs portfolio.

1999: Texas Pacific group acquires 70 percent of Punch; Punch acquires Inn Business Group and Vanguard (Allied Domecq) pubs.

2000: Punch Taverns places its leased and tenanted pubs into a new company, Punch Pubs, and begins the re-branding of its managed pub portfolio.

2002: The company spins off its managed pubs as the Spirit Group and launches a public offering on the London Stock Exchange.

2003: Punch Taverns acquires 283 pubs from Honeycombe Leisure, Greene King, Conquest Inns, and others and acquires the 3,115-pub group Pubmaster.

2004: The company launches Punch Taverns as a new global identity, replacing Punch Pubs, and acquires Innspired Group.

2005: The company sells 545 pubs from the Innspired Group and announces plans for future acquisitions.

the highly successful Pizza Express chain, and Roger Myers, who had built the Café Rouge chain of restaurants, formed a partnership to acquire the Bass portfolio for some £600 million. The Bass purchase was not the first deal orchestrated by Osmond and Myers. In November 1996, the pair had acquired the Wellington Pub Company, with its portfolio of 845 freehold pubs, from Nomura, an investment bank based in Japan that had become the United Kingdom's leading pub owner.

Prior to the completion of the sale, Bass dropped some 30 of the least profitable pubs from the portfolio. The reshuffling still left Punch with just under 1,400 pubs at the deal's completion in April 1998. Punch then launched a £40 million-per-year investment program, most of which was targeted at providing training for the group's pub operators in order to help them increase their profitability. Punch also encouraged pub owners to expand their food and catering offerings. In this way, Punch anticipated a wider industry trend in the 2000s that saw pub customers shift their consumption from purely beverages to an increasing focus on food.

While providing training, design, and purchasing support, Punch also replaced its operators' contract with a new range of contracts, providing a greater flexibility for operators in terms of their relationship with the company. At the same time, Punch moved to end the guest beer offerings at its pubs. Since the company was not a brewer, it was not bound to the obligation to offer guest beers. Nonetheless, the company's pubs continued to offer guest beers on a more limited scale.

Targeting the Pub Market Lead in the 2000s

From the outset, Punch announced its intention to take the company public in order to step up its expansion into the new century. Until then, the company sought other means of financing. In 1999, Osmond and Myers sold out most of their holding the company to American investment group Texas Pacific, which specialized in investments in the European market. Texas Pacific's share of Punch stood at 70 percent.

The sale to Texas Pacific was made in large part in support of Punch's bid to move into the U.K. pub market's big leagues. The late 1990s saw a flurry of large-scale pub portfolios come on the market as pub groups and brewers began tuning and reshuffling their pubs' operations for specific target markets and specialties.

Punch now began seeking the right fit among the many opportunities, launching an active acquisition program in 1999. The company's first purchase came in September 1999, when it acquired the 650 smaller pubs of the Inn Business group. Yet Punch was already preparing a larger acquisition. In 1999, beverage and restaurant powerhouse Allied Domecq had been in

negotiations to sell to Whitbread its pub operations, some 2,300 managed and leased pubs grouped as Vanguard. When the British Mergers and Monopolies Commission blocked the sale, Punch stepped in with its own winning bid of some £3 billion.

The addition of Vanguard boosted Punch into the top ranks of the British pub sector, with more than 4,000 pubs in its portfolio, including more than 1,000 managed pubs. The company at first expected to sell the managed pubs but instead decided to have a try at pub management. In 2000, Punch began re-branding the pubs under several trial brands, including the Big Room Bar, Beerhouse, and Copper Bowl. The company also operated the Big Steak pub and restaurant brand.

Nevertheless, Punch's real interest lay in its estate of leased and tenanted pubs. In 2000, these were all brought under a single business, called the Punch Pub group. By 2002, the company had decided to refocus itself as leased and tenanted specialist and de-merged its managed houses into a new and independent company, the Spirit Group. Following that operation, the company listed its stock on the London Stock Exchange in a successful offering that valued the company at nearly £600 million.

The offering, which allowed Texas Pacific to cash out some two-thirds of its holdings, also gave Punch the capital backing to continue its acquisition program. The company's next targets were more modest, however. By mid-2003, the company had added nearly 300 more pubs, mostly through the acquisitions of Honeycombe Leisure, a portfolio of tenanted estates from Spirit Group, Greene King, and Conquest Inns, for a total price of £121 million.

Punch moved into the United Kingdom's number two position at the end of 2003 when it announced its acquisition of rival pub group Pubmaster for £1.2 billion. The purchase added more than 3,100 pubs to Punch's portfolio, boosting its total past 7,400.

In 2004, Punch Taverns performed a new branding exercise, changing the name of its Punch Pub holding to Punch Taverns as well. The company followed this operation with a new large-scale acquisition, buying up the Innspired Group and its nearly 1,100 pubs for £335 million. Following that purchase, however, the company reviewed its now 8,300-strong portfolio, and in January 2005 disposed of 545 pubs, largely from the Innspired estate. That sale raised some £162 million for the company.

Later in 2005, Punch launched a refurbishment effort that it expected to rollout throughout its entire network of more than 7,800 pubs, backed by an investment expected to cost some £1 million per week. At the same time, the company announced its continued interest in expanding through acquisition. In January 2005, however, the company lost out on its bid for 364 Spirit pubs. Instead, the company turned its attention toward a new possibility, the 62-pub chain of Mill House Inns, expected to come up for sale in the early part of the year. Punch Taverns intended to keep making its way to the top of the U.K. pub market.

Principal Subsidiaries

GRS Inns Ltd; Pubmaster Finance Ltd; Punch Centrum Loan Company Ltd; Punch Funding II Ltd; Punch Taverns (Centrum) Ltd; Punch Taverns (CMG) Ltd; Punch Taverns (Jubilee); Punch Taverns (Offices) Ltd; Punch Taverns (PGRP) Ltd; Punch Taverns (PM) Ltd; Punch Taverns (PML); Punch Taverns (PPCF) Ltd; Punch Taverns (PPCS) Ltd; Punch Taverns (PTL) Ltd; Punch Taverns (Red) Ltd; Punch Taverns (SPML) Ltd; Punch Taverns (VPR) Ltd; Punch Taverns Finance plc.

Principal Competitors

Enterprise Inns Plc; Spirit Group; Limited Compass Group PLC; Whitbread PLC; Compass Roadside Ltd.; J D Weth-erspoon PLC; Wolverhampton and Dudley Breweries PLC; Mitchells & Butlers plc; Greene King PLC; Luminar PLC; Ascot PLC; SFI Group PLC.

Further Reading

Duckers, John, "Punching Above Its Weight," *Birmingham Post*, February 25, 2005, p. 24.

——, "Raise Glass to Pounds 3.5m," *Birmingham Evening Mail*, March 10, 2005, p. 62.

Fuquay, Jim, "Fort Worth, Texas-Based Group Buys British Pub Owner," *Knight Ridder/Tribune Business News*, May 19, 1999.

Hall, Amanda, "Pleased as Punch," *Sunday Telegraph* (London), May 12, 2002, p. 9.

Hobday, Nicola, "Punch IPO Hits Comeback Trail," *Daily Deal*, May 21, 2002.

Hope, Christopher, "Pubs Group's About-turn Gives New Heart to Nervy IPO market; Punch Taverns Relaunches Flotation at Lower Price," *Herald* (Glasgow), May 21, 2002, p. 19.

Johnson, Andrew, "Better Late Than Never for Punch in 600m Knockout," *Express* (London), May 23, 2002, p. 68.

Maitland, Alison, "Entertainer Unafraid of Confrontation," *Financial Times*, March 24, 1999.

"Punch Taverns Buys Pubmaster Estate," *Caterer & Hotelkeeper*, November, 13, 2003, p. 12.

Waller, Phil, "Punch's Growth Loses Fizz," *Birmingham Post*, January 27, 2005, p. 25.

Walsh, Dominic, "Punch in U-turn over Pubs," *Times* (London), September 8, 1999, p. 25.

——, "Punch Keen for Acquisitions," *Times* (London), January 27, 2005, p. 61.

Waples, John, "Punch Sets up Whitbread for Pounds 3bn Knockout Blow," *Sunday Times* (London), July 4, 1999, p. 1.

Wheeler, Brian, "Punch Develops Branded Pubs from Allied Estate," *Marketing Week*, June 8, 2000, p. 9.

—M.L. Cohen

Quovadx Inc.

6400 South Fiddler's Green Circle
Englewood, Colorado 80111
U.S.A.
Telephone: (303) 488-2019
Toll Free: (800) 723-3033
Fax: (303) 488-9738
Web site: http://www.quovadx.com

Public Company
Incorporated: 1997 as XCare.net, Inc.
Sales: $71.6 million (2003)
Stock Exchange: NASDAQ
Ticker Symbol: QVDX
NAIC: 511210 Software Publishers

Quovadx Inc., a global software and services firm based in Englewood, Colorado, serves thousands of companies in the fields of healthcare, financial services, telecommunications, manufacturing, and life sciences. The company assists customers worldwide to develop, extend, and integrate applications based on open standards. Quovadx is made up of three principal components. The first is its Integration Solutions division, which offers vertically specific solutions to improve processes and leverage existing technology systems. The other two components are its subsidiaries CareScience, Inc. and Rogue Wave Software, Inc. CareScience offers care management services and analytical solutions to hospitals and health systems and is a pioneer in community-wide data sharing and regional healthcare information organization solutions. Rogue Wave Software provides reusable software components and services that facilitate application development.

Origins

The story of Quovadx began in 1997 in Albuquerque, New Mexico. That year, a group of venture capital investors tried to save Mpower Solutions, Inc., a near-bankrupt healthcare software company. After a nationwide search for a new chief executive officer, the investors hired Lorine Sweeney, an expert in healthcare technology. Sweeney agreed to take the position provided she could relocate the company to Colorado. At 39, Sweeney's background included time at Microsoft, five years at Great West Life, and experience in the oil and gas industry, including briefly running a small oil and gas software company. In order to save the company, Sweeney hired a new team, formulated a new strategy, and started over in Colorado, recruiting ten executives with whom she worked at Thompson Healthcare, a Denver health care software firm. She renamed the company XCare.net, Inc. and began to search for badly needed venture capital. In 1999, when the company needed to raise $17 million to keep it afloat, Colorado's lack of experienced managers and engineers proved to be an obstacle. Sweeney's pitch to more than 100 venture capital firms was well received, but potential investors expressed little confidence that a Colorado company could attract top talent that would enable it to grow quickly.

Sweeney then switched strategies, spreading out the company's operations and adding a research and development facility in Silicon Valley to mollify investors. As a result, the company raised the $17 million and made an initial public offering in February 2000, which brought in $104 million. The company was already making considerable strides in the integrated software and services business, reporting 1999 revenues of $51.4 million, up from $10 million the year before. Unlike the plunging fortunes of other information technology companies after the stock market crash starting in the spring of 2000, XCare.net continued on the upswing. It signed a major a deal with MedUnite, a consortium of the nation's seven largest health insurers, to provide an Internet-based system for faster processing of medical claims, authorizations and referrals. In addition, since going public the company expanded its number of employees from 60 to 600 professionals in Atlanta, Georgia; Dallas, Texas; Charleston, South Carolina; Columbus, Ohio; Albuquerque, New Mexico; Islandia, New York; Los Angeles and San Carlos, California; and Honolulu, Hawaii. Moreover, sales had grown twelve-fold to $63 million, and the company's share price had doubled to more than $12.

Growth through Acquisitions

With cash from its public offering, XCare.net began to acquire companies as a primary part of its fast-growth strategy.

At the same time, it began to move beyond healthcare and into the entertainment industry to help companies automate digital distribution of films and music. In order to enter this new market, in 2000 XCare.net bought Integrated Media, a small New York company that created online movie promotions for film studios, including Paramount and Miramax. Xcare.net also opened a 15-person Los Angeles office and recruited Afshin Cangarlu, the former chief technologist for DreamWorks, the film studio founded by Steven Spielberg.

To reflect its new business direction, the company changed its name to Quovadx Inc. in September 2001. The change in name followed the acquisitions in June 2001 of Confer Software, Inc., a developer of e-business process management and workflow applications, and, in August, of Healthcare.com Corporation, a leading provider of enterprise application integration tools. Quovadx bought Confer for $6.6 million, including primarily an exchange of 592,453 shares of Quovadx common stock for the outstanding shares of Confer capital stock. The Healthcare.com acquisition totaled $93.1 million, which comprised 10,702,043 shares of Quovadx common stock issued in exchange for all outstanding shares of Healtchcare.com capital stock and $4.5 million in merger-related fees. Industry and financial analysts agreed with Quovadx's direction, especially since integration software was anticipated to fulfill a vital and profitable need in the marketplace that was expected to grow to $27.1 billion by 2004. Nowhere was this need greater than in the healthcare market, in which the company had built a substantial customer base that included such leading healthcare organizations as MedUnite, Healthnet, HCA, AMR/Kaiser, and the Medical University of South Carolina.

In December 2001, Quovadx concluded the acquisition of Pixel Group, a provider of integration and connectivity software with offices in the United Kingdom and Atlanta, for $7.3 million in cash and common stock. Pixel specialized in providing a wide range of integration products and had sold over 1.3 million integration and connectivity software licenses to hundreds of organizations in more than 50 countries, including to such customers as Dow Jones, Federated Department Stores, John Deere, IBM, Brooks Brothers, and British Telecom. A former distributor of Pixel's products for over a year, Quovadx accounted for about one-third of its $3 million in 2001 revenue. At the same time, editors of *InfoWorld* selected Quovadx as one of its top 100 innovators of 2001, exemplifying the creativity necessary to confront issues of fewer employees with larger workloads and declining budgets amidst the technology downturn.

In January 2002, the company announced both the expansion of its management team and the retirement of its chief

operating officer, Robert Murrie. Afshin Cangarlu, formerly executive vice-president of services, replaced Murrie, while the company added several positions, including executive vice-president and general counsel, vice-president of human resources, and chief medical officer and senior vice-president of clinical trials, to its executive team at Quovadx's Denver-area headquarters.

Quovadx's expansion of its management team reflected its rising profitability. Revenue of 2001, for example, totaled $52.3 million, an increase of 307 percent over revenue of $12.9 million for 2000. The company's had significantly expanded its presence in the fourth quarter of 2001 alone, signing a record 120 contracts worth $102 million. These contracts included such name brand clients as Gambro Healthcare, Baylor Healthcare, Methodist Health Care System, Medical University of South Carolina, McGraw-Hill Companies, Cable and Wireless, and Standard and Poor's. During 2001, Quovadx also took steps to broaden its distribution network, entering into strategic partnerships with Per-Se Technologies, Quadramed, Sun Microsystems, Microsoft, and MedUnited Service Paks.

In March 2002, the company sold its Advica Health Resources subsidiary to Royal Health Care of Long Island for $475,000 in cash and 4.6 percent of the outstanding equity in Royal. The terms of the asset sale agreement stipulated that Royal assume the operation of Advica's medical management services business, including personnel and property, and selected assets comprising key contracts, personnel, and equipment. Quovadx would retain Advica's core systems and information technology, which it would provide to Royal under a separate seven-year, $5 million services agreement.

On March 27, 2002, Quovadx purchased all of the outstanding capital stock of Outlaw Technologies, Inc., a leading provider of Healthcare Relationship Management (HRM) solutions to healthcare payer organizations. The purchase price, totaling $2.7 million, included 138,575 shares of Quovadx common stock and $1.8 million in cash and professional fees associated with the acquisition. With the acquisition, Quovadx could provide HRM to its customers and offer its own integrated software products to Outlaw's clients. Founded in 1999 in Boulder, Colorado, Outlaw Technologies was a privately held company that provided products which enabled clients to manage, control, and measure the direct and indirect relationships they had with their members, providers, groups, and agents. The acquisition marked yet another diversification of its operations into new niches in the healthcare market.

In September 2003, Quovadx announced it completed the purchase of CareScience, Inc., one of the nation's leading healthcare management companies. The deal was structured as an exchange offer, comprising $1.40 in cash and 0.1818 shares of Quovadx common stock for each share of CareScience common stock. The cost, totaling $30.1 million, included 2,415,900 shares of Quovadx common stock and $4.7 million in cash in exchange for all outstanding shares of CareScience and $2.3 million in merger related fees. Quovadx believed that CareScience's expertise in care management and clinical knowledge would complement its own medical management product offerings in the healthcare provider and payer segments.

The company's rapid revenue growth of 2,704 percent from 1998 to 2002 won it the ranking of 133 on the 2003 Deloitte Technology Fast 500, a ranking of the fastest-growing technology companies in North America. However, Quovadx lost $104 million on sales of $63.7 million in 2002, as the company could not entirely escape the telecom downturn. Within the first two quarters of 2003, nevertheless, the company increased its revenue and cut its loss by more than 70 percent to $858,000 during the quarter that ended in June.

In December 2003, Quovadx bought Rogue Wave Software, Inc. of Boulder, Colorado, a leader in C + + programming, for $79.1 million. The acquisition included an exchange offer in which Rogue Wave stockholders received a fixed exchange rate of $4.09 in cash and 0.5292 shares of Quovadx common stock for each share of Rogue Wave common stock. With the acquisition, Quovadx gained about 18,000 customers and over 300,000 software licenses. The deal brought the company an established product line and better positioned Quovadx to compete in both the Web services and application-development markets.

Troubled Times

On March 15, 2004, Quovadx said it was restating its 2003 financial results because it failed to collect payment from Infotech Network Group, a consortium of 15 information technology companies in India. The restatement caused Quovadx's stock to plunge 29 percent and forced the company to cut its revenue to $71.6 million from $82.9 million. In addition, its net loss widened to $14.7 million from $5 million. The restatement prompted several class action lawsuits alleging the company had violated security laws by issuing false and misleading financial results. Just days later, on March 19, the company also disclosed that securities regulators were conducting an informal investigation into its Infotech contract and other business deals from the third quarter in 2002.

However, when federal securities regulators gave notification that they were transforming their informal probe into a full-fledged investigation of the software maker's accounting practices, Quovadx's chief executive and chief financial officer resigned. The resignations marked the end of Lorine Sweeney's seven-year tenure as chief executive officer. With a weakening stock price and under pressure from the securities probe, in May 2004 a new management team cut 8 percent of the company's work force in a move to reduce costs. At the same time, NASDAQ notified Quovadx that it was in danger of being de-listed because of the delay in filing its 10-Q financial report.

Quovadx Positions Itself for the Future

To forestall the possibility of being de-listed by NASDAQ, the troubled software maker erased from its books $2.1 million in inflated revenue for 2002 and 2003 and issued delayed financial results for 2004 that showed red ink for the first six months. As a result of the restated financials, the Securities and Exchange Commission (SEC) ended its investigation and allowed Quovadx to regain compliance with NASDAQ.

In October 2004, Quovadx formalized the appointment of Henry A. Wagner as chief executive officer and president of the company. Wagner, then 63, had been serving as acting president and CEO since May 2004 after the company's two top executives abruptly resigned following the accounting irregularities that triggered the formal SEC probe. Before joining Quovadx, Wagner was executive vice-president and chief financial officer of Miran Corporation. After guiding the Quovadx through difficult times, Wagner had succeeded in repositioning the company to grow its software revenues by focusing on improving sales and expanding into new markets.

Principal Subsidiaries

CareScience, Inc.; Rogue Wave Software, Inc.

Principal Divisions

Integration Solutions.

Principal Competitors

SeeBeyond; Tibco Software; Vitria Technology.

Further Reading

"Denver Maker of Health-Care Software Changes Name, Direction," *Knight Ridder/Tribune Business News*, October 5, 2001.

"Englewood, Colo-based Software Maker Restates Earnings," *Knight Ridder/Tribune Business News*, August 18, 2004.

"Mounting Problems for Colorado Software Maker Quovadx," *America's Intelligence Wire*, May 14, 2004.

"Quovadx Acquires Rogue Wave Software for $71 Million," *eWeek*, November 4, 2003.

"Quovadx Announces Acquisition of Outlaw Technologies," *PR Newswire*, March 28, 2002.

"Quovadx Announces Changes to Management Team," *Business Wire*, April 12, 2004.

"Quovadx Announces Informal SEC Inquiry," *Business Wire*, March 29, 2004.

"Quovadx Announces Management Team Expansion," *PR Newswire*, January 10, 2002.

"Quovadx Announces Sale of Assets of Advica Health Resources to Royal Health Care, LLC," *PR Newswire*, March 11, 2002.

"Quovadx Completes CareScience Acquisition," *Business Wire*, September 19, 2003.

"Quovadx Completes Rogue Wave Acquisition," *Business Wire*, December 19, 2003.

"Quovadx, Inc. Announces Acquisition of the Pixel Group and Confirms Fourth Quarter 2001 EPS Guidance," *PR* Newswire, January 10, 2002.

"Quovadx Is the 133rd Fastest-Growing Technology Company in North America," *Business Wire*, October 14, 2003.

"Quovadx Ranked Among 2001's Top 100 Tech Innovators," *PR Newswire*, December 3, 2001.

"Quovadx Ranked Second in Deloitte & Touche Technology Fast 50 for Colorado," *Business Wire*, October 3, 2003.

"Quovadx Regains Compliance with Nasdaq Listing Requirements," *Business Wire*, August 23, 2004.

"Quovadx to Acquire CareScience in Stock and Cash Exchange Offer Valued at $2.09 Per Share," *Business Wire*, August 14, 2003.

"Quovadx to Buy CareScience," *Rocky Mountain News*, August 15, 2003, 3B.

"Quovadx Says SEC Probing Accounts of Failed India Deal," *Rocky Mountain News*, March 19, 2004, 4B.

"Software Maker Quovadx Delays Report," *The America's Intelligence Wire*, May 14, 2004.

"Troubled Quovadx Cuts 44 Jobs," *Rocky Mountain News*, May 5, 2004, 3 B.

"Two Top Quovadx Execs Quit CEO and CFO Resign as SEC Opens Formal Accounting Inquiry," *Rocky Mountain News*, April 13, 2004, 2B.

"XCare.net Has Changed Name to Quovadx, Inc.," *PR Newswire*, September 25, 2001.

—Bruce Montgomery

RANBAXY

Ranbaxy Laboratories Ltd.

19 Nehru Place
New Delhi
110 019
India
Telephone: +91 11 2645 2666
Fax: +91 11 2600 2091
Web site: http://www.ranbaxy.com

Public Company
Incorporated: 1962
Employees: 6,797
Sales: $1.18 billion (2004)
Stock Exchanges: India
Ticker Symbol: 500359.BO
NAIC: 325412 Pharmaceutical Preparation Manufacturing;
    325411 Medicinal and Botanical Manufacturing;
    325620 Toilet Preparation Manufacturing

Ranbaxy Laboratories Ltd. is the largest pharmaceutical company in India, and one of the world's top 100 pharmaceutical companies. Long a specialist in the preparation of generic drugs, Ranbaxy is also one of the world's top 10 in that pharmaceutical category as well. Yet, with India's agreement to apply international patent law at the beginning of 2005, Ranbaxy has begun converting itself into a full-fledged research-based pharmaceutical company. A major part of this effort has been the establishment of the company's own research and development center, which has enabled the company to begin to enter the new chemical entities (NCE) and novel drug delivery systems (NDDS) markets. In the mid-2000s, the company had a number of NCEs in progress, and had already launched its first NDDS product, a single daily dosage formulation of ciprofloxacin. Ranbaxy is a truly global operation, producing its pharmaceutical preparations in manufacturing facilities in seven countries, supported by sales and marketing subsidiaries in 44 countries, reaching more than 100 countries throughout the world. The United States, which alone accounts for nearly half of all pharmaceutical sales in the world, is the company's largest international market, representing more than 40 percent of group sales. In Europe, the company's

purchase of RPG (Aventis) S.A. makes it the largest generics producer in that market. The company is also a leading generics producer in the United Kingdom and Germany and elsewhere in Europe. European sales added 16 percent to the company's sales in 2004. Ranbaxy's other major markets include Brazil, Russia, and China, as well as India, which together added 26 percent to the group's sales. Ranbaxy posted revenues of $1.18 billion in 2004. The company, which remains controlled and led by the founding Singh family, is listed on the National Stock Exchange of India in Mumbai.

Moneylending Luck in the 1960s

Ranbaxy Laboratories had its origins in the early 1960s when Ranjit Singh and Gurbux Singh, two employees of a Japanese pharmaceutical company operating in India, formed their own pharmaceutical preparations company in Amritsar, in Punjab state. The two merged their names to form the name for their company, Ranbaxy.

Through the 1960s, India's pharmaceutical market remained dominated by foreign drug makers. The domestic pharmaceutical manufacturing industry was limited in large part to the dosage preparation, packaging, and distribution of existing formulations. Like many Indian drug companies of this period, Ranbaxy linked up with a European pharmaceutical company, and began production in 1962.

Ranbaxy's owners sought additional financing and turned to a local moneylender, Bhai Mohan Singh. By 1966, the pair had built up debts to Singh of more than the equivalent of $100,000. When Singh, a native of Pakistan who had arrived in India at the beginning of that decade, came to collect, the Ranbaxy partners offered to turn over their company to him instead.

Singh agreed to the deal and launched the Ranbaxy family on the path toward building one of India's largest business empires. Under Bhai Mohan Singh, Ranbaxy initially maintained its course of preparing and packing existing branded pharmaceutical products for the Indian market. The entry of Singh's eldest son, Parvinder, into the company in 1967, however, set the company on a new course to become a fully independent pharmaceutical company.

Company Perspectives:

The endeavour at Ranbaxy is to provide value. Value through pioneering work, research & development and quality pharmaceuticals across the globe.Ranbaxy keeps alive this endeavour as it steps into the new millennium, and reaffirms its commitment to the environment, the people and a healthier future.

Parvinder Singh had just graduated with a PhD in chemistry from the University of Michigan. The younger Singh's background in chemistry complemented his father's business flair. Yet Parvinder Singh himself quickly displayed a talent for business and was credited, in large part, with guiding the company into the ranks of the global pharmaceutical leaders.

Ranbaxy's good fortune came in 1970, when the Indian government passed legislation that effectively ended patent protection in the pharmaceutical industry. Indian pharmaceutical manufacturers were now able to produce low-cost, generic versions of popular, yet expensive drugs, revolutionizing the drug industry in India and in much of the world. The Singhs quickly took advantage of India's large, highly trained, yet inexpensive workforce, building up a strong staff of chemists and chemical engineers.

The company struck pay dirt early on, when it launched Calmpose, a generic formulation of the hugely popular Roche discovery, Valium. Released in 1969, Calmpose immediately placed Ranbaxy on India's pharmaceutical map. The company expanded quickly, and by 1973, Ranbaxy opened a new factory, in Mohali, for the production of active principal ingredients (APIs). This facility enabled the company to expand its range of generic medications and ingredients. To finance its growth, the company listed on the Indian Stock Exchange that year.

Ranbaxy's ability to produce generic medications at far lower cost than its branded competitors placed the company in a strong position for international expansion, especially in less developed markets. The company began its internationalization early on, launching a joint venture in Nigeria. That operation opened a production facility in Lagos in 1977.

Developing Research Expertise in the 1980s

Ranbaxy expanded its production at home as well, opening a new state-of-the-art dosage plant in Dewas in 1983. In 1987, the company became India's leading antibiotic and antibacterial producer when it completed a new API plant in Toansa, in Punjab, that year. The Toansa facility backed up Ranbaxy's plans to enter the U.S. market, and in 1988, the Toansa plant received Food and Drug Administration (FDA) approval.

Ranbaxy formulated a new strategy, that of becoming a full-fledged pharmaceutical company. The driving force behind the company's new direction was Parvinder Singh, who was named the company's managing director in 1982. Nonetheless, Bhai Mohan Singh remained in control of the company.

As part of its new strategy, Ranbaxy launched its own research and development center in 1985. The company also stepped up its marketing efforts, launching a new dedicated marketing subsidiary, Stancare, that year. By 1990, the company had a new product to sell, when Ranbaxy was granted a U.S. patent for its doxycycline antibiotic preparation. The following year, the company was granted a U.S. patent for its cephalosporin preparations, and the company built a new state-of-the-art facility for their production in Mohali.

A major milestone for the company came in 1992, when it reached a marketing agreement with Eli Lilly & Co. The companies set up a joint venture in India to produce and market Lilly's branded pharmaceuticals for the domestic market. At the same time, Lilly agreed to begin marketing Ranbaxy's generic medications in the United States. In this way, Ranbaxy gained widescale access, backed by the highly respected Lilly, into the world's single largest drugs market.

Parvinder Singh took over as head of the company—ousting his father in what was described as a family feud—in 1992. By then, Ranbaxy had grown into one of India's largest pharmaceutical companies on the basis of its generics production. Yet as pressure grew on India to begin enforcing international drug patents, the company itself appeared to have reached a crossroads—whether to remain focused on copying generic molecules, or to begin developing new drugs in-house. The company chose the latter, and in 1993 adopted a new corporate mission to announce its reformulated ambitions: "To become a research-based international company."

Global Branding for the New Century

Ranbaxy made good on its mission—by the middle of the next decade, nearly 80 percent of its sales came from outside of India. As a first step, the company launched a new joint venture, in China, backing its entry into that market with a production facility in Guangzhou. The following year, the company established subsidiaries in London, England, and in Raleigh, North Carolina. In 1995, the company stepped up its U.S. presence with the purchase of Ohm Laboratories Inc., which gave the company its first manufacturing plant in that market. Ranbaxy then launched construction of a new state-of-the-art manufacturing wing, which, completed that year, gained FDA approval.

This new facility enabled Ranbaxy to step up its presence in the United States, and in 1998 the company began marketing its generic products under its own brand name. That year, in addition, the company filed an application to begin Phase I clinical testing on its first in-house developed NCE. The following year, the company's NDDS efforts paid off as well, when Bayer acquired the rights to market Ranbaxy's single daily-dosage ciprofloxacin formulation.

Ranbaxy's international expansion continued as well, with the launch of marketing operations in Brazil. As the largest pharmaceuticals market in Latin America, that country was the cornerstone of the company's plans to expand throughout the region. Ranbaxy also expanded in Europe, with the agreement in 2000 to acquire Bayer's Germany-based generics business, Basics. The company also added production plants in Malaysia and Thailand.

Parvinder Singh died in 1999 and longtime righthand man D.S. Brar took over as company leader, naming family outsider Brian Tempest as company president. The new management team continued Singh's expansion strategy, opening a new manufacturing plant in Vietnam in 2001.

Key Dates:

1962: Ranjit Singh and Gurbux Singh incorporate Ranbaxy to market pharmaceuticals in Amritsar, India, and borrow funding from moneylender Bhai Mohan Singh.

1966: Bhai Mohan Singh takes over Ranbaxy in lieu of repayment of the loan.

1967: Son Dr. Parvinder Singh joins the company, which begins producing generic drugs.

1969: Calmpose, a Valium generic, is launched, becoming the company's first success.

1973: Ranbaxy goes public and builds a new API chemicals facility in Mohali.

1977: The company begins production in Lagos, Nigeria through a joint venture.

1983: The company opens a dosage plant in Dewas.

1987: The company builds a state-of-the-art API facility in Toansa in preparation for entry into the U.S. market.

1988: The Toansa facility receives FDA approval.

1992: The company launches a joint marketing agreement with Eli Lilly.

1993: A joint venture is launched in China; a new research-driven NCE and NDDS strategy is launched.

1994: The company opens a new research and development facility in Gurgaon, India.

1995: The company acquires Ohm Laboratories in the United States and builds a new FDA-approved production facility.

1998: Ranbaxy begins marketing its own branded drugs in the United States; the company launches clinical trials on the first in-house developed molecule.

2000: Ranbaxy acquires Basics, Bayer's generics business in Germany; the company enters Brazil.

2003: Ranbaxy successfully completes the first NCE phase I clinical trial; the company acquires RPG (Aventis) in France, becoming the leading generics manufacturer for that market.

2005: The company launches a new $100 million production facility in Brazil.

Ranbaxy also sought new alliances, and in 2003 the company reached a global drug discovery and development partnership with GlaxoSmithKline. That agreement called for Glaxo to handle the later-stage development process for Ranbaxy created molecules. The company's international expansion also took a major step forward at the end of 2002, when it agreed to acquire RPG (Aventis) in France, that country's leading generic drugs producer.

Ranbaxy's sales had by then topped the $1 billion mark, placing the company not only as the leader in India's pharmaceuticals industry, but also among the ranks of the world's top 100 pharmaceuticals companies. Ranbaxy also boasted a place among the world's top ten generic drugs producers. In addition, the company had advanced a growing number of its own NCE and NDDS molecules into clinical testing. The company's transition into research-based product development was seen as crucial as India announced its intention to enforce international drug patents at the beginning of 2005.

Ranbaxy appeared prepared to meet this challenge, however, and confidently set its sights on boosting its annual sales past $2 billion by 2007 and to more than $5 billion by the beginning of the next decade. International growth remained an essential part of that strategy. The company began negotiations for a major acquisition in Germany at the end of 2004, which was expected to be completed in 2005. The company also launched construction of a new $100 million production facility in Brazil. Meanwhile, Ranbaxy continued to increase its research and development budget, with the goal of generating as much as 40 percent of its revenues from its in-house innovations by the 2010s. Ranbaxy expected to remain India's drug leader into the new century.

Principal Subsidiaries

Basics GmbH (Germany); Gufic Pharma Ltd. (98%); Ohm Laboratories Inc. (United States); Ranbaxy (Hong Kong) Ltd.; Ranbaxy (Malaysia) Sdn. Bhd. (56.25%); Ranbaxy (Netherlands) B.V.; Ranbaxy (S.A.) Proprietary Ltd.; Ranbaxy (UK) Ltd.; Ranbaxy Do Brasil Ltda.; Ranbaxy Drugs and Chemicals Company; Ranbaxy Drugs Ltd.; Ranbaxy Egypt Ltd.; Ranbaxy Europe Ltd. (United Kingdom); Ranbaxy Farmaceutica Ltda. (Brazil; 70%); Ranbaxy Fine Chemicals Ltd.; Ranbaxy France SAS; Ranbaxy Ireland Ltd.; Ranbaxy Nigeria Ltd. (84.89%); Ranbaxy Panama, S.A.; Ranbaxy Pharmaceuticals Inc. (United States); Ranbaxy Poland Sp. z.o.o.; Ranbaxy PRP (Peru) S.A.C.; Ranbaxy Unichem Company Ltd. (Thailand; 88.56%); Ranbaxy USA, Inc.; Ranbaxy Vietnam Company Ltd.; Ranbaxy (Guangzhou China; 83%); Ranbaxy, Inc. (United States); Ranchem Inc. (United States); Ranlab Inc. (United States); RanPharm Inc. (United States); Rexcel Pharmaceuticals Ltd.; Solus Pharmaceuticals Ltd.; Unichem Distributors (Thailand; 99.96%); Vidyut Investments Ltd.; Vidyut Travel Services Ltd.

Principal Competitors

RPG Enterprises; GlaxoSmithKline Consumer Healthcare Ltd.; East India Pharmaceutical Works Ltd.; Dr. Reddy's Laboratories Ltd.; Cipla Ltd.; Concept Pharmaceuticals Ltd.; Khandelwal Laboratories Ltd.; Dabur India Ltd.

Further Reading

Bhandari, Bhupesh, *The Ranbaxy Story: The Rise of an Indian Multinational,* Calcutta: Penguin Books India, 2005.

Datta, P.T. Jyothi, "Ranbaxy Setting Up Plant in Brazil," *Business Line,* October 7, 2004.

Einhorn, Bruce, and Manjeet Kripalani, "A Little Lab Work—and A Lot of Lawyers," *BusinessWeek,* January 28, 2003.

Joly, Julie, "Un tigre dans la pharmacie," *L'Express,* December 20, 2004.

Mohan, N. Chandra, "Tempestuous Times Ahead for Ranbaxy," *Financial Express,* December 25, 2003.

"Ranbaxy Buys Aventis' Generics Unit in France," *Business Line,* December 14, 2003.

"Ranbaxy Restructures Top Management," *Times of India,* January 22, 2005.

"Ranbaxy Ties Up with Israeli Teva," *Press Trust of India,* December 20, 2004.

"Ranbaxy Turns into Billion Dollar Company," *India Business Insight,* February 2004.

Subrakanian, Nithya, "Ranbaxy's Tempest Upbeat on 2005," *Business Line,* January 19, 2005.

—M.L. Cohen

Rathbone Brothers plc

159 New Bond Street
London
W1S 2UD
United Kingdom
Telephone: +44 20 7399 0000
Fax: +44 20 7399 0011
Web site: http://www.rathbones.com

Public Company
Incorporated: 1742
Employees: 78
Operating Revenues: £109.95 million ($211.82 million)
   (2004)
Stock Exchanges: London
Ticker Symbol: RAT
NAIC: 523120 Securities Brokerage; 523920 Portfolio
   Management

While Rathbone Brothers plc (Rathbones) dates its history to a 1742 founding as a Liverpool-based shipping business, the company eventually came to be best known for providing financial services, with a focus on the investment management and unit trust markets. Rathbones operates from offices in London and Liverpool—the latter city is also the site of the group's backoffice operations—as well as six regional offices, including an office in Scotland. Since the late 1990s, the bank has built up a growing offshore presence, with operations in Jersey and Geneva, Switzerland, and in the British Virgin Islands. Rathbones also has grown through a series of acquisitions, as well as through the hiring of individual investment managers and their client portfolios. The United Kingdom remains by far the group's primary market. The United Kingdom also represents nearly 90 percent of the more than £7 billion of total funds under the group's management at the beginning of 2005. Investment management and banking accounts for approximately 80 percent of the group's operations, with trust services providing the remainder. Although the founding Rathbone family remains associated with the company, Rathbones has been listed on the London Stock Exchange since the mid-1980s. Former and current company employees hold about 25 percent of the group's stock. The company is led by Chairman Mark Powell, CEO Roy Morris, and CFO Andy Pomfret.

Shipping Dynasty Until the 20th Century

Rathbone Brothers was founded in 1742 by William Rathbone II. Born in 1696 in Gawsworth, a village near Macclesfield, England, Rathbone went to work in Liverpool, then a fast-growing British port, starting his professional life as a sawyer. By 1742, Rathbone had launched a business trading timber.

Rathhbone's son, William III, inherited his father's business and built it into a major international trading company. The younger Rathbone continued the local timber trading business, but extended its activities to encompass a wider range, adding new goods, and especially, new foreign trading routes. By the end of the century, the Rathbone family counted among the most prominent of Liverpool's rising shipping industry. William III was later joined by his son, William IV.

Much of the family's operations took place through a series of partnerships into the early 19th century. The company took on its more permanent form only in 1824, when brothers William V and Richard Rathbone, together with James Powell, formed a new partnership under the name of Rathbone Brothers & Co. By then, the company had established prominence for itself as a leading trader of cotton from the United States.

Over the following decades, Rathbone Brothers added additional partners, including William VI and his brother Samuel Greg Rathbone, who joined the company in 1842 and 1847, respectively. Another important figure in the company's development was Henry Wainwright Gair. By the 1840s, Rathbones had begun importing grain from the United States as well as cotton. The company, which built up an important fleet during this period, also profited from its trade with the United States by launching shipments of tea and coffee to the United States. India, too, represented an important trading market for the company, particularly for cotton and textiles. In 1841, the company's interests in India were strengthened when it became the official Liverpool trading agent for the giant East India Company.

Company Perspectives:

Independence is an increasingly rare phenomenon, especially today where large financial institutions often deliver "one-solution-for-all" services. At Rathbones we value our independence as it gives us the freedom to develop investment strategies that are right for our clients whatever their financial goals and risk profile. Independence also gives us the confidence to deal with change. While our firm has its roots in the 18th century, our approach is very much of today. We understand the vagaries of the world economies and are always ready to adapt individual investment strategies to meet the ever-changing circumstances of our clients. It is vital to have the experience, the insight, the technology and, of course, the presence of mind to do so—rapidly and decisively. And, finally, independence allows us to deliver a genuinely personal service that is based on an investment manager developing an investment solution that is individual to each client.

To support its growing trade interests, Rathbones established an agency in New York in the 1840s, initially under the leadership of Henry Wainwright Gair. At the same time, the company extended its reach to China, opening two agencies in Shanghai and Canton. Launched by Samuel Greg Rathbone, the company's Chinese branch began operating under the name of Rathbone, Worthington and Co. The company began exporting tea and silk from China, and importing British products to the country. Other Rathbone operations launched during the second half of the century included salted beef from South America; wheat, corn, and cotton from Egypt; and coffee from Brazil. The increasing reach of the company's operations prompted it to establish a new agency in London. Originally operated under the leadership of Rathbones partner William Lidderdale, the London branch began the base of operations for a new generation of Rathbones, William Gair Rathbone VII.

Changing Focus in the 20th Century

Like many of the great British trading houses, Rathbones' fortunes dwindled toward the turn of the 20th century. Increasing competition, including the appearance of a new generation of powerful companies in the United States, cut deeply into Great Britain's former trade dominance. At the same time, the appearance of new technologies, including steam and internal combustion engines, and the first intercontinental communications services, increasingly pushed the trading house toward obsolescence.

By 1890, Rathbones had begun to struggle to retain its profits. By 1898, the company's difficulties had forced it to shut down its London agency altogether. Rathbones' financial problems continued into the new century, and by 1912, the company was forced to restructure its operations. From that point, Rathbones progressively abandoned its trading operations in favor of a new field, that of financial management.

Entering the 20th century, the Rathbone family had become one of the country's most prominent. The Rathbones also had gained a reputation for their social and political advocacy. William IV had lead the way, taking the stand against British involvement in the slave trade, despite Liverpool serving as a major hub in that traffic. William V had fought corruption in the city's government, while William VI had been responsible for founding the area's District Nursing program. The family's social commitment continued into the new century, donating its family's Greenbank estate—home to the Rathbones since the late 18th century—to the University of Liverpool starting in the 1930s.

The Rathbone partnership in the meantime began a new, quieter life providing asset management services to the Rathbone family. Rathbones evolved into an accredited bank over the next decades, although the company did not develop typical banking products, such as checking accounts and other services. Instead, the company focused its operations on treasury management, in large part based on clients' excess assets. Rathbones also retained fairly closed operations. Into the early 1980s, the company's client base remained mostly limited to the Rathbone family and their friends and contacts.

Reforms to Britain's banking sector in the 1980s, coupled with the Thatcher government's pro-capitalistic stance, encouraged Rathbones to become interested in expanding its business. As part of that effort, the company abandoned its partnership status in 1984, and instead listed its stock as a public limited company (plc) on the London Stock Exchange that year. Nevertheless, Rathbones maintained certain aspects of its partnership past, such as the granting of equity shares in the business to its employees. By the dawn of the 21st century, former and current Rathbone employees held more than 25 percent of the company's shares. This helped lend a partnership-like feel to the company's corporate culture.

Leading U.K. Private Banker in the 21st Century

Yet Rathbones' public listing also exposed it to shareholder pressure. Into the late 1980s, the company appeared relatively inefficient, achieving only slender profit margins. Rathbones responded to the situation by agreeing to merge with another financial planning company, Comprehensive Financial Services Ltd., or CFS.

CFS was founded in 1971 by Oliver Stanley, with backing from a number of institutional investors. The London-based company initially acted as a consultancy, providing financial planning services. In 1975, however, after Stanley led a management buyout of the firm, it began expanding its services, not only in the United Kingdom, but also to a foreign clientele. In 1984, the company placed a number of its shares on the London exchange's Unlisted Securities Market. This in turn permitted the group to expand its operations into the discretionary fund management market through the acquisition of CFS (Investment Management) Ltd. That firm was owned and led by two former Dunbar Fund Managers, Micky Ingall and Jonathan Ruffer. Into the late 1980s, CFS enjoyed strong profits.

Although half the size, in terms of assets under management, as Rathbones, CFS proved twice as profitable. The merged company, which retained the Rathbone Brothers name, was able to exploit the complementary geographic scope of both companies, as well as Rathbones' coveted status as a full bank. The

Key Dates:

1742: William Rathbone II establishes a sawyer business and timber trading company in Liverpool.

1824: William Rathbone V and brother Richard Rathbone form a new partnership with James Powell, called Rathbone Bros. & Co.

1841: Rathbones becomes the principal trading agent in Liverpool for East India Company.

1847: Samuel Greg Rathbone becomes partner and expands operations with offices in Shanghai and Canton, China; Rathbones also opens an office in New York and, later, an office in London to handle increasing trade in tea and silk from China.

1898: Financial problems lead to the closing of the London agency.

1912: Rathbones restructures and converts its focus to financial management.

1971: Oliver Stanley founds a financial services consultancy in London, which later becomes CFS.

1975: Stanley leads a management buyout and expands the range of services offered by CFS.

1984: Rathbones lists on the London Stock Exchange; CFS places shares on the Unlisted Securities Market.

1985: CFS acquires CFS (Investment Management) Ltd.

1988: Rathbones and CFS merge, under the Rathbone Bros. name.

1990: Rathbones expands to Geneva and the British Virgin Islands.

1995: The company acquires the Laurence Keen investment management firm.

1996: The company acquires the Nielson Cobbold investment management firm.

1998: Keen and Cobbold are merged into a single, unified business; the company acquires Curzon Secretaries & Trustees Ltd. in Jersey.

2000: The company acquires Nigel Harris Trust Company Ltd. in Jersey.

2005: Rathbones forecasts total assets under management to top £8 billion by the end of the year.

larger Rathbones portfolio benefited from CFS's tighter efficiency; at the same time, the company also could take advantage of Rathbones' presence in Liverpool, which offered far lower overhead costs than CFS's London-based business.

Going forward, Rathbones began making a series of small acquisitions, including adding individual fund managers and the client portfolios, as well as small trust and other asset management firms. Rathbones also moved to establish a European presence ahead of the lowering of trade barriers among EU countries in 1992. As part of that effort, the company established an office in Geneva, Switzerland in 1989. Initially a partnership, Rathbones acquired full control of its Geneva branch in 1990, giving the bank an important entry into the underdeveloped unit trust management market in Switzerland. In that year, also, Rathbones established an office in the British Virgin Islands, increasing the scope of its trust and company services.

Rathbones made two significant acquisitions in the mid-1990s. In 1995, the company acquired investment management firm Laurence Keen. That purchase was followed up by the acquisition of Nielson Cobbold at the end of 1996. Operations of the three firms were then combined into a single entity in 1998, based around Rathbones' London and Liverpool centers. By expanding the company, Rathbones was also able to expand its geographic scope, with regional centers appearing in Edinburgh, Bristol, and Worcester, and elsewhere in Great Britain. Acquisitions continued to play an important role in Rathbones' growth, with additional purchases including the smaller firms of Albyn Investments and Walsham Consultants.

Rathbones also had moved onto the Channel Islands, allowing its customers to take advantage of the liberal tax laws there by establishing a dedicated Unit Trusts business. In 1998, the company expanded its Channel Islands presence with the acquisition of Curzon Secretaries & Trustees Ltd., which was subsequently renamed as Rathbone Jersey Ltd. Following that acquisition and the amalgamation of Lawrence Keen and Nielson Cobbold into the company, Rathbone launched a massive redevelopment of its administrative systems, creating a single, unified investment management computer system.

That process was completed, in large part, in 2000. The new system not only permitted the company a significant cost savings, notably by greatly reducing administrative tasks, but also provided a low-cost platform for further expansion. The company then launched a new round of acquisitions, including the 2000 purchase of Jersey-based Nigel Harris Trust Company Ltd. Other purchases by the company included Galsworthy & Stones and Oaktree Investment Management, as well as a number of individual investment managers.

Despite the difficult economic climate of the early 2000s, Rathbones maintained its strong growth. Between 2001 and the end of 2002, the company's assets under management portfolio grew by more than £1 billion ($1.6 billion). That growth continued toward mid-decade. By 2003, the company's total assets under management topped £5 billion. By the end of 2004, the group's total funds under management stood at nearly £7 billion ($13.6 billion), and the company expected its total assets portfolio to top £8 billion by the end of 2005. In this way, Rathbones, with a history stretching back more than 260 years, entered the new century as one of the United Kingdom's leading independent investment management banks.

Principal Subsidiaries

Rathbone Bank (BVI) Ltd. (British Virgin Islands); Rathbone Investment Management (C.I.) Ltd. (Jersey); Rathbone Investment Management Ltd.; Rathbone Jersey Ltd. (Jersey); Rathbone Stockbrokers Ltd.; Rathbone Trust Company (BVI) Ltd. (British Virgin Islands); Rathbone Trust Company B.V. (Netherlands); Rathbone Trust Company Jersey Ltd. (Jersey); Rathbone Trust Company Ltd.; Rathbone Trust Company S.A. (Switzerland); Rathbone Unit Trust Management Ltd.

Principal Competitors

Fortis N.V.; AEGON N.V.; CDC IXIS Capital Markets; Westpac Banking Corporation; Landesbank Berlin–Girozentrale;

DnB NOR ASA; BNP Paribas Arbitrage; Caisse Interfederalc de Credit Mutuel; UniCredit Banca Mobiliare S.p.A.; Mediobanca S.p.A.

Further Reading

Avery, Helen, "The Bald Truth About Rathbones," *Euromoney,* November 2004, p. 6.

Nottingham, Lucie, *Rathbone Brothers: From Merchant to Banker 1742–1992,* London: Rathbone Brothers PLC, 1992.

Owens, Martin, "The Rise of Rathbones," *Private Banker International,* December 2004, p. 11.

—M.L. Cohen

RCN Corporation

105 Carnegie Center
Princeton, New Jersey 08540
U.S.A.
Telephone: (609) 734-3700
Toll Free: (609) 746-4726
Fax: (609) 734-6164
Web site: http://:www.rcn.com

Public Company
Incorporated: 1997
Employees: 2,537
Sales: $484.9 million (2003)
Stock Exchanges: Over the Counter
Ticker Symbol: RCNI
NAIC: 513310 Wired Telecommunications Carriers

RCN Corporation is a Princeton, New Jersey-based company known as an "overbuilder" in the cable television industry. It establishes a cable and communications network in markets already served. However, unlike previous overbuilders that simply relied on cable, RCN has attempted to succeed by adding other revenue streams such as high-speed internet, local telephone, and long distance telephone and by offering their services in an attractively priced bundle to pry customers away from their long-time cable and communications providers. RCN operates in select, densely populated markets, serving more than one million customer connections in Boston, New York, Philadelphia, Washington, D.C., Chicago, Los Angeles, and San Francisco. Once a high-flying company able to attract investments from the likes of Hicks, Muse, Furst Inc., and Paul Allen of MicroSoft fame, RCN has been derailed by the meltdown of the tech sector in 2000. With its stock selling for just pennies on an over-the-counter basis, RCN underwent a Chapter 11 bankruptcy reorganization in 2004.

Founder Starts out in Construction in the 1980s

The man behind the rise of RCN, David C. McCourt, was born in Boston. He was the youngest of seven children, and his father was a construction contractor. As a teenager, McCourt aspired to be a hockey player or a policeman. When he went to college at Georgetown University, he decided to become a social worker. After graduating in 1979, he worked for 18 months as a probation officer's aide in a tough neighborhood in Washington, D.C. Reevaluating his career options, he returned home to Boston in 1981, went to work for his father, and by the end of the year had launched his own construction business. He became interested in telecommunications by sheer chance. "I was doing a $3,000 job pumping muck out of manholes so Time Warner could pull cable through," he told *Business News New Jersey* in 1998, recalling how he began laying coaxial cable for Time Warner and Cablevision in the Boston area. "Thinking that pumping muck made me a cable TV contractor, I submitted a bid and got the job."

Ambitious by nature, McCourt was not content for long to be a mere contractor and soon decided to lay telephone cable for himself. His new company, Corporate Communications Network (CCN), bypassed the local telephone provider by creating small local networks aimed at high-volume business customers. His efforts caught the attention of Peter Kiewit Sons, a major Omaha-based construction company, which had similar aspirations for Boston through a venture called Metropolitan Fiber Systems, later renamed MFS Communications. Kiewit and McCourt decided to join forces, resulting in MFS buying CCN to create MFS/McCourt. McCourt then set his sights on the United Kingdom, where telephone competition was in its infancy. He worked on his own for a year, then Kiewit again teamed up with him, becoming a partner in McCourt Kiewit International. He oversaw Kiewit jobs designing and building residential telephone and cable systems in Europe. The venture was eventually sold to MFS, which in turn was acquired by WorldCom in 1996 for $14.4 billion.

Having earned a reputation as a telecommunications maverick, McCourt returned to the United States and forged his third partnership with Kiewit. In 1993, they formed a Kiewit subsidiary called RCN Corporation to invest in the residential telephone and cable television industries. In October of that year, the company closed on its first deal, the $196 million purchase of a controlling interest in C-TEC, a Wilkes-Barre,

Company Perspectives:

RCN's goal is to be the dominant provider of residential communications services to the most densely populated markets in the country via out own network.

Pennsylvania-based telephone and cable-television outfit that had $257 million in revenues the prior year. McCourt was installed as C-Tec's chief executive officer and chairman, and RCN and C-Tec then formed a joint venture, Residential Communications Network Inc. to provide telecommunications services to the residential market. In August 1994, McCourt relocated the business to Princeton, New Jersey, in an effort to attract what he called "younger, more aggressive" employees.

Telecommunications Act of 1996 Offers Opportunities

The telecommunications landscape changed dramatically with the Telecommunications Act of 1996, which broke down the regulatory divisions between local telephone companies, long-distance providers, and cable television companies. As a result, a multitude of start-ups emerged to compete with the Baby Bells in offering communication services, mostly targeting business customers promising a higher-margin payoff than residential customers. Cable companies, on the other hand, were saddled with expensive one-way networks and were reluctant to invest the necessary capital to recast their infrastructure in order to enable it to accommodate two-way transmission. RCN took a different approach from that of most of the firms looking to exploit the openings provided by the change in law. It would go after residential customers, building a full-service fiber-optic network, market by market, with the plan of eventually achieving a national presence. The key to making this overbuilding approach work was to offer customers an attractively priced bundle of services: telephone, cable, and high-speed Internet.

In conjunction with the enactment of the Telecommunications Act of 1996, McCourt restructured C-Tec, splitting it into three separate public companies: Commonwealth Telephone Enterprises, which received C-Tec's Pennsylvania telephone operations; Cable Michigan, Inc., which took over all of the Michigan cable systems as well as a 62 percent stake in Mercom, operator of cable systems in Michigan and Florida; and Residential Communications Network, the communications network building entity that started out with 90,000 cable subscribers in New York and New Jersey. RCN then acquired Residential Communications Network to form the foundation for McCourt's new vehicle to take on the entrenched telecommunications industry. When the realignment was complete in October 1997, RCN lost little time in raising $575 million in junk bonds to start building its communications network. The initial focus was on a corridor that stretched from Boston to Washington, D.C., a potential market of some 25 million households. McCourt's ambitious goal was to make customers out of nine million of them. Given that it would cost from $1,200 to $1,400 to wire each household, RCN was looking at a $12 billion price tag to build the Northeast network.

RCN jump-started it expansion plan in 1996 with the acquisition of Liberty Cable, a company providing television services to New York City buildings through Multichannel Multipoint Distribution Service (MMDS) antennas. Launched in 1991, Liberty had 40,000 subscribers. RCN also gained toeholds in Boston and Washington, D.C., by forging joint ventures with Boston Edison in Boston and Potomac Electric in Washington. Because telephone and cable companies were loathe to have an upstart competitor string its network from already crowded utility poles or underground electric conduits, RCN gained right-of-way from the electric companies, sharing space on the top rung of the utility pole, reserved for electric power lines, and pulled next to power lines in underground conduits.

RCN showed early promise, due in large part to the heritage of telephone and cable companies, neither of which had developed much expertise in marketing during their days as monopolies. The cable companies were also limited financially by having piled up massive debt while acquiring other systems at inflated prices during buying sprees in the 1980s and 1990s. Furthermore, they were saddled with outmoded technology in the form of copper coaxial cable, which to upgrade would require a great deal of capital. As a result, they were hard pressed to complete with RCN in terms of both price and product. Additionally, unlike cable companies, whose franchise required that they virtually cover an entire market, RCN could be selective and cherry-pick the neighborhoods it wanted to wire, avoiding sparsely populated, high-income areas in favor of lower-income, densely populated neighborhoods that watched more television. In New York, the company was especially aggressive in building on the business Liberty Cable had established, which now gave RCN the advantage of offering both cable television and telephone service to residential developments. The company was also willing to accommodate landlords, not only in terms of service but in revenue-sharing plans that returned a percentage of gross revenues realized from a property.

In February 1998, RCN strengthened the data side of its business by acquiring a pair of Internet service providers (ISPs). It paid approximately $45 million for Virginia-based Erols Internet, Inc., serving more than 293,000 customers, and another $7.7 million for Boston-based UltraNet Communications with another 32,000 customers. Four months later, RCN added New York City-based Interport Communications at a cost of $8.5 million in cash and stock. Interport served 10,000 dial-up and 500 dedicated line Web hosting customers. Also in June 1998, RCN spent $13.4 million in cash and stock to add Springfield, Massachusetts-based JavaNet, Inc., which enjoyed success linking high schools and colleges to the Internet, boasting 30,000 dial-up and 400 dedicated line and Web hosting customers. As a result of the pickups, RCN was now the largest ISP in the northeast and one of the ten largest in the country. Also of significance in 1998, RCN won approval from the Federal Communications Commission to be an open-video system (OVS) operator in 109 Pennsylvania and 33 Northern California communities. By law, an OVS operator must lease large portions of its system channel capacity to third parties to provide cable television services. Cable companies contended that RCN misused the OVS provision to bypass local cable franchising rules and thereby gain access to a market, while in communities that offered an accommodating franchising authority, RCN was more than willing to seek a cable license. Yet despite the protestations of the competition, RCN was able to enter the markets it targeted. In Boston, Cablevision System Corporation was especially aggressive in its opposition, taking Boston Edison to court in 1998 and charging illegal competitive practices. RCN won and Cablevision's appeal to the U.S. Court of Appeals in Boston was rejected in September 1999.

RCN generated sales of $211 million in 1998, a significant improvement over 1997's $127.3 million, but the company's losses also began to mount, growing from $49.2 million in 1997 to nearly $205 million in 1998. However, given the large amount of capital required to establish a fiber optic network, losses were expected to continue. The prospects of RCN succeeding in its mission were given a boost in 1999 by the major investors it was able to attract. Dallas-based Hicks, Muse, Tate & Furst Inc. furnished $1.25 billion through loans and the purchase of stock. Later in the year, Microsoft's billionaire co-founder, Paul Allen, agreed to buy $1.65 billion in RCN stock. Thus, even as its net loss increased to $355 million in 1999, on sales of $276 million, RCN was in good financial shape, possessing ample cash to carry on.

The 1990s End on a High Note

Late in 1999, RCN spent some of its largesse to enter the Chicago market, acquiring 21st Century Telecom Group Inc. at a cost of $260 million in stock and the assumption of another $250 million in debt. Although 21st Century brought just 40,000 customers, it provided RCN with a toehold in a market that included 3.1 million homes. All told, in 1999 RCN laid more than 3,600 miles of fiber, an increase of 156 percent over the previous year. In 2000, the company was eying such new markets as Portland, Seattle, and Los Angeles. At this time, there were also rumors that RCN was likely to soon be acquired by a major cable or television company, such as Paul Allen's Charter Communications cable venture or MCI WorldCom. As a result, the price of RCN stock soared in 1999 and early 2000, but within a matter of weeks perceptions would change as the telecom sector began to falter and the price of RCN joined the downturn.

Investment money dried up and by the end of 2000 RCN, whose stock had lost more than 80 percent of its value, was forced to put on hold its plans to develop new markets. Instead, it took a step back, electing to conserve cash and focus on its existing seven markets and the one million homes its network passed, far short of the 15 million homes McCourt had originally targeted. Moreover, the customer base was not large enough to generate the kind of cash flow needed to keep up with operational expenses and interest payments. Because it was trying to drum up additional business in mature markets, RCN faced an even tougher task, compounded by management's inability to gain tighter control over costs. Investors reacted poorly to the retrenchment plan, and the company's stock was bid down even further, to less than $4 a share before it rebounded somewhat.

To better control costs, McCourt hired a pair of senior executives charged with focusing on expenses and RCN's field technicians. The company's accounting operation was also notorious for failing to bill some of its customers. To rectify this situation, RCN bought a new billing and customer management system in 2001. The company, saddled with a suffocating level of debt, also began negotiating with creditors to gain some relief. Nevertheless, while a number of short-term solutions were arranged, they merely postponed a day of reckoning.

The price of RCN stock fell below the $1 mark in 2002. To raise desperately needed cash, the company agreed in August of that year to sell its central New Jersey cable systems, a non-core asset, for $245 million. In an agreement reached with lenders, RCN could then reinvest the proceeds into the business. At the same time, the company continued in its efforts to control costs, which included laying off 3,000 employees, or half of its work force. The company's debt at this stage totaled approximately $1.7 billion, and at the end of 2002 RCN reported a net loss of $1.57 billion.

RCN continued in its efforts to build up its customer base in 2003. One bright spot was its average monthly revenue per customer, $90, a significant edge over the industry average of $55. However, the company was still burdened by the combination of a heavy debt load and poor stock price. In early 2004, RCN hired a restructuring specialist, then elected not to pay a $10 million interest payment, instead announcing that it would file for Chapter 11 bankruptcy protection. A restructuring plan negotiated with creditors called for two-thirds of its debt to be replaced with 100 percent of equity, while existing shares of stock, now worth pennies, would be "extinguished," leaving other investors out of luck. RCN filed for bankruptcy in May 2004, and by July McCourt announced he was stepping down as CEO, although he planned to remain as chairman and help in the search for a new chief executive. When the company emerged from Chapter 11 protection at the close of the year, however, McCourt was ousted as chairman as well. Whether new leadership would be able to fulfill his dream of building a national communications network was a question to be answered in the next chapter of RCN's brief but eventful history.

Principal Subsidiaries

RCN Internets Services, Inc.; RCN Telecom Services of Massachusetts, Inc.; RCN Telecom Services of Philadelphia, Inc.; RCN Telecom Services of Washington, D.C., Inc.; 21st Century Telecom Services, Inc.

Principal Competitors

Cablevision Systems Corporation; Time Warner Cable; Verizon Communications Inc.

Further Reading

Colman, Price, ''RCN Takes on the Big Guys,'' *Broadcasting & Cable*, March 9, 1998, p. 58.

''Face Value: Stand and Deliver,'' *Economist*, April 18, 1998, p. 65.

Goldblatt, Dan, ''RCN Is Building the Future of Telecom,'' *Business News New Jersey*, February 8, 1998, p. 1.

Higgins, John M., ''RCN's High-Wire Act,'' *Broadcasting & Cable*, May 8, 2000, p. 22.

Kennedy, Sam, ''Princeton, N.J.-Based Cable System to Filc for Bankruptcy,'' *Morning Call*, February 22, 2004.

Roth, Daniel, ''RCN's High-Wire Ace,'' *Forbes*, December 29, 1997, p. 88.

—Ed Dinger

Reading International Inc.

550 South Hope Street, Suite 1825
Los Angeles, California 90071
U.S.A.
Telephone: (213) 235-2240
Fax: (213) 235-2229

Public Company
Incorporated: 2001
Employees: 1,453
Sales: $93.7 million (2003)
Stock Exchanges: American
Ticker Symbol: RDI
NAIC: 7111320 Promoters of Performing Arts, Sports, and Similar Events without Facilities; 512131 Motion Picture Theaters, Except Drive-Ins; 525990 Other Financial Vehicles; 531120 Lessors of Nonresidential Buildings (Except Miniwarehouses); 551112 Offices of Other Holding Companies

Reading International Inc., is focused on the ownership and development of real estate assets, concentrating its efforts on the development, ownership, and management of cinema and live theaters. Reading International owns and operates a chain of multiplex theaters in Australia and New Zealand, where the company controls 18 theaters with 124 screens. The company owns a chain of multiplex cinemas in Puerto Rico, operating six theaters with 48 screens. In the United States, Reading International owns a chain of art-house cinemas located in New York City, Dallas, and Houston that operate under the name Angelika Film Center & Café, a chain consisting of nine cinemas with 53 screens. Reading International also owns seven off-Broadway style theaters in New York and Chicago.

Origins

On New Year's Eve, 2001, three separate, publicly traded companies joined together to form Reading International. The merger fused the corporate histories of the three constituents into one, giving the modern-day Reading International an eclectic background, one described by an incongruous medley of businesses that at one point represented the largest corporation in the world. Reading International's convoluted past involved coal mining, shipbuilding, a massive railroad business, a savings and loan institution, citrus farming, medical device manufacturing, and a supermarket chain, all of which, over the course of nearly 200 years, led to the company's manifestation in the 21st century as an operator of multiplex cinemas and off-Broadway theaters. The story of Reading International's development branched off into numerous, divergent directions, but the start of its story began at one point, in Pennsylvania in 1833.

Reading International took its name from the railroad known to anyone familiar with the board game Monopoly. Reading Railroad was established as The Philadelphia & Reading Railroad in 1833, founded to transport anthracite coal mined in Pennsylvania to destinations in Pennsylvania, New Jersey, and Delaware. At the time, coal was a major source of energy in the United States, making The Philadelphia & Reading one of the most important and wealthy companies in the country. The railroad poured its profits into other businesses, delving into coal mining, iron making, shipbuilding, and a host of other businesses. By the 1870s, The Philadelphia & Reading, which owned the P & R Coal and Iron Company, ranked as the largest corporation in the world.

By the end of the 19th century, The Philadelphia & Reading's greatest threat was from the federal government. Antitrust legislation aimed at breaking up monopolies prompted the railroad's owners to create a holding company, a company named Reading Company, which, on paper, owned The Philadelphia & Reading and P & R Coal and Iron Company. The tactic worked for a while, but eventually the U.S. Supreme Court ordered the company to separate itself into distinct entities. The breakup of the company in 1924 created the new version of Reading Company, a company solely devoted to operating the railroad.

Reading Railroad, like a handful of other railroad companies, began a gradual downward spiral after World War II. Coal's value as an energy source waned, replaced by oil, and competition in the freight-hauling business intensified, as railroads, particularly those operating in the eastern United States, lost substantial ground to the trucking industry. Between 1967 and 1972, six major northeastern railroads declared bankruptcy, and Reading was one of the moribund pack, filing for Chapter 11 in 1971. The operation of the rail lines controlled by Reading and those of its fallen brethren were consolidated by a federal government agency and given to the Consolidated Rail Corporation, or Conair, a government-sponsored company that began operating in 1976. Reading, meanwhile, was reduced to making its living primarily by developing some of its historic railroad properties, which consisted, in large part, of real estate holdings. It would be nearly 20 years before Reading sold its last railroad real estate asset, the Reading Terminal Headhouse in downtown Philadelphia, which was sold in 1993.

1980s–90s: A Prelude to Merger

As Reading gradually untangled itself from more than a century of being in the railroad business, its path crossed with that of another company, a company led by James J. Cotter. Cotter, described in the May 22, 1995, issue of the *Los Angeles Business Journal* as "a figure legendary in Southland big-money circles," figured as one of the principal leaders of Reading International and, to an extent, the inspiration for its creation. For decades, Cotter had served as a financial lieutenant to the Beverly Hills-based Forman family, a family whose fortune exceeded $500 million. Cotter served as the head of finance and operations for a chain of drive-in movie properties developed by the Forman family between the 1940s and 1960s. (The Forman family purchased real estate near proposed freeway off ramps, a business strategy that proved to be enormously lucrative as a labyrinth of freeways developed in southern California.)

In 1985, Cotter took control of a company named Craig Corporation. Craig Corporation was known primarily for its involvement in eight-track stereos and for developing an early version of what Sony Corporation unveiled as the Sony Walkman, but Cotter had different ideas for the publicly traded company. When he took the helm in 1985, Cotter converted Craig Corporation to a shell corporation to invest in other companies, emulating the model of famed investor Warren Buffet and his holding company, Berkshire Hathaway. "When you buy Craig today," an analyst remarked in a May 22, 1995 interview with the *Los Angeles Business Journal,* "you are really betting on Jim Cotter." Cotter used Craig Corporation to acquire stakes in a variety of companies, including a 50 percent interest in Stater Bros, a California-based supermarket chain. By the mid-1990s, Cotter's investments, held by Craig Corporation, included a 47 percent stake in Reading Company. Cotter also held an equity position in another company, the third member of the 2001 merger that created Reading International, Citadel Holding Corporation.

Citadel was a holding company similar to Cotter's Craig Corporation. The company was formed in 1983, counting as its major asset a Glendale, California-based savings and loan, or thrift, named Fidelity Federal Bank. Fidelity Federal's main line of business was in real estate, specifically owning and operating commercial real estate. The thrift also provided real estate advisory services. One of its clients was Reading, which by this point described itself as a Pennsylvania-based real estate development company.

Fidelity Federal began to flounder during the early 1990s. The thrift, which held $4 billion assets and operated 42 branch offices, was losing millions of dollars and in danger of being seized by its regulators. To cut itself free from the impending collapse of Fidelity Federal, Citadel spun off the thrift in August 1994 and began looking for better investments elsewhere. Among the investments made by the holding company was a substantial stake in a California citrus farm named Big 4 Ranch, which Citadel acquired in 1997. The following year, the company took an equity position in a California-based medical devices manufacturer, Gish Biomedical, Inc. In 2000, Citadel entered new investment territory by acquiring real estate properties occupied by movie theaters and theaters that staged off-Broadway productions. The move, one similar to the move made by Reading during the 1990s, set the stage for the 2001 merger creating Reading International.

While Citadel re-positioned itself after Fidelity Federal's fortunes faded, Reading pursued the development of its real estate business. The company began acquiring, developing, and operating real estate properties during the 1990s, focusing its efforts on properties occupied by cinema exhibitors and live theater operators. The majority of the company's holdings were located thousands of miles away from the company's historical native ground of Pennsylvania's coal mines. Reading entered Australia in 1995 and New Zealand in 1997, developing a chain of multiplex cinemas that operated under the Reading banner and exhibited mainstream films. Domestically, Reading pursued a more offbeat business direction, acquiring an art-house theater in Manhattan in 1996 that operated under the name Angelika Film Center. The company also grafted its oceanic operating strategy onto Puerto Rico, acquiring and expanding a chain of multiplex cinemas on the U.S. commonwealth island.

Merger in 2001

At the beginning of the 21st century, Reading Company, Craig Corporation, and Citadel, each intertwined with one another on some level, decided to join together and eliminate the substantial overlap in stock ownership, management, and control among the companies by becoming one company. The companies decided to focus on the business strategy pursued by Reading, fashioning itself as a cinema and live theater exhibition company with a strong focus on the development and holding of real estate assets. For experience in this area, the consolidated companies turned to Cotter, who had been involved in the movie theater business for decades. Cotter was named chairman and chief executive of the merged company, owning 30 percent of the new entity. When the merger, or the "consolidation transaction," was completed, Citadel, technically, was the surviving entity, but the name of the merged company became "Reading International Inc." because the majority of the operating assets initially belonged to Reading. In the wake of the merger, those businesses beyond the new company's scope were sold. In 2002, the stake in Big 4 Ranch was divested, followed by the sale of Gish Biomedical in 2003.

With Cotter at the helm, Reading International began building on the business foundation established at the beginning of 2002. There was, however, one area of the company's business that it no longer cared to develop further. Reading International executives decided to abandon plans for further expansion in Puerto Rico, where the company owned and operated six cinemas. After a competing cinema chain gained control of more than 80 percent of the Puerto Rican market, Reading International officials decided to exit the market and, as soon as the right opportunity presented itself, sell the company's Puerto Rican assets, which totaled $3.1 million. Reading International intended to focus on expanding its business in the United States, Australia, and New Zealand.

As Reading International entered the mid-2000s, the company stood as a nearly $100 million-in-sales company. By the end of 2003, its presence in Australia and New Zealand consisted of 18 cinemas with 124 screens. In the United States, the Angelika Film Center in Manhattan represented the flagship of what had become a small chain operating under the name Angelika Film Center & Café. By the end of 2003, the Angelika chain consisted of nine cinemas with 53 screens, maintaining a presence in New York City, Dallas, and Houston. The company's live theater properties consisted of seven off-Broadway style theaters located in New York City and Chicago.

Reading International planned to augment its holdings through internal means for the most part, rather than by acquiring properties. The company's activity in 2004 served as a blueprint for its future expansion, with much of its efforts focused on developing real estate. During the year, Reading International was building an 82,000-square-foot shopping center in Newmarket, Australia, a suburb of Brisbane. The company also was finishing the construction of a 150,000-square-foot retail and art-house project in Wellington, New Zealand. Outside Melbourne, in the suburbs of Moonee Ponds and Burwood, construction was under way on two retail and cinema properties. Although no major projects were undertaken in the United States during 2004, Reading International intended to expand on both fronts, extending its reach in the United States, Australia, and New Zealand.

Principal Subsidiaries

AHGP, Inc.; AHLP, Inc.; Angelika Film Centers (Dallas), Inc.; Angelika Film Centers LLC; Australia Country Cinemas Pty. Ltd.; Bayou Cinemas LP; Burwood Developments Pty. Ltd.; Citadel Acquisition Corporation; Citadel Cinemas, Inc.; Citadel Distribution Services, Inc.; Citadel Realty, Inc.; Cliveden Ltd.; Copenhagen Courtenay Central Ltd.; Craig Food & Hospitality; Craig Management, Inc.; Darnelle Enterprises Ltd.; Dimension Specialty, Inc.; Entertainment Holdings, Inc.; Hope Street Hospitality Hotel; Newmarket Pty. Ltd.; J.J. Cotter Associates; Liberty Theaters, Inc.; Liberty Theatricals, LLC; Craig Corporation; Minetta Live, LLC; Newmarket Properties Pty. Ltd.; Orpheum Live, LLC; Liberty Live, LLC; Port Reading Railroad Company; Puerto Rico Holdings, Inc.; Railroad Investments, Inc.; Reading Australia Leasing Pty. Ltd.; Reading Capital Corporation; Reading Cinema Properties Ltd.; Reading Cinemas Courtenay Central Ltd.; Reading Cinemas NJ, Inc.; Reading Cinemas of Puerto Rico, Inc.; Reading Cinemas Puerto Rico LLC; Reading Cinemas USA LLC; Reading Cinemas, Inc.; Reading Company; Reading Courtenay Central Ltd.; Reading Entertainment Australia Pty. Ltd.; Reading Exhibition Pty Ltd.; Reading Holdings, Inc.; Reading International Cinemas LLC; Reading Investment Company, Inc.; Reading Licenses Pty. Ltd.; Reading New Zealand Ltd.; Reading Pacific LLC; Reading Properties Pty. Ltd.; Reading Real Estate Company; Reading Realty, Inc.; Reading Resources, Inc.; Reading Theaters, Inc.; Reading Transportation Company; RG-I, Inc.; RG-II, Inc.; Ronwood Investments Ltd.; Royal George, LLC; Trenton-Princeton Traction Company; Tington Investments Ltd.; Tobrooke Holdings Ltd.; Trevone Holdings Ltd.; Twin Cities Cinemas, Inc.; US International Property Finance Pty Ltd.; Washington and Franklin Railway Company; Western Gaming, Inc.; Whitehorse Property Group Pty. Ltd.; Wilmington and Northern Railroad.

Principal Competitors

Village Roadshow Ltd.; Greater Union/Birch Carroll & Coyle; Hoyts Cinemas.

Further Reading

Cole, Benjamin Mark, "Traders Ponder What Craig Corp. Plans to Do with All Its Money," *Los Angeles Business Journal,* May 22, 1995, p. 4.
Mullen, Liz, "Citadel Holding Shares Ride Waves of Speculation Fueled by Sale Rumors," *Los Angeles Business Journal,* September 20, 1993, p. 5.
Walsh, James, "Where Size Doesn't Matter," *California Business,* October 1991, p. 66.

—Jeffrey L. Covell

Regis Corporation

7201 Metro Boulevard
Edina, Minnesota 55439
U.S.A.
Telephone: (952) 947-7777
Fax: (952) 947-7600
Web site: http://www.regiscorp.com

Public Company
Incorporated: 1954
Employees: 50,000
Sales: $1.92 billion (2004)
Stock Exchanges: New York
Ticker Symbol: RGS
NAIC: 812112 Beauty Salons; 812113 Nail Salons

Regis Corporation is the world's largest owner and operator of mall-based hair and retail salons. Atypical of the industry, the company owns, rather than franchises, the vast majority of its salons, which are operated under six divisions: Regis Salons, Promenade Salon Concepts, MasterCuts, Trade Secret, SmartStyle Family Hair Salons, and International.

Family Business Roots

Regis Corporation's history began with Russian-born barber Paul Kunin, who set up business in 1922. He built a chain of about 60 shops located in leased space in smaller-city department stores. "My father was never in the top department stores in Minneapolis. He was in the good places in Fargo," said Myron Kunin in a November 1985 *Corporate Report* article. Although Kunin had grown up working in the shops, it was his father's real estate ventures that he found intriguing.

Myron Kunin and his sister Diana bought the business in 1954. Their father kept the real estate holdings, however, and Kunin had to settle for being in the hair care business. Kunin eventually bought his sister's share of Regis Corporation and began trimming back the number of downtown department salons. In the mid-1960s, he began opening salons in the enclosed malls that were beginning to spring up in the suburbs

of middle-sized and small-sized cities around the country. The new salons had an upscale image and upscale prices. By 1975 Regis Corporation owned 161 salons, and sales for the fiscal year were $10.6 million.

Regis was an anomaly in an industry that was, according to William Swanson, "better known for its small-time mom-and-pop operations, managerial unevenness and generally meager earnings." Whereas the other hair care chains generally were franchised, Regis owned and operated its salons, which allowed for more control over the business. Compound annual sales grew by 29 percent and earnings per share grew by 32 percent for the period between 1978 and 1983.

Public Ownership in 1983

Regis became publicly owned in April 1983. The company operated more than 300 salons at the time. Piper, Jaffray & Hopwood analyst Dick Pyle, cited by Swanson, said Regis's success as a salon owner and operator was most likely due to factors such as knowledge of the business, good site selection, favorable leases, steady growth, fair treatment of employees, and consistency of image. Its Regis Hairstylists salons catered to a mostly female clientele—women who were willing to pay upper-end prices for trend-setting services and products.

In 1984, Regis bought a chain of about 60 shops that targeted male customers. But according to a 1989 *Fortune* magazine article by Julianne Slovak, write-offs related to the Your Fathers Mustache purchase cut into earnings for two years, and Regis converted the salons to other concepts.

Executive Vice-President Peter Fudurich, who joined the company in the 1960s when the California chain he worked for was purchased by Kunin, was in line to succeed Kunin as president. Kunin trusted Fudurich and the management team to oversee daily operation of the company. Kunin, already in 1985, had a number of interests outside of Regis Corporation, including television stations and real estate holdings and developments. He was also well known as an art collector, having spent millions on works by 20th-century American painters. Fudurich's illness and death, however, forced Kunin back into day-to-day involvement in the business.

Company Perspectives:

Our objective is to continue double-digit growth in sales and profits. We plan to enter the twenty-first century as a billion-dollar company. Our locations are prime. Our associates are the best trained in the industry. Continuing strong results reflect both sound strategy and good execution. We are fashioned for profitable growth.

In 1987, Kunin brought on board Paul Finkelstein, who had worked for both his family's Glemby International Hairstyling Salons and their chief rival, Seligman & Latz. Anthony Carideo wrote in 1988, ''Paul Finkelstein, Regis' savvy new president, is adding profits to the bottom line after several years of rapid expansion but erratic earnings comparisons.'' Finkelstein helped profits by restructuring commissions and emphasizing product sales. Sales for fiscal year 1988 were $192 million. Net income was $7.9 million, up 42 percent from the previous year.

Regis purchased the assets of more than 500 Seligman & Latz salons in August 1988. The nation's second largest department store beauty chain had Essanelle Salons in about 60 stores, including Saks Fifth Avenue and Neiman Marcus. Regis was granted exclusive rights to run the beauty salons in Saks stores.

Back to Private Ownership in 1988

Regis owned about 700 salons when the company returned to private ownership in October 1988. Wall Street's expectations regarding their short-term performance and the company's desire to reward new company managers through equity ownership were among the reasons cited for the change. Public shareholders held 30 percent of stock and received $17.70 per share—a price driven up by protests that the initial offering was too low.

Regis Corp. was merged into Regis Acquisition Corp., a subsidiary of Curtis Squire Inc., a venture capital firm controlled by the Myron Kunin family. The company incurred $113 million in debt to finance the buyout, pay a $33 million cash dividend to Curtis Squire, and purchase the Essanelle Salons. Unfortunately, the highly leveraged financing quickly became a huge stumbling block.

Kunin and Finkelstein had planned a big expansion into the department store salon business. But because of the debt load and changing financial climate, the company was refused new loans. Kunin personally funded the 1989 purchase of Maxim's Beauty Salons, a chain started by his uncle. Regis intended to purchase Glemby, which produced about $260 million in annual revenues, but could not do so without outside financing.

Banker and Minnesota Twins owner Carl Pohlad was introduced to the scenario. Pohlad and financier Irwin Jacobs were among the owners of MEI Diversified Inc.—a company that, according to Eric J. Wieffering, ''made a lot of investors wealthy'' in a 1986 bottling company sale to PepsiCo but had been less than successful in subsequent deals. Kunin and Pohlad began discussions regarding an MEI ownership stake in Regis in 1989, but failed to reach an agreement.

A Bad Hair Deal and a Return to Public Ownership in the Early 1990s

Operating income had been improving, but Regis failed to make some of its loan payments, and the terms were renegotiated at much higher interest rates. The hair salon company needed to reduce its debt, so Kunin returned to Pohlad. A deal with MEI was finally struck early in 1990. MEI agreed to purchase the New York-based Glemby Co. Inc., the nation's largest department store hair salon chain, and Regis's Maxim's Beauty Salons Inc. and Essanelle Salon Co. for a total of about $50 million.

MEI held an 80 percent share of the newly formed MEI-Regis Salon Corporation. Kunin and Regis owned the remaining 20 percent, and the company received a contract to manage the salons. More than 2,000 salons were included in the joint venture and had combined annual sales of about $400 million. Regis retained sole ownership of its Regis Hairstylists and MasterCuts salons.

Analysts and investors reacted positively when the MEI-Regis pairing was announced. Wieffering wrote in *Corporate Report Minnesota*, ''Here, they said, was the perfect match: a company with a lot of cash to invest and a business being run by one of the best operators in the industry.'' But the deal went sour when the department store salons' performance failed to meet MEI's expectations.

In May 1991, MEI filed a lawsuit against Glemby Co. Inc. claiming in U.S. District Court that the financial conditions and prospects of the business had been misrepresented. MEI had paid about $30 million for Glemby. Finkelstein, as a member of the founding family, initially was named in the suit but later was dropped from the list of defendants. Seeking to reduce its own debt further, Regis had been making plans to return to public ownership. That action was jeopardized when MEI announced that it also paid too much for the Regis salon chains it had purchased.

Despite building friction, the dispute between MEI and Regis was settled. The two companies agreed on a lower purchase price, and the MEI-Regis hair salons management contract was extended. MEI continued, however, to pursue the suit against Glemby.

The plan to go public proceeded after Regis found debt financing for $92 million in bank loans remaining from the buyout. The June 1991 public offering fell short of expectations: The 3.2 million shares sold for $2 off the asking price of $15, and the company raised only about $42 million. The sale reduced Kunin's share of Regis to 56 percent. Regis ended fiscal year 1991 with revenues of $307.7 million and net losses of $3.2 million.

The Regis and MEI partnership continued to deteriorate. MEI took over the management of the joint venture salons early in 1992 and changed the name of the operation to MEI Salon Corporation. MEI claimed Regis had mismanaged the stores, but Regis said the poorer-than-expected financial showing of the joint venture was due to the Gulf War and the economic recession. The hair business had been considered recession proof, but sales were sharply down, especially in department

Key Dates:

1922: Paul Kunin goes into business; his chain of salons eventually numbers 60.

1954: Myron Kunin and Diana Kunin purchase the business from their father.

1975: Regis owns 161 salons; sales total $10.6 million.

1983: Regis goes public.

1988: The company returns to private ownership and merges with Curtis Squire Inc. to form Regis Acquisition Corp., under the control of Myron Kunin.

1990: The company merges with MEI Diversified Inc. to form MEI-Regis Salon Corp.

1991: Regis goes public.

1992: The company purchases Trade Secret and enters the franchising business.

1993: A troubled relationship with MEI is settled after lawsuits and MEI's bankruptcy.

1996: Regis purchases salons operating in Wal-Mart stores.

2002: The company enters the beauty career education business with the purchase of four Vidal Sassoon academies.

2004: The company purchases Hair Club for Men and Women and enters the hair replacement industry.

stores where most of the MEI-Regis salons were located. A rash of department store bankruptcies forced the closure of 150 to 200 of the MEI-Regis salons. In May 1992, Regis sued MEI for expenses related to the management of the MEI-Regis salons. MEI countered with a $150 million suit against Regis alleging fraud, racketeering, and contract violations.

As the legal battle raged on, Regis continued to grow. In December 1992, the company purchased Consumer Beauty Supply, a mall-based beauty product retailer that complemented its service-oriented chains. Regis purchased a similar concept from Trade Secret Development Corp. the next year. Both the chains sold brand-named products such as Nexxus and Redken as well as the Regis line. Jennifer Waters wrote, "Both Trade Secret and Beauty Express are considered cash cows of the hair salon industry because of the growth in retail sales in recent years." The Trade Secret purchase put Regis into the franchising business for the first time.

In the meantime, MEI's series of losses had forced the company to file for Chapter 11 bankruptcy protection; the dispute with Regis was settled through the U.S. Bankruptcy Court in December 1993. Regis agreed to loan Toronto-based Magicuts Inc. $5.9 million for the purchase of the MEI salons. The settlement, which also included the transfer of Regis stock to MEI, cost Regis about $15 million. The legal battle hit the company's stock price as well. Regis stock fell from the $13 public offering price to the $6 to $9 range and stayed there until the suit was settled. The stock was trading in the mid-teens in the beginning of 1995.

Changes had been taking place in the hair salon industry. "To stave off competitors such as the publicly traded Supercuts, which has aggressively franchised its way to 850 sa-

lons, Regis has been building its own discount chain by adding 35 to 40 stores to its MasterCuts Division for the last two years," wrote Jagannath Dubashi in a 1994 *Financial World* article. MasterCuts, established in 1985 to cater to men, young adults, and children, had grown to 257 salons by the end of fiscal 1994 and contributed 16 percent of total revenues. In comparison, the company owned about 800 Regis Hairstylist salons, which generated more than half of total revenues.

Regis had begun operating hair care salons in Mexico in 1988 and in the United Kingdom in 1990. In 1993, the company held 260 international salons: 217 in its U.K. subsidiary, 35 in Canada, and eight in Mexico. Sales from the U.K. subsidiary, which also included salons in South Africa, contributed 9.4 percent of total company sales for the 1993 fiscal year. In 1995, Regis acquired Essanelle Ltd., which operated 79 upscale salons located in British department stores such as Harrods. The purchase also included some salons in Switzerland. The addition of 91 salons in the next year made Regis the United Kingdom's dominant hairstyling firm.

Building for the Future at the End of the 20th Century

In May 1996, Regis created a fifth area of operation with the purchase of 154 National Hair Care Centers LLC salons operating in Wal-Mart stores. The salons had total annual revenues of about $28 million. Susan Feyder wrote that according to Piper Jaffray Inc. analyst Saul Yaari, "The deal is significant because of the relationship Regis will have with Wal-Mart as it puts hair salons into new stores." The giant retailer expected to build 100 supercenters in 1996. Regis hoped to land spots in 30 to 50 of them.

Regis spent $30 million on acquisitions in fiscal 1996. Company revenues climbed to $499 million, and net income was $19 million, up 31 percent from the previous year. The company also brought its debt-to-capitalization ratio down to 37 percent from around 60 percent four years earlier. Kunin retired as chief executive officer at the end of the fiscal year, but retained his position as chairman of the board. Regis President and Chief Operating Officer Finkelstein succeeded him.

In July 1996, Regis announced plans to purchase SuperCuts, Inc., a pioneer in the discount haircut market, in a deal that exceeded $100 million. Founded in 1975, the franchiser was purchased by an investor group in 1987 and taken public in 1991. Revenues tripled between 1991 and 1995. A rapid expansion of corporate-owned stores, however, resulted in a $7.1 million loss in 1995. Regis stock fell 20 percent to around $26 per share, when news of the purchase was made public. Piper Jaffray analyst Yaari said in a July 1996 article by Sally Apgar, "I think the merger is a good fit, but the price was rich and, therefore, the risk is higher." Yaari also thought Wall Street might view the company, which now had six business areas, as spreading itself too thin.

New Directions in the Early 2000s

In December 2002 Regis entered into a significant new enterprise with the purchase of four Vidal Sassoon beauty academies. The schools were acquired with 25 Vidal Sassoon salons in Canada, the United States, the United Kingdom, and Germany for an undisclosed amount. The transaction was expected to add $25 million in revenues during the fiscal year ending June 30, 2003, and $49 million in revenues during fiscal year 2004. In June 2004 Regis purchased Blaine Beauty Career Schools, which operated six academies in Massachusetts, in a deal that was expected to generate $15 million in revenues during fiscal year 2005. The curricula at the Vidal Sassoon and Blaine academies included programs in cosmetology, nail art, and aesthetic services such as makeup, facials, massage, waxing, and reflexology, among others.

Regis anticipated that the acquisition and planned expansion of its education business would continue to be profitable for many years because continued high unemployment rates in the United States and Europe promised a steady stream of students, and Regis's ability to place graduates in its salons encouraged students to stay on for the two- to three-year duration of training programs. Since all of the programs at its schools were certified for Title IV student financial assistance in the United States, students in that country could count on getting tuition aid to attend the Vidal Sassoon or Blaine training centers. Academies also generated a 20 percent operating income, more than the company's core salon businesses generated. This income promised to raise the per-share earnings of the company's stock. Although the new business was expected to account for slightly less than 5 percent of the company's revenues by 2009, the academies fit well with the company's focus on employee training as a means of reducing operating costs, maintaining high-quality service, and increasing product sales. In fiscal year 2004, for example, Regis employed 140 artistic directors and spent $16 million on training for 53,600 stylists.

In December 2004, the company entered another new market with the purchase of 89 Hair Club for Men and Women hair replacement centers for $210 million in cash. The business differed from Regis's salons in that the operations were not in such high-visibility locations as malls or strip centers. With a single exception, Hair Club outlets were found in office buildings, professional buildings, or medical buildings that provided customers with a degree of privacy and a comforting, clinic-like setting. Regis planned to change the Hair Club's aggressive, hard-sell advertising strategy to emphasize privacy and use subtler, soft-sell tactics. The business was expected to add $50 million in revenues in 2005 and $115 million in 2006 by reaching customers in the over-40 age group, 40 percent of whom experience hair loss. As the baby boom generation aged, Regis anticipated the number of Hair Club clients would increase steadily.

Having already captured approximately 2 percent of the $150 billion worldwide hair care market by the end of fiscal 2004, the company maintained a robust acquisitions program to spur continued growth. Between 1994 and 2004 Regis bought 7,400 salons worldwide in 293 transactions, which added an estimated $25 million to its revenues. Among the acquisitions were 328 BoRics salons, nearly 400 First-Choice Haircutters salons, 1,200 Jean Louis David salons, the French franchisor St. Algue, 550 Haircrafters salons, 280 Opal Concepts salons, 153 Holiday Hair salons, and 980 The Barbers, Hairstyling for Men and Women salons. The average acquisition during the ten-year period involved about ten salons and was funded with operating cash, debt, the issue of common stock, and/or assumption of the acquisition's liabilities. The yearly expenditure for acquisitions rose

nearly 20 percent in the first four years of the 21st century, from $5.8 million in 2000 to more than $110 million in 2004. Regis hoped to double its size from 10,000 salons by 2010 or 2012.

Approximately half of the company's 13.9 percent compound annual growth in revenues during the early years of the 21st century was attributed to its acquisitions. Organic growth (construction of new stores and increases in sales at existing operations) accounted for the other half of its growth. Regis's agreement with Wal-Mart continued to be lucrative. At the beginning of 2005, there were 1,516 of the company's salons situated in high-traffic, high-visibility Wal-Mart locations. Although revenues continued to increase, such imponderables as a severe hurricane season in 2004 and unemployment rates of 5 percent or more in the United States and Europe had a marked effect on Regis's salon business. Closures and property damage due to storms put a $4 million dent in revenues. At the same time customers were lessening the frequency of their visits to salons because lack of work tightened their budgets. Despite setbacks, however, the company remained positive about its prospects, noting an increasing number of salons available for purchase and a vast, untapped market along the Pacific Rim, particularly in Asia.

Principal Divisions

Regis Salons; Promenade Salon Concepts (includes Supercuts, Cost Cutters, First Choice Haircutters, Magicuts, BestCuts, BoRics, Hair Masters, Saturday's, Style America, and Holiday Hair); MasterCuts; Trade Secret (includes Beauty Express); SmartStyle Family Hair Salons; International (European salons Jean Louis David, Vidal Sassoon, Regis Hairstylists, Supercuts, and St. Algue).

Principal Competitors

HCX Salons International LLC; Mascolo Ltd.; Cool Cuts 4 Kids Inc.

Further Reading

Apgar, Sally, "Regis Plans to Acquire Supercuts," *Star Tribune* (Minneapolis), July 16, 1996, p. 1D.
——, "Salon Chain Regis Corp. to Buy Products Retailer," *Star Tribune* (Minneapolis), December 8, 1992, p. 3D.
"Bad Weather Hurts Sales and Profit for the Quarter," *Wall Street Journal*, December 27, 2000, p. B8.
Brook, Steve, "MEI Settles with Regis in Hair Salon Dispute," *St. Paul Pioneer Press*, May 24, 1991.
Brookman, Faye, "Regis' Formats Meet Many Needs," *WWD*, July 11, 2003, p. 12.
Carideo, Anthony, "MEI Diversified, Regis on Brink of a Split," *Star Tribune (Minneapolis)*, March 7, 1992, p. 3D.
——, "Some See Regis Buyback Offer As Low," *Star Tribune* (Minneapolis), March 28, 1988, p. 8D.
Cecil, Mark, "Acquisitive Regis: No Beauty School Dropout," *Mergers & Acquisitions Report*, June 14, 2004.
——, "Regis Wields Its M&A Scissors Over Opal (Regis Corp. Acquires Opal Concepts Inc.)," *Mergers & Acquisitions Report*, June 2, 2003.
Dubashi, Jagannath, "Myron's Makeovers," *Financial World*, April 26, 1994, pp. 48–49.

"Edina, Minn.-Based Hair Salons Operator Sees Stock Fall After Lowering Forecast," *Knight Ridder/Tribune Business News,* January 6, 2005.

Feyder, Susan, "Edina-Based Regis Corp. Is Planning to Buy 154 Wal-Mart Hair Salons," *Star Tribune* (Minneapolis), May 10, 1996, p. 3D.

Gallagher, Leigh, "Lather, Rinse, Repeat," *Forbes,* October 27, 2003, p. 66.

Gentry, Connie Robbins, "Retailers on a Roll: Regis Corp. and Haircolorxpress Canvass Domestic and International Markets," *Chain Store Age,* July 2002, p. 116.

"Global Giants," *Hairdresser's Journal International,* July 2, 2004, p. 6.

"Hair Club Joins Regis in $210M Deal," *Daily Deal,* November 16, 2004.

"Hair Salon Company Regis Settles EEOC Discrimination Case for $3.5 Million," *Knight Ridder/Tribune Business News,* August 14, 2003.

Jones, Jim, "Tress Chic—The Twin Cities Hair-Care Industry Regis," *Star Tribune* (Minneapolis), February 17, 1991, p. 3D.

Jones, John A., "Regis Expands Its Hair Salon Empire in U.S. and Europe," *Investor's Business Daily,* June 5, 1996.

Jones, Sandra, "Regis Looks to Add Volume to Sassoon; Studio Salons Aiming for Broader Market," *Crain's Chicago Business,* June 21, 2004, p. 28.

Marcotty, Josephine, "Edina-Based Regis Corp. Plans to Acquire European Hair-Salon Operator for $6 Million," *Star Tribune* (Minneapolis), August 17, 1995, p. 1D.

"Minneapolis-Based Regis Grows to Global Salon Chain Giant," *Asbury Park Press* (Asbury Park, N.J.), September 27, 2002.

Nettleton, Pamela Hill, "Hair Today," *Twin Cities Business Monthly,* September 1995, pp. 68–73.

Peltz, James F., "Combing for Cash," *Los Angeles Times,* July 16, 1996.

Peterson, Susan E., "Regis Plans to Acquire Hair Club; Salon Giant Expanding into Hair Replacement Business," *Star Tribune* (Minneapolis), November 16, 2004, p. 1D.

Pyle, Richard E., "Periscope: Regis Corporation," *Corporate Report Minnesota,* October 1983, p. 118.

"Regis Acquires 328 Hair Salons," *Wall Street Journal,* July 16, 2002, p. D3.

"Regis, a Hair Salon Operator and Franchise, Has Named Paul Finkelstein, President and CEO, As Their New Chairman," *Corporate Financing Week,* May 10, 2004, p. 4.

"Regis, Biggest Owner of Hair Salons, Buys 328 Shops," *New York Times,* July 16, 2002, p. C11.

"Regis Buys Vidal Sassoon Beauty Salons and Academies," *New York Times,* December 19, 2002, p. C4.

"Regis Corp. (Buys GGG Group)," *New York Times,* October 23, 2001, p. C4.

Reuthling, Gretchen, "Regis, Owner of Beauty Parlors, Will Buy Hair Club," *New York Times,* November 16, 2004, p. C4.

Slovak, Julianne, "Companies to Watch: Regis Corp.," *Fortune,* January 2, 1989, p. 96.

Swanson, William, "Beauty and the Business," *Corporate Report Minnesota,* November 1985, pp. 92–96.

Tellijohn, Andrew, "Regis Adds Teen Concept: Mia & Maxx," *City-Business* (Minneapolis, Minn.), December 7, 2001, p. 1.

"U.S. Hair-Care Giant to Open Salons in Britain, *Daily Mail* (London), December 22, 2002.

Waters, Jennifer, "Regis Cuts Deal to Buy Trade Secret," *Minneapolis/St. Paul CityBusiness,* November 12, 1993, p. 3.

Wieffering, Eric J., "Two Sharks in a Bathtub," *Corporate Report Minnesota,* August 1992, pp. 57–62.

Youngblood, Dick, "Regis Looks Like Winner, By Well More Than a Hair," *Star Tribune* (Minneapolis), January 30, 1995, p. 2D.

—Kathleen Peippo
—update: Jennifer Gariepy

Reliance Steel & Aluminum Company

Reliance Steel & Aluminum Co.

350 South Grande Avenue, Suite 5100
Los Angeles, California 90071
U.S.A.
Telephone: (213) 687-7700
Fax: (213) 687-8792
Web site: http://www.rsac.com

Public Company
Incorporated: 1939 as Reliance Steel Products Company
Employees: 5,400
Sales: $2.94 billion (2004)
Stock Exchanges: New York
Ticker Symbol: RS
NAIC: 423510 Metal Service Centers and Other Metal
   Merchant Wholesalers

The Reliance Steel & Aluminum Company is one of the leading metals processing and distribution companies in the United States. Reliance operates more than 100 metals service centers in 30 states and in a few foreign countries (Belgium, France, and South Korea). The company buys steel and non-ferrous metals in bulk from primary producers and cuts it to size for smaller buyers. Reliance distributes more than 90,000 metal products to 95,000 customers in various industries. Carbon steel accounts more than half of sales; aluminum has been the next best-selling commodity with 24 percent of sales.

The company's pride is service, so decision-making is more decentralized than at other national rivals. Individual sales tend to be relatively small (about $900 or so) and typically require delivery within a day. The company often works with small job shops and traditionally has avoided the notoriously low-margin auto industry.

In an industry dominated by small, family-owned businesses, Reliance grew from a single metals-processing center in Los Angeles into a major corporation by acquiring dozens of competitors. In an interview with an industry publication in 1992, Joe D. Crider, then president and chief operating officer, explained, "You can pay the bill [for higher market share] through price cutting, or through paying goodwill to buy a competitor. In cutting prices, you often trash the marketplace. So over time, the latter route is usually the less expensive, as long as you buy at a reasonable price."

Growth through Acquisition: 1939–87

Reliance Steel & Aluminum Company was founded in Los Angeles on February 3, 1939 by Thomas J. Neilan. Originally named Reliance Steel Products Company, the business made and sold steel reinforcing bars (rebar) for the construction industry. In 1944, the name was shortened to Reliance Steel Company.

In 1948, Reliance Steel also began manufacturing products of aluminum and magnesium. As William T. Gimbel, Neilan's nephew who joined the company as a trainee in 1947, later told *Metal Service News,* "We started out (in 1939) with the dirty, old, down-in-the-gutter carbon steel, but that became a world commodity. So we decided that we wanted to upgrade into something that had a little bit more pizzazz, and we picked aluminum and magnesium."

Gimbel, who started as a warehouse man, succeeded Neilan in 1957 as president of the company, a year after its name was changed to Reliance Steel & Aluminum Company. Under Gimbel, Reliance began its long-running territorial expansion, naming a resident sales agent in Phoenix in 1958. Two years later, Reliance acquired a small Phoenix-based competitor, the Effron Steel Company. With the purchase of another competitor, the Westates Steel Company, in Santa Clara, Reliance Steel expanded into Northern California in 1961.

In 1963, Reliance continued its growth through acquisition by purchasing the Drake Steel Supply Company, which operated metals service centers in Fresno and San Diego, California. With the purchase, Reliance also acquired the services of Joe D. Crider, who had joined Drake in 1949 as a billing clerk and worked his way up to Fresno sales manager. After several years as manager of Reliance Steel's Los Angeles division, Crider was named executive vice-president in 1975, teaming up with Gimbel to form what *Metal Service News* would later call "perhaps the best known management team in the service center industry."

Company Perspectives:

We are excited about the improved operating environment and our ability to take full advantage of these opportunities. However, our most important challenge going forward is to fully pass through the significantly higher costs of our metals to our customers. We are hopeful that we will experience additional increases in customer demand levels in the foreseeable future.

In 1966, Reliance extended its reach into Texas by acquiring metals service centers in Dallas and San Antonio from Delta Metals, Inc. Two years later, the company bought out another Los Angeles competitor, the Catalina Steel Company, its fifth acquisition in ten years. By then, Reliance Steel had also established SupraCote, a coil-coating division, in Cucamonga, California. It became a separate subsidiary in 1973, and was sold to a management group in 1980.

Reliance Steel acquired Southern Equipment & Supply Company, San Diego's oldest metals service center, in 1972, and immediately launched a $1.8 million project to double the size of the San Diego facility. Two years later, the rapidly growing company announced a $4 million expansion in Los Angeles.

Reliance Steel also wanted to strengthen its position in Texas, and, after attempting to acquire a Houston business, temporarily abandoned its acquisition philosophy and opened a new metals service center in the port city in 1975. Gimbel told *Metal Service News,* "We had spent probably two years trying to buy out somebody, but at the time there was a big boom there, and everyone felt the streets of Houston were paved with gold. We just could never make a deal to buy someone. So we started our own company." Reliance closed the Houston center in 1984 due to a slump in the oil industry.

Reliance ventured into the eastern part of the United States for the first time in 1975 when it acquired the Purchased Steel Products Conmpany, in Atlanta. The move never panned out, however, and Reliance sold the center in 1987. Gimbel told *Metal Center News,* "We learned a lesson in Atlanta. If we're going to go further east, that probably means the Chicago area. And you don't move into Chicago on a shoestring."

Specialty Metals Since the Late 1970s

After more than three decades of operating full-service metals service centers, Reliance opened its first "specialty store" in 1976, forming the Tube Service Company, in Santa Fe Springs, California. The subsidiary specialized in tubular products. A second Tube Service opened three years later in Milpitas, California. In 1977, Reliance also acquired Bralco Metals, in Pico Rivera, California, which specialized in brass, aluminum, and copper. To manage its aluminum, magnesium, and stainless steel products, Reliance created a nonferrous metals division, Reliance Metalcenter, in 1980.

Also in 1980, Reliance also acquired Foucar, Ray & Simon, a specialty tube distributor in Hayward, California, with a branch in Portland, Oregon. The Hayward center was eventually merged into the Reliance center in Santa Clara. The Portland operation foundered and then closed in 1984. Gimbel told *Metal Service News* the acquisition had been a mistake. "Foucar was probably the second oldest service center in California, with a good reputation. They'd done well over the years, but I guess they'd gotten rigor mortis. We thought that we could change all that. We tried and tried to change it, and it didn't work. So we had to admit defeat and close up the place."

The setback, however, did not slow the company's aggressive growth. In 1981, Reliance purchased the Cd'A Service Center in Salt Lake City, Utah, from Spokane-based Cd'A Steel Service Center. The company then acquired Circle Metals in Carson, California, in 1983, and Tricon Steel & Aluminum in Fremont, California, and Arnold Engineering in Fullerton, California, in 1984. Arnold Engineering was renamed Arnold Technologies, Inc. and relocated to Anaheim. In the mid-1980s, Reliance gobbled up assets of the Ducommum Metals in Phoenix and Los Angeles, the Lafayette Metal Service Corp. in Long Beach, California, and the assets of the Livermore, California, metals service center from Capitol Metals Company. The company also acquired the Valex Corporation in Ventura, California, which made stainless steel components for electronic and pharmaceutical applications, the Dallas/Forth Worth Russell Steel Division of the Van Pelt Corp., and the Morris Steel & Aluminum Company in Albuquerque, New Mexico. In 1988, Reliance also acquired the Los Angeles Sheet & Steel Division from Earle M. Jorgensen Company.

The acquisitions certainly fueled growth. By 1988, the company's 50th year, sales topped $350 million. Nevertheless, Reliance continued to expand. Over the next two years, it acquired the assets of Albuquerque, New Mexico-based Smith Pipe & Steel and the Los Angeles and Phoenix operations of Lusk Metals. Other acquisitions in the 1990s included Affiliated Metals, an aluminum and stainless steel specialty center in Salt Lake City, Utah, and the Wichita, Kansas, operations of National Steel Service Center Inc., which stocked aluminum plate, sheet, and coil for the aerospace industry. The National Steel acquisition marked Reliance Steel's first foray into the Midwest.

Going Public in 1994

In 1994, after 55 years as a closely held operation, Reliance issued its first public stock. At the time, the company had about 180 stockholders, most of them employees or relatives of founder Thomas J. Neilan. Reliance had previously considered, and rejected, going public several times. In 1984, Gimbel told *Metal Service News,* "We'd go and talk to the brokers, but, unfortunately, anything with the name steel in it didn't get them very excited." In its prospectus, Reliance also signaled its intention to continue growth through acquisitions, stating, "Traditionally, metals service centers have been small, family-owned businesses that lack the diversity of experience and successful operating techniques of Reliance and thus have and may in the future become candidates for acquisition or consolidation."

A year after the initial public offering, Reliance acquired a 50 percent interest in American Steel, L.L.C. for $19 million, its largest purchase to date. (This shareholding was raised to 50.5

Key Dates:

1939: Reliance Steel Products Company is formed in Los Angeles to produce steel reinforcing bars (rebar).

1948: Reliance begins manufacturing aluminum and magnesium products.

1957: William T. Gimbel succeeds company founder Thomas J. Neilan as president.

1960: Phoenix competitor Effron Steel is acquired.

1961: Norther California's Westates Steel is acquired.

1963: Drake Steel Supply of Fresno and San Diego are acquired.

1966: Texas metals service centers are bought from Delta Metals, Inc.

1968: Rival Catalina Steel is acquired.

1972: San Diego's Southern Equipment & Supply metals service center is acquired and expanded.

1975: A new metals service center is opened in Houston.

1976: The company's first "specialty store" is set up in Santa Fe Springs, California, through its Tuber Service Company subsidiary.

1977: California's Bralco Metals is acquired.

1980: SupraCote coil-coating subsidiary is sold to management; tube distributor Foucar, Ray & Simon is acquired.

1984: The company's Houston service center is closed.

1988: Sales exceed $350 million.

1994: Initial public offering is made.

1995: A half-interest in American Steel is bought for $19 million.

1996: Reliance enters the Southeast with the purchase of Tennessee-based Siskin Steel & Supply Company for $71 million.

2001: Pitt Des Moines (PDM) is acquired for $97.5 million.

percent in May 2002). That was followed in 1996 with the acquisition of VMI Corporation, an 11-year-old nonferrous metals service center in Albuquerque, New Mexico, and CCC Steel, Inc., which operated carbon-steel service centers in Los Angeles and Salt Lake City. Reliance also announced the acquisition of the Siskin Steel & Supply Company, Inc., with metals service centers in Chattanooga and Nashville, Tennessee; Spartanburg, South Carolina; and Birmingham, Alabama. Reliance Steel paid $71 million for the company, which had revenues of $151 million and would operate as a wholly owned subsidiary. Siskin Steel & Supply had been formed in 1949 as the service center division of a scrap metal business established in 1900. David H. Hannah, then president, called the acquisition "an integral part of our strategy to become a national company with operations extending beyond the Western half of the United States."

In 1997, Reliance reported net income of $29.8 million on record sales of $654 million. It was the sixth consecutive year of record financial results. The company also acquired Amalco Metals, Inc., a metals service center company in Union City, California, that specialized in processing and distributing aluminum plate and sheet, and AMI Metals, Inc., a Brentwood, Tennessee, company that specialized in processing and distrib-

uting aluminum plate, sheet, and bar products for the aerospace industry. AMI operated service centers in Fontana, California; Wichita, Kansas; Brentwood, Tennessee; Fort Worth, Texas; Kent, Washington; and Swedesboro, New Jersey.

Crider, who became chairman in early 1997, succeeding Gimbel, who remained on the board of directors as chairman emeritus, said in interviews that he expected Reliance Steel to continue growing through acquisitions. Industry analysts expected Reliance to focus its expansion on the strengthening Midwest market.

Soaring in the Late 1990s

A secondary public offering in November 1997 raised $94 million to fuel further acquisitions. A $150 million private placement followed a year later.

Reliance continued to invest in the aerospace business, acquiring Service Steel Aerospace Corp. of Tacoma, Washington, in October 1997. The industry thrived until a dramatic falloff in orders in 1999.

Reliance bought Phoenix Metals of Atlanta for $21 million in January 1998. It had sales of $120 million a year. The company acquired a smaller Atlanta company, Georgia Steel Supply, around the same time. Georgia supply had revenues of $22 million a year.

Other 1998 acquisitions included Baltimore's Durrett Sheppard Steel Company (with annual sales of $47 million), Chatham Steel Corporation, Lusk Metals, Engbar Pipe & Steel Company, and Steel Bar Corporation. During the year, Reliance also reached an agreement to buy 50 percent of American Metals Corporation of West Sacramento, California, which was formerly part of the American Steel joint venture with Portland-based American Industries.

Company president David Hannah succeeded Joe D. Crider as CEO in February 1999. Crider remained chairman. Chairman emeritus William T. Gimbel had died in December 1998.

Liebovich Bros. Inc., a Rockford, Illinois, supplier of carbon steel products, was acquired in March 1999. It had sales of $130 million. Other 1999 acquisitions included Allegheny Steel Distributors Inc., Dallas-area aluminum distributor Arrow Metals, and Hagerty Steel of Illinois. Pennsylvania's Toma Metals Inc., a small specialty stainless supplier, was added in 2000.

The company's Valex unit dominated the U.S. market for electropolished stainless steel tubing and fittings used to build semiconductor plants. Expanding overseas, in 1999 Valex opened a distribution center in France and formed a manufacturing joint venture in Korea. Valex shut down its Phoenix distribution site in 2003.

RSAC Management Corp. was formed as a holding company in 1999. The corporation also performed administrative and management tasks for the metals service centers. Reliance ended the decade with sales of nearly $1.6 billion a year.

The metals service business was large and still highly fragmented in the late 1990s. *Forbes* described it as a $45 billion industry, while *American Metal Market* calculated the number of competitors had fallen to 3,400 from 7,000 in the 1980s.

Still Consolidating after 2000

Reliance's acquisitions continued in the 2000s, even as the economy was beginning to slow and, as CEO David Hannah told *American Metal Market,* the number of suitable potential acquisitions was thinning. (Reliance still avoided suppliers to the notoriously low-margin auto industry).

Reliance bought United Alloys Inc.'s aerospace division in August 2000. Founded in 1971, it had sales of $18 million a year. The acquisition added titanium products to Reliance's lineup.

The Midwest continued to be a focus for acquisitions. Viking Materials Inc., a Minneapolis-based processor and distributor of flat-rolled carbon steel products, was bought in early 2001. Viking had been formed in 1973 and had 1999 revenues of $83 million as well as 155 employees and facilities in Illinois and Iowa.

Reliance was also adding to its operations in the South. East Tennessee Steel Supply Inc. was added to Reliance's Chattanooga-based Siskin Steel unit in early 2001. It had revenues of $6.6 million in its 2000 fiscal year.

Pitt Des Moines Inc. (PDM) was purchased for $97.5 million in the summer of 2001. Pitt had sales of $260 million a year at seven locations, most in the West.

Reliance acquired assets of Central Plains Steel Company in April 2002. Based in Kansas, the business had net sales of about $27 million in 2003. Denver metals service center Olympic Metals, Inc. was acquired at the same time. Olympic specialized in aluminum, copper, brass, and stainless steel and had sales of $7 million in 2003.

Certain assets of a unit of bankrupt Metals USA, Inc. were purchased in September 2002 for $30 million. The unit subsequently began operating under its original name, Pacific Metal Company. Its sales were $70 million in 2003.

Purchasing magazine called 2002 the worst market for metal service centers in 20 years. An aggravating factor was the dramatic drop-off in commercial airliner orders following the September 11, 2001 terrorist attacks on the United States.

The U.S. government imposed tariffs on imported steel in early 2002. This made the price of hot-rolled carbon steel rise and Reliance's shares fall, observed the *Los Angeles Business Journal.* The tariffs were lifted in December 2003 after complaints by U.S. automakers.

Subsidiary AMI Metals, Inc. opened a European business in January 2003. Based in Gosselies, Belgium, AMI Metals Europe, SPRL focused on the aerospace industry. AMI closed its Atlanta area facility during the year while opening a new on in St. Louis.

Acquisitions in 2003 included Precision Strip, Inc., a fee-based or "toll" processor of carbon steel, aluminum, and stainless steel products. Reliance paid $250 million in cash and

assumed $26 million of debt in the deal, which closed in July. Precision Strip had sales of $122 million in 2002 and had facilities in the Midwest and the South.

Revenues skyrocketed 56 percent to $2.9 billion in 2004, and the company's net income of $170 million was four times that of 2003. The immediate future looked good, as the aviation industry was expected to begin to recover from its post-9/11 slump.

Principal Subsidiaries

Allegheny Steel Distributors, Inc.; Aluminum and Stainless, Inc.; American Metals Corporation; American Steel, L.L.C. (50.5%); AMI Metals, Inc.; CCC Steel, Inc.; Central Plains Steel Company; Chatham Steel Corporation; Durrett Sheppard Steel Co., Inc.; Liebovich Bros., Inc.; Lusk Metals; Pacific Metal Company; PDM Steel Service Centers, Inc.; Phoenix Corporation; Precision Strip, Inc.; RSAC Management Corp.; Service Steel Aerospace Corporation; Siskin Steel & Supply Company, Inc.; Toma Metals, Inc.; Valex Corporation (97%); Viking Materials, Inc.

Principal Competitors

Earle M. Jorgensen Company; Gerdau AmeriSteel Corporation; Integris Metals Inc.; Ryerson Tull, Inc.; Steel Technologies Inc.; ThyssenKrupp Materials North America Inc.; Worthington Steel Co.

Further Reading

Berry, Charles, "Reliance Takes the Road Less Traveled," *Metal Center News*, December 1992.

——, "The Art of the Deal: Growth by Acquisition," *Metal Center News*, December 1992.

Biddle, RiShawn, "Reliance Steels for Growth as Lifting of Tariffs Drives Shares," *Los Angeles Business Journal*, January 5, 2004, p. 22.

Chase, Martin, "Reliance Plans to Continue Acquisition Strategy," *American Metal Market*, September 19, 2001, p. 4A.

Cole, Benjamin Mark, "Man of Steel (Aluminum, Brass Too)," *Los Angeles Business Journal*, June 17, 1996, p. 17.

——, "Reliance Steel Plans $51.7 Million IPO; Plans Listing on Big Board," *Los Angeles Business Journal*, October 3, 1994.

Haflich, Frank, "As Targets Thin, Reliance Recasts Growth Rx," *American Metal Market*, June 9, 2000, p. 1.

——, "Reliance Continues Its Acquisition Spree," *American Metal Market*, October 9, 1998, p. 4.

——, "Reliance Debt Deal Seen as Commitment to Growth," *American Metal Market*, November 10, 1998, p. 4.

——, "Reliance Moving into New Niche in East," *American Metal Market*, May 16, 2000, p. 6.

——, "Reliance Still in Buying Mood," *American Metal Market*, May 22, 1998, p. 2.

——, "Reliance Will Lean More on Midwest," *American Metal Market*, January 27, 2000, p. 1.

——, "Today's Reliance Steel Bears Stamp of Late Chairman Gimbel," *American Metal Market*, December 18, 1998, p. 2.

Joch, Alan, "Tube Service Co.: A Generalist's Specialist," *Metal Center News*, December 1984.

——, "When Entrepreneurs Manage Entrepreneurs," *Metal Center News*, December 1984.

MacKey, William, "Flatrolled Vendor to the High-Tech Market," *Metal Center News*, December 1984.

Nelson, Brett, "Reliance Steel & Aluminum Move That Iron," *Forbes*, January 10, 2000, p. 152.

Petry, Corinna C., "Acquisition Fever Key to Reliance's Offering," *American Metal Market*, October 16, 1997, p. 2.

——, "Consolidation's Dynamic Duo," *Metal Center News,* October 1999, p. 28.

"Reliance MetalCenters: A History of Innovation," *Metal Center News*, December 1984.

"Reliance to Purchase Viking Materials, East Tennessee Steel Supply," *Metal Center News*, January 2001, p. 14.

"Siskin Celebrates Its Centennial," *Metal Center News*, April 2000, p. 20.

Stundza, Tom, "Worst Market in Two Decades Zaps Sales: Top 100 Metal Service Centers," *Purchasing*, May 2, 2002, pp. 16B1ff.

Triplett, Tim, "MCN Top 50: Service Center Industry Giants," *Metal Center News*, September 2004, pp. 18ff.

"The Web? There's No Reason to Rush," *Business Week*, May 15, 2000, p. 38D.

—Dean Boyer
—update: Frederick C. Ingram

Rewards Network Inc.

2 North Riverside Plaza, Suite 950
Chicago, Illinois 60606
U.S.A.
Telephone: (312) 521-6767
Toll Free: (877) 491-3463
Fax: (312) 521-6769
Web site: http://www.rewardsnetwork.com

Public Company
Incorporated: 1984 as Transmedia Network
Employees: 400
Sales: $93.25 million (2004)
Stock Exchanges: American
Ticker Symbol: IRN
NAIC: 561499 All Other Business Support Services

Rewards Network Inc. operates reward and loyalty programs for the hospitality and credit card industries. In 2004, Rewards Network's 3.8 million card members could choose from nearly 22,000 restaurants and merchants. Rewards Network's main U.S. regions of operation are New York City (which typically accounts for 40 percent of its revenues) and southern Florida. Rewards is headquartered in Chicago and has a support center in Miami.

The company provides restaurants with interest-free loans in exchange for blocks of meals sold to Rewards Network for half price. The company also has a program for restaurants to offer discounts on specific off-peak times. In addition to straight discounts on restaurant meals, members receive reduced hotel room rates and frequent flyer miles.

From Security Alarms to Media Barter: 1963–84

The founder of Rewards Network Inc., Melvin Chasen, took the long road to success. Beginning as a young entrepreneur in Colorado, Chasen had experimented with everything from selling security alarms to running a mergers-and-acquisitions firm before he settled on the media barter concept that became Rewards Network's business model.

In 1963, while still in his early thirties, Chasen founded his first company, Midway Enterprises Inc., in Colorado. Within five years, it had evolved into Pike's Peak Turf Club and by 1974 became Pike's Peak American Corporation. In the early 1980s, Chasen, with the help of ad agency executive Hank Seiden, entered the media barter industry. In media barter, companies buy up blocks of advertising from media outlets such as newspapers, radio, television and exchange them with companies for their excess merchandise or services. Often such companies will get an advertising equivalent to the wholesale price of their goods or services rather than having to settle for the heavily discounted price they would charge in a closeout sale.

To capitalize on the media barter idea, in 1983 Chasen renamed his business Transmedia Network and located it in New York City, where he began arranging advertising-for-services exchanges between radio stations and potential radio advertisers who needed ready cash. The majority of these companies were restaurants, which because of the dining industry's notoriously high turnover and thin profit margins were often unable to get loans from banks. Early on, Transmedia also operated as a media placement firm, earning 15 percent commissions on ad space purchased from such publications as *New York* magazine.

By lining up $500,000 in investment capital through the private placement market, Chasen financed Transmedia's early growth and merged the company into a public shell corporation in 1984. In exchange for financing his new business, Chasen's investors insisted that he run it, and in 1983 Chasen introduced the Transmedia card through which restaurant goers could receive 25 percent off meals at restaurants that had bartered meals for blocks of advertising. Chasen soon discovered, however, that restaurants much preferred cash to advertising space, and despite his own tight cash reserves he began offering pure cash advances to restaurants that agreed to accept the Transmedia card. The change in strategy paid off immediately and cash-strapped restaurants began lining up for Transmedia loans.

The amount of money Transmedia loaned restaurants was based on their reputation and capital needs as well as the amount of time Chasen estimated it would take Transmedia's cardholders to "pay off" the loan through restaurant visits. In exchange for a $5,000 interest-free loan to a restaurant (the standard amount Transmedia loaned to a new restaurant), Transmedia received $10,000 in meal credits, which Chasen anticipated would be used up by Transmedia cardholders within six months. Since restaurants' actual cost for food and beverages ranged from only 30 to 40 percent of the cost charged to customers, Chasen's major obstacle was not in finding restaurants willing to participate, or investors willing to loan Transmedia capital, but in getting consumers to believe they could get 25 percent dining discounts without some "catch." When even ads offering to waive the $50 membership fee for new members failed to do the trick, Chasen began hawking the Transmedia card to teachers' unions, law and accounting firms, police departments, and other professional groups to widen Transmedia's member base.

Working in Transmedia's favor were the features that made its card an improvement over earlier incarnations of the discount dining concept; no coupons had to be clipped and presented, maitre d's and waiters did not have to be forewarned that the customer intended to pay with the Transmedia card (though large parties had to make reservations in advance through Transmedia), and there were no limits on dining times or menu choices. As a Transmedia executive later recalled to the *Los Angeles Times,* "We designed the card so that there would be no restrictions, no coupons, no negatives."

Building a Franchise: 1985–91

The first directory listing the restaurants that honored Transmedia's "Executive Savings Card" (41 in all) was issued to Transmedia's 225 New York City members in 1985, just as a new competitor, In Good Taste (IGT), entered the meal barter/discount card market. In 1986, with revenues approaching $1 million, Chasen issued Transmedia shares in a public stock offering that infused $1 million of much-needed expansion capital into the business. By 1987, Transmedia had posted revenues of $1.8 million but suffered a net loss of $422,000. In July, Chasen reincorporated Transmedia (which, as an outgrowth of Chasen's earlier ventures, had been a Colorado corporation) in Delaware.

By painstakingly expanding consumer awareness of the card and marketing the Transmedia concept to the ever-growing pool of new cash-starved restaurants, Chasen realized a net income of $35,000 in 1988 on sales of $2.9 million. The Transmedia card generated traffic for restaurants, filling up empty seats and conferring an image of popularity on struggling startups in the business. Despite the heavy two-for-one price of the Transmedia loan, restaurant owners began embracing the idea of cash-on-the-spot loans that never had to be repaid in cash and offered the prospect for increased word-of-mouth traffic as Transmedia card users brought in new customers. Although the risk that a new restaurant would fold before customers used up its meal credits was unavoidable, in 1990 Transmedia wrote off only $109,000 in meal credit losses.

In its sixth year in business, Transmedia's sales vaulted to more than $4.4 million and net income nearly tripled to $99,000. To expand his business even further, Chasen began offering Transmedia franchises for sale in 1990, and by 1991 its first franchisee was offering the Transmedia card for restaurants throughout the New Jersey area. With 13 employees (nine of whom were independent sales staff under contract), 500 participating restaurants, and 25,000 cardholders in 1990, Chasen opened a Cardholder Service Center in North Miami and saw sales rise 70 percent to almost $7.5 million.

In 1991, the torrid pace of Transmedia's growth began to draw the attention of Wall Street and the national media. The *Wall Street Journal* boosted the company's profile with a favorable piece describing happy Transmedia cardholders pocketing $50 a month in savings and *Business Week* listed Transmedia as one of its top "Hot Growth Companies" in the spring. Not coincidentally, Transmedia's shares rose from $3 in February 1991 to $12 by late summer. By the end of 1991, Transmedia's staff had grown to 21, membership had risen to 50,000 cardholders, and sales had climbed to $13 million.

Competition and Growth: 1992–93

With his company now servicing New York, New Jersey, Connecticut, and Florida, Chasen offered 500,000 shares in a private placement stock offering in 1992 that generated close to $5 million in additional capital. In 1990 and 1991, a new entrant in the discount dining market, The Signature Group of Chicago, began negotiating with Transmedia for a joint licensing agreement in which the companies would honor each other's cards. Chasen allowed the talks to collapse, however, and the stage was set for Signature's entrance as a new player in the industry in June 1993. Already, in 1992, a fourth discount card service, A la Carte International Inc., had begun offering restaurantgoers a discount dining card plan. By 1993, the discount dining card market was ruled by Transmedia, Executive IGT (In Good Taste), and a new participant, Entertainment Publications. Each offered variations on the others' program, tweaking the discount card business model to strike the right balance with consumers.

In August 1991, Transmedia had optimistically predicted its membership would reach 100,000 by 1992. When 1992 closed, however, more than 112,000 members were actually toting Transmedia cards, which were now honored at 1,449 restaurants. With sales approaching $24 million, Transmedia moved its corporate headquarters from New York to Miami and contin-

Key Dates:

1984: Colorado entrepreneur Melvin Chasen relocates Pikes Peak American Corp. to New York and renames it Transmedia Network Inc.

1986: Transmedia meal barter/discount revenues approach $1 million.

1991: A New Jersey franchise is launched.

1993: A European subsidiary is incorporated; co-branded cards are started.

1997: Real estate magnate Samuel Zell invests in Transmedia.

1999: Dining A la Card is acquired from Montgomery Ward.

2000: IDine online venture is launched.

2002: Transmedia is renamed iDine Rewards Network.

2003: A hotel reward program is started, and the company's name is shortened to Rewards Network Inc.

ued its national expansion. By the end of 1993, Transmedia was adding 200 new restaurants a month, had extended its program throughout most of the East Coast, and had established franchise beachheads in San Francisco and Chicago. To extend the Transmedia concept overseas, in late 1992 Chasen announced a $1.25 million deal with Boston-based merchant bankers Conestoga Partners Inc. to license Transmedia's service in the United Kingdom and Europe. In February 1993, Transmedia Europe (comprising Transmedia Europe plc, Transmedia UK plc, and Transmedia UK Inc.) was incorporated to extend the Transmedia cards' reach from the British Isles to Turkey and the former states of the Soviet Union.

In late 1993, Chasen began a policy of partnering Transmedia with selected U.S. companies in order to broaden the company's offerings beyond restaurant dining. Among the first to sign on was the *New York Times,* which allowed Transmedia customers to take advantage of the benefits of its "Times Card" discount and membership program through a co-branded Transmedia/Times card. Transmedia also absorbed the restaurants honoring the Times card into its own network. The program had produced 64,000 new Transmedia cardholders by mid-1994 and spawned a series of co-branding, "retail loyalty" deals with such direct mail catalog merchants as The Sharper Image and Jos. A. Bank Clothiers and eventually even cruise lines like Carnival. Moreover, by the end of the year Chasen had announced plans to introduce the Transmedia program to Los Angeles, Texas, Georgia, Arizona, and Mississippi. With close to 200,000 cardholders and 2,300 participating restaurants, Transmedia's sales had swept past the $36 million mark by the end of its 1993 fiscal year, and its stock could boast two- and five-year total returns of 205 and 2,732 percent, respectively, placing it 14th on *Business Week*'s 1993 annual "Hot Growth Company" ranking.

Doubts and a Falling Stock: 1994–95

In March 1994, Transmedia struck a $1.25 million deal with Conestoga Partners II to allow them to license Transmedia's program in Australia and New Zealand and to sublicense it

elsewhere on the Pacific Rim under the name Transmedia Asia-Pacific. With more than 222,000 cardholders and 2,467 participating restaurants, Transmedia struck agreements with Cellular One, the cell phone service provider; Prodigy Services, the commercial online service provider; Amtrak; credit card issuer MBNA America Bank; and cable company Comcast to market the Transmedia card to the four companies' customers. Transmedia picked up 4,500 new card members when Cellular One offered its San Francisco customers the card as a premium, and Comcast generated another 3,500 members through a similar program. Prodigy made a blanket offer of the Transmedia card to any of its 700,000 subscribers who lived within 20 miles of a Transmedia-affiliated restaurant, and in July 1994 Amtrak began binding the card into copies of its on-board magazine on its East Coast routes. Aided by a new federal tax law that reduced the allowable business meal deduction from 80 to 50 percent, which forced many business people to look for cheaper ways to wine and dine clients, Transmedia went ahead with plans to expand outside Los Angeles into Orange County and basked in the glow of a *Financial World* magazine article that ranked it as America's third-best growth company. As Chasen doubled his staff to 90 employees, Transmedia finished the year with a net income of $4.4 million on sales of $48.6 million.

The year 1995 marked a watershed in the company's history. On the one hand, it expanded its network to 5,330 restaurants and almost 600,000 cardholders, began trading on the New York Stock Exchange, established a literacy-promoting philanthropic program called "TransReadia," and continued to expand its offerings beyond restaurant discounts. In an agreement with GE Capital it offered cardholders substantial discounts on long-distance phone calls and initiated a new program called Transmedia Dollars that allowed cardholders to forego the 25 percent discount on meals in exchange for credits toward the purchase of airline tickets. Members could also use the Transmedia card for discounts at a growing number of hotels, ski resorts, and spas.

On the other hand, the shimmer was beginning to fade from Transmedia's growth story. Although Transmedia cardholders charged $85 million on their cards in 1995, 70 percent of that volume came from New York City members alone. Its attempt to franchise its license was also proving costly, and in July it repurchased its Chicago franchise and waited for its so far unprofitable Denver and Phoenix programs to turn the corner. Moreover, two new competitors, CUC International's Premier card and the Florida-based Gusto card, were offering new competition, and in June Transmedia announced that its upcoming quarters would show earnings below Wall Street's estimates. Although revenues grew by 20 percent in 1995, that pace marked the slowest increase in the company's short history and net profits remained stagnant. *Forbes* magazine questioned Transmedia's business concept as a kind of restaurant-punishing sleight of hand and wondered aloud, "How far can Transmedia go on this marketing ploy?" Transmedia responded that its further expansion into the Midwest, the Gulf Coast of Florida, and the Southwest augured well for its future revenue growth and that its less than stellar performance in 1995 could be blamed on the late mailing of a marketing campaign that would have attracted even more new customers. The rarely spoken doubts behind four years of media hype seemed to come to a head all at once in late 1995, when Transmedia's stock began a harrowing decline from which it still had not recovered more than 18 months later.

The seeds of investors' concerns could perhaps be traced to worry over Transmedia's pell-mell expansion, but the media suggested that the company's trouble might involve the very core of its business scheme. By requiring restaurants to cough up meal credits valued at twice the amount of Transmedia's loans to them, the company was making it all but impossible for some of its restaurants to greet Transmedia customers with a welcoming smile. For every three new restaurants added to Transmedia's bimonthly directory, on average one would drop out or go out of business within a year. Although some restaurants found that as many as 40 percent of their first-time Transmedia customers came back, others complained that though the card attracted new customers, it also encouraged existing full-paying customers to switch to the Transmedia card as well, cutting even deeper into margins. Still others groused that the typical Transmedia customer was rarely a big spender and that by buying into the Transmedia program restaurants were announcing to the community that they were in trouble, so desperate for cash that they were willing to sacrifice profits. As one of Transmedia's competitors frankly admitted, ''The nature of the business is that successful restaurants don't need us.''

Retrenching in the Mid-1990s

Chasen and Transmedia fought back against Wall Street's doubts on multiple fronts. In January 1996, it struck a deal with Continental Airlines and United Airlines to allow cardholders to earn ten free miles for every $1 charged (versus the two to three miles earned by other charge cards). Its two overseas units reached an agreement to gain access to the 6-million-member database of British discount service provider Countdown Holding, and Transmedia began offering some of its customers a ''free-for-life'' Transmedia card to bolster card holder retention. Chasen also reached an agreement with Western Transmedia, his franchisee in the western United States, to reacquire control of its unspectacular programs in California, Oregon, Washington, and Nevada. Transmedia also began to exploit the global marketing potential of the Internet by creating its own Web site and marketing itself through the online site of the ''Diner's Grapevine'' service. Moreover, Chasen announced plans to spend $2.6 million in 1997 on computer software to modernize Transmedia's transaction processing operations, thus enabling it to perform the transaction processing for major credit card companies in addition to its own programs. Finally, in December 1996, Transmedia sold $33 million of its restaurant meal credits (known as ''rights to receive'') as securities to a group of investors in a private placement offering that promised to generate needed capital. Describing the deal as ''a major milestone'' in the company's history, Chasen excitedly characterized the newly capitalized Transmedia as a ''powerful cash machine'' now able to fund its future growth without having to take on new debt or sell shares of stock to the public.

In a sign of Chasen's commitment to returning Transmedia to its glory days, in February 1997 he recruited Stephen Lerch, a financial specialist from accounting firm Coopers & Lybrand, to become his right-hand man under the title executive vice-president. The same month, Transmedia's two overseas units, Transmedia Europe and Transmedia Asia Pacific, announced an agreement to combine forces, subject to shareholder approval. Despite an aborted attempt to acquire the operations of competitor, Gusto, in June 1997, with more than 1.2 million cardholders worldwide and agreements with more than 7,000 restaurants and over 400 hotels, Transmedia remained a force to be reckoned with, and Chasen announced that Transmedia's belt-tightening measures would begin to bear financial fruit during the summer of 1997.

Backing and Direction from Zell: 1997 and Beyond

Equity Group Investments Inc., an investment group led by well-known real estate entrepreneur Samuel (Sam) Zell, acquired an initial 20 percent holding in Transmedia in November 1997 for $10.6 million. Equity Group managing director F. Philip Handy succeeded company founder Melvin Chasen as Transmedia's chairman.

In 1999, Transmedia acquired its chief rival, the Dining A La Card (DALC) business of Montgomery Ward subsidiary The Signature Group. According to *Forbes,* the price was $35 million in cash and $6 million of Transmedia stock. Transmedia became the country's largest dining reward program, with more than two million members, via the DALC acquisition.

DALC's system did not require consumers to brandish a separate discount card at restaurants, which some felt embarrassing. Instead, transactions were tracked using credit card numbers. Transmedia switched to this method after the acquisition.

Around this time, Transmedia also began offering frequent flyer miles as incentives. Instead of a monetary refund, users could opt to receive ten miles for each dollar spent.

Zell and CEO Gene M. Henderson directed a turnaround at Transmedia, which lost money from 1997 to 2000. The company's shares migrated from the Big Board to the American Stock Exchange in April 2001.

The company had been taking control back from affiliates for a few years. Its licensing agreement with Transmedia Europe and Transmedia Asia Pacific ended in 2000.

A new online venture, iDine.com Inc., was launched in May 2000. IDine.com allowed upscale restaurants to set designate off-peak times as discount periods. The site was limited to the Chicago area at first. Wolfgang Puck casual restaurants eventually signed up for the iDine program.

The company was renamed iDine Rewards Network in 2002, reflecting the name of its new Internet-based restaurant rewards program. It was growing fast, increasing from $196 million in 2001 to about $285 million in 2002. IDine had 2.3 million members and 9,500 participating restaurants at this time.

Management was changed in late 2002, with George Wiedemann succeeding Gene Henderson as president and CEO. Sam Zell took the position of chairman following the resignation of Sheli Rosenberg. Wiedemann was founder of the direct marketing agency GreyDirect Marketing Group, Inc. and had also led Responsys Inc., a direct marketing technology supplier.

The company's headquarters was relocated from Miami to Chicago, Zell's traditional base of operations, in 2003. A large call center remained in Miami. The company's name was shortened to Rewards Network Inc. in December 2003 to reflect its breadth of offerings beyond dining.

During the year, IDine launched a rewards program geared toward independent hotels. The program was expanded in October 2003 in partnership with travel distribution company Travelweb LLC, which also represented major hotel chains. By the end of the year, 6,940 hotels were participating.

Sales were flat at $93 million in 2004, though active accounts rose from 3.4 million to 3.8 million. The number of participating merchants was also up, about 4,000, to 21,941. Net income slipped from $15.7 million to $13.2 million. Company president George S. Wiedemann said he expected results to improve as the company promoted new dining products while containing costs.

Principal Subsidiaries

iDine Media Group Inc.; Rewards Network Canada GP Corp.; Rewards Network Canada LP; Rewards Network Establishment Services Inc.; Rewards Network International, Inc.; Rewards Network Services Inc.; RTR Funding LLC; TMNI International Inc.; TNI Funding I Inc.

Principal Divisions

Dining; Hotels.

Principal Competitors

Hospitality Marketing Concepts; Hotels.com, L.P.; IGT Services Inc.

Further Reading

Beyer, Leslie, "A Flash in the Pan?," *Credit Card Management*, December 1999, p. 14.

Bongiorno, Lori, "The Class of ''95: Where Are They Now?," *Business Week*, May 26, 1997, p. 104.

Chandler, Michele, "Miami-Based iDine Names New Chairman," *Miami Herald*, September 24, 2002.

Coulton, Antoinette, "Card Exec Still Dining out on His Discount Idea," *American Banker*, February 13, 1997, p. 26.

——, "Transmedia, a Dining Card Firm, Expands Its Reach with U.K., Australia Deals," *American Banker*, September 19, 1996, p. 13.

DuPont, Dale K., "Miami-Based Dining Rewards Program Names New Chief Executive," *Miami Herald*, September 27, 2002.

——, "Miami-Based Online Restaurant Discounter on Track for Continued Strong Growth," *Miami Herald*, December 18, 2002.

Fickenscher, Lisa, "Dining Discounter Plans to Swallow Registry Firm," *American Banker*, August 18, 1998, p. 17.

——, "Transmedia Network, Signature Group Offer Dining Programs for Frequent-Flier Customers," *American Banker*, January 23, 1996.

Gibbs, Lisa, "Chasing Chasen," *Florida Trend*, October 1998, p. 12.

"Gusto-Transmedia Merger Discussion Ended," press release, North Miami, Fla.: Transmedia Network Inc., June 16, 1997.

Heimlich, Cheryl Kane, "Dining Cards: Will Work for Food," *South Florida Business Journal*, August 5, 1996.

Hutheesing, Nikhil, "Keeping the Seats Warm," *Forbes*, January 1, 1996, pp. 62–63.

Jenkins, Kathie, "Hollywood's New Calling Card Is Gray," *Los Angeles Times*, August 14, 1994, p. F16.

Knecht, G. Bruce, "A Charge Card That Buys a Cheap Meal and a Loophole," *Wall Street Journal*, February 9, 1994, p. B1.

Levin, Gary, "Discount Dining Card Makes Tasty Premium," *Advertising Age*, June 4, 1994.

Marcical, Gene G., "Queuing up for Deals on Meals," *Business Week*, August 26, 1991.

Mariani, John, "The Art of the Meal," *Worth*, February 1994.

Miracle, Barbara, "Looking for Big Eaters," *Florida Trend*, April 1997, p. 34.

Ostrowski, Jeff, "Ex SafeCard Exec Eyes Transmedia," *South Florida Business Journal*, November 28, 1997, pp. 1f.

"Plastics Tasty Trend," *Credit Card Management*, February 1994, p. 8.

Reed, Keith T., "Discounter Sells Out," *Baltimore Business Journal*, July 28, 2000, p. 8.

Ring, Trudi, "The Quest for High-Calorie Perks," *Credit Card Management*, March 1997, p. 129.

Rose, Barbara, "Internet Venture Set to Help Chicago Restaurants Fill Empty Seats," *Knight Ridder/Tribune Business News*, August 2, 2000.

Seemuth, Mike, "They'll All Dine with iDine Chairman Zell," *Miami Daily Business Review*, February 13, 2003, pp. A1f.

Stern, Gary M., "A Guide through Discounting Minefield," *Restaurant Hospitality*, February 1993.

Stieghorst, Tom, "Chicago Investor Becomes Head of North Miami, Fla.-Based Dining Rewards Firm," *Sun-Sentinel* (Fort Lauderdale), September 27, 2002.

Swafford, David, "Dining Card Savings—From Hotels to Haircuts," *Business Week*, October 9, 1995, p. 159.

Tannenbaum, Jeffrey A., "Issuer of Restaurant Discount Cards Tastes Success," *Wall Street Journal*, April 23, 1991.

Teitelbaum, Richard S., "Good Food Cheap? Pick a Card!," *Fortune*, March 18, 1996, p. 133.

"Transmedia Acquires Spinoff's Operations," *American Banker*, January 13, 1997.

"Transmedia Adds Phone Call Feature," *American Banker*, March 28, 1995.

"Transmedia Network Agrees with Estimates on First-Period Net," *Wall Street Journal*, January 18, 1993.

"Transmedia Program Going Down Under," *American Banker*, March 23, 1994, p. 15.

"Transmedia Stock Listed on New York Exchange," *American Banker*, July 7, 1995.

"Up and Down Wall Street," *Barron's*, March 15, 1993, p. 43.

Vardi, Nathan, "No Free Lunch," *Forbes*, February 3, 2003, p. 70.

Walker, Elaine, "Miami-Based Dining Rewards Company Boosts Perks to Attract Members," *Miami Herald*, May 7, 2001.

White, George, "Hungry for Bargains," *Los Angeles Times*, October 27, 1993, p. D1.

—Paul S. Bodine
—update: Frederick C. Ingram

Rhino Entertainment Company

3400 West Olive Avenue
Burbank, California 91505
U.S.A.
Telephone: (818) 238-6200
Fax: (818) 562-9242
Web site: http://www.rhino.com

Wholly Owned Subsidiary of Warner Music Group
Incorporated: 1977
Employees: 160
Sales: $80 million (1999)
NAIC: 334612 Prerecorded Compact Disc (Except
Software), Tape, and Records; 512110 Motion Picture
and Video Production; 512230 Music Publishers

Rhino Entertainment Company produces novelty records, archival reissues, definitive musical anthologies, and various artists series. Rhino considers itself to be a pop culture archive company, proclaiming that "Rhino Records is the label that collects records so that you don't have to." Others have called Rhino the top catalog development company in the business. Rhino is known for its distinctive packaging, which has garnered a number of industry awards. The company's themed boxed sets have been known to include extensive liner notes, elaborate graphics, 3D elements, and novelties such as jigsaw puzzles and fuzzy dice. Rhino does design work on Warner projects as well as for third party record companies.

Record Store Origins

The story of Rhino Entertainment is largely the story of its president, Richard Foos, and managing director, Harold Bronson. Avid music listeners and collectors, Foos was a sociology student at the University of Southern California in the late 1960s, when Bronson worked at the University of California, Los Angeles (UCLA) as a student representative for Columbia Records. Attending a local swap meet, Foos was inspired when he met a dealer who had purchased hundreds of records at a used record store for $3. The vendor was selling each LP for a dollar, turning a healthy profit. Foos went to the same record store, Aaron's, and

bought his own $3 pile of records. His entrepreneurial venture began out of the trunk of his car, driving to flea markets to try to sell the old jazz and blues recordings. Rhino Records was born in October 1973, when Richard Foos opened a store on Westwood Boulevard, a few blocks south of UCLA. Harold Bronson began working at the store as an employee.

A lack of traffic in the early days gave Foos and Bronson time to brainstorm about promotions. Bronson began to implement customer-attraction events exhibiting the slightly offbeat Rhino flair, such as Polka Day, Redneck Day, and Hassle the Salesman Day. Two years later, as a 1975 promotion, the first actual Rhino record—a vinyl 45 rpm release entitled "Go to Rhino Records" sung by the eccentric Wild Man Fischer, a street singer discovered by Frank Zappa some years earlier— was issued and given away for free in the store. When local radio stations began to play the record, Rhino earned an underground following, and business picked up.

By 1978, the Rhino label was officially launched by Fischer with a full-length album, *Wildmania,* recorded partially at Dodger Stadium and produced by Harold Bronson for $500. In November 1978, Rhino carved a niche for itself with its first reissue: a picture disc by the 1960s pop band The Turtles. This disc was the first step in plans to reissue the entire Turtles catalog. The philosophy behind re-releases of novelty tunes and past hits was to create records which did not yet exist that partners Foos and Bronson would want to buy. Reissues were to be a goldmine for Rhino, and the company was off to a good start. The label grossed nearly $60,000 in its first year. Although financial success was upon them, Foos and Bronson maintained a low-budget environment, taking small salaries, using the copy machine at a local stationery store rather than buying one, and even instituting an employee schedule for cleaning the bathrooms.

Growth continued, and in 1983 Rhino was a $2 million company. Employees have always been an integral part of Rhino's philosophy and operations, presenting Rhino's unique take on popular culture and music to the customer. Foos and Bronson were careful to hire people who shared their passion for popular culture and met with them every six months in order to run the company democratically. Employees were encouraged to develop product ideas based on their own musical tastes, and the Big Ideas program offered a bonus to employees who presented innovative ideas. Over the years, employee-centered rituals such as Open Forum meetings were instituted. A portion of every employee's salary was tied to company performance, and credits on Rhino products listed employees who worked directly on that release. Thus, invested in a number of ways in the company's future, employees played a uniquely involved role in the success story of Rhino.

Another unique aspect of Rhino's corporate identity was its emphasis on social responsibility. Back covers of releases were often devoted to information on issues ranging from AIDS to homelessness to animal overpopulation. Further, Rhino's merchandising of reissues was placed in the context of social consciousness, using commercial release of cultural icons as a tool for understanding the not-so-distant past. Proceeds from album sales were often donated to relevant charities, and Rhino has been involved over the years with national causes (such as the Rock the Vote campaign and the "ban the box" campaign for CDs) as well as the local community (specifically the Wooten Center, a Los Angeles inner-city recreation and education center).

Rhino stepped out on another limb in April 1984, releasing *Three Faces of Al,* a CD by the legendary comedy quartet the Firesign Theatre. The company also released greatest hits collections from The Turtles and Jerry Lee Lewis. The next year marked the debut of Rhino Home Video with the release of *My Breakfast With Blassie,* a satire of the Louis Malle film *My Dinner with Andre,* featuring comedian Andy Kaufman and wrestler Freddie Blassie. By the fall of 1985, Rhino was ready to end its independent distribution, signing with Capitol Records for distribution through CEMA.

A Golden "Moment" in 1987

In 1987, Rhino had its first number one hit when Billy Vera's pop-soul ballad "At This Moment" reached the top of the Billboard Hot 100 singles chart. By February, the song was Rhino's first RIAA (Record Industry Association of America) gold single, and by March the entire album (*By Request: The Best of Billy Vera & The Beaters*) became Rhino's first gold album. The company was selling 50,000 copies of the album each day, and its success almost became a recipe for disaster. Foos and Bronson spent a year trying to come up with another gold single, relenting only after they had wasted significant earnings.

Reissues continued to serve Rhino's consumer market, and the company went back to focusing on what had made it successful in the first place. In 1990, Rhino took advantage of, or perhaps fueled, the nostalgia trend for the 1970s that was sweeping the nation. Rhino released the first five volumes of a 1970s retrospective entitled *Have a Nice Day: Super Hits of the '70s.* This series was so popular that, by 1996, it would com-

prise 25 volumes. Another landmark issue that year looked further back in time to the Beat Generation. Launching Rhino Word Beat, a spoken-word label, *The Jack Kerouac Collection* was a three-volume box set which earned Rhino Grammy nominations for Best Historical Album and Best Liner Notes. Expanding to reach the country music audience, Rhino also released vintage material by country artists Johnny Cash, Willie Nelson, Merle Haggard, and Buck Owens in 1990.

Children became a new market for Rhino in 1991. Aiming to please the children of America and their music-shopping parents, the Kid Rhino label was launched in February of that year, licensing classic songs from Hanna-Barbera.

A worldwide distribution agreement was forged with Atlantic Records (distributed by Warner/Elektra/Atlantic Corporation, or WEA) in 1992 that entailed cooperative reissues of Atlantic's releases, especially from the 1950s through the 1970s. This deal gave Atlantic a 50 percent interest in Rhino.

The "Atlantic Launch" was Rhino's biggest undertaking to date in terms of promotions and releases. The company also entered into an agreement to distribute Avenue Records, including seven albums by the 1960s group War that had been out of print for a decade. That year, the company earned its second RIAA gold album with *The Righteous Brothers Anthology (1962–1974),* a two-volume retrospective. Two Rhino releases earned places in the Library of Congress's American Folk Life list of recommended 1992 titles: *Jubilation! Great Gospel Performances* and *Blues Masters: The Essential Blues Collection Vols. 1–5.* Revenues were boosted in the fourth quarter by best-selling box sets including *Aretha Franklin, Queen of Soul: The Atlantic Recordings* and *Monterey International Pop Festival.* The Aretha Franklin set earned the company its first Grammy, capturing the 1992 award for liner notes. The Monterey boxed set contained previously unpublished photos, interviews with festival participants, performance notes, and background on the festival. Net proceeds were donated to charitable organizations. Overall, 1992 was Rhino's most successful year to date, grossing over $55 million for the company.

One reason for Rhino's 1992 success may have been its unprecedented act of going on the road without its artists. Strictly as a name-recognition maneuver, Rhino took a 19-city tour of summer music festivals, investing somewhere from $60,000 to $100,000 to sell the idea of Rhino's institutional identity. Booths were set up at festivals in Austin, Texas; Telluride, Colorado; Boston; Philadelphia; Yosemite Park, California; and elsewhere, with each booth offering catalogs and promotional material and mailing list sign-up sheets. Rhino followed up the festival, sending prize packages of Rhino samplers, merchandise, and fliers to those on the new mailing list.

Several partnerships brought Rhino's product to larger audiences in 1993. The company took on a line of spoken-word tapes from apparel manufacturer Esprit that featured recordings from social issues lecturers such as Gloria Steinem and Jeremy Rifkin. With the clothing, craft, and accessories chain Putumayo, Rhino released a series of world music albums which were sold in Putumayo retail outlets. Kid Rhino and McDonald's embarked upon a new partnership in 1993, working together to create recordings starring McDonaldland characters such as Ronald Mc-

Key Dates:

1973: Richard Foos opens a Rhino Records store near the University of California, Los Angeles campus.
1977: A record label is formed.
1985: Rhino Home Video is formed.
1987: Rhino has its first gold single and album.
1991: Kid Rhino label is launched.
1992: Rhino wins a Grammy in the category of liner notes.
1993: Putumayo world music series is started.
1998: Warner Music Group acquires Rhino.
2001: Rhino becomes part of WMG's Warner Strategic Marketing division.

Donald. *Ronald Makes It Magic,* the first product of the partnership, was released the next year. A mega-licensing deal was made with Warner Bros. Animation, securing the rights for Kid Rhino to release audio titles using voices of the classic Looney Tunes characters as well as three new kids on the block (Yakko, Wakko, and Dot). This deal resulted in a highly successful first album which included wacky songs from Steven Spielberg's *Animaniacs* (a Fox Children's Network TV Show).

Reviving the folk festival tradition, Rhino joined Ben & Jerry's and Concert Associates to present a two-day "Troubadours of Folk Festival" at UCLA in the summer of 1993, inspired by Rhino's anthology of the same name and featuring performances by over 30 folk artists of the past and present. The festival later became a PBS special and was released by Rhino Home Video in 1994 and 1995. Marking the first folk festival of its magnitude in the Los Angeles area in 25 years, the event featured folk artists along with a crafts festival and 200 vendors.

The company was lauded as a serious film producer in 1993 when *The Panama Deception,* a Rhino Home Video co-production, received an Academy Award for Best Documentary. Adding to the company's laurels, Rhino International received its first gold record, the French release of Aretha Franklin's *20 Greatest Hits.* Other new steps were the FORWARD label, which focused on new music by established contemporary artists such as BeauSoleil, Todd Rundgren, Richie Havens, and NRBQ, and the restoration of the Atlantic Records jazz catalog. The company also released the first major retrospective of late 1970s and early 1980s punk, power pop, and new wave music, a nine-volume set called *DIY (Do It Yourself).* This set was targeted at both older fans who remembered the songs and younger consumers aged 16 to 30 who were part of the punk revival that spawned the Seattle "grunge" sound, with groups like Nirvana, Pearl Jam, and Soundgarden.

Rhino turned Sweet 16 in 1994, and the company threw a birthday party in the form of a national identity-promoting tour. Accolades for Rhino releases were plentiful in 1994. A third RIAA gold album was certified: *Billboard's Greatest Christmas Hits (1955–Present).* Two Grammy nominations were received that year: BeauSoleil's *La Danse de la Vie* was nominated for the Best Contemporary Folk Grammy and the Monterey International Pop Festival box set earned a nomination for Best

Historical Album. Finally, *The Best of War ... And More* received RIAA gold certification.

In the spring of 1994, Rhino and the Library of Congress signed a deal enabling Rhino to compile and release anthologies of historic recordings from the national archive, with the first project slated as a box set of presidential speeches. This agreement was the first large-scale licensing and production deal between a label and the Library of Congress. Rhino also acquired the rights to the Monkees catalog, and videos of the group's TV series and specials were subsequently released, along with the movie *Head,* a Monkees feature film, and reissues of all nine original Monkees albums with previously unreleased bonus tracks and new liner notes. Two new divisions were established—Rhino Films and Rhino Books. As the 1980s receded further into the past, Rhino unveiled the first five volumes of *Just Can't Get Enough: New Wave Hits of the '80s.* Looking to the future as well as the past, Rhino went online in October of 1994 on CompuServe. Sales for the year were record-breaking, surpassing $65 million.

New ventures continued in 1995, when Rhino launched its partnership with Turner Entertainment Co., issuing classic movie soundtrack albums from films released by Metro-Goldwyn-Mayer (MGM). Rhino Movie Music would release soundtracks in conjunction with the Turner Classic Movies cable television network, including *Doctor Zhivago, Show Boat, Meet Me In St. Louis, Easter Parade, North By Northwest, That's Entertainment! The Ultimate Anthology of M-G-M Musicals,* and *Lullaby of Broadway: The Best of Busby Berkeley at Warner Bros.* Turner/Rhino's *The Wizard of Oz* soundtrack collection was a big seller for the company, and the box set release of John Coltrane recordings in *The Heavyweight Champion: The Complete Atlantic Recordings* was a highly acclaimed jazz event. A new catalog arrangement with Elektra Entertainment resulted in the release of *Love Story, 1966–1972,* a double-CD anthology of the 1960s psychedelic band Love. Making its debut in the movies, Rhino Films was preparing to complete shooting of its first original production, *Plump Fiction,* featuring Julie Brown, Sandra Bernhard, Tommy Davidson, Paul Dinello, Dan Castellaneta, Paul Provenza, and Colleen Camp.

Having achieved a high level of success with its longstanding pop culture audience, Rhino began to tap other markets for its existing releases in 1995. The company directed attention to developing its market in the black community, launching the "Deep in the Groove" campaign to emphasize existing releases and new various-artists series such as Phat Trax and Smooth Grooves. The latter, a four-volume classic romantic rhythm-and-blues series, reached gold status by Rhino standards through the sale of over 500,000 units in 1995. The company also debuted an urban marketing campaign, dubbed "Rhino, Baby! You Didn't Know? Now You Know!," to familiarize young urban music fans with Rhino's existing catalog of R&B, soul, funk, and early hip-hop.

Rhino Home Video had a landmark year in 1995 with its first gold certification, earned for the classic Jimi Hendrix film *Rainbow Bridge.* The company also earned its fifth RIAA gold album certification for *Billboard's Greatest Christmas Hits (1935–1954).* Overwhelming advance orders for Rhino Home

Video's *The Monkees Deluxe Limited-Edition Box Set* caused the item to sell out before the end of the year. The Word Beat label, Rhino's Library of Congress partnership, released its first box set, *The Library of Congress Presents: Historic Presidential Speeches (1908–1993)*. Revenues surged again, with more than $70 million in 1995 sales, and the company still had no major debt. The company played an active role in royalty reforms, joining Sony, Atlantic, MCA, EWMI, and Denon to urge a fair share for older artists whose catalog material was reissued.

In 1996, Rhino Home Video began to be distributed by WEA. The company continued to explore new technology, placing a Rocky Rhino site on the World Wide Web. New releases of a Curtis Mayfield retrospective, a National Lampoon Radio Hour box set, *Youth Gone Wild: Heavy Metal Hits of the '80s,* and John Wesley Harding's *New Deal* were accompanied by the 23rd through 25th volumes of the *Have a Nice Day: Super Hits of the '70s* series. Partnership with the Starbucks coffee chain resulted in the production of two special CDs for its caffeinated customers.

U.S. Secretary of Labor Robert Reich visited Rhino's Los Angeles headquarters in 1996 and praised its continuing democratic attitude toward employee involvement, bestowing Rhino with a corporate citizenship award. (Rhino then had about 140 employees.) Foos simultaneously sent an ironic letter to Bob Dole, who had recently criticized rap music, offering him a copy of Rhino's *White Men Can't Wrap,* a compilation of pop hits spoken by actors of the 1950s and 1960s.

The name "Rhino" was selected by Richard Foos when he opened that original record store on Westwood Boulevard in Los Angeles to signify the way in which he opened the doors and blindly charged ahead. In 1996, according to *Success,* only 10 percent of the records produced in the United States were profitable, while 90 percent of Rhino's products earned profits. This track record placed Rhino in the rare position of having no debt and no history of significant earnings loss over the years. With spirit, daring, and unique flair, Rhino has continued to charge ahead with a finely focused vision of how to succeed in the entertainment industry.

The Rhino Musical Aptitude Test (RMAT), a trivia quiz modeled after college entrance exams, was launched in 1997. The RMAT turned into a yearly event taken by thousands of participants. In August 1999, Rhino put on its first RetroFest, a three-day retro concert and memorabilia festival.

Warner Buys Rhino in 1998

Warner Music Group (WMG) acquired the remaining shares of Rhino Entertainment Company from Rhino Records Inc. in May 1998. The deal did not include Rhino's film or book operations or retail stores. Rhino Home Video, which then had a staff of just five people, was included. WMG had previously owned 50 percent of Rhino Entertainment through Atlantic Records. Rhino co-founders Richard Foos and Harold Bronson remained with the company as president and managing director, respectively. The deal brought responsibility for most of the back catalog of WMG's many record labels, including Warner Bros., Elektra, Atlantic, and their imprints and subsidiaries.

Rhino continued to reign as the king of kitsch. *'70s Party Killers* featured such cringe-worthy hits as "Afternoon Delight," "Feelings," and Sammy Davis, Jr.'s "Candy Man." One popular series of "lounge music" recalled 1960s cocktail parties. Other genres were chronicled, including "power pop." More serious fare was offered in collections relating to Shakespeare and gospel music. Rhino expanded to comedy albums in the late 1990s, releasing career-long retrospectives of comics such as Stan Freberg.

Rhino was also helping put together futuristic music compilations for *Wired* magazine. Other music and video co-branding partners included the Hard Rock Café, Comedy Central, Discovery Communications, Nickelodeon, Playboy Enterprises, and VH1. These deals aimed to extend Rhino beyond its typical young music enthusiast customer. Rhino Entertainment Ventures was formed in late 1997 to develop joint projects.

Brandweek remarked that the label had the strongest brand identity since Motown. Sales were more than $80 million in 1999, when the company had 160 employees. Its catalog was exceeding 2,500 titles in print. The most elaborate collections, such as the aptly-named *Brain in a Box* sci-fi music retrospective, retailed for about $100 thanks to its elaborate packaging. The Rhino Handmade imprint was launched in 1999 to provide limited edition titles to collectors.

Rhino Entertainment became a part of WMG's new Warner Strategic Marketing division in September 2001. Warner Strategic Marketing also included Warner Special Products and a commercial marketing unit and was headed by Sony Music veteran Scott Pascucci. Pascucci told the *Los Angeles Business Journal* it was getting harder to license songs from other labels, leading Rhino to focus on Warner's catalog.

Rhino's distinctive packaging continued to win industry recognition. (Some of its retrospective collections were released under the original recording labels.) According to *Medialine,* its designers were also tapped for other Warner Music Group projects, such as music DVDs.

Rhino co-founder Harold Bronson left the company in October 2001. CEO and fellow founder Richard Foos followed five months later. Foos soon formed a competing label, Shout! Factory (Retropolis, LLC). Rhino's offices moved to Burbank, California, in December 2002 to share a roof with other Warner marketing operations. An executive told *Billboard* Rhino was working on 250 titles that year, fifty more than in 2001.

Rhino Vinyl, an imprint dedicated to that most retro of formats, was launched in April 2003. A trio of Grateful Dead LPs were first to be released, followed by other classic rock albums of the early 1970s such as *The Yes Album* and T. Rex's *Electric Warrior.*

Rhino had been working with Turner Classic Movies for ten years to produce soundtrack compilations for old films. In the fall of 2004, the partnership began offering dozens of these online through the iTunes Music Store.

Rhino Home Video was also busy, releasing DVDs of the 1971 "Soul to Soul" concert in Ghana and the 70th anniversary celebration at Harlem's history Apollo Theater recorded in

2004. The complete first season of 1980's sitcom *Too Close for Comfort* was another offering.

Technology provided more new outlets. In June 2004, Rhino Records inked a deal to supply Electronic Arts with music for its EA SPORTS video games. At the same time, Rhino and Verizon Wireless announced the Rhino Retro Club service for downloading ringtones and wallpapers to mobile phones.

Principal Competitors

BMG Strategic Marketing; Retropolis, LLC; Sony Music Entertainment Inc.

Further Reading

Beirne, Mike, "Brand on the Run," *Brandweek*, October 30, 2000, p. 40.

Bessman, Jim, "Rhino Compilation Recalls Monterey Fest," *Billboard*, August 29, 1992, pp. 10–11.

——, "Rhino Rolls Out Major Atlantic Catalog Push," *Billboard*, July 18, 1992, pp. 8–9.

——, "Rhino, Discovery Link for Music Product," *Billboard*, June 6, 1998, p. 71.

——, "Tom Lehrer Boxes Up His 'Remains' for Warner/Rhino," *Billboard*, April 15, 2000, p. 15.

Borzillo, Carrie, "Labels Mate Music, Crafts, Cosmetics," *Billboard*, May 15, 1993, pp. 10–11.

"Boxed CD Sets Paint True-to-Life Portraits," *Packaging Digest*, May 2000, p. 64.

"Brainy Design Has Observers Reeling," *Packaging Digest*, December 1, 2000, p. 6.

"Consumer Friendly, the Rhino Chain Succeeds," *Billboard*, July 3, 1993, pp. 45–46.

Davies, Barbara, "Rhino Takes Its Name on Tour; Info Booth Rides 19-City Fests Schedule," *Billboard*, August 1, 1992, p. 40.

"Eighteen Excellent Reasons to Feature Rhino Entertainment," Los Angeles: Rhino Entertainment Company, 1996.

Eyman, Scott, "Retro Rules! Old Hits. Obscure Bits. Rhino Records Is the Label Where Retro Fits," *Palm Beach Post*, October 29, 2000, p. 1J.

Fixmer, Andy, "Rhino Facing Extinction under Warner," *Los Angeles Business Journal*, April 28, 2003, p. 3.

Friend, Tad, "Rhinophilia: Consumed," *New Republic*, August 17, 1992, p. 9.

"Great Moments in Rhino History," Los Angeles: Rhino Entertainment Company, 1996.

Gutman, Barry, "Rhino Takes Video to the Web," *Video Business*, October 8, 2001, p. 25.

——, "Rhino Entertainment: Really Big on Catalog," *Video Business*, February 25, 2002, pp. 38f.

Holland, Bill, "Rhino Enters Label Venture with Library of Congress," *Billboard*, November 5, 1994, pp. 14–15.

——, "Sony, Rhino Plan Royalty Reforms for Older Artists," *Billboard*, March 4, 1995, pp. 10–11.

Jaffee, Larry, "Rhino: 'Better Packages Because We Need To,'" *Medialine*, June 1, 2003, p. 18.

Jeckell, Barry A., "Rhino Gets Back to Vinyl Roots," *Toronto Star*, April 10, 2003, p. G13.

Kava, Brad, "Rhino Records Charges toward the Future by Repackaging Music's Past," *Pittsburgh Post-Gazette*, March 22, 1999, p. F6.

McCormick, Moira, "Rhino Favorite MFLP Re-Ups Deal," *Billboard*, August 4, 2001, p. 58.

Morris, Chris, "New Rhino Records Location Has Unique Personality," *Billboard*, February 16, 2002, p. 55.

——, "Warner Focuses Catalog Strategy," *Billboard*, March 30, 2002, p. 8.

Nathan, David, "Rhino Looks to Bring Home Higher Visibility to R&B Releases," *Billboard*, December 17, 1994, pp. 14–15.

Nelson, Chris, "A Label Works Unlikely Territory, Searching for Gold," *New York Times*, October 20, 2003, p. C8.

Olson, Catherine Applefeld, "Wired, Rhino Celebrate 'Futurists,'" *Billboard*, January 23, 1999, p. 77.

Paige, Earl, "Rhino, Esprit Team for Spoken Tapes," *Billboard*, April 24, 1993, p. 23.

Reece, Doug, "WMG Acquires Rhino Entertainment Co.," *Billboard*, May 30, 1998, p. 10.

"Rhino's New Business Safari," *Brandweek*, July 13, 1998, p. 22.

Rosen, Craig, "Avenue/Rhino Deal Good for War Reissues," *Billboard*, September 5, 1992, pp. 10–11.

——, "Rhino Spearheads Multiple-Act L.A. Summer Folk Fest," *Billboard*, May 22, 1993, pp. 12–13.

——, "Rhino Takes Excursion into Poptopia! Label to Issue 3-Disc Power Pop Retrospective," *Billboard*, April 19, 1997, p. 11.

Russell, Deborah, "Rhino Series Harks Back to the Punk Era," *Billboard*, January 23, 1993, pp. 1–2.

Sherber, Anne, "Creativity, Branding Deals Keep Rhino Home Video on Its Toes," *Billboard*, March 1, 1997, pp. 53ff.

Skierka, Tom, "Laughs Start Here; Rhino Shows It's Not About to Pronounce Comedy Albums Dead Yet," *Spokesman Review* (Spokane, Washington), December 23, 1999, p. D3.

Waddell, Ray, "Rhino Records Planning to Take Old Show on Road," *Milwaukee Journal Sentinel*, December 20, 2000, p. 3E.

Warshaw, Michael, "How the Rhino Brothers Trained Their Instincts and Turned $3 into $70 Million," *Success*, October 1996, pp. 28–30.

Wener, Ben, "The Brains Behind the Box; Ever Wonder How Rhino Records' Collections Come to Be—And Manage to Sell? So Did We," *Orange County Register*, November 24, 2000, p. 1.

Whipp, Glenn, "Leader of the Packs: Box-Set Innovator Rhino Records Is About to Release Its Most Ambitious Project Yet," *Orange County Register*, August 29, 2000, p. F4.

—Heidi Feldman
—update: Frederick C. Ingram

Robert Half International Inc.

Robert Half International Inc.

2884 Sand Hill Road
Menlo Park, California 94025
U.S.A.
Telephone: (415) 854-9700
Fax: (415) 954-9735
Web site: http://www.rhi.com

Public Company
Incorporated: 1948 as Robert Half Inc.
Employees: 182,300
Sales: $2 billion (2004)
Stock Exchanges: New York
Ticker Symbol: RHI
NAIC: 541612 Human Resources and Executive Search
Consulting Services; 561310 Employment Placement
Agencies

Robert Half International Inc. (RHI) is a leading provider of temporary, full-time, and contract employees, and is the oldest and largest specialist company placing accounting, finance, and information technology professionals. RHI operates seven divisions and one subsidiary. Accountemps places accountants and other financial professionals in temporary positions; Robert Half Finance & Accounting provides permanent, full-time personnel in the fields of accounting, banking, and finance; Robert Half Technology supplies contract information technology professionals; OfficeTeam specializes in high-end temporary administrative personnel; Robert Half Legal supplies attorneys, paralegals, and legal support personnel for temporary, project, and full-time positions; Robert Half Management Resources provides accounting, banking, and finance professionals on a project basis; and The Creative Group provides creative, advertising, marketing, and Web design professionals on a freelance basis. The subsidiary Protiviti specializes in independent internal audit and business and technology risk consulting. At the end of 2004, RHI had more than 330 offices in 43 states, the District of Columbia, Belgium, Canada, the Czech Republic, France, Germany, Ireland, Italy, Japan, the Netherlands, New Zealand, Singapore, and the United Kingdom. Revenues for 2004 totaled $2 billion.

Origins

Robert Half was a pioneer in the employment services industry, founding Robert Half Inc. in 1948 as an employment agency for accountants. He eventually created Accountemps to supply accountants and other financial professionals to firms needing those skills on a temporary basis, while continuing to place permanent employees through his Robert Half offices. Following the success of his business in California, Half began franchising the concept around the country. The temporary personnel industry grew slowly during the 1960s and 1970s, then began to expand rapidly during the 1980s. By 1985, there were 150 independent Robert Half and Accountemps franchises.

The second half of the decade saw major changes in the company. In 1985 Harold M. "Max" Messmer, Jr., assumed the presidency of Robert Half Inc. In July 1986, Boothe Financial Corporation acquired all the outstanding stock of the company and Messmer almost immediately began a program to buy all the franchises in the Robert Half system. In 1987, after being divested by Boothe, Robert Half International Inc. went public, and Messmer became chief executive officer as well as president. The following year, he became chairman of the board.

During 1989, the company began opening new offices, and Gibbons, Breen, Van Amerongen, L.P., a merchant banking concern, bought 3.1 million shares of the company's stock, approximately 27 percent of the outstanding common shares. As the decade ended, RHI had revenues of $234.5 million, a 29 percent increase from 1988.

The temporary staffing industry experienced double-digit expansion during the 1980s, and many people believed temporary employment firms would survive any national recession. As a result of rapid consolidation, the number of larger, national firms increased, and competition for contracts was intense. This led to a price war which began in the general clerical segment of the industry but soon spread to the specialized areas such as accounting.

Recession and Recovery in the Early 1990s

In 1990, RHI's concentration on accounting and financial temporary placements helped avoid much of the price war, and the company could afford to acquire Wayne S. Mello & Associates, a financial recruiting firm in Florida. Robert Half, the permanent placement operations, reached a peak in its revenues of $450 million. However the employment recession which began that year did have an effect on the company, with revenues growing by only 9 percent, a big drop from 1989.

In a normal year, Robert Half's permanent placement activity accounted for 15 to 20 percent of the company's total revenues. This meant that RHI was more dependent on permanent placements than most temporary staffing firms, and as the demand for permanent employees fell as a result of corporate downsizing and restructuring, RHI's business began to weaken.

Management's reaction to the situation was a "go slow" strategy. They reduced overhead, cut and focused the advertising budget, and improved cash management. The poor economy also made it easier for the company to acquire Robert Half and Accountemps franchises, which were suffering, and to buy a Seattle-based temporary employment firm, which placed accounting and data-processing employees.

Management also decided the time was right to test a move away from their traditional financial placements. Late in 1991 they started a new division, OfficeTeam, placing temporary high-end, office administrative personnel. This start-up business was in response to requests from longtime clients for help when they needed temporary employees with administrative, word processing, and office management skills. To keep overhead low, RHI placed an OfficeTeam salesperson in a few Accountemps offices. That year the new division brought in $2 million in revenues. That was a bright spot in a year in which revenues dropped by 16 percent and earnings per share by more than 50 percent.

In 1992, its second year, OfficeTeam revenues increased to $12 million, and accounted for nearly 5 percent of the company's total bookings. The permanent placement business, however, brought in only $22 million, less than half the amount it generated in 1990. The company responded by merging most Robert Half offices with Accountemps facilities or combining satellite offices into a single hub office to serve an area.

Company revenues began to turn up towards the end of 1992 as employers felt confident enough to add temporary employees to their workforces. Having expanded into administrative placements through OfficeTeam, the company decided to explore making placements in the legal field, and acquired The Affili-

ates, a firm in Southern California that placed temporary and permanent paralegal, legal administrative, and other legal support personnel.

During 1993, RHI expanded to the East Coast with the purchase of Key Financial, a Washington, D.C., firm that placed accountants, and opened offices in France, Belgium, and the United Kingdom. The company also completed placing an OfficeTeam salesperson in each of its 135 domestic offices. The temporary administrative placement service had turned into a very successful undertaking as it brought in nearly $41 million that year, more than 13 percent of total revenue. RHI found it had little competition in this area from the national giants such as Kelly or Manpower since most OfficeTeam placements were with longstanding clients who needed only a few workers at a time. Company revenues for the year reached $306.2 million.

Total employment in the United States began to grow in the last half of 1993 and RHI's permanent placement business finally started to improve as a result. As the economy strengthened and corporate downsizing and restructuring slowed, the temporary staffing industry found itself thriving. Employers wanted the flexibility to respond quickly to changing market conditions and to avoid overstaffing. Where traditionally employers hired temporary workers primarily to fill in during busy periods, now there was a growing demand for professionals with skills not usually associated with temporary work—home health care, prison management, scientists, and technicians.

New Directions in the Mid-1990s

RHI responded to the demand for additional specialized placements by creating RHI Consulting, a new division providing systems analysts, computer engineers, and other information technology specialists to clients on a contract basis. Specialized staffing in the IT area became very popular among temporary employee firms during the mid-90s. Not only was the demand there, but the assignments were for longer durations than many other types of placements and, perhaps most importantly, the margins were higher.

As RHI was branching into other areas, it continued to pull together its core business. By March 1994, the company had acquired all but four of the original 150 Robert Half and Accountemps franchises. According to a Kidder Peabody analyst's report that month, "Management believed that centralized ownership would help reduce costs, aid the funding and implementation of advanced data processing systems, and bring more sophisticated marketing, accounting and legal practices to former stand-alone operations." The company completed its franchise buyback in 2003.

The temporary help industry continued its explosive growth. According to the National Association of Temporary Staffing Services (NATSS), in 1995, 2.16 million people worked as temporary employees each day, up from 185,000 in 1970. They represented 1.78 percent of total employment, holding one out of every 56 jobs, compared to one out of every 100 jobs in 1990 and one out of every 384 jobs in 1970.

Furthermore, NATSS estimated that nearly a quarter (24.2 percent) of the total temporary personnel payroll was made up of specialized professionals, including accountants and infor-

Key Dates:

1948: Accountemps and Robert Half Finance & Accounting are established.
1985: More than 150 Robert Half and Accountemps franchises are operating independently in the United States.
1987: Company goes public.
1989: Company begins opening new offices in response to temporary-staffing industry boom.
1990: Recession hits, slashing RHI's growth.
1991: Robert Half and Accountemps offices merge to cut costs; company acquires The Affiliates, renaming it Robert Half Legal.
1993: Company expands operations to Europe.
1999: Continuing strong economy taxes RHI's ability to place job candidates; stock price drops by half; company is revamped to meet changing market conditions.
2001: Stock value jumps to three times its 1999 low.
2002: Protiviti is founded.
2003: Company completes its franchise buyback program.

mation technology specialists. The industry itself generated $39.2 billion in 1995, almost twice as much as it had five years before, when receipts were $20.5 billion.

For RHI, 1995 was an outstanding year. Revenues increased by 41 percent to $628.5 million, all through internal growth. OfficeTeam had revenues of $147 million, and the two-year old RHI Consulting brought in $39 million through its 38 locations. The company was ranked 18th among all NYSE companies based on total return to investors for the 1993 to 1995 period.

The industry credited its growth to several factors, benefiting both employers and employees. The primary advantage to both parties was greater flexibility. Employers were able to manage their workflow and workforce more effectively by using temporary help to complete special projects, fill short-term vacancies, and avoid overstaffing. For the employees themselves, taking temporary assignments afforded, according to Edward Lenz, "flexibility, independence, supplemental income, skills training, "safety-net' protection while between permanent jobs, and the opportunity to find permanent work." RHI also offered its temporary employees a competitive benefit package.

In addition to its employment activities, RHI was a recognized research authority. Its annual national and regional salary guides were used by the U.S. Department of Labor in the preparation of the Occupational Outlook Handbook, and the company's accounting and information technology Hiring Indexes provided important hiring projections. A variety of surveys kept executives, managers, and temporary employees informed about issues as diverse as why companies hire temporary help to the length of the average executive's workday.

Both Max Messmer and the company's founder, Robert Half, published books and articles on hiring and job search practices. Half's books included *The Right Way to Get Hired in Today's Job Market, Making It Big in Data Processing, How to*

Get a Better Job in This Crazy World, and *Finding, Hiring and Keeping the Best Employees*. In 1995, Messmer wrote Job Hunting for Dummies, part of the . . . *For Dummies* series published by IDG Books. He also wrote *50 Ways to Get Hired and Staffing Europe*.

The company's reputation also was enhanced by endorsements from leading professional associations, including the American Payroll Association, the National Association of Credit Management, the American Institute of Professional Bookkeepers, and Professional Secretaries International. It also had worldwide marketing alliances with major accounting and word processing software publishers and major CPA review course companies.

Business continued to be good for the company through 1996. It had a two-for-one stock split and reported record revenues of nearly $900 million and income of over $61 million.

The temporary staffing industry was a growing segment of the economy. But with some 7,000 firms supplying their clients with temporary help, big national or international companies had the edge. As CEO Messmer explained in a 1996 *Barron's* article, "Smaller outfits don't have the clout to attract professionals—accountants, medical workers, technicians, programmers—who can deliver the highest margins for the temp company, because the smaller firms don't offer jobs across the country."

In just over ten years, Robert Half International had grown from a small franchiser to a leading international company in this market. It had created successful specialized niches that connected with its longtime core business of accounting and financial placements, and had paid for its expansion through internal growth. The demand for accountants and auditors remained high; the Bureau of Labor Statistics projected a 32 percent increase in those jobs over the next decade. The number of computer and information technology jobs was expected to double over the same period, many of which could be expected to be filled by contract staffers. All of these factors made the future look good for RHI.

A Downturn and a Comeback in the 2000s

In 1999, however, a continued strong economy and record low unemployment rates slowed the company's growth after nearly a decade of steadily rising revenues. Robert Half's placement services had difficulty finding people to fill their clients' open jobs. Although revenues increased by 16 percent and profits rose 7 percent, the value of the company's stock dropped by a full 50 percent. Standard & Poor's 500 companies averaged 15 percent growth during the 1990s, but Robert Half averaged about 38 percent growth, more than twice the rate of the S & P 500, and wary investors reacted swiftly to the company's sharp slowdown. "We were too slow to see it coming," CEO Max Messmer told Victoria Murphy of *Forbes,* adding "It was embarrassing to tell (clients) we had no one to fill their empty spots."

Messmer made up for lost time by switching his company's focus away from getting new clients to finding job candidates to meet clients' needs. The ratio of spending in its placement divisions had traditionally been $40 million for marketing to

$20 million for recruiting. Messmer reversed the proportions, hired 400 new recruiters, and began paying cash incentives of up to 33 percent of recruiter bonuses based on number of hires made. He also made significant changes in the company's approach to doing business, placing job postings on the Internet career site Monster.com and investing $44 million to improve communication networks between branch offices and give all employees computers and Internet access. To improve employee retention in the tight job market, Robert Half offered stock options with a short vesting period and established Web sites where temps could check payroll and look for work. By 2001, investors appeased by the success of the new direction tripled RHI's stock value from its 1999 low.

Messmer also began to diversify and reorganize along new lines to meet the demands of a rapidly-changing marketplace. As of 1992, Accountemps and Robert Half Finance & Accounting drew 90 percent of the company's revenues. In the late 1990s Robert Half Technology expanded the company's services to provide information technology professionals, and Robert Half Legal extended the business to provide temporary, project, and full-time attorneys, paralegals, and legal support personnel. The Creative Group was formed to supply creative, advertising, marketing, and Web design professionals on a freelance basis. Following the Enron and WorldCom accounting scandals of 2001 and 2002, the company hired 760 former members of the consulting and risk-management practice of the accounting firm Arthur Andersen, which was devastated by convictions for obstruction of justice in the Enron case and stripped of its U.S. accounting license. With these new employees Robert Half founded the subsidiary Protiviti, an independent internal audit and risk management consulting practice. The new venture broke even in 2003, earning $133 million, 7 percent of Robert Half's revenues during the year. This accomplishment placed Protiviti just behind the Big Four accounting firms Ernst & Young, Deloitte & Touche, KPMG, and PricewaterhouseCoopers. By the end of 2002 a full 50 percent of the company's $1.9 billion revenues derived from new divisions and Protiviti, which had not existed a decade before.

Legislation resulting from the Enron and WorldCom scandals provided another new avenue of business for the company. The Sarbanes-Oxley Act, signed into law July 30, 2002, ordered fundamental changes in accounting practices for all publicly-traded corporations doing business in the United States in order to prevent the sorts of abuses that brought about the downfall of a number of large corporations around the turn of the 21st century. Compliance with the act required the intensive work of highly-skilled professionals in a number of disciplines, many of whom had to be independent of the corporations for which they did Sarbanes-Oxley-mandated work. By the end of the third quarter of 2004, Sarbanes-Oxley compliance work accounted for 15 to 20 percent of Robert Half's consolidated revenues for the year. Although the dead-

line for compliance fell on December 31, 2004, the company expected that the tighter controls and testing regimens mandated by the act would result in a continued need for more accounting professionals. In addition, the New York Stock Exchange began requiring all companies trading on its board to have an internal audit function. Some companies traded on the NASDAQ voluntarily instituted internal audits, as well, all of which was expected to provide Robert Half with a steady growth in client base and revenues into the future.

Principal Subsidiaries

Protiviti.

Principal Divisions

Accountemps; The Creative Group; OfficeTeam; Robert Half Finance & Accounting; Robert Half Legal; Robert Half Management Resources; Robert Half Technology.

Further Reading

Brandstrader, J.R., "It's an Ill Wind," *Barron's,* March 25, 1996, p. 18.
Byrnes, Nanette, et al., "The Good CEO," *Businessweek,* September 23, 2002.
Caldwell, Douglas E., "The New Economy's Gold Digger," *Silicon Valley/San Jose Business Journal,* March 16, 2001, p. 38.
Desloge, Rick, "Robert Half, Kelly Services Share in Temp Firm Growth," *St. Louis Business Journal,* December 1, 1997, p. 24.
Fleming, Eric C., "Job-Recruiter Blues: Will Paltry Demand Drain Robert Half Shares?," *Barron's,* November 11, 2002, p. T8.
Jordon, Steve, "New Risk-Consulting Firm Lures Ex-Andersen Employees," *Omaha World Herald,* June 6, 2002.
Lenz, Edward. "Flexible Employment: Positive Work Strategies for the 21st Century," *Journal of Labor Research,* 1996.
Marsh, Ann, "We're Your Talent Agent," *Forbes,* August 10, 1998, p. 104.
"Morningstar Names Max Messmer of Robert Half International as 2003 CEO of the Year," *Morningstar,* January 6, 2004.
Murphy, Victoria, "Robert Half International: Everyone Need Apply," *Forbes,* January 8, 2001, p. 106.
Robson, Douglas, "Half's Measures: Robert Half Harnesses Outsourcing Trend to Prove that Even Big Businesses Can Grow Quickly," *San Francisco Business Times,* April 18, 1997, p. 5A.
Siwolop, Sana, "Renting the Workers, But Buying the Stock," *New York Times,* December 15, 1996.
"Staffing Firm Founder Robert Half Dead at 82," *Accounting Today,* September 24 2001, p. 56.
Svaldi, Aldo, "California-Based Staffing-Services Firm Hires 760 Andersen Accountants," *Denver Post,* June 6, 2002.
"Temporary Help Services Continue Growth; Several Factors Cited," Alexandria, Va.: National Association of Temporary Staffing Services, June 17, 1996.

—Ellen D. Wernick
—update: Jennifer Gariepy

Sanders Morris Harris Group Inc.

600 Travis, Suite 3100
Houston, Texas 77002
U.S.A.
Telephone: (713) 224-3100
Toll Free: (800) 900-4611
Fax: (713) 993-4677
Web site: http://www.smhg.com

Public Company
Incorporated: 1999 as Pinnacle Global Group Inc.
Employees: 317
Sales: $103.90 million (2003)
Stock Exchanges: NASDAQ
Ticker Symbol: SMHG
NAIC: 523120 Securities Brokerage

Sanders Morris Harris Group Inc. is a financial services firm that ranks as the largest investment bank in the southwestern United States. Through its subsidiaries, the company offers a broad range of services, including investment banking, asset management, securities brokerage, investment advisory services, and fiduciary services. Sander Morris Harris manages more than $6 billion in client assets. The company maintains offices in Houston, Dallas, Denver, Fort Worth, Los Angeles, and New York.

Origins

The process by which Sanders Morris Harris Group arrived at its name involved numerous mergers and acquisitions. It also charted the evolution of a small, Texas-based, private equity placement firm into the largest investment bank in the Southwest. The series of mergers and acquisitions that led to the creation of Sanders Morris Harris Group at the turn of the 21st century brought together more than a half-dozen financial services executives, their surnames constituting the corporate titles of their businesses. For example, when Sanders Morris Mundy merged with Harris Webb & Garrison, the transaction joined together Don Sanders, Ben Morris, John Mundy, Robert Garrison, Titus Harris Jr., and Richard Webb. The one name missing from this group, however, was the most distinguished of the lot, Sanders Morris Harris Group's chairman, George L. Ball.

Ball was regarded as a wunderkind during the 1970s, earning a sterling reputation that had not faded by the turn of the 21st century. A New Jersey native, Ball earned an economics degree at prestigious Brown University in 1960 and then spent the next two years serving in the U.S. Navy. After leaving the military, Ball joined E.F. Hutton, one of the largest financial services companies in the country. Ball worked as stockbroker at E.F. Hutton, joining the retail side of the company's business. He quickly made a name for himself, besting his contemporaries by a wide margin, and quickly rose through the firm's executive ranks. Ball was 39 years old when he was named president of E.F. Hutton, gaining promotion to the number two position at the firm at a remarkably young age.

When Ball was promoted to president in 1977, he began working alongside E.F. Hutton's chairman, Robert Fomon. Fomon concentrated on corporate strategy and investment banking, while Ball took charge of the firm's retail brokerage business. Ball excelled in his responsibilities. "Ball was like a big brother to us," an E.F. Hutton broker said in a February 29, 1988 interview with *Fortune* magazine. He was "a leader, a Napoleon," the broker added. "He kept us together, created an esprit de corps." Ball assembled an exceptionally skillful team of salespeople, leading a brokerage force that generated more commission per account than any competing firm. By 1980, E.F. Hutton's brokerage business was generating $1.1 billion in revenues, more than any firm in the country save Merrill Lynch.

E.F. Hutton was immensely successful under Ball's leadership. The company's collapse after his departure only added to the luster of his reputation. In mid-1982, in what the June 6, 1983 issue of *Forbes* magazine termed a "celebrated defection," Ball left E.F. Hutton to serve as president and chief executive officer of Prudential-Bache Securities, Inc. Not long after Ball left, E.F. Hutton deteriorated, rocked by a scandal that led to the company's guilty plea in 1985 to 2,000 felony charges involving a massive check-overdraft scheme. The company collapsed, primarily because of its conviction for fraud, but many in Wall Street were quick to point out that E.F. Hutton was never the same after Ball left the firm.

Company Perspectives:

Sanders Morris Harris Group's focused vision is to maintain a solid regional presence and offer an extensive menu of services to meet the diverse needs of high net worth individuals. The Company will continue to seek new ways to achieve even higher service levels, enhanced by our time-proven expertise, impressive performance, experienced team of professionals, an award-winning research team and respected corporate stability.

Ball's career progressed at Prudential-Bache. In 1986, he was elected to the position of chairman, holding the three top posts (chairman, chief executive office, and president) until his resignation in 1991. Next, Ball spent a year working as a consultant before joining Smith Barney Shearson Inc. in 1992 as the firm's senior executive vice-president. Meanwhile, the company that would later count him as its chairman, Sanders Morris Harris Group, was beginning to take shape as the numerous corporate entities that constituted its operations began to join together.

The earliest predecessor Sanders Morris Harris Group was formed in 1987. That year, three financial services executives started their own firm, Sanders Morris Mundy Inc. The principal figures involved were Don Sanders, Ben Morris, and John Mundy, two of whom, Sanders and Morris, served in executive capacities at Sanders Morris Harris Group at the turn of the 21st century. Morris, a certified public accountant, started his career at what later became PricewaterhouseCoopers, LLP, and served in several executive capacities at Mid American Oil and Gas, Inc., eventually becoming the company's president. Sanders was a familiar face to George Ball, joining E.F. Hutton while Ball was enrolled at Brown University. Sanders spent 28 years at E.F. Hutton, where he ranked as one of the firm's leading brokers, resigning in 1987 to co-found Sanders Morris Mundy.

Sanders Morris Mundy represented of the principal firms that later formed Sanders Morris Harris Group. The firm provided corporate equity financing and money management services to a wealthy clientele. Sanders Morris Mundy participated as co-underwriter on numerous initial public offerings (IPOs), helping several Texas-based companies such as Houston's USA Waste Services Inc. and Leviathan Gas Partners convert to public ownership. In 1996, in a deal that played a significant part in the creation of Sanders Morris Harris Group, the firm acquired Williams MacKay Jordan & Co. A Houston-based firm, Williams MacKay specialized in providing institutional brokerage services and public company research, exhibiting a particular expertise with companies based in the Southwest and with companies involved in the energy sector. According to several analysts, it was Sanders Morris Mundy's acquisition of Williams MacKay, specifically its institutional business, that made the company an attractive candidate for inclusion within Sanders Morris Harris Group.

While Sander Morris Mundy broadened its business scope, another Houston-based firm was expanding as well. The firm of Harris Webb & Garrison represented another principal firm that

eventually created Sanders Morris Harris Group. The retail brokerage and investment bank was started in 1994 by Titus Harris, Jr., Richard "Rit" Webb, and Robert Garrison II. Harris and Garrison played leading roles in the formation and management of Sanders Morris Harris Group. Harris, who worked at E.F. Hutton during Ball's tenure, served as senior vice-president of Lovett Underwood Neuhaus & Webb, a division of Kemper Securities Group, Inc., between 1983 and 1991. Garrison also worked for a division of Kemper Securities, serving as managing partner of Lovett Mitchell Webb & Garrison. The same year he co-founder Harris Webb & Garrison, he also helped start Pinnacle Management & Trust Co., the third principal company behind the formation of Sanders Morris Harris Group.

1999 Merger Creates Pinnacle Global Group

It was from Garrison's side of the corporate family that Sanders Morris Harris Group's formation began. In 1999, Garrison's firm and Pinnacle Management & Trust merged with three companies, PGG Capital, Spires Financial, and TEI Inc. TEI was a publicly held environmental services company that sold its assets before the merger. Pinnacle Global Group was formed as a holding company to house the merged entities, becoming a publicly held concern itself by virtue of absorbing TEI. Pinnacle Global Group represented the most direct descendant of Sanders Morris Harris Group. In October 1999, Pinnacle Global Group announced its agreement to acquire Sanders Morris Mundy, which by this point was led by George Ball. After a dozen years in business, Sanders Morris Mundy had developed an institutional sales and research team that covered more than 150 companies in the Southwest, for which Pinnacle Global Group was willing to pay $40 million to acquire. Pinnacle Global Group, reportedly, was particularly attracted to the assets Sanders Morris Mundy acquired in its 1996 purchase of Williams McKay Jordan & Co.

At the time the acquisition was announced, Pinnacle Global Group stood as a $136.4 million-in-assets financial services holding company. Garrison and his fellow senior executives decided to merge Sanders Morris Mundy into Harris Webb & Garrison. When the transaction was completed, the merger, which led to Ball's appointment as chairman of Pinnacle Global Group, created Sanders Morris Harris, a Pinnacle Global Group subsidiary and the largest Texas-owned and Texas-based investment bank. To this profile were added two more acquisitions completed before the end of 2000, the purchase by Sanders Morris Harris of Blackford Securities, a Garden City, New York-based prime brokerage company, and the joint Pinnacle Global Group and Sanders Morris Harris acquisition of Cummer/Moyers, a fixed income manager based in Fort Worth, Texas.

A new identity for Pinnacle Global Group became the notable event of 2001, an event that brought the company back to the roots of its earliest predecessor. Sanders Morris Harris, an investment bank with more than $2 billion in assets in its private client group, was the most well known of all the businesses operating under the Pinnacle Global Group umbrella. Ball hoped to end confusion by adopting Sanders Morris Harris as the new name for the entire organization, explaining his reasoning in a June 1, 2001 interview with the *Houston Chronicle*. "There are eight corporations that publicly trade as Pinnacle-something," he said. "Pinnacle Global got confused with a few

pany entered the mid-2000s suggested its senior executives had yet to satisfy their ambitions.

Sanders Morris Harris Group completed two important acquisitions in 2003 and 2004 that provided momentum for the company's future expansion. In 2003, the company merged its Pinnacle Management & Trust Co. subsidiary into Salient Partners LP, a manager of $670 million in assets held by high-networth investors. Sanders Morris Harris Group retained a 50 percent stake in the merged entity, bringing assets under its management to $5.2 billion. In 2004, the company acquired Crest Advisors, an investment advisory firm based in New York City. Founded in 1996, Crest Advisors focused on the telecommunications, media, and technology sectors. Its acquisition by Sanders Morris Harris Group represented an integral component of the company's strategy to sell financial services and products to middle-market companies, that is, those with annual revenues ranging between $25 million and $500 million, a section of the market that Ball and his team hoped to exploit as the decade progressed.

troubled Pinnacles, one of which is in Chapter 11, and some others are dot-coms not doing so well right now.'' Accordingly, Pinnacle Global Group changed its name to Sanders Morris Harris Group Inc., changed its ticker symbol from PING to SMHG, and rebranded its subsidiaries. Blackford Asset Management became SMH Asset Management; PPG Capital became SMH Capital; and Cummer/Moyers became SMH Capital Advisors.

Sanders Morris Harris Expands in the Early 2000s

In the wake of Pinnacle Global Group recasting itself as Sanders Morris Harris Group, the company broadened the scope of its activities, expanding largely through acquisitions. In April 2001, Sanders Morris Harris announced its acquisition of Kissinger Financial Services Inc., a financial planning firm based in Maryland. Kissinger, with $300 million in assets under management and $2.4 million in annual revenues, retained its name after the acquisition, becoming a wholly owned subsidiary of Sanders Morris Harris Group. In 2002, the company waged a bidding war with five West Coast-based banks and one New York-based bank for the 23-person institutional equity group of Sutro & Co. Sanders Morris Harris Group emerged as the winner, gaining a Los Angeles-based sales team that expanded the company's research coverage, moving it into new sectors such as entertainment, media, satellites, and wireless.

As Sanders Morris Harris Group entered the mid-2000s, the company was cementing its reputation as an insightful research organization that adhered to a pragmatic, conservative investment strategy. ''We have not been marching around with a high school band behind us,'' the company's research director remarked in a May 2002 interview with *Buyside*. Nevertheless, the company, albeit quietly, had grown into a formidable, respected force in the Southwest's financial community. With Ball serving as chairman, Sanders serving as vice-chairman, and Morris and Garrison holding the titles of chief executive officer and president, respectively, the company pressed ahead with its growth plans. The acquisitions completed as the com-

Principal Subsidiaries

SMH Private Equity Funds; Salient Partners & Pinnacle Trust Co.; SMH Captial Advisors, Inc.; SMH Asset Management.

Principal Competitors

Morgan Keegan & Co., Inc.; Stephens Inc.; SWS Group, Inc.

Further Reading

Apte, Angela, ''Let's Make a Deal,'' *Houston Business Journal*, February 11, 2000, p. 2B.
Buggs, Shannon, ''Houston Financial Services Holding Company Changes Name, Retires Ticker,'' *Houston Chronicle*, June 1, 2004, p. 7.
——, ''Sanders Morris Harris Group Bolsters Investment Bank Arm,'' *Houston Chronicle*, April 23, 2004, p. 54.
Carlsen, Clifford, ''A Small Texas Biotech Fund with Grand Designs,'' *Daily Deal*, October 1, 2001, p. 32.
Chensvold, Christian M., ''Sense & Sensibility: Sanders Morris Harris Group Blends the Styles of Value and Pragmatism with Growth and Momentum,'' *Buyside*, May 2002, p. 69.
Fowler, Tom, ''Venture Capital Fund Created to Help Smaller Biotech,'' *Houston Chronicle*, September 28, 2001, p. 4.
Gordon, Sarah, ''Texas Boutique Acquires Sutro Equity Group,'' *Wall Street Letter*, January 7, 200, p. 1.
Greer, Jim, ''Pinnacle Drops Name in Favor of Subsidiary's Recognized Moniker,'' *Houston Business Journal*, May 25, 2001, p. 8A.
''Investment Group Credits Management, Banking Arms,'' *Houston Chronicle*, November 5, 2004, p. 9.
Rulison, Larry, ''Timonium Financial Firm Sells to Texas Gaint,'' *Baltimore Business Journal*, April 13, 2001, p. 17.
Serva, Sandy, ''Rooted in Research,'' *Buyside*, May 2003, p. 57.
''Texas Investment Banks to Merge,'' *American Banker*, October 14, 1999, p. 7.

—Jeffrey L. Covell

Sean John Clothing, Inc.

525 7th Avenue, Suite 1009
New York, New York 10018
U.S.A.
Telephone: (212) 869-6422
Fax: (212) 869-4133
Web site: http://www.seanjohn.com

Wholly Owned Subsidiary of Bad Boy Worldwide
  Entertainment Group
Incorporated: 1998
Employees: 75
Sales: $450 million (2004)
NAIC: 424320 Men's and Boys' Clothing and
  Furnishings Merchant Wholesalers; 424330 Women's,
  Children's, and Infants' Clothing and Accessories
  Merchant Wholesalers; 448110 Men's Clothing
  Stores; 448120 Women's Clothing Stores

Owned by Sean "P. Diddy" Combs's Bad Boy Entertainment Group, Sean John Clothing, Inc. is a designer and marketer of men's, boy's, and women's apparel. Sean Jean Clothing caters to customers aged between 12 and 45, selling its apparel through retailers such as Bloomingdale's, Macy's, Belk's, Carson Pirie Scott, Bernini, and Fred Segal. The company also operates its own store in New York City, the first of what is expected to be a chain of company-owned retail outlets.

Origins

Sean John Combs's eponymous apparel company represented one facet of a business empire that ranked the hip-hop mogul as the wealthiest entertainer under 40 in the United States. Combs's rise in the business world was exceptionally quick and boundless in scope, beginning with an internship that, a decade later, evolved into annual salary of more than $300 million. Sean John Clothing represented a sizeable portion of that fortune. The company was an expression of the personality and vision of its founder, and, as such, the history of Sean John Clothing was one part of the story of Sean John Combs's remarkable rise in the business world.

Combs was born in Harlem in 1969, the son of Melvin and Janice Combs. Melvin Combs was killed when Sean was two years old, the victim of a homicide, which prompted Janice Combs to take Sean and his sister Keisha to a safer environment. Janice Combs moved the family to Mt. Vernon, New York, where she worked three jobs to support her two children. Sean Combs attended Mount Vernon Montessori School and Mount Saint Michael Academy, where he earned a nickname that millions of music fans would come to know a decade later. When he was playing football, Combs had a tendency to expand his chest in an effort to intimidate others, a habit that led his teammates to call him "Puffy."

After leaving Mount Saint Michael, Combs enrolled at Howard University in Washington, D.C. He began pursuing a business degree, but an internship at Uptown Records in New York City diverted his attention away from his studies, prompting him to leave Howard University after two years. Combs now focused entirely on making a name for himself at Uptown Records, and in the process he quickly becoming a driving force in the city's hip-hop scene. One year, after starting as an intern at the company, Combs served as Uptown Records' director of A&R (Artists and Repertoire), a position that made him responsible for scouting, signing, and promoting music talent. At 21 years old, he was charged with ensuring that the debut albums of artists Jodeci and Mary J. Blige were hits. Combs succeeded, lending his vision of urban youth to help create a new niche within the hip-hop genre, making Jodeci and Mary J. Blige the new stars of hip-hop soul.

Combs left Uptown Records in 1993, ready to start his own business in the music industry. He signed an exclusive agreement with Clive Davis of Arista Records to distribute the recordings of artists signed to his newly formed record label, Bad Boy Entertainment, a business that began in Combs's home. Starting out, Combs had two artists, Craig Mack and his friend and frequent collaborator Christopher Wallace. Craig Mack's album was the first recording released by Bad Boy Entertainment and sold more than one million copies. However, the breakthrough moment for Combs's record label arrived with the introduction of Wallace's monikers to the record-buying public. *Ready to Die* marked the debut release by "Notorious

B.I.G.,'' one of the names (''Biggie Smalls'' was the other) used by Wallace. This release sold well over one million copies, earning the ''multi-platinum'' distinction used by the recording industry.

The success of *Ready to Die* confirmed Combs's reputation as a skillful producer, arranger, and manager in the recording industry. Soon after, he was inundated with requests from other artists to lend his touch to their work. Mariah Carey turned to Combs for production help, as did TLC, Lil Kim, and Usher, fanning the legitimacy and expansion of Bad Boy Entertainment. Combs's growing reputation and power gave his company the leverage to negotiate a 1996 joint venture with Arista Records that resulted in a rarely heard of 50–50 split between the two labels. Continuing to rise in professional stature, Combs signed, developed, and produced albums for a string of artists such as Faith Evans, the female trio Total, and the male vocal group 112, all of which earned the platinum designation. Combs then began a recording career himself, releasing his first single, *Cant Nobody Hold Me Down,* in January 1997 under the name ''Puff Daddy.'' His next venture involved forming an apparel company that operated under the corporate umbrella of Bad Boy Entertainment Group, the corporate entity that governed all of Combs's business ventures.

Combs's ambition found a new release with the creation of Sean John Clothing in 1998. A significant component of his electric rise in the music industry involved nuances of style and image making, and this naturally led to Combs's interest in fashion. Combs formed Sean John Clothing to bring his vision of urban streetwear to the mainstream men's clothing market, hiring an executive from Ralph Lauren, Jeffrey Tweedy, to help him create what *Newsweek*, in its February 12, 2001 issue, referred to as a ''hip-hop-meets-Liberace'' apparel label. ''Understand,'' Combs wrote on the Sean Jean Web site, ''that we are not in the clothing business for a quick hit, but we are truly committed to the expansion and growth of the men's marketplace and will use all of our resources to ensure quality in both design and production of Sean Jean always exceeds your expectations. I didn't want to over use my celebrity,'' he added. ''I just call it Sean Jean, which is my fashion alter ego and real name.''

Debut in 1999

The Sean John men's sportswear line debuted in the spring of 1999. The company's first shipment of apparel was sold in department and specialty stores across the nation, appearing in retail shops controlled by Bloomingdale's, Macy's, Belk's, Carson Pirie Scott, Bernini, and Fred Segal. The line was an enormous, immediate success, attracting a wealth of customers and earning admiration from the fashion world. In 2000, Combs was nominated for a Council of Fashion Designers of America Award as menswear designer of the year. The nomination, which was uncommon for a designer after only a year in busi-

ness, represented the equivalent of an Academy Award nomination, putting Combs within the exclusive circle of elite designers such as Anna Sui, Todd Oldham, and Marc Jacobs. Combs failed to win the coveted award, losing to Marc Jacobs, but the nomination by itself confirmed Sean John Clothing as an apparel label of merit.

Combs earned another nomination for a Council of Fashion Designers of America Award in 2001, a year that included several momentous events for both the man and the company. Combs spent much of early 2001 sitting a court room, standing trial for charges of gun possession and bribery. The charges, stemming from an incident at Club New York in December 1999, led to a six-week trial that found Combs not guilty of all five counts brought against him. (Shortly thereafter, Combs held a press conference announcing he was changing his nickname from ''Puff Daddy'' to ''P. Diddy''). The trial did nothing to tarnish Combs's image among the high-fashion elite or among the legions of customers who flocked to stores to buy his clothing. Sales shot past $100 million, quickly becoming the financial driving force within Bad Boy Entertainment Group. Kal Ruttenstein, the influential fashion director at Bloomingdale's, expressed nothing but praise for Sean John's line. ''It's not just kids who are buying it,'' Ruttenstein explained in a February 12, 2001 interview with *Newsweek*. ''It's their dads in the suburbs who don't know Puffy that are buying because of the quality too. I wear Sean John like crazy, and I'm no spring chicken.''

Sean John Clothing succeeded by winning over two distinct realms of the apparel industry. The company's runway shows were extravagant affairs attended by celebrities and the arbiters of what was high-fashion and what was not. Combs's skills as a producer, promoter, and showman gave his company a decided edge in this area. In 2001, for instance, Sean John Clothing made fashion history when it became the first designer to have its runway show broadcast live on television, a two-hour event simulcast by the E! Style networks. On display at the company's runway events were showcase apparel items, pieces of clothing such as a $5,000 pair of rhinestone-studded jeans that were well beyond the apparel budgets of ordinary consumers. Sean John Clothing did not make its revenue by selling rhinestone-studded jeans or opulent furs, instead, the company's commercial success came from attracting ordinary consumers. The sale of the company's simple casual separates, leather jackets, and suit blazers provided the majority of its sales. Combs made his reputation on the runway, earning nominations for Council of Fashion Designers of America Awards for three consecutive years, but his company made its living on the streets.

Sean John Clothing's unmitigated success as a designer of menswear provided the encouragement to develop a line of apparel for boys and women. Sales increased robustly, approaching $400 million by 2003, when the Sean John brand was sold in more than 2,000 retail locations throughout the country. Combs's achievements in the music industry during the 1990s, many observers noted, had helped popularize East Coast-style hip-hop, cultivating a mass-market audience for the genre. His success with Sean John Clothing produced a similar effect, bringing urban streetwear to the suburban market, although

Key Dates:

1998: Sean John Clothing is formed.
1999: The first line of apparel bearing the Sean John label is introduced.
2001: The runway show for the Sean John Clothing line is broadcast live on television.
2004: The company opens its first retail store in New York City.

Combs, in a May 21, 2003 interview with *South Florida Sun-Sentinel*, stressed, "I think the mainstream is coming to what we are doing at Sean John rather than the other way around."

Sean John Clothing Moves into Retail in 2004

In 2003, Combs directed Sean John Clothing's progression to the next step in the apparel business. He began working on plans for the company's own retail store, a flagship unit located on Fifth Avenue in New York City. Construction of the store was underway before the end of 2003, leading to its grand opening in June 2004. The Manhattan location was expected to be the first of a chain of Sean John Clothing stores, as Combs revealed plans to open ten stores in selected markets throughout the country by the end of 2005. At roughly the same time the flagship store opened, Combs entered into a joint venture agreement with a young designer named Zac Posen, making an undisclosed investment in Posen's three-year-old company, Outspoke LLC. "I see Zac as someone who shares the same drive and vision that I have," Combs said in an April 21, 2004 interview with *WWD*. "I also saw an opportunity for Sean John to make an impact with Zac Posen by giving him the tools and resources that he needed for his business to grow and mature."

As Sean John Clothing prepared to launch its assault on the retail front, the company's prospects were bright. During its first five years in business, the apparel designer demonstrated a consistent ability to succeed both on the runway and at the cash register. Although mistakes, particularly in the capricious world of fashion, were inevitable, the company possessed the financial strength of its founder and chief executive officer to support its future development as a retailer and designer. In 2004, *Fortune* magazine named Combs the wealthiest U.S. entertainer under the age of 40, estimating his income for the year at $315 million. Sean John Clothing represented a substantial percentage of that income, making its success critical to the success of Combs.

Principal Subsidiaries

Sean John Marketing.

Principal Competitors

Karl Kani Infinity Inc.; Phay Fashions LLC; Rocawear, Inc.

Further Reading

Bustard, Dan, "P. Diddy Clothing Makers Visit Vermont for Protest with Congressman," *Eagle Times*, November 13, 2003, p. A3.

"Combs Says He Will Look into Sweatshop Accusation," *St. Petersburg Times*, October 29, 2003, p. 2B.

Davis, Alisha, "Puffy's fur Is Flying," *Newsweek*, February 12, 2001, p. 32.

Doyle, Tim, "Diddy Bo. 1 on Rich List," *Mirror*, September 10, 2004, p. 17.

English, Simon, "P. Diddy Wraps Ups Clothes Divestment," *Daily Telegraph*, September 17, 2003, p. C3.

"Ex-Employee Raps Work Conditions," *Houston Chronicle*, October 29, 2003, p. 3.

Hagwood, Rod Stafford, "Sean John Clothing Line Making Some Noise," *South Florida Sun-Sentinel*, May 21, 2003, p. B2.

Malone, Scott, "Kernaghan, Worker Detail Diddy Claims," *WWD*, October 29, 2003, p. 12.

Morris, Valerie, "P. Diddy's Sean John Clothing Empire Forms Joint Venture with Designer Zac Posen," *America's Intelligence Wire*, April 22, 2004, p. 13.

Porter, Charlie, "Hip Shop Baby Phat," *Guardian*, September 15, 2003, p. 11.

Raftery, Brian M., "Hit and Runway," *Entertainment Weekly*, February 23, 2001, p. 12.

"Sean John Seeks New Shop Sites," *New York Post*, April 29, 2004, p. 40.

Wilson, Eric, "Combs Hopes to Score Hit with Posen," *WWD*, April 21, 2004, p. 3.

Wynn, Kelli, "Fired Hondurans Describe Sweatshop," *Dayton Daily News*, November 4, 2003, p. B3.

—Jeffrey L. Covell

Sierra Nevada Brewing Company

1075 East 20th Street
Chico, California 95928
U.S.A.
Telephone: (530) 893-3520
Web site: http://www.sierranevada.com

Private Company
Incorporated: 1980
Employees: 365
Sales: $100 million (2005 est.)
NAIC: 312120 Breweries; 722110 Full-Service Restaurants

Sierra Nevada Brewing Company is one of the top ten beer makers in the United States and the country's largest privately owned "craft brewery." The firm's beers include its best seller, the distinctively hop-flavored Pale Ale, as well as Porter, Stout, and Wheat varieties. In addition to these year-round brews, Sierra Nevada produces the seasonally available Summerfest, Celebration, and Bigfoot, as well as others which are available on tap at select locations, including the company's own restaurant and pub, located next to its brewery in Chico, California. The firm is owned and run by founder Ken Grossman.

Beginnings

The Sierra Nevada Brewing Company was founded in 1979 by Ken Grossman and Paul Camusi in the town of Chico, California, some 175 miles northeast of San Francisco in the Sacramento Valley. Both men had enjoyed brewing their own beers at home, and three years earlier one-time chemistry student Grossman had opened a store that sold home-brewing and winemaking supplies.

At the time they decided to go into business, there were only a handful of small breweries in the United States, notably Anchor Steam in San Francisco and New Albion in Sonoma, California, that produced the kind of flavorful, hand-crafted beers which the pair wanted to make. The bland lager-style offerings of industry leaders Anheuser-Busch, Miller, Pabst, Stroh, and Coors had come to closely resemble each other, and

the availability of American-brewed traditional varieties like ale, porter, and stout had almost become a thing of the past.

Grossman and Camusi were motivated to start their new company by the simple desire to brew good beer and expected to sell no more than 3,000 barrels a year, not even a drop in the bucket in an industry whose leaders brewed millions, in some cases tens of millions, of 31-gallon barrels each year. In 1979, the pair started construction of their brewery on a gravel road outside of Chico, using equipment scavenged from a dairy, a soft-drink bottler, and closed breweries. The new company was named after backpacker Grossman's favorite hiking spot, the nearby Sierra Nevada mountain range, and financed with $100,000 borrowed from the partner's parents.

On November 15, 1980, the first batch of Sierra Nevada Pale Ale was brewed. However, Grossman and Camusi were not satisfied with the result, and they threw out the first nine batches (at a cost of $1,000 each) before commencing production in 1981. In addition to pale ale, they brewed several other varieties, including a darker porter and stout. In its first year, the company sold just 500 barrels.

Unlike the industry's leaders, and even most home brewers, Grossman and Camusi used whole hops instead of hop pellets or extracts, as well as top-fermenting yeast, which resulted in a rich, highly distinctive flavor. The beer was also "bottle conditioned," which meant that a small amount of yeast was added to the unpasteurized beer as it was bottled, resulting in a secondary fermentation and natural carbonation. Few brewers of any size used this process because it was difficult to get consistent results, and the vast majority simply pumped carbonation into their pasteurized beers before bottling. Beer aficionados prized the firm's methods, which yielded a fresher, richer flavor and also caused Sierra Nevada's beer to age better than mass-produced brews, giving it a longer shelf life in the process.

With production underway, Sierra Nevada's first employee, Steve Harrison, was put in charge of marketing and sales, and he went out to local stores and beverage distributors to try to get them to carry the firm's brews. He had a hard time persuading them to take on the new, unfamiliar beer, however, and those who did sometimes saw it gather dust on the shelf.

Company Perspectives:

"Back in 1980, I founded the Sierra Nevada Brewing Company with one simple goal in mind—to produce the finest ales and lagers possible. To achieve this goal we have always used the highest quality and most natural brewing ingredients while utilizing the very best brewing practices. This allows us to create ales and lagers with superior flavor, aroma, balance and character. You can personally measure our success in this endeavor by enjoying our fine beers!" (Ken Grossman—Master Brewer, Owner, Founder, and President of Sierra Nevada Brewing Company)

Sales Take off in Mid-1980s

Gradually sales began to grow in Chico, where the large population of students at California State University had a healthy thirst for beer. Distribution was later extended to San Francisco, where the beer was discovered by Grateful Dead guitarist Jerry Garcia. When word got out that Garcia loved the firm's porter, many of the band's loyal fans began to seek out Sierra Nevada's beers. A May, 1984 profile of the brewery in the *San Francisco Chronicle*'s *Sunday Magazine* gave the firm another boost, as did an article in New York's *Village Voice,* which helped create demand for the beer on the East Coast.

With the company's beers beginning to attract attention in the media, Sierra Nevada Pale Ale, Porter, and Stout started to appear more frequently alongside imports like Heineken and Lowenbrau in specialty beer stores and even in some supermarkets such as Safeway, whose head beverage buyer had been introduced to the beer when visiting his daughter at college. The company had gotten its start at a time when there were few competitors and when growing numbers of Americans were seeking out the richer flavors of imported beer. In 1984, there were just 15 microbrewers (under 10,000 barrels) and 25 regional brewers (under 500,000 barrels) in the United States.

By 1987, Sierra Nevada was distributing its beers to seven states, and production had increased to 12,000 barrels per year. To handle this growth, a larger brewery was needed, and in 1988 the firm completed one which featured a 100-barrel brewhouse, four open-barrel fermenters, and 11 68-barrel secondary fermenters. The year after the new brewery was operational, the company also added a restaurant and pub to serve its beers, including some special brews not available elsewhere.

The firm was now reaching a wider customer base than the largely male college students and beer aficionados it had begun with, one that included more women and mainstream beer drinkers who were willing to give the company's beers a try. By 1989, production had jumped to 30,500 barrels, and expansion of the new brewery had already begun. This growth was especially remarkable given the fact that the firm eschewed the use of advertising, relying solely on word of mouth and occasional media coverage. Sierra Nevada also did not research consumer desires and trends in an attempt to reach a larger market but instead focused strictly on brewing quality beers.

The 1990s saw expansion continue at a rapid rate, with production hitting six figures in 1993, when 104,325 barrels were brewed. By now, the microbrewery segment had begun to explode, with more than 300 small brewers operating in the United States, including more than 70 in California alone. Part of this count included brewpubs, which made beer for consumption on the premises only.

In 1995, with the company's production continuing to mushroom, Grossman decided it was time to install a new bottling line. The firm had been using one built in 1962 for the makers of Rolling Rock beer in Pennsylvania, which was now outmoded. After much research, he selected a new system that removed almost all of the air from a bottle before filling, virtually eliminating the oxygen that could degrade a beer's flavor. The company installed it in February 1996 after arranging the brewing schedule so that production was disrupted for only two days. The line's $2 million cost was funded by a Bank of America loan. During the year, the firm, which now employed 80, produced 265,000 barrels of beer.

New Brewery Added in 1998

The company needed more than just a new bottling line to keep up with demand, however, and in 1997 Sierra Nevada began construction on a second plant based on the design of the existing one but on a larger scale. The new brewery had a capacity of 600,000 barrels of beer per year, with the capability for future expansion built in. Because making the firm's beers involved using the more complicated method of bottle-conditioning, it maintained a state-of-the-art testing laboratory with a staff of ten to assure quality. A case of beer from each batch was stored and tested after six months. Then it was tested again a year later. The environmentally conscious firm also added a wastewater treatment plant to the new facility.

By this time, the craft beer segment of the marketplace had reached a period of reevaluation that some were calling a shake-out. Distributors were being pressured by the largest beer makers to focus more on their own products, while the proliferation of small breweries had led to a flood of similar beers vying for the consumer's attention, forcing stores to drop slower-moving brands. Makers of imported beer, once the trend-setters in the premium beer market, had also launched aggressive new marketing campaigns, while liquor distillers were beginning to successfully divert younger drinkers away from beer and wine. The craft industry itself had also been hurt by the inconsistent output of some brewers, occasional deterioration of products due to lack of proper rotation in stores, and the loss of "fair-weather" microbrew drinkers, who briefly tried the more expensive brews, which typically cost one and one-half to two times as much as mainstream beer, before returning to their old familiar lager or lite beer. Additionally, several specialty beers had been launched by the major brewing companies that were less expensive than a true craft beer but were packaged to look as though they came from a small brewery. These included Anheuser Busch's Pacific Ridge Pale Ale, which had been clearly patterned after Sierra Nevada. All of these factors made succeeding in the business difficult, and a number of small brewers folded while others cancelled expansion plans.

Key Dates:

1979: Ken Grossman and Paul Camusi start building a brewery in Chico, California.
1981: Output totals 500 barrels in the company's first year in business.
1988: The rapidly expanding company opens a new brewery.
1989: The company opens a restaurant and pub.
1993: Production tops 100,000 barrels per year.
1996: A $2 million bottling line is installed.
1998: A new brewery comes on line with a capacity of 600,000 barrels per year.
2000: ''The Big Room'' concert hall opens.
2004: Sierra Center Stage televised concert series debuts.

Despite such challenges, Sierra Nevada's position as the leading independently owned maker of specialty beers in the United States insulated it from many of the industry's woes, and the company's sales continued to surge. Output in 1997 had been 302,734 barrels, and this jumped to 382,050 in 1998 and 420,000 in 1999. By this time, Ken Grossman had bought out Paul Camusi to become sole owner of the firm.

''The Big Room'' Opens in 2000

In 2000, the company opened a no-expense-spared 350-seat auditorium called The Big Room at its brewery, which soon began hosting concerts by local and nationally known folk, blues, and world-music performers. A full kitchen and bar were attached, and the space was made available to rent for banquets and other events.

Tours of Sierra Nevada's brewery had long been a popular tourist attraction in Chico, and many fans of the company's beers went out of their way to visit the area for this purpose. To accommodate their requests for souvenirs, the company had opened a store that sold a variety of Sierra Nevada logo merchandise. Its offerings included a line of beer-based mustards which the firm had also begun to market around the country.

Though Sierra Nevada beer had been distributed nationally for some time, sales were still strongest on the West Coast. In 2000, 57 percent of the firm's beer was sold in California, with 43 percent purchased in the northern half of the state. New York was far behind in second place, with 3.4 percent, followed by Nevada with 2.7 percent and Colorado with 2.6 percent.

In 2001, Ken Grossman bought the shuttered Fun World amusement park adjacent to the company's plant. The defunct amusement park was then torn down in anticipation of Sierra Nevada's future expansion. During the year, production topped 541,000 barrels, up from just under 500,000 the year before.

In 2003, Sierra Nevada began limited distribution to England. The firm had previously resisted exporting its beers, in part because the rapid growth in the U.S. market had consumed all of its output. The following year, Sierra Nevada Pale Ale won the ''Champion Beer'' award and the gold medal in the International Keg Ales category at the Brewing Industry International Awards in England, considered the ''Oscars'' of brewing. The year 2004 also saw the debut of a series of televised concerts taped at the firm's Big Room. Sierra Center Stage, as the program was known, was shown on a number of public television stations.

In 2005, the company began preparations to install four Direct Fuel Cell (DFC) generators to supply electrical power to its plant. The generators used natural gas, but the company was also exploring the possibility of using anaerobic digester gas from its brewery. The expensive DFC units were more efficient than standard combustion-based generators, and their purchase was part of the company's ongoing commitment to being good stewards of the environment.

In 25 years, Sierra Nevada Brewing Company had risen from humble origins to a leading position in the American beer industry. The firm had benefited from its position as one of the first modern craft breweries, but its success was also the result of astute management and a deep commitment to quality. With export sales just beginning, further growth seemed assured.

Principal Competitors

Boston Beer Co.; New Belgium Brewing Co.; Redhook Ale Brewery; Widmer Brothers Brewing Co.; Deschutes Brewing Co.; Pyramid Brewing Co.; Pete's Brewing Co.

Further Reading

''The Big Room,'' *Chico News & Review*, February 1, 2001.
Birdwell, Scott, ''Sierra Nevada: Going to the Source,'' *Houston Chronicle*, June 4, 1999, p. 14.
''California Classic,'' *Modern Brewery Age*, May 16, 1994, p. S20.
''Interview with Ken Grossman,'' *Modern Brewery Age*, May 10, 1999.
Schlachter, Barry, ''One Little Brew and How It Grew,'' *Fort Worth Star-Telegram*, August 15, 2001, p. 4.
''Sierra Nevada Installs $2 Million Packaging Plant,'' *Erickson Report*, March, 1996.
''Sierra Nevada Puts a New Spin on Its Business,'' *Modern Brewery Age*, May 18, 1998, p. 36.
''Sierra Nevada to Install Fuel Cell Powerplants Late Next Year,'' *Modern Brewery Age*, June 7, 2004, p. 2.
Speer, Robert, '' 'Stage' Presence,'' *Chico News & Review*, May 6, 2004.
Stratton, Brad, ''Brewing up Success,'' *Quality Progress*, March 1, 1997, p. 5.
Waddell, Dave, ''Chico, Calif.-Based Brewing Company Takes Pride in Quality Product,'' *Sacramento Bee*, August 19, 2001.

—Frank Uhle

Siskin Steel & Supply Company

1901 Riverfront Parkway
Chattanooga, Tennessee 37408
U.S.A.
Telephone: (423) 756-3671
Toll Free: (800) 756-3671
Fax: (423) 756-9641
Web site: http:///www.siskin.com

Wholly Owned Subsidiary of Reliance Steel & Aluminum Co.
Founded: 1900
Employees: NA
Sales: $159.2 million (2003 est.)
NAIC: 423510 Metal Service Centers and Other Metal Merchant Wholesalers

A subsidiary of Reliance Steel & Aluminum Company, Siskin Steel & Supply Company is a Chattanooga, Tennessee-based company that processes and distributes steel and aluminum products. Siskin serves customers throughout the southeastern United States from four service centers located in Chattanooga and Nashville, Tennessee; Spartanburg, South Carolina; and Birmingham, Alabama. Siskin is also responsible for two other Reliance subsidiaries: Georgia Steel Supply Company, located in Atlanta, and East Tennessee Steel Supply Inc., located in Morristown, Tennessee. Aluminum products include angles, cast plates, sheets, channels, handrail pipe, square tubing, and tread plate. Stainless steel products include angles, plates, sheets, rounds, flats, and squares. Carbon steel products include hot-rolled angles, round pipe, hot-rolled tees, a variety of tubing, cold-finished products, and hot-rolled products. Siskin employs integrated computers to offer value-added processing services, such as smooth, fast oxyfuel, plasma and laser cutting; the ability to shear up to three-quarters of an inch thick and 20 feet long; and sawing capabilities for beams as wide as 36 inches.

Company Roots: The Dawn of the 20th Century

The history of Siskin Steel was typical of America a century ago, essentially the immigrant success story of Robert Hyman Siskin. Born in Lithuania he came to America in a cattle ship in 1890, and like so many others, he was fleeing religious persecution. He knew little about America and after passing through Ellis Island in New York harbor he moved to Chattanooga, Tennessee, because someone on the cattle boat who was bound for the city convinced Siskin to be his travel companion. Siskin took up one of the few trades open to the newly arrived. He became an itinerant peddler. Unable to afford a horse and wagon, he carried his wares on his back and hiked to outlying rural communities in a 75-mile radius west of Chattanooga to sell his goods, only returning when his pack was empty. Like many immigrants, he saved his money until he could send for his family. In 1900 Siskin was then able to set up a business and put his peripatetic days behind him. With just $6 he and a partner launched a scrap metal business—Rubin and Siskin Iron and Metal—on a rented lot in Chattanooga.

Siskin bought out Rubin in 1910 and changed the name of the business to R.H. Siskin and Sons, although his eldest boy, Mose, was just ten years old, and Mose's brother Garrison was seven. But the boys already had contributed to the family's finances by selling milk from the family cow and hawking newspapers. The extra money was welcome, given that the 20-man scrap business operated out of a small dirt-floor shack and could not afford to buy any equipment until 1924, when Siskin bought the first company truck. Mose and Garrison did what they could, fashioning a wagon out of a soap box, and scouring the neighborhoods for scraps of metal as well as bottles, rags, and other salvageable junk.

Money may have been tight, but Robert Siskin always kept a cigar box for spare change, which he then shared with anyone in need. Just as the business was beginning to prosper, however, Siskin died in 1926, leaving the scrap metal operation in the hands of his now grown-up sons. It was Mose and Garrison Siskin who would begin to reap what their father had sewn, as the company began to experience steady growth. By the mid-1930s, despite the Great Depression, the company was doing well enough to build a new office, although in the meantime it operated out of a converted street car. With the advent of World War II came a great need for scrap metal services, as the country was desperate for supplies to convert into armaments.

It was also during the war, in 1942, that an incident took place that would alter the lives of the Siskin brothers. Garrison injured himself during a train trip when he stepped out to stretch his legs at a stop. But as he was about to reboard, the train lurched, and a steel platform cover struck his leg, causing a blood clot that became life-threatening. Given little chance to survive, Garrison was told that if he was to have any chance to live his leg would have to be amputated. Deeply religious, he spent a night in prayer, and according to family lore he asked that his life and his leg be spared in exchange for devoting the rest of his life to helping others. After he made a complete recovery, Garrison kept his word and was joined by his brother, who declared, "If it's your promise, it's my promise, and we will keep it together." Like their father they had a cigar box where they kept petty cash, and over the next few years they often drew on those funds to help people in need, to pay for groceries or to meet a doctor's bill. They also helped many people by employing them at Siskin Steel. In one case, the company installed a Braille switchboard to facilitate the hiring of a blind person. In 1950 they formalized their philanthropy by establishing the Siskin Memorial Foundation, in memory of their parents. Over the years, the foundation funded college scholarships, built wheelchair ramps to public buildings, donated playground equipment, and paid for the construction of a number of buildings close to the University of Tennessee at Chattanooga, which in addition to housing the foundation's offices was home to an outpatient clinic, a school for special children, a religious museum, and other charitable institutions. Because of Garrison Siskin's experience, the foundation placed a great deal of emphasis on physical rehabilitation. The downtown buildings eventually became the University of Tennessee Chattanooga Physical Therapy School, and in 1959 the foundation launched the 365 Club, which raised money to provide physical rehabilitation services to both children and adults. The program asked residents to donate money for 365 days of the year, even if it was just a penny. People of all ages in Chattanooga participated in what became an area institution. In 1986 a separate nonprofit corporation was established by the foundation to develop a rehabilitation hospital. The Siskin family's efforts of nearly half a century came to fruition in 1990 with the opening of the Siskin Hospital for Physical Rehabilitation in Chattanooga.

Post-World War II Move into Distribution

Following World War II, with the economy humming following a brief postwar lull, Siskin Steel continued to grow at a rapid clip. In 1949 the brothers moved beyond the scrap metal business by launching Chattanooga Steel and Supply Company to distribute new steel and related products. In time the two companies were merged, forming Siskin Steel and Supply.

Siskin expanded beyond Chattanooga during the 1960s, opening a sales office in Atlanta in 1963. It was around this time that the company was forced to relocate its scrap yard to make way for a new highway. As a result, Siskin moved to a new 40-acre lot where it kept 100 people employed. To keep pace

with the company's growing distribution business, Siskin expanded and modernized its Chattanooga warehouses in the 1970s, so that they encompassed more than 400,000 square feet. Having outgrown its headquarters, the company in addition built a new office building, which opened in 1978. It was also during this period that a third generation took charge of Siskin Steel. Mose's son Robert Siskin and Garrison's son-in-law Mervin Pregulman. In 1978 Pregulman was named president and chief executive officer, the same year that Mose Siskin died. A year later, Garrison died as well.

By 1980 Siskin was generating about $50 million in annual revenues. Over the next 15 years that amount would triple, due to an effort launched in the mid-1980s to expand the company throughout the Southeast. In 1985 Siskin bought Birmingham, Alabama-based Steel Supply Company, which subsequently took on the Siskin name and became the company's first branch operation. Next, Siskin built a 100,000-square-foot steel service center from scratch in Nashville in 1989 to cut transportation costs and accommodate Nissan and Saturn auto plants in the area. Altogether the company now served seven southern states. To better focus on the steel service center industry, Siskin elected in 1990 to exit the original business, selling its ferrous and non-ferrous scrap-processing assets to Commercial Metals Co.

With its attention and resources now fully committed to the distribution of new steel products, Siskin quickly moved to fill out its product offerings, adding a wide range of new sizes and grades. The company then sought to continue its geographic expansion, in particular eyeing Charlotte, North Carolina, and nearby markets. At that same time, Southern Steel Company, located in Greenville, South Carolina, was looking to be acquired. A medium-sized company, it lacked the resources necessary to grow to the next level, falling uncomfortably between the cracks—not specialized enough to compete with niche operations, and too small to go up against larger companies that could take advantage of economies of scale to offer lower prices. Although it was not certain which party first approached the other, Siskin and Southern Steel were a good fit, and a purchase price was agreed to in December 1991. Southern Steel adopted the Siskin name and began serving the North Carolina and South Carolina markets. The Greenville operation was primarily a hot-rolled sheet distributor, but under Siskin it greatly expanded its product offerings. As a result Greenville outgrew its facility, leading to the construction of a new state-of-the-art 91,000-square-foot plant in Spartanburg, South Carolina, which opened as a replacement in 1995.

A Successful Marketing Program in the Early 1990s

In the meantime, Siskin also looked to upgrade one of its Chattanooga plants, made necessary because an aggressive marketing program launched in the early 1990s proved highly successful. Sales increased significantly in such product lines as tubing, and hot-rolled, cold-rolled, stainless, aluminum, and alloy bars. As a result the company needed to expand its inventory levels. But because of the plant's location, sandwiched between a highway and tracks of the Norfolk & Southern Railroad, expansion was a challenge. Fortunately the railroad agreed to move some of the tracks, which were seldom used, allowing Siskin to find enough room to add about 20,000 square feet to its plate and structural bays on the north side of the facility. On the other side, however, where tubing and bar

---

Key Dates:

1900: Rubin and Siskin Iron and Metal is formed to deal in scrap.
1910: Robert Siskin buys out his partner.
1926: Siskin dies and is succeeded by sons Mose and Garrison.
1949: A new steel distribution business is launched.
1978: Mose Siskin dies, and the third generation takes over.
1990: The original scrap business is sold.
1996: Reliance Steel acquires Siskin.
2000: Siskin celebrates its 100th anniversary.

---

products were stored, there was no hope of moving the highway. Siskin solved this problem by tearing down the 45-year-old tubing warehouse and replacing it with a more efficient warehouse, thus expanding the tubing storage area by 20,000 square feet. The company still had a problem storing bar products, with no easy solutions available until it learned about a new automated, bar-code driven storage and retrieval system offered by a German company. Siskin became the first U.S. service center to purchase the new system. All told, Siskin spent about $8 million expanding the Chattanooga plant.

In fiscal 1995 Siskin posted sales of approximately $151 million. The company now reached a crossroads. The steel industry was undergoing a period of consolidation and in order to remain competitive and continue to grow, Siskin needed to join forces with a larger company. Like Southern Steel, it found itself in the difficult position of being too big to be small but not big enough to get bigger. Over the years, Siskin had been courted by a number of suitors. Then in 1996 it found a company that appeared to be a good fit, Reliance Steel & Aluminum, which it approached about an acquisition. In October 1996 Reliance agreed to buy Siskin for $71 million.

Reliance was 40 years younger than Siskin, founded in Los Angeles in 1939 by Thomas J. Neilan as Reliance Steel Products Co. It originally produced steel reinforcing bars for the construction industry, then in 1948 added aluminum and magnesium products. The company adopted the Reliance Steel & Aluminum name in 1956 and launched an expansion program, relying primarily on acquisitions. In 1966 Reliance moved into Texas and in 1975 attempted to enter the southeastern United States, but an Atlanta operation did not work out and was sold in 1987. Other acquisitions in the 1980s proved more successful, as Reliance bought companies located throughout California, as well as Utah, Arizona, New Mexico, and Kansas. In 1994 the company went public, using the proceeds and its stock to fuel

further acquisitions. A major part of Reliance's bid to expand beyond the western half of the United States was the purchase of Siskin, which was the company's largest acquisition, by far eclipsing the $25 million purchase of CCC Steel Corp. several months earlier.

Reliance was more than happy to allow Siskin to continue under its current management. Reliance President David Hannah told the *Chattanooga Times,* "Siskin is a well-managed company and we're going to try to stay out of their way and let them continue to grow." A fourth generation of the founding family stayed on to run the company in the form of John Pregulman, Mervin Pregulman's son, who was named president and chief operating officer. In 2000 Siskin reached its 100-year anniversary still under family management having grown from two employees to 600. With its new corporate parent, the company had the resources to continue growing. In 2000 it acquired East Tennessee Steel Supply Inc., a Morristown, Tennessee-based company that processed and distributed carbon steel plate, bar, and structurals.

With the economy struggling in the early years of the new century, Reliance and Siskin did not enjoy the best of times. Nevertheless, they fared better than many in their industry, remaining profitable and continuing to grow market share. In 2002 John Pregulman left Siskin, replaced as CEO by Jerry Pearson, leaving only one member of the founding family involved in the business: Assistant Vice-President in Accounting David Binder, grandson of Mose Siskin.

Principal Subsidiaries

Georgia Steel Supply Company; East Tennessee Steel Supply Inc.

Principal Competitors

Olympic Steel, Inc.; O'Neal Steel, Inc.; Shiloh Industries, Inc.

Further Reading

Anderson, Lee, "Siskin—'Only in America,'" *Chattanooga Time Free Press,* October 1, 1996.

Flessner, Dave, "California Firm Buys Siskin Steel," *Chattanooga Times,* October 1, 1996.

Haflich, Frank, "Reliance Steel Set to Purchase Siskin," *American Metal Market,* October 3, 1996, p. 2.

Regan, James G., and Michael Marley, "CMC to Buy Siskin Units," *American Metal Market,* August 7, 1990, p. 1.

"Siskin Celebrates Its Centennial," *Metal Center News,* April 2000, p. 20.

—Ed Dinger

San Jose
Water
Company

SJW Corporation

374 West Santa Clara Street
San Jose, California 95196
U.S.A.
Telephone: (408) 279-7800
Fax: (408) 279-7934
Web site: http://www.sjwater.com

Public Company
Incorporated: 1866 as San Jose Water Company
Employees: 301
Sales: $149.7 million
Stock Exchanges: American
Ticker Symbol: SJW
NAIC: 221310 Water Supply and Irrigation Systems

SJW Corporation, based in San Jose, California, is a holding company for three subsidiaries. The primary business is the San Jose Water Company, a public utility serving the metropolitan San Jose area, comprised of 138 square miles and home to about 1 million people. SJW Land Company primarily owns and operates parking facilities located close to the water company's headquarters, in addition to owning some commercial buildings and undeveloped land in San Jose as well as parcels in Florida and Connecticut. The third SJW subsidiary is 75-percent owned Crystal Choice Water Service, which provides water softening and purification systems to residential customers. SJW also owns 1.1 million shares of California Water Service Group, a San Jose-based water company serving customers in California, New Mexico, and Hawaii. SJW is a public company trading on the American Stock Exchange.

Mid-19th Century Origins

Because of plentiful supplies of water, the San Jose area of the Santa Clara Valley was well populated by Native Americans even before the Spanish established a settlement there in the 1770s. The Spanish built a network of *acequias,* essentially open ditches of flowing water, which served the growing population until the mid-1800s. However, the water supply was subject to floods and droughts and proved a ready place for mosquitoes to breed and spread cholera and typhoid. In 1854, the first artesian well was dug in San Jose, providing a safe supply of potable water. A local foundry owner named Donald McKenzie recognized that the delivery of water offered a business opportunity. He build two water tanks at the San Jose Foundry, and in February 1865 acquired the rights to provide water to the residents of San Jose and Santa Clara, 400 people in all, and agreed to also provide water for fire protection. With partners John Bonner and Anthony Chabot, he then incorporated the San Jose Water Company in November 1866 to operate the 25-year franchise. With $100,000 in capital, the company quickly installed water mains, prompting instant demand for service. The demand was so strong that it soon became apparent that artesian wells, because they were subject to effects of dry weather, were not a reliable enough water source to support expansion of the company. The company now looked to the Santa Cruz Mountains, which offered a potentially vast supply of water if rainfall could be trapped and stored in reservoirs.

In December 1868, San Jose Water was reincorporated and its capital stock increased to $300,000, the extra funds needed to build the company's first reservoirs. The effort was overseen by Nathaniel Mason, McKenzie's replacement as company president, in 1869. The Seven-Mile Reservoir was completed in 1870, followed a year later by the Three-Mile Reservoir. Also in 1871, the Tisdale Reservoir, named for local banker William Tisdale opened. It was a joint venture with the Los Gatos Manufacturing Company, a flour mill that relied on water power and had already built dams and reservoirs for its own purposes. The two companies worked closely together until 1886, at which point Los Gatos Manufacturing became a competitor by purchasing the Los Gatos Water Company. In 1890, San Jose Water resolved the conflict by acquiring Los Gatos Manufacturing, in the process adding Los Gatos water customers.

In 1874, Edward Williams became company president, a post he held until the end of the century, except for a two-year stint, 1894 to 1896, when banker Tisdale held the job. During William's tenure, San Jose Water expanded steadily. In the 1870s, the company opened a pair of reservoirs, Lake McKenzie and Lake Kittredge, followed by Lake Cozzens in 1882. Lake Williams Reservoir opened in 1895 under Tisdale's watch. Also in 1895, the company lost the Santa Clara business when that community elected to build a municipal water works. When Williams returned as president, the company made up for the loss in 1899 by acquiring Mountain Springs Water Company.

Steady Expansion through the 1970s

Williams' successor, George W. Cozzens, continued a policy of buying land along the key Los Gatos Creek, but he soon faced a major challenge involving another area stream known as Coyote Creek. Water from this and other streams fed a plentiful artesian belt around San Jose, and starting in 1903 San Jose Water began digging wells to tap into for additional water supplies to meet its growing need. However, another enterprise, the Bay Cities Water Company, saw an opportunity to siphon off 80 million gallons a day for sale to San Francisco and Oakland, and thus bought 1500 acres of land in the Coyote watershed. San Jose Water and valley ranchers vigorously opposed the idea, leading to a two-year court fight that they ultimately won in 1905.

Due to poor health, Cozzens resigned in 1907, replaced by George McKee, during whose five-year term San Jose Water beefed up its infrastructure, adding nine wells and pumping stations. Joseph Ryland took over as president in 1912, a post he held until 1928. During his tenure, the company's 50-year charter of incorporation expired in 1916, leading to the creation of San Jose Water Works, which took over all the franchises controlled by San Jose Water. Also during Ryland's 16 years, the company picked up additional water rights along Los Gatos Creek from Pacific Gas and Electric Company and in 1919 acquired Cottage Grove Water Works and Cherryhurst Water Company. In 1928, Ryland added another 300 customers through the purchase of Willow Glen Water Works. By the time Ryland was succeeded as president by Seymour Kittredge in 1928, San Jose Water was serving 23,000 customers.

During Kettredge's nine-year term, San Jose Water experienced a number of noteworthy changes, as did the water industry as a whole due to an acquisition spree of eastern utility holding companies, which bought up water companies and other utilities during the late 1920s. In 1929, General Water Works and Electric Company bought a controlling interest in San Jose Water for $5.1 million, but management remained unchanged and the company carried on as before. A major effort during this period was the replacement of a wooden flume, more than 50 years old, that connected Los Gatos Creek to Jones Dam. The new metal flume constructed by the company would now be able to direct some ten million gallons of water a day to its distribution system. During the 1930s, San Jose Water continued its land purchases. The most notable deal was the 1936 purchase of the entire town of Wrights, located in the Santa Cruz mountains.

In 1937, San Jose Water hired a new president, Ralph Elsman, who was to hold the job longer than any person in

company history, serving 31 years until 1968. He also became president and general manager of California Water Service Company, a General Water subsidiary that in 1940 moved its offices to the newly enlarged building that housed San Jose Water's headquarters, although it remained independently operated. Early in Elsman's tenure, a bid to place San Jose Water under municipal ownership was defeated by a public vote and the company remained commercially owned. After World War II, Elsman left his mark on the company in a number of ways. After San Jose Water gained its independence from General Water in 1945, Elsman placed it on a more secure financial footing by reorganizing the company and taking it public. During his three decades at the top, he also oversaw the spending of $60 million in capital improvements and an increase in the amount of surface water the company could store by two billion gallons. This expansion of the utility plant was made all the more necessary by tremendous economic growth in the Santa Clara Valley. Much of that additional storage capacity came from the Austrian Dam, built in 1951. Demand for water grew so strong that despite the addition of new wells and hundreds of miles of new mains installed, San Jose Water was unable to keep pace. In the mid-1960s, the company began drawing on water imported to the valley to supplement supplies. Before leaving the company, Elsman saw computers become involved in the running of the utility. In 1965, a computerized operations system was installed to monitor water levels and make optimum use of pumps.

In 1968, Nathaniel Kendall, the company's chief engineer who had been responsible for the construction of the Austrian Dam, succeed Elsman as president of San Jose Water. During his six-year stint, there was renewed interest from the city of San Jose to acquire the company, but nothing came out of the many talks the parties held on the subject. Kendall's replacement, J.W. Weinhardt, took over in 1974 and saw San Jose Water through the rest of the century in a career with the company that lasted nearly 40 years. His first contact with San Jose Water came in 1959 when he worked as an accountant for Peat Marwick Mitchell and conducted an audit of the utility. In 1963, he was recruited by San Jose Water to become chief controller. He accepted the job and worked his way up through the ranks over the next decade.

Changes and Growth through the Mid-1990s

During Weinhardt's tenure, San Jose Water's distribution system was put to the test by a drought that lasted from 1976 to 1977. Although the company was able to meet demand, it instituted a water conservation program, distributing kits to customers that included showerhead flow restrictors, toilet displacement bottles, and dye tablets to detect leaks. The program showed immediate results, as water usage decreased by 23 percent from 1976 to 1977. During this period, the company also improved its customer service capabilities by installing an online computer information system in 1977 that replaced manual ledgers and provided customer service representatives with up-to-the-moment billing information on a computer screen. Because San Jose Water's infrastructure was aging, with a large number of mains over 100 years old and too small to keep up with contemporary demands, Weinhardt devoted much of his attention to upgrading the distribution system. He also ex-

Key Dates:

1866: San Jose Water Company is formed to serve Santa Clara and San Jose.
1895: Santa Clara builds a municipal water system.
1913: The company is reorganized as San Jose Water Works.
1929: General Water Works and Electric Company acquires the company.
1937: Ralph Elsman begins a 31-year-tenure as president.
1951: Austrian Dam is built.
1974: J.W. Weinhardt is named president.
1985: Holding company JSW Corporation and subsidiary SJW Land Company are formed.
2001: Crystal Choice Water Service is launched.
2002: Weinhardt retires.

panded the company through acquisition. In 1980, the 5,300 customers of the Campbell Water Company were added to the 190,000 customers San Jose Water already served.

In 1983, the company changes its name from San Jose Water Works to San Jose Water Company. Two years later, in February 1985, the company's shareholders agreed to create a holding company called SJW Corporation to provide the company with greater flexibility to engage in non-utility business. In July 1985, SJW acquired San Jose Water in a stock exchange, with the stock of the holding company now trading on the American Stock Exchange in place of San Jose Water. Then, in October, SJW created SJW Land Company, which subsequently acquired real estate assets from San Jose Water. About one-third of SJW was owned by Roscoe Moss Company, a Los Angeles water drilling company that had been slowly buying up the stock since 1978. Roscoe Moss and his brother George Moss each sat on the SJW board and were open about their desire to one day gain majority control of SJW. Far from a hostile takeover, the effort was friendly and leisurely paced. Finally, in 1992, Roscoe Moss and SJW merged, and in the process SJW added the business of Western Precision Inc., a Sunnyvale, California, metal machining company. SJW held onto the company until 1995 when Western Precision's management team bought the business for $2 million. Through the merger, SJW also picked up a 9.7 percent stake in California Water Services.

Surviving in the Late 1990s and Beyond

In 1997, San Jose Water took over the operation of the City of Cupertino's water system under the terms of a 25-year lease. By the end of decade, the company served more than 970,000 customers. It was at this point that SJW's management hired Morgan Dean Witter to explore strategic options, including the sale of the company, which had an estimated market value of approximately $265 million. However, it was likely to command a much higher price in light of consolidation taking place in the water industry, spurred by the buying sprees of French companies Vivendi and Suez Lyonnaise, which had emerged as international giants in recent years. In less than a month, SJW agreed to a $390 million offer, plus the assumption of $90 million in debt, from New Jersey-based American Water

Works, one of America's largest investor-owned water utilities. Already in 1999, it had completed 16 acquisitions, but gaining approval from the California Public Utilities Commission for the SJW deal proved problematic. Regulators continually postponed the date for making a final decision on the application. In February 2001, frustrated that the deadline had now been pushed back to September 2001 (almost two years after a tentative agreement had been struck), American Water Works walked away from the deal, fearful that in September the decision would once again be kicked down the road. As a result of the commission's lack of action, the suitors that had once lined up to bid for SJW shied away. In the meantime, Weinhardt stepped down as chief executive in 1999, replaced by W. Richard Roth, although he remained as chairman.

Another deal that went awry was San Jose Water's attempt in 2002 to take over the operation of San Jose's municipal water system, which served the 20 percent of area residents not covered by San Jose Water. The matter became a contentious political issue, but despite intense lobbying by San Jose Water the plan never came to fruition. During the early 2000s, SJW enjoyed success on other fronts, however. In 2001, after a year of test marketing, it launched Crystal Choice Water Service LLC, a 75 percent majority-owned joint venture with Kinetico Incorporated. It offered San Jose Water customer's a chance to rent or purchase Kinetico's total home water treatment system, which combined in a single unit chlorine removal, water softening, and a reverse osmosis process to produce drinking water. San Jose Land also began to develop property near the HP Pavilion in downtown San Jose.

In May 2002, Weinhardt retired as chairman and was succeeded by Drew Gibson, a director since 1986. Weinhardt's departure marked the end of an era for San Jose water and its parent SJW, as his tenure spanned almost a third of the company's history. Although SJW was a relatively small company, generating revenues of close to $150 million and net income of $18.7 million in 2003, there was every reason to expect it to continue on as a profitable concern for years to come.

Principal Subsidiaries

San Jose Water Company; SJW Land Company; Crystal Choice Water Service LLC (75%).

Principal Competitors

American States Water Company; American Water Works Company, Inc.; Southwest Water Company.

Further Reading

Barry, David, "J. W. Weinhardt: Neither the Drought Nor the Arid Regs Have Withered His Spirit," *Business Journal*, June 18, 1990, p. 12.

Roberts, Ricardo, "Bidders Won't Wash up on SJW's Shores," *Mergers & Acquisitions Report*, March 5, 2001.

Roberts, Timothy, "Water Deal: Pipeline to Profits," *Silicon Valley/San Jose Business Journal*, August 16, 2002, p. 1.

Whaley, Sharon, ed., *San Jose Water Company 125th Anniversary*, San Jose: SJW, 1992, 32 p.

—Ed Dinger

Sterling European Airlines A/S

Kommanditaktieselskab
Copenhagen Airport South
2791 Dragoer
Denmark
Telephone: (+45) 70 33 33 70
Fax: (+45) 70 33 23 23
Web site: http://www.sterling.dk

Private Company
Incorporated: 1994
Employees: 612
Sales: DKK 1.25 billion (2003)
NAIC: 481111 Scheduled Passenger Air Transportation;
481112 Scheduled Freight Air Transportation; 481212
Nonscheduled Chartered Freight Air Transportation;
481211 Nonscheduled Chartered Passenger Air
Transportation; 48819 Other Support Activities for
Air Transportation

Sterling European Airlines A/S (SEA) is Scandinavia's leading low-fare airline. It was created in 1994 from the ashes of Sterling Airways, which had once been the world's largest charter airline. SEA's predecessor pioneered low-fare routes from Denmark to southern Europe and North America, and Sterling European is also known for its budget emphasis. Sterling is 50–50 owned by Ganger Rold ASA and Bonheur ASA, both of whose shares trade on the Oslo Stock Exchange. About 1.8 million people flew Sterling in 2004. SEA also has significant cargo and maintenance operations. The airline has a fleet of about a dozen Boeing 737s. Based in Copenhagen with Norwegian ownership, Sterling operates from all three Scandinavian countries: Denmark, Sweden, and Norway.

Origins

The history of Sterling European Airways can be traced back to Rev. Ejlif Krogager, dubbed the "Flying Vicar" by some. Krogager was a Lutheran priest in the village of Tjaereborg in West Jutland, Denmark. In the 1950s, he began taking parishioners on bus tours to Spain and other southern European destinations. This developed into the Tjaereborg Rejser group, which specialized in budget holidays. By the early 1960s, notes a 1992 obituary of Krogager in the *Times* (London), the group had 80 buses.

In May 1962, Krogager established the original Sterling Airways, a charter airline, with two prop-driven DC-6s acquired from Swissair. Flights began that July. In 1965, the airline began flying modern Caravelle jets.

Sterling became the world's largest private charter airline in the 1970s. In the late 1970s, Sterling filed a complaint with the EEC against the monopoly by government-sponsored SAS on scheduled routes from Scandinavia to European capitals. A decade later, Sterling was pioneering charter flights from Denmark to North America, also against resistance from SAS.

Sterling Airways was spun off from the Tjaereborg group in 1986. At the time of its 25th anniversary in 1987, according to company records, the airline had a fleet of 19 aircraft and nearly 1,300 employees. Sterling's sales were then about DKK 2 billion. It was flying around 800,000 passengers a year.

Sterling Airways managing Director Ejnar Lundt led a management buyout of the airline and its flight catering unit Aero Chef in 1988. An investment group paid DKK 754 million ($118.4 million) to acquire the company. Danish investors, including Sterling employees, held 51 percent of shares, with Sweden's Reso Travel Group taking up the rest. A new company, Sterling Holding, was formed for the transaction. Company founder Ejlif Krogager retired from the Tjaereborg travel company at this time. He had left the clergy in 1972 and died in 1992.

Sterling ended the 1980s with 1,800 employees. Sales were DKK 2.1 billion with a pre-tax profit of DKK 101 million in the fiscal year ending March 1989. The fleet included ten Boeing 727s, five Caravelles, two Corvettes, and two new Boeing 757s.

Liberalization in the 1990s

Sterling built a giant new hangar, and in 1990 the company won the rights to set up a European maintenance center for

Company Perspectives:

Through more than 40 years, the Sterling name has been dear to the Scandinavians' heart. Millions of Scandinavian tourists have enjoyed the effective transport and good service of the airline to and from holidays, primarily in Southern Europe, which have added much to experience. The legendary founder of Tjæreborg Rejser, Rev. Ejlif Krogager, founded Sterling Airways. He got the inspiration to the Sterling name from his mother, who always used Sterling silver for presents because, to her, it was a symbol of quality. This attitude still lies behind the special Sterling spirit, which has been created through decades: The essence of dynamics and drive focusing on safety, quality and service.

refitting Boeing 727s with hush kits. Around the same time, a merger with small charter carrier A/S Conair was discussed but not consummated.

In 1991, Sterling joined two other independent Scandinavian airlines in an alliance as the European aviation market neared liberalization (deregulation). Its partners in the TransNordic Group were Stockholm-based Transwede Airways and Oslo's Norway Airlines. Sterling had acquired 33 percent of the shares of both of these airlines. The three were all affiliated with Stockholm's NRT Nordisk Group, which was partly owned by the Reso Travel Group. Sterling was providing flight training and catering services for its TransNordic partners.

According to *Flight International World Airline Directory*, in 1993 Sterling was operating only one scheduled route, between Copenhagen and Luxembourg. The airline had a dozen planes, mostly Boeing 727s, and 1,000 employees.

Sterling European Formed in 1994

Sterling's years as an independent company were numbered, however. On September 22, 1993, the airline was pronounced bankrupt. It had 722 employees at the time.

A new charter airline, Sterling European Airlines (SEA), was formed on January 1, 1994 following the demise of the original Sterling Airways. It started charter operations with Boeing 727 airliners leased from Sterling Airways in May 1994. There were about 180 employees. Startup capital was just DKK 5 million.

SEA posted a gross profit of DKK 45 million for its first fiscal year, which was eight months long. Turnover for this period was DKK 265 million.

In January 1995, Sterling European underwent a management buyout. Lars Svenheim of Sweden, who owned 52 percent of the company, was the managing director, while chairman Keld Ditlev Petersen held 16 percent.

The next year, in 1996, Ganger Rolf ASA and Bonheur ASA acquired 90 percent of the company's shares. Both Ganger Rolf and Bonheur, an affiliate of the Fred Olsen group, were based in

Norway and publicly traded. They bought out Sterling European's remaining shares in 1999.

In 1998, SEA began phasing out its Boeing 727s in favor of Next Generation Boeing 737s. The airline was leasing the new planes. By this time, SEA had begun operating dedicated 727 freighters for TNT Airways.

Perceiving a gap in the transatlantic air cargo market, in November 1999 the airline's Sterling Cargo unit began operating a leased Boeing 747 freighter on a twice-weekly service from Copenhagen and Stockholm to New York, Chicago, and Los Angeles. It also started a weekly service to Dubai. SEA posted a loss of DKK 55 million in 2000, which was doubled the next year.

Sterling European expanded, rather than contracted, its services in the uncertain travel environment following the September 11, 2001 attacks on the United States. Several new routes to southern Europe were added by the end of the year. Another 21 routes were opened in 2002, including connections to Oslo and Stockholm. Sales were DKK 881 million.

Repositioned in 2002

By this time, the carrier had repositioned itself as Scandinavia's first low-fare airline. A survey by the Swedish newspaper *Aftonbladet* soon pronounced Sterling European to be the best low-cost airline in Scandinavia. Unlike some budget rivals, Sterling preferred to fly to major airports. The survey found Sterling offered better shopping opportunities than Snowflake (SAS's budget offshoot) and Ryanair. In 2004, a group of Swedish travel agents also voted Sterling the best low-cost airline in the region. Sterling operated from all three Scandinavian countries.

Sterling European's passenger count rose a colossal 40 percent in 2003, to 1.35 million. Sales were DKK 1.25 billion. The airline opened almost a dozen new routes during the year as the fleet was increased from six to eight Boeing 737 aircraft, the popular mid-size jet that was a favorite of budget airlines along the Southwest Airlines model in the United States.

At the forefront of an industry trend, Sterling European introduced "super-flexible" ticket rules in the spring of 2004. Passengers could cancel or change tickets up to two hours before departure without penalty. This could even be done online. In December of the year, Sterling announced a partnership with Hostelworld, an online reservations company, to offer low-cost lodgings in Europe.

Sterling introduced a unique development to low-cost travel in September 2004: missed departure insurance. This coverage, developed with Europæiske Rejseforsikring, provided reasonable reimbursement for additional airfare and hotel fees in the case of a delay in the first of two connecting flights. This took some of the risk out of combining flights on budget airlines with those on traditional airlines.

In the fall of 2004, there were press reports that German travel group TUI AG was interested in acquiring Sterling European, though this did not happen. Sterling added another four planes to its young fleet during the year, bringing the total to

Key Dates:

1962: Sterling Airways is launched by Tjaereborg founder Rev. Ejlif Krogager.
1988: Management buys out Sterling Airways.
1991: TransNordic alliance is formed with Transwede Airways and Norway Airlines.
1993: Sterling Airways goes bankrupt.
1994: Sterling European Airlines is formed.
1995: Sterling European undergoes a management buyout.
1996: Ganger Rolf ASA and Bonheur ASA acquire control of SEA.
1998: SEA begins to update its fleet with Next Generation Boeing 737s.
1999: Boeing 747 freighter service to the United States and Dubai begins.
2002: SEA is repositioned as a low-fare carrier.
2004: Passenger count rises 36 percent in spite of a difficult aviation environment.

a dozen Boeing 737s. About 1.8 million people few the airline in 2004, a 36 percent improvement over the previous year, in spite of a difficult environment that saw several bankruptcies in the world's aviation industry.

Sterling European was in discussions with several small low-price airlines over the possibility of creating an international alliance to compete with the majors. The company began cooperating with Norway Airlines on several European routes beginning in February 2005. Together, they were able to increase flight frequency to up to 12 flights a day on the vital Copenhagen-Oslo route. Sterling European was continuing to expand in 2005, adding new destinations such as Edinburgh, Scotland, and Montpellier, France.

Principal Competitors

Maersk Air A/S; flynordic; Ryanair Holdings plc; Snowflake.

Further Reading

"Air Fares; Sterling Work," *Economist*, February 11, 1978, p. 58.
Barnes, Hilary, "Danes Spark Row on Scandinavian Air Traffic Rights," *Financial Times* (London), August 27, 1987, p. 4.
——, "Sterling Airways Sold Off," *Financial Times* (London), March 11, 1988, p. 26.
Barrett, Frank, "Obituary: Eilif Krogager," *Independent* (London), January 10, 1992, p. 13.
"Cargo Airline Sterling European Opts for Internet," *Reuters News*, July 30, 1999.
"Cheap Airfares: Coming in on a Wing and a Prayer," *Economist*, October 27, 1979, p. 73.
"Conair and Sterling Airways Are to Merge," *Børsen*, August 7, 1990, p. 1.
Cooper, Richard, "Sterling European Signs for 737—Reluctant to Go for Airbus," *Airclaims*, June 26, 1997.
Hailey, Roger, "Sterling Cargo Fills Gap in Northern Europe Airfreight Market," *Lloyd's List*, August 16, 1999, p. 6.
Jensen, Karin, "Budget Airlines Alliance a Possibility Long Term; Might Threaten SAS," *AFX.COM*, September 25, 2003.
Kj, Max, "Sterling Lines up New 737 Fleet," *Flight International*, July 16, 1997, p. 10.
"Pastor Eilif Krogager," *Times* (London), January 10, 1992.
Shifrin, Carole A., "Scandinavian Carriers Form Alliance to Exploit Post-1992 Marketplace," *Aviation Week & Space Technology*, September 30, 1991, p. 38.
"Sterling Airways' Airline Division to Become Separate Company," *Børsen*, December 31, 1993, p. 3.
"Sterling Airways Could Continue Operating Until 1999—Administrator," *Børsen*, June 20, 1994, p. 2.
"Sterling Airways Has Published Its Final Results for 1988/89," *Textline Multiple Source Collection (1980–1994)*, September 2, 1989.
"Sterling Airways Sells Airline Unit," *Børsen*, January 11, 1995, p. 2.
"Sterling European Airlines Achieves 1994 Year-End Surplus," *Børsen*, July 3, 1995, p. 7.
"Tjaereborg Fonden of Denmark Has Sold Sterling Airways and Its Aero Chef Subsidiaries to Mr Ejnar Lundt, the Managing Director of Sterling Airways," *Textline Multiple Source Collection (1980–1994)*, November 20, 1987.
"TUI in Talks to Buy Danish Airline Sterling European Airways—Sources," *AFX European Focus*, September 3, 2003.
"TUI No Longer Interested in Danish Budget Airline Sterling," *Agence France Presse*, November 12, 2003.

—Frederick C. Ingram

Stratagene Corporation

11011 North Torrey Pines Road
La Jolla, California 92037
U.S.A.
Telephone: (858) 535-5400
Fax: (858) 535-0071
Web site: http://www.stratagene.com

Public Company
Incorporated: 1984 as Stratagene Holding Corp.
Employees: 334
Sales: $69.7 million (2003)
Stock Exchange: NASDAQ
Ticker Symbol: STGN
NAIC: 334516 Analytical Laboratory Instrument
Manufacturing; 511210 Software Publishers

Stratagene Corporation is a developer, manufacturer, and marketer of specialized life science research and diagnostic products, including reagents, kits, cell-derived products, nucleic acid purification and analysis products, and gene-sequencing software and analysis tools. Stratagene's life sciences research division supports advances in science by inventing, manufacturing, and distributing products that simplify, accelerate, and improve research. These products are designed for academic, industrial, and government research applications in fields spanning molecular biology, genomics, proteomics, drug discovery, and toxicology. The company's diagnostic division develops and manufactures products for urinalysis as well as advanced automated instrument and reagent systems that use blood samples to test for more than 1,000 different allergies and autoimmune disorders. By combining its expertise in diagnostics and molecular biology, Stratagene Corporation pursues opportunities to expand its range of products to include molecular diagnostics kits and instrumentation.

Origins

Founded in 1984, Stratagene became the first company to develop and commercialize a new technology that promised to replace standard monoclonal antibody technology. Anticipated to have a significant effect on the pharmaceutical industry, the new technology enabled researchers to produce monoclonal antibodies inexpensively, in less time, and without the sacrifice of thousands of animals. The technology used recombinant DNA in bacterium E. coli to create collections of millions of distinct monoclonal antibodies, which were screened to uncover monoclonals with the greatest potential for important diagnostic and therapeutic uses. The new bacterial technology allowed researchers to produce pure human antibodies, replacing reliance on foreign animal protein that could elicit a more dangerous immune response.

The technology was invented by Dr. Richard A. Lerner of the Research Institute at Scripps Clinic and Dr. Joseph Sorge, founder of Stratagene. Sorge earned his B.S. degree in biology and chemistry at the Massachusetts Institute of Technology and an M.D. degree at Harvard Medical School. He received postdoctoral training in molecular biology at Cold-Spring Harbor Laboratories, was an assistant member at the Scripps Research Institute, and was an adjunct member of Scripps Clinic and Research Foundation. As a result of the Lerner and Sorge breakthrough, Stratagene formed a subsidiary in 1989 called Stratacyte Corporation to commercialize, license, and pursue applications for the new technology. Stratacyte intended to apply the technology to the development of therapeutic agents for cancer, autoimmune and infectious diseases, the refinement of diagnostic tests, and the development of enzymes for medical and industrial processes.

New Products in the Early 1990s

In March 1992, the company settled litigation with the biotechnology firm Ixsys, Inc. and its vice-president and chief scientific officer, Dr. William D. Huse, a former scientist at Stratagene. The litigation involved ownership rights over the newly developed method of creating recombinatorial libraries of monoclonal anti-bodies, the so-called "magic bullet" of the immune system. Under the terms of the settlement, the parties agreed that the two companies, together with the Scripps Research Clinic, could freely pursue this technology on their own. In addition, Stratagene granted to Ixsys a non-exclusive license

303

under the patents governing the recombinant antibody technology. In return, Ixsys agreed to pay Stratagene royalties on any revenues received under the license.

In May 1993, Stratagene and GenPharm International Inc. of Mountain View, California, announced the development of a new transgenic mouse for mutagenesis and tumorigenesis research. The ''new'' transgenic mouse provided flexibility and new opportunities for study in the fields of toxicology, molecular biology, and medicine, enabling scientists for the first time to discern the relationship between DNA frequency and the development of tumors within the same animal model. It was also another achievement for a worldwide biotechnology company that had developed over 1,000 gene characterization and transfer products and instruments for laboratory research in the fields of molecular biology, biochemistry, cell biology, immunology, and biomedical science. This development was one of many that represented a fundamental shift away from conventional studies to the use of transgenic animals as models to investigate disease processes, develop new therapeutic drugs, and screen toxic and mutagenic substances. The use of animal models carried the enormous benefit of being low risk in a market that was anticipated to grow well into the next century.

In May 1995, Stratagene and the Perkin-Elmer Corporation signed an agreement authorizing Stratagene's RoboCycler temperature cyclers to be used in the patented polymerase chain reaction (PCR) process. Under the agreement, Stratagene became Perkin-Elmer's first U.S. supplier of thermal cyclers, which were used in the PCR process with authorized reagents (enzymes), including Stratagene's Taq, TaqPlus, and Pfu DNA polymerases. In June 1998, Stratagene also entered into an exclusive distribution agreement with Lexicon Genetics Incorporated. The agreement provided that Stratagene distribute Lexicon's 50-plus gene targeting products in the Americas, Europe, and Asia.

Stratagene Reorganizes and Extends Global Reach

In the late 1990s, Stratagene initiated major organizational changes to better coordinate research and development, improve and expand manufacturing capabilities, and more efficiently allocate sales and marketing resources. Beginning in 1997, the company significantly increased recruitment of experienced sales representatives for its domestic and overseas sales territories. Stratagene also reorganized its European operations by establishing a centralized office in the Netherlands and expanding its direct sales efforts. In 1998, the company began

moving its storage and shipping operations, and most of its production and customer service operations from La Jolla, California, to a new facility in Austin, Texas. The move to Austin, completed in 1999, was made because of the quality of the labor pool in the area. Stratagene also significantly increased funding in research and development. This was done primarily to develop new capabilities and products in the areas of nucleic acid purification and analysis and genomics and bioinformatics.

In 1997, Stratagene began pursuing the discovery and cataloging of unique single nucleotide polymorphisms. Because this field represented a departure from its core business, Stratagene formed a new company, Phenogenex, to pursue research and development opportunities in this area. When it became clear that other firms with greater resources were entering the field, however, Stratagene discontinued the project in 1999.

In June 1999, Cambridge Antibody Technology (CAT) announced that it signed a settlement agreement with Stratagene and the Scripps Research Institute concerning interference with patent applications in the United States owned by the Medical Research Council (MRC). The parties agreed the patent applications would be co-owned by the MRC, Scripps, and Stratagene. In addition, the parties agreed that CAT would be the sole exploiter of all the parties' intellectual property rights under the various patent applications, subject to certain rights reserved by the MRC, Scripps, and Stratagene and their pre-existing licensees. The settlement also provided that CAT pay $1.25 million to Stratagene and Scripps.

In July 2000, Stratagene signed a strategic licensing agreement for worldwide exclusive rights to sell Avigen, Inc.'s kits for making recombinant adeno-associated virus (AVV) vectors for research purposes. As a global leader in the discovering, engineering, and supplying of biotechnology research reagents and with a direct sales force in the United States and a network of independent distributors worldwide, Stratagene was well positioned to market Avigen's technology. In November 2000, Stratagene also considered going public but abruptly withdrew due to pronounced declines in the stock market. Stratagene became a casualty of the nation's ailing IPO market that only months earlier had been flooded with over priced initial public offerings, some of dubious value. With the beginnings of the stock market decline in 2000, technology investors fled pricey internet stocks, some into biotechs, causing an enormous run up in their share prices. In 2000, biotechnology companies raised approximately $36 billion compared to $7.7 billion in 1999. In addition, between October 1999 and September 2000, 55 biotech companies raised $5.5 billion alone through IPOs. By late fall of 2000, however, the IPO market was vanishing along with the fortunes of the stock market.

Nonetheless, by 2000 the company was marketing its products in 45 countries worldwide. Stratagene sold its products directly to customers in the United States, Canada, Germany, France, the United Kingdom, and 14 other countries. In addition, the company used specialized distributors in more than 25 other countries. Stratagene's customers included most of the major pharmaceutical and biotechnology companies, such as Merck, Pfizer, Amgen, and Genentech. The company also served leading academic research laboratories, including Harvard University, Stanford University, and the University of

Key Dates:

1984: Stratagene Holding Corporation is founded by Dr. Joseph Sorge.
1989: The company forms Stratacyte as a subsidiary to pursue new bacterial technology.
1992: The company settles litigation with Ixsys, Inc.
1993: Stratagene and GenPharm International announce the development of new transgenic mouse.
2000: The company withdraws its initial public offering.
2003: Stratagene signs a merger agreement with Hycor Biomedical, Inc.
2004: Stratagene acquires the assets of BioCrest Holding.

California system. In addition, Stratagene continued to develop new products, including its Mx4000 multiplex quantitative PCR instrument system, which was introduced in February 2001. The Mx4000 system was designed to create a new standard for genotyping and gene expression analysis in the rapidly developing field of genomics.

In June 2000, Stratagene was sued in U.S. District Court by Invitrogen Corporation, which alleged infringement on one of its patent claims concerning R Nase H minus reverse transcriptase enzymes. Invitrogen's motion for a preliminary motion was denied, and the case was stayed pending trial in a related action involving Invitrogen and a third party concerning the same patents. Invitrogen appealed the denial of an injunction and the stay to the Federal Circuit Court of Appeals. In February 2002, the Court of Appeals upheld the district court's decision. In March 2001, Invitrogen also sued Stratagene for patent infringement related to the making, using, and selling competent *e.coli* cell products, but the courts found in favor of Stratagene.

Company Looks to Future Growth

In July 2003, Stratagene and Hycor Biomedical Inc. of Garden Grove, California, a developer, manufacturer, and marketer of clinical diagnostic instrument systems and reagents, announced the signing of a definitive merger agreement. With the acquisition of Hycor, concluded in June 2004, the company offered diagnostic products and life sciences research tool products to the international academic, pharmaceutical, clinical, and government laboratory markets. The agreement provided for Hycor to operate as a wholly owned subsidiary of the new company. In the stock-for-stock transaction, shareholders of Hycor received 0.6158 of a share of Stratagene Corp. for each share of Hycor Biomedical. By acquiring the publicly traded Hycor, the company became a public company with 21.9 million common shares outstanding and changed its name to Stratagene Corporation in September 2004.

Upon closing the Hycor deal, Stratagene acquired all the assets of BioCrest Holding (BCH), a limited liability company that was treated as a partnership for income tax purposes. In exchange, Stratagene forgave all of the outstanding intercompany indebtedness owed by BCH and its subsidiaries to Stratagene of approximately $5.5 million. As part of the acquisition, Stratagene acquired BCH's interests in its subsidiaries,

which included Phenogenex, LLC, Iobion Informatics, LLC, and an investment in a joint venture consisting of a 49 percent interest in a limited partnership that operated a research lab. As a result of the acquisition, Stratagene owned 100 percent of Phengenex and about 78 percent of Iobion

In September and November 2004, Stratagene was sued by Third Wave Technologies, Inc. and Applera Corporation in separate actions. Third Wave's suit claimed patent infringement concerning its invasive cleavage structure chemistry used to analyze nucleic acid, the foundation of genetic materials and infectious agents. As a result, Third Wave sought a court order that would block the sale of certain Stratagenc products. Applera's suit alleged patent infringement covering instruments for the performance of real-time PCR, including Stratagene's Mx4000 and Mc3000P instruments and certain related reagents. Aside from the specifics of each case, the lawsuits represented a highly competitive environment in which rapid technological change and frequent new product introductions were typical. Stratagene looked to its future knowing that sustaining its success would depend on continuous, timely development of new products that addressed evolving markets in the life sciences field. Many of Stratagene's competitors possessed greater financial, operational, and sales and marketing resources as well as more research and development experience. Nonetheless, Stratagene had a record of innovation and seemed well positioned to capitalize on future opportunities.

Principal Subsidiaries

Hycor Biomedical Inc.

Principal Competitors

Applied Biosystems Broup; Bio-Rad Laboratories Inc.; Qiagen N.V.

Further Reading

Crabtree, Penni, ''Tepid Market Sours Elitra; S.D. Biotech Files to Cancel $86 Million IPO,'' San Diego Union-Tribune, *November 22, 2000.*
''Dr. Huse and Ixsys Win Appeal Dismissing Stratagene's Suit against Them,'' PR Newswire, *May 22, 1991.*
''Gertzen, Jason, ''Madison, Wis.-based Biotechnology Firm Files Suit Against California Company,'' Milwaukee Journal Sentinel, *September 16, 2004.*
''Hycor and Stratagene Announce Definitive Merger Agreement,'' Business Wire, *July 24, 2003.*
''Hycor and Stratagene Complete Merger,'' Business Wire, *June 2, 2004.*
''Invitrogen Patent Limited by Court; Stratagene Files Counterclaims,'' Business Wire, *September 24, 2001*
''Lexicon Signs Exclusive Distribution Agreements with Stratagene and Takara Shuzo Co., Ltd. for Gene Targeting Reagents, Business Wire, *June 11, 1998.*
''Perkin-Elmer Authorizes Use of Stratagene RoboCycler Temperature Cyclers in PCR Process,'' Business Wire, *May 2, 1995.*
Somers, Terri, ''La Jolla, Calif-Based Firm Acquires Hycor Biomedical, Goes Public,'' San Diego Union-Tribune, *June 3, 2004.*
——, ''Merger in Works for Stratagene, Hycor Biomedical,'' San Diego Union-Tribune, *July 26, 2003.*
''Stratacyte Succeed in Producing Human Anti-Body Fragments in Bacteria,'' Business Wire, *October 14, 1990.*

''Stratagene and Ixsys Announce Settlement of Technology Litigation,'' PR News, *March 24, 1992.*

''Stratagene Announces Invitrogen's Reverse Transcriptase Patent Severely Limited,'' Business Wire, *October 23, 2001.*

''Stratagene Announces Launch of Mx4000 Multiplex Quantitative PCR System,'' PR Newswire, *February 21, 2001*

''Stratagene Spinoff to Commercialize Third-Generation Monoclonal Anti-Bodies,'' Business Wire, *December 8, 1989.*

''Texas Court Holds That Stratagene's Competent Cell Products Do Not Infringe Invitrogen Patent,'' Business Wire, *November 8, 2001.*

''Third Wave Files Patent Infringement Suit against Stratagene,'' PR Newswire, *September 15, 2004.*

—Bruce P. Montgomery

SWH Corporation

17852 17th Street
South Building, Suite 108
Tustin, California 92780-2142
U.S.A.
Telephone: (714) 544-4826
Toll Free: (866) 566-4647
Fax: (714) 544-7663
Web site: http:www.mimiscafe.com

Wholly Owned Subsidiary of Bob Evans Farms Inc.
Founded: *1978*
Employees: *7,695*
Sales: *$240.5 million (2003)*
NAIC: 722110 Full-Service Restaurants

A subsidiary of Bob Evans Farms Inc., SWH Corporation is a Tustin, California-based company that operates the Mimi's Café chain of more than 90 full-service restaurants. Mimi's Café combines a New Orleans-style French bistro with a family-friendly casual-dining concept. Although units are found in 13 states, spread from the West Coast to Florida, most Mimi's Cafés are found in California, where the first restaurant opened in 1978. Mimi Café has rarely spent money on advertising or promotions, preferring instead to devote resources to offering quality food and relying on repeat business and strong word of mouth. The restaurants, opened for breakfast, lunch, and dinner, feature a menu of some 100 items, with an emphasis on such American fare as meat loaf, pot roast, pork chops, pot pies, and hamburgers. Steaks and pastas are also available, as well as some Creole-inspired dishes. In addition, the chain offers a lengthy children's menu, while also serving beer and wine.

Origins in the 1940s

SWH was founded by Arthur J. Simms and his son, Thomas Simms. The elder Simms served as a bombardier and navigator in the European theater during World War II. After the war, he became involved in the restaurant business, an area in which he had some familiarity. His own father ran small hotels and cafés in Chicago during the 1920s and 1930s. Simms moved to Los Angeles, where he ran the commissary at MGM Studios. A dashing and somewhat flamboyant man given to wearing pink sport coats, Simms was well suited for Hollywood. He opened his first restaurant in 1952 with partner Bob Ehrman, a coffee shop called Ben Frank's which would form the basis of SWH. Two more Ben Frank's would open in the Los Angeles area, and Simms also ran another coffee shop chain called the Wooden Shoes. Thomas Simms had no intention of following his father into the restaurant business. Rather, he earned an aeronautical engineering degree from the University of California at Santa Barbara in 1970. However, he graduated during poor economic conditions, and, unable to find an engineering job, he opted to join his father. Among their ventures was a sidewalk café called the French Quarter, which they opened in West Hollywood in 1974. Two years later, SWH acquired an upscale coffee shop, The Kettle, located in Manhattan Beach. Unfortunately for the father-son enterprise, the prosperous days for coffee shops were beginning to fade, primarily due to higher rents that resulted in the need for a higher level of sales.

Arthur and Tom Simms, along with partners Brian Taylor and Paul Kurz, recognized that there was an opening in the market for a restaurant that was part coffee shop and part dinner house, combining the atmosphere of the latter with the value of the former, a niche that would one day be classified as casual dining. They turned to their French Quarter restaurant as a starting point for creating an eatery that essentially Americanized the European café. For a name they chose Mimi's Café. According to company lore, Mimi was a French woman Arthur Simms met during World War II. Purportedly, he flew dangerous spy missions over occupied France, but near the end of the war he was on the ground with the troops liberating a small French town. Here Simms met Mimi, with whom he had a one-night love affair. Although they would never see each other again, he would never forget her, and naming the new restaurant after her was a tribute to their short-lived romance. In 1996, a reporter for the *Orange County Register* asked Simms about the tale: "He looked surprised, whistled twice like a parrot, waggled his white eyebrows. 'That's press stuff.'" He explained that while he was serving as a bombardier and navigator, hardly a spy, he was in France in 1944 because his plane had delivered a general there. At a hotel party in a newly liberated French town, he did have an affair with a woman named Mimi, but it was far from an all-consuming romance. ''I had girls in London, too!'' he said, ''I had a girl in Chicago.'' As for paying homage to Mimi by naming the new restaurant after her, Simms recalled telling his son, '' 'What're we gonna call it, Mimi's or Gigi's?' Flipped a coin and it was Mimi's.''

Mimi's Café Launched in the Late 1970s

The first Mimi's Café opened in December 1978 in Anaheim, California, near Disneyland. The restaurant was a major success, leading SWH to open a second Mimi's Café in 1981 in Garden Grove, California, followed by others in 1982 and 1983. The company then accelerated the pace for the next several years, opening a new Mimi's Café every eight months. By 1989, SWH had 11 of the restaurants in Southern California generating close to $30 million in revenues. The company also continued to operate Ben Franks, French Quarter, and The Kettle, which combined accounted for another $8 million in sales. There was no desire to franchise the concept of Mimi's Café, the partners preferring instead to maintain tight control. Because Mimi's Café was not an easy concept to execute, in the early 1990s SWH implemented a training program called Mimi's University. The five-day program of lectures, books, and exams was geared toward new front-of-the-house employees. Not only did the program instill the chain's philosophy and provide detailed information about the menu and how dishes were prepared, it served to weed out people who were not likely to fit in with the culture. As a result, Mimi's Café dramatically decreased its staff turnover rate.

Mimi's Café reached 16 units in 1993, at which point SWH decided to accelerate the pace of expansion. The company took on debt and opened another five restaurants over the next two years. During this period, SWH also began to update its decor. When the chain was founded, marketing studies showed that women were the key decision makers on where to dine, and, in keeping with these findings, Mimi's Café featured a lot of pastel colors, which also worked well in the high-density areas where the early units operated. However, as the chain expanded into suburban and rural markets, the color scheme no longer worked as well, especially with men. As a result, the chain went for a mainstream look, opting for more earth tones and primary color accents. Pink tablecloths and floral curtains were now replaced with green-and-white checked tablecloths and white curtains featuring stripes of primary colors. The chain also went for an even more rustic exterior look.

With an accelerated expansion pace came a need to move beyond the Southern California market, where finding appropriate real estate became more difficult. SWH first looked to

Arizona, opening a restaurant in Scottsdale, then made plans to open a Mimi's Café in northern California, in San Jose. By this stage, at the end of 1995, the Mimi's Café chain was posting sales of about $50 million. SWH began harboring plans to spread the concept even further, perhaps taking it nationally, but such aspirations required help. In 1996, SWH found a partner in Saundera Karp & Megrue, a Stamford, Connecticut-based private merchant bank that had previously owned the Marie Callender's chain and other restaurant companies and was known to take a supportive, yet hands-off approach with its assets. SKM bought about 65 percent of SWH, allowing the elder Simms, Kurz, and Taylor to cash out. Thomas Simms, on the other hand, retained his 35 percent stake and continued to run the operation.

Over the next five years, the Mimi's Café chain more than doubled in size, entering 2001 with 49 stores, as sales topped $141 million. In addition to entering the northern California market, the chain spread to Nevada, Texas, and Colorado. In targeting new markets, SWH looked for family-oriented suburban areas with a high density of 35- to 64-year olds, markets where the company could potentially build a cluster of restaurants. Management continued to eschew the idea of franchising, instead securing partners with extensive restaurant experience in the area who were given incentives for growing the business.

New Owners and New Leadership in the 2000s

In October 2000, Arthur Simms died at the age of 82, marking the end of an era. By this point, his son Thomas was reaching the limit of his ability to manage a chain exceeding 50 units with national aspirations. Simms told *Nation's Restaurant News* in 2003 that the business exceeded his operational expertise ''when the brand pushed into Texas in 1999, opening four restaurants in 13 months. 'Texas was my Waterloo,'' he admits, explaining, ''My capabilities ended when we got out of the Southwestern region.'' He now sought out the services of an executive able to take the Mimi's Café chain to the next level. In 2001, he recruited and hired Russ Bendel to serve as president and chief executive officer, while he stayed on as chairman of the board.

Bendel first worked in restaurants when he was just 15. A native of Philadelphia, Pennsylvania, he earned a degree in accounting from Florida International University and gave that field a try before deciding to return to the food service industry. He moved back to the North, where he became a manager at the Copper Door restaurant in Rockville, Maryland, and then for four years managed several restaurants in Philadelphia owned by an investment group. Next, he spent 12 years working for Marriott Corporation, becoming involved in a number of acquisitions and mergers and gaining a nationwide familiarity with the restaurant industry. After W.R. Grace Company acquired Marriott, he took a position with one of the owner's restaurant operations, in 1991 becoming vice-president of operations for El Torito Restaurants in Southern California. Bendel was then recruited by Outback Steakhouse in 1995 and helped the chain to establish a presence in the Southern California market. He next became involved in a joint venture between Outback and Roy's Restaurants in Hawaii, working in that capacity from 1999 to 2001. At this point, a former colleague at El Torito, Ed Bartholemy, who had become the chief financial officer for

SWH, suggested that Simms meet with Bendel. The two men hit it off and Bendel was hired to shepherd Mimi's Café throughout he next stage of its development.

When Bendel took over in June 2001, the Mimi's Café chain numbered 53 units. Over the next three years, the company added another 27 units, moving into such new markets as Kansas City and St. Louis, Missouri; Tampa, Florida; Salt Lake City, Utah; Oklahoma City and Tulsa, Oklahoma; Albuquerque, New Mexico; and Colorado Springs, Colorado. For 2003, revenues grew to $240.5 million. To achieve this growth, SWH had to take on debt, which by 2004 had grown to more than $75 million. In May 2004, the company filed papers with the Securities and Exchange Commission to make an initial public offering of stock in the hopes of raising $85 million to pay down its debt. Piper Jaffray, CIBC World Markets, and Banc of America Securities were set to underwrite the offering, but it was not to be conducted.

In July 2004, SWH was sold to Columbus, Ohio-based Bob Evans Farms for $182 million, a price which included the assumption of the company's debt. The deal was considered a surprise development, but in truth Bob Evans' CEO, Stewart Owens, had been talking to Thomas Simms for three years. For Bob Evans, acquiring the Mimi's Café chain made sense because it occupied a different place in the market from that of the Bob Evans chain, plus it offered a unique concept that promised to be a strong growth vehicle while also being a good cultural fit. From the point of view of SWH, the sale to Bob Evans provided it with a deep-pocketed partner with a solid infrastructure, and it avoided the requirements and pressures that came with being a public company. The company would also be allowed to operate as an independent operation. Moreover, Mimi's Café's national aspirations were well served by its connection to Bob Evans, which was already operating in markets that the chain wanted to enter, in particular the eastern part of the country. In early 2005, the first Ohio unit opened. All told, the chain planed to open 15 restaurants in 2005.

Mimi's Café had achieved consistent growth for more than 25 years without the benefit of regular advertising. That situation was likely to change as the chain entered the next stage of its development as a subsidiary of Bob Evans. In December 2004, SWH hired Lowell Petrie to serve as its vice-president of marketing. Petrie had enjoyed tremendous success in raising the profile of the Denny's restaurant chain, which previously had been seen as little more than a breakfast joint. His immediate task at Mimi's Café, on the other hand, was to boost the breakfast business. Overall, he was likely to serve an essential role in building brand awareness for Mimi's Café as the chain entered new markets and continued to pursue its greater ambitions.

Principal Competitors

Applebee's International, Inc.; Brinker International, Inc.; Darden Restaurants, Inc.

Further Reading

Balmain, Melissa, ''Man Behind Mimi's Has Taste for Life,'' *Orange County Register*, March 18, 1996, p. B1.

Bellantonio, Jennifer, ''Mimi's Café Rides French Wave to Growth,'' *Orange County Business Journal*, November 17–November 23, 2003, p. 1.

Bernstein, Charles, ''Family Business: Tom Simms Has Raised Mimi's From a Small Restaurant into a Growing Force in Casual Dining,'' *Chain Leader*, September 2003, p. 58.

Berta, Dina, ''Unique Mimi's Café Dinnerhouse Chain Poised for National Growth,'' *Nation's Restaurant News*, August 20, 2001, p. 32.

Doss, Lori, ''Regional Powerhouse Chains: Mimi's Café,'' *Nation's Restaurant News*, January 28, 2002, p. 132.

Rogers, Monica, ''From-Scratch Success,'' *Chain Leader*, September 2001, p. 39.

Spector, Amy, ''Russ Bendel,'' *Nation's Restaurant News*, September 22, 2003, p. 54.

—Ed Dinger

Swissport International Ltd.

Zuerich-Flughafen, 8058
Switzerland
Telephone: (+41) 812 4950
Fax: (+41) 811 1001
Web site: http://www.swissport.com

Private Company
Incorporated: 1996
Employees: 22,000
Sales: CHF 1.17 billion ($950 million) (2003)
NAIC: 488119 Other Airport Operations; 488190 Other
    Support Activities for Air Transportation; 488510
    Freight Transportation Arrangement; 541614 Process,
    Physical Distribution, and Logistics Consulting
    Services; 551112 Offices of Other Holding Companies

Swissport International Ltd. is the world's largest ground handling company. It boasts operations at 170 stations in 34 countries, and handles three million tons of cargo a year. Swissport's activities encompass everything an airline needs on the ground to move passengers and cargo efficiently and safely. The company also performs such services as line maintenance, aircraft cleaning, and fueling. Swissport began as the ground handling operations of Swissair AG and became an independent company in 1996. It underwent a management buyout in 2002 as Swissair underwent bankruptcy. Swissair's successor, Swiss International Air Lines Ltd. (SWISS), is the company's largest client.

Origins

Swissport International Limited became an independent company in 1996. Formerly known as Swissair Ground Services, the operation had provided ground handling for Swissair AG since the mid-1950s.

Swissport immediate set out upon global expansion, creating international subsidiaries and joint ventures. In January 1997, the company acquired a 40 percent holding in Munich Airport's Airport Services Muenchen GmbH unit and began providing ground services at London Heathrow Airport. By the end of the

year, Swissport's operations had spread to Israel, Brazil, Puerto Rico, and Kenya.

Revenues were CHF 420 million in 1997. Swissport had 3,000 employees at the time and operations at just three stations. In the late 1990s, operations were expanded to South Africa, Turkey, France, the Netherlands, the Philippines, Peru, and the United States.

In 1999, Swissport acquired the ground handling operations of Aer Lingus at London's Heathrow Airport. About the same time, the European Union required airports to open up their ground handling activities to competition, clearing the way for regional expansion.

World's Largest in 1999

Another acquisition, in the United States, boosted Swissport's employment to 15,000 people and made it the world's largest ground handler. The company paid about $155 million (CHF 240 million) to buy DynAir Holdings Inc. from Alpha Airports Group Plc of the U.K. in July 1999. DynAir operated at 55 U.S. airport stations.

Revenues exceeded CHF 1 billion in 2000, when there were 17,000 employees working for Swissport. The number of stations served was up to 127, as the company opened, acquired, or bought into units in Greece, Spain, Mexico, Saudi Arabia, Tanzania, Argentina, and the Dominican Republic. The company operated in 22 countries altogether. Swissport posted an operating result of CHF 84 million for the year.

London investment firm Candover Partners Limited acquired a controlling interest in Swissport in 2002. Candover paid CHF 580 million for its 85 percent holding. Previous owner SAir Group was then in bankruptcy, having folded within weeks of the September 11, 2001 attacks on the United States. (*Ground Handling International*'s October 2003 issue featured a detailed discussion of the deal with Charlie Green, a director of Candover Partners who helped oversee the management buyout.) Established in 1980, Candover had backed over 100 companies but this was its first investment in the ground handling business.

During 2002, subsidiaries in the Netherlands and Puerto Rico were shut down, while Swissport opened units in Honduras and acquired Benelux handlers Cargo Service Center BV and CS-Lux. Cargo Service Center, formerly owned by D Logistics AG of Germany, operated at 61 stations in 15 countries and had annual revenues of about CHF 200 million. The CS-Lux buy brought Swissport into Luxembourg, an important cargo hub, where it competed with the handling operations of freight carrier Luxair.

The year 2003 saw the opening of units in Uruguay and India. Swissport also took over the Geneva operations of Cargologic and entered the PrivatPort joint venture with PrivatAir. PrivatPort, based in Geneva, offered ground handling, catering, and VIP services for executive jets. This market was expected to grow due to the inconvenience to passengers of airline security measures.

Swissport also acquired a majority stake in the new Unitpool container venture. Unitpool, based in Zurich, was a world-leading supplier of shipping containers for air cargo.

Swiss International Air Lines Ltd. (SWISS) was the company's largest client, and in June 2003 Swissport announced it was cutting about 350 jobs at its three bases in Switzerland due to downsizing at SWISS. Swissport had employed about 3,000 people at airports in Zurich, Basel and Geneva. Revenues were up to CHF 1.2 billion ($950 million) in 2003, when Swissport employed about 20,000 people. Operating result was CHF 93 million.

New Frontiers in 2004 and Beyond

Zurich-based Protectas Aviation Security Ltd. was acquired in early 2004. It had operations in Switzerland and Africa and 240 employees providing security for about two-dozen airlines. Security was seen as an important growth market after the September 11, 2001 terrorist attacks.

In 2004, Swissport also acquired Groundstar Ltd. from rival 3i Group. Groundstar, which had 2,000 employees, offered ground handling at five U.K. airports beyond Swissport's grand handling operation at Heathrow and cargo facility in Manchester.

Swissport had led a wave of industry consolidation. It was also pioneering new ways of working with clients. A new five-year global cooperation agreement with KLM Royal Dutch Airlines was seen as the way of the future between ground handlers and carriers.

Swissport streamlined its regional divisions from five to three in April 2004. The company was focusing on the fast-

growing Asian market. The company won a ten-year license to become Changi Airport's third ground handler beginning in July 2005.

Swissport shut down its subsidiary at London's Heathrow Airport in November 2004 after several years of losses. The operations at five other U.K. airports were not affected.

Swissport broadened its range of ground services offerings in Zurich and Geneva by acquiring aircraft moving and de-icing services from SR Technics. Swissport, which was aiming to be a single-source ground services supplier for airlines, expected to derive considerable synergies from the new tasks. Swissport was also opening its first fueling operation outside the United States, at Newcastle International Airport.

Swissport sought to streamline the frustrating airport check-in experience through its new "Secure Check" system developed with ICTS International N.V. Secure Check began a trial run at Zurich Airport in December 2004.

In January 2005, Swissport announced it was divesting its operations at France's Toulouse and Nice airports to MAP-Handling. Swissport held on to its stations at Paris Charles de Gaulle and several other French airports.

Swissport was reentering freight handling operations at Amsterdam's Schiphol Airport in March 2005. Schiphol was Europe's third largest air cargo hub. Swissport's earlier joint venture there had closed in 1999. Swissport was also expanding capacity at its other Benelux stations.

Another part of Swissport's plans was a potential initial public offering in 2005. The company seemed positioned to do well. Analysis in the trade publication *Airline Business* suggested that carriers would continue to outsource aviation services in order to focus on customer management issues.

Principal Subsidiaries

Checkport Schweiz AG; Dar es Salaam Airport Handling Company Ltd. (DAHACO) (Tanzania; 51%); Havas Havaalanlari Yer Hizmetleri AS (Turkey; 40%); PrivatPort (joint venture with PrivatAir); Q.A.S. Quality Airport Services Israel Ltd. (50%); S. Stuttgart Ground Services (joint venture with Stuttgart Airport); Swissport Baggage Sorting AG; Swissport Dominicana SA (34%); Swissport GBH Peru SA (49%); Swissport Hellas SA (Greece; 50%); Swissport USA, Inc.; Unitpool.

Principal Divisions

Division Americas; Division Asia/Africa; Middle East & Cargo; Division Europe.

Principal Operating Units

SCS (Swissport Cargo Services); SEA (Swissport Executive Aviation); SFS (Swissport Fueling Services); SMS (Swissport Maintenance Services).

Principal Competitors

GlobeGround GmbH; Menzies Aviation Group; Servisair plc; Worldwide Flight Services, Inc.

Further Reading

Bulkeley, Andrew, "Swissport to List Shares," *Daily Deal*, September 1, 2004.

"Changes to Top Management At Swissport International," *Hugin*, February 24, 2004.

"Candover in Swissair Talks," *European Venture Capital Journal*, September 2001, p. 83.

Done, Kevin, "Swissport Cuts 750 Jobs in Heathrow Shutdown," *Financial Times* (London), November 17, 2004, p. 2.

Edwin, Wilfred, "Gov't Offloads Its DAHACO Shares," *All Africa*, April 11, 2003.

Gill, Tom, "Ground Handling Goes Acquisition Crazy," *Airline Business*, August 31, 1999, p. 11.

"Huge Interest as Swissair's Parent Starts Big Sell-Off," *Evening Standard*, March 26, 2001.

"In or Out? When Swissport's Management Wanted to Realise a Dream They Approached an Equity Investor for Help," *Ground Handling International*, October 2003, pp. 44ff.

Mathew, James and M. Ahmed, "Swissport May Take over Cambata Aviation," *Business Standard* (India), January 16, 1999, p. 11.

O'Toole, Kevin, "The New Leaders in Handling: Ground Handling Is Developing a Higher Profile in the Industry, Attracting a New Style of Leadership," *Airline Business*, January 2000, p. 78.

Paisner, Guy, "Candover Moves to Reassure as Swissport Heathrow Collapses," *eFinancialNews.com*, November 16, 2004.

"SAirGroup Unit Expands in Africa, South America," *Neue Zuercher Zeitung*, June 15, 2000, p. 12.

"Schiphol Handling Company Dutchport to Close End January," *Reuters News*, December 5, 2001.

Sreenivasan, Ven, "Swissport Is Changi's Third Ground-Handler; It Beats Worldwide Flight and Will Start Ops in July 05," *Business Times Singapore*, June 30, 2004.

"Swissair Sister Company Eyeing Local Catering/Cruise Ship Services," *Caribbean Business*, November 13, 1997, p. 2.

"Swissport Acquires Groundstar Ltd. from 3i to Enhance Its Position in the UK Ground Handling Market," *Hugin*, April 8, 2004.

"Swissport Acquires Key Ground Services Functions from SR Technics at Zurich and Geneva Airports," *DPA-AFX*, November 19, 2004.

"Swissport Acquires Luxembourg-Based CS-Lux and Gains Access to One of Europe's Key Air Cargo Hubs," *Hugin*, October 15, 2002.

"Swissport Acquires Protectas Aviation Security Ltd. and Establishes Itself in the Global Airline and Airport Security Business," *Hugin*, February 9, 2004.

"Swissport and EDS Sign Long-Term Strategic Agreement," *Market News Publishing*, April 30, 2004.

"Swissport and KLM Conclude Multi-Year Worldwide Ground Handling Agreement," *Hugin*, April 1, 2004.

"Swissport and PrivatAir Co-Found Ground Handling Company in Geneva for Executive Private Jets and Lay Plans for a Global Cooperation," *Hugin*, May 6, 2003.

"Swissport Awaits Final Nod on DynAir," *Ground Handling International*, July 1999, p. 2.

"Swissport Buy-Out Completed," *International Financial Law Review*, March 1, 2002, p. 10.

"Swissport Chosen to Provide Fuelling Operations at Newcastle International Airport," *Europe Intelligence Wire*, November 18, 2004.

"Swissport Continues Global Push," *Airports International*, April 1, 2000, p. 17.

"Swissport International Ltd Continues to Grow (Weiterer Wachstumssprung Bei Swissport), *Neue Zurcher Zeitung*, November 23, 1999.

"Swissport Reports Interesting Business Developments In France and the UK," *Europe Intelligence Wire*, January 21, 2005.

"Swissport's Container Venture," *Ground Handling International*, October 2003, p. 68.

"Swissport to Merge German Ops with AHS," *Reuters News*, February 22, 2000.

Swissport to Start Cargo Operations st Amsterdam Airport, Gaining Access to Europe's Third-Biggest Airfreight Hub," *Hugin*, January 27, 2005.

"Trading Places: Management Buy-Outs Ultimately Look to Be Sold On; and Groundstar's Sale Has Come at a Propitious Moment, Reckons CEO Nigel Daniel," *Ground Handling International*, June 2004, pp. 48f.

Turpin, Andrew, "Menzies Stalking Swissport," *Scotsman* (Edinburgh), January 31, 2005, p. 2.

"Universal Teams with Swissport to Offer Ground Handling in France," *Weekly of Business Aviation*, January 8, 2001, p. 18.

—Frederick C. Ingram

Tacony Corporation

1760 Gilsinn Lane
Fenton, Missouri 63026-0730
U.S.A.
Telephone: (636) 349-3000
Fax: (636) 349-2333
Web site: http://www.tacony.com

Private Company
Founded: 1946
Employees: 500
Sales: $150 million (2003 est.)
NAIC: 335228 Other Household Appliance Manufacturing;
    335212 Household Vacuum Cleaner Manufacturing

Based in Fenton, Missouri, privately owned Tacony Corporation manufactures, imports, and sells sewing machines, vacuum cleaners, ceiling fans, janitorial equipment, and accessories. The company is comprised of more than a dozen divisions. The Amazing Designs Embroidery division offers 3-dimensional embroidery designs to hobbyists by way of CD, floppy disk, or memory card. Baby Lock USA Sewing Products manufactures and sells the popular Baby Lock line of sergers, sewing, and embroidery machines. Blakeman's Floor Care Parts & Equipment is a wholesaler of floor care equipment and parts. CFR Carpet Cleaning Machines manufactures commercial carpet cleaning equipment. Elna USA Sewing Products manufactures and retails home sewing machines and accessories. Industrial Sewing Products imports and distributes major brands of industrial sewing machines. Nancy's Notions is a sewing, quilting, and embroidery catalog company launched by Nancy Zieman, host of PBS's "Sewing With Nancy" television series. Origins Software provides the kind of software required by contemporary home embroiderers and is capable of making embroidery designs from any number of sources, including original art work. Tacony Sewing Central is a wholesaler of home and industrial sewing machine parts, as well as notions and accessories. Powr-Flite Commercial Floor Care Parts & Equipment manufactures and distributes vacuums, carpet dryers, floor machines, and other commercial janitorial equipment.

Regency Ceiling Fans designs and distributes high-end ceiling fans, ceiling fan lighting, and accessories. Riccard American Sewing & Vacuum Products manufactures high-end sewing machine and vacuum cleaners sold through its dealer network. Simplicity Sewing Machines serves the hobbyist market. Simplicity Vacuum Cleaners offers both canister and upright vacuum cleaners sold through independent retailers. Tacony's 103,000-square-foot headquarters includes a warehouse, sewing lab, and company training center. Tacony also maintains an in-house advertising and printing operation. The company is headed by Ken Tacony, the son of founder Nick Tacony.

Tacony Launched in Postwar Era

Tacony Corporation was founded in 1946 in St. Louis by Nick Tacony, who invested his entire savings to begin buying sewing machine parts for servicing sewing machines and fixing up some for resale. He originally set up shop in his basement, but by the end of the decade was able to move into a storefront location in St. Louis. During the 1950s, he expanded his business by directly importing sewing machines, replacement parts, and accessories from Europe and Asia, then selling them wholesale to Midwest sewing machine retailers. Tacony took his business national by acquiring a pair of East Coast competitors.

In 1970, Tacony was joined by his son, Ken, who had just completed a four-year stint in the U.S. Air Force after earning a degree in business administration. At this stage the company was generating some $3 million in annual sales. Much of its growth during the 1970s was the result of Tacony Corporation introducing the Baby Lock, the first serger for home sewers. Like the industrial "overlocker" sewing machine, the multi-needle home serger could perform three functions in one pass: sewing, trimming the seam allowance, and overcasting. The Baby Lock proved so popular that it revitalized a declining sewing market and led to industry-wide growth. It would also prepare the ground for the rise of the hobbyist market.

In 1984 Nick Tacony died and his son took over the family business. Sales had now reached $23 million, but the company faced an uncertain future due to societal changes. An increasing number of women were now working outside the home, leaving

Company Perspectives:

The company's mission is to profitably grow our leadership position in the industries we serve, creating success for our customers, our associates and all others that depend on us.

many without the time or inclination to use sewing machines to mend or make clothing. As a result, the sale of sewing machines in America was trending downward, and it was becoming clear that if Tacony Corporation was to maintain growth it would have to make some adjustments to its core sewing business while taking steps to diversify beyond it.

Diversity Sought in 1980s

In 1985 Tacony became a licensee of Simplicity sewing machines to tap into the market for less expensive sewing machines, priced under $300. Studies indicated that most sewing machine sales in the United States now took place at the lower price point. Tacony also reorganized its efforts to distribute parts and accessories with increased customer support. In 1989 it formed the Tacony Sewing Central sales division. The idea behind it was to offer a wide selection of sewing machine parts for both home and industrial machines, as well as accessories and notions—25,000 items in all—supported by a staff of specialists. The new unit was also positioned to sell proprietary sewing products as Tacony acquired or developed them, setting the company up to sell into foreign markets using the Sewing Central infrastructure. Also during the 1980s, Tacony supplemented its sewing business while achieving diversity by acquiring Riccar America Company in 1988. The California-based company not only produced a superior sewing machine, it also manufactured a high-end line of vacuum cleaners. A year later, Tacony built on its new vacuum cleaner business by using the Simplicity name to launch a new line of quality vacuum cleaners.

The success of Ken Tacony's efforts during the 1980s were demonstrated on the balance sheet. Sales had virtually doubled since he took over for his father, and the company was ready to enjoy even greater growth in the 1990s. Not only was Tacony ready to build on its non-sewing product lines, it began benefiting from an unexpected change in the sewing marketplace. The sewing machine, which made its mark in the 1800s as an everyday household tool, now became the province of the hobbyist. Rather than sewing because they had to, people were now sewing for fun. The craft niche grew out of the introduction of embroidery machines in the early 1990s. They were more expensive, offering a higher margin to sellers, and the more features the machines offered, the more features customers wanted. They became high-tech machines capable of completing the most complex of designs. In turn, embroidery designs also became a profit center, as an array of new looks and patterns were offered on floppy disks, CDs, and memory cards. There was also the rise of heirloom sewing—the production of ornate clothing and other items, such as pillow cases and bags—intended to be kept as family heirlooms. The growth of the embroidery market was also spurred by the rise of the Internet. People could download designs and communicate with fellow enthusiasts. Rather than passing a sewing machine on to

the next generation, people were trading up after a few years, as well as buying computer upgrades. The sheer number of embroidery machines in use may have paled in comparison to the penetration of the traditional sewing machine in America in years past, but the margins were excellent and the possibility for accessory sales seemed endless. With Sewing Central in place, Tacony was able to quickly tap into this explosive new market and offer a range of product lines: specialty threads, stabilizers, memory cards, and sewing machine software.

By making strategic acquisitions in the 1990s, Tacony took advantage of the resurgence in sewing while continuing to pursue its efforts at diversification. In 1991, it acquired Blakeman's to enter the wholesale floor care parts and equipment field. Tacony then completed a pair of acquisitions in 1996. By purchasing Elna USA, Tacony added the well known Elna brand. Founded in Switzerland in the 1930s, Elna developed the first portable sewing machine to rely on a free arm. Tacony would apply the Elna name to a wide range of sewing machines and related products, including a broad range of sewing and embroidery machines, sergers, sewing and serger feet with added capabilities, an Heirloom sewing kit, and software. Also in 1996, Tacony added to its janitorial products and growing floor care business by acquiring Texas-based Powr-Flite, which manufactured and distributed products such as floor scrubbers, burnishers, sanders, sweepers, commercial vaccums, wet/dry vacuums, extractors, dryers, and ozone generators used to eliminate odors in cleanup efforts. Another new product area for Tacony in the 1990s was ceiling fans, the result of the acquisition of Regency Ceiling Fans. Regency designed and distributed a wide range of commercial and home ceiling fans, including children's fans and patio fans, as well as blades, shades, light kits, and an assortment of accessories such as remote controls, pull chains, and specialty bulbs. Tacony's efforts at changing its product mix were so successful that in 1996 sewing machines and related products accounted for just 51 percent of sales, with the floor care sector contributing 38 percent and ceiling fans 11 percent.

Ever since the late 1980s, Tacony began to realize the necessity of manufacturing its own vacuums rather than rely on imports from Taiwan, fearful that growing direct marketing operations would significantly cut into the business of distributors. However, it was not until the Powr-Flite acquisition that management decided to investigate more deeply the idea of manufacturing vacuum cleaners in the United States. The example of Powr-Flite's Fort Worth plant was a key selling point. It employed about a dozen assemblers and without the benefit of computers was able to produce about $20 million in annual sales. Tacony turned to Mid-America Manufacturing Technology Center, a service organization that helped small and mid-sized manufacturers, for assistance in evaluating whether it was wise, given high labor costs in the United States, to launch a large-scale domestic manufacturing operation. Some of the data MAMTC uncovered was eye opening. Other than the plastic housing, Taiwan manufactured none of the parts it assembled into vacuum cleaners. In fact, most were made in the United States, which meant that Tacony could save some money in this regard by manufacturing at home. Moreover, MAMTC estimated that the costs of shipping from Taiwan, as well as duties, accounted for 6.5 percent of the cost of vacuums made in Taiwan. With these cost savings factored in, Tacony was wil-

Key Dates:

1946: Nick Tacony starts a wholesaling sewing machines and parts company in St. Louis.
1970: Nick Tacony's son Ken joins the business.
1984: Ken Tacony succeeds his father upon Nick Tacony's death.
1988: Vacuum cleaner manufacturer Riccar America Company is acquired.
1996: Elna USA is acquired.
2000: CFR Corporation is acquired.
2003: Nancy's Notions is acquired.

ling to test the idea of bringing manufacturing back to the United States. It hedged its bet somewhat by forming a joint venture in 1997 with its Taiwanese partner. They launched USA Vacuum Industries and opened a plant located some 90 minutes south of St. Louis in St. James, Missouri. The subsidiary was an immediate success, due in large measure to the high number of less-expensive plastic parts available locally. Tacony now transferred all of the manufacturing for Simplicity and Riccar vacuums to St. James, then in 1999 bought out its partner. With the help of MAMTC, Tacony also added product designers to develop its own lines of vacuum cleaners.

Major Upgrades in the 2000s

Despite making a number of advances in the 1990s, Tacony experienced a loss in momentum late in the decade. Sales of $119 million in 1999 were only a slight improvement over 1998. In response, Tacony upgraded its computer infrastructure and modernized its warehousing operations, while speeding up product development. In addition, it opened a new plant in Fort Worth, Texas, to manufacture commercial janitorial equipment. Sales grew to more than $130 million in 2000 and the company was set up for further growth in the new century. Tacony added to its janitorial equipment business by acquiring Texas-based CFR Corporation in 2000. Founded in 1985, CFR manufactured a state-of-the art line of high-end commercial carpet cleaning equipment. It pioneered the concept of recycling and filtering cleaning solutions for an environmentally sound cleaning system. CFR's list of products grew to include vacuums, a blower/dryer, and an ozone generator. Tacony also expanded on its core sewing business in 2000. It acquired six-year-old The Finishing Touch Thread Co., a Knoxville, Tennessee-based company that distributed embroidery products aimed at the hobbyist. In addi-

tion, Tacony introduced the Origins line of home embroidery software, capable of creating designs from a range of sources, including scanned images and original artwork. The patented digitizing software translated the original into an embroidery design, complete with stitch type, stitch sequence, design segments, color sequencing, and color match. Tacony then bolstered its presence in the embroidery marketplace in 2003 with the acquisition of Nancy's Notions, the catalog operation of Nancy Zieman, host of the popular PBS television series *Sewing With Nancy.*

Aside from embroidery, there was another growing hobby in America that might have an influence on Tacony's future: "scrapping." Estimated as a $2.5 billion industry in 2004, scrapping involved the decoration of scrapbooks that contained family photos and other memorabilia. Rather than an individual activity, scrapping was emerging as a modern day version of the quilting bee, an excuse for women to get together and socialize while at the same time preserving family history. It grew out of the same heirloom tradition associated with embroidery, prompting Tacony to modify some of its embroidery machines so that they were also capable of personalizing paper scrapbook pages. Whether scrapping would ever have a major impact on Tacony's revenues, which grew to some $150 million in 2003, remained to be seen. However, as had been the case throughout its history, Tacony was nimble enough to change with the times and as a result was likely to prosper for the foreseeable future.

Principal Subsidiaries

Baby Lock USA; Blakeman's Floor Care Parts & Equipment; CFR Corporation; Elna USA; Nancy's Notions; Regency Ceiling Fans; Riccar America Company.

Principal Competitors

Singer N.V.; Hirsch International Corp; Necchi S.p.A.

Further Reading

"Kenneth Tacony, Tacony Corp.," *St. Louis Business Journal*, June 20, 1997.

Korbblum, Rachael, "Tacony Adds Embroidery Line with Acquisition," *St. Louis Business Journal*, June 19, 2000, p. 9.

"Sewing Enters the Computer Age," *Associated Press*, July 23, 2001.

Stamborski, Al, "Tacony Corp. May Be MAMTC's Poster-Child Firm," *St. Louis Post-Dispatch*, October 9, 2000, p. 12.

"Tacony Corp.," *St. Louis Business Journal*, March 27, 2000, p. A72.

—Ed Dinger

Talk America Holdings, Inc.

12020 Sunrise Valley Drive, Suite 250
Reston, Virginia 20191
U.S.A.
Telephone: (703) 391-7500
Fax: (703) 391-7525
Web site: http://www.talk.com

Public Company
Incorporated: 1989 as Tel-Save Inc.
Employees: 1,300
Sales: $382.7 million (2003)
Stock Exchanges: NASDAQ
Ticker Symbol: TALK
NAIC: 517110 Wired Telecommunications Carriers;
    517910 Other Telecommunications

Talk America Holdings, Inc., sells local and long-distance telephone services in 25 states, primarily in Georgia, Louisiana, Michigan, Pennsylvania, Ohio, and Texas. In a business climate of falling long-distance rates, Talk America has transformed itself from a reseller of long-distance to a provider of facilities-based long-distance services to a bundler of local and long-distance services. The company carries most of the traffic on its own network of switches and other owned or leased facilities. Talk America also has grown through using the Internet as its principal marketing tool, attributing much of its subscriber base to a former promotional marketing agreement with America Online, Inc., which was terminated in 2001.

Origins

Talk America was originally founded in 1989 under the name Tel-Save Inc. by former cable construction veteran Daniel Borislow to resell AT&T long-distance services. Within several years, Tel-Save became one of AT&T's largest wholesalers, offering steep discounts on selected services for companies with dedicated and switched access. In 1994, company president Borislow and ten Tel-Save employees became ensnared in a scandal involving illegal campaign contributions to U.S. Con-gressman Jim Greenwood. Each had donated $1,000 to Greenwood's campaign committee on the same day, raising the specter that Borislow was trying to buy influence from Greenwood, who sat on a powerful House committee that oversaw regulations governing the contentious telecommunications industry. After a probe by the Federal Election Commission (FEC), the eleven Tel-Save associates agreed to pay a $30,000 civil penalty for illegal campaign contributions. The FEC concluded that Borislow knowingly and willfully violated federal campaign law by laundering a corporate contribution through individuals.

A Name Change and an Innovative Marketing Deal

In 1995, the company went public, changing its name to Tel-Save Holdings. By this time, the company was providing long-distance telecommunications services to more than 215,000 small and medium-sized businesses located throughout the United States. Most of Tel-Save's success relied on riding the coat tails of AT&T, which under the 1984 consent decree was mandated to provide other companies "equal access" to its long-distance facilities. With the Federal Communications Commission (FCC) considering rewriting the regulations governing the telecommunications industry in 1996, Tel-Save sought to position itself as a viable competitive enterprise in case the equal access rule was eliminated. The firm planned on using its offering proceeds to buy or lease switching and transmission equipment from AT&T to cut costs and offer steeper discounts under its One Better Network name.

Upon starting its own network, Tel-Save Holdings needed new subscribers for its long distance services, a prospect it found tougher than expected. As a result, in January 1997 the 36-year old Borislow approached top executives at America Online's headquarters in Dulles, Virginia, with an innovative marketing plan and a $50 million check. Borislow's approach proved to be impeccable timing for the ailing AOL, which was on the verge of ruin. The switch to flat-price billing weeks earlier resulted in constant busy signals for subscribers, generating class action suits, intense media criticism, and attempts by competitors to pick up disgruntled customers. AOL promised $350 million in network upgrades to keep its subscribers, but it was forced temporarily to reduce its marketing and advertising

Company Perspectives:

Talk America is a leading integrated communications service provider with programs designed to benefit the residential and small business markets. Talk America has a state-of-the-art telecommunications network, and real-time online billing platform and provides savings to its customer base.

over concern it could not accommodate new customers. AOL needed cash and favorable press. Tel-Save could provide both, leading AOL executives to gamble on Borislow's offer. As a result, Borislow wrote a new check for $100 million to launch the new business in December 1997.

Borislow's plan included billing customers directly online via credit card, eliminating paper, postage, and check cashing costs. With its $100 million, Tel-Save received exclusive rights to sell long-distance phone service to AOL's 14-million customers and got top status among AOL's advertisers. Through its marketing alliance with AOL, Tel-Save attracted 500,000 new long-distance customers in less than four months. AOL saw advantages in the deal as a way of advertising the cheapest long distance service, conveniently billed, and serving as an impressive retention tool for millions of its customers. The simple billing idea that allowed AOL users to view and pay phone bills online stunned the entire industry with its cost efficiencies, leading AT&T, MCI, and others to offer similar services to their own Internet customers. The deal with AOL also attracted potential buyers looking to acquire Borislow's company. Although Wall Street estimated the company's worth at $1.2 billion, Borislow ran Tel-Save as a stripped down operation with only one assistant and shared a bullpen office with six of the company's 235 employees, including his president and chief financial officer.

Reorganization and Two More Name Changes

In July 1997, Tel-Save agreed to acquire Share Technologies Fairchild Inc., the largest U.S. provider of shared telecommunication services, for $511 million, or $11.25 per share. Tel-Share founder and chief executive officer Dan Borislow viewed the transaction as catapulting the company into the local exchange business with over 110,000 local access lines and creating a full-service, facilities-oriented telecommunications provider with local operations in 28 major markets nationwide. With the deal, Tel-Save also would get 475 buildings, 1,200 employees, and half a million customers. In November 1997, however, Intermedia Communications Inc. made a surprise bid of $366 million in cash and a $274 million assumption of debt for Shared Technologies, topping Tel-Save's friendly offer. Intermedia's bid broke up the Share Technologies' planned merger with Tel-Save two weeks away from closing. Tel-Save elected not to make a counteroffer, subsequently collecting $237.3 million in breakup fees from Intermedia. However, one month later, in December 1997, Tel-Save signed a definitive agreement to acquire Symetrics Industries, Inc., a diversified electronics company that served both the defense and telecommunications industries. The agreement provided that Tel-Save acquire all of the outstanding shares of Symetrics for $15 per share.

In 1998, the company changed its name to Tel-Save.com, Inc. and named Gabriel Battista as chairman, chief executive officer, and president. Prior to joining Tel-Save, Battista was chief executive officer of Network Solutions, Inc., an e-commerce company whose stock was one of the top performing Internet issues in 1998. Battista took over the company's reins at a time when its future appeared to be dimming. Borislow's innovative AOL deal that promised windfall profits proved to be only a limited success. Although Tel-Save attracted 1.8 million customers, recruiting them was expensive. The company's earnings also plunged, causing its stock to drop from $27 in February 1998 to $5³⁄₁₆ in October. Borislow's pronouncements about offering the company for sale, and then changing his mind, contributed to Tel-Save becoming one of Wall Street's most controversial telecom stocks. With its prospects waning, Tel-Save's board of directors recruited Gabriel Battista to give the company new direction.

Under Battista's leadership, Tel-Save.com, Inc. changed its name to Talk.com in April 1999 to emphasize the company's new beginning as a hub for online and offline communications. Talk.com said it would continue to offer long-distance services on the Internet and provide such features as real-time call detail, various sorting capabilities, downloads, and interactive customer service. Battista also recruited a new senior management team to complete the company's turnaround as the leader in leveraging the power of the Internet to bill, service, and market telecom services. Its marketing agreement with AOL having broken new ground for Internet use, Talk.com worked to further its leadership position through marketing partnerships with other top Internet service providers, including Prodigy, Wired Digital, and Compuserve.

Entry into the Local Phone Market and Another Name Change

In October 1999, Talk.com said it would also begin providing local phone service to small and medium-sized businesses nationwide. With this aim in mind, in March 2000 Talk.com announced a merger agreement with Access One Communications, a privately held local telephone company that provided service in nine southeastern states, in a stock deal valued at $208 million. The company anticipated the merger to propel it into the new, emerging local services market and considerably expand its geographical reach. With the acquisition of Access One, which posted 1999 revenues of $50 million, Talk.com would get 55,000 local-service customers in Bell South territory, as well as have the capacity to offer local service to its already 300,000 long-distance customers in the region. The acquisition would provide little business overlap, since most of Access One's customers were small businesses, while Talk.com's customers were largely residential. With the conclusion of the acquisition in August 2000, Ken Baritz, former chief executive officer of Access One, became president of Talk.com. Gabriel Battista remained as chairman and chief executive officer. As a result of repositioning itself in the local telephone market, Talk.com began a more aggressive strategy of selling a bundled package of telecommunications services that included local, long-distance, and Internet services along with building more brand name awareness to acquire more customers.

Separately, Talk.com announced an agreement with Soros Private Equity to invest $80 million in the company for 80,000

```
┌─────────────────────────────────────────────┐
│              Key Dates:                       │
│                                               │
│ 1989:  Tel-Save, Inc. is founded.             │
│ 1995:  The company goes public and changes    │
│        its name to Tel-Save Holdings, Inc.    │
│ 1997:  The company launches a major marketing │
│        agreement with America Online.         │
│ 1998:  The company changes its name to        │
│        Tel-Save.com, Inc.                     │
│ 1998:  Founder Daniel Borislow leaves the     │
│        company and is replaced by Gabriel     │
│        Battista.                              │
│ 2000:  The company acquires Access One        │
│        Communications.                        │
│ 2001:  The company changes its name to Talk   │
│        America Holdings, Inc.                 │
│ 2002:  Talk America restructures its debt.    │
│ 2003:  Talk America signs a deal with Kingdom │
│        Ventures, Inc., a rapidly growing      │
│        church development company, to market  │
│        telecommunications services to         │
│        faith-based organizations and their    │
│        members.                               │
└─────────────────────────────────────────────┘
```

shares of 7 percent convertible preferred Talk.com stock and warrants for 200,000 shares of the company's common stock at $17.91 per share. As part of the agreement, a partner of Soros Private Equity would join Talk.com's board of directors. Talk.com planned to use the investment proceeds for working capital and other corporate operations.

In April 2001, chairman and chief executive officer Gabriel Battista announced another name change for the local and long-distance service provider to Talk America Holdings, Inc. to better reflect its coast-to-coast reach. The company had recently expanded its network of bundled telecommunications services to California, establishing a presence in 13 states.

Legal and Financial Turbulence

Talk America's more aggressive marketing campaign, however, led regulators in ten states to begin making inquiries and launch legal proceedings against the company after receiving thousands of consumer complaints for "slamming," or switching phone service without consent, and overcharging for service. The complaints also prompted the Federal Communications Commission to initiate an investigation of Talk America's business practices and marketing activities. Despite denying the charges, one state had already fined Talk America, which lost $61.8 million in 2000 on revenue of $544.5 million. In Florida, regulators received 1,200 complaints, while consumers lodged 300 complaints in Tennessee, 554 in Georgia, 260 in North Carolina, 200 in Mississippi, 139 in Alabama, and 171 in Pennsylvania. In August 2001, the California Public Utilities Commission began its own investigation of the company for allegedly switching customers' phone service without their consent and billing them for services they never approved. Talk America also came under scrutiny for millions of promotional checks it sent to customers of other local and long-distance phone companies. When people cashed the checks, Talk America switched their service. Although the tactic was not illegal, regulators criticized the company for failing to make clear the

terms of the promotional offer. As a result of the multi-state investigations and litigation, Talk America paid cash settlements in several states with the added requirement that it clean up its customer base.

With the steep telecommunications downturn, and under mandated requirements to clean up its customer base, in August 2001 Talk America reported a second-quarter loss 62 times greater than its first-quarter deficit. The company lost $62.7 million compared to $891,000 for the same quarter in 2000. The company's marketing agreement with AOL was also terminated. By August 2002, however, Talk America was turning a surprise profit at a time when other telecommunications firms were going bankrupt. The company managed to repair its finances by twice restructuring its debt. The debt restructuring plan came after the company's share price collapsed from a high of $30 in February 1998 to $0.33 a share in the fourth quarter of 2001 as investors fled over concerns of the company's high debt load and troubles with its local telephone service. By pushing out 95 percent of its immediate debt obligations to the year 2007 and negotiating a restructuring deal with MCG Finance Corp. and its largest shareholder and creditor, AOL Time Warner Inc., Talk America managed to show a profit amidst the greater telecommunications collapse. As a result, Talk America's stock rose an extraordinary 500 percent.

Part of the company's success stemmed from selling local phone service by leasing lines from the Baby Bells at very attractive prices, putting it at a competitive advantage to take local market share. Like AT&T and WorldCom Inc.'s MCI Group, Talk America and others also were expanding their use of leased land lines to compete with the Bells in various states. With the Bells mandated to provide all the connection services, competing carriers needed to invest little capital to add lines beyond state-required leasing charges. In this way, Talk America and other carriers could add thousands of new lines each month at minimal expense. The company already had 244,000 lines by the end of the second quarter of 2002 with plans to have eventually two to four million in service. With each line earning between $40 and $60 in monthly revenue, Talk America had the potential to make billions in annual sales. Nonetheless, the company had plenty of skeptics who believed Talk America was too dependent on the FCC and noted that the Baby Bells were responding to competition by offering bundled services similar to Talk America's with fewer subscribers leaving. Nevertheless, the company was succeeding in a difficult environment amidst the telecom downturn, posting five consecutive quarters of sales growth and seven quarters of profits by July 2003.

Surviving in a New Telecom Environment

In July 2003, Talk America and Kingdom Ventures, Inc., a rapidly growing church development company, signed a deal enabling Kingdom Ventures to market telecommunications services to faith-based organizations and their members. With continued growth in its bundled customer base, Talk America reported second quarter 2004 revenue of $114.9 million, up 23 percent over second quarter revenue in 2003. Second quarter highlights also included the launch of dial-up Internet service to existing customers, plans to offer broadband service, a cash balance that exceeded total debt by $9.9 million, and the addition of 49,000 bundled service customers, which spurred strong revenue growth. However, the company was dealt a heavy blow when new FCC regulations resulted in its losing access to the Baby Bells' local networks at attractive prices, causing some investors to jettison its stock. Investor concerns over this reversal evaporated after the company posted solid third quarter results, reporting a 21 percent increase in revenue to $120.5 million. With the close of 2004, Talk America had weathered the worst of the telecom downturn, offering new bundled services to an expanding customer base nationwide. As a result, Talk America could look forward to further positioning itself to take advantage of a recovering telecommunications market.

Principal Competitors

AT&T Corporation; SBC Communications Inc.; MCI Inc.; Sprint Corporation.

Further Reading

Abrahms, Doug, "Telephone Company Offer Deals on Internet," *Washington Times*, March 31, 1998, p. B8.

Autorino, Anthony D., "Shared Technologies Fairchild to Merge into Tel-Save," *Business Wire*, July 17, 1997, p. 1.

"California Commission to Investigate Phone Firm for 'Slamming,' " *Knight Ridder/Tribune Business News*, August 21, 2001.

Cochran, Thomas N., "Offerings in the Offing," *Barron's*, September 11, 1995, p. 41.

Devlin, Frank, "Greenwood, Murray Spar Over Finances," *Morning Call*, July 20, 1994, p. A1.

Deutsch, Claudia, "Talk.com Plans to Acquire Access One," *New York Times*, March 27, 2000, p. C 11.

Frank, Devlin, "New Hope to Pay Fine for Illegal Campaign Funding," *Morning Call*, August 23, 1995, p. A1.

Garner, Dudley E., "Symetrics Industries Inc to be Acquired by Tel-Save Holdings Inc," *PR Newswire*, December 19, 1997, p. 1.

Madigan, Sean, "Talk America," *Washington Business Journal*, August 10, 2001, p. 23.

Marcovitz, Hal, "Greenwood's Actions Are Noticed Here," *Morning Call*, July 27, 1994, p. B 1.

Mills, Mike, "AOL Deal Would Empower Long-Distance Firm Tel-Save," *Washington Post*, June 19, 1998, p. F3.

"The Nation's Largest Provider of E-Commerce Telecom Services Changes Name from Tel-Save.com to Talk.com; The Start of a New Beginning," *PR Newswire*, April 26, 1999, p. 1.

"Reston, Va.-Based Phone Service Marketer Faces Multistate Scrutiny," *Knight Ridder/Tribune Business News*, June 14, 2001.

"Shares Rise for Reston, Va. Based Local Telephone Service Provider," *Washington Times*, July 8, 2003.

"Surprise Bidder Seeks Shared Technologies Fairchild," *New York Times*, November 18, 1997, p. D4.

"Talk America, Others Threaten the Baby Bells' Market Share: A Restructuring of Debt Has Enhanced Its Image on Wall Street, but at lease One Analyst Sees Risk in the Dramatic Change," *Grand Rapids Press*, August 24, 2002.

"Talk America Reports Solid Second Quarter Earnings," *Business Wire*, August 3, 2004, p. 1.

"Talk.com Completes Acquisition of Access One Communications," *Business Wire*, August 9, 2000, p. 1.

"Talk.com Names Ed Meyercord Chief Financial Officer; Key Executive Appointment Completes Company's New Senior Management Team," *PR Newswire*, August 13, 1999, p. 1.

Waxler, Caroline, "Not-So-Cheap Talk," *Forbes*, March 9, 1998, p. 230.

Weber, Thomas E., "Telecommunications: Facing Big Loss, An Online Player Sees Hopes Dim," *Wall Street Journal*, November 17, 1998, p. B1

—Bruce P. Montgomery

Terrena L'Union CANA CAVAL

BP 199
Ancenis
F-44155 Cedex
France
Telephone: (+33) 2 40 98 91 11
Fax: (+33) 2 40 98 91 64
Web site: http://www.terrena.fr

Cooperative Company
Incorporated: 2004
Employees: 12,600
Sales: EUR 2.98 billion ($2.5 billion)
NAIC: 311511 Fluid Milk Manufacturing; 111332 Grape Vineyards; 112111 Beef Cattle Ranching and Farming; 112112 Cattle Feedlots; 112120 Dairy Cattle and Milk Production; 112210 Hog and Pig Farming; 112340 Poultry Hatcheries; 112390 Other Poultry Production; 311119 Other Animal Food Manufacturing; 311512 Creamery Butter Manufacturing; 311513 Cheese Manufacturing; 311514 Dry, Condensed, and Evaporated Dairy Product Manufacturing; 311611 Animal (except Poultry) Slaughtering; 312130 Wineries

Terrena L'Union CANA CAVAL is one of France's top three cooperatives and one of the country's leading agro-industrial groups. Through its Gastronome subsidiary, Terrena is also France's third-largest poultry products producer. Formed through the union of three cooperatives (CANA, CAVAL, and GCA) at the beginning of 2004, Terrena is backed by more than 35,000 farmer members, and, including its various subsidiaries, has more than 12,600 employees. Terrena operates in a number of major agricultural markets, including cereals, seeds, vineyards, milk and dairy products, eggs, beef, pork, poultry, rabbit, and animal feed. Together, agricultural production represents the majority of the cooperatives annual sales (19 percent crops and vineyards, 31 percent meats and poultry, and 13 percent milk and dairy products). Terrena supports these operations through a network of 350 agricultural supply stores and specialized distributors, providing fertilizers, seeds, and equipment to its members and others, repre-

senting 20 percent of the group's sales. Terrena also operates a number of consumer-oriented garden centers and food markets under the Gamm Vert and Espace Terrena names. Terrena's consumer brands include Paysan Breton (butter), Soviba (beef and pork); Valepi (cereals and flours); wine labels including Les Vignerons des Terroirs de la Noelle, Anjou Villages, Coteaux d'Ancenis, and Muscadet; and, through its Gastronome prepared foods subsidiary, Douce France and Fermier d'Ancenis. Groupe Terrena consists of the Terrena cooperatives (organized geographically into Terrena Loire, Terrena Atlantic, and Terrena Poitou) and its subsidiary operations. The cooperative part of the business contributed nearly EUR 1 billion to the group's total EUR 2.98 billion ($2.5 billion) in sales in 2003.

Beginnings in the late 19th Century

The grouping of cooperatives that resulted in the creation of Terrena at the beginning of 2004 covered the French agricultural heartland of the Loire Atlantic, Vienne, and Poitou regions in the west of France. Terrena's earliest component had originated in Anjou in the late 19th century. The cooperative movement, which had originated in England during the mid-19th century, had rapidly gained popularity throughout the European continent, spawning branches in the banking, grocery, and other industries. The cooperative movement proved an ideal solution for the agricultural sector as well, creating a structure for often highly independent farmers to join forces across the country.

Cooperatives remained highly local efforts throughout the 19th and into the 20th century, typically grouping farmers in a limited region. Such was the case with the creation of the Syndicate Agricole et Viticole d'Anjou, in the Loire Valley region, created in 1887. This cooperative grouped a number of the Anjou region's farmers and wine growers in the Anjou area. Over the next decades, the region saw the appearance of a number of new cooperatives, such as a seed cooperative founded in 1926. This cooperative also became a founding member of the later CAVAL (Cooperative Angevine du Val du Loire), created in 1967 through the merger of seven local cooperatives. The Syndicate Agricole joined the CAVAL cooperative in 1971.

By then, the cooperative movement in France had begun to consolidate into larger, more economically powerful groups. A major stimulus to this movement was the rise of the supermarket sector in the country. During the 1960s and 1970s, the retail food sector began its shift away from the small grocer model. In its place appeared a smaller number of large-scale, nationally operating supermarket groups. These companies actively encouraged the creation of large-scale agro-industrial operations, if only to simplify and ensure the consistency of their own supply needs, as well as to respond to consumer demand for lower food prices. Yet the rising purchasing clout of the supermarket groups and their constant pressure on farmers and food producers to lower their prices encouraged the food producers and the cooperatives behind them to build scale on their own in order to resist more effectively the pricing pressures from the retail groups.

Another fast-growing cooperative in the west of France was CANA. That cooperative had its origins in 1932, when Yves Le Gouais, a prominent local landowner and agronomist, brought together nine local farmers and vineyard owners to form the Saint-Mars-La-Jaille cooperative. The cooperative grew in its importance to the region and its farmers and in 1952 set up its own offices on a six hectare estate in the village of Ancenis, between Nantes and Angers. The move prompted a change in name to the Cooperative Agricole La Noëlle Ancenis, or CANA.

CANA quickly began to add its production systems. In 1955, for example, the cooperative installed a feed mill in order to produce its own animal feed. The cooperative also built a wine storage facility, supporting the casking and fermentation operations of its wine-growing members. CANA next branched out into poultry production, installing a slaughtering facility during the 1970s. A second slaughtering and boning facility, for beef, was opened in Le Lion d'Angers in 1981.

Dairy products represented another strongly growing activity for CANA. In 1977, the company built a butter production plant, which led to the launch of a nationally recognized brand, Paysan Breton. In 1980, the cooperative expanded its dairy production with the construction of a cheese factory as well, and CANA began producing its own branded line of cheeses. In this way, CANA established an early market for itself on the nation's supermarket shelves.

Mega-Cooperative for the New Century

During the 1980s, CANA developed several national brands, including Laiterie du Val d'Ancenis for its milk and dairy products and Gastronome. The company's beef, and later pork,

production started marketing under the Soviba label and quickly rose to become one of France's leading meat brands.

CANA continued to expand during the 1980s. The group's beef and pork business grew strongly, and Soviba began exporting to other European countries in the middle years of the decade. By 1988, the cooperative had added slaughtering and cutting operations on an industrial scale, providing fresh and processed products such as hamburgers, sausages, and kebabs to its large-scale distribution group customers.

In the late 1980s, CANA expanded its Soviba subsidiary through a number of takeovers, including a slaughtering facility at Chemillé in the Maine et Loire department in 1989. In 1992, the company took over a beef slaughtering and processing facility in Saint Maixent L'Ecole, in the Deux Sevres, then expanded that business to include pork as well. CANA also diversified its operations in the 1990s, entering the food ingredients market with the launch of Epi Ingredients, a joint-venture with Coopagri Bretagne. CANA's Laïta joint venture with Coopagri Bretagne and the Even cooperative became major producer of dairy products, especially French cheeses, building up exports to some 70 countries and total sales of nearly EUR 300 million. In 1998, CANA created the ARCA partnership with another cooperative, ARCO.

Meanwhile, CAVAL had been growing as well, notably through its merger with another prominent regional cooperative, CVL, the Cooperative Vienne Loire, in 1993. In 1998, CAVAL expanded again, this time by forming an umbrella cooperative, the Union Poitou Anjou, with Groupe Centre Atlantique, or GCA. Covering farmers in the Poitou region, GCA had been founded in 1936 in the Vienne department.

The late 1990s saw a major shift in the French food sector. Competition among European markets had been steadily intensifying since the lowering of trade barriers in the early 1990s. The concentration of the supermarket sector into a handful of major players had drastically reduced the range of potential customers, while the French cooperatives had to face increasing price pressures, especially from their often lower-priced competitors in Spain, North Africa, Italy, and elsewhere. In response, the French cooperatives had no choice but to gain scale in order to compete and to achieve a profit from the razor-thin margins allowed them by the large supermarket chains.

The outbreak of Bovine Spongiform Encephalitis (BSE, also known as "mad cow disease") in France in the late 1990s sparked a new crisis in France's agricultural sector, particularly in the market for beef. The sudden drop in beef consumption forced beef producers such as Soviba to respond by expanding its exports. In order to do this, Soviba acquired a new slaughtering facility, in Villers Bocage, in 1997.

These factors combined to spark a wave of consolidation in the French cooperative movement as well as in the agricultural and food production sectors in general. CANA and CAVAL joined in this trend, forming a number of partnerships, notably in the beef sector (CANA with GIBEV and CAVAL with GERAP). In 2000, CANA and CAVAL announced their intention to form a new cooperative structure between them. That union, which did not for the time being include GCA, took on the name of Terrena in 2001.

Key Dates:

1887: An agricultural and vintner's cooperative is created in Anjou.
1926: A seed cooperative is created in Anjou.
1932: Yves Le Gouais leads the founding of Saint Mars La Jaille cooperative.
1936: An agricultural cooperative is founded in the Vienne region.
1942: Saint Mars La Jaille cooperative begins dairy production.
1952: Saint Mars La Jaille acquires a site in Ancenis and becomes CANA.
1967: CAVAL is formed through the merger of seven Loire Valley cooperatives.
1971: The agricultural and vintner's cooperative in Anjou joins CAVAL.
1977: CANA constructs a butter production facility.
1978: CANA constructs a poultry slaughtering facility.
1981: CANA begins operating a beef slaughtering and boning facility and launches Soviba beef brand and subsidiary.
1988: Soviba adds a modern slaughtering facility in Le Lion d'Angers.
1993: CAVAL merges with CVL.
1998: CAVAL forms UPA with GCA.
2000: CAVAL and CANA agree to merge.
2003: The merger of CAVAL and CANA into Terrena is agreed.
2004: Group Terrena is founded and Ter'elevage partnership is formed.

CANA and CAVAL began moving closer together in the early years of the 2000s, and by the end of 2003 their members had voted to proceed with a full merger of the two cooperatives. Soon after, the members of GCA voted to join Terrena. CANA, CAVAL, and GCA became known, respectively, as Terrena Atlantic, Terrena Loire, and Terrena Poitou. A new umbrella entity, Groupe Terrena, acted as a holding company for the group's cooperatives, on the one hand, and its production, retail, and other subsidiaries on the other. Terrena voted to make the merge retroactive to the beginning of 2003, enabling it to post its first full year of combined sales at EUR 2.98 billion ($2.5 billion).

As it moved toward the mid-2000s, Terrena represented a new mega-cooperative in France, claiming the position of the country's third-largest agro-industrial group. Terrena's momentum appeared to attract additional consolidation in the industry. In January 2004, after merging the CANA and CAVAL beef production units, Terrena announced the formation of a new cooperative union, Ter'elevage, grouping Terrena's operations with its partners GIBEV and GERAP. Also during 2004, Terrena merged with two of its pork production partners, SEPMA and Teldis Porc, which were absorbed by Terrena Porc. As one of France's leading agro-industrial cooperative, Terrena had gained the scale it needed in order to remain a player in the highly competitive European agro-industrial industry.

Principal Subsidiaries

Epi Ingredients (50%); Espaces Gamm Vert; Gastronome; Laïta (33%); LVA; Soviba; Terrena Loire; Terrena Atlantique; Terrena Poitou; Terrena Viande.

Principal Competitors

Lactalis; Bongrain S.A.; Even; Coopagri Bretagne; Agrial; UNICOPA; Entremont S.A.; Yoplait S.A.S; CEDILAC S.A; Cooperative Laitiere Ploudaniel.

Further Reading

Coquin, Louis, "Terrena, mastodonte de la coopération," *Nouvel Ouest*, December 2003.
Favreau, Adrien, "La Cana étudie la création de 400 emplois en un an grâce à la loi Robien," *Monde*, March 2, 1997.

—M.L. Cohen

Toll Brothers Inc.

250 Gibraltar Road
Horsham, Pennsylvania 19044
U.S.A.
Telephone: (215) 938-8000
Fax: (215) 938-8010
Web site: http://www.tollbrothers.com

Public Company
Incorporated: 1986 as Toll Brothers Inc.
Employees: 4,655
Sales: $3.86 billion
Stock Exchanges: New York Pacific
Ticker Symbol: TOL
NAIC: 236110 Residential Building Construction; 236115
New Single-Family Housing Construction (Except
Operative Builders); 236116 New Multifamily
Housing Construction (Except Operative Builders);
236117 New Housing Operative Builders; 237210
Land Subdivision; 522310 Mortgage and
Nonmortgage Loan Brokers; 524127 Direct Title
Insurance Carriers; 561621 Security Systems Services
(Except Locksmiths)

Toll Brothers Inc. is a leading U.S. homebuilder, constructing some 8,000 homes annually. Most are single-family luxury residences. Toll is distinguished in its industry by a long record of profitability and revenue growth. Subsidiaries produce homebuilding supplies such as lumber products and offer a variety of consumer services ranging from insurance to cable television. Toll is active in about 300 communities in 20 states and is strongest in the Mid-Atlantic.

1967 Origins

Toll Brothers was founded in 1967 by brothers Robert I. (Bob) and Bruce E. Toll. Bob Toll was only 26 years old at the time and had received his B.A. from Cornell University as well as a law degree from the University of Pennsylvania. Bob served a brief stint as an attorney at a firm called Wolf, Block, Shorr and Solis before determining that his future didn't lie in the legal profession. Both Bob and Bruce had been exposed to the construction business by their father, Albert, who built homes, and Bob believed that industry had more to offer.

In 1967 Bob teamed up with his brother to start building houses. Bruce, who had an accounting degree from the University of Miami, was 24 years old at the time. Their educational backgrounds were a comfortable fit; Bob had a good foundation in principles related to buying land and conducting legal transactions, while Bruce held a firm grip on the basics of the financial side of the business. They started out buying land and building homes in southeastern Pennsylvania—their first deal was the sale of two colonial-style houses—and would continue to build solely in that territory for more than a decade. The brothers built about 30 homes annually during the start-up years, and gradually increased that number throughout the 1970s to become a dominant homebuilder in Pennsylvania. (According to *Newsweek,* their first houses sold for $17,990 each.)

The Toll brothers' success during the 1970s was the result of several factors. From the start, they emphasized quality construction and customer satisfaction. Their efforts would eventually earn them a reputation as the "dream house" builder in their markets. Just as importantly, the brothers determined early on that they were going to pursue a conservative financial strategy that would allow them to evade the homebuilding cycles that so commonly wreaked havoc on the industry. To that end, they tried to keep construction costs to a minimum and were careful not to invest heavily in land that might become overpriced when the economy soured.

1980s Expansion

By the end of the 1970s the Toll brothers' annual home sales were approaching the $50-million mark. After spending nearly 15 years constructing houses only in southern Pennsylvania, they decided that it was time to branch out geographically. In 1982 they began building homes in central New Jersey. Success in that region augmented ongoing gains in their core Pennsylvania market. By the mid-1980s Toll Brothers had become a respected builder in the upscale central New Jersey housing

Company Perspectives:

As the nation's leading luxury home building company, we take pride in creating homes that are as beautiful to look at as they are comfortable to live in. Each Toll Brothers home offers a combination of quality materials and superior design, where every detail is meticulously crafted and every enhancement you select is seamlessly added to create a customized home that is uniquely yours.

market. Revenues climbed rapidly, growing nearly 300 percent between 1982 and 1987 to more than $137 million.

The Toll brothers' gains during the mid-1980s resulted from factors other than geographic expansion. Indeed, a serious decline in earnings in 1984 convinced the pair that they were going to have to make some radical changes in their management style if they were going to succeed in the evolving and increasingly competitive homebuilding industry. They instituted tighter operating and financial controls and began hiring top-flight managers to handle individual projects. Each development was run by a manager who operated largely autonomously. Most of the recruits were quite young and often sported advanced degrees in law, engineering, or business.

Besides top-flight management and strict controls, Toll benefited from a savvy marketing strategy during the mid-1980s. Toll billed itself as a designer of luxury homes, but it did not build custom homes. Instead, it offered customers a variety of floor plans with customized options. Thus, Toll effectively brought the efficiencies of the mass homebuilding sector to the luxury segment. Toll was able to build the luxury homes for less money than custom builders because of its high-volume purchasing power and computerized construction cost controls. To cut costs further and to ensure quality, Toll also operated its own lumber and panel plant that supplied trusses and other prefabricated units for its homes. The company also maintained a separate mortgage affiliate to serve its clients.

In May 1986 the Tolls incorporated a successor company in Delaware as Toll Brothers, Inc., and went public for the first time with an offering on the New York Stock Exchange that raised about $40 million. They used that money to begin branching into other regions of the Northeast. In 1987 they expanded into northern Delaware and Massachusetts and in 1988 tapped the Maryland market. They typically entered new markets by building their mid-range homes, called "Executive" models. The Executive homes were priced from $170,000 to about $300,000, sported 2,400 to 3,000 square feet, and were located on lots ranging from one-quarter to three-quarters of an acre in size.

Once the brothers established the Toll Brothers name in an area with their Executive homes, the company would start building its lower-end and high-end models. Its low-end line of houses, were also considered move-up homes with 1,700 to 2,000 square feet of space and usually situated on lots of about 10,000 square feet or less. Dubbed the Glen line, they were priced from $120,000 to $170,000. In contrast, the high-end, or Estate, line of homes were often priced around half a million

dollars and ranged in size from 3,000 to 4,500 square feet. They were located on three-quarters to three acres of land and offered such features as two-story foyer entries, curved staircases, walk-in closets, and whirlpool master baths.

As a result of geographic expansion and some of the highest profit margins in the industry, Toll Brothers managed to boost sales from about $76 million in 1985 to more than $200 million in 1988, while net income climbed from less than $4 million to more than $24 million during the same period. Toll Brothers even received *Professional Builder* magazine's coveted "Builder of the Year" award in 1988. Going into 1989 the company was in the process of building hundreds of homes throughout much of the Northeast.

Unfortunately, the housing boom of the mid-1980s went bust in 1989. Many homebuilders were forced out of business, while even the most financially conservative companies experienced severe slumps. Toll Brothers was not exempt from the shakeout. For the first time in its 22-year history the company failed to show a rise in net income. In fact, profits slumped to about $13 million for the year as sales slipped to $177 million.

Although Toll was hurt by the downturn, it was recognized as one of the healthiest survivors. It continued to post a profit and even managed to secure several new building contracts. In fact, Toll used the slump as an opportunity to invest its excess cash in land that stressed developers and banks were trying to unload at significantly depressed prices. Toll would later be praised for this savvy strategy. It loaded up on land when other companies were trying to get rid of it at low prices, and it developed and sold the properties at inflated prices when housing markets recovered. The company was able to execute the tactic because, unlike many other builders, it only built homes after they were sold and it refused to pay too much for a property.

Indeed, following the late 1980s and early 1990s housing slump, Toll further tightened its controls and became even more conservative in its building strategy. The company's land buyers perused literally hundreds of properties and purchased only a small fraction of them. Its pursuit of devalued properties allowed it to expand into other regions in the Northeast and Mid-Atlantic.

Booming in the 1990s

In 1992 Toll began building in Connecticut and Virginia before cracking into New York in 1993. In addition to its land and building interests, Toll began operating a subsidiary called Toll Advisors in 1990. That company was set up as a consulting firm to help other financiers and developers work out their problem development projects.

Toll's ability to profit throughout the recession was partly attributable to the health of its market niche. By the early 1990s Toll had become the largest homebuilder in the nation that specialized in luxury homes. During the slump in homebuilding, the segment least fazed was the upscale housing market. Toll geared its homes to high-income move-up buyers between the ages of 35 and 55. That segment of the population continued to post household income gains and was increasing its proportion of the national wealth going into the mid-1990s. Furthermore, those buyers were less affected by interest rate volatility because they typically had large amounts of money to put down on a new home (from equity in their previous home). That cash also made it easier for them to qualify for a new mortgage loan.

The overall result was that demand for upscale housing stayed strong, and Toll was positioned to benefit. Furthermore, housing markets strengthened going into the mid-1990s and Toll Brothers started developing many of the properties it had purchased a few years earlier. Revenues bounced up to a record $281 million in 1992 before jumping to $395 million in 1993 and then to $504 million in 1994. Meanwhile, net income rose from a low of $5 million in 1991 to more than $36 million in 1994.

Encouraged by gains in its core markets, Toll made plans in 1994 to expand out of the Northeast and into Orange County, California, and Raleigh, North Carolina. In early 1995, moreover, Toll announced its intent to expand into Palm Beach County, Florida; Charlotte, North Carolina; and Dallas, Texas. Furthermore, Toll Brothers reached an agreement to acquire its first company in 1995, announcing plans to purchase Geoffrey H. Edmunds & Associates, Inc., a Scottsdale, Arizona-based builder of luxury homes.

Despite a decline in housing starts, Toll managed to boost construction activity during 1995 and increase sales and profits. It accomplished that feat by pursuing the same basic strategy that it had followed for several years: build large numbers of high-quality, upscale homes at the lowest prices and keep a close eye on costs. By 1995 the average cost of Toll's move-up home line had increased to a range of $175,000 to about $400,000, while its mid-range Executive homes were going from about $230,000 to $425,000. Its high-end Estate homes sold for as much as $665,000, or more in some instances. The company was also constructing some attached homes, including townhouses, "carriage homes," and "villas" priced from $100,000 to more than $400,000.

Threatening Toll Brothers' dominance of the upscale housing segment in several regions in the mid-1990s were several other national and regional homebuilders that were mimicking its operating and marketing strategy. Furthermore, industry insiders wondered whether Toll would be able to recreate in other regions the success it had achieved in the Northeast, where the company's inventory of land and low cost structure provided a benefit less attainable in some other regions. Despite critics' doubts, Bruce and Bob Toll, who were still running the com-

pany and remained the primary stockholders, expected to expand successfully in their existing markets and to branch out into new regions.

Toll's web site, launched in 1996, would become an important marketing tool. The company added a "Design Your Home Feature" to engage prospective buyers. Toll sold 2,109 homes worth $759 million during the 1996 fiscal year.

The geographic progression of the company's activities continued into the late-1990s. Toll was becoming a truly national company. Las Vegas and Nashville markets were entered in 1997. The next year, the Toll Brothers Realty Trust was formed to back commercial development. Toll also launched its own insurance company in the late 1990s.

Toll was also moving into different types of residences. It began its first homes for active senior communities in New Jersey in 1998. The next year, it partnered with Marriott Senior Living Services in developing an assisted-living community in Reston, Virginia.

In its fiscal 1999 annual report, Toll announced the creation of a new broadband venture, Advanced Broadband, L.P. This unit was formed to install fiber optic lines in Toll communities to supply Internet and cable service. Income was $101.5 million on sales of $1.46 billion in 1999.

Sustained Growth After 2000

In 2000 and 2001, Toll entered the Rhode Island, New Hampshire, and Colorado markets. A country club community was begun in 2002 near Hilton Head, South Carolina—another new territory.

During this time, mortgage rates were reaching unprecedented lows, prompting a boom in housing starts. At the same time, the bust in tech stocks made real estate seem like an even better investment. Toll's business was expanding, but CEO Robert Toll lamented to CNNfn the difficulty of finding new property to develop in certain states in the Mid-Atlantic and in California. Toll's $2.2 billion in 2001 gross home sales made it the eighth largest builder in the United States at the time, according to *Builder* magazine.

Toll bought Richard R. Dostie, Inc., a builder in Jacksonville, Florida, in 2003. The Manhattan Building Company was also acquired, marking Toll's interest in urban development.

Sales surged 40 percent to $3.9 billion in the fiscal year ended October 2004. Net income rose 58 percent to $409 million. During the year, the company partnered with Pinnacle Ltd. to begin developing waterfront condominiums in Hoboken, New Jersey, at the site of the former Maxwell House coffee plant. Similar developments were soon underway in Philadelphia, San Francisco, San Jose, and South Florida (Singer Island).

A slight rise in interest rates in late 2004 would not be considered good news for homebuilders, CEO Robert Toll told *Investor's Business Daily*. However, he noted that Toll Brothers had thrived in 1995 as mortgage rates reached 9 percent. *Investor's Business Daily* noted that Toll's upscale dwellings, priced at an average of $650,000, were less sensitive to interest rate swings. Toll told the paper that, percentage-wise, twice as many families (15 percent) were making more than $100,000 a year in the United States than had been true two decades earlier.

While it continued to build for affluent baby boomers and empty nesters, the company was also returning to the multifamily market after a 20-year absence. Toll was building about 8,000 homes a year. With 30-year mortgage rates under 6 percent in early 2005, the housing industry continued to surge—and Toll Brothers continued to ride the crest of the wave.

Principal Subsidiaries

Advanced Broadband L.P.; Westminster Insurance Agency, Inc.; Westminster Mortgage Corporation; Westminster Title Company, Inc.

Principal Competitors

Centex Corporation; D.R. Horton, Inc.; KB Home; Lennar Corporation; Pulte Homes Inc.; Ryland Group Inc.

Further Reading

Alva, Marilyn, "Toll Bros., Huntingdon Valley, Pennsylvania; CEO of Home Builder Has Heard It All Before," *Investor's Business Daily,* December 22, 2004, p. A10.

Bady, Susan, "Reach Out: Connecting with Anxious Buyers Will Get Trickier in the Year Ahead," *Builder,* December 2001, p. S24.

Butler, Betsy, "Large Firms Find a Home in Unique Local Market," *Business First—Columbus,* June 8, 2001, p. 12.

"CEO Portrait: Robert I. Toll," *Philadelphia Business Journal,* July 2, 1999, p. 12.

Covaleski, John, "Toll Brothers Jumps in on the Business of S&L Crisis," *Philadelphia Business Journal,* September 10, 1990, Sec. 2, p. 7B.

——, "Toll Takes Some Lumps, Looks for Opportunity," *Philadelphia Business Journal,* May 28, 1990, Sec. 2, p. 17B.

Croghan, Lore, "The Careful Carpenter: Why Home Builder Toll Brothers Thrives when Most Others Don't," *Financial World,* August 29, 1995, p. 36.

Donohue, Gerry, "Toll Brothers (America's Best Builders & the Lee Evan's Award for Business Management Excellence)," *Builder,* January 1996, p. 308.

Ellman, Steve, "Covenant Keepers: Developer Challenges Subdivision Review Panel," *Miami Daily Business Review,* December 27, 2002, p. A1.

Goodspeed, Linda, "New England Tastes Mean a Tough Market for Homebuilders," *Boston Business Journal,* September 22, 1995, Sec. 2, p. 4.

Kostelni, Natalie, "Toll Brothers Spawns Multimedia Subsidiary," *Philadelphia Business Journal,* February 11, 2000, p. 12.

——, "Toll Out to Steer Group Into Path of Investors," *Philadelphia Business Journal,* September 1, 2000, p. 10.

Lelen, Kenneth, "Looking for Profits in the Old Pumpkin Patch," *Business for Central New Jersey,* June 12, 1989, p. 10.

Lurz, William H., "How Toll Makes Money on Luxury Homes," *Professional Builder,* January 1997, p. 72.

——, "Robert I. Toll: The 'Sky's the Limit' as Toll Brothers Targets Baby Boomers Moving Up to Bigger and Better Homes," *Professional Builder,* February 1998, p. 52.

Maynard, Roberta, "Who Will Build Tomorrow's Homes?," *Builder,* January 2000, p. 193.

McGinn, Daniel, "Betting Against a Housing Bust," *Newsweek,* August 26, 2002, p. 38.

Moore, Paula, "Pa. Home Builder Scouts Denver Market," *Denver Business Journal,* October 7, 1994, p. 17.

Murdock, James, "All in the Family: Detached-Home Giants Expanding Their MH Presence," *Multi-Housing News,* November 2004, p. 1.

Orrin, Spellman, "Toll Brothers Broadens Market in Northeast," *Focus,* March 2, 1988, p. 38.

Ostrowski, Jeff, "New Breed of Home Builders Mix Luxury and High Volume," *South Florida Business Journal,* July 25, 1997, p. 10.

Phillipidis, Alex, "Toll Brothers on Building Spree," *Westchester County Business Journal,* August 21, 1995, p. 1.

Richmond, Iris, "The Producers: A Bullish, High-Profile Performance by the Public Builders Positions Them to Pull Away from the Pack," *Builder,* May 2002, p. 33.

Romans, Christine, "Toll Brothers—CEO, CNNfn," *CEOWire,* September 17, 2003.

"Toll Brothers Announces Record Sales Level," *Delaware Business Review,* May 25, 1992, p. 18.

"Toll Brothers Dominates Philadelphia," *Professional Builder,* December 30, 2004, p. 71.

"Toll Brothers Emerges as Luxury Builder," *Mercer Business,* May 1988, p. 72.

"Toll Brothers Expansion Will Tap Into Urban Development Boom," *Real Estate Weekly,* November 5, 2003, p. C9.

Varney, Stuart, "Toll Brothers—Chmn. & CEO Interview," *CEOWire,* February 23, 2005.

Walsh, Thomas J., "Toll: Stock Price Drop Just 'Herd Mentality'," *Philadelphia Business Journal,* October 9, 1998, p. 4.

—Dave Mote
—update: Frederick C. Ingram

Tosoh Corporation

3-8-2 Shiba, Minato-ku
Tokyo
105-8623
Japan
Telephone: (+81) 3 5427 5118
Fax: (+81) 3 5427 5198
Web site: http://www.tosoh.com

Public Company
Incorporated: 1935
Employees: 9,167
Sales: ¥484 billion ($4.7 billion) (2004)
Stock Exchanges: Tokyo
Ticker Symbol: 4042
NAIC: 325181 Alkalies and Chlorine Manufacturing;
325131 Inorganic Dye and Pigment Manufacturing;
325188 All Other Inorganic Chemical Manufacturing;
325211 Plastics Material and Resin Manufacturing;
325311 Nitrogenous Fertilizer Manufacturing; 325312
Phosphatic Fertilizer Manufacturing; 325320 Pesticide
and Other Agricultural Chemical Manufacturing;
325998 All Other Miscellaneous Chemical Product
Manufacturing; 326299 All Other Rubber Product
Manufacturing; 327310 Cement Manufacturing;
331111 Iron and Steel Mills; 334419 Other Electronic
Component Manufacturing; 334516 Analytical
Laboratory Instrument Manufacturing

Tosoh Corporation is one of Japan's leading manufacturers of industrial and specialty chemicals. With origins as a producer of soda ash and caustic soda, Tosoh remains a major producer of chlor-alkali chemicals. Since the 1990s, the company has also focused on building up its vinyls production and other petrochemicals capacity, and in the 2000s Tosoh has begun to emphasize its development of chemicals for the biosciences field. The company also produces materials for the electronics and semiconductor industries, including quartz, electrolytic manganese dioxide, and zirconia. At the same time, as a partner in the Holland Sweetener joint venture, Tosoh is one of the world's top producers of the artificial sweetener aspartame. The company's operations are grouped under three primary divisions: Petrochemicals, which represents 28.9 percent of group revenues; Basic, including chlor-alkali and cement, which adds 28.6 percent to the company's annual revenues; and Specialty Chemicals, including organic chemicals, quartz products, scientific instruments, and other specialty materials, which contributes some 34 percent to group sales. A highly vertically integrated company (at its main site, Tosoh operates its own coal-fired power plant producing more than 525,000 kW), Tosho's Services division provides transportation, warehousing, IT, and other support services. In addition to its operations in Japan, Tosoh has established a global presence, with some 50 foreign subsidiaries in the United States, the Netherlands, the United Kingdom, the Philippines, Singapore, Malaysia, China, Switzerland, Greece, and elsewhere. In 2004, the Tokyo Stock Exchange-listed company's revenues topped ¥484,389 billion ($4.7 billion). Madoka Tashiro serves as company chairman and CEO.

Origins in the Soda Ash Industry

Tosoh Corporation was founded in 1935 as Toyo Soda Manufacturing Corporation in order to produce sodium carbonate, better known as soda ash. The company built its first factory in the Yamaguchi prefecture, near Tokyo. The plant's location on the Japanese coast gave it a ready source of brine, from which both soda ash and caustic soda are produced. The site remained the later Tosoh Corporation's main production facility, one of the largest in Japan, into the 21st century, boasting more than 3.7 million square meters of production space, it's own port facility, and even it's own coal-fired power generating plant, which ultimately reached a capacity of more than 525,000 kW.

Production at the plant, known as the Nanyo Manufacturing Complex, began in 1936. The company's initial production was geared toward the glass industry. As its soda ash production increased over the next decade, Toyo began looking for means to make use of its production byproducts. One offshoot of the group's soda ash production was the development of a cement manufacturing arm, using the ash waste from the soda ash production process. In 1942, the company began producing bromine as well, an element naturally occurring in brine and the only liquid nonmetallic element. The following year, Toyo expanded its production again, this time launching production of sodium hydroxide, or caustic soda.

In the years following the war, as the Japanese economy revved up to become one of the world's most vibrant, Toyo continued to expand both its production capacity and its range of products. During the next decades, Toyo's range of products expanded to include fused phosphate, chlorinated paraffin, ammonium chloride, and phosphoric acid. The company's product expansion also led it to build a second facility, at Yokkaichi, in 1971. That plant, in addition to the production of caustic soda and chlorine derivatives, also played a major role in Toyo's diversification into the petrochemicals sector. Among the petrochemical products developed at the Yokkaichi Manufacturing Complex were petroleum resins, polyethylene, and propylene.

International Growth Begins in the 1960s

Toyo's expansion meanwhile had taken it to the United States, where it opened its first sales office in New York in 1964. The following year, Toyo formed a joint venture with Stauffer Chemical Co. Ltd., based in the United States. That operation, originally known as Toyo Stauffer Chemical Co., launched production of dicalcium phosphate in 1966, before adding titanium trichloride in 1967 and alkyl aluminiums in 1969. Other products added by the joint venture included Solvay catalysts in 1977 and electronic grade metal alkyls in 1982. After merging with the Netherlands' Akzo, the joint venture became known as Tosoh Akzo in 1987, before adopting the name Tosoh Finechem.

In the early 1970s, the company also entered Europe, launching a joint venture with Mitsubishi Corp. to produce and distribute electrolytic manganese dioxide, used in the production of automotive batteries. Formed in 1973, the company built a plant in Thessaloniki, Greece. Production was launched in 1975. In that year, Toyo grew by acquisition, taking over fellow Japanese producer Tekkosha Co. Ltd., a company founded in 1925.

In 1976, Toyo added a European sales and marketing subsidiary called Amto International, based in Amsterdam. That subsidiary changed its name to Tosoh Europe BV in 1987. The company also began seeking new production opportunities. In 1975, it launched a polyvinyl chloride operation in a joint venture with

Mitsui Co. in Indonesia. That subsidiary, PT Standard Toyo Polymer, began production of PVC at a plant in Merak, on the island of Java, in 1976. In another joint venture, Delamine BV, created with Akzo Nobel, the company began producing ethylene amines in Amersfoort, in the Netherlands, in 1978.

In 1979, Toyo established a full-fledged subsidiary in the United States, which later became known as Tosoh USA. That subsidiary then became the company's primary sales and marketing arm in the United States. In the 1980s, the company, which formally adopted the name Tosoh Corporation in 1987, launched a drive to establish a manufacturing presence in the United States as well.

The company launched a joint venture with Rohm and Haas Company in the United States. TosoHaas, as the new company was called, enabled Tosoh to enter the production of bioseparations in 1987. The following year, a joint venture with the Netherlands' DSM, called Holland Sweetener Corporation, brought Tosoh into the production aspartame. The joint venture, initially created in 1985, became the leading European producer of the artificial sweetener by the turn of the 21st century.

Major Japanese Chemicals Producer in the 2000s

Acquisitions and joint ventures played an important role in Tosoh's expansion, particularly its growth overseas. Acquisitions also enabled the company to carry out an expansion of its product lines. In the late 1980s, the company extended its operations into silica glass, quartz, zirconia, and related materials used for the electronics and semi-conductor industries. In 1989, for example, the company acquired Nippon Silica Glass USA, a leading producer of quartz and other silica glass materials. That purchase also brought Tosoh into the production of zirconia grinding media, used for manufacturing multi-layer ceramic capacitors. The company's zirconia range included zirconia powder, fully integrated zirconia, and zirconia ceramics. Under Tosoh, the division, already one of the world's leading producers of zirconia, expanded its production capacity from 200 metric tons per year to more than 620 metric tons per year at the turn of the century. By then, Tosoh claimed 60 percent of the global market for zirconia and 90 percent of the market for high-grade zirconia used in fiber optics and related high-technology applications.

Other late 1980s acquisitions included the purchase of the specialty metals division of Varian Associates in 1988. Renamed Tosoh SMD, the company produced sputtering targets and high purity thin film deposition materials for the semiconductor industry.

Tosoh also entered Malaysia and the specialty resins market with the purchase of a stake in that country's Industrial Resins (Malaysia) Sdn. Bhd. In 1989, Tosoh acquired a stake in Weiss Scientific Glass Blowing Co. Based in Oregon, with operations in the United Kingdom, the company had been founded in 1970 by Gunther Weiss, producing quartz products for the newly developing semiconductor industry. By the mid-1970s, the Weiss company boasted a production facility of more than 12,000 square feet. With Tosoh's involvement, that plant was expanded to 60,000 square feet in 1989.

Tosoh acquired 100 percent control of the Weiss company in 1993. The company then set out to expand its silica glass

Key Dates:

1935: Toyo Soda Manufacturing Co is founded to produce soda ash for Japan's glass industry.
1942: The company begins production of bromine.
1943: Production of caustic soda is launched.
1964: The company opens its first foreign sales office in the United States.
1966: Toyo Stauffer Chemical Co. (ultimately Tosoh FineChem) joint venture is formed and production of dicalcium phosphate is launched.
1971: Production at a second facility, Yokkaichi Manufacturing Complex, begins.
1975: The company acquires Tekkosha Co. of Japan and enters into a joint venture in Greece.
1976: The company founds Amto International (later Tosoh Europe) in the Netherlands.
1979: Tosoh USA is founded.
1987: The company changes its name to Tosoh Corporation and forms a joint venture Holland Sweetener Company to produce aspartame in the Netherlands.
1988: A Specialty Metals Division is acquired from Variant; the company enters Malaysia through a stake in Industrial Resins (Malaysia) Sdn Bhd.
1989: The company acquires a stake in Weiss Scientific Glass Blowing in Oregon.
1990: A stake in Eurogenetics in Belgium is acquired.
1992: The company purchases a stake in General Chemical (Soda Ash) Company in New Jersey.
1993: Full control of Weiss Scientific is acquired.
1994: Full control of Eurogenetics is acquired.
1995: The company establishes a production subsidiary in Korea.
2000: Full control is gained of Nippon Silica Glass, TosoHaas (renamed Tosoh Biosep) and Tosoh Akzo (renamed Tosoh Finechem).
2003: The company unifies all biosciences operations under the Tosoh Bioscience name.

with Mitsubishi, the Bank of the Philippine Islands, and Mabuhay Vinyl Corporation. That company was named Philippine Resins Industries.

Asia became a particular target market for growth in the late 1990s and early 2000s for Tosoh. The company launched a subsidiary in South Korea in 1995 and also added new operations in Indonesia, called PT Satomo Indovyl Polymer. The following year, Tosoh entered Singapore through its Tosoh SMD division.

In 2000, Tosoh acquired full control of both Nippon Silica Glass and Tosoh Akzo, the latter company becoming Tosoh Finechem. Also in 2000, Tosoh expanded its sputtering targets business with the purchase of California's SET, renamed as Tosoh SET. Tosoh also took full control of its joint venture with Rohm and Haas, TosoHaas, which was by then a leading producer of bioseparations and chromatography materials, renaming the company Toosh Biosep.

At the beginning of 2003, Tosoh moved to unify all of its biotechnology operations under a single banner, Tosoh Bioscience. This process involved the re-branding of the group's various diagnostic and scientific-oriented companies, which included Eurogenetics, Tosoh Biosep, and San Francisco-based Tosoh Medics.

Turning toward mid-decade, Tosoh announced its intention to step up its chlor-alkili production in response to the fast-growing demand in the Asian region. In May 2003, Tosoh spent ¥17 billion to add some 150,000 tons of aniline production capacity, which would enable the production of raw materials used in making polyurethane. In February 2004, the company acquired majority control of its Philippines resins joint venture with Mitsubishi in order to solidify its position as a dominant chlor-alkili producer in the region.

In the meantime, Tosoh's entered the Chines market with the establishment of a sales subsidiary in Shanghai in April 2004. This move provided Tosoh with a vast new market for its chemicals range. The company also made plans to begin manufacturing in China itself. In December 2004, the company neared approval for launching a project to build a polyvinyl chloride plant in Guangzhou with a capacity of 200,000 metric tons per year. Tosoh hoped to have that plant operational by 2006. From a small producer of soda ash, Tosoh Corporation had grown into a leading Japanese and global producer of diversified materials.

capacity, forming the joint venture Nippon Silica Glass Europe, which launched production at its own facility in 1996. The company acquired Cryco Quartz Inc. in 1995, and then expanded its Oregon production site to 100,000 square feet in 1998. In 2001, Tosoh merged Weiss Scientific, Cryco Quartz, and NSG Europe into a single entity, Tosoh Quartz Inc.

Back at home, Tosoh grew in 1990 through the acquisition of Japanese rival Shin-Daikyowa. That company had been founded in 1968, then merged with Chubu Chemical Co. in 1978. Shin-Daikyowa had acquired a styrene monomer plant that year and grew into a prominent Japanese petrochemicals producer.

Tosoh's growth remained strong throughout the 1990s. The company acquired a stake in New Jersey-based General Chemical (Soda Ash) Company in 1992, which followed on the purchase of shares in Eurogenetics NV, based in Belgium, in 1990. By 1994, Tosoh had completed its acquisition of Eurogenetics. The company had formed a new joint venture in the Philippines

Principal Subsidiaries

Delamine B.V. (Netherlands); General Chemical (Soda Ash) Partners (USA); Holland Sweetener Company V.O.F. (Netherlands); Holland Sweetener North America, Inc. (USA); Mabuhay Vinyl Corporation (Philippines); P.T. Satomo Indovyl Polymer (Indonesia); P.T. Standard Toyo Polymer (Indonesia); Philippine Resins Industries, Inc.; Tosoh (Shanghai) Co., Ltd. (China); Tosoh America, Inc.; Tosoh Bioscience GmbH (Germany); Tosoh Bioscience LLC (USA); Tosoh Bioscience N.V. (Belgium); Tosoh Bioscience Srl. (Italy); Tosoh Bioscience U.K.; Tosoh Bioscience, A.G. (Switzerland); Tosoh Bioscience, Inc. (USA); Tosoh Europe B.V. (Netherlands); Tosoh Hellas A.I.C (Greece); Tosoh Polyvin Corporation (Philippines); Tosoh Quartz Co., Ltd. (Taiwan); Tosoh Quartz Ltd. (U.K.); Tosoh Quartz, Inc. (USA); Tosoh SET, Inc. (USA); Tosoh SGM USA, Inc. (USA); Tosoh Singapore, Pte., Ltd. (Singapore); Tosoh SMD Korea, Ltd.; Tosoh SMD Taiwan Co., Ltd; Tosoh USA, Inc. (Ohio).

Principal Divisions

Petrochemicals; Basic; Specialty Chemicals.

Principal Competitors

Shandong Ocean Chemical Company Ltd.; Dalian Chemical Industry Co.; Bangladesh Chemical Industries Corp.; Solvay S.A.; Zigong Honghe Chemical Company Ltd.; Celanese AG; Kaneka Corp.; Hebei Tangshan Soda Factory; Entreprise Miniere et Chimique S.A.; Formosa Plastics Corp.; Hanwha Chemical Corp.

Further Reading

"Anniversary Celebration," *Pharmaceutical Technology Europe*, November 16, 2004, p. 7.

Hariharan, Malini, "Tosoh Corp Faces Rising Costs," *ACN: Asian Chemical News*, March 22, 2004, p. 6.

Hunter, David, and Mollet, Andrew, "Tosoh Stays the Course," *Chemical Week*, October 24, 2001, p. 33.

McPadden, Michael, "Tosoh Sees Further Change After Difficult Fiscal First Half," *Chemical Market Reporter*, December 17, 2001, 23.

Sutton, Susan, "Growing with Demand," *Ceramic Industry*, June 2001, p. 18.

"Tosoh Announces Global Brand Name," *Ceramic Industry*, February 2001, p. 12.

"Tosoh Corp. Unifies Companies," *LC-GC North America*, March 21, 2003, p. 238.

"Tosoh Doubles PVC Capacity," *ACN: Asian Chemical News*, December 6, 2004, p. 21.

"Tosoh Hunted on TSE on New Virus Detection Method," *Jiji*, December 24, 2004.

—M.L. Cohen

Tuesday Morning

Tuesday Morning Corporation

6250 LBJ Freeway
Dallas, Texas 75240
U.S.A.
Telephone: (214) 387-3562
Fax: (214) 387-1974
Web site: http://www.tuesdaymorning.com

Public Company
Incorporated: 1974
Employees: 7,950
Sales: $565 million (2004)
Stock Exchanges: NASDAQ
Ticker Symbol: TUES
NAIC: 452990 All Other General Merchandise Stores

In spite of its name, Tuesday Morning Corporation does not always open its stores on Tuesday mornings. For about half the year the stores are closed entirely. During its four annual ''sales events,'' which cover the peak shopping seasons, most of the company's stores are open seven days a week. Tuesday Morning sells upscale items at deeply discounted prices. Its merchandise, which the company describes as ''first-quality, famous-maker giftware,'' generally goes for 50 to 80 percent below original retail prices. The company keeps its overhead costs in check by locking its doors during off-peak times of the year and by maintaining a no-frills atmosphere in its stores.

1970s Origins As Upscale Garage Sale

The name and concept for Tuesday Morning came from company founder, Chairman, and Chief Executive Officer Lloyd Ross. He came upon the idea for a part-year store while working for Rathcon, Inc., a manufacturer and importer of gift merchandise, in the early 1970s. Ross noticed that manufacturers had no reliable way to dispose of their surpluses of high-end inventory. He began purchasing excess merchandise from top-name manufacturers and selling it to department and specialty stores at a nice profit. The process worked so well that Ross decided to try selling a variety of products at what amounted to a single gigantic garage sale in a rented warehouse in north

Dallas. The sale was a huge success, and it left no doubt in Ross's mind that there was a place in the retail world for an operation specializing in upscale closeout items. Naming the company was easy. Ross had wanted to run a company named after a day of the week ever since he was a teenager delivering copies of the *Saturday Evening Post*. He picked Tuesday because in his opinion, ''Tuesday morning is the first positive day of the week,'' according to company press materials.

Soon after the initial success of his concept, Ross settled on the four-sales-a-year schedule. The sales quickly gained a loyal following. In addition to offering prestigious items at low prices, limiting the time during which they were available created a sense of anticipation and excitement for many customers. For its first several years, the company continued to operate out of temporary locations, such as vacant supermarkets or warehouses. New employees were hired for each season. Before long, however, a core group of returning sales personnel made up the bulk of the staff. Tuesday Morning soon began to expand geographically, primarily in the South and West. Eventually the company settled into permanent locations. Tuesday Morning management, however, avoided locating their stores in the posh malls of the well-known department stores that often sold the same merchandise for twice the price. Tuesday Morning stores have always been no-frills operations, relying on the merchandise rather than decoration to create their atmosphere. The typical Tuesday Morning customer was an upper middle-class woman who might otherwise shop at a place like Nieman Marcus. Many of those women purportedly transferred their Tuesday Morning purchases into big-name department store boxes when they got home.

Profitable Throughout the 1980s

Tuesday Morning went public in 1984, and by the following year there were 56 stores in the chain, generating sales of about $37 million. Sales events were handled by 1,400 part-time workers as well as 60 administrative personnel at company headquarters and 110 warehouse employees. Meanwhile, certain company policies kept Tuesday Morning on good terms with the manufacturers of their merchandise and even with the department stores that it was undercutting. Tuesday Morning generally did not include manufacturers' names in its advertising since some manufacturers felt that association with a discount chain devalued their products. If a brand name was used in an ad, it was only with the manufacturer's explicit permission. If a competing department store became upset about a markdown on a product it was still carrying, Tuesday Morning usually would take it off the shelves.

Tuesday Morning's sales and profits grew each year for the rest of the 1980s, with the exception of 1988, when earnings were held in check by a temporary increase in expenses, including the construction of a new warehouse. By 1987 there were 81 large, no-frills Tuesday Morning outlets operating in 16 states, still mostly in the South. To keep rental costs low, the company continued to locate its stores mainly in strip malls in outer ring suburbs, rather than in indoor malls or city centers. Labor costs also remained low since each store had only one permanent full-time employee, the store manager. The chain's army of part-timers were mainly housewives, who were often motivated by the opportunity to get first crack at the closeout merchandise offered at each sales event, not to mention a 20 percent discount. In 1987 the company earned $3.7 million on revenue of $66 million.

Company sales passed the $100 million mark in 1990. By the following year there were 132 stores in the Tuesday Morning chain, with locations in 21 states. Although still primarily a force in the South and Southeast, there were eight Tuesday Morning outlets in Chicago and ten in the Washington, D.C. area by this time. One of the company's strengths continued to be the loyalty of its employees. This applied not only to returning sales personnel, but to the company's growing permanent staff as well. As of 1991, 10 percent of Tuesday Morning's store managers had been with the company for more than ten years, and 400 salespeople had worked there for at least five years. As the company's reputation in the retail industry grew, buying became easier as well, since manufacturers now came to Tuesday Morning with their closeout items rather than the company having to seek out bargain merchandise. Since Tuesday Morning was able to maintain high quality standards for the merchandise it sold, the stigma attached to having products sold by a deep discounter was no longer as powerful.

As the Tuesday Morning chain continued to grow, its methods became more sophisticated. Although it still relied heavily on word of mouth to generate new customers, the company also compiled a mailing list containing two million names. Attractive, four-color brochures were sent to customers on the list just before the beginning of each sales event. An experiment in television advertising a few years earlier had proven to be almost too successful. Stores in the markets targeted by the ads were cleaned out of merchandise almost immediately. New TV and radio campaigns were more carefully prepared for. Most ads featured the company's tag line, "Gifts. 50% to 80% off everything. It's true and it's guaranteed." Tuesday Morning also experimented with a phone-order catalog, which was initially sent to a 170,000-name subset of its regular mailing list. In addition, the company's distribution center in North Dallas was equipped with cutting-edge computer equipment, which allowed for instantaneous communications between stores, warehouse, and trucks. Unlike its stores, Tuesday Morning's distribution center was active 12 months a year.

New Technology in the 1990s

Explosive growth made it necessary to completely refurbish the company's warehouse technology during the early 1990s. Prior to the upgrade, the company had relied on sheer manpower—in the form of 400 extra employees—to handle the crush of work during peak periods. Merchandise was arriving at the company's lone warehouse in such quantities that tracking it was becoming next to impossible. By 1992 the warehouse system was in utter disarray. The transition began early in 1993, when Tuesday Morning President and Chief Operating Officer Jerry Smith moved his office into the warehouse facility in order to observe the process more closely.

After months of examination, suggestions, planning, and design, a new computer system was unveiled in February 1994. The new system employed up-to-date gadgetry such as hand-held scanners, point-of-sale terminals, and radio-frequency technology. It was now possible to locate a single specific box from among the tens of thousands of items in the system at any given time with pinpoint accuracy. With the new tracking system, which included an innovative software package called "DC Wizard," worker productivity improved threefold. The system allowed Tuesday Morning's warehouse to handle up to 450,000 pieces worth $1 million per day with only 135 people, compared with the 500 people it took to process just $650,000 worth of merchandise using the old system. Once employee training was completed, the need for temporary help during peak periods, and the massive cost associated with it, was reduced dramatically. After incurring a $1.1 million loss in 1993, the first losing year in the company's history, Tuesday Morning earned $2.7 million in 1994. Company management was quick to credit the turnaround to the technological overhaul, which was completed two years ahead of schedule. For 1994 the company reported sales of about $190 million.

By 1995 the Tuesday Morning mailing list contained more than three million names, and the number of stores in the chain was approaching 250. That year, sales passed the $200 million mark, and the chain's geographical range covered 31 states. There were 271 Tuesday Morning stores in operation by the middle of 1996. Amazingly, no serious competitor selling similarly prestigious merchandise at deep discounts had emerged in the 20-plus years since Tuesday Morning was established. Now

Key Dates:
1974: Lloyd Ross holds his first ''garage sale.''
1975: Tuesday Morning is incorporated.
1984: The company goes public.
1988: A new warehouse facility is built.
1990: Sales exceed $100 million.
1994: A sophisticated computer system is implemented to control merchandise traffic.
1997: Tuesday Morning is taken private.
1999: The company is taken public.
2003: The company begins remodeling all outlets.

that the chain was truly national in scope, it was difficult for such a competitor to establish a foothold in the market.

Into the 21st Century

In 1997, Tuesday Morning was taken private by a group composed of the company's management, the investment firm Madison Dearborn, and some unaffiliated investors, who purchased all of the company's capital stock for approximately $325 million. The company operated on a private basis until April 1999, when it made an initial public offering of 13.2 million shares of common stock at a starting price of $15 per share. The net profit of $76.1 million realized from the sale was used to pay down debts incurred during the 1997 privatization.

From 1999 through 2004, the company experienced steady sales growth due to several factors: more high-ticket items, such as furniture and rugs, were offered to customers; advertising and direct-mail campaigns expanded the client base among the company's usual market of middle-aged, upper-middle-class women; and the successful development of e-mail notification lists began drawing younger women into the stores. This expansion sparked the need for infrastructure improvements. Beginning in 2003, the company began enlarging and remodeling stores. By July 2004 about half the Tuesday Morning outlets had been completed, with another 300 scheduled for remodeling in January 2005. The 1994 overhaul of the company's warehousing and distribution system continued to reap savings for the corporation as management and workers grew accustomed to new systems and fine-tuned operations to improve product allocation and reduce time spent moving product onto sales floors.

In the early years of the 21st century, the Tuesday Morning Corporation was named a defendant in several lawsuits. Three complaints were filed in 2001 and 2002 by workers who alleged that they were not properly compensated for overtime wages. In October 2003, the company settled out of court with a group of these workers, management trainees. The settlement agreement was approved by the court on April 2, 2004, but the case continued through appeals into the following year. In December 2003, another complaint was filed on behalf of workers who alleged a number of labor issues, including failure to pay for

minimum reporting time, travel time, split-shift premiums, and meal periods. In addition to labor disputes, the Tuesday Morning Corporation was named in a suit filed by Liz Claiborne Inc. and L.C. Licensing Inc. over costume jewelry sales. The suit was resolved amicably in September 2004; details of the settlement were not released. In June 2004 the Thomas Kinkade Company filed a suit against Tuesday Morning that alleged copyright infringement and false advertising on goods sold in the second quarter of 2004.

Despite its legal issues, Tuesday Morning continued to enjoy increasing sales and a widening customer base at the beginning of 2005. At that time, the company focused on opening more stores, expanding its range of high-ticket items, offering goods to attract younger clients, and realizing cost savings by improving efficiency. By the third quarter of 2004, the company had 641 stores in the United States and Canada and appeared to be on track for continued expansion in the future.

Principal Subsidiaries

Friday Morning, Inc.; Tuesday Morning, Inc.; TMI Holdings, Inc.; TMIL Corporation.

Principal Competitors

Target Corporation; Bed Bath & Beyond Inc.; Pier 1 Imports Inc.; The TJX Companies Inc.

Further Reading

Chanil, Debra, ''The Last Great Treasure Hunt,'' *Discount Merchandiser,* October 1995, pp. 42–44.
Fisher, Christy, ''If It's Tuesday Morning, the Store May Be Open,'' *Advertising Age,* January 29, 1990, p. S2.
——, ''New TV Ads to Dawn for Tuesday Morning,'' *Advertising Age,* February 20, 1989, p. 67.
Hall, Cheryl, ''Controlled Chaos,'' *Dallas Morning News,* August 13, 1995, pp. 1H-2H.
Helliker, Kevin, ''If There's Hardly Anything Left to Buy, It's Tuesday Morning on Christmas Eve,'' *Wall Street Journal,* December 23, 1991, p. B1.
Keefe, Lisa M., ''Keep the Customers Waiting,'' *Forbes,* September 21, 1987, p. 74.
Mayer, Caroline E., ''If It's Tuesday, This Must Be a Sale,'' *Washington Post,* November 19, 1984, p. 9.
Slom, Stanley, ''Less is More,'' *Stores,* January 1992, pp. 134–36.
——, ''Tuesday Morning DC Set for Expansion,'' *Chain Store Age,* May 1991, pp. 232–34.
——, ''Tuesday Morning Sells 185 Mornings,'' *Chain Store Age,* April 1991, pp. 26–28.
Swisher, Kara, ''Tuesday Morning, with Discounts Almost Daily,'' *Washington Post,* February 21, 1991, p. C10.
''Tuesday Morning Upgrade Raises Productivity,'' *Chain Store Age,* March 1996, pp. 36–37.
Wojahn, Ellen, ''Closed for Business,'' *Inc.,* April 1985, p. 118.

—Robert R. Jacobson
—update: Jennifer Gariepy

Uno Restaurant Holdings Corporation

100 Charles Park Road
West Roxbury, Massachusetts 02132
U.S.A.
Telephone: (617) 323-9200
Fax: (617) 323-4252
Web site: http://www.unos.com

Private Company
Incorporated: 1943 as Pizzeria Uno
Employees: 8,200 (est.)
Sales: $265 million (2004 est.)
NAIC: 722110 Full-Service Restaurants; 533110 Lessors of Nonfinancial Intangible Assets (Except Copyrighted Works)

Uno Restaurant Holdings Corporation is the controlling body for a group of companies that operate and/or franchise a chain of casual dining restaurants known as Pizzeria Uno ... Chicago Bar & Grill. Specializing in Chicago-style deep-dish pizza, Pizzeria Uno restaurants are full-service establishments that also offer a broad range of other menu items, including pastas, appetizers, salads, and desserts. In addition to its responsibility for approximately 150 restaurants around the United States, Canada, Puerto Rico, and Korea, Uno Restaurant Holdings Corporation also controls a consumer food products division that produces and distributes Uno food items for retail sale in supermarkets and convenience stores.

Deep-Dish Pizza: A New Concept for the 1940s

The Uno concept dates back to 1943, when Ike Sewell decided to open a pizzeria in Chicago with his friend, Ric Riccardo, founder and owner of Riccardo's Restaurant. Riccardo had just returned from a trip to Italy and was hoping to capitalize on a relatively new item on the American scene: pizza. The two men utilized space in the basement of a Chicago mansion to create Pizzeria Uno, where they began showcasing a pizza creation that came to be known as Chicago-style deep-dish.

For 12 years, Sewell and Riccardo's establishment continued to perfect its pizza, which was a thick-crusted version baked for almost an hour in a deep pan. While Sewell continued at his position as an executive for Standard Brands and Riccardo managed his other restaurant endeavor, their deep-dish pizza product gained immense popularity throughout Chicago. In 1955 they opened another restaurant just blocks away from the original, naming it Pizzeria Due.

Ten years later both restaurants were undeniable successes, and Sewell retired from his position with Standard Brands at the age of 62. He decided to open a third restaurant in the Chicago area, this time with a different focus. Su Casa began operating in 1965 and was regarded by many to be the first upscale Mexican restaurant in Chicago.

Nationwide Expansion in the 1970s and 1980s

In 1975, a man by the name of Aaron Spencer was in Chicago on business and ate dinner at Pizzeria Uno. As the owner of 24 New England Kentucky Fried Chicken units, Spencer was well versed in the restaurant industry, and recognized that Sewell and Riccardo possessed a product capable of success on a national level. He contacted them with an offer to purchase franchise rights for Pizzeria Uno, but was rejected initially, as had been all other franchise offers throughout the years.

Three years later, however, Spencer was still interested in expanding Pizzeria Uno nationally. He finally convinced Sewell to allow one test unit to be opened in Boston, and it was an immediate success. Based on that unit's proven prosperity, Sewell agreed to sign a full franchise deal giving Spencer complete expansion rights, and by 1979 the deal was set. Sewell maintained control of his three restaurants in Chicago, while Spencer created a company called Pizzeria Uno to manage his new restaurants in Boston, and Uno Restaurants, Inc. to manage all other franchised units. Although Sewell never took an active part in the management of the newly formed Uno chain, he continued to manage his own restaurants and served as a director for Spencer until his death in 1990.

In 1984, Spencer decided to sell his Kentucky Fried Chicken units in order to concentrate solely on strengthening his blossoming Uno business. Three years later, Uno had expanded so much that Spencer formed a new body called Uno Restaurant Corporation to preside over the two existing divisions housing

Company Perspectives:

Uno is well positioned for continued growth. We have established a distinctive niche in the restaurant industry, as the only full-service, casual dining restaurant with a signature product—Chicago deep-dish pizza. We have built on the widespread popularity of this product to broaden the appeal of our concept, while leveraging our expertise to create additional opportunities through retail sales, new initiatives, and an expanding franchise system.

the company-owned and franchised operations. Stock in the new Uno Restaurant Corporation was offered to the public, helping to earn approximately $6.2 million to fund future expansion efforts.

By 1988, Uno Restaurant had grown to include 15 company-owned restaurants and 26 franchised units, with a strong concentration in the Boston area. Prospective franchisers were continuing to make offers to Spencer, whose company made efforts to select new owners based mainly on the potential of the location. After choosing new sites, Uno Restaurants collected a one-time $40,000 fee from new franchisees and then offered them support in starting operations and implementing the Uno concept program. The program, known as "Going for the T.O.P.," (an acronym for Train, Operate, and Promote), was created in an effort to ensure a consistent level of service and management throughout the rapidly growing chain. The program was instituted by a committee known as the Number One Club, composed of three of the top franchise operators and three company owners.

Diversifying and Regrouping in the Early to Mid-1990s

After ten years of building Pizzeria Uno into a strong presence across the Eastern Seaboard, Spencer began to widen the restaurant's scope. A diverse assortment of new items designed to satisfy a wide variety of customers was added to the Uno menu. The decision also was made to begin selling Uno's prepackaged deep-dish cheese pizza in supermarkets and convenience stores throughout the New England area.

Entering the 1990s, the restaurant industry was hit especially hard by a weakened economy, which meant less money was available for consumers to spend on dining out. Pizzeria Uno, however, fared extremely well in comparison with its competitors, which had come to be other full-service chains such as Chili's and Applebees, rather than other pizza makers. Uno and its prospects looked so good, in fact, that it began to attract other important players in the restaurant industry as franchisees. New owners included Art Gunther, former Pizza Hut president; J. Jeffrey Campbell, former Pillsbury Restaurant Group chairman; Jeff Grayson, former president of General Mills; Louis Neeb, former chairman of Burger King; and Stanley Nippon, a former executive at McDonald's.

By mid-1990, Uno Restaurant was responsible for the operation of 75 restaurants, after experiencing a remarkable 84 percent increase in profits over the previous four years. Average per-unit sales were significantly more than $1 million, and the

demand for Uno's retail pizza product was rapidly increasing. The company made attempts to keep pace by purchasing a processing plant near Boston, which enabled it to expand its retail pizza offerings to include pepperoni and sausage varieties as well as the cheese pizza already being sold. Prior to that acquisition, all retail production had been done out of the kitchen of one of the Boston restaurants. This new division began operating as Uno Foods, Inc.

Meanwhile, in response to a recession brought on by the Gulf War, Uno tried to counter the downturn in sales within its major markets of Boston and New York by offering different specials and promotions. It advertised specially priced deals during the lunch hours, and lowered prices on its children's menu in an effort to capture more families as patrons. Furthermore, the restaurants continued to expand their menu items, serving pizza, pasta, sandwiches, and salads, in addition to a full array of appetizers and desserts. One popular addition to the menu was the plizzetta, a light, thin-crusted gourmet pizza that accounted for 15 percent of the chain's sales by 1992.

Based on the success of the Uno pizza retail line following the purchase of the new production facility, the company decided to test a new takeout concept in selected restaurant locations. It began offering fresh, refrigerated unbaked pizzas for customers to pick up and take home, which allowed people to enjoy the product at home without Uno having to implement a delivery service. Another benefit of the takeout pizzas was the availability of all topping combinations, as compared with the limited offerings available in supermarkets.

In 1992, almost 50 years after Sewell and Riccardo entered the pizza business, Uno Restaurant acquired all of the outstanding shares of the three original restaurants in Chicago. The Pizzeria Uno chain had grown to include 109 restaurants throughout the United States, Canada, the United Kingdom, and Australia. Uno also was experimenting with the hotel foodservice market by offering its pizzas as room-service items at selected Hiltons and Marriotts in the United States.

Unfortunately, the chain's push to expand its menu beyond its pizza roots had not yet proved as successful as had been anticipated. While Uno's signature deep-dish pizza was a unique high-quality item, many of the restaurant's additional items did little to set Uno apart from other restaurants. Therefore, in 1993 Uno launched a $2.5 million effort to upgrade its units' kitchens, adding saute stations, charbroilers, grills, and fryers, enabling them to produce dishes of the same high quality as the pizza. The menu shifted slightly from its "Italianized" base, and the chain's restaurant units took on the name Pizzeria Uno . . . Chicago Bar & Grill.

Meanwhile, franchise expansion slowed for a short time while Uno tried to deal with an unsolicited $100 million acquisition bid by Morrison Restaurants, owner of the successful Ruby Tuesday restaurant chain. When Morrison originally initiated the offer, Uno's yearly sales were approximately $84 million; by the time Morrison backed away a year later, Uno's sales figures had far surpassed the $100 million mark for the first time in the company's history. In addition, Uno Foods, Inc. had just landed a contract with American Airlines to put its pizza aboard selected flights, and was benefiting from increased distribution into supermarkets in the East.

In 1994, as Uno was completing its restaurants' kitchen renovations and beginning to see success from marketing Uno as an eatery with a diversified menu, the company made an acquisition that coincided with the new focus. Uno Restaurant purchased all rights to three Bay Street Seafood restaurant units in Illinois, New Jersey, and Pennsylvania. A far stretch from Uno's early beginnings in pizza, the restaurants further diversified the company's offerings in the dining industry.

Entering the late 1990s, Uno Restaurant was well positioned for continued growth in each of its divisions. The company was composed of 150 full-service restaurants, including 86 company-owned and 64 franchised establishments, and was finalizing plans to enter new markets. In 1996, as it entered into negotiations with franchisees overseas, the company created Pizzeria Uno International and hired Bruce Raba to act as president of the division. Later that year, Spencer passed down his duties as CEO to Craig Miller, who had been president since 1986.

New Dishes, New Partners, New Growth in the Late 1990s

In the second quarter of 1996 Uno's comparable store sales, an important measure of a retail business's health, dropped 1.2 percent compared with the second quarter of fiscal 1995. The company lost $2.64 million on sales of $40.29 million. At the end of March 1996, the company posted a loss of $2.10 million for the first six months of fiscal 1996, despite the fact that revenue was up 10.6 percent to $80.85 million compared with the first half of fiscal 1995. The loss included a pretax charge of $3.94 million taken to write down the value of certain assets. Among these assets were the three Bay Street Seafood outlets opened in 1994 and three Uno Pizza Takery carryout operations. These ventures had lasted three years in all at a loss of $3.3 million and delayed rollout of Uno's efforts at kitchen and dining room remodeling and menu revision.

In 1996 the company began in earnest to change over from pizza parlor to full-service casual dinner house. The word "pizzeria" was shrunk and finally eliminated from the restaurant's logo. The look of Uno outlets was changed from a traditional pizzeria décor to what the company described as a "Chicago warehouse look." Modeled on old industrial buildings converted to restaurant use, the new design incorporated rough-finish brick veneer walls, exposed pipes and ductwork overhead, and low-hanging Tiffany-style lamps on chains. Service-station-type doors were used to divide smoking and nonsmoking sections and as storefront windows, adding to the industrial look. A comprehensive beverage program aimed at marketing premium beers and liquors in larger portions—15-ounce beers and 20-ounce frozen cocktails—was implemented. New training for bartenders was instituted and showy four-color comprehensive beverage menus for each table were introduced to spur sales. In 1998, the company experimented with opening a microbrewery under the name Pizzeria Uno Restaurant and Brewery to add to the perception of its beverage menu's emphasis on premium quality. Randy Clifton, formerly franchise system developer for the restaurant chain T.G.I. Friday's, was brought in during 1998 to move Uno away from urban outlets with high rents and small spaces to suburbia. He was charged with finding franchisers willing to open multiple suburban Uno restaurants and weeding out franchisers who were unwilling to commit to the chain's new look and suburban focus.

The repositioning efforts broadened Uno's customer base from its former "20-something" clientele to 25- to 40-year-olds with children who visited at least twice a month. Nonpizza items comprised 65 percent of sales, and by 1999 check averages were up 4 percent to $11.80. Higher traffic and larger check averages resulted in steady sales growth. Net income reached $9.8 million in 1999, up 63 percent from the previous year, on revenues of $214.23 million, a revenue increase of 12 percent over 1998. From 1996 to 1999, however, the company's stock valuation continued to suffer. Despite Uno's strong comeback in 1996, stock prices hovered around $7 per share. Small cap stocks in general experienced the same difficulties at the time because Wall Street investors perceived smaller companies as poor risks. Concerns about the economy drove buyers away from the restaurant trade. In an interview quoted by Paul Frumkin in the November 15, 1999 issue of *Nation's Restaurant News,* Bank of America securities analyst Stacey Jamar commented: "[R]estaurant stocks have performed fairly poorly over the last several months. . . . I think there is a concern in the marketplace that the economy will slow either from rising interest rates or pressure from inflation, and that will hurt consumer spending and subsequently hurt restaurant sales and restaurant stocks. . . . I think it's a little overdone . . . eating out in the U.S. has become less of a discretionary expenditure and more sort of a way of life. . . . I think the stocks have been pressured unduly.''

The illiquidity of Uno stock hampered plans to expand the business to 1,000 units, a number Uno executives felt was easily possible given the necessary capital. The company was able to grow a certain degree using internal funding. In 1997, Uno went international, concluding agreements with franchisees in Korea, Indonesia, Pakistan, and the United Arab Emirates (U.A.E.). The Korean firm Kolon Express & Tour Co. signed a ten-restaurant deal that included first refusal rights for Japan and Singapore. Pt. Nadya Vincent Indotama signed on to build ten units over ten years in Indonesia, with the first to open in Jakarta, and Jason Foods LLC agreed to open 12 outlets in Pakistan, starting in Lahore. Al Bannai Enterprises in the U.A.E. completed a deal to open 22 restaurants over seven years in the U.A.E., Saudi Arabia, Egypt, Kuwait, Jordan, Oman, Qatar, Bahrain, and Lebanon. As the 21st century approached, it became apparent that Uno could not look to Wall Street to keep expansion plans rolling. In April 2001, Uno Chairman Aaron Spencer and four of the company's executive officers took the company private, purchasing stock for $9.75 per share from shareholders, an approximately $41 million deal. Four years later, Uno found the backing for which it was looking. It sold a controlling interest in the company to the New York investment firm Centre Partners Management LLC for an undisclosed sum. According to Paul Frumkin, writing in the January 24, 2005 issue of *Nation's Restaurant News,* Centre Partners managing director David Blatte cited Uno's potential for growth as an important element in concluding the sale, and Aaron Spencer remarked, ''I would expect [the number of units] to double, at least.'' At the same time, Uno welcomed Frank Guidara as its new chief executive, replacing Craig Miller, who left Uno in 2001. Guidara, formerly president and CEO of Au Bon Pain, was known for his successful turnaround of that company. As CEO at Uno, Guidara was expected to focus on improving the chain's food quality. As of 2005, Uno had systemwide revenues of $500 million, drawn from 203 outlets, 123 of which were company-owned.

Principal Subsidiaries

Uno Foods, Inc.

Principal Divisions

Mid-Atlantic Division; New England Division; Western Division; Metro & Upstate New York Division.

Principal Competitors

Darden Restaurants Inc.; Rock Bottom Restaurants Inc.; Carlson Restaurants Worldwide Inc.; California Pizza Kitchen Inc.; Pizza Inn Inc.

Further Reading

Allen, Robin Lee, ''More Than Pizza: Uno Emerges from Long Dinner-House Overhaul,'' *Nation's Restaurant News,* February 14, 2000, p. 4.

——, ''Pizzeria Uno Launches Microbrew Concept,'' *Nation's Restaurant News,* April 27, 1998, p. 3.

Autry, Ret, ''Companies to Watch: Uno Restaurant,'' *Fortune,* July 16, 1990, p. 75.

Backas, Nancy, ''Bigger Is Better at Pizzeria Uno,'' *Cheers,* May 2000, p. 14.

Bell, Alexa, ''Betting on Pizzeria Uno,'' *Restaurant Business,* July 20, 1989, p. 170.

Brumback, Nancy, ''Upper Crust,'' *Restaurant Business,* March 15, 2002, pp. 55–62.

Farkas, David, ''Bound for the Burbs,'' *Chain Leader,* June 2000, p. 44.

Frumkin, Paul, ''Growth Gurus: Pizzeria Uno's Strong Operations and Phenomenal Growth Have Wooed Industry Luminaries,'' *Restaurant Business,* July 20, 1989, p. 164.

——, ''Multichain Investor Centre Partners Buys Control of Uno,'' *Nation's Restaurant News,* January 24, 2005, p. 1.

——, ''Pizzeria Uno Charts Its Course for Smoother Times Ahead,'' *Nation's Restaurant News,* April 15, 1991, p. 35.

——, ''Pizzeria Uno Eyes Retail Expansion,'' *Nation's Restaurant News,* May 28, 1990, p. 1.

——, ''Uno Withdraws from Secondary Offering,'' *Nation's Restaurant News* 33, no. 46, November 15, 1999, p. 1.

Frydman, Ken, ''Pizzeria Uno: More Than Just Another Fast-Food Pizza Place,'' *Nation's Restaurant News,* November 16, 1987, p. 3.

Gatlin, Greg, ''Uno Serves Up Growth As Company Hones Strategy,'' *Boston Herald,* June 2, 1999, p. 038.

Hodges, Dave, ''Public's Appetite for Pizza Keeps Franchise Searching for Sites,'' *Orlando Business Journal,* October 1, 1989, p. 1.

Mack, David, ''Pizzeria Uno's New Look Leaves Behind Its Checkered Past,'' *Nation's Restaurant News,* May 8, 2000, p. 26.

Mehlman, William, ''Boston Doldrums Not Likely to Derail Uno Restaurants,'' *Insiders' Chronicle,* April 23, 1990, p. 1.

Papiernik, Richard, ''Uno Sales, Profits Heat Up Through 6 Mos. in FY 2000,'' *Nation's Restaurant News,* June 19, 2000, p. 11.

Papiernik, Richard L., ''Stock Price, Profits Spark Uno Buyout-Bid Speculation,'' *Nation's Restaurant News,* January 11, 1999, p. 1.

——, ''Uno Restaurant Corp. Earnings Grow 98% for 6 Months in '99,'' *Nation's Restaurant News,* April 26, 1999, p. 12.

Paul, Ronald N., ''Going for the Top,'' *Restaurant Hospitality,* April 1988, p. 162.

Peters, James, ''Wall Street Not Impressed As Uno Pursues Strong Growth Track,'' *Nation's Restaurant News,* September 4, 2000, p. 11.

''Pizzeria Uno Eyes Expansion in Middle East, Indonesia,'' *Nation's Restaurant News,* October 6, 1997, p. 58.

''Pizzeria Uno to Open 10 New Locations in Korea,'' *Nation's Restaurant News,* July 15, 1996, p. 92.

''Pizzeria Uno to Shed Bay Street Grill Restaurants,'' *Nation's Restaurant News,* January 6, 1997, p. 80.

Prewitt, Milford, ''Pizzeria Uno Founder Sewell Dies,'' *Nation's Restaurant News,* September 3, 1990, p. 3.

''Uno Cites New Prototype As It Seeks to Stem Losses,'' *Nation's Restaurant News,* June 10, 1996, p. 12.

''Uno Lists Merger-Related Costs As It Prepares to Go Private,'' *Nation's Restaurant News,* July 30, 2001, p. 12.

''Wage Inflation, Utility Costs Hamper Uno 6-Month Profits,'' *Nation's Restaurant News,* April 30, 2001, p. 12.

Zuber, Amy, ''Pizza Chains: Those in the Dough Rise to the Top on Wall Street,'' *Nation's Restaurant News,* June 21, 1999, p. 4.

—Laura E. Whiteley
—update: Jennifer Gariepy

Vanguard Health Systems Inc.

20 Burton Hills Boulevard
Suite 100
Nashville, Tennessee 37215
U.S.A.
Telephone: (615) 665-6000
Fax: (615) 665-6099
Web site: http://www.vanguardhealth.com

Private Company
Incorporated: 1997
Employees: 14,300
Sales: $1.78 billion (2004)
NAIC: 524114 Direct Health and Medical Insurance
    Carriers; 621491 HMO Medical Centers; 621493
    Freestanding Ambulatory Surgical and Emergency
    Centers; 621498 All Other Outpatient Care Centers;
    621999 All Other Miscellaneous Ambulatory Health
    Care Services; 622110 General Medical and Surgical
    Hospitals; 622310 Specialty (except Psychiatric and
    Substance Abuse) Hospitals; 923130 Administration
    of Human Resource Programs (except Education,
    Public Health, and Veterans' Affairs Programs)

Vanguard Health Systems Inc. acquires nonprofit hospital systems and converts them to investor-owned status. The company is active in several markets, including Phoenix, Arizona; Orange County, California; Greater Chicago, Illinois; San Antonio, Texas; and Massachusetts. Vanguard typically buys bankrupt or near-bankrupt facilities, then invests in capital improvements to help upgrade service. A series of regional boards provides more local input than at other corporate hospital chains.

Origins

Vanguard Health Systems was formed in July 1997 by group of healthcare executives led by Charles Martin, Jr. Martin, an Alabama native, had started successful companies before. He helped launch General Care Corp., a small nursing home firm that Hospital Corporation of America (HCA) acquired for $78 million in 1980. He then worked for HCA, one of the predecessor companies of industry leader Columbia/HCA Healthcare Corp., eventually taking over 104 poorly performing hospitals spun off as Healthtrust. Martin was chairman and CEO of OrNda HealthCorp. (formerly Republic Health Corp.) from 1992, when it was bankrupt, to its $3 billion acquisition by Tenet Healthcare Corp. in January 1997.

Many nonprofit hospitals were struggling to meet their capital requirements in the changing healthcare industry. Vanguard foresaw the potential for consolidation in areas other consolidators were avoiding. "The name 'Vanguard' means literally the foremost or leading position in a trend," said Martin in a January 1998 statement.

With $1.5 billion in backing, mostly from Morgan Stanley Capital Partners of New York City. Vanguard aimed to consolidate community hospitals into investor-owned systems where the conditions were favorable. It was focused primarily on smaller markets within urban areas. What made the company unique, reported *Modern Healthcare,* was its governance by regional advisory boards, each comprised of both eight hospital and three Vanguard representatives.

First Acquisition in 1998

Vanguard acquired its first hospital, Maryvale Samaritan Medical Center of Phoenix, from the nonprofit Samaritan Health System in 1998. Maryvale had 213 beds.

Several early acquisition attempts failed, including that of New Jersey's Barnert Hospital. A deal to acquire six Philadelphia-area hospitals from the bankrupt Allegheny Health, Education and Research Foundation (AHERF) also fell apart.

Vanguard's revenues for the fiscal year ended June 30, 1999 were $91.5 million, twelve times those of the previous year. The company lost $6.4 million in fiscal 1999 and $2.6 million in fiscal 1998. The net loss was narrowed to $1.4 million in fiscal 2000, when revenues were up to $304.7 million. Vanguard was profitable in fiscal 2001, with net income of $10.7 million on revenues of $667.8 million.

Company Perspectives:

Vanguard Health Systems aspires to be the pre-eminent organization of market-leading, top quality healthcare provider systems preferred by communities, patients, physicians, payers, employers and employees.

In late 1999, Vanguard acquired hospitals in Anaheim and Huntington Beach, California. West Anaheim Medical Center had 219 beds, while Huntington Beach Hospital had 130. The seller was Triad Hospitals, a Dallas-based spin-off of Columbia/HCA.

Vanguard boosted its Arizona operations with the acquisition of the 222-bed Phoenix Baptist Hospital in 2000. The company also expanded into major new markets. MacNeal Health Network, which included a 333-bed hospital in the Chicago suburb of Berwyn, Illinois, was added during the year. MacNeal, a nonprofit facility, had net income of $11.6 million on revenues of $268 million in fiscal 1998.

Also in 2000, La Palma Intercommunity Hospital of Orange County, California, was acquired from Long Beach-based Memorial Health Services. Vanguard had attempted to buy La Palma a year earlier but had lost out to Memorial, which had acquired La Palma along with another hospital from Catholic Healthcare West. La Palma lost $4.5 million on net patient revenues of $36.1 million in fiscal 1998. In 2001, Vanguard opened the Magnolia Surgery Center in Orange County.

An HMO Acquired in 2001

A 2001 acquisition brought Vanguard its first HMO. Vanguard paid $39 million for bankrupt PMH Health Resources. PMH owned the 195-bed Phoenix Memorial Health system as well as the Phoenix Health Plan, a Medicaid HMO with 43,572 members and annual revenues of $107 million. It was rare for an investor-owned hospital chain to own a Medicare HMO, noted *Modern Healthcare*. A company executive told the publication it made sense for Vanguard to own an HMO due to the high numbers of Medicaid patients its Phoenix area hospitals treated.

Company cofounder William "Larry" Hough was promoted to president in mid-2001. Martin retained the titles of chairman and CEO. Hough had been an executive vice-president and chief operating officer for Martin both at Vanguard and at OrNda HealthCorp.

In 2002, Vanguard entered a joint venture with the University of Chicago Hospital Health System to buy the 200-bed Louis A. Weiss Memorial Hospital on the Windy City's North Side.

Vanguard opened the West Valley Hospital in Goodyear, Arizona, in 2003. This and the other Phoenix area (Maricopa County) facilities were grouped under the Abrazo Health Care banner.

The San Antonio-area Baptist Health System was acquired in 2003 in a deal worth $306 million. It had five acute care

Key Dates:

1997: Vanguard Health Systems is founded by a group of healthcare executives.
1998: Phoenix's Maryvale Samaritan Medical Center is acquired.
1999: Three hospitals are acquired in Anaheim and Huntington Beach, California.
2000: MacNeal Health Network (Illinois), La Palma Intercommunity Hospital (California), and Phoenix Baptist Hospital are bought.
2001: Vanguard opens Magnolia Surgery Center in Orange County, California; Phoenix Memorial and Phoenix Health Plan are acquired.
2002: Vanguard enters a joint venture with the University of Chicago Hospital Health System to buy Louis A. Weiss Memorial Hospital.
2003: West Valley Hospital opens in Goodyear, Arizona; San Antonio's Baptist Health System is acquired.
2004: Three hospitals are acquired in Massachusetts; Blackstone Group invests in Vanguard.

hospitals with a total of 1,537 licensed beds. Vanguard won the bid against spirited competition. It committed to invest $200 million in capital and soon set out renovating and expanding the Southeast Baptist Hospital, North Central Baptist Hospital, and Northeast Baptist. The area was booming and needed more capacity, reported the *San Antonio Express-News*.

Revenues for the fiscal year ended June 30, 2004 were $1.78 billion, up 33 percent largely due to the San Antonio acquisitions. Net income rose 137 percent to $40.1 million.

Blackstone Backing in 2004

Vanguard announced a major investment from the Blackstone Group in July 2004. Blackstone acquired two-thirds of the company's equity. The deal valued Vanguard, which then had 16 hospitals, at $1.75 billion. Morgan Stanley and Vanguard managers retained 30 percent.

At the end of calendar 2004, Vanguard acquired three Massachusetts acute care hospitals from Tenet Healthcare Corporation. These included the 348-bed Saint Vincent Hospital at Worcester Medical Center and the 420-bed MetroWest Medical Center, which was made up of two campuses: Natick's Leonard Morse Hospital and Framingham Union Hospital. Vanguard paid $100 million for the assets. Vanguard had reportedly been interested in MetroWest since 1998, when it was majority owned by Columbia/HCA Healthcare Corp. Saint Vincent had once been owned by Martin's previous firm, OrNda. In the mid-2000s, Vanguard was proceeding with a course of acquisitions that had kept the company growing since its inception and would likely continue to do so for the foreseeable future.

Principal Operating Units

Abrazo Health Care; Baptist Medical Center; Huntington Beach Hospital; La Palma Intercommunity Hospital; Louis A. Weiss

Memorial Hospital; MacNeal Hospital; Magnolia Surgery Center; MetroWest Medical Center; North Anaheim Surgicenter; North Central Baptist Hospital; Northeast Baptist Hospital; St. Luke's Baptist Hospital; Saint Vincent Hospital; West Anaheim Medical Center.

Principal Competitors

HCA Inc.; Iasis Healthcare Corp.; Tenet Healthcare Corp.; Triad Hospitals, Inc.

Further Reading

Bellandi, Deanna, "Finally in the Vanguard: Following String of Failed Bids, Nashville Hospital Company Boosts Acquisition Total to Four," *Modern Healthcare*, October 11, 1999, p. 24.

"CEO Interview: Keith Pitts—Vanguard Health Systems Inc.," *Wall Street Transcript*, February 2, 2002.

Galloro, Vince, "A Juicy Stake; Equity Firm Buys Majority Share of Vanguard," *Modern Healthcare*, August 2, 2004, p. 10.

Gedan, Benjamin, "Hospital Buyer Seen as Viable; Backers Cite Financial Health, Reputation," *Boston Globe*, October 24, 2004, p. 1.

Goldstein, Josh, "Nashville, Tenn., Firm Exits Deal to Buy Struggling Philadelphia Hospital," *Philadelphia Inquirer*, October 14, 2004.

Hammel, Lee, "Vanguard Gets Local Boost to Buy Hospital; City Leaders Turn Out for State Hearing," *Worcester Telegram & Gazette*, November 9, 2004, p. A1.

Hoffman, David, "Vanguard's Martin: Industry Needs Creative Management," *Bond Buyer*, November 3, 1999, p. 6.

Johnson, Linda A., "Barnert Hospital Backs out of Potential Sale to For-Profit System," *Associated Press Newswires*, September 17, 1998.

Kievra, Bob, "Waiting in the Wings; St. Vincent a Familiar Landscape for Vanguard CEO," *Worcester Telegram & Gazette*, September 19, 2004, p. E1.

Kirchheimer, Barbara, "Acquisition: It's All in How You Look at It," *Modern Healthcare*, November 1, 1999, p. 48.

——, "Vanguard: The Midwest and Beyond; Hospital Chain Is Looking to Buy Hospitals and Practices in Dayton, Ohio, and Phoenix," *Modern Healthcare*, May 22, 2000, p. 24.

——, "On Again, Off Again," *Modern Healthcare,* August 28, 2000, pp. 36f.

——, "Exception to the Rule; Vanguard Health Systems to Buy HMO; Proves Providers Can Run Health Plans," *Modern Healthcare*, April 23, 2001, p. 22.

——, "Vanguard Explores IPO; Three-Year-Old System Needs Cash for Bigger Deals," *Modern Healthcare*, July 2, 2001, p. 28.

Klein, Sarah A., "Buyout Will Mean Cash Infusion for Tired Weiss: But Some Fear for Community Ties," *Crain's Chicago Business*, December 17, 2001, p. 29.

Limbacher, Patricia B., "Martin's New Gambit: Ex-OrNda Chief Unveils For-Profit with Unique Structure," *Modern Healthcare*, January 26, 1998, p. 14.

——, "Vanguard's Slow Start Reflects Market," *Modern Healthcare*, February 9, 1998, p. 17.

——, "Vanguard Gets Slow Start: System Struggles with Mounting Failed Acquisitions," *Modern Healthcare*, October 19, 1998, p. 24.

Moon, Susanna, "Taking Cost off Supply Shelf; Healthcare Turning to Supply Chain Management Techniques Honed by Retail, Manufacturing to Limit Inventory, Slash Expenses," *Modern Healthcare*, November 22, 2004, p. 26.

Poling, Travis E., "Bidding Intensifies for San Antonio Hospital Group," *San Antonio Express-News*, May 24, 2002.

——, "Health System Owner to Pump Money Into Aging San Antonio Hospital," *San Antonio Express-News*, October 9, 2003.

——, "Hospitals Expanding to Keep Up with Growth," *San Antonio Express-News*, February 13, 2005.

Rosenbush, Steve, "Blackstone's Vanguard Ambitions," *Business Week Online*, July 21, 2004.

Serb, Chris, "Money for Mission," *H&HN: Hospitals & Health Networks*, April 20, 1998, pp. 57f.

Sharpe, Anita, "Entrepreneurs Look to Profit on Nonprofit Hospitals," *Wall Street Journal*, February 2, 1998, p. B4.

Shrinkman, Ron, "Vanguard Jilted Again as Seller Flees Altar," *Modern Healthcare*, June 28, 1999, p. 21.

——, "Soft Landing," *Modern Healthcare*, March 19, 2001, pp. 36ff.

——, "First, the Bad News," *Modern Healthcare*, April 9, 2001, pp. 14f.

Somasundaram, Meera, "Vanguard Watches for More Hospital Buys," *Crain's Chicago Business*, April 24, 2000, pp. 4f.

Stark, Karl, "Nashville, Tenn., Hospital Firm Executive Has Record of Successes," *Philadelphia Inquirer*, March 13, 1998.

——, "Nashville, Tenn.-Based Vanguard Health Systems to Buy a North Jersey Hospital," *Philadelphia Inquirer,* July 2, 1998.

"Vanguard Completes the Acquisition of Baptist Health System," *Managed Care Weekly Digest*, January 27, 2003, p. 34.

"Vanguard Health Systems Launched to Partner with Non-Profit Multi-Hospital Systems," press release, Nashville, Tenn.: Vanguard Health Systems Inc., January 26, 1998.

—Frederick C. Ingram

Vicat S.A.

6 Place De L Iris
92400 Courbevoie
France
Telephone: (+33) 01 58 868 686
Fax: (+33) 01 58 868 686
Web site: http://www.vicat.fr

Public Company
Incorporated: 1853
Employees: 5,700
Sales: EUR 1.46 billion ($1.27 billion) (2003)
Stock Exchanges: Euronext Paris
Ticker Symbol: VCTP
NAIC: 327310 Cement Manufacturing; 327410 Lime
    Manufacturing

Vicat S.A. is France's third-largest producer of cement, concrete and granulates, and also holds a strong share in these markets in the United States, through its National Cement Company subsidiaries in Alabama and California. Vicat produces more than 17 million tons of cement per year in 12 factories, including five in France, two in the United States, two in Turkey, and one each in Senegal, Egypt, and Switzerland. The company also operates grinding plants in France and Italy. Each year, the company produces more than seven million cubic meters of concrete in nearly 210 sites in France, the United States, Switzerland, and Turkey, and more than 15 million tons of granulates in 57 locations in France, Turkey, Switzerland and Senegal. The company's products include its Prompt brand of fast-setting cement. Vicat has also extended its operations over the years into a number of complementary activities, including specialty concrete coatings; prefabricated concrete products, including sewage and drainage pipes; transportation and logistics of concrete and other building materials; wholesale distribution of concrete and other building products through a chain of ten depots; and paper through Les Papeteries de Vizille, which produces 30,000 tons of specialty papers per year, especially paper and packaging for the construction industry, including cement sacks. These operations accounted for nearly 20 percent of the group's sales, which neared EUR 1.5 billion ($1.3 billion) in 2003. Cement added approximately 40 percent to the group's sales, while concrete, including ready-mix and granulates, added nearly 41 percent. France remains the group's primary market, at nearly 50 percent of sales. International sales topped 50 percent for the first time in 2003, with the United States, at 22 percent, representing the company's second-largest market. The company was founded by the son of Louis Vicat, the inventor of artificial cement, and the family remains the company's largest shareholder, with some 53 percent of shares. CEO Jacques Merceron-Vicat is the sixth generation to lead the company. Quoted on the Euronext Paris Stock Exchange, Vicat's other major shareholder is Heidel-bergCement, which controls 35 percent of its shares.

Beginnings in the 1850s

Cement making had remained relatively unchanged from the Roman period into the early 19th century. However, traditional cement techniques, mixing limestone with hardened clay fragments and furnace slag, were not as suitable for underwater use. When Louis Vicat, a graduate of France's prestigious Ecole Polytechnique, received an order to construct a bridge over the Dordogne River in 1812, he began searching for an alternative method for producing cement.

Vicat's research led him to test various materials and combinations as well as methods for mixing them. Over the next four years, he searched throughout France, finding a great number of limestone deposits. Vicat also identified the components of natural cements, that is, clay and lime, and recognized a cement mixture's holding power relied on the type and quality of the clay.

By 1816, Vicat had developed and published his "theory of hydraulicity," in which he identified the hydraulic forces generated through mixing the appropriate proportions of lime and clay. Vicat also developed a classification system based on the hydraulicity of various substances and the proportions needed to create an artificial cement. As Vicat wrote: "Since we know how and why the hydraulic power changes, depending on the respective contents of limestone and clay, therefore we know how to produce artificial mixes at will and with accuracy." By 1817, Vicat had perfected the method and introduced the world's first artificial cement.

To his credit, Vicat did not seek to patent his artificial cement, nor did he launch the production of cement on any kind of scale. Yet Vicat's invention was to have a dramatic effect on building techniques in the 19th century, making possible construction on a vastly larger scale, inspiring a great deal of innovation, and literally laying the foundation for the Industrial Revolution.

The Vicat family remained closely linked to Louis Vicat's invention. Vicat's son Joseph, who had also attended the Ecole Polytechnique, decided to launch the first large-scale industrial production of artificial cement. Vicat built his first cement factory in 1853, in Genevrey-de-Vif in the Isere region. Vicat's company took advantage of the clay deposits in the Chartreuse hillside, in particular a vein yielding a particularly fine clay. The company was to continue to exploit that vein for more than 150 years, enabling it to develop its fast-setting Prompt cement.

The Vicat company remained in the family and became incorporated as SNC Ciments Merceron-Vicat et Cie in 1863. The company later changed its status, incorporating as a limited liability company in 1919. By then, Vicat's invention had inspired further new materials, such as Portland cement and ready-mix concrete. Vicat had also expanded its operations, adding on a number of complementary operations, such as production of concrete-based products, including sewage and drainage pipes and foundation blocks. Vicat also began producing concrete coating and facings.

A growing number of competing producers arose in the wake of Vicat's success. Yet the company remained a leading player in the sector throughout the 20th century. In 1922, the company succeeded in building France first large-scale cement production plants, in Montalieu and in La Grave de Peille. The launch of production at these sites helped boost the company's total yearly production to more than 2.5 million tons.

International Growth in the 1970s

Into the 1960s, the French cement and concrete industry remained highly fragmented. This was due in large part to the difficulty and high cost of transporting cement and concrete, a situation that favored the development of a highly localized industry. Yet the small scale of the majority of cement producers made it difficult to carry out the investment needed to expand and modernize their facilities. In Vicat's case, production rose only slightly into the middle of the decade, just topping three million tons per year.

The need for scale, along with French government pressure, encouraged the first wave of consolidation in the cement and concrete sector in the late 1960s. Vicat quickly emerged as a leader in the consolidation movement. The company's first acquisition came in 1967 with the purchases of Société Méditerranéenne des Chaux et Ciments Portland Artificiels. The following year, the company expanded its own operations, establishing a new cement plant in Créchy.

Vicat made its next purchase in 1969, taking over Société des Ciments de Xeuilley. In 1970, the company added Ciments de Voreppe et Vouvesse and Ciments de la Porte de France. These were followed by the acquisition of Ciments de Pont-à-Vendin in 1971. In 1973, Vicat added a wholesale and distribution business, l'Auxiliaire des Matériaux de Construction Auximaco.

While Vicat continued seeking out new acquisition targets in France, its attention turned to the international market in the mid-1970s. In 1974, the company made its first foreign acquisition, buying up the National Cement Company of America in Ragland, Alabama. That company had started producing cement around the turn of the 20th century and became the leading cement producer in Alabama. The addition of the Ragland facility, along with Vicat's other acquisitions, helped boost its total production to nearly six million tons that year.

The recession of the 1970s slowed down Vicat's growth. In 1980, however, the company renewed its expansion drive, turning first to Société des Ciments Chiron. Vicat also continued seeking to diversify its business with complementary activities. In 1983, the company acquired Les Papeteries de Vizille, which produced specialty printing and writing papers. While the paper mill maintained that activity under Vicat, it also began producing papers for packaging, especially large-size Kraft-paper sacs for building materials such as the company's own concrete and cement products, as well as other products, including fertilizers and chemicals. The Vizille site eventually expanded its packaging production to some 80 million sacks per year.

Vicat simplified its name to Vicat SA in 1984 and once again began scouting for a foreign acquisition. The company returned to the United States in 1987, buying up the Lebec cement factory in Los Angeles, launching Vicat's National Cement Company of California subsidiary. The purchase strategically placed Vicat in what was by then the largest cement market in the United States. At the same time, Vicat's top French competitors, Lafarge and Ciments Française, had also entered the U.S. market. The three French groups combined to claim the leading share of a market that had come to be dominated at more than 75 percent by foreign interests.

Foreign Focus in the 2000s

Vicat added a new complementary business in 1989 when it purchased SATM, a specialist in transporting cement, concrete, and granulates for large-scale construction projects. SATM, founded in 1958, gave Vicat a network of ten branch offices throughout France.

Key Dates:

1817: Louis Vicat publishes a method for the production of artificial cement.

1853: Joseph Vicat constructs a factory to produce cement using his father's method.

1863: The company is incorporated as SNC Ciments Merceron-Vicat et Cie.

1919: SNC Ciments Merceron-Vicat et Cie converts its status to a limited liability company.

1922: The company builds its first two large-scale cement production sites in France.

1967: Société Méditerranéenne des Chaux et Ciments Portland Artificiels is acquired.

1968: The company builds a new cement plant in Créchy.

1969: Société des Ciments de Xeuilley is acquired.

1970: The company buys Ciments de Voreppe et Vouvesse and Ciments de la Porte de France.

1971: Ciments de Pont-à-Vendin is acquired.

1973: The company enters the wholesale and distribution market with the purchase of l'Auxiliaire des Matériaux de Construction Auximaco.

1974: The company enters the United States with the purchase of Ragland plant in Alabama.

1980: Société des Ciments Chiron is acquired.

1983: The company diversifies into paper and packaging with the purchase of Les Papeteries de Vizille.

1984: The company changes its name to Vicat SA.

1987: Lebec cement factory in Los Angeles area is acquired.

1989: Vicat acquires SATM, a transporter of aggregates, cement, and concrete.

1991: Konya Cimento, in Turkey, is acquired.

1994: Bastas Baskent, in Ankara, Turkey, and SOCOCIM, in Senegal, are acquired.

2001: Vigier, in Switzerland, is acquired.

2003: Cementi Centru Sud, in Italy, and Sinai Cement Company, in Egypt, are acquired.

2004: Materiaux SA, in France, and Biedermann, in Switzerland, are acquired.

In the 1990s, Vicat widened the scope of its international interests. The company first turned to Turkey, where it acquired Konya Cimento in 1991. The addition of that plant, located in Central Anatolia, boosted Vicat's total production past nine million tons. Vicat returned to Turkey in 1994, buying a majority stake in Bastas Baskent, the leading cement producer in the Ankara market. The company continued to broaden its Turkish operations, adding a ready-mix facility and sites in Karaman and Manavgat on the Mediterranean coast.

Vicat continued building its capacity in the United States, notably through the installation of a ready-mix plant in Alabama. This investment helped win the company a number of major contracts from the city of Atlanta as it prepared for the 1996 Olympic Games. The company next turned its attention to Senegal, where it acquired SOCOCIM in 1994. That company was not only the leader in the Senegalese market but also held a leading position supplying cement to neighboring markets. The company's investment and acquisitions helped it top 13 million tons per year by the mid-1990s.

Vicat's next major acquisition came in 2001, when it acquired Switzerland's Vigier. That company had been founded in 1871, in Luterbach, and later built a cement plant in Rechcnette. The addition of Vigier also gave the company control of Créabéton Matériaux, with five factories producing a variety of prefabricated cement products such as cinder blocks, walls, and paving tiles. Vigier also helped raise Vicat's production capacity past 15 million tons that year.

In 2003, Vicat turned to Italy, where it acquired Cementi Centru Sud, then to Egypt, where it purchased the Sinai Cement Company. These purchases helped the company top 17 million tons that year. Vicat then returned to Switzerland, buying aggregates and concrete producer Biedermann in 2004. Also in that year, Vicat launched a new aggregates joint-venture in Senegal and built a new rock crushing facility there as well, launching operations in February 2004.

Back in France, Vicat expanded its domestic operations with the purchase of Matériaux SA, a leading aggregates producer in the Metz, Nancy, and Thionville regions, with operations reaching to Luxembourg as well. The addition of Matériaux's business boosted Vicat's aggregates production by another one million tons. By then, Vicat had clearly set its future growth prospects on its continued international expansion. As a pioneer in the world cement market, Vicat's future rested on a solid foundation.

Principal Subsidiaries

Annecy Béton Carrières; Atelier du Granier; Béton Travaux; Bétons Granulats du Centre; Builders Concrete (United States); Cementi Centro Sud Spa (Italy); Condensil; Kirkpatrick (United States); Matériaux Centre France; Monaco Béton; National Cement Company (United States); National Cement Company of California (United States); National Ready Mixed (United States); Sablières du Grésivaudan; Sigma Béton; United Ready Mixed (United States); Vicat; Vicat International Trading.

Principal Competitors

IFI; Lafarge S.A.; CRH plc; Cementos Apasco S.A. de C.V.; Taiheiyo Cement Corporation; Fomento de Construcciones y Contratas S.A.; HeidelbergCement AG; Grupo Ferrovial S.A.; Cemex S.A. de C.V.; Italmobiliare S.p.A.; Italcementi S.p.A.; CEMEX.

Further Reading

Homer, Eric, "Heavy: Cement Concern Vicat Sets up $400 million Via Credit Lyonnais," *Private Placement Letter*, July 28, 2003.

"Vicat Clinches stake in Sinai," *MEED Middle East Economic Digest*, April 4, 2003, p. 16.

"Vicat Acquires Swiss Cement Group Vigier," *European Report*, January 31, 2001.

—M.L. Cohen

Vilmorin Clause et Cie

BP 1
Chappes
F-63720
France
Telephone: (+33) 4 73 63 41 95
Fax: (+33) 4 73 63 41 80
Web site: http://www.vilmorinclause.com

Public Company
Incorporated: 1998 as Vilmorin Clause & Cie.
Employees: 3,029
Sales: EUR 492.2 million ($594.7 million) (2004)
Stock Exchanges: Euronext Paris
Ticker Symbol: RIN
NAIC: 111421 Nursery and Tree Production; 424910
    Farm Supplies Merchant Wholesalers

Vilmorin Clause & Cie is the world's leading supplier of seeds for the professional gardener and the consumer home garden markets. Based in France, and majority held by agro-industrial cooperative Groupe Limagrain, Vilmorin has developed a strong international presence built around a network of subsidiaries, including Ferry-Morse and Harris Moran in the United States; U.K. leader Suttons Seeds; Nickerson Zwaan in the Netherlands and Germany; a majority stake in Israel's Hazera Genetics, world leader in tomato seeds; Flora Frey and, since 2004, Sperling in Germany; Kyowa Seeds ni Japan, as well as Vilmorin, Oxadis and Clause Tézier in France. These companies oversee a stable of brands, including Vilmorin, Henderson Seeds, Clause, HM, Top Green, Kyowa, Flora-Frey, Suttons, Sperli, and Ferry-Morse. Over two-thirds of the group's sales come from outside of France. Of this amount, Europe, excluding France, represents 48 percent; the Americas add 30 percent; and the Asian Pacific region adds 10 percent. Vilmorin operates nearly 40 production site globally, supported by 46 research laboratories throughout its zones of operation. Eighty percent of the group's sales, which topped EUR 492 million, derives from the sale of seeds, including vegetable, flower, and lawn seeds for the consumer market and vegetable seeds for the professional market. The company also distributes related gardening items, as well as pet foods. Listed on the Euronext Paris Stock Exchange, Vilmorin Clause & Cie has been part of Groupe Limagrain since 1975. That company also remains Vilmorin's majority shareholder, with more than 51 percent of its stock.

From 18th Century Origins through the 1980s

Vilmorin's connection to the world of botany and the modern seeds industry stretches back to the mid-18th century. In 1743, Madame Claude Geoffrey, known as the "maitresse grainetière" in Paris, opened a boutique for plants and seeds on the city's Quai de la Mégisserie with her husband, Pierre d'Andrieux, then the chief seed supplier and botanist for King Louis XV.

Geoffrey and Andrieux's daughter later married Philippe Victoire de Vilmorin, who joined the business in 1775. The boutique added Vilmorin's name, becoming Vilmorin-Andrieux. The company was to continue operating under this name for more than 200 years. De Vilmorin recognized the need for a means of communicating and describing the variety of seeds available to horticulturists, farmers, and others, and collaborated with a natural history specialists to produce the first seed catalog.

The Vilmorin name gained international stature in the 19th century through the efforts of Louis de Vilmorin. Born in 1816, the grandson of Philippe de Vilmorin spent his professional life as a biologist and chemist, with a focus on the breeding and cultivation of plants. Louis de Vilmorin began developing a theory of heredity in plants and recognized that it was possible to select certain characteristics of a plant and transmit them to successive generations in order to develop a new variety of that plant. In 1856, de Vilmorin published his "Note on the Creation of a New Race of Beetroot and Considerations on Heredity in Plants," establishing the theoretical groundwork for the modern seed-breeding industry.

Botany remained at the center of the de Vilmorin family's occupations through succeeding generations. The family played an important role in a number of theoretical and technical advances such as developing the principles of genealogical breeding programs, improving seed quality through cross-breeding initiatives, and creating disease-resistant and hybrid varieties of plants.

In 1972, Vilmorin-Andrieux was bought up by René Hodée, a farmer from the Anjou region. Hodée moved the company to La Ménitré. Three years later, Hodée sold Vilmorin-Andrieux to Limagrain. Based in the Limagne plains of the Auvergne region, Limagrain had been founded in 1942 as a cooperative specialized in producing and selling seeds. Limagrain formally adopted its name in 1965 and developed a specialty focus on developing corn seeds and varieties. By 1970, the cooperative had succeeded in developing its corn LG 11, which quickly became the top-selling corn seed variety of the period and laid the foundation for the Limagrain's growth into a major agro-industrial group.

The purchase of Vilmorin-Andrieux represented an important extension of Limagrain's operations into the markets for flowers, ornamental plants, and fruits and vegetables seeds. Limagrain made two more major acquisitions into the 1980s. In 1979, the group acquired France's Tézier, a specialist in seeds for the professional gardening sector. The acquisition of Tézier already helped establish Limagrain as one of the world's top sources for seeds for both the professional and consumer markets.

In 1981, Limagrain turned to the United States, buying Ferry-Morse Co. That company was the result of the 1930 merger of the D.M. Ferry Co., founded in 1856, and the C.C. Morse and Co., founded in 1874. Over the following decades, Ferry-Morse grew into a major supplier to the North American home garden seed market.

Forming a Garden Seeds Specialist in the 1990s and Beyond

At the end of the 1980s, Limagrain began taking steps to restructure its garden seeds business for both the professional and consumer markets. In 1989, the company formed an umbrella structure for its consumer vegetable seeds operations, called Oxadis. This subsidiary became the marketing and distribution wing for the group's Vilmorin and Tézier seed brands. Oxadis also handled the group's pet foods and supplies operations, which was seen as a natural extension to the seeds business because the company's Home Garden customers tended to own pets.

In 1990, Limagrain acquired 80 percent of Germany's Flora-Frey, the leader in that market. That purchase encouraged Limagrain to create a dedicated subsidiary to include all of its vegetable and flower seeds operations. Also in 1990, the cooperative created a new holding structure, Ceres, which took over Vilmorin S.A. (the company's name since 1986) as well as Tézier, Oxadis, Flor-Frey, and Ferry-Morse. In 1992, however, Limagrain renamed its gardening seeds subsidiary as Vilmorin & Cie.

Vilmorin & Cie acquired the other members of the former Ceres, becoming the holding company for Limagrain's gardening seeds operations. In 1992, Vilmorin & Cie listed its shares on the Paris Stock Exchange. Limagrain nonetheless retained majority control of the company and into the mid-2000s continued to hold more than 50 percent of the company.

The public offering enabled Vilmorin to begin an expansion drive that continued throughout the 1990s. Acquisitions accounted for a major part of the group's growth during the period, starting with the purchase of a 25 percent stake in Australia's Triagro and the acquisition of the leading garden seeds group in the United Kingdom, Suttons. Suttons own history dated back to its founding in Reading in 1806 by John Sutton. The company established its own laboratory as early as 1840, eighty years before British law required seeds testing.

In 1995, Vilmorin stepped up its stake in Flora-Frey, to 90 percent, then opened a subsidiary of that company in Austria. The following year, Vilmorin made two more significant acquisitions: Clause, based in France, and Harris Moran Seeds Inc., of the United States. The Clause brand specialized in providing seeds for the professional gardeners circuit. In 1990, Clause was purchased by Rhone Poulence, which also bought the Harris Moran, based in the United States, that year. The two companies were operated independently of each other. Following their acquisition by Limagrain, Clause was merged with Tézier, forming Clause Tézier, while Ferry-Morse was merged into Harris Moran, becoming a subsidiary of the larger company. Following the Clause acquisition, Vilmorin changed its name, becoming Vilmorin Clause & Cie. It then transferred Clause's home garden operations into Oxadis.

Vilmorin continued its expansion into the end of the decade. The company moved into the Benelux region with the purchase of Nickerson Zwaan, founded in 1976 in the Netherlands. Nickerson Zwaan then took over Clause's Germany business in 1998. That year, also, the group established a Polish subsidiary for Flora-Frey. In another move, Vilmorin merged its holding in Triagro into a new joint venture, called the Henderson Seeds Joint Venture Trust. Vilmorin had also been building up a presence in Japan, notably through a stake in Mikado. By 1997, Vilmorin's share in that company had risen to 20 percent.

Vilmorin's presence in Japan took a step up in 2000 with the purchase of that country's Kyowa Seeds. The following year, Vilmorin returned to the Netherlands, acquiring a 20 percent share of Bio Seeds, the holding company for biotechnology and plant genomics specialist Keygene. That purchase was complemented in 2002 by the acquisition of another Dutch company, Van den Berg.

Key Dates:

1743: Madame Claude Geoffrey and husband, Pierre d'Andrieux, then the chief seed supplier and botanist for King Louis XV, open a plant and seed boutique in Paris.

1775: Philippe de Vilmorin the joins business, which becomes Vimorin-Andrieux.

1856: Louis de Vilmorin publishes "Note on the Creation of a New Race of Beetroot and Considerations on Heredity in Plants," establishing the theoretical groundwork for the modern seed-breeding industry.

1975: Limagrain acquires Vilmorin-Andrieux.

1979: Limagrain acquires the vegetable seed group Texier.

1981: Limagrain acquires Ferry-Morse in the United States.

1986: Vilmorin-Andrieux changes its name to Vilmorin SA.

1989: Limagrain establishes Oxadis.

1990: Limagrain acquires 80 percent of Germany's Flora-Frey, then sets up a holding company, Ceres, for its garden seeds operations.

1992: Ceres becomes Vilmorin & Cie.

1993: Vilmorin goes public on the Paris Stock Exchange and acquires Suttons (U.K.) and 25 percent of Australia's Triagro.

1995: Flora-Frey Austria is established.

1997: The company purchases Clause Semense, Clause Jardin, and Harris-Moran Seed Company from Rhone Poulenc as well as Nickerson Zwaan (Netherlands) and forms the Henderson Seeds Joint Venture Trust in Australia.

1998: The company forms a strategic alliance with Israel's Hazera and acquires a 12.6 percent stake in the firm.

2000: Kyowa Seeds (Japan) is acquired.

2001: The company acquires a stake in Keygene (Netherlands).

2003: The company boosts its share in Hazera to 55 percent, making it the world leader in the tomato seeds segment.

2004: Vilmorin acquires Germany's Sperling GmbH and establishes Marco Polo Seeds Thailand as a spearhead for future Southeast Asia expansion.

Into the mid-2000s, Vilmorin continued to seek expansion opportunities, with a special focus on new technologies and markets. In 1998, for example, the company launched a strategic partnership with Israel's Hazera, one of the world's leading producers of tomato seeds, founded in 1939. As part of their alliance, Vilmorin acquired 12.6 percent of Hazera. The partnership resulted in a research agreement with the American firm of Agrinomics in 2000 and paved the way for a closer relationship between the two companies. In July 2003, Vilmorin boosted its share of Hazera to 55 percent. The purchase also gave Vilmorin control of Hazera's subsidiaries in Spain, China, and the United States.

Vilmorin's expansion drive continued into 2004. In that year, the company added Carl Sperling & Co. Founded in Hamburg in 1788, the Sperling company was one of the oldest of its kind in Germany and the largest home garden firm in Europe. Sperling brought Vilmorin its specialty in vegetable seeds and its strong Sperli brand.

By the end of 2004, Vilmorin had transformed itself into a truly international company. Nearly 70 percent of the group's sales, which topped EUR 492 million that year, were generated outside of France. While Europe and North America continued to account for the vast majority of the company's foreign sales, Vilmorin had begun to make headway in its new frontier: the Asian markets. In 2004, the company established a new subsidiary, Marco Polo Seed Thailand, as a spearhead for its future expansion in the region. Vilmorin Clause & Cie had planted the seeds for its future growth.

Principal Subsidiaries

American Bio Corporation Inc. (USA); Clause Tezier; Flora Frey GmbH (Germany); Harris Moran Seeds Inc. (USA); Hazera Genetics Ltd. (55%, Israel); Henderson Seeds JV (50.65%, Australia); Kyowa Seeds (Japan); Marco Polo Seed Thailand; Nickerson Zwaan BV (Netherlands); Nickerson Zwaan GmbH (Germany); Nickerson Zwaan India; Nickerson Zwaan Ltd. (U.K.); Oxadis; Sperling GmbH (Germany); Suttons (U.K.); Top Green; Vilmorin.

Principal Competitors

Syngenta International AG; Sapporo Holdings Ltd.; VBA; Groupe Euralis; Samhall AB; Advanta B.V.; Seminis Inc.; Sakata Seed Corp.; Kaneko Seeds Company Ltd.

Further Reading

Barnier, Benjamin, "Vilmorin Clause devient le numero un mondial des semences de tomates," *Monde*, July 15, 2003.

Goldberg, Nir, "Vilmorin Mulls Expanding Investment in Hazera," *Israel Business Arena*, November 24, 2002.

Lorelle, Veronique, "Limagrain, le cooperative auvergnate rivale de Monsanto," *Monde*, August 25, 2001.

"Vilmorin Acquires 20% Stake in Dutch Bio Seeds Group," *European Report*, July 18, 2001.

"Vilmorin Clause affiche une meilleure sante," *Echos*, October 14, 2002.

—M.L. Cohen

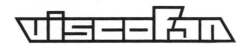

Viscofan S.A.

C/Iturrama 23 entreplanta
Pamplona
E-31007
Spain
Telephone: +34 948 19 84 44
Fax: 34 948 19 84 31
Web site: http://www.viscofan.com

Public Company
Incorporated: 1975 as Viscofan S.A., Industria Navarra
    de Envolturas Celulosicas
Employees: 3,573
Sales: EUR 371.3 million ($506.6 million) (2003)
Stock Exchanges: Madrid
Ticker Symbol: VIS
NAIC: 311612 Meat Processed From Carcasses; 221122
    Electric Power Distribution; 551112 Offices of Other
    Holding Companies

Viscofan S.A. is the world's largest manufacturer of artificial casings, the sleeves that hold sausages. Viscofan is also one of the most diversified casings producers, producing four of the six different types of meat casings: edible and inedible collagen; plastic; and cellulose. (The remaining categories are natural and fibrous casings.) By extending its production into multiple casing categories, and by positioning itself as a low-cost producer, Viscofan has captured a global market share of some 40 percent. This places it ahead of its two main competitors, Viskase, in the United States, and Devro, in the United Kingdom. Viscofan's casings are distributed to more than 80 countries worldwide. Based in the Navarro region of Spain, Viscofan supports its international sales through a network of manufacturing plants, including two each in Spain and Brazil, and plants in Germany, the Czech Republic, the United States, Peru, and Mexico. The company also operates sales and distribution subsidiaries in the United Kingdom, Thailand, Canada, Costa Rica, Russia, and Poland. The company's casings production plants are operated by Viscofan itself, and by its subsidiary, Naturin, based in Germany, which specializes in edible and non-edible collagen-based casings. In addition to its casings business, Viscofan also operates IAN S.A. (Industrias Alimentarias de Navarra), which produces and cans asparagus, olives, and tomatoes for pastes and sauces under the Carretilla brand name. Viscofan is listed on the Bolsa de Madrid and is run by founder and Chairman Jaime Echevarría Abona and CEO Juan Ignacio Villegas Díaz. Paper producer Iberpapel holds a 35 percent stake in Viscofan.

Converting to Casings in the 1970s

In the early 1970s, Viscofan was a tiny company based in Spain's Navarro region producing cellulose-based pastes. Yet toward the middle of the decade, the company faced a dwindling market for this product. As the company's founder Jaime Echevarría Abona explained to *United Press International:* "We were the first in making cellulose paste. When we realized it was an obsolete product, we started making casings."

Casings, the wrappers used for shaping sausages and other meat products, were traditionally made using the linings from animal intestines. Yet natural casings presented large variations in thickness and strength and thus did not lend themselves to automated production techniques. At the same time, natural casings were often in short supply. In the 1920s, the rising industrial food groups began seeking new materials and methods for producing sausages and, in the United States, especially frankfurters. In the 1920s, the later Viskase group developed a method for producing casings from cellulose, which could then be removed from the sausage, resulting in the "skinless" frank.

Echevarría began adapting the technology for producing cellulose casings. In 1975 Echevarría incorporated his company as Viscofan S.A., Industria Navarra de Envolturas Celulosicas. The company, which based its own production process on Viskase's patented methods, nonetheless required several years to perfect its method. As Echevarría pointed out: "It's easy to make a perfect meter of cellulose casing, but it's a whole different issue to produce them by the millions."

Finally, in 1979, Viscofan was ready to launch full-scale production of its own cellulose-based casings. Over the next several years, the company perfected its technology and by the mid-1980s Viscofan emerged as the lowest-cost producer of cellulose casings in the world. Despite the low pricing of its casings, Viscofan was able to generate relatively high margins, in large part due to the efficiency of its production process. These high margins allowed the company to reinvest in boosting its capacity while continuing to improve its efficiency. Into the mid-1980s, the company's sales surged forward, and by the middle of the decade the company was on its way toward claiming a 30 percent share of the global market outside of the United States.

Viscofan capitalized on its growing market position by expanding its operations onto an international scale. The company began opening sales and distribution subsidiaries in a number of key markets, such as Russia and elsewhere in Eastern Europe where sausage sales were traditionally strong. The United States and Canada, however, remained off-limits to the company due to patent restrictions. To fuel its growth, Viscofan went public in 1986, listing on the Bolsa de Madrid.

Viscofan posted impressive growth through the end of the 1980s. From a global market share of just 6 percent in 1986, the company's rise was dramatic. By the end of the decade, Viscofan claimed a 17 percent share of the world cellulose casings market. Yet cellulose casings remained just one of several casings segments which included such newly developed and fast-growing categories as collagen-based and fibrous casings.

At first, Viscofan responded to this situation by diversifying into other product areas. In 1988, the company acquired Industrias Alimentarias de Navarra (IAN), a producer of canned vegetables, especially asparagus and tomato paste and sauces, but also, at the time, artichokes and cooked vegetables. Under Viscofan, IAN refocused its own production around a core of tomato products and asparagus. The latter activity was boosted in 1990 when IAN established a subsidiary in Peru dedicated to the growing and canning of asparagus. The new facility gave Viscofan access to Peru's year-round asparagus growing season.

In 1989, Viscofan added to its new foods division with the purchase of Industrias Muerzas. That company produced a line of canned fruits and preserves under the popular Bebe brand, then the Spanish leader with a 12 percent market share. Meanwhile, IAN also produced and canned black olives through its Comaro subsidiary. Some 95 percent of Comaro's production went toward the export market, particularly to the United States and Canada, Germany, and Japan.

Adding Casing Technologies in the 1990s

Fast-growing Viscofan took a major step toward market dominance in 1990, when it acquired Germany's Naturin GmbH. That company, roughly four times Viscofan's size, stemmed from experiments in the 1920s that sought to produce artificial casings using collagen found in the lining under a cow's hide. The founders of Naturin developed a process for producing a collagen-based gel, which could then be extruded as a casing. Collagen offered a number of advantages, not the least of which was a greater strength and consistency than natural casing. Like cellulose, the original collagen casing was inedible.

By 1933, Naturin had perfected its production process. The company opened a factory in Weinheim, Germany and took on the name of Naturin-Werks Becker & Co. Production started that year. Naturin continued to develop its technology, and in 1962 launched a revolution in the sausage market, that of an edible collagen-based casing.

In the 1970s, Naturin became interested in adapting new materials for its casings production. In 1970, the company constructed a new facility for production of polyamide-based casings. Naturin's research and development efforts paid off again toward the end of the decade, and in 1978 the company launched the first biaxially oriented plastic casing. Into the mid-1980s, further development with collagen led to the début of the first food-industry grade collagen film, in 1983.

Naturin had expanded onto the international market as well, establishing sales subsidiaries in the United States, Canada, the United Kingdom, and Switzerland. Naturin also developed major markets in the Eastern European countries. The company's exposure to these markets brought it into difficulties at the end of the 1980s, however. At the same time, Naturin's technology had fallen behind the industry as whole. Meanwhile, its production lines had increasingly become antiquated.

Viscofan paid DEM 260 million for Naturin. The acquisition quadrupled Viscofan's sales and enabled it to expand its casings range into four of the six casings segments, including a world-leading position in the collagen-based casings market. Following the acquisition, Viscofan began restructuring Naturin. This process, hampered by the ongoing conversion to the free market system in Eastern Europe and by a lingering recession, was only completed by the late 1990s. Nonetheless, the acquisition of Naturin proved to be of strategic importance in Viscofan's rise to global dominance of the casings market.

Global Casings Leader in the New Century

Viscofan turned its attention to the Latin American market—the world's largest market for artificial casings, accounting for some 40 percent of all sales. In 1991, the company established a sales and distribution subsidiary in Brazil, itself the largest casings market in South America. Viscofan soon deepened its Latin American presence, building a cellulose shrilling plant in Brazil in 1993. Shrilling involved a process of compressing and pleating casings so that they could be used in high-speed sausage stuffing equipment.

In 1995, Viscofan added a second cellulose casings factory in Brazil, acquired from Hoechst. That purchase gave the company capacity in casings extrusions. In 1999, the company built a third facility in Brazil, adding further extrusion capacity. The new facility not only allowed Viscofan's Brazilian subsidiary to become autonomous, it also enabled the company to claim leadership in the Latin American market.

Key Dates:

1975: Viscofan begins developing cellulose-based casings production in Pamplona, Spain.
1979: The company launches large-scale production.
1986: The company lists on the Bolsa de Madrid as sales of cellulose casings surge.
1988: The company acquires IAN and diversifies into canned vegetable production.
1989: The company acquires Industrias Muerzas and its Bebe brand of conserves and canned fruit.
1990: The company acquires Naturin, leading producer of collagen-based casings; IAN opens an asparagus production and canning facility in Peru.
1991: The company opens a sales subsidiary in Brazil.
1993: The company opens a shrilling plant in Brazil.
1994: The company begins sales of cellulose casings in Canada and the United States; a sales subsidiary is opened in Moscow.
1995: The company acquires Gamex in the Czech Republic and Hoechst's cellulose casings business in Brazil.
1998: A cellulose casings production plant is built in Montgomery, Alabama.
2000: A new production facility is launched in the Czech Republic.
2001: A sales subsidiary is established in Thailand.
2002: A sales subsidiary is established in Poland.
2003: The company sells the Bebe conserves brand; a cellulose casings production plant is launched in Mexico.

In the meantime, Viscofan continued its international expansion elsewhere. The ending of patent restrictions in North America allowed Viscofan to begin selling its casings in Canada, followed by the United States, by 1994. The move came at a crucial moment, as Viscofan's two primary competitors in the United States—Devro, of the United Kingdom, and especially Viskase—had both run into financial difficulties. Viscofan's highly efficient, low-cost production allowed the company to undercut its competitors, and the established presence of Naturin in the North American market gave Viscofan a ready distribution network.

Into the late 1990s, Viscofan's operations in the United States had outpaced its ability to import casings. In 1998, therefore, the company established a production facility in Montgomery, Alabama, in order to supply the North American market.

Viscofan also had successfully turned around its Naturin subsidiary by then. Part of this effort came with the relocation of the group's conversion facility to the Czech Republic, a move made with the acquisition of that country's Gamex in 1995. In 1999, Viscofan expanded its Czech operations with the establishment of Viscofan CZ, and the construction of new extruding and shrilling facilities.

Viscofan also boosted its market position through the opening of new foreign sales and distribution subsidiaries. In 1994, the company opened a subsidiary in Moscow, which also provided support for the company's sales in the Far East. In 2000, however, Viscofan set up a dedicated Asian sales subsidiary in Thailand.

Closer to home, the company added a sales subsidiary in Poland in 2002. At the same time, Viscofan continued to develop its presence in the Latin American market. In 1999, the company established a dedicated sales subsidiary for the Central American market in Costa Rica. Meanwhile, the rising demand for Viscofan's casings in the region led it to begin construction of a new production facility, which opened in Mexico in 2003. Viscofan had successfully grown from a small, Spanish-focused producer into the world's leading producer of artificial casings in the new century.

Principal Subsidiaries

Gamex CB S.R.O. (Czech Republic); IAN Peru S.A.; IAN S.A.; Naturin Canada; Naturin GmbH; Naturin Ltd. (U.K.); Viscofan Centroamerica; Viscofan CZ S.R.O. (Czech Republic); Viscofan de Brasil Ltd.; Viscofan Mexico; Viscofan Moscu (Russia); Viscofan Poland; Viscofan Thailand; Viscofan USA Inc.

Principal Competitors

Devro PLC; Viskase Companies, Inc.; Hormel Inc.

Further Reading

Gutierrez, Miren, "The Case of Spain's Sausage King," *United Press International,* September 11, 2002.
"Naturin Ltd.," *Food Trade Review,* February 2004, p. 92.
"Strong Profit Growth for Viscofan," *Food Production Daily,* February 26, 2003.
"Viscofan vende mermeladas Bebe a Helios por 15 millones de euros," *El Pais,* April 29, 2003.

—M.L. Cohen

Walkers Snack Foods Ltd.

1600 Arlington Business Park
Theale, Reading
Berkshire RG7 4SA
United Kingdom
Telephone: (+43) 0 118 930 6666
Fax: (+43) 0 118 930 3152
Web site: http://www.walkers.co.uk

Wholly Owned Subsidiary of PepsiCo, Inc.
Incorporated: 1948
Employees: 4,000
Sales: £600 million (2005 est.)
NAIC: 31191 Snack Food Manufacturing; 311919 Other
  Snack Food Manufacturing

Walkers Snack Foods Ltd., a unit of PepsiCo, Inc., is the United Kingdom's leading manufacturer of crisps, or potato chips. Every day about 11 million people bite into one of the company's products, which are manufactured at 15 sites around the country. Walkers grew from a regional Midlands brand to one of the biggest in the United Kingdom after being acquired by Pepsi in 1989. Other key brands of the company include Quavers, Monster Munch, Dippas, and Sensations.

Origins

The Walkers story begins with Mr. Henry Walker, a successful butcher from Mansfield, England, who relocated in the 1880s to run a shop in Leicester. Walker's operation eventually began making meat pies. It was moved to Cheapside in 1912.

Walker started a new sideline when postwar rationing made meat scarce. Under the guidance of managing director R.E. Gerrard, in 1948 the firm began frying potato slices in a fish fryer. When meat rationing ended in 1954, the company continued making its popular crisps, introducing its best-selling cheese and onion-flavored variety the same year.

PepsiCo Buys Walkers in 1989

By the end of the 1980s, snacks were a £1 billion industry in the United Kingdom. By this time, Walkers was owned by Nabsico, which also held the Smiths, Tudor, and Planters brands. Walkers was still then primarily a regional brand in the Midlands, while Smiths crisps had national distribution. Each had a share of about 19 percent of the United Kingdom's salty snack market, though Smiths' emphasis was on low prices.

The French group acquired Walkers when it bought all of RJR Nabisco's European biscuit (cookie and cracker) and snack interests (five companies in all) for $2.5 billion in June 1989. (RJR had been acquired by buyout firm Kohlberg Kravis Roberts & Co.)

A month later, PepsiCo, Inc. acquired Walkers Crisps and Smith Foods from BSN (later Danone) for $1.35 billion (£900 million). Walkers and Smiths, which had a combined turnover of about £290 million ($460 million), were merged in March 1993. The combined entity was called Walkers Smiths Snack Foods until January 1994, when it was renamed Walkers Snack Foods.

A 1992 Euromonitor survey pegged Walkers with a 33.5 percent share of the £835 million British crisp market. According to the *Wall Street Journal,* the United Kingdom's snack food market was second only to that of the United States. There seemed to be room for innovation, as the idea of large multi-serving bags had not yet caught on in the United Kingdom, noted an analyst quoted in *USA Today.* The United Kingdom was also more or less free of corn snacks such as Frito's and Doritos. Americans ate twice as much snack food as Brits, according to *Marketing Week,* and corn products accounted for the difference.

Doritos Launched in 1994

PepsiCo had attempted to introduce the Cheetos brand in the United Kingdom through an unsuccessful $8 million launch in 1990. Two years later, the company ended up renaming them Chester Snacks and halving the price. Ruffles, a PepsiCo brand of ridged potato chip, also faltered in its attempt to cross the pond, so PepsiCo replaced it with the new Walkers Crinkles brand.

The acquisition of Walkers and Smiths made PepsiCo Europe's largest snack producer and allowed it to position its Frito-Lay brands for entry into the Common Market after 1992. As PepsiCo's snack company in the United Kingdom, Walkers

Company Perspectives:

The UK's largest food brand, we're also the fourth largest business within the jaw-droppingly dynamic PepsiCo group. Already some 11 million Walkers packets are hungrily opened every day but the fact is, we've hardly scratched the surface of what's possible. There's massive potential to develop both the market, and our already huge share of it, still further.

Key Dates:

1948: Walkers begins frying potato chips.
1954: Best-selling cheese and onion flavor crisps are introduced.
1989: PepsiCo acquires Walkers.
1993: PepsiCo merges Walkers and Smiths.
1994: Doritos are successfully introduced in the United Kingdom.
2002: Sensations sub-brand is launched.

launched the Doritos brand in that country in 1994. PepsiCo spent $18 million on a new crisps plant in Coventry (the largest in the world) to support the Doritos rollout and another $9 million on marketing, noted *Snack World.* The company gave away seven million bags of chips as part of the promotional campaign.

By the end of 1994, Doritos had a 3 percent share of the United Kingdom's £1.8 billion snack market. PepsiCo introduced Doritos to continental Europe, Asia, and Latin America the following year. Walkers introduced salsa dips in the mid-1990s to help spur sales of larger bags of Doritos.

Walkers Smiths, as the merged company was briefly known, was turning around its loss-making private label manufacturing by making these lines more accountable. Private label still accounted for just 3.5 percent of profits in 1994, noted *Marketing.*

The company introduced some quality-related refinements to its packaging in the mid-1990s. Foil packaging was brought out for Quavers, a brand acquired via Smiths, in 1993. Foil maintained freshness better than plastic. Monster Munch, also from Smiths, switched to foil in 1995. (An unrelated Australian snack food company called Smiths was owned by competitor United Biscuits.) Walkers began using nitrogen-filled bags in 1996, another move aimed at preserving freshness.

Walkers sold off its Planters Nuts business to management in 1996. Its sales had slipped by half to £13 million from its peak since the brand's U.K. introduction in 1977.

Martin Glenn was named president and CEO of Walkers in September 1998. As a marketing executive, he had previously overseen the rollout of Doritos. He replaced Tony Illsley, who was leaving to lead the U.K. cable company Telewest Communications. He had worked for Pedigree Petfoods before joining Walkers in 1992.

Walkers' crisps sales from April 1997 to April 1998 were calculated at £410 million, according to IRI Infoscan. This was down about £20 million.

Walkers updated its crisps packaging in 1998, adding the logo of Frito-Lay, the PepsiCo unit that was Walkers' corporate parent. Package sizes were adjusted at the same time. Walkers also launched a television advertising campaign featuring soccer star Gary Lineker. The ads played off Lineker's mild-mannered image with the theme "No More Mr. Nice Guy."

The company spent £50 million relaunching its namesake brand and making improvements to other lines, Martin Glenn (then marketing vice-president) told *Brand Strategy,* including £15 million spent on facilities in northern England.

Brand Strategy observed that the only growing product for the once-dominant Smiths brand was Salt 'n Shake crisps, which contained separately packaged salt.

Walkers brought out a new brand of ridged potato chip in 1999. It shared the name "Max" with Pepsi's sugar-free name in the United Kingdom. With flavors like Screaming Salt and Vinegar, Punching Paprika, and Hard Cheese and Onion, Max chips were expected to appeal to teenagers. According to Glenn, 70 percent of the potato chips sold in the United Kingdom were seasoned.

The £10 million Evening Snacking campaign of 1999–2000, centered on Doritos Dippas, sought to win a higher share of that market for Walker's chips and dip. In 2001, Walkers added a pickled onion flavor to its Monster Munch brand geared for children. This variety made consumers' tongues turn blue.

Advertising and a stream of instant-win promotions built awareness of Walkers in the last half of the 1990s. One survey ranked Walkers as the United Kingdom's second best-selling brand after Coca-Cola. The popularity prompted an expansion of facilities such as the former Tudor plant near Durham, in northeast England.

New Flavors in the 2000s

Walkers entered the £120 million Irish snack market in 2000. The company was profitable and had 3,000 employees.

Walkers joined HJ Heinz in developing a co-branded, ketchup-flavored variety of crisps in 2001. Even more exciting developments were around the bend in the form of the new Sensations sub-brand launched in May 2002. These chips featured exotic-sounding flavors such as Thai Lemongrass. An appeal for summertime snacking was built around limited edition Fish & Chips flavor fries. Walkers also unwrapped Great British Takeaways crisps in 2003, which featured Chicken Tikka Masala and Chinese Spare Rib flavors. Walkers unveiled a number of new crisps flavors later in the year: Baked Ham & Mustard, Lamb & Mint Sauce, Roast Beef & Yorkshire Pudding, and, in time for Christmas, Roast Turkey with Paxo Sage & Onion Flavour. Walkers supported Sensations with star power, including appearances by Gary Lineker and socialite Tara Palmer Tomkinson. By the end of 2003, reported *Food Manufacture,* Sensations alone were a £60 million business.

Packaging and logo were redesigned in early 2004. The company was expanding, adding a £5.5 million warehouse in County Durham. Annual sales were estimated at £600 million.

Principal Competitors

Golden Wonder; KP Foods UK Ltd.; Tayto Ltd.

Further Reading

"Attack on Snacks—Somerfield and Walkers," *SuperMarketing*, August 2, 1996, p. 57.

Beale, Claire, "TMC Scoops All Walkers Media," *Marketing*, October 28, 1993, p. 5.

Bond, Cathy, "Marketing Technique: When Crisps Go Critical," *Marketing*, April 27, 1995, p. 38.

Brackey, Harriet Johnson, "PepsiCo Buys Top U.K. Snack Firms," *USA Today*, July 5, 1989, p. 2B.

Bradbury, Amanda, "Response File—Walkers Snack Foods," *Precision Marketing*, April 8, 1996, p. 6.

"Category Champion," *In-Store Marketing*, September 6, 2000, p. 20.

"Company CV: Walkers Snack Foods," *Marketing*, April 1, 2004, p. 50.

Conley, Clare, "Walkers Launches Max Crisps," *Marketing Week*, August 27, 1998, p. 5.

Cork, Laura, "Crisp Performance," *Works Management*, September 1, 2001, pp. 30–31.

"Glenn Demands Better Creativity," *Marketing Week*, April 5, 2001, p. 9.

"The Guardian Has Looked at the State of the Market for Crisps, Nuts and Savoury Snacks," *Guardian*, April 29, 1988, p. 10.

"High Profile: Walkers Trips the Lites Fantastic," *Grocer*, November 30, 1996, p. 36.

Hone, Lucy, "BMP DDB Relaunches Walkers with New Lineker Epic," *Campaign*, April 10, 1998, p. 4.

Marsh, Harriet, "Below-the-Line: Walkers Resurrects Copycat Brands War," *Marketing*, January 25, 1996, p. 11.

Murphy, Claire, "Agencies Line up for a Taste of Walkers," *Marketing Week*, March 25, 1994, p. 10.

——, "£3.5M Push for Doritos Launch," *Marketing Week*, May 13, 1994, p. 11.

——, "How Walkers Made a Packet," *Marketing,* November 21, 1996, p. 19.

Nicholas, Ruth, "Walkers Picks O'Leary for Top Job," *Marketing Week*, April 16, 1993, p. 5.

Oram, Roderick, "Crisp Makers Pack a Pog to Attract Younger Munchers," *Financial Times*, February 3, 1996, p. 20.

——, "When It Comes to the Crunch—The Global Snacks Battle Between UB and PepsiCo Is Highly Instructive," *Financial Times*, Management Sec., February 5, 1996, p. 8.

Pears, Chris, "Walkers Expands in Shifts Shake-Up," *Northern Echo*, August 15, 2001, p. 10.

Pendrous, Rick, "A Model of Good Warehouse Design and Operation," *Food Manufacture*, April 2004, p. 25.

"Pepsi Kills 2nd Global Brand," *Euromarketing*, June 29, 1993.

Richards, Amanda, "Doritos' Glenn Takes Lead Role—Walkers Smiths," *Marketing*, September 15, 1994.

"Roy Keane Gives Walkers an Irish Welcome," *Irish Marketing and Advertising Journal*, March 1, 2000.

Schiffman, James R., and E.S. Browning, "PepsiCo Buys Two BSN Firms, Moves into Nothern Europe Snack-Food Field," *Wall Street Journal*, July 5, 1989.

Seymour, Tony, "Food for Thought—Walkers Snack Foods' Personal Development Programme," *Northern Echo*, April 4, 1996, p. 16.

Smith, Alison, "A Mission to Make Europeans Eat Snacks," *Financial Times*, April 28, 1997, p. 18.

"Smiths and Walkers Crisp Companies Go to Pepsi in Surprise $1.3bn Deal," *Grocer*, July 8, 1989, p. 10.

"Snacks Get into Shape for 1995," *SuperMarketing*, January 6, 1995, p. 19.

"The Vineyard Studio Has Been Commissioned to Create a New Corporate Identity for Walkers Crisps (RJR Nabisco) and Revamp the Company's Packaging," *Design Week*, May 6, 1988, p. 5.

"Walkers Keeps Promotions Topped Up," *Grocer*, July 4, 1998, p. 34.

"Walkers' New Look Brings It into Line with International Parent," *Brand Strategy*, March 20, 1998, p. 3.

"Walkers Sells Planters," *Eurofood*, May 8, 1996, p. 12.

"Walkers Smiths' Private Label Is Boost to Profits," *Marketing*, October 27, 1994.

"Walkers to Launch Heinz Ketchup-Flavoured Crisps," *Marketing Week*, May 17, 2001, p. 7.

"Warning for the Brands," *Grocer*, October 29, 1994, p. 12.

"What You Really Really Want Is a Bag of Crisps," *Grocer*, July 12, 1997, p. 8.

Whitworth, Mick, "Strictly for the Grown-Ups," *Food Manufacture*, NPD Supplement, Winter 2003, pp. 12–13.

——, "The Price Is Right: Walkers Snack Foods," *Grocer*, October 28, 1995, p. 34.

—Frederick C. Ingram

wet *seal*

The Wet Seal, Inc.

26972 Burbank
Foothill Ranch, California 92610
U.S.A.
Telephone: (714) 583-9029
Fax: (714) 583-0715
Web site: http://www.wetsealinc.com

Public Company
Incorporated: 1962
Employees: 6,656
Sales: $517.6 million (2004)
Stock Exchanges: NASDAQ
NAIC: 448120 Women's Clothing Stores

A nationwide specialty retailer of moderately priced apparel for women, The Wet Seal, Inc. operates three chains under the "Contempo Casuals" and the "Wet Seal" and "Arden B." banners. During the mid-1990s, Wet Seal operated 363 retail stores in 34 states and Puerto Rico, with the majority of the company's stores located in California. After decades of unassuming prosperity, Wet Seal recorded explosive growth during the 1980s but began faltering in the 1990s. To restore profitability, the company acquired a 237-store retail junior women's chain named Contempo Casuals, Inc. in 1995. The acquisition nearly tripled the size of Wet Seal and greatly expanded the company's geographic scope. However, by the early 2000s, Wet Seal was struggling due to various internal and external factors, and in 2005 looked to its new CEO, Joel N. Waller, for a turnaround.

Origins

Wet Seal was established in late 1962 in California as a beachwear retailer, though its development into the 300-unit retail chain in operation during the mid-1990s occurred only after the company had significantly broadened its beachwear merchandise mix. During the first two decades of its existence, Wet Seal had developed into a $5-million-in-sales, 17-store chain, with all retail units located in California. Size, however, was not the chain's problem. Although Wet Seal's diminutive stature left it

lost among the larger apparel retailers in California, its profitability stood out as its most glaring handicap. The company was awash in debt. The sweeping changes that transformed the company into one of the darlings of the California retail apparel industry during the 1980s occurred midway through the decade when the struggling chain gained new management and a new owner. In 1984, a Canadian retail store chain named Suzy Shier acquired Wet Seal, paying $2 million for the struggling and little-known business. The purchase marked the beginning of years of robust growth and Wet Seal's ascendancy to prominence in the fiercely competitive California retail market.

1980s Growth

The chief architect of Wet Seal's prolific rise was Ken Chilvers, head of Suzy Shier's operations. When Suzy Shier acquired Wet Seal in 1984, Chilvers left Toronto and moved to California to steward the fortunes of money-losing Wet Seal. For assistance in arresting the chain's financial slide, Chilvers turned to Kathy Peckham, a former Jordan Marsh merchandising executive. Peckham's changes were pervasive, essentially abolishing the strategy that had guided Wet Seal's existence during the 1960s and 1970s. She put together a merchandising mix designed to attract a much larger customer base, adding junior sportswear apparel items that quickly drew flocks of customers to the stores. Flowered denim, mini-skirts, colorful Aztec prints, and psychedelic bikinis graced Wet Seal's racks and shelves from the mid-1980s forward, drawing teenage girls in packs. Surprisingly, their mothers came as well, unafraid to don the youthful fashion trends of the day.

The metamorphosis worked, bringing in teenage customers and women in their late 40s. During the exponential growth that ensued, Chilvers was granted autonomy from his silent partners at Suzy Shier, gaining full control over all Wet Seal operations. Peckham, meanwhile, ascended to Wet Seal's executive vice-president and general merchandising manager posts, earning recognition for sparking growth that dazzled industry analysts. While describing the chain's meteoric rise, one member of the business press who cited Joseph Magnin and Contempo Casuals as the retail success stories of the 1960s and 1970s, respectively, hailed Wet Seal as the "retail phenom" of the 1980s, a distinction that few could discount given what the company had

---

Company Perspectives:

In the business of fashion, as with fashion itself, putting the right combination together is essential. Wet Seal and Contempo Casuals have done just that, and the result is definitely ... us. We're more than just an outfit, we're an inspiration.

---

achieved during the latter half of the 1980s. Between 1985 and 1989, annual sales mushroomed more than 900 percent, approaching the $100 million plateau; the number of stores jumped from 17 to 78; and sales per square foot rose from $150 to $420. Most important, the company's profitability was restored, underscoring the importance of Chilvers' and Peckham's work.

By the end of the 1980s, Wet Seal's stature within the California retail industry had grown dramatically and Chilvers was intent on keeping the momentum. He invested heavily in increasing the size of each store, raising the average square footage of a Wet Seal unit from 2,500 to 4,000. Inside the stores, considerable capital had been invested as well. The enlarged units contained wide center aisles flanked by walls with merchandise stacked to the ceiling. Behind the central cash registers, massive computer-driven video walls played the latest rock music videos, accentuating the trendy appeal of Wet Seal merchandise.

By all accounts a successful formula had been created, but it was a formula that had yet be tested outside of California. That changed in 1989 when Wet Seal established its first stores outside of California, opening stores in Las Vegas and Phoenix that registered success commensurate with the company's California stores. Not stopping there, Chilvers looked to expand elsewhere and signed a lease in the summer of 1989 for a store in Hawaii, announcing concurrently that he planned to establish at least five stores in Hawaii by the following year. Ambitious plans were slated for Florida as well, where Chilvers anticipated establishing a minimum of 30 stores. For Chilvers, the success achieved during his first five years as Wet Seal's leader prompted him to map out ambitious plans for the company's future. However, for those industry pundits alarmed by the chain's rapid expansion, Chilvers had an answer. "We are taking a cautious approach," Chilvers explained to a Women's Wear Daily reporter in 1989. "We will do 25 to 30 new stores next year and, let's face it, there were a lot of people who came before us that went from 65 stores to 100 and then were dinosaurs at 300."

As the company entered the 1990s, it appeared the only hazard on the horizon was Chilvers' fear of expanding too rapidly. Store sales continued to climb, the company's merchandise was widely popular, and its march across California's borders was meeting with encouraging, uninterrupted success. As Chilvers perceived it, the greatest danger of excessively rapid expansion was sacrificing the quality and "look" of Wet Seal stores in order to save money to finance the establishment of additional stores. To combat this potential problem Chilvers refused to cut corners while expanding. He invested roughly twice the industry average for each store opening and continued

to create hip havens for his customers. To fuel expansion, Chilvers took the company public in July 1990, raising $37 million from an initial public offering that was used to trim debt and finance the establishment of additional stores. By the end of the year, 20 new stores had been added to the chain, giving Wet Seal a total of 93 stores scattered across five states.

One year after moving out of California—where the company had been confined for 27 years—Wet Seal operated in Arizona, Nevada, Hawaii, and Florida. The 20 stores opened in 1990 helped lift sales over $100 million for the first time and the company's net income reached a record $7.1 million, providing tangible evidence that the prodigious expansion completed during the year had not negatively affected Wet Seal's performance. The company's financial performance, in fact, was particularly remarkable considering the state of the national economy during the early 1990s, as the first stirrings of a national recession signaled the beginning of hard times for retailers across the country. By 1991, the severity of the recession was intensifying, but unlike many of its competitors Wet Seal was moving forward, unchecked. *Time* magazine featured the company as one of the few retailers able to buck the trend spreading across the country that left many retailers pulling at their wrists as store sales plummeted and profits sagged. By constantly turning over its merchandise, which Wet Seal executives dubbed "multigenerational," and by awarding weekly bonuses to employees for inventory turnover, Wet Seal was exhibiting a financial vibrancy that distinguished it from rivals and lent credence to the statement that the company might be the "retail phenom" of the 1990s as well.

By the end of 1991 there were 112 stores composing the Wet Seal chain. Sales were up from the $107 million generated in 1990, climbing to $120 million, and although profits slipped to $4.2 million, the company's financial health was sound. As the company continued with its expansion plans in 1992, adding 13 stores during the year, industry observers were surprised by the announcement of Chilvers' departure in March. Forty-five years old at the time, Chilvers had opted to take early retirement, explaining that his reasons for leaving were "private and personal, relating to my health and my family, and do not bear upon my relationship with Wet Seal or its directors, which had always been excellent." Chilvers exit paved the way for Kathy Peckham, now Kathy Bronstein.

Financial Woes During the 1990s

With Bronstein in charge, Wet Seal pressed on with expansion for the remainder of 1992, but by the end of the year, when the company reported its second consecutive decline in annual profit totals, signs of trouble were evident. Sales for the year reached an all-time high of $150 million, but Wet Seal's net income slipped from $4.2 million to $3.6 million. Following this disheartening news, the company expanded only modestly in 1993, adding four stores as sales throughout the chain began to dip. By the end of the year, alarms were blaring loudly at the company's headquarters. Annual sales dropped to $140 million and, most disconcerting, the company's net income slipped into the red. Wet Seal lost $2.4 million in 1993 and another $1 million in 1994, as the years of explosive growth shuddered to a stop.

Key Dates:

1962: Wet Seal is established in California as a beachwear retailer.
1984: Canadian retail store chain Suzy Shier acquires Wet Seal.
1991: The Wet Seal chain comprises 112 stores.
1995: Neiman Marcus Group sells its floundering Contempo Casuals chain to Wet Seal.
1996: Limbo Lounge, a "unisex" outlet featuring urban clothes for teenaged men and women, is launched.
1997: Wet Seal acquires 17 stores and one lease from the Los Angeles-based clothing retailer/manufacturer Rampage.
1998: The company acquires stores from Britches Great Outdoors and Mothers Work Inc.; Arden B. chain is launched.
2001: The company purchases 18 Zutopia stores from the children's wear retailer Gymboree Corporation.
2003: Following years of financially lackluster performance on the part of Wet Seal, CEO Kathy Bronstein is forced out of the company; Peter Whitford takes over as CEO and Allan Haims is named president of the Wet Seal division.
2004: Whitford and Haims resign from the company.
2005: Joel N. Waller is named CEO.

"It was a huge shock to be that hot and then turn sour," Bronstein reflected to a reporter from *Women's Wear Daily.* "It taught that even when you're doing well," she went on to explain, "there's only a limited time you have before you have to change. You've got to know when to pull the plug." During the two-year financial malaise, Bronstein and other Wet Seal executives searched for a solution, a way to restore the company's former luster. While expansion had continued, bringing the company's store count total up to 133 by the end of 1994, consumers had lost interest in junior apparel, sending a shock wave throughout the industry. Fashion tastes had changed and Wet Seal had not foreseen the shift, a mistake that thrust the company into a precarious position as it entered the mid-1990s.

In early 1995, the company discovered what it perceived as a solution to its financial woes, a solution Bronstein described as an "unbelievable break." In April, Chestnut Hill, Massachusetts-based Neiman Marcus Group agreed to sell its floundering Contempo Casuals chain to Wet Seal. Wet Seal, as its 1995 annual report declared, "went shopping for just the right fit" and Contempo Casuals, a specialty women's retail chain that had flourished during the 1970s, was selected. With 237 stores scattered throughout 34 states and Puerto Rico, Contempo Casuals represented a significant addition to Wet Seal's operations, nearly tripling the company's size and immediately transforming it into a genuine national retailer. Expected to be completed by the end of May, the deal was concluded in July for stock valued at $1 million.

Although some industry analysts questioned the benefits of combining Contempo Casuals, which lost $37 million on $303 million in sales in 1994, and Wet Seal, a money loser itself,

Bronstein was confident the right move had been made, noting in *Women's Wear Daily,* "We saw that without adding significant overhead we could make ourselves instantly profitable." On the heels of the Contempo Casuals acquisition, the company continued to tinker with its business approach, testing a new concept store during late 1995 called "The Girl's Room," which featured apparel and accessories such as novelty toys, cosmetics, candles, and books. Positive early results prompted the company to push forward with the concept and make plans to incorporate "The Girl's Room" into 160 stores nationwide. Other plans for the late 1990s included the establishment of as many as ten new stores in 1996, but the primary focus after the Contempo Casuals acquisition was on improving sales and profitability. With this as its chief objective, Wet Seal entered the late 1990s intent on wielding its new-found national power to become a dominant force in the U.S. retail industry.

Comebacks Fizzle

In 1996, it appeared that Wet Seal was indeed on the brink of a new era of profitability. For the first time since 1992, the company was back in the black, thanks largely to its Contempo Casuals division. Net income for the year totaled $15.3 million on sales of $375 million, compared to $5.8 million in earnings on sales of $266.7 million in 1995. In November 1996, Wet Seal introduced a new store concept, Limbo Lounge, a "unisex" outlet that featured urban clothes for teenaged men and women in an "entertainment" setting that included TV screens, Internet access, and in one case, a juice bar. Two locations were opened in California. The following year, Wet Seal acquired 17 stores and one lease from the Los Angeles-based clothing retailer/manufacturer Rampage, which had filed for Chapter 11 bankruptcy protection; the terms of the deal were not disclosed. Wet Seal planned to continue operations under the Rampage brand name. In July 1998, the company acquired 102 more stores including 78 from Herndon, Virginia-based Britches Great Outdoors for an undisclosed sum and 19 Episode stores from Philadelphia maternity wear chain Mothers Work Inc. for $2.8 million. The acquisitions poised Wet Seal for the opening of Arden B., a new chain devoted to slightly upscale clothing for 20- to 40-year-old women, in November 1998.

By the end of 1998, Wet Seal showed income of $26 million, an 18 percent gain over the previous year. Sales rose 15 percent to $485.4 million over 1997. This success evaporated in 1999 when bad merchandising decisions sent Wet Seal stores customers to competitors. Attempting to cash in on the successful formula of khakis and polo shirts that had paid off for such competitors as Abercrombie & Fitch, J. Crew, and American Eagle Outfitters, the company remerchandised its flagship stores with preppy casual wear in place of the trendy clubwear styles it had long relied upon. Although sales totaled $524.4 million, an 8 percent increase over the previous year, net income plunged from $25.9 million in 1998 to $14.2 million in 1999, a drop of 45 percent. Some analysts attributed the company's woes to resources spread too thinly among its Wet Seal/Contempo Casuals, Limbo Lounge, and Arden B. divisions. A Wet Seal catalogue first issued in 1998 was discontinued after a single year. Sales remained weak in 2000 despite modest improvements in March and November. Wet Seal decided to cease acquisitions for a time, close down its Limbo Lounge outlets, now 26 in number, convert nearly all of its 200 Contempo Casuals stores into Wet Seal locations, and refocus on female fashion. Both Wet Seal stores and Arden B. locations underwent a makeover. Wet Seal outlets were brightened up with open ceilings, more lighting, and glossy pink, blue, and white walls. Some stores opened shoe departments and added mannequins. A separate merchandising and management team was put in place for Arden B., and the chain's concept was honed to differentiate it from the Wet Seal concept. The efforts paid off; sales increased 10.6 percent to $580 million in fiscal year 2000; income jumped 37 percent to $19.5 million.

In 2001, the company resumed acquisitions. Wet Seal paid an undisclosed amount to purchase 18 Zutopia stores from the children's wear retailer Gymboree Corp. Zutopia extended Wet Seal's target market to include 5- to 12-year-old children. CEO Kathy Bronstein told Kristin Young of *Women's Wear Daily,* "Strategically, it's our vision to pick [a customer] up when she's [age] five or six and drop her off somewhere between 50 and 60." By the end of the third quarter of fiscal 2001, sales were up 4.4 percent for the quarter and net income had jumped 70 percent to $6.8 million from the third quarter of the previous year. Commentators noted that the company was performing exceptionally well in an economic climate that had other specialty apparel retailers struggling. Product placements on the popular WB network reality show *Popstars* pushed Wet Seal's brand exposure. Through an exclusive deal, Wet Seal attired the cast and carried clothes modeled on those worn on the television show in stores under the Popstars brandname. Kathy Bronstein told Marianne Wilson of *Chain Store Age* that the company's strategy would hinge on pricing. "We are very recognizant of the onslaught of competition, new and existing, that can impact our business," Bronstein remarked. "Our job as a retailer is to make sure that if the customer is responding to fashion at a price, we are offering it."

The upswing of 2001 did not last into 2002. Factors including a slowing economy, rising unemployment, decreasing mall traffic, and lessening consumer confidence eroded retail sales industry wide during the first half of the year. A California dockworkers lockout interfered with merchants' ability to move inventory from offshore sewing contractors into stores, further complicating Wet Seal's increasingly bleak picture by causing shortages of key items, especially seasonal pants. Wet Seal continued to rely on the "bohemian" and "peasant-look" fashions that had scored sales successes a year earlier, although the market was saturated with such styles. In July, Wet Seal was able to report modest increases in sales (10.7 percent, or $302.8 million) and fair performance on income ($12.4 million, an increase of 38.7 percent), but it lowered its earnings estimates from 17 cents per share to 12 to 14 cents per share and warned investors that the third and fourth quarters might show no growth at all. At the end of 2002, the company showed an overall drop in income of 86.3 percent to $4.2 million. Sales during 2002 increased only 1.1 percent to $608.5 million. Wet Seal reported losses of $2.5 million in the third quarter of the year and $5.6 million in the fourth quarter, effectively wiping out the comeback of the previous year.

The economic recession dragged into 2003. David Moin of *Women's Wear Daily* called the early months of the year "a season of pink slips," as retailers showed numerous executives the door. Kathy Bronstein, having reported two weak quarters in a row, was abruptly forced out at Wet Seal. She retaliated with a lawsuit charging "wrongful termination, gender discrimination, emotional distress," and other offenses. The lawsuit was settled out of court in a deal that included $2.2 million in cash, a retirement plan with a surrender value of more than $915,000, $125,000 in attorney fees, 4,422 shares of stock, and stock options worth an estimated $4.2 million, with taxes on the cash settlement to be paid out of the stock distribution.

Australian-born Peter Whitford, formerly president-worldwide of The Disney Stores, replaced Bronstein as CEO in May 2003. In August, he brought in colleagues from Disney to fill key positions in the executive offices, including Joseph Deckop, who was appointed to the new post of executive vice-president of central planning and allocation, and Allan Haims, who became president of the Wet Seal division. As senior vice-president and creative director of the Wet Seal division, the company brought in designer Victor Alfaro, noted for his upscale women's couture.

In January 2004, the company closed down its Zutopia division, citing a need to refocus on its core business. Cautioning that spring and summer 2004 would be the earliest that the new leadership's influence would be felt, Wet Seal's management set about making changes in its marketing strategy. The company conducted in-store contests to find "stylizers," trendy teenage girls who would appear in its advertising and give feedback about the stores' merchandise. Sources inside and outside the company agreed, however, that Wet Seal needed to make a strong showing during the crucial back-to-school season in autumn 2004. In its quarterly SEC (Securities and Exchange Commission) filing of June 2004, Wet Seal noted that "potential reorganization under Chapter 11 of the U.S. bankruptcy code" was a looming possibility. The report also noted that vendors and factors had tightened the company's credit because of its poor showing over the previous two years. Industry analyst Liz Pierce of the firm Sanders Morris Harris commented to Kristin Young and Vicki M. Young of *Women's Wear Daily* that merchandise presentation was not working as planned. "Some of the [fall] product is coming [in stores] on an item-by-item basis. That's not merchandised like they told us it was going to be. They said it's going to be a compelling selling presentation." Wachovia Securities analyst Joseph Teklits pointed out that inventory issues and the departure of in-house talent, including Arden B. president Greg Scott, were making business worse for Wet Seal. "We have learned that Wet Seal's woes are deepening on all fronts," he wrote. Amidst these troubles, designer Alfaro departed the company in August 2004, just as his new line of "vintage angels" and "granny chic" looks was hitting stores.

The season did not go well. Sales declined 15.9 percent in the third quarter compared to the same period in 2003. Overall sales for the year showed a drop of 20.1 percent from 2003. Analysts noted that Alfaro's fashions were simply out-of-step with the big sellers of the season. In November, Whitford and Haims resigned, and the company once again looked for a change in marketing strategy that would save it from Chapter 11. In December 2004, amid speculation that bankruptcy proceedings were not far, the company announced the closure of 150 Wet Seal stores—a full third of the division's outlets—and the elimination of 2000 jobs. Relief came, however, in the form of a cash infusion from the New York firm S.A.C. Capital Management, which signed a deal to give $40 million in exchange for convertible notes. In late December, Joel N. Waller, formerly chairman of Wilsons Leather, was named CEO effective February 1, 2005. Michael Gold, a veteran of the company who had run more than 400 of its stories in the U.S. and Canada, was appointed as retail consultant. Despite these changes, industry opinion remained guarded as to Wet Seal's eventual fate.

Principal Divisions

Arden B.; Contempo Casuals; Wet Seal.

Principal Competitors

The Gap, Inc.; Abercrombie & Fitch Co.

Further Reading

Bellantonio, Jennifer, "Major Expansion Fuels Rebound for Apparel Firm Catering to Teens," *Los Angeles Business Journal*, December 17, 2001, p. 12.

——, "Retailer Wet Seal Trying to Fashion Return to Vogue," *Los Angeles Business Journal*, November 24, 2003, p. 7.

"Bronstein Settles with a Wet Seal," *Women's Wear Daily*, September 17, 2003, p. 38.

"Bronstein Succeeds Chilvers as Wet Seal's President, CEO," *Women's Wear Daily*, March 24, 1992, p. 20.

Cecil, Mark, "Wet Seal: Wandering toward a Takeout?," *Mergers & Acquisitions Report*, September 13, 2004.

Choi, Amy S., "Wet Seal Names Waller CEO," *Women's Wear Daily*, December 20, 2004, p. 2.

Derby, Meredith, "Wet Seal: Shopping Arden B.?," *Women's Wear Daily*, October 14, 2004, p. 3.

Fallon, Kathryn Jackson, "Wet Seal and Whale Songs," *Time*, June 3, 1991, p. 45.

Ginsberg, Steve, "Wet Seal Makes Waves," *Women's Wear Daily*, August 9, 1989, p. 14C.

Greenberg, Julie, "Wet Seal Starts New for Back-to-School," *Women's Wear Daily*, June 10, 2004, p. 10.

Hazel, Debra, "Wet Seal Makes a Splash with Teens," *Chain Store Age*, March 1997, pp. 43–45.

"In Limbo," *Women's Wear Daily*, November 7, 1996, p. 11.

Klepacki, Laura, "Wet Seal Color Pulled after 6-Month Test," *Women's Wear Daily*, September 27, 2002, p. 13.

Kletter, Melanie, and Kristin Young, "Thomas Leaves Wet Seal," *Women's Wear Daily*, October 5, 2000, p. 15.

Kletter, Melanie, "Margin Drop Hits Wet Seal," *Women's Wear Daily*, March 20, 2000, p. 2.

——, "Profits Surge at Hot Topic, Wet Seal, Urban Outfitters," *Women's Wear Daily*, August 20, 1998, p. 4.

——, "Wet Seal Inks Deal to Acquire Zutopia," *Women's Wear Daily*, January 5, 2001, p. 12.

——, "Wet Seal Stock Drops as Sales Sag in Third Quarter," *Women's Wear Daily*, October 27, 1999, p. 23.

Kolbenschlag, Michael, "Ken Chilvers Knows How to Manage a Fast-Growing Company," *California Business*, November 1989, p. 80.

Marlow, Michael, "West Coast Junior Chains: Trend Catchers," *Women's Wear Daily*, June 29, 1995, p. 6.

Miller, Paul, "Wet Seal to Reenter Catalog Business," *Catalog Age*, April 1, 2002.

Moin, David, "Kathy Bronstein Exits Wet Seal," *Women's Wear Daily*, February 7, 2003, p. 2.

Montgomery, Tiffany, "California Teen Retailer's Chief Executive Steps Down," *Orange County Register*, November 10, 2004.

——, "Foothill Ranch, Calif.-Based Teen Fashion Retailer to Cut Jobs, Stores," *Orange County Register*, December 29, 2004.

——, "Struggling California Teen Retailer Will Focus on Price," *Orange County Register*, November 24, 2004.

"Neiman's to Sell Contempo Casuals," *Daily News Record*, April 4, 1995, p. 11.

"Retailer Grows into Sophisticated Concept," *Shopping Center World*, April 1999, p. 42.

"Retailer to Shutter 150 Stores, Cut 2,000 Jobs," *New York Post*, December 29, 2004, p. 33.

Rozhon, Tracie, "The Teenage Crush on Wet Seal Stores Is So Over," *New York Times*, September 3, 2004, p. C1.

Sarkisian-Miller, Nola, "Haims, Alfaro Brought into Wet Seal Inc.," *Women's Wear Daily*, August 21, 2003, p. 3.

Tyree, Michelle Dalton, "Wet Seal CEO out as Firm Secures Funds," *Women's Wear Daily*, November 10 2004, p. 2.

"USA: Wet Seal Faces Series of Class-Action Lawsuits," *just-style.com*, September 1, 2004.

"USA: Wet Seal's President Allan Haims Quits," *just-style.com*, November 24, 2004.

Weitzman, Jennifer, "Comp-Store Declines Lead Wet Seal to Loss," *Women's Wear Daily*, March 21, 2003, p. 11.

——, "Limited Brands and Wet Seal Add to Chilly Outlook for Fall," *Women's Wear Daily*, August 23, 2002, p. 1.

——, "Wet Seal Net Gushes," *Women's Wear Daily*, March 22, 2001, p. 10.

——, "Wet Seal Sags on Soft Sales, *Women's Wear Daily*, March 19, 2004, p. 13.

——, "Wet Seal Style Changes Pay off," *Women's Wear Daily*, November 20, 2000, p. 22.

"Wet Seal Agrees to Buy 17 Stores from Rampage," *Women's Wear Daily*, August 14, 1997, p. 14.

"Wet Seal Settles Wage Dispute Suit," *Women's Wear Daily*, January 22, 2004, p. 4.

"Wet Seal to Buy 24 Episode Stores from Mothers Work for $2.8M," *Women's Wear Daily*, September 22, 1998, p. 26.

"Wet Seal to Close 150 Stores and Cut 2,000 Jobs," *New York Times*, December 29, 2004, p. C3.

"The Wet Seal Will Pay $1.28 Million to as Many as 500 Store Managers in California Who Claimed They Were Denied Overtime Wages," *Chain Store Age*, March 2004, p. 22.

Wilson, Marianne, "Wet Seal's Primo Performance," *Chain Store Age*, November 2001, p. 50.

Young, Kristin, "Wet Seal's Fashionable Redo," *Women's Wear Daily*, April 16, 2001, p. 23.

——, "Zutopia: No Utopia," *Women's Wear Daily*, January 8, 2004, p. 9.

Young, Kristin, and David Moin, "Wet Seal Names Peter Whitford CEO," *Women's Wear Daily*, May 30, 2003, p. 2.

Young, Vicki M., and Kristin Young, "Sinking or Swimming? Back-to-School Key for Struggling Wet Seal," *Women's Wear Daily*, June 29, 2004, p. 1.

Young, Vicki M., "Wet Seal Closing Units, Cutting Jobs," *Women's Wear Daily*, December 29, 2004, p. 2.

——, "Wet Seal Sales Slump Hinders Earnings," *Women's Wear Daily*, November 25, 2002, p. 16.

Zaczkiewicz, Arthur, "Wet Seal Loss Widens in Third," *Women's Wear Daily*, December 2, 2004, p. 19.

—Jeffrey L. Covell
—update: Jennifer Gariepy

WFS Financial Inc.

23 Pasteur
Irvine, California 92618
U.S.A.
Telephone: (949) 727-1000
Toll Free: (800) 289-8004
Fax: (949) 727-2313
Web Site: http://www.wfsfinancial.com

Wholly Owned Subsidiary of Western Financial Bank
Incorporated: 1988 as Western Consumer Service
Employees: 2,094
Total Assets: $1.05 billion (2004)
Stock Exchanges: NASDAQ
Ticker Symbol: WFSI
NAIC: 522291 Consumer Lending; 522110 Commercial
    Banking; 541613 Marketing Consulting Services

WFS Financial Inc. is one of the nation's largest independent auto finance companies, specializing in originating, securitizing, and servicing new and pre-owned prime and non-prime credit quality automobile contracts through its nationwide network of 8,000-odd car dealers. The company offers refinancing and end-of-term leasing options directly to consumers. WFS Financial has headquarters in Irvine, California, and operates 39 offices nationwide. As a subsidiary of Western Financial Bank, a federal savings bank exempt from state laws, it is the only independent automobile lender to enjoy federal preemption, or exemption from state licensing and laws governing lenders.

From a Statewide to a Nationwide Market: 1973–96

In 1973, Earnest S. Rady, chairman of Westcorp, the parent company of Western Financial Bank, founded an independent lending company to provide car and truck loans to consumers. The company, which provided an alternative to loans from manufacturers' lending arms, began operations with one dealer in California. It securitized its contracts through sales of investment-grade securities on Wall Street, with the company servicing its loans.

The company grew quickly for the remainder of the 1970s and throughout the 1980s, expanding its territory and making auto loans to consumers through automobile dealerships. In 1988, it incorporated as Western Consumer Service, a wholly owned consumer finance subsidiary of Western Financial Bank, to provide non-prime automobile finance services. This market was one not serviced by the bank's automobile finance division. In 1990, Western Consumer Service changed its name to Westcorp Financial Services.

During the first half of the 1990s, WFS underwent steady growth that almost doubled its size. By 1991, the company had 32 offices. Within the next few years, it was originating contracts in seven, primarily western, states. By 1995, WFS had a network of 14 dealer centers and 63 branch offices that covered 13 states, including two states in which the company did not have offices. That year, Western Financial Bank transferred its auto finance division to WFS, which changed its name again to WFS Financial Inc. and made an initial public offering.

Also in 1995, Joy Schaefer became president and chief operating officer of WFS Financial. An accounting major at Wesleyan University, Schaefer graduated magna cum laude in the early 1980s and had joined Westcorp in 1990 after working with Liberty National Bank and Illinois National Bank and as an audit manager with Ernst & Young LLP. At Westcorp, she rapidly worked her up in the company, occupying several positions at there and at Westcorp's subsidiary, Western Financial Bank.

As president and chief operating officer of WFS Financial, Schaefer was instrumental in orchestrating its growth and development. Competition with other lenders for borrowers increased in the mid-1990s, pushing loan rates downward, and WFS Financial, along with other auto financers, began to stretch its standards, taking on more risk for less return by making loans to people with tarnished credit. From 1996 to 1997, Schaefer enacted a strategy for aggressive expansion based on focusing more on the non-prime market.

During the second half of the 1990s, "WFS Financial continue[d] to experience increasing loan volumes due to its geographic expansion and continued growth in existing markets," according to Schaefer in a company release. By 1997, the company had issued loans in 32 states, with non-prime loans accounting for fully 50 percent of the loans issued.

Unfortunately, these non-prime loans resulted in a sharp rise in the company's loan losses and delinquencies in 1997. "Bankruptcies are at an all-time high," Lee Whatcott, the company's chief financial officer, remarked in a February 1998 *Orange County Register* article. "We are tightening our underwriting to make sure we get paid for the risks we take." At the end of 1997, loan losses at WFS Financial reached a record high of 3.4 percent, and the company's earnings took a beating. Profits decreased 19 percent to $31.3 million. At the end of 1998, the company posted losses of $16.6 million.

Other auto lenders that also specialized in non-prime loans were similarly struggling with rising delinquency rates and increased competition, and many did not survive. WFS Financial took stock of where it stood and made the decision to slow down its growth with fewer loan originations.

Corporate Restructuring: 1997–2000

In 1997, Schaefer, at the age of 38, succeeded Earnest S. Rady as chief financial officer of WFS Financial. That year, she also led the company on a corporate restructuring plan. Having added 15 states a year to its base of operations between 1994 and 1996, WFS Financial's operations were scattered, and the company was plagued by redundancies. Schaefer's plan aimed to reduce these overlaps, improve leadership, and reorganize operations.

In 1997 and 1998, WFS Financial spent $40 million on new technology and replaced all but two top-tier executives. Beginning in 1998, the company combined its 15 prime lending dealer centers and 44 non-prime lending branch offices in the western states into 12 regional business centers and 15 satellite offices. Later that same year, the company extended its organizational streamlining to WFS Financial's operations in the central and eastern United States. As part of this restructuring, WFS Financial cut about 20 percent of its workforce, or 400 positions, and eliminated 96 offices. Upon completion of the plan, the company operated through 21 regional business centers and 26 satellite offices nationwide. The intent of the streamlining was to provide dealers with a single point of contact, but it also had an unexpected side-effect. After the firings and office closings, droves of employees who were concerned about the com-

pany's financial problems quit, leaving behind a plethora of positions to be filled.

By 1999, WFS Financial's turnaround was complete, and the company filed to sell two million shares of common stock, leaving its parent, Western Financial Bank, with an 80 percent share of the company. Between 1985 and 1999, WFS Financial had securitized more than $14 billion of automobile contracts, becoming the fourth-largest issuer of automobile loans in the United States. In 1999, the company set a new mark when the automobile contracts it serviced totaled about $5 billion.

The year 2000 was a good one for WFS Financial. Rising non-prime loan volume triggered new records in sales and profits, and revenues increased 26 percent to $4.2 billion from $3.3 billion in 1999. Net income surged 42 percent to $75 million. The company securitized $16.6 billion of auto contracts. It also entered into agreements to provide lending services for two leading online auto buying services, CarsDirect.com and StoneAge.com. WFS Financial became the finance arm for the latter's newest program, the "StoneAge Driver."

Changes in 2002 and Beyond

By 2001, with nearly 6,000 franchised dealers in WFS Financial's portfolio, including five of the ten largest dealer groups, WFS was one of the five largest issuers of auto loans in the country. (The Big Three automakers were the top three.) That year, the company made $8.2 billion in car loans, and revenue was $602 million. This figure represented an almost 200 percent increase in sales over a three-year period. WFS Financial also acquired an interest in DealerTrack Holdings, Inc., an Internet business-to-business portal that brought together finance companies and dealers in 2001. However, WFS Financial's stock price continued to decline, leading Westcorp to decide in 2002, that it intended to acquire the outstanding 16 percent of common stock. The board later recanted this position when critics objecting, saying that such a move would be bad for the company's shareholders.

Schaefer resigned unexpectedly in 2002 and left its board scrambling to find her replacement. It settled on Tom Wolfe, who had been with the company since 1998 and was then WFS Financial's president. When, during the second half of 2002, consumers, encouraged by low loan rates, embarked on a credit-fueled spending spree, WFS experienced an increased demand for its auto loans. By this point, only 20 percent of the company's loans were non-prime. WFS Financial's customers, on average, earned $50,000 a year and borrowed $16,000 to buy a two-year old Honda or Toyota. Still, the company contracted with Balboa Life & Casualty in mid-2002 for creditor-placed insurance that transferred credit risk off of WFS Financial.

In 2003, industry experts estimated that the automobile finance group was the second-largest consumer finance industry in the country, with more than $684 billion of loan originations that year. However, there was some slowing in sales growth due to the weakening economy. WFS Financial, which still offered its services to a wide range of consumers, from those with excellent credit ratings to those with some credit challenges, announced that it had "seen an increase in non-performing loans in line with the weak economy and the drop in used car prices," according to a 2002 *Knight Ridder Tribune Business News* article.

Key Dates:

1973: Earnest S. Rady founds an independent automobile loan company.
1988: The company incorporates in California as Western Consumer Service.
1990: The company changes its name to Westcorp Financial Services.
1995: Western Financial Bank transfers its auto finance division to WFS; WFS changes its name again to WFS Financial Inc. and makes an initial public offering; Joy Schaefer becomes president and chief operating officer of WFS Financial.
1999: WFS Financial sells two million shares of common stock.
1997: Schaefer succeeds Earnest S. Rady as chief executive officer of WFS.
2000: WFS Financial enters into agreements with CarsDirect.com and StoneAge.com.
2001: WFS Financial acquires an interest in DealerTrack Holdings, Inc.
2002: Schaefer resigns and is replaced by Tom Wolfe.
2004: Westcorp arranges to acquire the 16 percent of WFS Financial not owned by Western Financial Bank.

In 2004, Westcorp and WFS Financial worked out the terms of an agreement whereby Westcorp would acquire the 16 percent of WFS Financial not already owned by its other subsidiary, Western Financial Bank. Before the acquisition, WFS Financial had to borrow from its parent company at third-party rates. However, once reabsorbed, the cost of funds would become the same as the cost to the bank. "We believe that this transaction makes sense for both companies and their shareholders," announced Rady, chairman of Westcorp, in a 2004 press release. The merger was unanimously approved by the boards of directors of both Westcorp and Western Financial Bank.

Although well-established throughout the country, WFS Financial continued to seek out opportunities to build its market share, especially in those states that it had entered since the mid-1990s. Its goals included increasing contract purchases from its current dealer base as well as developing new relationships with dealers, especially those doing a high volume business or ones with multiple locations. WFS Financial also sought to expand its market share of pre-owned automobile contracts.

Principal Subsidiaries

WFS Financial Auto Loans, Inc.; WFS Financial Auto Loans 2, Inc.; WFS Investments, Inc.; WFS Funding, Inc.; WFS Receivables Corporation; WFS Receivables Corporation 3; WFS Web Investments.

Principal Competitors

DaimlerChrysler Services; Ford Credit; General Motors Acceptance Corporation.

Further Reading

Armstrong, Douglas, "Judge Exempts California Lender from Wisconsin Laws," *Milwaukee Journal Sentinel*, December 4, 1999, p. 1.

Hieger, Jennifer, "Irvine, California-Based Lender Back in Profitable Shape after Turn-around," *Orange County Register*, September 17, 1999.

Kelleher, James B., "Irvine, California-Based Firm Wants Stake in Auto-Loan Unit Back," *Knight Ridder Tribune Business News*, July 18, 2002, p. 1.

"Nonprime Surge Helps WFS Financial Sales Boost," *Ward's Dealer Business*, June 2001, p. 9.

Sanders, Edmund, "California Auto Lender Will Cut Jobs by 20 Percent," *Orange County Register*, February 11, 1998.

——, "WFS Financial Posts Loss for First Quarter," *Orange County Register*, April 23, 1998.

Vyas, Rajiv, "Auto Loans Power Growth of WFS Financial, Westcorp," *Orange County Business Journal*, October 29–November 4, 2001, p. 28.

—Carrie Rothburd

Wienerberger AG

Wienerbergstr 11
Vienna
A-1100
Austria
Telephone: (43) 1 601 920
Fax: (43) 1 601 92466
Web site: http://www.wienerberger.com

Public Company
Founded: 1819
Employees: 12,000
Sales: EUR 1.76 billion ($2.2 billion) (2003)
Stock Exchanges: Vienna
Ticker Symbol: WIE
NAIC: 327331 Concrete Block and Brick Manufacturing;
    327390 Other Concrete Product Manufacturing;
    551112 Offices of Other Holding Companies

Wienerberger AG is the world's leading manufacturer of bricks, including hollow bricks and facing bricks. The company dominates the brick market, with a number one position in hollow bricks worldwide, the lead in the European facing brick market, and the number two spot in facing bricks in the United States. Wienerberger produces its hollow bricks under the Porotherm and Poroton brands in Europe. Facing bricks are marketed under the Terca brand in Europe and through subsidiary General Shale in the United States. Wienerberger is also one of the world's leading manufacturers of concrete pavers. The company's Semmelrock division holds the number one position in Europe for that segment. In the mid-2000s, Wienerberger added a second core operation, roofing systems, in order to balance out its bricks business. To this end, the company acquired Belgium's Koramic, the leading roofing systems company in Europe, in 2004. Other roofing systems subsidiaries include ZZ Wancor, in Switzerland, and Bramac and Tondach Gleinstatten, both of which are active in Central and Eastern Europe. Wienerberger has a manufacturing presence in nearly 25 countries, with a total of some 235 plants under operation in 2005. The company has been engaged on an active expansion program. In 2004 alone the company spent approximately EUR 540 million on investments and has announced plans to spend at least EUR 250 million in 2005. Wienerberger is listed on the Austrian Stock exchange. In 2004, the company posted revenues of 1.76 billion.

Austrian Industrial Giant in the Early 19th Century

Alois Miesbach was 29 years old when he decided to launch a company manufacturing bricks in 1819. A native of Mähren, Miesbach built a factory on the Wienerbergstrasse in Vienna. Over the next 40 years, Miesbach's company developed into one of the region's largest and became a primary source of employment for workers from the Böhmen region. As his business grew, Miesbach continued to add new capacity, and during this period the company built Europe's largest brickworks. By the time Miesbach died in 1857, his company operated nine brickworks, a clay plant, and several coal mines. Miesbach's company also entered the construction sector, building a number of homes and buildings in the Vienna area.

Miesbach's nephew, Heinrich Drasche, took over at the company and continued its expansion. Among other achievements, the company added more than 400 new houses outside of the city center, as well as ten new houses on Vienna's exclusive Ringstrasse, under Drasche's leadership. Other buildings constructed by the company using its bricks was the famed Heinrichhof, built in 1868. That building was destroyed during World War II.

The Wienerberger Ziegelfabriks- und- Bausgesellschaft, as the company came to be known, incorporated as a limited liability company in 1869, and became one of the first Austrian companies to list its stock on the Vienna Stock Exchange. Joining the company's board of directors at this time was architect Heinrich Freiherr von Ferstel. The association with von Ferstel led the company to build such important Viennese structures as the Wiener Votivkirche and the Palais Ferstel.

In addition to brick manufacturing and construction, Wienerberger added a number of other businesses, including that of ornamental sculptures. These sculptures became a major export product for the company and were found in many European capitals. This activity continued until World War II.

Challenges and Achievements in the 20th Century

The 20th century represented an extended period of ups and downs for Wienerberger. Into the new century, the company continued expanding, adding plants beyond Austria and into such regions as Czechoslovakia, Croatia, and Hungary. Yet with the end of World War I and the collapse of the Austro-Hungarian Empire, Wienerberger lost most of its foreign operations. The company rebuilt around its core Austrian holdings, especially its huge Wienerbergstrasse factory. This facility was bombed during World War II, however, resulting in the deaths of many company employees as well as the destruction of much of its manufacturing plant.

The postwar years, and the reconstruction of Austria amid a general economic boom, brought new growth to Wienerberger. By the mid-1950s, the company had rebuilt its production capacity and had begun achieving record levels. In the early 1970s, Wienerberger began branching out, buying up Bramac, a manufacturer of concrete tiles in 1972. The company also expanded its production capacity in general, with 11 factories in operation at the end of the decade.

On the whole, however, the company appeared to have lost its momentum, particularly during the economic downturn of the 1970s. At the end of the decade, Wienerberger, despite being a major Austrian industrial company, remained almost entirely focused on its domestic market. Meanwhile, the difficult recession years had led Wienerberger to seek financial backing, and during this time the company came under majority control of Bank Austria Creditanstalt.

The company's fortunes began to change in the early 1980s, when a new management team launched a restructuring of the company's operations and developed a new expansion strategy that targeted a leading position in the European market. After consolidating its Austrian presence, the company turned toward the international market in the middle of the decade.

A significant point in the group's development came in 1986, when Wienerberger acquired Germany's Oltmanns-

Gruppe. With that purchase, Wienerberger became a major player in the European brick market, with more than 200 factories. Meanwhile, Wienerberger had been diversifying its operations, expanding into such areas as the manufacturing of clay pipe. The company's interests in piping were expanded in 1989 with the launch of its Pipelife joint venture. That year, Wienerberger also entered the metallurgy and abrasives market with the purchase of a stake in Treibacher Chemische Werke. In addition, Wienerberger purchased the OAG Group, a wholesaler of sanitary fixtures.

Acquisitions played an important role in Wienerberger's growth into Austria's largest industrial group. Into the 1990s, the company made a number of significant acquisitions, including a stake in paving systems specialists Semmelrock, based in Austria. In the early 1990s, Wienerberger targeted expansion in the newly opening Eastern European markets, starting with Hungary in 1990.

New management at the beginning of the 1990s put in place a new strategy emphasizing, on the one hand, Wienerberger's continuing expansion and, on the other hand, a streamlining of its operations around a narrower core of bricks and paving tiles. As part of the effort, the company divested much of its diversified holdings, including the OAG Group in 1994, Treibacher Schleifmittel in 1997, as well as real estate assets and other operations. The sale of a parking garage business, Wipark, and the remainder of Treibacher Industries in 2000, completed Wienerberger's transformation into a pure play building materials business.

The mid-1990s saw Wienerberger's push into the global big leagues. In 1995, the company went to France to purchase the Sturm Group, followed by the acquisition of Terca. That purchase gave the company the leading share of the facing brick market in Belgium and the Netherlands. Also in 1996, the company acquired majority control of Semmelrock.

By the end of the decade, Wienerberger claimed the number one position in the European brick market. In 1999, the company shot to the top of the global ranks after acquiring the U.S. firm General Shale Inc. as well as Switzerland's ZZ Wancor, and, through its Pipelife joint venture, Mabo, which focused on the Scandinavian market.

Continued Expansion in the 2000s

Wienerberger boosted its U.S. presence in 2000, acquiring Cherokee Sanford, based in Sanford, North Carolina, then the largest privately owned brick manufacturer in the United States. The purchase added five brick plants, with a total capacity of 375 million bricks per year.

Wienerberger showed no sign of letting up the pace into mid-decade. In 2001, the company bought Optiroc's brick division, the leading producer of bricks in the Scandinavian region. That year, the company also acquired Germany's number two producer, Megalith, for EUR 47 million. These acquisitions were followed up by the purchase of family-owned Brada Baksteen NV in the Netherlands and the continental European brick business of Hanson Plc in 2002. Also in that year, Wienerberger made its entry into the United Kingdom, buying up that country's number three brick maker, thebrickbusiness.

Key Dates:

1819: Alois Miesback founds a brick factory on Wiener-bergstrasse in Vienna.

1857: Nephew Heinrich Drasche takes over after Miesbach's death.

1869: The company reincorporates as a public limited liability company, Wienerberger Ziegelfabriks-und- Bausgesellschaft, and becomes one of the first firm to list on the Vienna Stock Exchange.

1918: Wienerberger loses its operations in Hungary, Poland, and elsewhere after the collapse of Austro-Hungarian Empire.

1945: Wienerbergstrasse is destroyed by bombs.

1972: The company acquires Bramac concrete tiles.

1986: Wienerberger begins internationalization with purchase of Germany's Oltmanns-Gruppe.

1989: The company attempts diversification with Pipelife joint venture and the acquisition of Trebacher Chemische Werke and OAG Group.

1990: Wienerberger expands into Eastern Europe.

1995: The company acquires Sturm Group in France.

1996: Wienerberger acquires Terca, in Belgium, and a majority stake in Semmelrock in Austria.

1999: The company acquires General Shale in the United States and becomes the world's leading brick manufacturer.

2000: Wienerberger divests itself of the last of its diversified holdings to become a pure play building materials group.

With its brick business now ranked number one worldwide, Wienerberger moved to create a second core business, that of roofing tile systems, in 2003. For this, the company bought a 50 percent stake in Koramic Roofing, the number two player in the European roofing systems sector. The company also announced its intention to acquire full control of Koramic in the near future. Wienerberger also moved toward becoming a free float company when main shareholder Bank Austria Creditanstalt sold its holding in the company, a process completed in 2004.

In the meantime, Wienerberger's expansion continued. In 2004, the company spent some EUR 540 million on acquisitions and further expansion, including the Koramic purchase and several new acquisitions in the United States, as well as a number of investments deepening the group's presence in Central and Eastern Europe. Wienerberger's transformation from a primarily domestic company to global player had been dramatic. By 2005, international operations accounted for 97 percent of the group's total revenues. Wienerberger made it clear that it expected its expansion to continue, announcing plans to spend "at least" EUR 250 million on new expansion in 2005.

Principal Subsidiaries

Bramac Dachsysteme International GmbH; General Shale Building Materials Inc. (United States); Koramic Roofing Products N.V. (Belgium); Pipelife International GmbH; Semmelrock Baustoffindustrie GmbH; Tondach Gleinstätten AG; Wienerberger Bricks B.V. (Netherlands); Wienerberger Bricks N.V. (Belgium); Wienerberger Ceramika Budowlana Sp.z.o.o. (Poland); Wienerberger cihlársky prumysl, a.s. (Czech Republic); Wienerberger Teglaipari Rt (Hungary); Wienerberger Ziegelindustrie GmbH; Wienerberger Ziegelindustrie GmbH (Germany); ZZ Wancor (Switzerland).

Principal Competitors

Anglo American plc; Lafarge S.A.; Central Pre-Mix Concrete Company Inc.; Fomento de Construcciones y Contratas S.A.; Hanson plc; Eurovia S.A; Glen-Gery Corporation; Imerys Ltd.; Rinker Group Ltd.; FLS Industries A/S; Tarmac Ltd.

Further Reading

Bulkeley, Andrew, "Brick Giant Bulks Up," *Daily Deal*, January 11, 2003.

Hall, Eric, and William Frey, "Wienerberger Seen as a Bid Target," *Financial Times*, April 17, 2000, p. 28.

Pesola, Maija, "Butterflies All Round as Brick Behemoth Stalks the Sector," *Financial Times*, October 9, 2004, p. 4.

Simonian, Haig. "Building on a Growth Strategy," *Financial Times*, October 25, 2004, p. 4.

——, "Rapid Expansion Boosts Wienerberger," *The Financial Times*, November 17, 2004, p. 28.

——, "Wienerberger on Hunt for acquisitions," *Financial Times*, February 16, 2005, p. 29.

"Wienerberger Plans to Expand in Germany," *Handelsblatt*, September 30, 2003.

"Wienerberger Storms into UK Brick Market," *Contract Journal*, October 6, 2004, p. 14.

—M.L. Cohen

Wolfgang Puck Worldwide, Inc.

1250 4th Street, Suite 310
Santa Monica, California 90401
U.S.A.
Telephone: (310) 319-1350
Fax: (310) 319-1350
Web site: http://www.wolfgangpuck.com

Private Company
Incorporated: 1983
Employees: 4,900
Sales: $375 million (2002 est.)
NAIC: 722110 Full-Service Restaurants; 722211 Limited-Service Restaurants; 722320 Caterers

Wolfgang Puck Worldwide, Inc., brings the trademark cuisine of one of America's most celebrated chefs to an audience far beyond the white tablecloths of Los Angeles' renowned Spago restaurant. Since arriving in the United States in the 1970s, Wolfgang Puck has become one of the wealthiest and possibly the most famous chefs in history, thanks in part to regular appearances on national television programs. Observers have described him as the first chef ever to successfully start and run his own chain of restaurants, while his company has been successful in capitalizing on his name in both mid-range restaurant chains, frozen foods, cookware, consumer packaged foods, and the home meal replacement category.

Puck's former wife, Barbara Lazaroff, has been instrumental in his success as she focuses on management details and designing the restaurant's unique interiors. Puck and Lazaroff's interests in their seven fine dining restaurants, each separate partnerships with other investors, were held under Puck Lazaroff Inc. These produced approximately $60 million of revenue in 1997. Puck and Lazaroff owned 30 percent of the Wolfgang Puck Food Company in 1998, which operated 21 casual restaurants (the full-service Wolfgang Puck Cafes and Oba-Chine, and the counter-service Wolfgang Puck Express) and Wolfgang Puck Packaged Foods. In 2001 Wolfgang Puck Worldwide, Inc. was founded to oversee the myriad activities of the Wolfgang Puck brand name, including not only its fine dining restaurants, but

casual dining restaurants, catering business, and packaged food products, but Puck's television shows, books, and syndicated newspaper column as well.

Birth of a Legend

Wolfgang Puck was born in St. Veit-Glan, Austria. His mother was an accomplished chef at a posh resort, and Puck began his culinary training at the age of 14. He apprenticed at L'Oustau de Baumaiere in Provence at 19, and later worked in several top Parisian restaurants such as Maxim's as well as the Hotel de Paris in Monaco. He reportedly dreamed of owning his own restaurant and becoming rich doing it.

In 1973, at the age of 24, Puck emigrated to Indianapolis, working at La Tour. A year and a half later he was co-owner of Hollywood's illustrious Ma Maison, where the celebrity of its clients seemed contagious and Puck became renowned for his skill and creativity. Puck prided himself on using the freshest and finest ingredients, and also displayed a flair for showmanship.

In 1979, Puck met Barbara Lazaroff, a Bronx native who was studying biochemistry. An outspoken contrast to the somewhat reticent Puck, Lazaroff quickly became his champion, urging him first to ask for a raise at Ma Maison and then guiding him into the limelight of television cooking shows. Puck's own cookbook, *Modern French Cooking for the American Kitchen* (1982), soon followed.

With the help of a few investors, in January 1982 Puck fulfilled a lifelong dream by opening his own restaurant in West Hollywood, Sunset Boulevard's illustrious Spago. Lazaroff was responsible for the striking design of the $512,000 restaurant, which featured an open kitchen illuminated like a stage. She reported taking up to four years, from concept to completion, to develop the eatery. At Spago, Puck perfected his trademark of topping pizzas with exotic gourmet ingredients such as duck sausage or smoked salmon.

A second, Asian-California fusion restaurant, Chinois on Main, was established in Santa Monica in 1983. This was opened as a buffer against the inconstant fashions of the food

Company Perspectives:

The name Wolfgang Puck, in the eyes of food lovers and experts alike, represents the ultimate in good cooking. That name now refers not only to the world-famous chef himself but also to the culinary empire he has built since the early 1980s: the group of fine dining restaurants through which he first rose to prominence, developed in partnership with Barbara Lazaroff; his extensive catering and events business, which gains international attention through its flagship event, the annual Governor's Ball following the Oscars; and Wolfgang Puck Worldwide, Inc., the corporation that controls the Wolfgang Puck brand in areas as diverse as casual and quick-service dining, consumer packaged foods, cookware, book publishing, television, radio and internet programming, and other franchising, licensing, and merchandising activities.

business, but it provided what many feel to be Puck's most creative outlet: mixing Asian and French cuisine with the assistance of chef Richard Krause. Lazaroff again designed the restaurant's interior, which also featured an open kitchen.

Birth of the Food Company in 1983

The Wolfgang Puck Food Company began in 1983 as the brainchild of Robert Koblin, a Beverly Hills heart specialist. Koblin's original concept was to offer healthful frozen dinners designed by a number of prominent chefs. Eventually the health aspect was minimized and Koblin settled on Puck alone as the chef.

The company's first products were frozen desserts, created by Spago's pastry chef Nancy Silverton. The quality of ingredients, however, seemed to price the company out of the market. In 1987 the company then tried frozen pizza but the company still quickly ran through its $3 million of start-up capital. Koblin's bankers subsequently replaced him as leader of the company with Selwyn Joffe.

According to the *New Yorker*, Joffe saw Puck as "the Armani of the food business," and imagined a range of lines for different budgets to parallel the eminent couturier's empire. Lower-priced restaurants and frozen foods would cash in on Puck's stature in the world of fine dining, where his star continued to shine. In 1989, Puck ventured outside of southern California with the opening of the Postrio in San Francisco. Opening the high-overhead Eureka in West Los Angeles in 1990, however, proved disastrous. Puck lacked control of the brewery to which the sausage house was attached and subsequently his restaurant shared its failure, losing $5 million. Puck himself owned 10 percent of the venture. Granita, an elaborate, $3 million Mediterranean-themed restaurant that opened in 1991 struggled to break even in its seasonal Malibu home.

Greener pastures were just around the bend. Though initially reluctant, Wolfgang Puck became one of the first eminent chefs to try his luck in Las Vegas with the opening of the Spago there in 1992. The most successful of the high-end restaurants, it eventually achieved $12 million in annual sales. Eventually a Cafe and an upscale Chinois restaurant followed.

Food Company Expanding in the 1990s

In 1991, the company opened its first, limited-menu, self-service Wolfgang Puck Express inside Macy's in San Francisco's Union Square. In 1993, the Wolfgang Puck Cafe, a less ambitious counterpart to Spago, opened in Universal Studio's Universal City. The Cafe featured table service and a larger menu than the Express. The Express and Cafe were originally designed to promote frozen foods, but they quickly became profit centers for the Food Company, thanks to their immediate appeal and high profit margins. The full-service Cafes annually generated between $2 and $4.5 million each. By 1995, there were ten Cafes in existence, half of them Express units.

Puck boasted of having more great chefs among his 1,400 employees than any other chain, and executives described the Cafes as more "chef-driven" than other chain restaurants. Menus were somewhat customized at each one, and the chefs cooked from scratch. The dining areas were individualized as well: seating at various Cafes ranged from 88 to 200. The company capitalized upon the success of Puck's Asian fusion creations by starting another chain in 1996. The first Oba-Chine opened in Beverly Hills; restaurants in Seattle and Phoenix soon followed.

Frozen foods, where the company squared off against giants such as Kraft, proved a much more difficult market to penetrate. Nevertheless, the Food Company claimed growth exceeding 50 percent a year in the mid-1990s. The scale of operations prompted the partners to choose Frank Guidara as the company's chief executive in September 1996. Unlike Joffe, Guidara possessed extensive experience in foodservice management, gained at steakhouse chains and fine dining restaurants. He soon induced new levels of consistency across the Food Company. Guidara's concept of the Wolfgang Puck brand included merchandising. A Florida entrepreneur licensed the right to make Wolfgang Puck cookware, but the Food Company itself offered a range of souvenir items from glasses to T-shirts.

The Food Company's packaged foods, managed by former Procter and Gamble executive Tom Warner, garnered sales of approximately $17 million in 1997. Under Warner, the company's expensive frozen products became more competitively priced. The costs of ingredients were trimmed to match consumer reality. From 1997 to 1998, the number of packaged items offered by the Food Company grew from 23 to 43. Aside from ten different types of pizza, Puck's lasagna, ravioli, tortellini, and cannelloni were also available in the freezer.

Completing the Empire in the Late 1990s

Puck and Lazaroff topped off their fine dining empire with a few new openings in 1996 and 1997. They licensed Spago branches in Tokyo and Mexico City. The third U.S. Spago opened in the River North section of Chicago in 1996. It adjoined a new Cafe. *Nation's Restaurant News* reported the new restaurant received 3,000 reservation requests per day. A new Chinois opened in Las Vegas in January 1997 as did a Spago in Palo Alto, California.

The Food Company opened a Grand Cafe, an expanded branch of the Wolfgang Puck Cafe, at Disney World in Orlando, Florida, in the summer of 1997. It also included a sushi bar

---

Key Dates:

1982: Wolfgang Puck opens his first restaurant, Spago, in West Hollywood.
1983: Wolfgang Puck Food Company is incorporated.
1989: The Postrio restaurant opens in San Francisco.
1991: The company opens its first Wolfgang Puck Express in San Francisco.
1992: Spago restaurant opens in Las Vegas.
1993: Wolfgang Puck Cafe opens in Universal Studio's Universal City.
1996: The Oba-Chine Asian restaurant chain is founded.
1997: Grand Cafe opens at Disney World in Orlando, Florida.
1998: Wolfgang Puck Catering & Events is formed.
1999: Wolfgang Puck canned soup is introduced.
2001: Wolfgang Puck Worldwide, Inc. is founded; the *Wolfgang Puck* television show debuts on the Food Network.
2003: *Wolfgang Puck's Cooking Class* television show debuts on the Food Network.

---

known as B's Bar. The 22,000-square-foot facility consisted of four separate areas: The Cafe for casual dining; The Dining Room for upscale dining; B's Lounge & Sushi Bar; and a Wolfgang Puck Express for quick casual service.

At the end of 1997, Puck and Lazaroff owned majority shares in several fine dining restaurants, which had grossed $56 million in 1996. These interests were kept separate from the Wolfgang Puck Food Company, however, of which they owned slightly more than a third. It collected revenues of $70 million in 1996. Revenues for 1997 were reported at $60 million for the Food Company, while the upscale restaurants grossed $56 million.

A New Direction in the Early 2000s

In 2001 the Wolfgang Puck Food Company was replaced by Wolfgang Puck Worldwide, Inc. The new corporation was established to oversee the use of the Wolfgang Puck brand name in all of its business activities. The new corporation had two subsidiaries: Wolfgang Puck Fine Dining Group, which operated the upscale dining restaurants, and Wolfgang Puck Catering & Events, which ran the extensive catering business, including the high-profile annual Academy Awards Governor's Ball. Wolfgang Puck Worldwide handled the casual dining restaurants, and the related brand products, such as the frozen pizza and entrees, coffee, canned soups, and cookware, as well as activities such as Wolfgang Puck's television programs, books, and newspaper column. In 2002 the company had estimated sales of $375 million.

Wolfgang Puck Worldwide announced in 2001 a partnership with ConAgra, the nation's second largest food company, that was intended to greatly expand the distribution of Wolfgang Puck packaged foods. The new partners introduced a line of wood fired frozen pizzas in 2002. That same year saw several other major developments for the company. Wolfgang Puck Worldwide acquired Cucina! Cucina!, a popular Italian restau-

rant chain with 21 locations in the Pacific Northwest; Kendall-Jackson Wine Estates announced the creation of a new line of wines created by Wolfgang Puck; and Crystal Cruises added several of Puck's Asian recipes to the menu of its Jade Garden restaurant aboard its Crystal Symphony cruise ship.

While the early years of the new century saw many positive changes for the company, there were also some personal setbacks for those behind the scenes. The original Spago restaurant in West Hollywood, opened by Puck and his wife Lazaroff in 1982, closed its doors in 2001. A year later it was announced that Puck and Lazaroff were getting divorced. The couple separated amicably and continued to be partners in the company.

Whereas Puck had long been a frequent guest on ABC's *Good Morning America* television program—and had appeared on other programs such as *The Late Show with David Letterman*, *The Tonight Show with Jay Leno*, *Frasier*, and *The Simpsons*—it was only in 2001 that he teamed with the Food Network and Weller/Grossman Productions to create the *Wolfgang Puck* show on the Food Network. In 2003, the Emmy Award-winning show was superseded by *Wolfgang Puck's Cooking Class*, a Food Network show in which Puck offered up-close cooking lessons to his viewing audience. These shows helped to popularize Puck's signature catch phrase, "Live, love, eat!" Puck turned to newspaper syndication in March 2003 when Tribune Media Services launched his weekly column, "Wolfgang Puck's Kitchen." The column offers expert cooking tips and recipes suitable for home preparation.

As of early 2005, Wolfgang Puck Worldwide operated 54 Wolfgang Puck Cafes and Wolfgang Puck Expresses in the United States, four in Japan, and one in Canada. An aggressive franchising program for the Wolfgang Puck Expresses called for some 300 new locations to be added in 2005 alone. The Wolfgang Puck Fine Dining Group operated 12 upscale restaurants, including Spago restaurants in Palo Alto, Beverly Hills, Las Vegas, and Maui; the Chinois restaurants in Las Vegas and Santa Monica; and the Postrio restaurants in Las Vegas and San Francisco. Wolfgang Puck Catering & Events not only catered the annual Academy Awards Governor's Ball, it was also the permanent catering service for the Chicago Museum of Contemporary Art, the University of Chicago's Gleacher Center, the St. Louis Science Center, the St. Louis Art Museum, and the St. Louis Contemporary Art Museum.

Principal Subsidiaries

Wolfgang Puck Fine Dining Group; Wolfgang Puck Catering & Events.

Principal Competitors

Ark Restaurants; California Pizza Kitchen; Levy Restaurants.

Further Reading

Barrier, M., "The Chef As Famous As His Customers," *Nation's Business,* July 1991.
Bertagnoli, Lisa, "Real Simple: Light on Decor and Awash in California Colors, the New Wolfgang Puck Express Focuses on Food," *Chain Leader,* April 2004, p. 28.

Butler, Charles, "Recipe for Success," *Sales and Marketing Management,* August 1998.

Cohen, Richard L., "Wolfgang Puck Invades Supermarkets," *Pizza and Pasta,* February 1996, p. 24.

Correa, Barbara, "Divorce Likely to Carve Up Chef Wolfgang Puck's Food Empire," *Daily News,* December 3, 2002.

Courtmanche, John, "Empire-Building Strategy Goes Global," *Daily Variety,* January 29, 2003, p. A6.

Cuthbert, Lauren, "Convenience and Taste Boost Frozen Sales," *Natural Food Merchandiser,* March 1998.

Daniels, Wade, "Wolfgang Puck: Trendsetting Chef Parlays His Name and Fame into an International Brand," *Nation's Restaurant News,* January 27, 2003, p. 150.

Elam, Shade, "Wolfgang Puck May Open Three Restaurants Here," *Atlanta Business Chronicle,* May 18, 1998.

Fixmer, Andy, "Failed Division Folded Under Puck Umbrella," *Los Angeles Business Journal,* September 27, 2004, p. 6.

——, "Puck Struggles to Find the Right Recipe," *Los Angeles Business Journal,* September 1, 2003, p. 1.

——, "Puck's Earliest Investors Get Steamed As Chef Remakes Menu of Companies," *Los Angeles Business Journal,* March 22, 2004, p. 1.

——, "Rival Chefs Under One Roof As Compass Buys Puck Stake," *Los Angeles Business Journal,* February 23, 2004, p. 7.

Gellene, Denise, "Breaking Bread: Puck Deal Indicative of American Express' Renewed Efforts," *Los Angeles Times,* May 8, 1996.

Howard, Theresa, "Wolfgang Puck," *Nation's Restaurant News,* February 1, 1996, p. 124.

Kessler, John, "Coming Soon: Celebrity Chef Wolfgang Puck's Dining Empire," *Atlanta Journal and Constitution,* May 29, 1998.

Komaiko, Leslee, "Puck Everlasting: Despite Growing Empire, Name Evokes Loyalty, Hands-on Attention to Detail," *Daily Variety,* January 29, 2003, p. A1.

Krummert, Bob, "The Partners of Puck Step Out," *Restaurant Hospitality,* May 2002, p. 15.

Kuh, Patrick, *The Last Days of Haute Cuisine,* New York: Viking Press, 2001.

"Lazaroff Seeks Divorce from Chef-Partner Puck," *Nation's Restaurant News,* December 16, 2002, p. 54.

Lempert, Phil, "America's Top Chefs Find Success in Retail Market," *Chicago Tribune,* October 8, 1997.

Lubow, Martin, "Puck's Peak," *New Yorker,* December 1, 1997, pp. 46–53.

"Marketing the Wolfgang Puck Latte Line," *Beverage Industry,* October 2003, p. 38.

Martin, Patricia, "Redefining Dining," *Las Vegas Business Press,* January 26, 1998.

Martin, Richard, "Frank Guidara," *Nation's Restaurant News,* January 1997, pp. 80–81.

——, "Wolfgang Puck Cafe," *Nation's Restaurant News,* May 22, 1995.

——, "Wolfgang Puck: Chef, Restaurateur, Celebrity, Los Angeles," *Nation's Restaurant News,* January 1995, pp. 159–60.

Morris, Kathleen, "Add a Dash of Show Biz and Stir," *Business Week,* May 19, 1997.

"NRN Names Puck, Lazaroff 1997 Innovator of the Year Recipients," *Nation's Restaurant News,* June 2, 1997, pp. 1, 4.

"Puck's Spago Hollywood Closes Doors, Sells Site to Miyagi Operator," *Nation's Restaurant News,* April 16, 2001, p. 80.

Puck, Wolfgang, *Adventures in the Kitchen with Wolfgang Puck,* New York: Random House, 1991.

——, *Live, Love, Eat!: The Best of Wolfgang Puck,* New York: Random House, 2002.

——, *Modern French Cooking for the American Kitchen,* New York: Random House, 1982.

——, *Pizza, Pasta & More,* New York: Random House, 2000.

——, *The Wolfgang Puck Cookbook: Recipes from Spago, Chinois and Points East and West,* New York: Random House, 1986.

——, *Wolfgang Puck Makes It Easy,* Nashville: Rutledge Hill Press, 2004.

Reckard, E. Scott, "Fifty-Eight More Workers Suspected by INS in Eatery Raids," *Los Angeles Times,* September 11, 1997, p. D1.

——, "INS Raids Shut Puck Cafe, Fellow OC Mall Eatery," *Los Angeles Times,* September 10, 1997, p. D1.

Reichl, Ruth, *Comfort Me with Apples,* New York: Random House, 2001.

Rothman, Cliff, "Style and Substance: Lazaroff Continues to Add Personal Touch to Puck Eateries," *Daily Variety,* January 29, 2003, p. A4.

Sheridan, Margaret, "Wolfgang Puck: A Pioneer in Restaurant and Food Innovation Reflects on What Has Driven His Career," *Restaurants & Institutions,* October 1, 2004, p. 22.

Specht, Jeff, "Live, Love, Eat," *Business Geography,* July/August 1996.

Spector, Amy, "Puck Sells 8 Cucinas, Shutters 4 Cafe Units, Spago Chicago," *Nation's Restaurant News,* January 12, 2004, p. 1.

Swetlow, Frank, "A Casual Interview with the King and Queen of Fine Dining in Los Angeles," *Los Angeles Business Journal,* October 27, 1997.

Walkup, Carolyn, "Spago Chicago Premiers As Puck Dining Portfolio Grows, Diversifies," *Nation's Restaurant News,* December 9, 1996.

"What's Cooking at the Wolfgang Puck Food Company," *California Centers,* Spring 1996, pp. 8–12.

Wolf, Barnet D., "Celebrity Chef Wolfgang Puck Opens First Ohio Restaurant in Columbus," *Columbus Dispatch,* October 7, 2004.

Wolfgang Puck: Amadeus of Our Age, Tokyo: Shibata Publishing, 2001.

"Wolfgang Puck Food Begins Flying on US Airways in the In-Flight Cafe," *Nation's Restaurant News,* January 19, 2004, p. 22.

—Frederick C. Ingram
—update: Thomas Wiloch

Workman Publishing Company, Inc.

708 Broadway
New York, New York 10003-9555
U.S.A.
Telephone: (212) 254-5900
Fax: (212) 254-8098
Web site: http://www.workman.com

Private Company
Incorporated: 1968
Employees: 250
Sales: $95.8 million (2003 est.)
NAIC: 511130 Book Publishers; 511199 All Other Publishers

Workman Publishing Company, Inc., is a leading independent publisher of non-fiction books, games, and calendars. The firm's biggest successes include pregnancy guide *What to Expect When You're Expecting*, the Brain Quest learning card game for children, and Page-A-Day calendars. Other popular Workman offerings include cookbooks; books that are packaged with toys; books, calendars, and toys based on B. Kliban's drawings of cats; and popular culture parodies like *The Official Preppy Handbook*. The company is owned and run by its founder, Peter Workman.

Beginnings

Workman Publishing was founded in New York City by Peter Workman, a 30-year-old Yale graduate who had previously held a number of publishing-related jobs, including working in sales at Dell Publishing, as a clerk at a bookstore, as a reader at a woman's magazine, and as a copy boy at the *New York Daily News*. In 1968, he decided to strike out on his own and formed a small company to package books for sale to larger publishers.

In 1972, the Workman company moved into publishing books of its own with Richard Hittleman's *Yoga: 28 Day Exercise Plan;* other lifestyle and humor books followed. The company's first major success was *The Toy Book* by Stephen Caney, which showed children how to make simple toys by themselves. Though Workman did not have the budget to advertise it, the author made hundreds of personal appearances, and the book went on to sell several hundred thousand copies over the next few years. Caney would later publish other children's activity books for Workman, including some that were packaged with toys and other related objects.

Workman published relatively few books per year and issued only titles in which the firm's owner himself believed. Unlike many large publishing houses, which focused on developing blockbusters and let slow-selling titles fall by the wayside, his company was persistent in promoting books until they caught on. One example of this was illustrator B. Kliban's *Cat*, which sold poorly on initial release. Seeking ways to gain exposure, Workman sent most of his staff to the annual Madison Square Garden cat show to sell copies and then printed up posters of Kliban's humorous cat illustrations to give to bookstores. When patrons started to steal them, the company got requests for copies to sell and reached a licensing agreement with Kliban to print them. Other *Cat* merchandise followed, including pillows, mugs, and calendars.

Page-A-Day Calendar Introduced in 1979

The success of its Kliban cat calendars led the company to create calendars with other themes, and in 1979 the Page-A-Day desk calendar debuted, with 365 tear-off pages, each with a different image. Workman was the first to market a whimsical calendar of this type, and it was received enthusiastically by the public.

Another Workman success of this period was 1980's *The Official Preppy Handbook*, which spoofed a popular style trend of the day. It topped the *New York Times* trade paperback bestseller list and remained in the rankings for many months.

In 1984, Workman published *What to Expect When You're Expecting*, written by a freelance medical writer along with her two daughters, one of whom was a nurse. The practical, information-packed guidebook took readers through pregnancy month-by-month, with illustrations and helpful hints. Though the company received only 6,800 orders from bookstores at first, it tried marketing ploys like offering a special deal to stores that ordered five or more copies and sent the authors to physi-

Company Perspectives:

Look at our offerings and you'll see not a company running on past successes, but one that works just as hard to launch the new idea as it does to keep the proven title selling—a company that works as hard to publish the best calendar as it does to publish the best book.

cians' conferences to encourage them to recommend it. Sales soon began to pick up, and the title became a steady seller, topping one million copies within six years' time. Its success spawned a number of additional books like *What to Eat When You're Expecting* and *What to Expect: The First Year.*

Purchase of Algonquin Books in 1988

In 1988, Workman bought Algonquin Books of Chapel Hill, North Carolina. Founded in 1982, Algonquin published both non-fiction and fiction titles, including well-regarded novels by Clyde Edgerton, Jill McCorkle, and Kay Gibbons. Its president, Louis P. Rubin, Jr. would remain in charge, while Workman would take on production, sales, and distribution chores.

The company had by now built a reputation for its unique publishing style. Workman books were known for their clever writing, their strong design, and their sometimes offbeat content. In addition to nonfiction titles, books of humor, and calendars, Workman also put out cookbooks like the best-selling *Silver Palate Cookbook* as well as children's titles. The firm typically issued a relatively modest twenty titles per year but kept more than 75 percent of its backlist in print, an unusually high rate for the industry. Its books, typically paperbacks, were often priced less than comparable titles from larger publishers.

Peter Workman received much of the credit for his firm's success, as it was his vision, attention to detail, and somewhat eccentric nature that had guided the choices of titles and helped nurture them to fruition. Workman was considered a difficult person by some and was well-known for changing cover designs and other details at the last minute, but he inspired loyalty among much of his staff and praise from industry observers who saw him and his company as the antithesis of the faceless, conglomerate-owned giants of the book trade.

In the fall of 1990, Workman published its first novel (*Good Omens: The Nice and Accurate Prophecies of Agnes Nutter, Witch*) while continuing to offer the usual range of *Cat* items, activity books by Caney, a book on AIDS for teens, and numerous calendars like one of teddy bears which featured photos selected from 20,000 sent in by the public. The company also issued titles on a variety of subjects, including herbs, dolls, and games. The firm's biggest hit of 1990 was Suzy Becker's parody *All I Need to Know I Learned from My Cat*, which sold 540,000 copies in just two months' time, making it the company's fastest-selling title ever.

Brain Quest Introduced in 1992

In June 1992, Workman began publishing Brain Quest, a children's knowledge card game which was licensed from Edi-

tions Play Bac, a French firm which had developed it and successfully marketed it in that country as "Les Incollables" ("Little Bits Of Knowledge"). The game, which was published in different editions for each grade from first through seventh, was intended to help kids learn while having fun. It was marketed with the slogan "It's OK to Be Smart." Promotion was accomplished via eye-catching displays in stores, a mailing to 20,000 school principals, and later a Brain Quest Challenge held at Walt Disney World in Florida.

At first, only 50,000 sets were published for each grade, but these quickly sold out. Though the company had a hard time keeping up with orders, by December 1.6 million had been sold. This amount doubled the next year, when preschool and kindergarten editions were published with colorful artwork featuring Ryan Lion and Amanda Panda, respectively, and the tagline "Get a Smart Start." A competitor, Western Publishing, introduced a similar game called "Ask Me!," and Workman filed suit, claiming that Western had broken an implied confidentiality agreement when it had looked at, and passed on, the Brain Quest concept in 1990.

In 1993, Workman made an offer to buy Stewart, Tabori & Chang, a publisher whose titles it distributed. Negotiations broke down in May, however, and at year's end Workman's distribution contract with the company expired.

Artisan Imprint Founded in 1994

In March 1994, Workman founded a new division called Artisan, which would publish twelve to fifteen illustrated books and calendars each year. The high-quality books, published on heavy paper, would cover such topics as cooking, sports, and gardening. The unit would be run by former Stewart, Tabori & Chang publisher Leslie Stoker.

The spring of 1995 saw the firm partner with Toronto-based Eating Well magazine publisher Telemedia to form Eating Well books. In July, Workman reached an out-of-court settlement with Western Publishing over its "Ask Me!" card series. Terms were not disclosed. In the fall, Workman teamed up with upscale garden products retailers Smith & Hawken to publish a series of gardening titles. The year also saw the company named Publisher of the Year by the American Wholesale Booksellers Association.

In May 1997, Workman went online for the first time with the Workman Electric Booksite, which featured information about its titles for retailers and consumers, a store locator, and several interactive entertainment features. That same month saw Ann Bramson named publisher of Artisan Books, replacing the departing Leslie Stoker. By this time, Workman was also distributing the books of two other publishers, Black Dog & Leventhal and Greenwich Workshop Press. The company had recently invested in Groupe Latingy of France to help that firm buy art book publisher Harry Abrams, as well.

In February 1999, Workman hired Bruce Harris to serve as publisher and chief operating officer of the firm. Harris had worked for 38 years at Crown Publishers and Random House, where he had most recently been president of trade sales and marketing. April of that year saw Workman license its Brain

Key Dates:

1968: Peter Workman begins packaging book projects for other publishers.
1972: The company publishes its first book, *Yoga: 28 Day Exercise Plan.*
1975: B. Kliban's *Cat* is published.
1979: Page-A-Day Calendars are introduced.
1984: *What to Expect When You're Expecting* is published.
1988: Algonquin Books is acquired.
1992: Brain Quest learning card game is released, and 1.6 million sets are sold.
1994: Artisan Books, a high-end imprint, is formed.
2001: Workman buys control of the trade and custom publishing units of Storey Publishing.

Quest concept to IBM, which would turn it into a series of software products for home and school use.

With more than 14 million sets of Brain Quest cards already in print, Workman launched a revised version of the series, which it had spent $1 million to prepare. The revamped cards featured full-color art and 50 percent new editorial material. A brightly painted yellow bus was sent around the country to promote it, with mascots Amanda Panda, Ryan Lion, and BQ the bull terrier on board.

The company was now reducing the number of titles it published annually, which had increased in recent years to more than 40, to focus more energy on promoting its backlist. Nearly one-third of all Workman titles had surpassed the 100,000 sales mark.

In September 1999, the company introduced the digital Page-A-Day calendar, which gave computer users a version of the popular calendar that contained many additional features like month-at-a-glance grids, the ability to type in appointments, pop-up reminders, and audio and video snippets. Purchasers of any of the firm's 47 print calendars could download a digital version for free. Popular titles of this period included *Audubon Birds, Fly Fishing, 365 Cats,* and *The 365 Stupidest Things Ever Said.* They were priced between $8.95 and $10.95. Also in the fall of 1999, Workman partnered with Boston public television station WGBH to publish *The Antiques Roadshow Primer,* based on the hit television series.

Over the years, Workman had published increasing numbers of what were known in the trade as ''books-plus,'' which tied a book to an interactive object. Examples included *How to Kazoo,* which came complete with instrument, and *The Bones Book,* which was accompanied by a small skeleton. Others came with marbles, jumpropes, magic tricks, music CDs, puzzles, and balls, while a Workman bird-watching guide was packaged in a bird feeder.

In July 2000, the firm's editor-in-chief, Sally Kovalchick, died suddenly of a heart attack. She had worked for the company for 26 years and helped put together a number of successful titles, including *The Official Preppy Handbook* and *Cat.* In

the fall, her place was taken by Susan Bolotin, a veteran of Random House and Simon & Schuster, who had most recently served as executive editor of *Good Housekeeping* magazine.

Acquisition of Storey Publishing in 2001

In June 2001, Workman bought a majority stake in the trade publishing and custom publishing units of Massachusetts-based Storey Publishing, which the firm distributed. Storey had published more than 560 books, primarily how-to titles on country living.

Following the September 11 terrorist attacks, Workman published a calendar which featured images of American flags photographed in the aftermath of the attacks. The proceeds were donated to the *New York Times'* 9/11 neediest fund and the American Red Cross. In the spring of 2002, the company released its third edition of *What to Expect When You're Expecting,* which had sold more than ten million copies in the United States alone. A *USA Today* poll reported that 93 percent of pregnancy guidebook readers had used it.

In April 2004, the firm named Walter Weintz chief operating officer, succeeding Bruce Harris, who left to become a consultant. Peter Workman's wife Carolan, who had served as director of international publishing for a number of years, also left during the year to be replaced by Kristina Peterson. With Peter and Carolan Workman now in their 60s, their daughter Katie was in line to take over, having been named associate publisher in 2003.

New titles for 2004 included *Nesting: It's a Chick Thing; How to Make Someone Love You Forever in 90 Minutes or Less; The S Factor: Strip Workouts for Every Woman;* and *How to Grill: The Complete Illustrated Book of Barbeque Techniques.*

For more than 35 years, Workman Publishing Company had issued a steady stream of distinctive, highly successful titles that included everything from pop-culture parodies and serious non-fiction books to calendars, cookbooks, children's activity books, and games. The firm's strong backlist, and its reputation for carefully-chosen and well-developed new titles, put it in a strong position for continued success.

Principal Competitors

Random House, Inc.; TimeWarner Book Group, Inc.; HarperCollins Publishers, Inc.; Simon & Schuster, Inc.

Further Reading

Cox, Meg, ''Publishing: Workman Finds Clever, Quirky Books, Marketed with Great Care, Bring Success,'' *Wall Street Journal*, July 19, 1990, p. B1.

Dahlin, Robert, ''Workman, Smith & Hawken Till Common Ground,'' *Publishers Weekly*, September 18, 1995, p. 36.

Donahue, Dierdre, ''2002 Calendar Glorifies the Flag Every Day,'' *USA Today*, October 15, 2001, p. D1.

O'Briant, Don, ''Agreement Turns Another Page in the History of Algonquin Books,'' *Atlanta Journal-Constitution*, October 20, 1988, p. D7.

''Peterson Joins Workman,'' *Publishers Weekly*, September 13, 2004, p. 20.

Rosen, Judith, ''Workman to Acquire Storey,'' *Publishers Weekly*, June 11, 2001, p. 9.

Stander, Bella, ''Q: Which Workman Phenomenon Has Sold 4.8 Million Units. A: The Brain Quest Card Series, Which Challenges Kids to 'Get a Smart Start,' '' *Publishers Weekly*, January 24, 1994, p. 24.

Weeks, Linton, ''Read It and Laugh: For Peter Workman, Publishing Is a Ticklish Business,'' *Washington Post*, February 8, 2000, p. C1.

''Workman, Western Settle Dispute,'' *Publishers Weekly*, July 17, 1995, p. 121.

—Frank Uhle

Yahoo! Inc.

---

701 First Avenue
Sunnyvale, California 94089
U.S.A.
Telephone: (408) 349-3300
Fax: (408) 349-3301
Web site: http://www.yahoo.com

Public Company
Incorporated: 1995
Employees: 5,500
Sales: $3.5 billion (2004)
Stock Exchanges: NASDAQ
Ticker Symbol: YHOO
SICs: 518111 Internet Service Providers; 518112 Web
  Search Portals; 516110 Internet Publishing and
  Broadcasting; 518210 Data Processing, Hosting, and
  Related Services

Yahoo! Inc. is one of the world's leading Internet media companies. Using its seemingly neverending compilation of links to other Web sites, as well as its extensive searchable database, the company helps Internet users navigate the World Wide Web. Anyone can access the Yahoo! Web site for free because it is funded not by subscriptions but by the advertisers who pay to promote products and services there. Yahoo! leads its competitors in the amount of user traffic at its site, with over 2.4 billion page views viewed through its 25 international sites in 13 languages each day. The company also offers Internet users other peripheral services, such as free e-mail accounts (Yahoo! Mail), online chat areas (Yahoo! Chat), and news tailored to each user's demographic or geographic area (Yahoo! News). The company's principal shareholders are the FMR Corporation with 12.5 percent of the stock, cofounder David Filo with 7.9 percent, cofounder Jerry Yang (6.7 percent), and CEO Terry S. Semel (1.2 percent). Yahoo! stock sold at around $35 a share during 2004.

Humble Beginnings

Yahoo! Inc. got its start in 1994 as the hobby of two Stanford University students who were writing their doctoral disserta-

tions. Jerry Yang and David Filo, both of whom were candidates in Stanford's electrical engineering doctoral program, spent much of their free time surfing the World Wide Web and cataloging their favorite Web sites. In doing so, they created a Web site of their own that linked Internet users to Yang's and Filo's favorite places in cyberspace. At that time, their site was called "Jerry's Guide to the World Wide Web."

As their Web site grew, both in size and in the number of links from which it was composed, the number of people who used the site also increased dramatically. Thus, Yang and Filo began spending more and more time on their new hobby, gradually converting the homemade list into a customized database that users could search to locate Web sites related to specific interests. The database itself was originally located on Yang's Stanford student computer workstation, named "akebono," while the search engine was located on Filo's computer, "konishiki" (the two computers were named after legendary Hawaiian sumo wrestlers).

As for the transformation of the database's name from "Jerry's Guide to the World Wide Web" to "Yahoo!," the two men became bored with the original tag and set about to change it late one night while bumming around in their trailer on the Stanford campus. Looking to mimic the phrase/acronym "Yet Another Compiler Compiler" (YACC), a favorite among Unix aficionados, Yang and Filo came up with "Yet Another Hierarchical Officious Oracle" (YAHOO). Browsing through the online edition of Webster's dictionary around midnight, they decided that the general definition of a yahoo—rude and uncouth—was fitting. Yang was known for his foul language, and Filo was described as being blunt. The two considered themselves to be a couple of major yahoos, and thus the name which would soon become a household brand was born.

It was not long before the Yahoo! database became too large to remain on the Stanford University computer system. In early 1995, Marc Andreessen, co-founder of Netscape Communications, invited Yang and Filo to move Yahoo! to the larger computer system housed at Netscape. Stanford benefited greatly from this move due to the fact that its computer system finally returned to normal after having been inundated by Yahoo!'s activity.

Company Perspectives:

Yahoo! Inc. is a leading global Internet communications, commerce and media company that offers a comprehensive branded network of services to more than 274 million individuals each month worldwide. As the first online navigational guide to the Web, www.yahoo.com is the leading guide in terms of traffic, advertising, household and business user reach. Yahoo! is the No. 1 Internet brand globally and reaches the largest audience worldwide. Headquartered in Sunnyvale, Calif., Yahoo! has offices in Europe, Asia, Latin America, Australia, Canada and the United States.

Expansion in 1995

Commercialization soon followed. Yang and Filo began selling advertisement space on their site in order to fund further growth. The duo soon realized that it was going to be too difficult to manage both the creative and the administrative aspects of the Yahoo! enterprise. They recruited Tim Koogle, also a former Stanford student, to come aboard as CEO. Prior to his arrival at Yahoo!, Koogle had put himself through engineering school by rebuilding engines and restoring cars and had then gone on to work at Motorola and InterMec Corporation.

One of Koogle's first moves as the company's CEO was to bring in Jeff Mallett as COO. Mallett was a former member of the Canadian men's national soccer team who, at age 22, began running the sales, marketing, and business development aspects of his parents' telecommunications company, Island Pacific Telephone, in Vancouver. Prior to joining the Yahoo! gang, he also gained experience in marketing at Reference Software and WordPerfect and acted as vice-president and general manager of Novell Inc.'s consumer division. Together, Koogle and Mallett began transforming Yahoo! from a homegrown list of interesting Web sites into the most popular stop along the information highway.

Koogle and Mallett soon became known as "the parents" at Yahoo!'s corporate headquarters. While Yang and Filo would arrive at work wearing T-shirts and sneakers, Koogle and Mallett preferred Italian silk ties. Many viewed the foursome's working relationship as that of kids with ideas and the adults that they found to put these ideas into practice. In the August 6, 1998, edition of the *San Francisco Chronicle*, analyst Andrea Williams of Volpe Brown Whelan & Co. referred to Koogle and Mallett as "Yahoo's equivalent of the Wizard of Oz, pulling the strings from behind the scenes. . . . Americans are captivated by the idea of two college kids like Yang and Filo starting an incredible service. But [Mallett] and [Koogle] have turned it into a business that advertisers and investors understand and respect."

The majority of Yahoo!'s revenue came through banner advertising deals. In basic terms, Yahoo! sold space on its Web pages to companies wishing to promote their products to the demographic that frequented the Yahoo! site. The purchased space not only acted as a visual advertisement, as in a magazine, but often served as a link to the advertiser's own Web site as well. Thus, a simple click on a banner ad by an Internet user could immediately transport that user to the advertiser's Web site. In this sense, banner ads were somewhat superior to other forms of advertisement in that no other purveyor of advertising (television, radio, magazines) had ever led consumers to a company quite so immediately.

As another means of generating revenue, Yahoo! struck up distribution deals with Web sites that were looking to increase their own traffic. For example, Yahoo!, while not itself an online retailer, boasted a lot of user traffic at its site. An online retailer, however, might have goods or services to sell but a need to first increase traffic at its own site in order to sell those goods. A distribution deal would pair the two sites, with Yahoo! leading its customer traffic to the retailer's site in exchange for a cut of the transaction revenues whenever customers made purchases. In this sense, Yahoo!, along with competitors such as Excite, Infoseek, and Lycos, came to be known as a "portal"— a gateway to the rest of the Internet.

Through banner advertising and distribution deals, Yahoo! was able to continue offering its services to Web surfers for free, as opposed to online services such as America Online (AOL), Prodigy, and Microsoft Network. The latter three charged monthly fees for the use of their offerings. Although these online service companies' offerings were often more graphically intricate and visually pleasing than the Yahoo! site, they were essentially providing the same thing as Yahoo! while at the same time charging for the service. According to Jonathan Littman in the July 20, 1998 edition of *Upside Today,* "Yahoo, much like Amazon.com, built a natural Internet brand through its simple desire to satisfy customers." It was not long before Yahoo!'s user base was comparable to that of industry giant AOL, even though its 1995 revenues topped off at only around $1 million.

The Birth of a Brand Name: 1996

In 1996, Yahoo! went public, offering shares of its stock for $13. In the first day of trading alone, the company's stock price sailed to $43, and its estimated valuation was quoted at upwards of $300 million, more than 15 times its eventual 1996 revenues of approximately $20 million. Around that time, Yahoo! decided to start promoting itself in through advertising. Another former Stanford graduate, Karen Edwards, was brought aboard as the Yahoo! "brand marketer," and she immediately lined up ad agency Black Rocket of San Francisco to handle Yahoo!'s account. Black Rocket was composed of four independent advertising executives who, ironically, owned no computers.

That spring, Yahoo! used almost its entire advertising budget for 1996 to run its first national-scale ad campaign on television. Luckily, the ad was an immediate hit. In the television spot, a fisherman used Yahoo! to obtain some baiting tips, then proceeded to land a number of gigantic fish. According to Jonathan Littman in a July 20, 1998 edition of *Upside Today,* "The faux testimonial captured the Net's spirit without being the least bit techie." From this campaign arose the company tagline "Do you Yahoo!?" Yahoo! executives hoped that the efforts would help their operation to blossom into a full-fledged media company.

The quest to turn the Yahoo! name into a major brand took a few wacky turns along the way. For example, Edwards decided that the Yahoo! name simply needed to be out in the public eye as much as possible, regardless of the manner in which it appeared. Yahoo! posters began appearing at many outdoor locations, such as sporting events, concerts, and even construction sites. The Yahoo! logo was placed everywhere, with one of the most notable places being a tattoo on the rear-end of a Yahoo!'s financial pages' senior producer, when he made good on a lost bet. It was also plastered on the side of the San Jose Sharks' Zamboni ice machine and printed onto items such as Ben & Jerry's ice cream containers and VISA cards. The yellow and purple Yahoo! logo even appeared shrink-wrapped onto five Yahoo! employees' cars, and one spring Edwards planted her flower garden at home in yellow gladioli and purple petunias.

Acquisitions and Further Expansion: 1997–98

As Yahoo! became a certifiable household brand name, the company began striving to further satisfy the needs of its users. Following the trend set by online service companies such as AOL, Yahoo! added services and features such as chat areas, Yellow Pages, online shopping, and news. The company also added a feature called ''My Yahoo!,'' which was a personalized front page for regular users that displayed information tailored to each user's interests. The company also teamed up with Visa to create an Internet shopping mall (an idea that was later aborted), with publisher Ziff-Davis to create ''Yahoo! Internet Life'' (an online and print magazine which never came to fruition), and with Netscape to develop a topic-based Internet navigation service to be used with the Netscape Communicator browser software.

By 1997, Internet surfers were using Yahoo! to view approximately 65 million pages of electronic data each day. That year, Yahoo! acquired online White Pages provider Four11 for $95 million. The purchase gave Yahoo! access to Four11's e-mail capabilities, which when integrated into Yahoo!'s offerings allowed the company to provide its users with free e-mail (Yahoo! Mail). By mid-1998, over 40 million people were logging on to Yahoo! each month, 12 million of whom had become registered Yahoo! e-mail users. To put those numbers into perspective, one can consider that at that time, only 30 million people were tuning in to network-leader NBC's top-rated show *ER* each week, and the number of Yahoo! e-mail users was comparable to that of online service giant AOL.

In July 1998, Yahoo! received a $250 million investment from Japan's Softbank Corporation, increasing Softbank's share of the

company to approximately 31 percent. Yahoo!'s market valuation at that time was $6.9 billion, which was much higher than that of most other media companies. As an emerging media company, Yahoo! began to move into the Internet access market that year through the launch of Yahoo! Online. To do so, the company initially formed a partnership with MCI WorldCom, but the arrangement deteriorated later that year. Subsequently, Yahoo! crafted a deal with communications giant AT&T to provide Internet access through AT&T's WorldNet service.

Also in 1998, Yahoo! replaced Digital Equipment's Alta Vista with California-based search engine specialist Inktomi as the supplier of Yahoo!'s search engine. Yahoo! then purchased Viaweb, a producer of Internet software programs. The acquisition resulted in the posting of a one-time $44 million charge in 1998. Yahoo! planned to use Viaweb's software to start a new service, which would allow its users to set up their own Web sites for the purpose of buying and selling goods online.

In October 1998, Yahoo! purchased Yoyodyne Entertainment for 280,664 shares of Yahoo! common stock. Yoyodyne added its permission-based direct marketing capabilities to Yahoo!, which also obtained the company's database of consumers, valuable demographic information, and other Yoyodyne assets. Prior to the acquisition, much of Yoyodyne's direct marketing was done through online games and sweepstakes at Internet sites such as EZSpree.com, GetRichClick.com, EZVenture.com, and EZWheels.com. Yahoo! announced that while those four sites would remain intact after the integration of Yoyodyne into Yahoo!, the former company's overall brand would be phased out.

By the end of the year, Yahoo!'s user traffic had increased considerably since 1997, with Web surfers viewing approximately 95 million pages of information through Yahoo! each day, a huge increase from the previous year's average.

Phenomenal Growth in the 2000s

By the end of the 20th century, the computer industry, and the Internet industry in particular, was becoming increasingly inundated with new players. In July 1998, NBC had purchased a 19 percent interest in Snap!, another portal operated by CNET Inc. Disney followed suit by grabbing a 43 percent stake in Infoseek Corporation. At Home Corporation purchased Excite, Inc., and Microsoft Corporation increased promotion of its MSN portal. Even America Online made moves to increase its scope through the acquisition of Netscape and its Netcenter portal. Nobody wanted to be left out of the Internet game, since many analysts predicted that it would be the next true media industry.

Yahoo! tried to maintain its large share of the market by continuing to focus on its users and their satisfaction. Recognizing that it would only take one click of a computer mouse for a Yahoo! user to defect to one of its competitors, the company began to provide its users with even more features and services. In January 1999, Yahoo! announced the purchase of GeoCities, the third most-visited Web site in December 1998 (directly behind top-rated AOL.com) and second-rated Yahoo.com. The GeoCities site was a creator of electronic communities for people. Based on people's interests, GeoCities allowed its users to set up their own personal home pages. Yahoo! hoped that the acquisition of GeoCities would bring many of that site's users to Yahoo!, and vice versa.

The new century saw a dramatic rise in both sales and profits for Yahoo! In 2001 the company had sales of $717 million; in 2002, $953 million; in 2003, $1.6 billion; and in 2004, $3.5 billion, a one-year increase of 120 percent. This period began with a loss of $92.8 million in 2001. In 2002, however, the company posted a net income of $42.8 million. This rose in 2003 to $237.9 million and to a healthy $839.6 million net income in 2004. Such phenomenal growth was fueled by a number of factors, including steady acquisitions of other Internet companies. During the years 2000 to 2004, Yahoo! acquired thirteen companies: Arthas.com, eGroups, Kimo, Sold.com, Launch Media, HotJobs, Inktomi, Overture Services, Beijing 3721 Technology Co. Ltd., FareChase, OddPost Inc., Music-Match, and Kelkoo. Web traffic increases have also played a part. As of March 2004, the Yahoo! network of properties received some 2.4 billion page views per day.

A flurry of new joint ventures also promised continuing growth for Yahoo! In November 2001, the company teamed with SBC Communications to offer co-branded DSL and Dial services. This partnership was reaffirmed in November 2004 when the two companies agreed to a multi-year extension of their venture. They planned to move beyond products offered only on a home computer to products for home television and audio systems, Cingular wireless phones, SBC FreedomLink Wi-Fi, and SBC Home Networking equipment. Yahoo! CEO Terry Semel explained: "The new services that will be developed out of this expanded relationship represent the next step in Yahoo!'s strategy to further deepen consumer relationships by extending our products and services beyond the desktop. SBC and Yahoo! are putting consumers in the driver's seat, delivering what they want—when, how and where they want it." In December 2004, the company teamed with Nextel Communications Inc. to offer a group of Yahoo! products and services, including e-mail, instant messaging, games, and news content, on Nextel handheld devices. The venture combined Yahoo!'s wireless messaging capabilities with Nextel's nationwide network. In January 2005, the company signed a deal with Verizon Communications Inc. to offer Verizon's broadband customers a new Verizon Yahoo! portal. "We are very excited to team up with Verizon, the largest communications company in the U.S., as their partner of choice, in order to provide Verizon's subscribers with a compelling new Verizon Yahoo! offering," said Dan Rosensweig, Yahoo!'s chief operating officer. With such ambitious plans for the future, growth projections for Yahoo! remained optimistic.

Principal Subsidiaries

HotJobs.com, Ltd.; Kelkoo S.A.; Musicmatch, Inc.; Overture Services, Inc.; Yahoo! Europe; Yahoo! Japan.

Principal Competitors

America Online, Inc.; About Inc.; Google Inc.; Microsoft Corporation.

Further Reading

Alden, Christopher J., "Kingmaker," *Red Herring*, August 1998.

Angel, Karen, *Inside Yahoo!: Reinvention and the Road Ahead*, New York: Wiley, 2002.

Delaney, Kevin J., "Forging Yahoo's Future; CEO Terry Semel Revitalized Web Portal, but Rival Google Could Complicate 'Phase Two,' " *Wall Street Journal*, June 24, 2004, p. B1.

Delaney, Kevin J., and Dennis K. Berman, "A Big Buy for Yahoo Isn't Likely; Company to Focus Spending Spree on Expanding Global Presence and Increasing Its User Base," *Wall Street Journal*, December 15, 2004, p. C1.

Gumbel, Andrew, "The Cyberpunks," *Independent*, March 24, 1999, p. BR5.

Hansell, Saul, "Yahoo to Acquire GeoCities," *New York Times*, January 28, 1999.

Himelstein, Linda, et. al., "Yahoo!: The Company, the Strategy, the Stock," *Business Week*, September 7, 1998.

Mittner, Greta, "Yahoo Plays Yoyodyne's Game," *Red Herring Online*, October 13, 1998.

Napoli, Lisa, "Yoyodyne Deal Signals Next Stage of Marketing," *New York Times*, October 14, 1998.

"SBC, Yahoo! Extend Pact," *Grand Rapids Press*, November 19, 2004, p. C3.

Schlender, Brent, "How a Virtuoso Plays the Web: Eclectic, Inquisitive, and Academic, Yahoo's Jerry Yang Reinvents the Role of the Entrepreneur," *Fortune*, March 6, 2000, p. F79.

Swartz, Jon, "Yahoo's Other Dynamic Duo," *San Francisco Chronicle*, August 6, 1998, p. D3.

"Winning on the Web," *Success*, February, 1996, p. 27.

"Yahoo! to Strengthen Investment in China," *Alestron*, January 31, 2005.

—Laura E. Whiteley
—update: Thomas Wiloch

INDEX TO COMPANIES

Index to Companies

Listings in this index are arranged in alphabetical order under the company name. Company names beginning with a letter or proper name such as Eli Lilly & Co. will be found under the first letter of the company name. Definite articles (The, Le, La) are ignored for alphabetical purposes as are forms of incorporation that precede the company name (AB, NV). Company names printed in bold type have full, historical essays on the page numbers appearing in bold. Updates to entries that appeared in earlier volumes are signified by the notation **(upd.)**. Company names in light type are references within an essay to that company, not full historical essays. This index is cumulative with volume numbers printed in bold type.

Aetna Life and Casualty Company, III
180–82, 209, 223, 226, 236, 254, 296,
298, 305, 313, 329; **10** 75–76; **12** 367;
15 26; **23** 135; **40** 199
Aetna National Bank, **13** 466
AF Insurance Agency, **44** 33
AFC. *See* Advanced Fibre
Communications, Inc.
AFC Enterprises, Inc., 32 12–16 (upd.);
36 517, 520; **54** 373
AFE Ltd., **IV** 241
Affiliated Computer Services, Inc., 61
12–16
Affiliated Foods Inc., 53 19–21
Affiliated Hospital Products Inc., **37** 400
Affiliated Music Publishing, **22** 193
Affiliated Paper Companies, Inc., **31** 359,
361
Affiliated Physicians Network, Inc., **45** 194
Affiliated Publications, Inc., 7 13–16; **19**
285; **61** 241
Affinity Group Holding Inc., 56 3–6
Affordable Inns, **13** 364
AFG Industries Inc., **I** 483; **9** 248; **48** 42
AFIA, **22** 143; **45** 104, 108
Afianzadora Insurgentes Serfin, **19** 190
AFK Sistema, **59** 300
AFL. *See* American Football League.
AFLAC Incorporated, 10 28–30 (upd.);
38 15–19 (upd.)
AFP. *See* Australian Forest Products.
AFRA Enterprises Inc., **26** 102
AFRAM Carriers, Inc. *See* Kirby
Corporation.
African Rainbow Minerals, **63** 185
Africare, 59 7–10
AFT. *See* Advanced Fiberoptic
Technologies.
After Hours Formalwear Inc., 60 3–5
AFW Fabric Corp., **16** 124
AG&E. *See* American Electric Power
Company.
AG Barr plc, 64 9–12
Ag-Chem Equipment Company, Inc., 17
9–11. *See also* AGCO Corporation.
AG Communication Systems Corporation,
15 194; **43** 446
Ag Services of America, Inc., 59 11–13
Agan Chemical Manufacturers Ltd., **25**
266–67
Agape S.p.A., **57** 82–83
Agar Manufacturing Company, **8** 2
Agatha Christie Ltd., **31** 63 67
AGCO Corp., 13 16–18; **67** 6–10 (upd.)
Age International, Inc., **62** 347
Agefi, **34** 13
AGEL&P. *See* Albuquerque Gas, Electric
Light and Power Company.
Agema Infrared Systems AB, **69** 171
Agence France-Presse, 34 11–14
Agency, **6** 393
Agency Rent-A-Car, **16** 379
Agere Systems Inc., 61 17–19
AGF. *See* Assurances Generales de France.
Agfa Gevaert Group N.V., III 487; **18**
50, 184–86; **26** 540–41; **50** 90; **59**
14–16
Aggregate Industries plc, 36 20–22
Aggreko Plc, 45 10–13
AGI Industries, **57** 208–09
Agiba Petroleum, **IV** 414
Agie Charmilles, **61** 106, 108
Agilent Technologies Inc., 38 20–23; **63**
33–34

Agip SpA. *See* ENI S.p.A.
Agiv AG, **39** 40–41; **51** 25
Agnew Gold Mining Company (Pty) Ltd.,
62 164
Agouron Pharmaceuticals, Inc., **38** 365
Agr. *See* Artes Grafica Rioplatense S.A.
Agra Europe Limited, **58** 191
AGRANA, **27** 436, 439
Agri-Foods, Inc., **60** 256
Agri-Insurance Company, Ltd., **63** 23
AgriBank FCB, **8** 489
Agribrands International, Inc., **40** 89
Agrico Chemical Company. *See* The
Williams Companies.
Agricole de Roquefort et Maria Grimal, **23**
219
Agricultural Minerals and Chemicals Inc.,
13 504
Agrifull, **22** 380
Agrigenetics, Inc. *See* Mycogen
Corporation.
Agrilusa, Agro-Industria, **51** 54
Agrobios S.A., **23** 172
Agroferm Hungarian Japanese
Fermentation Industry, **III** 43
Agrologica, **51** 54
Agromán S.A., **40** 218
AGTL. *See* Alberta Gas Trunk Line
Company, Ltd.
Agua de la Falda S.A., **38** 231
Agua Pura Water Company, **24** 467
Agusta S.p.A., **46** 66
Agway, Inc., 7 17–18; **21** 17–19 (upd.);
36 440
Aherns Holding, **60** 100
AHI Building Products. *See* Carter Holt
Harvey Ltd.
AHL Services, Inc., 26 149; **27** 20–23; **45**
379
Ahlstrom Corporation, 53 22–25
Ahmanson. *See* H.F. Ahmanson &
Company.
AHMSA. *See* Altos Hornos de México,
S.A. de C.V.
Ahold. *See* Koninklijke Ahold NV.
AHP. *See* American Home Products
Corporation.
AHS. *See* American Hospital Supply
Corporation.
AHSC Holdings Corp. *See* Alco Health
Services Corporation.
Ahtna AGA Security, Inc., **14** 541
AI Automotive, **24** 204
AIC. *See* Allied Import Company.
AICA, **16** 421; **43** 308
AICPA. *See* The American Institute of
Certified Public Accountants.
Aid Auto, **18** 144
Aida Corporation, **11** 504
AIG. *See* American International Group,
Inc.
AIG Global Real Estate Investment Corp.,
54 225
AIG/Lincoln International L.L.C., **54** 225
Aigner. *See* Etienne Aigner AG.
Aiken Stores, Inc., **14** 92
Aikenhead's Home Improvement
Warehouse, **18** 240; **26** 306
AIL Technologies, **46** 160
AIM Create Co., Ltd. *See* Marui Co., Ltd.
AIM Management Group Inc., **65** 43–45
AIMCO. *See* Apartment Investment and
Management Company.
Ainsworth Gaming Technologies, **54** 15

Ainsworth National, **14** 528
AIP. *See* Amorim Investimentos e
Participaço.
Air & Water Technologies Corporation,
6 441–42. *See also* Aqua Alliance Inc.
Air BP, **7** 141
Air By Pleasant, **62** 276
Air Canada, 6 60–62; **23** 9–12 (upd.); **29**
302; **36** 230; **59** 17–22 (upd.)
Air China, 46 9–11
Air Compak, **12** 182
Air de Cologne, **27** 474
Air Express International Corporation,
13 19–20; **40** 138; **46** 71
Air France. *See* Groupe Air France; Societe
Air France.
Air Global International, **55** 30
Air-India Limited, 6 63–64; **27** 24–26
(upd.); **41** 336–37; **63** 17–18; **65** 14
Air Inter. *See* Groupe Air France.
Air Inuit, **56** 38–39
Air Jamaica Limited, 54 3–6
Air La Carte Inc., **13** 48
Air Lanka Catering Services Ltd. *See* Thai
Airways International.
Air Liberté, **6** 208
Air Liquide. *See* L'Air Liquide SA.
Air London International, **36** 190
Air Mauritius Ltd., 63 17–19
Air Methods Corporation, 53 26–29
Air Midwest, Inc., **11** 299
Air New Zealand Limited, 14 10–12; **24**
399–400; **27** 475; **38** 24–27 (upd.)
Air NorTerra Inc., **56** 39
Air Pacific Ltd., 70 7–9
Air Products and Chemicals, Inc., I
297–99, 315, 358, 674; **10** 31–33
(upd.); **11** 403; **14** 125; **54** 10
Air Pub S.à.r.l., **64** 359
Air Russia, **24** 400
Air Sahara Limited, 65 14–16
Air Sea Broker AG, **47** 286–87
Air Southwest Co. *See* Southwest Airlines
Co.
Air Taser, Inc. *See* Taser International, Inc.
Air Transport International LLC, **58** 43
Air Wisconsin Airlines Corporation, 55
10–12
Airborne Freight Corporation, 6 345–47
345; **13** 19; **14** 517; **18** 177; **34** 15–18
(upd.); **46** 72
Airbus Industrie, **7** 9–11, 504; **9** 418; **10**
164; **13** 356; **21** 8; **24** 84–89; **34** 128,
135; **48** 219. *See also* G.I.E. Airbus
Industrie.
AirCal, **I** 91
Airco, **25** 81–82; **26** 94
Aircraft Modular Products, **30** 73
Aircraft Turbine Center, Inc., **28** 3
Airex Corporation, **16** 337
AirFoyle Ltd., **53** 50
Airgas, Inc., 54 7–10
Airguard Industries, Inc., **17** 104, 106; **61**
66
AirLib. *See* Société d'Exploitation AOM.
Airline Interiors Inc., **41** 368–69
Airlines of Britain Holdings, **34** 398; **38**
105–06
Airlink Pty Ltd. *See* Qantas Airways Ltd.
Airmark Plastics Corp., **18** 497–98
Airopak Corporation. *See* PVC Container
Corporation.
Airpax Electronics, Inc., **13** 398
Airport Leather Concessions LLC, **58** 369

General Electric Mortgage Insurance Company, **52** 244

General Electric Railcar Wheel and Parts Services Corporation, **18** 4

General Electric Venture Capital Corporation, **9** 140; **10** 108

General Elevator Corporation, **25** 15

General Export Iron and Metals Company, **15** 116

General Felt Industries Inc., **I** 202; **14** 300; **17** 182–83

General Finance Corp., **III** 232; **11** 16

General Finance Service Corp., **11** 447

General Fire Extinguisher Co. *See* Grinnell Corp.

General Foods Corp., **I** 608, 712; **II** 530–34, 557, 569; **V** 407; **7** 272–74; **10** 551; **12** 167, 372; **18** 416, 419; **25** 517; **26** 251; **44** 341

General Foods, Ltd., **7** 577

General Furniture Leasing. *See* CORT Business Services Corporation.

General Glass Corporation, **13** 40

General Growth Properties, Inc., 57 155–57

General Host Corporation, 7 372; **12** 178–79, **198–200**, 275; **15** 362; **17** 230–31

General Housewares Corporation, 16 234–36; **18** 69

General Injectables and Vaccines Inc., **54** 188

General Instrument Corporation, 10 319–21; **17** 33; **34** 298; **54** 68

General Insurance Co. of America. *See* SAFECO Corporation.

General Leisure, **16** 33

General Maritime Corporation, 59 197–99

General Medical Corp., **18** 469

General Merchandise Services, Inc., **15** 480

General Mills, Inc., II 501–03; **10 322–24 (upd.)**; **36 234–39 (upd.)**; **44** 138–40; **50** 293–96; **62** 269; **63** 250, 252

General Motors Acceptance Corporation, **21** 146; **22** 55

General Motors Corporation, I 171–73; **10 325–27 (upd.)**; **36 240–44 (upd.)**; **64 148–53 (upd.)**; **65** 59, 62

General Nutrition Companies, Inc., 11 155–57; **24** 480; **29 210–14 (upd.)**; **31** 347; **37** 340, 342; **45** 210; **63** 331, 335

General Office Products Co., **25** 500

General Packing Service, Inc., **19** 78

General Parts Inc., **29** 86

General Petroleum Authority. *See* Egyptian General Petroleum Corporation.

General Physics Corporation, **13** 367; **64** 166

General Portland Cement Co., **III** 704–05; **17** 497

General Portland Inc., **28** 229

General Printing Ink Corp. *See* Sequa Corp.

General Public Utilities Corporation, V 629–31; **6** 484, 534, 579–80; **11** 388; **20** 73. *See also* GPU, Inc.

General Radio Company. *See* GenRad, Inc.

General Railway Signal Company. *See* General Signal Corporation.

General Re Corporation, III 258–59, 276; **24 176–78 (upd.)**; **42** 31, 35

General Rent A Car, **25** 142–43

General Research Corp., **14** 98

General Sekiyu K.K., IV 431–33, 555; **16** 490. *See also* TonenGeneral Sekiyu K.K.

General Shale Building Materials Inc. *See* Wienerberger AG.

General Signal Corporation, 9 250–52; **11** 232

General Spring Products, **16** 321

General Steel Industries Inc., **14** 324

General Supermarkets, **II** 673

General Telephone and Electronics Corp. *See* GTE Corporation.

General Telephone Corporation. *See* GTE Corporation.

General Time Corporation, **16** 483

General Tire, Inc., 8 206–08, **212–14**; **9** 247–48; **20** 260, 262; **22** 219; **56** 71; **59** 324

General Transistor Corporation, **10** 319

General Turbine Systems, **58** 75

General Utilities Company, **6** 555

General Waterworks Corporation, **40** 449

Generale Bank, II 294–95

Générale Biscuit S.A., **II** 475

Générale de Banque, **36** 458

Générale de Mécanique Aéronautique, **I** 46

Générale de Restauration, **49** 126

Générale des Eaux Group, V 632–34; **21** 226. *See* Vivendi Universal S.A.

Generale du Jouet, **16** 428

Générale Occidentale, **II** 475; **IV** 614–16

Générale Restauration S.A., **34** 123

Generali. *See* Assicurazioni Generali.

Génération Y2K, **35** 204, 207

Genesco Inc., 14 501; **17 202–06**; **27** 59

Genesee & Wyoming Inc., 27 179–81

Genesee Brewing Co., **18** 72; **50** 114

Genesee Iron Works. *See* Wickes Inc.

Genesis Health Ventures, Inc., 18 195–97; **25** 310. *See also* NeighborCare, Inc.

Genesse Hispania, **60** 246

Genetic Anomalies, Inc., **39** 395

Genetics Institute, Inc., 8 215–18; **10** 70, 78–80; **50** 538

Geneva Metal Wheel Company, **20** 261

Geneva Pharmaceuticals, Inc., **8** 549; **22** 37, 40

Geneva Rubber Co., **17** 373

Geneva Steel, 7 193–95

Geneve Corporation, **62** 16

GENEX Services, Inc., **52** 379

Genix Group. *See* MCN Corporation.

Genmar Holdings, Inc., 45 172–75

Genoc Chartering Ltd, **60** 96

Genosys Biotechnologies, Inc., **36** 431

Genovese Drug Stores, Inc., 18 198–200; **21** 187; **32** 170; **43** 249

Genpack Corporation, **21** 58

GenRad, Inc., 24 179–83

Gensec Bank, **68** 333

GenSet, **19** 442

Genstar, **22** 14; **23** 327

Genstar Gypsum Products Co., **IV** 273

Genstar Rental Electronics, Inc., **58** 110

Genstar Stone Products Co., **15** 154; **40** 176

GenSys Power Ltd., **64** 404

GenTek Inc., **37** 157; **41** 236

Gentex Corporation, 26 153–57; **35** 148–49

Gentex Optics, **17** 50; **18** 392

Genting Bhd., 65 152–55

GenTrac, **24** 257

Gentry Associates, Inc., **14** 378

Gentry International, **47** 234

Genty-Cathiard, **39** 183–84; **54** 306

Genuardi's Family Markets, Inc., 35 190–92

Genuin Golf & Dress of America, Inc., **32** 447

Genuine Parts Company, 9 253–55; **45 176–79 (upd.)**

Genung's, **II** 673

Genus, **18** 382–83

Genzyme Corporation, 13 239–42; **38 203–07 (upd.)**; **47** 4

Genzyme Transgenics Corp., **37** 44

Geo. H. McFadden & Bro., **54** 89

GEO SA, **58** 218

Geo Space Corporation, **18** 513

GEO Specialty Chemicals, Inc., **27** 117

geobra Brandstätter GmbH & Co. KG, 48 183–86

Geodis S.A., 67 187–90

Geofizikai Szolgáltató Kft., **70** 195

Geographics, Inc., **25** 183

GEOINFORM Mélyfúrási Információ Szolgáltató Kft., **70** 195

Geomarine Systems, **11** 202

The Geon Company, 11 158–61

Geon Industries, Inc. *See* Johnston Industries, Inc.

GeoQuest Systems Inc., **17** 419

Georesources, Inc., **19** 247

Georg Fischer AG Schaffhausen, 38 214; **61 106–09**

Georg Neumann GmbH, **66** 288

George A. Hormel and Company, II 504–06; **7** 547; **12** 123–24; **18** 244. *See also* Hormel Foods Corporation.

George A. Touche & Co., **9** 167

George Booker & Co., **13** 102

George Buckton & Sons Limited, **40** 129

The George F. Cram Company, Inc., 55 158–60

George H. Dentler & Sons, **7** 429

The George Hyman Construction Company, **8** 112–13; **25** 403

George J. Ball, Inc., **27** 507

George K. Baum & Company, **25** 433

George P. Johnson Company, 60 142–44

George R. Rich Manufacturing Company. *See* Clark Equipment Company.

George S. May International Company, 55 161–63

George Smith Financial Corporation, **21** 257

George Weston Limited, II 631–32; **36 245–48 (upd.)**; **41** 30, 33

George Wimpey plc, 12 201–03; **28** 450; **51 135–38 (upd.)**

Georges Renault SA, **III** 427; **28** 40

Georgetown Group, Inc., **26** 187

Georgetown Steel Corp., **IV** 228

Georgia Carpet Outlets, **25** 320

Georgia Cotton Producers Association. *See* Gold Kist Inc.

Georgia Federal Bank, **I** 447; **11** 112–13; **30** 196

Georgia Gas Corporation. *See* Atlanta Gas Light Company

Georgia Gulf Corporation, 9 256–58; **61 110–13 (upd.)**

Georgia Hardwood Lumber Co.,. *See* Georgia-Pacific Corporation

Georgia Kraft Co., **8** 267–68

INDEX TO INDUSTRIES

Index to Industries

AEROSPACE

AIRLINES

AUTOMOTIVE

CONSTRUCTION

FOOD PRODUCTS

PERSONAL SERVICES

PETROLEUM

TOBACCO

TRANSPORT SERVICES

WASTE SERVICES

GEOGRAPHIC INDEX

Geographic Index

Ireland

Israel

Italy

Jamaica

Japan

NOTES ON CONTRIBUTORS

Notes on Contributors

ATKINS, William Arthur. Illinois-based writer.

BRENNAN, Gerald E. California-based writer.

COHEN, M. L. Novelist and business writer living in Paris.

COVELL, Jeffrey L. Seattle-based writer.

DINGER, Ed. Bronx-based writer and editor.

GARIEPY, Jennifer. Editor and artist in Detroit, Michigan.

GREENLAND, Paul R. Illinois-based writer and researcher; author of two books and former senior editor of a national business magazine; contributor to *The Encyclopedia of Chicago History* and *Company Profiles for Students.*

HALASZ, Robert. Former editor in chief of *World Progress* and *Funk & Wagnalls New Encyclopedia Yearbook;* author, *The U.S. Marines* (Millbrook Press, 1993).

HAUSER, Evelyn. Researcher, writer and marketing specialist based in Arcata, California; expertise includes historical and trend research in such topics as globalization, emerging industries and lifestyles, future scenarios, biographies, and the history of organizations.

INGRAM, Frederick C. Utah-based business writer who has contributed to *GSA Business, Appalachian Trailway News,* the *Encyclopedia of Business,* the *Encyclopedia of Global Industries,* the *Encyclopedia of Consumer Brands,* and other regional and trade publications.

JONES, Howard A. Writer and editor.

MONTGOMERY, Bruce P. Curator and director of historical collection, University of Colorado at Boulder.

ROTHBURD, Carrie. Writer and editor specializing in corporate profiles, academic texts, and academic journal articles.

SHEPHERD, Kenneth R. Michigan-based writer and editor.

UHLE, Frank. Ann Arbor-based writer; movie projectionist, disc jockey, and staff member of *Psychotronic Video* magazine.

WILOCH, Thomas. Author whose most recent title is *Crime: A Serious American Problem* (2005); regular contributor to *Rain Taxi Review of Books;* associate editor with *Sidereality.*